British Hotels & Inns

Dog-friendly Breaks in Britain

French Bed & Breakfasat

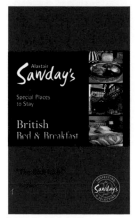

British Bed & Breakfast

Alastair
Sawday's
Special Places to Stay

Twelfth edition
Copyright © 2015
Alastair Sawday Publishing Co. Ltd
Published in 2015
ISBN-13: 978-1-906136-73-4

Alastair Sawday Publishing Co. Ltd,
Merchant's House, Wapping Road,
Bristol BS1 4RW, UK
Tel: +44 (0)117 204 7810
Email: info@sawdays.co.uk
Web: www.sawdays.co.uk

Series Editor Alastair Sawday
Editorial Gwen Vonthron
Consultant Editor David Hancock
Production coordinator Sarah Frost Mellor,
Lianka Varga
Editorial Assistance George Eaton, Louise
Phipps, Lianka Varga, Sam Wiltshire
Senior Picture Editor Alec Studerus
Picture Editor Ben Mounsey
Writing David Hancock, David Ashby,
Tom Bell, Jo Boissevain, Vincent Crump,
Sarah Frost Mellor, Becca Harris,
Allen Stidwill, Andy Turvill, Mandy Wragg
Inspections David Hancock,
David Ashby, Tom Bell, Colin Cheyne,
Vincent Crump, Mary Dixon, Tom
Fahay, Becca Harris, Paul Hennessy,
Brian Jones, Allen Stidwill, Andy Turvill,
Mandy Wragg
Thanks also to others who did an inspection or two.
Marketing & PR
Emily Enright 0117 204 7801
marketing@sawdays.co.uk

Alastair Sawday has asserted his right to
be identified as the author of this work.

Production: Pagebypage Co. Ltd
Maps: Maidenhead Cartographic Services
Printing: Pureprint, Uckfield
Distribution: The Travel Alliance, Bath
Diane@popoutmaps.com

Front cover photo credits
1. The Museum Inn, entry 206 2 & 3. The King's Head, entry 268

Back cover photo credits
1. Admiral Codrington, entry 395 2. The White Hart, entry 534 3. Woolpack Inn, entry 272

Spine cover photo credit
Charles Bathurst, entry 715

Alastair Sawday's

Special Places

Pubs & Inns
of England & Wales

4   Contents

Worth a Visit   547–573

We have some extra gems for you at the back of the book – pubs numbered 797-1026 and ordered by county – that haven't quite made a full entry. Perhaps they have just opened or changed hands or are simply on our radar as ones worth watching. They certainly merit a visit so why not drop in on them and let us know how you get on.

Photo: Tom Germain

How important ARE pubs, really? Things are changing, at hectic speed. The old greasy-spoon is almost gone, Soho's seedier dives are to go, the seaside boarding house is a rare relic, dingy pubs and transport cafés are almost gone, all replaced by gleaming purveyors of latte, cocktails, WiFi, hip-dom and hedonism. Why lament the hemorrhaging of traditional pubs? This, surely, in the great scheme of things, is small beer. But is it? And the news on the pub front is not quite that bad, anyway.

Let's start with the growth of the micropub. A Micropub, is a 'small freehouse which listens to its customers, mainly serves cask ales, promotes conversation, shuns all forms of electronic entertainment and dabbles in traditional pub snacks'. We salute their success.

Pubs are becoming more informal too, breaking conventions about, for example, meal-times. Many even serve breakfast and tea. Craft breweries are on the rise, teaming up with local pubs. Some pubs even make their own soft drinks and use their own herbs in their cocktails. There are now enterprising young gin-makers (eg Chase, and Sipsmith) and spirits are used imaginatively in food – such as gin-cured salmon.

Another trend is for pubs to sell their own take-away food, and they cater better, now, for vegetarians. There is, also, more food from countries such as Korea, Peru, Scandinavia and Canada. Bar food is better and better, too – almost tapa-like.

Competition has spurred pubs on to greater imaginative efforts, so now you can find a five-room tree-house in Devon and other crazily wonderful ideas for pub bedrooms. The pop-up concept has reached pubs, too – with an old Morris van taking the Richmond Arms to Old Bosham harbour. There are bakeries in pubs, fish and chip shops, and others; all is possible.

Roll on the willingness to re-invent an old tradition. That way lies the salvation of the great British pub. Let us hope that much of this will come at prices within everyone's reach.

Alastair Sawday

Those who are familiar with our Special Places series know that we look for originality and authenticity, and disregard the anonymous and the banal. We also place great emphasis on the welcome – as important to us as the setting, the architecture, the atmosphere and the food.

The notion of 'special' is at the heart of what we do, and is highly subjective. We also recognise that one person's idea of special is not necessarily another's so there is a big variety of places in this book, from rural rustic to urban chic, from gastropub to cider house.

Inspections and subscriptions

We have visited every entry in this guide. We pick up those details that cannot be gleaned over the internet or by phone, and we write the descriptions ourselves, doing our best to avoid misinterpretation. If a pub is in, we think it's special, and the write-up should tell you if it's your sort of special.

Owners pay to appear in this guide. Their fee goes towards the high costs of inspecting, of maintaining our website and producing an all-colour book. We only include places that we find special for one reason or another, so it is not possible for anyone to buy their way onto these pages. Nor is it possible for the owner to write their own description. We say if the bedrooms are small, or if a main road is near. We do our best to avoid misleading people.

Photo: The Old House Inn, entry 606

Feedback

Many of the pubs with rooms that appear in this guide are on our website, too. If you would like to tell us about your visit to any of these places, find them there and follow the link to the feedback form. For those that don't feature on our website, please email us with your feedback and tell us about your visit – the food, ales, staff and, crucially, the atmosphere. Write to info@sawdays.co.uk.

A lot of the new entries in each edition are recommended by our readers, so keep telling us about new places you've discovered, too.

Disclaimer

We make no claims to pure objectivity in choosing these places. They are here simply because we like them. Our opinions and tastes are ours alone and we hope you will share them. Do remember that the information in this book is a snapshot in time and may have changed since we published it; do call ahead to avoid being disappointed.

You should know that we don't check such things as fire alarms, kitchen hygiene or any other regulation with which owners of properties receiving paying guests should comply. This is the responsibility of the owners.

Finding the right place for you

Drink, eat, sleep A growing number of pubs and inns combine atmosphere with good food and bedrooms to match – and at lower prices than many hotels. It's true that some pubs are virtually indistinguishable from some small hotels, but a lively bar serving real beer should put them into the classic inn category. Some pubs with rooms are more modest village affairs where the enthusiasm to get things right in the bar extends upstairs. (If you are worried about noise at weekends, you can ask for a room at the back or a room across the way.) So the next time you take a weekend or business break, dismiss those roadside lodges and impersonal hotels in favour of a friendly country inn.

Gastropubs and country dining pubs Our best pubs are luring foodies away from pricier restaurants as a wave of casual dining enfolds the nation. Many backstreet boozers have been transformed, the fruit machines and beer-stained carpet being replaced by

Photo left: Sign of the Angel, entry 670
Photo right: The Crescent Inn, entry 707

chalked-up menus and chunky tables. In the countryside, too, old-fashioned locals are being rejuvenated by landlords and chefs who believe that gastronomy is rooted in the soil and that food should be fresh, seasonal and sourced from the best local suppliers.

Our favourite food pubs in England and Wales are described within these pages; all strike a happy balance between restaurant and pub. (Note that booking is not always a given and you may have to take your chance with a table.)

Maps

The maps at the front of the book show the approximate position, via a series of coloured flags, of each of our pubs and inns. Red flags indicate pubs with rooms, gold flags the award winners, blue flags the pubs without rooms, dark grey flags the Worth a Visits. The maps are for guidance only; use a detailed road map or you could lose yourself down a tangle of lanes.

Symbols

Below most entries you will see a line of symbols, which are explained at the very back of the book. They are based on the information given to us by the owners but things do change, so use the symbols as a guide rather than an absolute statement of fact. Please note that the symbols do not necessarily apply to the bedrooms. Double-check anything that is

Photo: The Queen's Inn, entry 329

important to you. A fuller explanation of some symbols is given below.

Children – The 🏃 symbol is given to pubs that accept children of any age. That doesn't mean that they can go everywhere in the pub, or that highchairs and special menus or small portions are provided. Nor does it mean that children should be anything less than well-behaved! Call to check details such as separate family rooms, whether children are allowed in the dining room and whether there is play equipment in the garden.

Dogs – The 🐕 symbol is given to places where your dog can go into some part of the pub, generally the bar and garden. It is unlikely to include eating areas.

Wheelchairs – We use the ♿ symbol if we've been told those in wheelchairs can access the bar and a wc. The symbol does not apply to accommodation.

Pub awards

Every year we choose those pubs that we think deserve a special mention. Our categories are: pubs serving local, seasonal and organic produce; authentic pubs; community pubs; pubs with rooms; and our favourite newcomers. More details are given on pages 15-20, and all the award winners have been stamped.

Opening times

We list the hours pubs are closed during the afternoon and whether or not

they are closed during particular lunchtimes and evenings. We do advise that you check before setting out, especially in winter.

Meals and meal prices

We give the approximate cost of main courses in the bar and/or restaurant. Note that some pubs charge extra for side dishes, which significantly increases the main course price. Note that many pubs do fixed-price Sunday lunches, and that prices in general may change. Check when booking. We also state days or sessions when no food is served.

Bedrooms, bathrooms and breakfasts

If you're thinking of staying the night in a simple pub or inn, bear in mind that an early night may not be possible if folk are carousing below. A few bedrooms do not have en suite bathrooms – please ask on booking – and pub room check-ins are often late, eg. from 6.30pm. Breakfasts are generally included in the room price, and most places serve breakfast between 8am and 10am.

Bedroom prices

Prices are per room for two people sharing. If a price range is given, then the lowest price is for the least expensive room in low season and the highest for the most expensive room in high season. The single room rate (or the single occupancy of a double room) generally

follows. Occasionally prices are for half board, ie. they include dinner, bed and breakfast. Do check.

Bookings and cancellations

Tables – At weekends, food pubs are often full and it is best to book a table well in advance; at other times, only tables in the dining rooms may be reserved. Tables in the bar may operate on a first-come, first-served basis. Some of the best gastropubs do not take reservations at all, wanting to hold on to their pubby origins. We applaud that, but it does mean you need to arrive early to bag a space. Always phone to double-check meal times.

Rooms – Most pubs and inns will ask for a credit card number and a contact phone number when you telephone to book a room. They may take a deposit at the time of booking, either by cheque or credit/debit card. If you cancel – depending on how much notice you give – you can lose all or part of this deposit unless your room is re-let. Ask the pub to explain their cancellation policy before booking so you understand where you stand; it may avoid a nasty surprise.

Payment

Those places that don't accept credit or debit cards are marked with a cash symbol.

Tipping

It is not obligatory but it is appreciated, particularly in pubs with restaurants.

Photo left: The King's Head, entry 268
Photo left: The Royal Oak, entry 244
Photo overleaf: The White Horse, entry 603

Sawday's Pub Awards 2015/16

We have chosen 15 absolute corkers for the annual Sawday's Pub Awards. Every single pub featured in this book is special but these 15 have been selected by our inspectors because they stand out in their particular category.

Award categories:

Local, seasonal and organic produce

Authentic pub

Community pub

Favourite newcomers

Pubs with rooms

Photos:
The Queens Arms, entry 533
The Bridge Inn, entry 296
Lord Crewe Arms at Blanchland, entry 215

Rat Inn   Entry 466
Northumberland

Local, seasonal and organic produce

Hearts sing when our inspectors find menus promoting regional and seasonal produce, home-reared and home-smoked meats, village-baked bread, fish from local catches, foraged finds, organic wines and ale from pubs' own microbreweries. This year's food champions are:

Jacobs Inn   Entry 501
Oxfordshire

The Queens Arms   Entry 533
Somerset

The Old Spot   Entry 248
Gloucestershire

Authentic pub

We have visited scores of simple, authentic, unspoilt gems and they are a diminishing breed. The ones we found particularly genuine are:

The Horseshoe Inn   Entry 683
Wiltshire

The Goodmanham Arms   Entry 732
Yorkshire

Blackwood Arms　　　　Entry 55
Buckinghamshire

Community pub

These are great little locals run by enterprising landlords who have succeeded in making their pub the hub of the community. Shining examples include:

The Jolly Sailors　　　　Entry 450
Norfolk

The Sheppey Inn　　　　Entry 548
Somerset

The Bridge Inn   Entry 296
Herefordshire

The Jolly Gardeners   Entry 407
London

Favourite newcomers

Nothing makes us happier than discovering a new Special Place to add to our collection, be it a tired old inn lovingly brought back to life by new owners or a hidden, little-known gem that we stumbled upon on our travels:

The Duncombe Arms   Entry 563
Staffordshire

The Anchor Inn   Entry 201
Dorset

Pubs with rooms

Our bunch of inns-with-rooms (which warrant full page entries) range from swish to charmingly rustic. We have visited more bedrooms than ever for this edition – and you can drink and eat very well at these places, too.

Lord Crewe Arms at Blanchland
Entry 215
Durham

The Shibden Mill Inn   Entry 708
Yorkshire

Alastair Sawday's

‘More than a bed
for the night…’

Britain
France
Ireland
Italy
Portugal
Spain

www.sawdays.co.uk

Self-Catering | B&B | Hotel | Pub | Treehouses, Cabins, Yurts & More

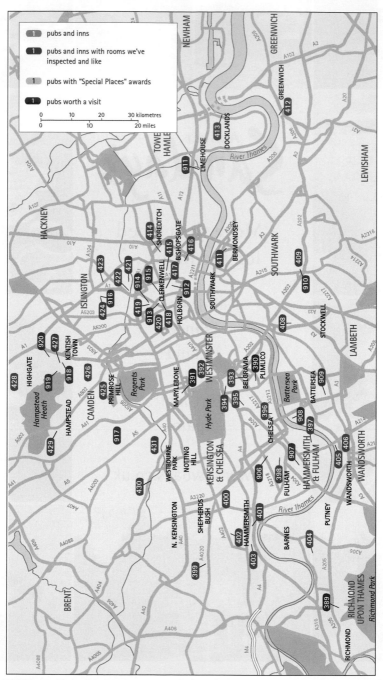

© Maidenhead Cartographic 2015

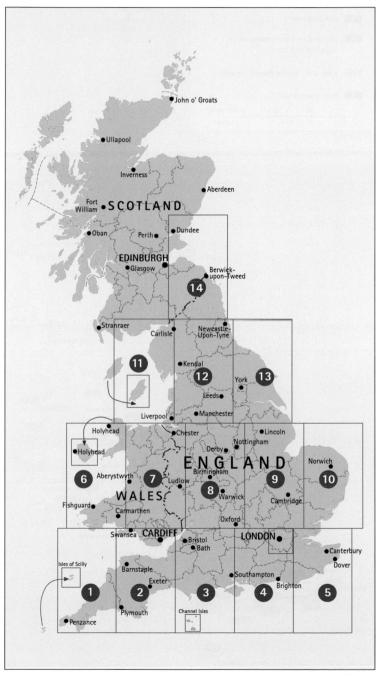

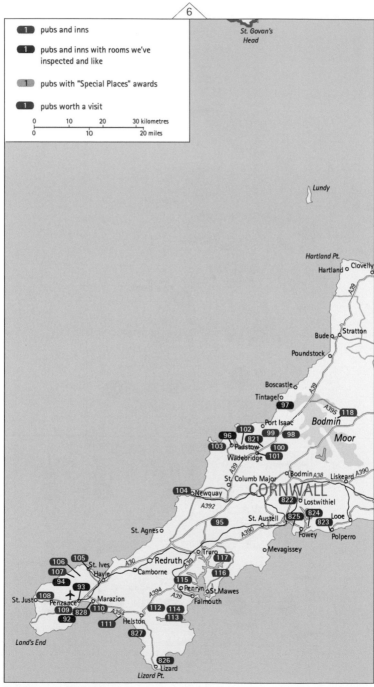

6

pubs and inns

pubs and inns with rooms we've inspected and like

pubs with "Special Places" awards

pubs worth a visit

| 0 | 10 | 20 | 30 kilometres |
| 0 | | 10 | 20 miles |

St. Govan's Head

Lundy

Hartland Pt.
Hartland   Clovelly
A39

Bude   Stratton

Poundstock

Boscastle
Tintagel
97

Port Isaac   Bodmin
102   99   98   A395   118
96   821   Moor
103   Padstow   100
Wadebridge   101
A39
St Columb Major   Bodmin A38   Liskeard A390
CORNWALL
104   Newquay   822   Lostwithiel
A392   825   824
95   St. Austell   823   Looe
St. Agnes   A390   Fowey   Polperro
Mevagissey
Truro   117
106   105   St Ives   A30   Redruth   116
107   Hayle   Camborne
94   115   A39
93   Penryn   St. Mawes
St. Just   108   Marazion   114   Falmouth
Penzance   112
109   828   110   A394   113
92   A39
111   Helston
827
Land's End

826
Lizard
Lizard Pt.

© Maidenhead Cartographic 2015

Map 2

25

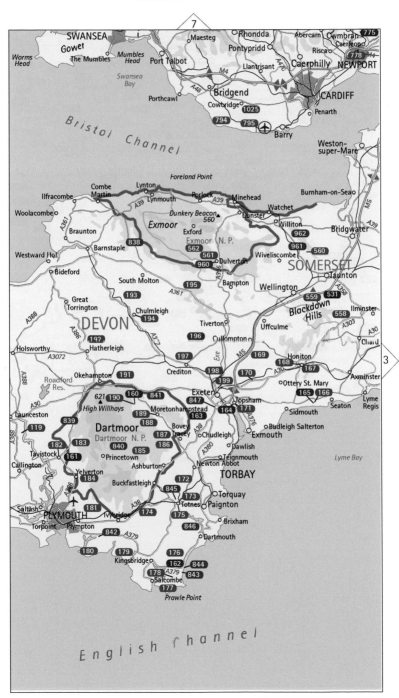

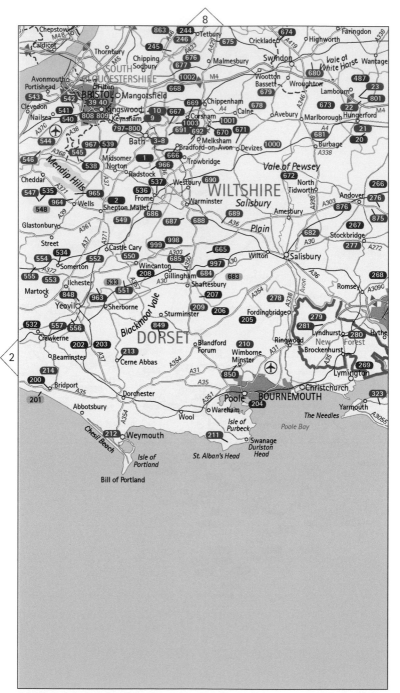

Map 4

27

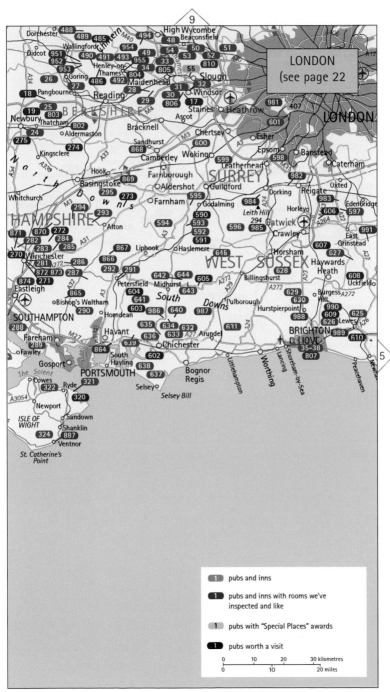

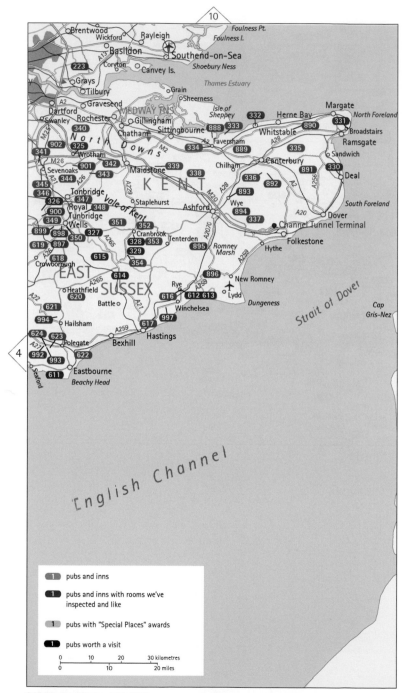

Map 6

29

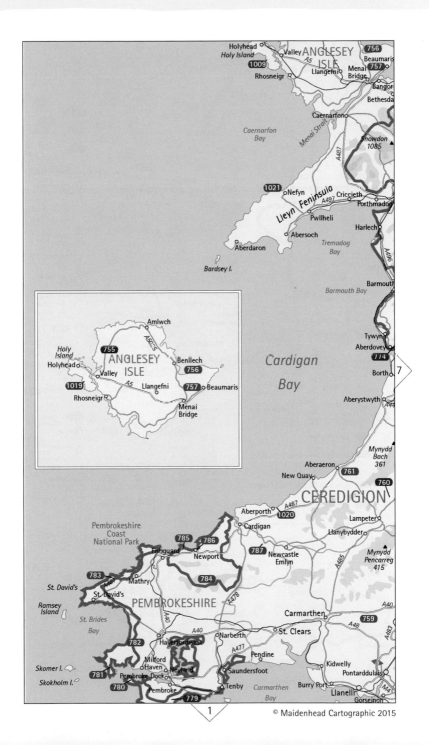

Holyhead
Holy Island
Valley
ANGLESEY
ISLE
756
Beaumaris
A5
757
1009
Llangefni
Menai
Bridge
Rhosneigr
Bangor
Bethesda
Caernarfon
Caernarfon
Bay
Menai Strait
A487
Snowdon
1085
1021
Nefyn
Criccieth
Lleyn Peninsula
A497
Porthmadog
Pwllheli
Harlech
A496
Abersoch
Tremadog
Bay
Aberdaron
Bardsey I.
Barmouth
Barmouth Bay

Amlwch
Tywyn
Holy
Island
755
A5025
Aberdovey
Holyhead
Benllech
774
ANGLESEY
ISLE
756
Borth
7
Valley
A5
1019
Llangefni
757
Beaumaris
Aberystwyth
A44
Rhosneigr
Menai
Bridge

Cardigan
Bay

Mynydd
Bach
361
Aberaeron
761
New Quay
760
CEREDIGION
Aberporth
A487
Lampeter
1020
Cardigan
Llanybydder
Pembrokeshire
Coast
National Park
785
786
Mynydd
Pencarreg
415
Fishguard
Newport
787
Newcastle
Emlyn
783
784
A485
St. David's
Mathry
A478
Ramsey
Island
St. David's
A40
PEMBROKESHIRE
Carmarthen
759
St. Brides
Bay
A48
A483
782
Narberth
St. Clears
A40
Haverfordwest
A477
Skomer I.
Pendine
Kidwelly
Milford
Haven
781
Saundersfoot
Pontarddulais
Skokholm I.
Pembroke Dock
Neyland
M4
780
Pembroke
Tenby
Burry Port
Llanelli
779
Carmarthen
Bay
Gorseinon
1

© Maidenhead Cartographic 2015

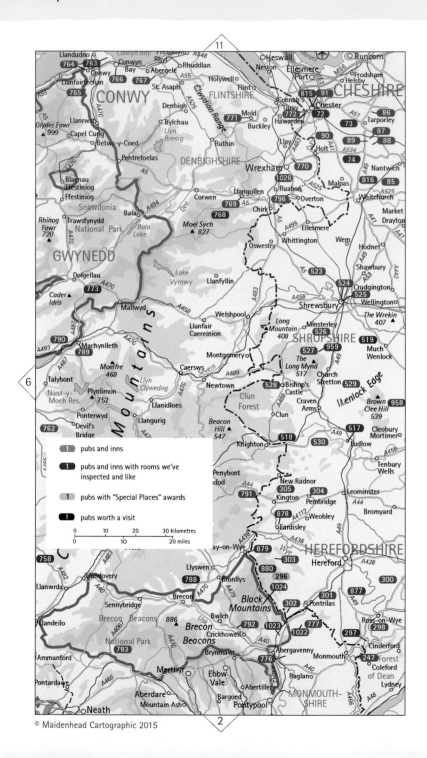

Map 8   31

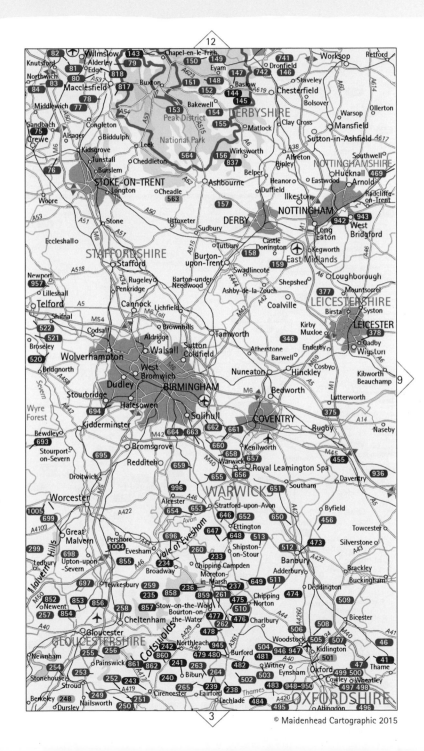

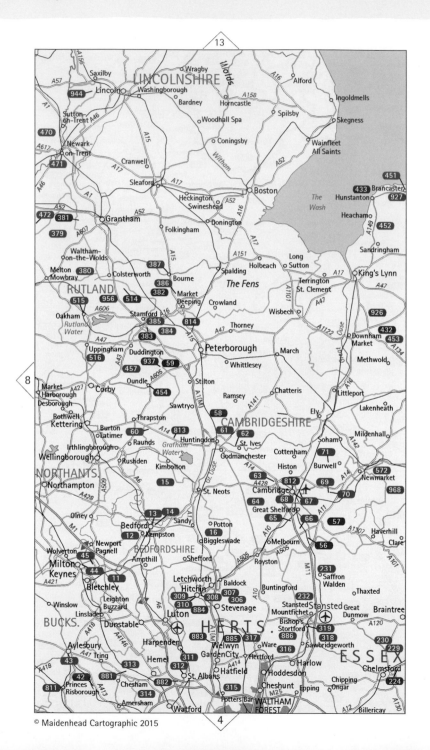

Map 10

33

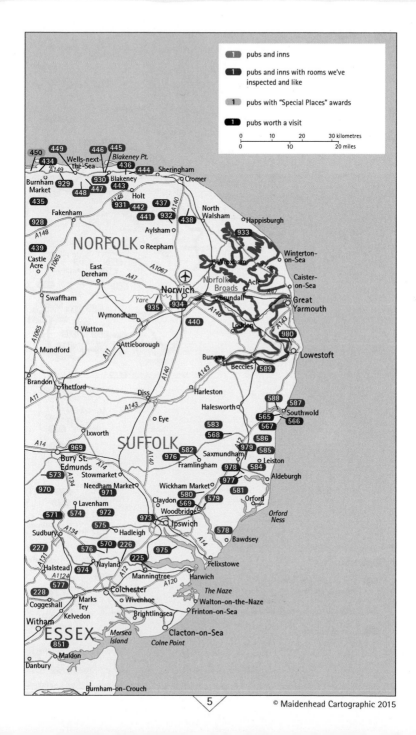

pubs and inns

pubs and inns with rooms we've inspected and like

pubs with "Special Places" awards

pubs worth a visit

0   10   20   30 kilometres
0   10   20 miles

450 449 446 445
434 Wells-next- Blakeney Pt.
A149 the-Sea 436 444 Sheringham
Burnham 929 930 Blakeney 443 Cromer
Market 448 447 Holt
435 Fakenham 931 442 437 North
928 441 932 Walsham Happisburgh
A148 Aylsham 438
439 NORFOLK Reepham 933
Castle East A1067 Winterton-on-Sea
Acre Dereham A47 Caister-on-Sea
Swaffham Norwich Norfolk Acle
Watton Broads
Mundford Wymondham 935 934 Brundall Great Yarmouth
Attleborough 440 A146 Loddon Yarmouth
Brandon 980
Thetford Bungay A143 Lowestoft
A11 Diss Beccles 589
Harleston
Halesworth 588 587
A143 588 Southwold
Eye 583 565 566
Ixworth 568 567
SUFFOLK 586
969 582 979 585
A14 976 Saxmundham 978 Leiston
Bury St. Framlingham 584 Aldeburgh
Edmunds 977
573 Stowmarket 580 581
970 Needham Market 569 579 Orford
971 Wickham Market Orford Ness
571 574 972 Claydon
575 973 Woodbridge
Sudbury Hadleigh Ipswich
227 570 226 578 Bawdsey
576 225 975
Halstead 974 Nayland Manningtree Felixstowe
228 577 Harwich
Coggeshall Colchester A120
Marks Wivenhoe The Naze
Witham Tey Kelvedon Walton-on-the-Naze
ESSEX Brightlingsea Frinton-on-Sea
851 Mersea Clacton-on-Sea
Danbury Maldon Island Colne Point

Burnham-on-Crouch

5

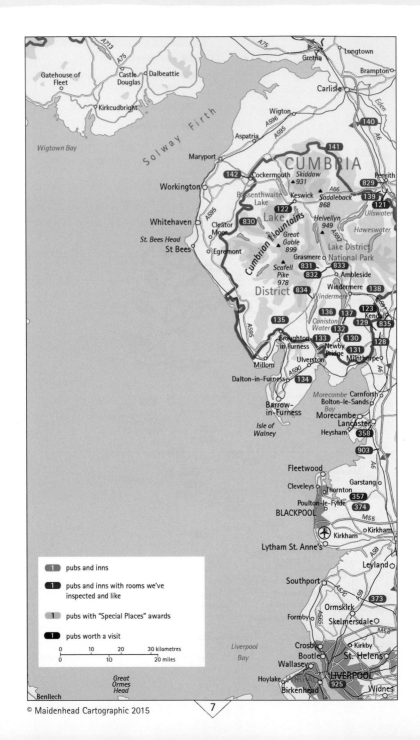

© Maidenhead Cartographic 2015

Map 12   35

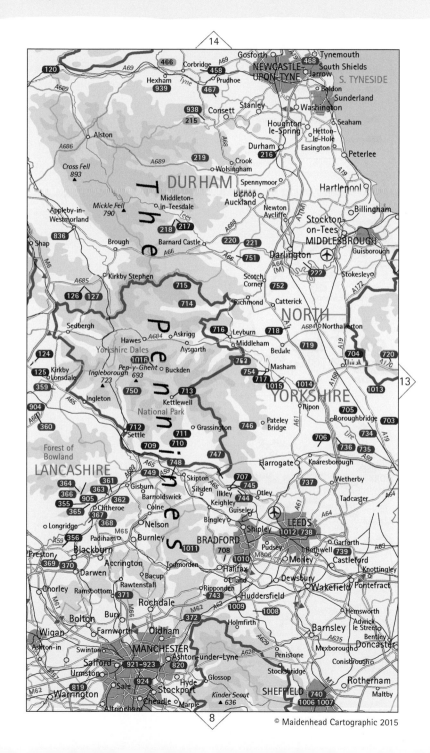

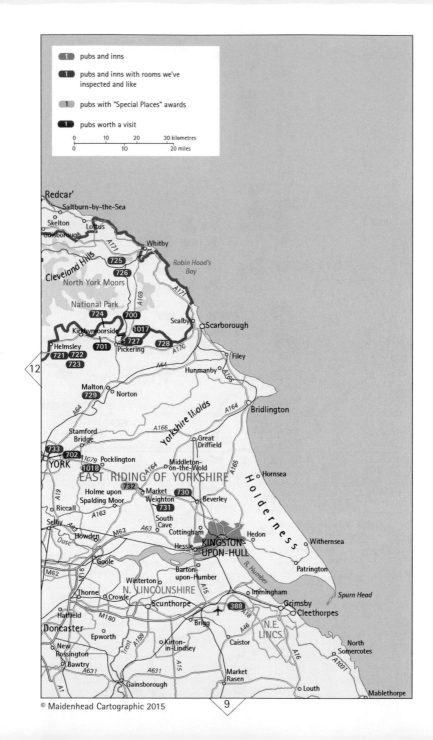

pubs and inns

pubs and inns with rooms we've inspected and like

pubs with "Special Places" awards

pubs worth a visit

Map 14

37

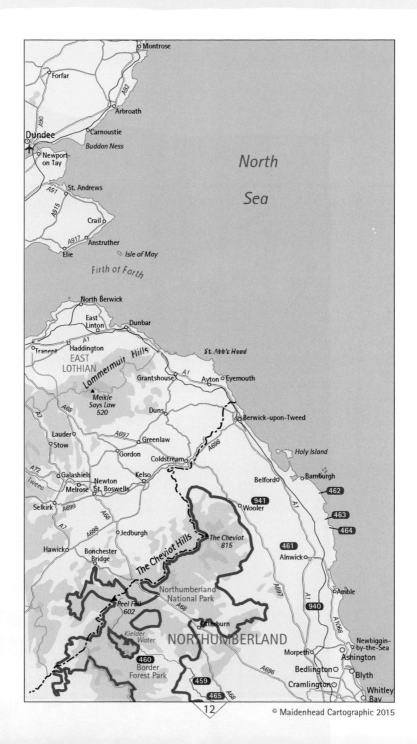

© Maidenhead Cartographic 2015

England

The Wheatsheaf Combe Hay
Combe Hay

A hidden valley, a pretty village, a gorgeous inn, three fabulous rooms. Views from the lush terraced garden — replete with veg plot and hens — stretch across to a fine ridge of trees, the manor house and church jutting out of the woods below. In summer there are barbecues, lazy lunches, horses clopping by. This is a 15th-century farmhouse with later additions — it's all but impossible to spot the join — whose exterior comes clad in Farrow & Ball creams. Gastropub interiors have neutral colours to soak up the light, sandblasted beams, halogen spotlights and Lloyd Loom wicker dining chairs. Steps outside lead down to three deeply comfy bedrooms in a stone building. All come in contemporary rustic style with light wood furniture, flat-screen TVs, Egyptian cotton and deluge showers; there are White Company oils and bathrobes too. Climb back up for seriously good food, perhaps pork belly with quince purée, skate wing with beetroot, parmesan and capers, and Valrhona chocolate fondant. Bath is a hike across the fields.

Rooms	3 doubles: £120–£150.
Meals	Lunch & dinner £16.50–£26.
Closed	Open all day.

Ian & Adele Barton
The Wheatsheaf Combe Hay,
Combe Hay,
Bath BA2 7EG

Tel	+44 (0)1225 833504
Web	www.wheatsheafcombehay.com

Oakhill Inn
Oakhill

The Digneys, owners of the much-loved King William and the Garricks Head in Bath, were the ones to give this old village inn a sympathetic brush up and a fresh look. There are still rugs on bare boards, bold red and green walls lined with local art, old sofas and rustic tables, and a cosy corner by the blazing log fire. Families and food and ale-lovers flock, for local ales from Newmans and Stonehenge breweries, and a well-priced menu of robust British dishes. Tuck into rump steak and horseradish sandwiches; beef and ale stew with curly kale; pot-roast partridge; beer-battered pollock and triple-cooked chips; and the most comforting of comfort puddings – warm treacle tart and winter nut crumble with custard, served seasonally, of course. The eclectic, very individual feel extends upstairs – the purple-painted master bedroom sports a big brass bed, crisp linen, bold lamps, a feature fireplace, quirky paintings and old furnishings, and a wood-floored bathroom with claw-foot bath, candles, thick towels, and a walk-in shower. Gorgeous all round.

Rooms	4 doubles, 1 twin/double: £90–£120. 1 family room for 4: £150–£190. Single £77.50. Extra bed £18. 2 rooms interconnect to create a suite: £180.
Meals	Bar meals from £4.95. Lunch from £10.95. Dinner from £11.95. Sunday lunch, 3 courses, £23.95.
Closed	Rarely.

Charlie & Amanda Digney
Oakhill Inn,
Fosse Road, Oakhill,
Radstock BA3 5HU
Tel +44 (0)1749 840442
Web www.theoakhillinn.com

Entry 2 Map 3

Bath & N.E. Somerset

The Garricks Head
Bath

This famous old pub next to the Theatre Royal has been a refuge for actors since 1720. Pretty tables outside on the alleyway, while a private terrace overlooks shoppers pottering up Westgate Street. Inside, turn left for the smart restaurant or right for the lively bar. You can eat wherever you want – locally sourced comfort food, perhaps pea and mint soup, beef and oyster pie, sticky toffee pudding. Owner Charlie used to work at the Anchor & Hope in Waterloo, so the style is robust English, with great produce and seasonality the hallmarks. The feel throughout is relaxed, with boarded floors, the odd leather sofa and a splash of colour on the walls. As for the beers, they mostly hail from small local breweries and change regularly. A long wine list offers much by the glass.

Meals	Bar meals from £6.45.
	Lunch & dinner from £10.95.
	Sunday lunch, 2 courses, £18.95.
Closed	Open all day.

Charlie & Amanda Digney
The Garricks Head,
8 St John's Place,
Bath BA1 1ET
Tel   +44 (0)1225 318368
Web   www.garricksheadpub.com

🏃 🐾 🍺 🍷 🔊

Bath & N.E. Somerset

The Old Green Tree
Bath

In Bath centre, the oldest pub in Bath hums with life even before midday. Tim, Nick and their staff are fanatical about real ale – at least six guest beers are chalked up on the board. Squeeze through the narrow planked bar into a cabin-like room undecorated since panelling was installed in 1928 – this pub is part of our heritage and has no intention of changing! In three little low-ceilinged rooms, a mosaic of foreign coins are stuck up in frames behind the bar, along with local artists' work. The lunch menu includes hearty old English dishes and a daily chef's special; the chutneys are homemade, the pâtés too. They have a devoted following and the drink is not limited to beer – there are malts, wines and hot toddies too.

Meals	Lunch £5.50-£10. Not evenings.
Closed	Open all day.

Tim Bethune & Nick Luke
The Old Green Tree,
12 Green Street,
Bath BA1 2JZ
Tel   +44 (0)1225 448259

 🍵

Bath & N.E. Somerset

The Marlborough Tavern
Bath

A pint's throw from the Royal Crescent, The Tav is one of Bath's best food pubs, loved by locals and visitors alike. The 18th-century interiors tick all the gastropub boxes with sage green paintwork, feature wallpapers, polished boards and smartly snug corners. Wines include a fashionable palette of rosés, perfect for sipping in the lovely walled courtyard garden. As for the food, it is driven by the produce: seasonal and local are the buzzwords with producers and provenance listed. There's Chew Valley smoked salmon, Neston Park Farm beef, local woodland pork and fruit and veg from seventh generation Eades greengrocers, just up the road. Fish arrives daily from Cornwall and Devon, Sunday lunches are the stuff of legend and booking is pretty much essential.

| Meals | Lunch & dinner, 2 courses, £12. |
| Closed | Open all day. |

Joe Cussens
The Marlborough Tavern,
35 Marlborough Buildings,
Bath BA1 2LY
Tel   +44 (0)1225 423731
Web   www.marlborough-tavern.com

Entry 5 Map 3

Bath & N.E. Somerset

The Chequers
Bath

A lovely little Georgian pub tucked away close to the Circus, the Assembly Rooms and Royal Crescent. Interiors come with mirrored panels, parquet flooring and cushioned pew benches. A pint of Butcombe waits at the bar, as do some rather good wines, many available by the glass. Do try salt and pepper squid, seared haunch of venison, plum tarte tatin – Head Chef Leigh Evans is a rising star. All locally sourced – the meat and vegetables from within 40 miles, while the fish comes from sustainable stocks off the Devon and Cornwall coasts. Sunday lunch runs from midday to 9pm by popular demand (booking advised). There's a smart little meeting room upstairs, too, which turns into a private dining space, perfect for families and friends. Add happy staff into the mix and you have a *bone fide* Bath gem.

| Meals | Lunch & dinner £6.95-£23.50. Sunday roast from £13.50. |
| Closed | Open all day. |

Joe Cussens
The Chequers,
50 Rivers Street,
Bath BA1 2QA
Tel   +44 (0)1225 360017
Web   www.thechequersbar.com

Entry 6 Map 3

Bath & N.E. Somerset

Bath & N.E. Somerset

The Star Inn
Bath

Listed on the National Inventory of Historic Pubs, a pub and museum piece wrapped into one. Active since 1760, it is partitioned into three numbered rooms, each furnished with rough planks, panelled walls, opaque toplights and ancient settles. A coal fire pumps out the heat and you can still get a free pinch of snuff from the tins on the ledge… you can almost imagine the old regulars pressing their lips to their tankards. To this day Bass is served in four-pint jugs which you can take away for a small deposit. No meals, just the odd bap from a basket on the bar. What counts is the beer — so much so that Alan has started his own brewery and has since scaled the heady heights of the world of real ale to win awards for his Bellringer tipple. A jewel.

King William
Bath

In a small corner of old England, as good a city pub as you are likely to find. It's tiny and candlelit, smiley and friendly, and the locals would revolt if a single thing changed. Known as the King Billy, it has a chilled café/bar vibe with some lovely wines and local beers. The food is deliciously tasty, you can eat downstairs or, more smartly, in two micro dining rooms up (booking advised). Dishes are simple, rustic, modern, and utterly irresistible. Try duck terrine with roast pears, beef stew with mash and greens, Dorset apple cake with raspberry ice cream. Bare boards, village hall furniture and background soul pull in a funky crowd. As for the gorgeous staff, where else do you chat about Ezra Pound's poetry while ordering a pint?

Meals	Baps from £2.20.
Closed	2.30pm-5.30pm.
	Open all day Sat & Sun.

Meals	Bar meals from £6.
	Lunch from £5.
	Dinner from £12.
	Sunday lunch, 3 courses, £25.
	Not Monday or Tuesday lunch.
Closed	3pm-5pm.
	Open all day Sat & Sun.

Alan Morgan
The Star Inn,
23 Vineyards,
Bath BA1 5NA
Tel   +44 (0)1225 425072
Web   www.star-inn-bath.co.uk

Entry 7 Map 3

Charlie & Amanda Digney
King William,
36 Thomas Street,
Bath BA1 5NN
Tel   +44 (0)1749 840442
Web   www.kingwilliampub.com

Entry 8 Map 3

Hare & Hounds
Bath

Ten-mile views, excellent food and cool interiors at this beautifully renovated Victorian inn above Bath, looking across the city to Solsbury Hill. A conservatory, decked terrace, sprawling garden and a vast mullioned window in the bar all face the right way – you gaze on fields where vegetables for the restaurant are grown. You might find goat's cheese and honey terrine, beer-battered haddock and hand-cut chips, dark chocolate mousse and clementine purée. At the bar, St Austell's Tribute and Hare & Hounds Ale stand side by side, backed up by excellent wines, many available by the glass. The pub is open all day, breakfast is served from 8.30am. There's a fire in the bar, a separate menu for children, and a private dining room for small parties. Perfectly located for those travelling to or from the M4 to the north of Bath. Gorgeous.

Meals	Lunch & dinner £10.50-£22. Sunday roast £13.50-£15.50.
Closed	Open all day.

Joe Cussens
Hare & Hounds,
Lansdown Road,
Bath BA1 5TJ
Tel   +44 (0)1225 482682
Web   www.hareandhoundsbath.com

Entry 9 Map 3

White Hart
Widcombe Hill

A short walk from Bath Spa station, in mellow stone Widcombe, this big imposing pub has a pleasant courtyard garden for supping summer pints. Despite its reputation as one of the best places to eat in town, it still feels pubby, with a jolly bar, a pleasingly plain dining room and a mixed bag of tables. On rugby day it heaves, as pints of Butcombe Bitter and RCH Pitchfork are downed. Chef Rupert Pitt has worked in some of Bath's best restaurants and his menu is short and to the point, with five starters and six mains. The food, well-priced and following the seasons, is delicious. Try the marinated feta with Mediterranean bulgur wheat salad, the baked sea bass with lemon and saffron butter, the tender slow-braised pork belly with cider gravy, the superb treacle tart.

Meals	Lunch & dinner £10-£13. Sunday lunch, 3 courses, £23. Not Sunday eve.
Closed	Sun evenings (in winter).

Rupert Pitt & Jo Parson
White Hart,
Widcombe Hill,
Bath BA2 6AA
Tel   +44 (0)1225 338053
Web   www.whitehartbath.co.uk

Entry 10 Map 3

Bedfordshire

The Black Horse
Woburn

The success of the Swan in sleepy Salford prompted Peach Pubs to take on the old Black Horse in posh Woburn. It looks every inch a small marketplace pub, yet the Georgian façade gives way to a big rambling interior. A lively front bar (wood floor and tables, high stools, Greene King ales) leads through to a big eating area, where red chairs, cushions and leather wall benches add colour to the beamed and informal dining room. Food combines classic pub dishes with modern brasserie meals and Peach's trademark deli boards: nibbles of cheese, charcuterie, fish and vegetarian treats, served with chutneys and artisan breads. Or choose potted duck livers; sea bass with lemon and fennel dressing, pear and blackberry crumble – best enjoyed in the secluded courtyard garden.

Meals	Lunch & dinner £10.75-£18.75.
Closed	Open all day.

Andrew Coath
The Black Horse,
1 Bedford Street,
Woburn MK17 9QB
Tel   +44 (0)1525 290210
Web   www.blackhorsewoburn.co.uk

♿ ⚲ 🐾 📖 🍷 🔊

Entry 11 Map 9

Bedfordshire

The Legstraps
Wootton

Card games in the Snug, newspapers by the door, blankets for outside on cool evenings. There's something really inviting about this little pub, on the corner of a country road just outside Wootton. It's run by two young blokes who like a pub to be a pub, but love to offer great food too, and chef Harry's friends from London's Borough Market tip up on Fridays for Market Night: that's how foodie they are. The interior is equally enticing. Step in to find slate floors, low ceilings, rich taupes, deep reds… leather sofas by the wood-burner and funky wing chairs. The dining room sparkles with downlighters and the open kitchen is behind the bar. Pop in for a pint of Adnams and a deli board of charcuterie or cheeses (Westcombe Cheddar, Wodehill Blue), or get stuck straight into braised lamb shoulder with a punchy orange glaze. Brilliant staff, too.

Meals	Starters from £5.
	Dinner from £10.
	Sunday roast £13.50.
Closed	Mon.
	3pm-5.30pm Tues-Thurs.
	Open all day Fri-Sat and
	12pm-6pm Sun.

Paul Collins
The Legstraps,
20 Keeley Lane, Wootton,
Bedford Mk439hr
Tel   +44 (0)1234 854112
Web   www.thelegstraps.co.uk

⚲ 🐾 📖 🍷

Entry 12 Map 9

Bedfordshire

The Embankment
Bedford

Peach Pubs snapped up this town-centre hotel in 2008; now it's their flagship inn. The strikingly timbered neo-Tudor building overlooks the leafy embankment of the Great Ouse. The style of its late-Victorian heyday has been recreated inside, so there are period fireplaces, big mirrors, wooden floors, leather wall benches and a semi-retro feel, from the airy front bar to the dining rooms at the back. Now a vibrant inn with a buzzy, laid-back bar and a modern all-day menu, the Embankment draws a lively crowd – prepare to drink, eat and make merry. You can drop in for breakfast (cosily in front of the fire); order a delicious coffee and cake; graze from the tempting deli board menu; or enjoy the daily roast. There's a super heated and semi-covered area outside at the front, and the riverside walks are gorgeous.

Bedfordshire

The Park
Bedford

In a residential suburb near the park, the uninspiring 1900s exterior conceals an interior with a funky feel, following an inspired refurbishment by a small and passionate pub company. Traditional fireplaces, flagstones, beams and wood panelling blend effortlessly with quirky fabrics and furnishings in trendy-retro dining rooms that converge onto the bar area; lounge on a cool leather sofa or nurse a pint at the bar. The kitchen delivers great pub food: rabbit, cured ham and pistachio terrine, pressed pork belly with black pudding croquettes, and mint chocolate parfait, while the market-fresh fish and daily specials are listed on a brown paper roll on the wall. Tip-top ales from Bedford's Charles Wells brewery and a verdant heated patio garden area complete a very promising picture.

Meals	Lunch & bar meals from £5. Dinner from £11. Sunday roast £13.50.	Meals	Lunch & dinner £11–£18.50. Sunday lunch, 3 courses, £20. Not Sunday eve.
Closed	Christmas Day.	Closed	Open all day.

Jonathan Taylor
The Embankment,
6 The Embankment,
Bedford MK40 3PD
Tel   +44 (0)1234 261332
Web   www.embankmentbedford.co.uk

Entry 13 Map 9

The Manager
The Park,
98 Kimbolton Road,
Bedford MK40 2PA
Tel   +44 (0)1234 273929
Web   www.theparkbedford.co.uk

Entry 14 Map 9

Bedfordshire

Bedfordshire

The Plough at Bolnhurst
Bolnhurst

A tavern has stood here since the 1400s. The last one burnt down, but tradition lives on in this unusually atmospheric reincarnation. Imagine nooks, crannies, stripped boards, blackened beams, leather armchairs, a bookcase stuffed with Sawday's tomes (yes!) and a welcome for all: foodies, families and old boys in for a pint. Chef-patron Martin Lee's grounding was with Raymond Blanc so the food, served in a barn open to the ceiling, is of note: crab risotto with chilli and parsley, Denham Estate venison, caramel soufflé with armagnac ice cream, and a beautiful platter of cheeses. The wines are impressive, though the Hopping Mad bitter also slips down a treat. All is loved and nurtured and that includes the garden, with its little pond and decking, and picnic rugs for summer. A bright light in Bedfordshire.

The John O'Gaunt
Sutton

It's worth crossing Sutton's trickling ford to reach the John O'Gaunt. Outside, a chalked blackboard welcomes everyone – wet feet or dry. Inside is a cosy bar, an open fire under a gleaming copper hood, and ales such as Woodforde's Wherry to accompany table skittles. On the other side of the bar, in the wood-clad restaurant and conservatory, happy punters tuck into Chef Jago's seasonal dishes: chicken liver parfait with toast and onion marmalade; Scottish mussels with Aspall cider and smoked bacon. The pudding list – warm chocolate fondant, anyone? – is tempting, but so is the Neal's Yard Dairy cheese menu on which each cheese is lovingly described. If you fall under the cheese 'spell' for too long, make sure your car is on the right side of the ford if it's raining!

Meals	Bar meals from £7.95. Lunch & dinner from £13. Sunday roast £21-£25.
Closed	3pm-6.30pm. Sun evenings & Mon.

Meals	Lunch & dinner £12.30-£16.
Closed	Mon (except Bank Holidays). 3pm-6pm Tues-Sat. Open midday-6pm Sun.

Martin & Jayne Lee & Michael Moscrop
The Plough at Bolnhurst,
Kimbolton Road, Bolnhurst,
Bedford MK44 2EX

Tel   +44 (0)1234 376274
Web   www.bolnhurst.com

Entry 15 Map 9

Jane & Jago Hurt
The John O'Gaunt,
30 High Street, Sutton,
Sandy SG19 2NE

Tel   +44 (0)1767 260377
Web   www.johnogauntsutton.co.uk

Entry 16 Map 9

The Winning Post
Winkfield

The old Cottage Inn has become Winkfield's hub, with a cute smokers' hut on the front terrace and a classy-rustic interior. This Upham Brewery pub is named (in part) after the stables that flank the drive, and there's a purpose-built extension with rooms at the back. Inside: dark planked floors and standing timbers, black lanterns fixed to low beams, a smattering of framed paintings, a roaring fire in the bar, copper pans by the wood-burner. It's nooked and crannied, cosy and inviting: a talented team has been at work. The staff are attentive and friendly; the food is flavourful modern European. Enjoy Newlyn crab with smoked salmon and crayfish, pork belly with black pudding mash, lemon posset with raspberry sorbet, and a liqueur coffee if you can find space. After a day at Henley Regatta it would be tempting to stay; ten rooms face the garden and one opens onto it; another is reached via outside steps. You get complementary tea, coffee, bottled water and fresh milk, the WiFi is fast, the beds are comfy, the rooms are peaceful, the kids are welcome, and breakfast is excellent.

Rooms	8 doubles, 2 twins: £85–£120.
Meals	Breakfast available. Lunch from £12. Dinner from £25.
Closed	Rarely.

Gregory Loison
The Winning Post,
Winkfield Street, Winkfield,
Windsor SL4 4SW

Tel	+44 (0)1344 882242
Web	www.winningpostwinkfield.co.uk

The Royal Oak
Yattendon

Handsome centrepiece of a handsome village, the Royal Oak sits at its crossroads – the quintessential country inn. The bar is a back-in-time proposition of original checkerboard tiles, beams, brick and panelling, four hearths ablaze, offering superb pints of Good Old Boy and Mr Chubbs from the West Berkshire Brewery. But time has not stood still. The lobby's leather sofas and gleaming wooden floors, made homely by patterned rugs, project a smartness that carries through to the restaurant's terracotta reds and chunky beech furnishings where the likes of five-spiced duck salad with chicory, cucumber and sweet chilli and beetroot risotto, crispy sage and parmesan reflect an inventive use of local ingredients. Stay over and snuggle down in big comfy bedrooms, some classically kitted out with antiques and rich fabrics, others more contemporary. Choose between pretty views across the square or the walled garden; the quietest are at the back and three are in the old staff house. A garden ringed with herbs, shrubs and trellises includes smart wicker seating and is a boon for summer. Pub quizzes and family suppers underlie links to the community.

Rooms	8 doubles, 2 twin/doubles: £90–£130.
Meals	Lunch & dinner £11–£18.
Closed	Open all day.

Rob McGill
The Royal Oak,
The Square,
Yattendon RG18 0UF

Tel   +44 (0)1635 201325
Web   www.royaloakyattendon.co.uk

The Bunk Inn
Thatcham

Tucked peacefully away on the outskirts of Curridge is a two-storey brick building painted a pretty dove grey, with modern extensions behind. Outside is a large enclosed terrace, a heated hut for smokers and ample topiary; inside is an inviting bar. Find stripped pine tables fronting leather and felt banquettes, a leather sofa by the brick fireplace, wooden stools flanking the polished bar, and wide wood boards on the floor. Dogs are welcome, families are encouraged, and the menus are chalked up on the board. If you want to go posh then head for the dining room down the passage, Farrow & Ball'd in smart country style with pale carpeting and stable door partitioning. You can have 'lager and lime' mussels with spiced frites, aged beef burger with sticky white onions, and pork loin with smoked potato and cider cream. Stay the night in one of nine rooms, comfortable and contemporary and varying in size, the creakiest, and the more characterful, in the old part. Some have outdoor patios, all have tea and coffee making facilities, flat-screen TVs, mood lighting and top-notch mattresses.

Rooms	7 doubles, 2 twins: £85–£120.
Meals	Dinner, 1 course, £15; 3 courses, £30.
Closed	Open all day.

Amanda J'Bair & Lewis Spreadbury
The Bunk Inn,
Curridge,
Thatcham RG18 9DS
Tel   +44 (0)1635 200400
Web   www.thebunkinn.co.uk

Entry 19 Map 4

The Dundas Arms
Kintbury

Charming new owners snapped up this delightful, old-fashioned Berkshire favourite in 2012. Realising its potential – it's in a stunning spot at the junction of the Kennet river and Kennet & Avon Canal – they have breathed new life into the place. Unused rooms have been opened up and the glorious riverside garden, once hidden and private, throngs in summer. Dabbling ducks entertain families while narrowboats glide by canal-side benches. Check out the papers by the log fire in the Library, a civilised space with leather wing chairs and sofas, or order a pint of Good Old Boy in the modern-traditional bar, all gleaming wood floor and pew benches, hunting prints and open fire. Choose a pork sharing board or fish and chips in the bar, or splash out on local game pie and whole baked sea bass from a seasonal dinner menu. Comfortable bedrooms are split between the inn and the converted stable block (dogs welcome), and French windows open to gorgeous riverside terraces. Follow the towpath to Hungerford (books, antique shops), then come back by train.

Rooms	8 doubles: £100–£140.
Meals	Light lunch from £6.95.
	Dinner, 3 courses, from £30.
	Bar snacks available.
Closed	Open all day.

Emily Carr
The Dundas Arms,
53 Station Road,
Kintbury RG17 9UT
Tel   +44 (0)1488 658263
Web   www.dundasarms.co.uk

Berkshire

Crown & Garter
Inkpen Common

Down winding country lanes is a red-brick beauty, with a long, trimmed beer garden overlooking the fields and an unexpectedly glamorous interior. There are gleaming floorboards, tartan curtains, a brick-lined hearth, bright pops of colour and atmospheric lighting. The bakery, from which croissants, cookies, cakes and breads flow, is a fabulous feature, and the café attracts the locals. As for the kitchen, it's led by Matthew Ambrose and the menu has something for all, from hearty club sandwiches for walkers to elegant butternut squash risotto for vegetarians to pan-fried sirloin of beef with fondant potatoes, served with ceremony from under silver cloches. Cockerels crow in the fields and in summer life spills onto a stone terrace. You can walk from the front door, try your luck at Newbury Races or watch the early morning gallops at Lambourn.

Meals	Bar meals from £6.95. Lunch & dinner from £9.95. Sunday roast £22. Not Sunday eve or Monday/Tuesday lunch.
Closed	3pm-5.30pm (5pm-7pm Sun). Mon & Tues lunch.

Gill Hern & Christopher Box
Crown & Garter,
Great Common Rd, Inkpen Common,
Hungerford RG17 9QR

Tel   +44 (0)1488 668325
Web   www.crownandgarter.co.uk

Entry 21 Map 3

Berkshire

Pheasant Inn
Shefford Woodlands

The spruced-up Pheasant is still a cracking old pub with a big reputation among the horse-racing set. The much-loved shabby gentility (rustic tiling, big mirrors, pine tables) has been retained and the TV remains tuned into the racing – often drowned out by the hubbub of jockeys and trainers. Ramsbury Gold and Two Cocks Cavalier help charge the atmosphere, backed up by several wines by the glass. As for food, good ingredients are used in comfortingly familiar ways. The menu delivers simple but careful home cooking: crispy salt and pepper squid with aïoli, chicken liver and pink peppercorn pâté with toasted brioche and red onion jam, pan-fried sea bass with potato rösti, crushed minted peas and a clam beurre blanc sauce and the famous Pheasant Inn burger. It's the best M4 pit-stop for miles.

Meals	Lunch & dinner £11.95-£21.95.
Closed	Christmas Day.

The Manager
Pheasant Inn,
Ermin Street, Shefford Woodlands,
Hungerford RG17 7AA

Tel   +44 (0)1488 648284
Web   www.pheasantinnlambourn.co.uk

Entry 22 Map 3

Berkshire

The Eastbury Plough Inn
Eastbury

West Berkshire is surprisingly rural, its sloping green fields studded with sheep – and the village of Eastbury is exceedingly pretty, with thatch cottages, trees and a dreamy river running through. The pub is cream-coloured with grey windows; its benches out the front gaze on the river, and its back garden has a climbing frame for children. Step into a traditional bar, just big enough not to be pokey, where a fire glows in a real old brick fireplace, horseshoes and hops decorate beams and shelves, and drinkers order new wave lagers from Fuller's; there are also good local beers. To the right an arch opens into a swirly carpeted dining room, much-loved by families and locals. The menu is busy and the portions are generous; tuck into king scallops with foie gras and black pudding; pavé of Royal Berkshire venison; sumptuous roasts on Sundays.

Meals	Lunch from £6, dinner from £12.
Closed	Mon all day.
	3pm-6pm Tues-Fri.
	(3.30pm-6pm Sat).
	Open all day Sun.

Graham White & Louise Powell
The Eastbury Plough Inn,
Eastbury,
Lambourn RG17 7JN

Tel	+44 (0)1488 71312
Web	www.eastburyplough.com

Berkshire

The Newbury
Newbury

Chef Clarke Oldfield, who helped set up the Albion in Bristol's Clifton village, has headed down the M4 to do the same for Newbury. With business partner Peter Lumber they have transformed the old Bricklayers Arms into a lively, laid-back and super-stylish venue. Expect vibrant colours, horse racing artwork, shelves groaning with cookery books (have a flick through), leather sofas for pints of Otter, and candles on sparkling wood tables. From an open kitchen Clarke delivers robust modern food – braised rabbit with pappardelle and parmesan; rib-eye with rocket and hollandaise sauce; rice pudding with fresh cherries. Pop in for coffee and pastries from 10am, super Sunday roasts, proper bar snacks (salt cod fritters, chorizo Scotch egg), and fresh bread and deli stuff to take home.

Meals	Lunch & dinner £11.50-£27.
	Sunday roast £9.50-£26.
	Not Sunday eve.
Closed	Open all day.

Peter Lumber
The Newbury,
137 Bartholomew Street,
Newbury RG14 5HB

Tel	+44 (0)1635 49000
Web	www.thenewburypub.co.uk

Berkshire

Berkshire

The Pot Kiln
Frilsham

An isolated country pub with stunning views and a long history. Interiors are almost ramshackle but nonetheless well looked after, and the staff are all smiles. Food is characterful because it's based on what the owner (TV chef Mike Robinson) shoots, forages or buys locally; there are no predictable clichés on the menu. This is a food-led pub with great beer and a huge local following, a dedicated drinking area and a historic feel: in the tiny, basic bar are bare tables, a dartboard and foaming pints of Brick Kiln Bitter. If it's lovely in summer – the front garden looks onto fields – it's a treat in winter, when log fires and a menu strong on game come into their own; try venison pie with mash, follow with plum and almond tart. The wine list is both serious and affordable. Do book.

The Bell Inn
Aldworth

The Bell has the style of village pubs long gone and has been in the family for 250 years. Plain benches, venerable dark-wood panelling, settles and an outside gents: it's an unspoilt place that visitors love. There's an old wood-burning stove in one room, a more impressive hearth in the main bar, and early evening drinkers cluster around a unique glass-hatched bar. Fifty years ago the regulars were agricultural workers; today piped music and mobile phones are fervently opposed. The food fits the image and they keep it simple: choose from warm rolls bursting with home-baked ham (or ox tongue or cheddar), treacle sponge and a winter soup of the day. Drink prices are another draw; the ales come from Arkell's and West Berkshire breweries. There's also a great big garden.

Meals	Bar meals £3.95-£10. Lunch & dinner £12.50-£16. Not Tuesdays.
Closed	3.30pm-6pm. Open all day Sat & Sun.

Meals	Bar meals £2.80-£6.50.
Closed	3pm-6pm (7pm Sun). Mon (except Bank Holidays).

Mike & Katie Robinson
The Pot Kiln,
Frilsham,
Thatcham RG18 0XX
Tel   +44 (0)1635 201366
Web   www.potkiln.org

Entry 25 Map 4

H E Macaulay
The Bell Inn,
Aldworth,
Reading RG8 9SE
Tel   +44 (0)1635 578272

Entry 26 Map 4

Berkshire

Miller of Mansfield
Goring

A jog from the Thames is a 1700s brick inn with beautiful bay windows and a big walled courtyard to the rear. Inside: stripped floors, exposed walls, sherry barrels, real fires by leather sofas, elegance, warmth and the odd walker's dog. It's not a glamorous pub, although it's far from scruffy, and it's not a gastropub either. But there's Nick Galer in the kitchen, who's learned from the industry's best, and a perfect front of house in the shape of Mary. Nick (ex Fat Duck) is a great cook who uses wonderful produce, then adds his inimitable spin, so you could find line-caught hake with clams, crushed peas, pea purée and fennel, and lemon meringue tart with Earl Grey ganache. The restaurant is neater and plusher, great for a family roast lunch. In short, we loved it all, from the real ales to the 14 wines by the glass to the superb nibbles.

Meals	Lunch from £12.50. Dinner from £20.
Closed	2.30pm-6.30pm Mon-Sat. Open midday-4pm Sun.

Nick & Mary Galer
Miller of Mansfield,
High Street, Goring,
Reading RG8 9AW
Tel   +44 (0)1491 872829
Web   www.millerofmansfield.com

Entry 27 Map 4

Berkshire

The Bell Inn
Waltham St Lawrence

Owned by Waltham St Lawrence village, deep in rural Berkshire, is a rare all-rounder. This 14th-century Wealden house, beamed inside and out, comes with low ceilings, creaking fireplaces, wattle and daub walls, a mishmash of furniture and candelabra lighting. It's a haven for ale fiends, five pumps rotating superbly kept local brews and a further six cask ciders held in cellar. A menu mounted above the hearth at midday and at 7pm offers one delicious constant – 'Bambi burger', minced on site from venison shot by a regular – alongside mallard with duck leg fritter and braised chard; juniper marinated venison with mash; quince crumble, dictated daily by season and produce. Regulars are a crew of colourful eccentrics, making the Bell Inn well-nigh perfect.

Meals	Lunch & dinner £10-£16.
Closed	3pm-5pm Mon-Fri.

Iain Ganson
The Bell Inn,
The Street, Waltham St Lawrence,
Twyford, RG10 0JJ
Tel   +44 (0)118 934 1788
Web   www.thebellwalthamstlawrence.co.uk

Entry 28 Map 4

The Beehive
White Waltham

Step into this unassuming brick pub in a Berkshire village, to enter a centre of culinary delight. Walk straight into the working bar to find pale tongue and groove panelling and two long wooden tables, cushioned banquettes and a mish mash of chairs, and four well-kept ales on pump. Pale-carpeted and spread across two rooms is the light-filled, open-plan restaurant, where chunky tables are set generously apart, unobtrusive pictures hang on pale walls and a fire burns away beneath a blackboard of specials. Snails from Dorset with gorgonzola and garlic butter, Cornwall-landed cod with tender beans and Morteau sausage, Yorkshire rhubarb trifle with custard... such was our lunch. It's really good food lovingly created from really good produce, and there's a dedicated menu for the under 12s.

The Royal Oak
White Waltham

Modest at first glance, there's star quality inside. Nick Parkinson (son of Michael) may have given this small inn a stylish lift, but he has managed to keep much of the traditional character... scrubbed wooden floors and stripped beams, timbers and panelling, the occasional music night. The bar is cosy and inviting, with solid wooden furniture, an open fire and a couple of armchairs, and the dining room's food, beautifully cooked by Dominic Chapman, is modern and classy, with a good choice of wines. Tuck into pickled South Devon mackerel with beetroot and watercress, peppered haunch of venison and creamy spinach, Yorkshire rhubarb trifle. And you can get a lovely pint of London Pride. The Royal Oak, friendly and well-run, opens its door to drinkers and diners with equal enthusiasm.

Meals	Dinner, 3 courses, £30.
Closed	3pm-5pm Mon-Sat. Open all day Sun.

Meals	Lunch & dinner £12.50-£24.
Closed	2.30pm-6.30pm. Sun evenings.

Dominic Chapman
The Beehive,
Waltham Road,
White Waltham SL6 3SH
Tel   +44 (0)1628 822877
Web   www.thebeehivewhitewaltham.com

Entry 29 Map 4

Nick Parkinson
The Royal Oak,
Littlefield Green, White Waltham,
Maidenhead SL6 3JN
Tel   +44 (0)1628 620541
Web   www.theroyaloakpaleystreet.com

Entry 30 Map 4

Berkshire

The Belgian Arms
Holyport

The thick creeper tangling across the face of this 200-year-old building hides a pub with a menu of classics cooked by a top-notch team. The grounds stretch down to the duck pond from a patio dotted with benches. The menus are co-written with a little Michelin starred consultation by Dominic Chapman, and link hearty pub staples with a selection of adventurous modern dishes; try hot smoked salmon, with beetroot and horseradish, followed by Cornish fish and chips. For pud, sticky toffee pudding. Prices are the same for lunch and dinner, but top-quality ingredients and preparation mean that expectations are easily matched. It's great to see a pub so competent in the kitchen welcoming drinkers, families and locals, rather than chasing awards.

Meals	No meals Sunday eves.
Closed	3pm–5pm Mon–Thurs.
	Sun 6pm–12am.

Nick Parkinson
The Belgian Arms,
Holyport Road, Holyport,
Maidenhead SL6 2JR
Tel   +44 (0)1628 634468
Web   www.thebelgianarms.com

Entry 31 Map 4

Berkshire

Two Brewers
Windsor

In Royal Windsor, next to the Cambridge Gate and the magnificent Long Walk, is a charming pub whose small quaint rooms meander around a panelled bar. One room with big shared tables has deep red walls and matching ceilings; others have intimate seating. There are magazines to dip into and walls crammed with press cuttings, pictures and mirrors; on a blackboard above the fire, anecdotes commemorating each day are chalked up in preference to menu specials. It's massively popular but reserve a table and you won't go hungry. The compact menu follows a steady pub line, with daily specials, roasts on Sundays, and tapas on Friday and Saturday nights. Choose between beer, champagne, fine wines… and pavement tables to tempt you after the rigours of the Big Tour. Dogs are welcome – but no under-18s.

Meals	Lunch & dinner £11–£19.50.
	Sunday roast £12.50.
Closed	Open all day.

Robert Gillespie
Two Brewers,
34 Park Street,
Windsor SL4 1LB
Tel   +44 (0)1753 855426
Web   www.twobrewerswindsor.co.uk

Entry 32 Map 4

Berkshire

Berkshire

The White Oak
Cookham

Behind the rosy-brick Cookham façade lies one of the finest food-led pubs in Britain. In a light, bright, charming restaurant (wooden floors, heritage colours) Clive Dixon cooks British produce-led food that is gimmick-free and consistently delicious. Accompanied – of course – by impeccable wines are a richly flavoured game pâté with a quince compote; a delicate crab and sweetcorn chowder; shepherd's pie made with Cornish lamb; Vacherin cheese and potato ravioli with sautéed chestnuts; and lardy cake – indulgent, perfectly made – with a salted whisky caramel and vanilla ice cream. This is serious cooking and those who know their food, flock. Book in advance, especially on BYO Mondays when there's a generous deal on Highland dry-aged steaks. You'll like the service too: attentive, fun, engaging.

The Crown
Burchett's Green

On the crossroads of a hamlet near Maidenhead is a very old pub with a fresh back-to-basics interior and a chef for whom food is a passion. The menu changes so often it has no time to make it to the website; instead, chalked up on the board, you find "Artichokes like when in Provence", "A Bowl of Arabic Grains with Harissa", "Berkshire Pig with its own Chipolata". Slaving away in the tiniest kitchen Simon Bonwick creates simple, gutsy, flawless classics inspired by market-fresh produce. The Ardennes pâté with gherkins, capers, shallots and home-baked bread was pink and robust; the salt marsh lamb rump was roasted with rosemary; the treacle sponge was as light as a cloud; and the Cashel Blue came with a beautiful Eccles cake. There are real ales, real ciders, and new front of house is son Dean – manning the bar, sorting the cellar. This is food of exceptional quality.

Meals	Lunch & dinner £12–£22.	Meals	Lunch from £10. Dinner, 3 courses, £20.
Closed	Sun evenings.	Closed	Please check before you visit.

Henry & Katherine
The White Oak,
The Pound, Cookham,
Maidenhead SL6 9QE
Tel +44 (0)1753 864294
Web www.thewhiteoak.co.uk

Entry 33 Map 4

Simon Bonwick
The Crown, Burchett's Green Road,
Burchett's Green,
Maidenhead SL6 6QZ
Tel +44 (0)1628 826184
Web www.thecrownburchettsgreen.com

Entry 34 Map 4

Brighton & Hove

Jolly Poacher
Brighton

Not much more than a mile from central Brighton, this electric blue Victorian corner pub sits quietly in a residential street, but don't let looks deceive you; the food really packs a punch. Chunky wooden tables are laid for dining, and there's room enough for drinkers at the front (note you might want to be careful on the spiral staircase to the loo). Local big-hitter Harveys is a regular at the pumps, joined regularly by one other regional brew, plus a good choice of wines by the glass. But it's Anthony Burns's cooking that lights up the place, with contented locals tucking into hearty and classically inspired stuff such as pork five ways (including crispy trotter), beer-battered cod and chips, or a roast rib of beef for Sunday lunch. Scrumptious!

Meals	Dinner, 2 courses, £14; 3 courses, £17.
Closed	Mon all day. Open 10am-11pm Tues-Sat & 10am-10pm Sun.

Kirsten Wass
Jolly Poacher,
100 Ditchling Road,
Brighton BN1 4SG
Tel   +44 (0)1273 683967
Web   www.thejollypoacher.com

Entry 35 Map 4

Brighton & Hove

The Chimney House
Brighton

When exploring the maze of streets behind arty Severn Dials you don't expect a Victorian redbrick pub in among the painted stuccoed houses. Enter and be seduced. Planked floors, dark polished furniture, high ceilings, sash windows... there's a contemporary feel and the space is big, airy and light. With excellent beers, including Harveys, and 14 wines by the glass, it's a popular hangout for locals. But it's the food that's the star. A daily-changing menu zooms in on pub classics (cottage pie, sausages and mash) and Mediterranean-style dishes (fish soup with grey mullet, mussels and cockles) that attract diners in droves – and there's a sensible kid's menu. Pop in at lunchtime for soup and sandwiches, pick up some homemade bread or jars of jam and chutney to take home.

Meals	Lunch from £4.95. Dinner from £10.50. Sunday roast £12.50.
Closed	3pm-5pm Tues-Thurs. All day Mon.

Helen & Andrew Coggings
The Chimney House,
28 Upper Hamilton Road,
Brighton BN1 5DF
Tel   +44 (0)1273 556708
Web   www.chimneyhousebrighton.co.uk

Entry 36 Map 4

The Ginger Pig
Hove

Everyone loves this pub minutes from the beach. The décor is fresh, contemporary and open-plan and the food is consistently brilliant. Whether it's poached skate wing terrine, a chargrilled rib-eye with hand-cut chips, or a blackboard special (slow-braised lamb with spiced cabbage and garlic mash perhaps) this is a serious destination for those who love British food. In spite of gastropubby leanings, the friendly team has created a balanced mix of drinking bar frequented by locals and dining area decked with modern art. It's all down to experienced restaurateur Ben McKeller who, in transforming this building, has created the first in the funky, family-friendly Gingerman group. The paved, sheltered garden is a little oasis.

Meals	Lunch & dinner £9.50–£18.
Closed	Open all day.

Ben McKeller
The Ginger Pig,
3 Hove Street,
Hove BN3 2TR
Tel   +44 (0)1273 736123
Web   www.gingermanrestaurants.com

Entry 37 Map 4

The Foragers
Hove

The laid-back Foragers in residential Hove combines the conviviality of a boozer with classy food from a talented team — you can glimpse the chefs at work from the front bar. Blackboard specials and printed menus are dependent on the seasons and raw materials are sourced from Sussex producers. There's a definite preference for organic, especially concerning meat (the Sunday roast always is). So everything bursts with flavour, from braised wild rabbit with buttered greens to Jerusalem artichoke and mushroom suet pudding; mash might be truffled or roast onion'd. There are sandwiches too, perhaps salt beef with dill pickle or steak with mayo, and Sussex Best Bitter to wash it all down. The interior revamp has created two distinct rooms with a relaxed, casual air — and the smart, decked all-weather garden is a popular draw.

Meals	Bar meals £4–£8.
	Lunch £6–£14.
	Dinner £14–£19.
	Sunday lunch, 3 courses, £21.
	Not Sunday eve.
Closed	Open all day.

Paul Hutchison &
Sara Rottner Hutchison
The Foragers,
3 Stirling Place, Hove BN3 3YU
Tel   +44 (0)1273 733134
Web   www.theforagerspub.co.uk

Entry 38 Map 4

Bristol

The Lion
Bristol

On one of the steep narrow streets in the cosy Bristol community of Clifton Wood is a little pub that the locals love. Grandad on his barstool keeps a friendly watchful eye – this is a family affair. Bath Ales and Tribute are on tap and the food is all made to order – perhaps pie of the day, a delicious burger, a tasty risotto. The Welsh Black steaks are good and the Sunday lunch is legendary – come with the keenest appetite! Irish music rocks in the back bar on Fridays, there's a pub quiz on Wednesdays, open fires in winter and a happy weekend throng: families, couples, groups, dogs. Note the terrace to the side and the mini community park for children next door. One super-comforting local.

Meals	Lunch from £4.75.
	Dinner from £7.25.
	Sunday roast £9.50.
Closed	Open all day.

Fiona & Charity Vincent &
David Waddilove
The Lion, 19 Church Lane,
Clifton Wood, Bristol BS8 4TX
Tel   +44 (0)117 926 8492
Web   www.thelionclifton.com

Entry 39 Map 3

Bristol

Kensington Arms
Bristol

At the end of a quiet street in leafy Redland, this Victorian corner pub with its decked front terrace – abuzz from lunch till late – is a popular local. Stylish and unpretentious, its painted panelling and planked floors are complemented by big mirrors and quirky touches. Fresh flowers and daily menus sit on scrubbed tables – so tuck into swordfish carpaccio in the bar (and delicious warm bread) or settle down to three scrumptious courses in the restaurant. This is modern food of the best kind, with a focus on provenance: pan-fried duck livers with bone marrow toast and persillade, home-smoked salmon fishcakes, pumpkin and pinenut gnocchi, hot chocolate fondant. Everything about the Kenny is lovely, and that includes the staff.

Meals	Lunch & dinner £9.50-£14.
Closed	Open all day.

Suzy Hislop
Kensington Arms,
35-37 Stanley Road,
Redland, Bristol BS6 6NP
Tel   +44 (0)117 944 6444
Web   www.thekensingtonarms.co.uk

Entry 40 Map 3

The Mole & Chicken
Long Crendon

In the middle of nowhere, hardish to find and absurdly picturesque (*Midsomer Murders* has been filmed here). Come on a damp Sunday and settle in for the day; come on a sunny one for an impressive decked terrace with barbecues and beautiful views. Inside, low beams, roaring fire, background music, squishy leather sofas. It's a relaxed, friendly sort of a place, with ales on tap and 12 wines by the glass. The restaurant feel takes over in several little rooms with chunky pine tables, 60s art and gleaming glasses, and we hear great reports of the food: Crendon Manor pork belly, scallops, black pudding, apple and pomme purée; a superb Sunday roast (thick, tender beef, fiery horseradish sauce, creamy celeriac, great Yorkshire pudding). With food this good it's worth staying the night and five charming rooms await in the adjoining cottage. Named after the colours used in them, they are immaculate, stylish and serene; 'Strawberry', the smallest, is Victorian, 'Duck Egg' is dreamy, 'Dairy Queen' is super-cosy, and 'Mustard' has a roll top in the bedroom itself.

Rooms	4 doubles: £110. 1 family room for 4: £140.
Meals	Lunch from £8. Dinner from £14.95.
Closed	Open all day.

Steve Bush
The Mole & Chicken,
Easington Terrace, Long Crendon,
Aylesbury HP18 9EY
Tel   +44 (0)1844 208387
Web   www.themoleandchicken.co.uk

Entry 41 Map 8

The Nags Head Inn
Little Kingshill

This was Roald Dahl's local – it features in *Fantastic Mr Fox*, half a mile out of Great Missenden. It's a beautiful old building built of red brick and flint under bright red pantiles, framed by the rolling hills of the Chilterns. At the back is a vast garden with plenty of trees under which to dream and picnic tables with umbrellas. Inside, a classic refurbishment from owner Alvin Michaels of the award-winning Bricklayers Arms, with food to match: the beloved 15th-century boozer has become a great dining pub. Now low dark beams and big inglenook blend with modern oak and lemon hues, there are salt and pepper mills on shining tables and boxed shelves guarding armagnacs. The food is faultless: try pan fried wood pigeon breast with black pudding and a dry sherry jus, or slow cooked pork hock on a bed of sweet & sour cabbage. Drinks cover every aspect of the grape and globe, plus London Pride, and young staff are attentive. Bedrooms above are equally good, their creams and whites complementing ancient timbers. There are ironing boards, toiletries and full-length mirrors, and the bed linen is delicious.

Rooms	3 doubles, 2 twins: £90–£130.
Meals	Lunch & dinner from £10.95. Sunday lunch, 3 courses, £23.95.
Closed	Christmas Day.

Alvin Michaels
The Nags Head Inn,
London Road, Little Kingshill,
Great Missenden HP16 0DG

Tel	+44 (0)1494 862200
Web	www.nagsheadbucks.com

The Bell
Stoke Mandeville

An attractive pub, built of brick around the turn of the last century, on the main road into Stoke Mandeville. Landlord James is engaging and affable, doing what he does best: creating a great name for The Bell. This is a pub where the food is the draw and the place was packed on a Tuesday lunch time in February. Beyond the big easy bar, with its dogs, WiFi and daily papers (reading glasses on tap!) is the dining room, large, lofty and light, a relaxed setting for modern, accomplished and seasonally-led food. Our guinea fowl with fondant potato, creamed cabbage and cep was top-notch. With a children's menu too, this is a brilliant venue for a family. Treat yourself to a pint of Bombardier by the log-burner, or a peach bellini in the lawned beer garden at the back.

The Swan
Salford

Peach Pubs have the knack of identifying a corner of countryside longing for a dining pub and finding just the right place. The gastronomic desert around Milton Keynes was their target; now this once ordinary Edwardian boozer in sleepy Salford has been given a new lease of life. The result is impressive: a main bar with wood floors, warm colours, leather chairs, upholstered curved benches – a laid-back modern feel. There's also a fabulous private dining room in a converted barn. Outside: a smart terrace, a kitchen garden and a smokehouse. Escape the M1 for great deli boards (antipasti with artisan breads) and enjoyable modern pub food served all day – duck liver pâté with mulled onion marmalade; venison with chestnut jus; rhubarb and custard trifle.

Meals	Lunch & dinner £11.75–£22.
Closed	Open all day.

Meals	Lunch from £6.50.
	Dinner from £13.75.
Closed	Christmas Day.

James Penlington
The Bell,
29 Lower Road, Stoke Mandeville,
Aylesbury HP22 5XA
Tel   +44 (0)1296 612434
Web   www.bellstokemandeville.co.uk

Entry 43 Map 9

Andrew Coath
The Swan,
2 Wavendon Road, Salford,
Milton Keynes MK17 8BD
Tel   +44 (0)1908 281008
Web   www.swansalford.co.uk

Entry 44 Map 9

Buckinghamshire

Swan Inn
Milton Keynes Village

A 13th-century beauty in the heart of a sprawling New Town; across roundabouts, through housing estates, to arrive at 'Milton Keynes Village'. Spruced up in a stylish gastropub style, keeping its beams, fireplaces and layout, the Swan has cool colours and scatter cushions, chic chairs in the snug and a glowing open fire in the bar. In the cosy dining room – wooden floors, chunky tables, open-to-view kitchen – a selection of sharing platters are on the menu alongside gammon, egg and chunky chips, or opt for a vegetarian treat of couscous-stuffed Romano pepper with goat's cheese croquette. Some produce comes from local allotments (in return for a pint or two), while imaginative evening meals might include dishes such as a gilt pork hock, Toulouse sausage and white bean cassoulet. In summer you can eat on the sun terrace or in the pretty orchard garden.

Buckinghamshire

The Hundred
Ashendon

With its walls of old brick and polished plaster and simple, soulful medley of furniture, it's not a swanky place and that is its charm. As if in sympathy with the inventive feel, local chef Matt (ex St John, London) knows how to make simple food taste special. Our dishes were spot on: a succulent starter of kohlrabi and pomegranate, another of squid, chilli and celery, then a robust beef and potato pie, and a melt-in-the mouth braised lamb. There's an honesty and confidence about the food that demonstrates a skilful hand – and you can't not love a pub with spotted dick and custard on the menu. The beers are Brill Gold and Tring, the wine list is short but very good. They say, "bring your kids, your pets, your mates, your boots, your nan, your boss, your lover". Brilliant!

Meals	Lunch & dinner £7–£16.
	Sunday roast £13.95.
Closed	Open all day.

Meals	Lunch & dinner £5.50–£15.50.
Closed	Mon all day. 3pm–6pm Tues–Fri.

Tyrone Bentham
Swan Inn, Broughton Road,
Milton Keynes Village,
Milton Keynes MK10 9AH
Tel   +44 (0)1908 665240
Web   www.theswan-mkvillage.co.uk

Entry 45 Map 9

Matt Gill & Pia Knight
The Hundred,
Lower End, Ashendon,
Aylesbury HP18 0HE
Tel   +44 (0)1296 651296
Web   www.thehundred.co.uk

Entry 46 Map 8

Buckinghamshire

The Pointer
Brill

The wine list is impressive, the beer is Pointer, the cider is local and the food is good modern British. Brill is a pretty village, and the handsome Pointer, an inn since 1702, stands close to the church. Next door is their own butcher's shop and deli, Longhorn cattle come from the local farm; their hide covers the cool bar stools and their meat goes into the burgers. Find sturdy oak beams and a reclaimed French oak bar, modishly upholstered sofas and pictures on pale-hued walls. The dining room overlooks the garden and has an open kitchen. Try seared grouse breast with watercress salad; wild mushroom risotto with parmesan; warm chocolate brownie with chantilly cream. It's a sophisticated place but you can still bring the dog, and the garden is large and enclosed.

Meals	Lunch £5.95–£13.95.
	Dinner £5–£21.
Closed	Open all day Tues–Sun
	& Mon from 2.30pm.

Alexa Pienaar
The Pointer,
27 Church Street, Brill,
Aylesbury HP18 9RT

Tel   +44 (0)1844 238339
Web www.thepointerbrill.com

Entry 47 Map 8

Buckinghamshire

The Old Queens Head
Penn

Run by the small and intimate Little Gems group, this pub by the green oozes character and charm; dating from 1666, its old beams and timbers blend perfectly with a stylish and contemporary décor in both the rambling bar and the dining rooms. Find rug-strewn flags, polished boards, classic fabrics, lovely old oak, and innovative seasonal menus and chalkboard specials. Choices range from 'small plates' – confit duck leg, bam hock and apricot terrine with toasted rye bread – to big dishes of slow-cooked shin of beef with saffron risotto, bone marrow crust and gremolata jus. For those who have room left, there's a tempting selection of puddings, raspberry Bakewell tart with clotted cream for one. To top it all, a parasol-strewn terrace, glorious summer garden, and walking in the ancient beech woodlands of Common and Penn Woods.

Meals	Lunch, bar meals
	& dinner £11.75–£19.75.
Closed	Open all day.

The Manager
The Old Queens Head,
Hammersley Lane, Penn,
High Wycombe HP10 8EY

Tel   +44 (0)1494 813371
Web www.oldqueensheadpenn.co.uk

Entry 48 Map 4

Buckinghamshire

The Royal Oak
Bovingdon Green

The old whitewashed cottage stands in a hamlet on the edge of the common – hard to believe that Marlow is just a mile away. It's one of a thriving small group of dining pubs (the Alford Arms, Herts, and the Swan Inn and Old Queens Head, Bucks). Beyond the terrace is a stylish open-plan bar, cheerful with terracotta walls, rug-strewn boards, cushioned pews and crackling log fires. Order a pint of local Rebellion and check out the daily chalkboard or printed menu. Innovative pub grub comes in the form of 'small plates' such as Wobbly Bottom goats' cheese with basil quinoa and walnuts, and main meals – slow-cooked beef cheek bourguignon or pan-roast venison loin; all is fresh and delicious. Indulge in a marshmallow parfait with banana, chocolate and honeycomb. The sprawling gardens are perfect for summer.

Meals	Lunch & dinner £11.75–£19.75.
Closed	Open all day.

David & Becky Salisbury
The Royal Oak,
Frieth Road, Bovingdon Green,
Marlow SL7 2JF
Tel   +44 (0)1628 488611
Web   www.royaloakmarlow.co.uk

Entry 49 Map 4

Buckinghamshire

The Jolly Cricketers
Seer Green

When the Jolly Cricketers came on the market, Seer Green residents Chris and Amanda couldn't resist. Now pretty plants clamber up the brickwork outside, while behind the bar, optics have been replaced by sweet shop jars filled with roasted nuts, olives and lollipops – a picture of individuality matched by a freehouse ale selection that shows off the best of local breweries. Ornate fireplaces, oddment-cluttered shelves and pine tables create an unpretentious backdrop for cider-braised ham, crispy poached egg, pineapple chutney and triple-cooked chips; or succulent beef rump, tongue and cheek with potato purée. Coffee mornings, book clubs and pub quizzes contribute to a community spirit but do nothing to dilute this pub's new-found dining status.

Meals	Bar meals from £10.50.
	Lunch from £6.50.
	Dinner from £12.50.
Closed	Open all day.

Amanda Baker & Chris Lillitou
The Jolly Cricketers,
24 Chalfont Road, Seer Green,
Beaconsfield HP9 2YG
Tel   +44 (0)1494 676308
Web   www.thejollycricketers.co.uk

Entry 50 Map 4

Buckinghamshire

The Swan Inn
Denham

Swap the bland and everyday for the picture-book perfection of Denham village and the stylish Swan. Georgian, double-fronted, swathed in wisteria, the building is now in the capable hands of the Little Gem pub group. It's inviting and charming with rug-strewn boards, chunky tables, cushioned settles, a log fire and a fabulous terrace for outdoor meals. Food is modern British; choose from the 'small plates' list – honey roast ham hock with baby gem and pea salad, soft boiled quail's egg with homemade salad cream. If you've nothing to rush for, enjoy pan-fried pork tenderloin with cider braised savoy cabbage and caramelised nectarine jus, accompanied by a pint of Rebellion IPA or one of 22 wines by the glass. The owners have thought of everything, and the gardens are big enough for the kids to go wild in.

Buckinghamshire

The Three Oaks
Gerrards Cross

At the point where Gerrards Cross gives way to countryside, this well-heeled country pub is an impressive stop on the foodie trail. Upon entering, the bar splits two ways: one towards the library-like drinking area, made for relaxing in by the fire with a pint of Rebellion IPA; the other towards a mishmash of dining tables and benches and stripped back floors... in subtle contrast to the more decorative formal dining room. Everywhere natural taste blends with traditional, including a sensible, seasonal menu. As in the Cripps' other pubs, this bears the stamp of Clive Dixon, the dishes come in generous portions and the set lunch is a steal. A little play has crept into toad-in-the-hole with merguez sausages, but the essentials are spot-on: warm and efficient staff, plentiful free bread, a promising wine list, super coffee.

Meals	Lunch, bar meals & dinner £11.75–£19.50.
Closed	Open all day.

Meals	Lunch & dinner £13.50–£22. Sunday roast £16.
Closed	Open all day.

	The Manager
	The Swan Inn,
	Village Road, Denham,
	Uxbridge UB9 5BH
Tel	+44 (0)1895 832085
Web	www.swaninndenham.co.uk

Entry 51 Map 4

	Henry Cripps
	The Three Oaks,
	Austenwood Lane,
	Gerrards Cross SL9 8NL
Tel	+44 (0)1753 899016
Web	www.thethreeoaksgx.co.uk

Entry 52 Map 4

Buckinghamshire

The White Horse
Hedgerley

In tiny Hedgerley village is a perfectly preserved slice of unspoiled pubbery. Whitewashed brick, horseshoes and cartwheels peer from shrubbery and window baskets, illuminated by ancient gas lamps on both street and façade. Inside, exposed wood is overlaid by carpet, while endless beams and supports for low ceilings are festooned with artefacts. As a serious ale house, seven ever-changing beers are drawn direct from cask and served via a hatch, the selection rotating on a seasonal basis. Food is from a pre deep-fryer age with ploughman's, quiches, cold meats and baps displayed at a chilled counter alongside the odd hot option of chunky lamb broth or maybe pheasant Wellington. A busy garden and marquee are a treat in summer – and house an aviary of finches.

Meals	Lunch £6-£10. Not evenings.
Closed	2.30pm-5pm.
	Open all day Sat & Sun.

Doris Hobbs & Kevin Brooker
The White Horse,
Village Lane, Hedgerley,
Slough SL2 3UY

Tel   +44 (0)1753 643225

Entry 53 Map 4

Buckinghamshire

The Chequers Inn
Wooburn Common

Perched on the rolling Chilterns (conveniently midway between the M4 and M40), this 17th-century coaching inn has been carefully and lovingly nurtured for 35 years by the Roehrig family. The classic bar stands at its heart, with a beamed ceiling, oak timbers, flagstone floor, lived-in sofas, cosy alcoves and a warming winter fire. Here you'll find Marlow Rebellion on tap and dad Peter chatting to the locals. Son Nicholas is now driving the business forward and, having added a smart contemporary restaurant a few years back, plans to spruce up the bar. Good fresh food takes in classic bar dishes (rib-eye steak, venison casserole, top-notch burgers) alongside inventive restaurant-style meals – scallops with pork belly and celeriac purée; lamb with wasabi and herb crust; sweet pistachio cake.

Meals	Set lunch £13.95-£17.95 (Mon-Sat).
	Sunday roast £22.95-£27.95.
	Dinner from £17.50.
Closed	Open all day.

Peter & Nicholas Roehrig
The Chequers Inn,
Kiln Lane, Wooburn Common,
Beaconsfield HP10 0JQ

Tel   +44 (0)1628 529575
Web   www.chequers-inn.com

Entry 54 Map 4

Buckinghamshire

Blackwood Arms
Burnham

This unassuming pub could be in the middle of the woods; indeed, it is near Burnham Beeches. There's a nose bag by the trees for horses, a dismounting block for riders and a dreamy garden bright with doves, pheasants and blackbirds that reaches down to a field of horses. Inside it is cottagey, quirky, full of character: plain boards, dark settles, hops on beams, old horsebrasses, stacked logs, and a basket of rugs for hardy drinkers. English Chancellors have patronised the Blackwood over the years (Profumo too) and 'My Week with Marilyn' was filmed here. Children are welcomed and so are dogs; Sunday lunch is like Crufts. Ales, ciders, gins, wines by the glass, it's all waiting for you along with game from local shoots, tasty seafood grills, juicy burgers, nursery puds and a Moroccan chef; the 'bourek' parcels are gorgeous.

Meals	Starters from £5.25.
	Lunch & dinner from £7.50.
Closed	Mon all day.

2015/16

Sawday's
PUB AWARD

Community pub

Sean Arnett
Blackwood Arms, Common Lane,
Littleworth Common, Burnham,
Slough SL1 8PP

Tel	+44 (0)1753 645672
Web	www.theblackwoodarms.net

Entry 55 Map 4

www.sawdays.co.uk/pubs

Red Lion Inn
Hinxton

In pretty, peaceful Hinxton, close to Cambridge, the rambling Red Lion is a popular stopover in an area deprived of good inns. And its secluded garden, replete with dovecote, arbour and patio, overlooks the church: a lovely spot for peaceful summer sipping. Another draw is the buzzy atmosphere Alex has instilled in the beamed bar with its deep green chesterfields, worn wooden boards, cosy log fire and ticking clock. Ales from City of Cambridge, Adnams and Woodforde's add to the appeal, as do eclectic menus that list a range of classic pub dishes and more inventive specials, all at good prices. Pop in for a beef and horseradish sandwich or linger over venison with blackberry jus or wild mushroom fettuccine; tuck into delicious roast Norfolk chicken on Sunday. Puddings are to die for: sticky toffee pudding with caramel sauce, lemon tart with mango coulis. Named after local beers and ciders, new-build rooms are comfortable and smart with a fresh, contemporary feel – lightwood furniture, wooden floors, crisp cotton on top-quality beds, fully tiled bathrooms. Breakfasts are a serious treat.

Rooms	3 doubles, 5 twin/doubles: £120–£140. Singles £95. Extra bed/sofabed £30 per person per night.
Meals	Lunch & dinner £11–£25. Bar meals £4.50–£10.50. Sunday roast £12.
Closed	Rarely.

Alex Clarke
Red Lion Inn,
32 High Street, Hinxton,
Saffron Walden CB10 1QY
Tel +44 (0)1799 530601
Web www.redlionhinxton.co.uk

Entry 56 Map 9

The Black Bull Inn
Balsham

Buoyed by the success of the Red Lion at Hinxton, Alex snapped up the 16th-century Black Bull in nearby Balsham. Unloved for years, it is back on track as a pretty thatched pub. The beamed and timbered bar is spruced up, a new bar servery has been added, wooden floors gleam and there's a smart mix of old dining tables and leather sofas fronting the glowing log fire; so cosy up with a pint of Rusty Bucket on a winter evening. The ancient, high-raftered and adjoining barn has been restored and refurbished to perfection and is the place to sit and savour some cracking pub food; try the lamb shank with roasted garlic mash and rosemary jus, or the smoked haddock with tarragon foam. In the bar, tuck into roast beef and horseradish sandwiches or a plate of Suffolk ham, plus eggs and hand-cut chips. Comfortable rooms in the annexe, some overlooking the car park, sport oak floors and hand-made furniture, and down duvets on king-size beds. Tiled bathrooms come with bath and shower. A peaceful backwater bolthole, handy for the A11/M11, Cambridge and the Newmarket Races.

Rooms	5 twin/doubles: £115–£135. Singles £90. Extra bed/sofabed £30 per person per night.
Meals	Bar meals from £6. Lunch & dinner from £12. Sunday roast £13.
Closed	Open all day.

Alex Clarke
The Black Bull Inn,
27 High Street, Balsham,
Cambridge CB21 4DJ
Tel   +44 (0)1223 893844
Web   www.blackbull-balsham.co.uk

The Abbot's Elm
Abbot's Ripton

Through force of personality and inspiration in the kitchen, John and Julia Abbey have managed to create a pub that caters for everyone without feeling like a compromise. Enter – passing a display case bearing tribute to John's carrying of the Olympic torch – to be faced with the deliciously tough decision of choosing between stylish pub grub in the bar and French-inspired cuisine in the restaurant. No fewer than 36 wines by the glass, including some made specially for the pub, will help you find something for any occasion: a quick lunch, a fancy evening out. The décor throughout the three-sectioned bar and the restaurant is smart and modern without being showy, while 17th-century character remains in the big beautiful hearth and towering beamed ceiling. The Abbot's Elm pulls a diverse crowd, from villagers to hikers to foodies. And if the brandy snap dessert means you end up wanting to stay, there are three ground-floor bedrooms available. Simple but smart, they have some antique items of furniture but comfort is favoured over grandiosity, and newly-built bathrooms come kitted out with bathrobes and stacks of towels.

Rooms	2 doubles, 1 twin/double: £75–£85.
Meals	Lunch & dinner from £9.50. Not Sunday eve.
Closed	Open all day.

John & Julia Abbey
The Abbot's Elm,
Abbot's Ripton,
Huntingdon PE28 2PA
Tel   +44 (0)1487 773773
Web   www.theabbotselm.co.uk

The Crown Inn
Elton

Conkers, hundreds of them, harden to a deep russet brown in the late summer sun by the front door and under the towering tree, beneath which huddles The Crown – an idyllic setting. The ancient sandstone inn looks across the green of this Wolds village that harbours beautiful Elton Hall. The bar, beamed, and painted in pastel hues, with a huge oak mantel and grate, is the epitome of Old England. Here you may enjoy a pint of Golden Crown and a light meal. In the 'snug', seated by the big log fire on a wintery night, what better than to settle in front of a chicken liver and brandy parfait (with homemade chutney), or a fillet of sea bass and red mullet with prawn and courgette risotto. For traditionalists, there's ale-battered haddock and chips, and beef, ale and mushroom pie. Weekend dining is in the circular conservatory, which opens to a large decked area in summer. As for the bedrooms, they're gorgeous (plantation-style shutters for privacy, king-size beds, great lighting) and come with snazzy en suites.

Rooms	6 doubles (with sofabeds), 2 twin/doubles: £120–£180. Singles from £55. Sofabed for 2, £30 per child.
Meals	Lunch & dinner £5–£25 (not Sunday night or Monday lunch). Restaurant closed first week January.
Closed	Open all day.

	Marcus Lamb
	The Crown Inn,
	8 Duck Street, Elton,
	Peterborough PE8 6RQ
Tel	+44 (0)1832 280232
Web	www.thecrowninn.org

Entry 59 Map 9

Cambridgeshire

The Pheasant
Keyston

This textbook country outpost does beams, open fires and comfy sofas better than anyone, yet never forgets it's a pub; two to three guest ales are on hand pump. John Hoskins bought the Pheasant in 2012 and chef/patron Simon Cadge is at the helm. The menu is English (give or take some gnocchi and tempura), the cooking is restorative, the meat is reared in the village, and if the mushroom man turns up with a colony of flavoursome fungi, then the menu will announce them. Add an enterprising list of wines and expertly kept ales and you have the Pheasant to a T. Try crab and prawn agnolotti, pork cheeks with puy lentils, parsnip purée and glazed brussels, and polenta cake with pineapple and coconut sorbet. If you don't want a full-blown meal, there's bar food instead. And beautiful unpasteurised British cheeses.

Meals	Lunch & dinner from £15.
	Sunday lunch, 3 courses, £25.
Closed	Open all day.

Simon Cadge
The Pheasant,
Village Loop Road, Keyston,
Huntingdon PE28 0RE
Tel   +44 (0)1832 710241
Web   www.thepheasant-keyston.co.uk

Entry 60 Map 9

Cambridgeshire

The Crown Inn
Broughton

There's been a pub-cum-saddler's shop in this little hamlet since medieval times. Villagers saved the Crown back in 2001; now you find one of Cambridgeshire's most-loved gastropubs. Huge terracotta floor slabs, oak beams and a long lightwood bar aimed at drinkers: no fewer than four local ales are on tap here, as well as 15 wines by the glass. Round the side of the chimney breast is a bright open dining room with fresh blooms, a mixture of old and new – all very 21st-century. The food, occasionally inventive but never showy, includes venison steak with parsnip purée, fish and chips with homemade tartare, mushroom and ale pie, and some very tasty Sunday roasts. Children have capacious (and stylish!) lawns to play on in summer, and conkers from huge chestnut trees to plunder.

Meals	Bar meals £6.50-£10.95.
	Lunch £6.50-£15.95.
	Dinner £6.95-£17.50.
	Sunday lunch, 3 courses, £18.45.
Closed	3pm-6pm Mon-Sat.
	Open all day Sun.

Mark Burrell
The Crown Inn,
Bridge Road, Broughton,
Huntingdon PE28 3AY
Tel   +44 (0)1487 824428
Web   www.thecrowninnrestaurant.co.uk

Entry 61 Map 9

Cambridgeshire

Cambridgeshire

The Cock
Hemingford Grey

A cracking country pub. First there's the pretty village that runs down to the river, then the tangle of footpaths and cycle tracks that wait beyond. As for this lovely 17th-century pub, it basks in its original simplicity – a bare-boarded bar, cosy low beams, a much-used log-burner, then four great ales from local breweries. Books and maps, the daily papers and happy staff all wait. For food, move into the airy restaurant where buttermilk walls and modern prints sit beautifully with wooden floors and tables. The menu is full of treats – crayfish cocktail, hake with chorizo, honey-glazed duck, roast plum crème brûlée. The chef makes his own sausages, there's local game in season, a fine cheese board and a much-praised Sunday lunch. Cambridge is close and you can walk across the fields to pretty St Ives.

Three Horseshoes
Madingley

From the outside, the thatched pub is old; push the door and you embrace the new. It is simple, stylish, open, with pale wooden floors and chocolate and cream paintwork; there is lightness and space yet the familiar features remain. The bar has Adnams bitter and a guest ale on tap, a contemporary open fire and a menu that focuses on Italian country dishes and imaginative combinations: chargrilled lamb with cavolo nero and braised beans; roast pork belly with fagioli beans, lemon and spinach; white chocolate, mascarpone and pistachio cheesecake. Relaxed but excellent service matches the atmosphere of the busy bar while formality and white linen come together in the conservatory dining room, popular with business lunchers. In both rooms the choice of wines is superb – pity the designated driver!

Meals	Lunch from £5.50. Dinner from 11.50. Sunday roast from £14.50.		Meals	Bar meals from £4. Lunch & dinner £12–£25. Sunday lunch, 3 courses, £26.
Closed	3pm-6pm (4pm-6.30pm Sun).		Closed	3pm-6pm. Open all day Sat & Sun in summer.

	Oliver Thain		Richard Stokes
	The Cock, 47 High St, Hemingford Grey, Huntingdon PE28 9BJ		Three Horseshoes, High Street, Madingley, Cambridge CB23 8AB
Tel	+44 (0)1480 463609	Tel	+44 (0)1954 210221
Web	www.cambscuisine.com/ the-cock-hemingford	Web	www.threehorseshoesmadingley.co.uk

Entry 62 Map 9

Entry 63 Map 9

Cambridgeshire

The Willow Tree
Bourn

Why use tea lights when you can stick candelabra on the table? Or light bulbs when you can hang four chandeliers above the bar? The Willow Tree mixes quirky design with heavenly food, a popular combination that has given the place a buzz. Expect a little metaphorical wrangling with the menu – you're going to want everything on it. From the bar order cocktails, mocktails, hot toddies, pints of Pegasus or a bottle of delicious French wine. As for the food, there's tapas (calamari, garlic prawns), sharing platters (venison and thyme meatballs), comfort food (fish pie, sausage and mash), pizzas, hot ciabattas, goat's cheese cake with beetroot crisps, venison stew with spiced red cabbage, mulled pear and fig tart with strawberry mascarpone. There are deckchairs under a willow tree in the garden and a take-out service for lucky locals. One of the best.

Meals	Lunch from £6.50.
	Dinner from £9.50.
Closed	Open all day.

Craig & Shaina Galvin-Scott
The Willow Tree,
29 High Street,
Bourn CB23 2SQ
Tel   +44 (0)1954 719775
Web   www.thewillowtreebourn.com

Entry 64 Map 9

Cambridgeshire

The Queen's Head
Newton

David and Juliet have run this legendary pub for nearly half a century and are joined by son Robert. There's a timeless appeal in the main bar where clattering floorboards, plain wooden tables and aged paintings are watched over by a vintage clock that keeps the beat; a tiny carpeted lounge with dark beams and well-worn furniture is a cosier alternative when the fire blazes. The whole interior is unusual and unspoilt, the perfect backdrop for shove ha'penny, cribbage and beef dripping on toast. Yes, the food is simple, but deliciously so: rare roast beef sliced wafer-thin, ripe stilton sandwiches, ham on the bone, a mug of rich brown soup – dispensed with slow deliberation and accompanied by Adnams ales straight from the barrel. A pub with a loyal following.

| Meals | Bar meals £3.50-£6. |
| Closed | 2.30pm-6pm (7pm Sun). |

David, Juliet & Robert Short
The Queen's Head,
Fowlmere Road,
Newton,
Cambridge CB22 7PG
Tel   +44 (0)1223 870436

Entry 65 Map 9

Cambridgeshire

The Tickell Arms
Whittlesford

Named after the original owner, a local Cambridge squire, this striking blue and white Gothic villa has long been cherished, for its flamboyant eccentricity and its garden. In 2012 Cambscuisine restored its pub status. Expect a smart rustic feel and a big dose of Gothic character in elegant fireplaces, gilt mirrors and French-arched doors. There are old dining tables and chapel chairs on wooden floors, cool-blue hues, bowler hat lampshades above a snug bar. A conservatory dining room and a flower-fringed terrace overlook the lily pond – perfect spots for summer lunch. Modern seasonal menus champion local suppliers, so enjoy potted ham hock, devilled rabbit leg with tarragon sauce, and mulled poached pears, all washed down with local Milton ales or a carafe of wine from a Languedocian list.

Meals	Bar meals from £5.
	Lunch, 2 courses, £14.
	Dinner main course from £11.50.
Closed	Open all day.

Oliver Thain
The Tickell Arms, North Road,
Whittlesford, Cambridge CB22 4NZ

Tel	+44 (0)1223 833025
Web	www.cambscuisine.com/
	the-tickell-whittlesford

Entry 66 Map 9

Cambridgeshire

The Punter
Cambridge

This is a pub that seems to wink conviviality. Maybe it's the suntrap courtyard at one side, with its flotsam of flowery crockery and pot plants, or the candles glowing in every window, enhancing the feeling that you are stepping back to an earlier age. Inside you'll find comely sofas, sturdy school chairs and and an artful jostle of kitschy paintings, with a matching mishmash of punters too – post-grads, dog lovers, creative types and determined townies who'll make the journey from across the river for their favourite dish at their favourite table. The regularly changing menu is a concise affair, blending quality pub staples with more eye-catching offerings: smoked eel with roast squash; venison sausages and mash; sea bass with hazelnut crumble; cod loin with bulgar wheat. Best to book.

Meals	Lunch from £5.
	Dinner £12.50-£16.
	Weekdays only.
Closed	Open all day.

Sarah Lee
The Punter,
3 Pound Hill,
Cambridge CB3 0AE

Tel	+44 (0)1223 363322
Web	www.thepuntercambridge.com

Entry 67 Map 9

Cambridgeshire

The Rupert Brooke
Grantchester

Hire a punt, or follow in the footsteps of Rupert Brooke and take the 'Grantchester Grind', that much-loved, meandering riverside path. However you choose to get to Grantchester, you'll find a "corner… that is forever England". And, at the end of the high street, a revitalized dining pub with sparkling sash windows. The interiors have been tastefully done: stylish pendants here, vintage armchairs there, photos of Brooke as a boy. There's a big lofty light-filled dining space with mushroom banquettes and an open-to-view kitchen, an elegant bar for pre-dinner drinks, a softly lit snug, and in summer you spill onto the terraces. Enjoy guest beers, ever-changing wines and seasonal menus that will tempt you: wild mushroom and truffle macaroni, baked camembert with honey, Red Poll steaks and burgers, a seafood curry, a pretty Kir Royale panna cotta.

Meals	Dinner & Sunday roast from £14.
Closed	Open all day.
	Kitchen closed Sun.

Paul Wicker
The Rupert Brooke,
2 Broadway, Grantchester,
Cambridge CB3 9NQ
Tel   +44 (0)1638 751818
Web   www.therupertbrooke.com

Entry 68 Map

Cambridgeshire

Hole in the Wall
Little Wilbraham

Hiding down a hundred lanes, this pretty village pub is in the inspired hands of Alex Rushmer, Masterchef winner 2010. It's clearly well-loved. Regulars drop by for a swift half in the big timbered bar – find horse brasses and country prints, junk-shop tables and log fires – or gather for lunch in the country room at the back. In contrast to all this old-fashioned rusticity the food is decidedly modern: ingredients as local and organic as can be and chalkboard specials changing regularly. Alex's cooking is inventive: seared scallops with Ibérico ham, cauliflower purée and apple jelly; Telmare Farm duck with potato and spring onion terrine and a spiced caramel sauce; hake with chorizo hash and Romesco sauce; Sunday roast rib with all the trimmings. On summery days, the front garden is glorious.

Meals	Lunch & dinner £10.50-£17.50.
Closed	3pm-6.30pm.
	Sun evenings & Mon.

Alex Rushmer & Ben Maude
Hole in the Wall,
Primrose Farm Road, Little
Wilbraham, Cambridge CB21 5JY
Tel   +44 (0)1223 812282
Web   www.holeinthewallcambridge.com

Entry 69 Map 9

Cambridgeshire

The Carpenters Arms
Great Wilbraham

A small, traditional, country pub where they brew their own beer and serve fabulous food, most of it French. Richard and Heather had an award-winning restaurant in France for six years, teaching the French a thing or two about food. Inside, the bar is authentic and characterful – low ceilings, bar billiards, padded pews, armchairs in front of the wood-burner. It's delightfully refreshing, a proper country local untouched by interior designers! Pick up a pint of Sauvignon Blond or Mild Manners, then fail to resist the menu. You might find Coquilles St Jacques with a Provençal sauce, slow-roasted pork with apple and sage, chocolate amaretto truffle mousse. On Sundays, in season, the roast pheasant comes with parsnips and chestnuts, magical stuff; there are good French wines to wash it down. Walks start from the front door with Cambridge waiting across the fields. Brilliant.

Meals	Dinner from £15.50.
Closed	Tues.
	Sun 3pm-12am.

Richard Hurley
The Carpenters Arms,
10 High Street,
Great Wilbraham CB21 5JD
Tel   +44 (0)1223 882093
Web   www.carpentersarmsgastropub.co.uk

Entry 70 Map

Cambridgeshire

Dyke's End
Reach

In a community hamlet in Fen country is a "splendid" pub (to quote the Prince of Wales), rescued from closure by the locals in 1997. Now privately owned, this former 17th-century farmhouse is a lovely old place, with log fires, scrubbed pine tables and a relaxing vibe in the snug, candlelit bar. George prides himself on serving beers from small regional breweries, and the pub even has a microbrewery at the back. After you've settled in for a pint, try one of the seasonal specialities from the oft-changing lunch and dinner menus. There's always fresh fish, as well as ever popular pub favourites such as local sausages and mash with onion gravy or beer-battered haddock and chips, and chef's daily specials. Finish with sticky toffee pudding with butterscotch sauce or crème caramel. There's al fresco dining on the lawn overlooking the village green, and memorable Sunday roasts – do book!

Meals	Lunch from £6.95.
	Dinner from £11.95.
	Sunday lunch, 3 courses, £21.95.
	No food Monday.
Closed	2pm-6pm & Mon lunch.
	Open all day Sat & Sun.

Catherine & George Gibson
Dyke's End,
8 Fair Green, Reach,
Cambridge CB25 0JD
Tel   +44 (0)1638 743816
Web   www.dykesend.co.uk

Entry 71 Map 9

Albion Inn
Chester

Welcome to Chester's last unspoilt Victorian corner pub, where many a young man would have spent his King's shilling after signing up for King and Country in the nearby Drill Hall. The Albion is all about the commemoration of The Great War 1914-1918, and with the Centenary this year, the pub is set to do its bit. To a background of William Morris wallpaper, soft lamps and a 1928 Steck Player piano that occasionally entertains, are four cask ales, a flurry of malts, decent wines and 'Trench Rations' in un-trench-like portions – lamb's liver with bacon and onions in cider gravy, perhaps, or monkfish, prawn and chorizo casserole. Yummy Staffordshire oatcakes from Tunstall with all sorts of fillings are a house special; desserts include spiced apple sponge and custard. Do stay; the bedrooms at the top (with a separate entrance) are compact, cosy and en suite, with good antique furniture and super-comfortable beds. You are welcome to bring the dogs (sausages available) but not the children. Michael, the landlord of this traditional city pub with an individual streak, has been at the helm for more than 40 years.

Rooms	1 double, 1 twin: £85. Singles £70.
Meals	Lunch & dinner £6.20–£10.70. Not Sunday eve.
Closed	3 days at Christmas, New Year's Eve and New Year's Day.

Michael Mercer
Albion Inn,
Park Street,
Chester CH1 1RN
Tel   +44 (0)1244 340345
Web   www.albioninnchester.co.uk

The Pheasant Inn
Higher Burwardsley

Pheasants scatter across the fields and the views, on a clear day, stretch to Liverpool. Gloriously positioned on a former farm in the Peckforton Hills, the Pheasant has been stylishly revamped. The old laid-back feel has survived the smartening up of dark beams in bustling bars where pots of jasmine scent the air and Weetwood Old Dog comes from the cask; for sheer cosiness, book a table by a fire (there are three). The food is more refined than your average pub grub, and is informally and delightfully served. Our lamb rump with broad beans, radish and apricots was full of flavour, our salmon with pancetta came with a creamy chive butter, and the sticky toffee pudding was pleasingly light. Deli boards and all-day hot beef sandwiches are also on the cards: just the job after hiking the Sandstone Trail. The staff are the best and if you are arranging to stay the night the 12 bedrooms, some traditional (soft carpeting, sumptuous drapes, dark oak furniture), some contemporary (wide oak boards, exposed stone walls, atmospheric lighting) are split between the inn, the stone barn and the 'stables'; go for one with a view.

Rooms	8 twin/doubles: £95–£124.
	3 suites for 2: £105–£140.
	1 family room for 4: £135–£170.
	Singles from £85.
Meals	Bar meals £3.95–£8.50.
	Lunch & dinner £6.75–£19.95.
	Sunday roast £12.50.
Closed	Open all day.

Andrew Nelson
The Pheasant Inn,
Higher Burwardsley, Tattenhall,
Chester CH3 9PF

Tel	+44 (0)1829 770434
Web	www.thepheasantinn.co.uk

The Cholmondeley Arms
Cholmondeley

As prim and proper as a Victorian schoolmistress on the outside, as stylish as Beau Brummell within: the sandblasted brick walls of this old school house rise to raftered, vaulted ceilings and large windows pull natural light into every corner. Shelves of gin hover above fat radiators, cartoons and photos nestle amongst old sporting paraphernalia, and oriental rugs sprawl beneath an auction lot of tables, pews and chairs. The glorious carved oak bar dominates the main hall and apart from the malted charms of Cholmondeley Best Bitter and Merlin's Gold there are a staggering 200 varieties of ruinously good gin to discover, with the aid of a well-thumbed guide or one of the many charming staff. And when the dinner bell goes study the menus on antique blackboards and opt for devilled lambs kidneys on toast, followed by baked cod with brown shrimps and lemon butter, or a spicy sausage and butternut squash hash cake. Rooms in the old headmaster's house behind are calm and civilised with all the comfort you need. Seldom has going back to school been this much fun.

Rooms	5 doubles, 1 twin: £60–£100.
Meals	Lunch & dinner £7.25–£17.95. Not Christmas Day.
Closed	Open all day.

Jess Turner
The Cholmondeley Arms,
Wrenbury Road, Cholmondeley,
Malpas SY14 8HN
Tel   +44 (0)1829 720300
Web   www.cholmondeleyarms.co.uk

Entry 74 Map 7

The Bear's Paw
Warmingham

Tucked into a pretty village is a dazzlingly refurbished 19th-century inn. There's an almost baronial feel to the Bear's Paw, thanks to the polished oak panelling, the huge fireplaces, the sweeping floors, the leather bucket chairs, bookshelves and old prints and vintage photos. No stuffiness here, just cheery staff making sure you are well-watered and well-fed. Six cask ales, several from Weetwood, all local, take centre stage on the bar; there are also premium brand spirits, 12 malts and an excellent wine list. At well-spaced wooden tables are menus that blend classics with modern twists. Try game and root vegetable pie served with hand-cut chips and pickled red cabbage; vegetarian lasagne with wild mushrooms, spinach and toasted pine nuts; posh poached egg with truffle sabayon. There are deli boards and fabulous sandwiches too. Staying the night? You have 17 superb bedrooms to choose from, each boutiquey, each flaunting funky fabrics, contemporary wallpapers, media hubs and designer fittings. Bathrooms are sleek with granite tops, rain showers, and the softest towels and robes.

Rooms	10 doubles, 7 twin/doubles: £80–£170.
Meals	Lunch & dinner £5.95–£19.95.
Closed	Open all day.

Andrew Nelson
The Bear's Paw,
School Lane, Warmingham,
Sandbach CW11 3QN
Tel   +44 (0)1270 526317
Web   www.thebearspaw.co.uk

Entry 75 Map 8

Cheshire

The White Lion
Barthomley

An inn since 1614 and a siege site in the Civil War, the character-steeped White Lion – wonky black and white timbers, thick thatched roof – stands beside a cobbled track close to a sandstone church. Step in to find three gloriously unspoilt rooms, all woodsmoke and charm, wizened oak beams, ancient benches and twisted walls, tiny latticed windows and quarry-tiled floors. No music or electronic wizardry here, just the crackling of log fires and a happy hubbub. Lunchtime food is listed on chalkboards as walkers and locals settle on ancient settles at scrubbed tables for hot beef and onion baguettes with chips, hearty ploughman's and Sunday roasts, all washed down with well-kept pints of Marstons and Jennings real ale. Summer seating is at picnic benches on the cobbles, with pretty views onto the village.

Meals	Lunch & dinner £4.75–£7.95.
Closed	Open all day.

Laura Condliffe
The White Lion,
Barthomley,
Crewe CW2 5PG
Tel   +44 (0)1270 882242
Web   www.whitelionbarthomley.com

Entry 76 Map 8

Cheshire

The Black Swan
Lower Withington

Think country cottage cum café cum pub and you are on the right track – sort of! Sip a pint of Mucky Duck on the tartan sofa as the bull's head gazes out from the large brick fireplace; elsewhere, upbeat wallpaper jostles with floral and patchwork fabrics and cosy nooks abound; there are two private rooms upstairs too. All is bright, uplifting and immensely friendly. Menus focus on the best of classic pub food with some lighter twists: the lamb hot pot with pickles, red cabbage and rustic bread was delicious and the mulled plum crème brûlée a perfect ending. The three-in-one pies are popular and the homemade soups fly. Outside is a pretty garden area with a wood-fired pizza oven lit on warmer days. Play boules, walks in the tranquil countryside. Very special.

Meals	Bar meals from £9.95.
	Lunch from £5.95.
	Dinner from £12.95.
	Sunday lunch, 2-3 courses, £20–£27.
Closed	Open all day.

Sarah Gibbs
The Black Swan,
Trap Street,
Lower Withington SK11 9EQ
Tel   +44 (0)1477 571770
Web   www.blackswancheshire.com

Entry 77 Map 8

Cheshire

Harrington Arms
Gawsworth

This red-brick building started life as a farmhouse in 1663 and could still be part of a working farm. The outside may have grown but the inside has barely changed – and it wasn't long ago that they were serving beer just from the cask. Off the passageway are a bar and a quarry-tiled snug – big enough for a settle, a table and an open fire. Then three more public rooms: the traditionally furnished Top Parlour, the Garden Room (with a magnificent baking range) and the Tap Room where Friday's folk club takes place. The Wightmans have changed little and that includes the quality of the ale: it's said you won't get a finer pint of Robinson's than at the Harrington. Home-cooked meals are locally sourced and range from soup to sirloin steak; look out for the homemade pies on the specials board!

Meals	Bar meals £3.95–£11.25. Sunday roast £8.25.
Closed	3pm–5pm, Mon–Fri.

Andy & Caroline Wightman
Harrington Arms, Church Lane,
Gawsworth, Macclesfield SK11 9RJ
Tel   +44 (0)1260 223325
Web   www.harringtonarmsgawsworth.
robinsonsbrewery.com

Entry 78 Map 8

Cheshire

The Lord Clyde
Kerridge

Surrounded by fields, a short drive from the former silk town of Macclesfield, a young Cheshire gem. Vanilla walls, a gleaming bar and a spotless dining room with a log fire make a modest setting for food that is exciting, challenging and delicious. On the autumn menu we found celeriac and chicory with buttermilk and prune; rabbit with parsnip, wild mushrooms and pressed potato; 35-day aged rib-eye with fat chips and peppercorn sauce; bitter chocolate and quince with custard and crisp mousse. Owner-chef Ernst has a pedigree, and that includes Noma in Copenhagen. So push the boat out and sample the nine-course tasting menu – allow a glorious three hours. The bar is still a drinkers' domain (always Speckled Hen), wife Sarah runs a happy team, and if you fancy a sandwich, order one: the sourdough bread is out of this world.

Meals	Lunch £7.95–£20.95.
Closed	Please check before you visit.

Sarah Richmond & Ernst Van Zyl
The Lord Clyde,
36 Clarke Lane, Kerridge,
Bollington SK10 5AH
Tel   +44 (0)1625 562123
Web   www.thelordclyde.co.uk

Entry 79 Map 8

Cheshire

The Wizard
Nether Alderley

The old coaching inn is backed by magnificent leafy National Trust woodland – and there's a wizard's well out there with a legend to match. You're a world away from bustling Alderley Edge and this large rambling pub has many good things to offer: stone floors with Indian rugs, scrubbed wooden tables, an eclectic mix of prints, paintings and photos, great fare. It's a cosy and intimate place run by a bright and cheery staff. Ales come in the form of Thwaite's Original or an award-winning Storm Brewing Company's beer (Silk of Amnesia and Looks Like Rain Dear being just two); all are magic in a glass. Foodies won't be unhappy either; we found the duo of beef with steamed Galloway mini suet pudding and a roast barrel-rump with beetroot purée a big treat. There's also a pretty sheltered patio for warm days. The Sunday roast is always popular so make sure you book!

Meals	Lunch & dinner £7–£13.95.
Closed	3pm–5.30pm.
	Open all day Sat & Sun.

Martin Ainscough
The Wizard,
Macclesfield Road, Nether Alderley,
Macclesfield SK10 4UB
Tel   +44 (0)1625 584000
Web www.ainscoughs.co.uk

Entry 80 Map 8

Cheshire

The Bull's Head
Mobberley

You feel the warmth as soon as you walk through the door. Candles glow on the tables of this pretty village pub, fires crackle, and the staff couldn't be nicer. Under a low-beamed ceiling, seven hand pumps dispense the finest local ales from Storm, Wincle and Redwillow as well as the inimitable Mobberley Wobbly – ale is king! Add in a Highland extravaganza of over 80 whiskies and other tempting brews and you have the makings of a celebration. Chef Steve cooks 'pub classics from the heart' with full English flavours; the steak and ale pie is a fully encased masterpiece in itself, and the Irish whisky sticky toffee pudding too indulgent for words. With outside tables for sunny days, this is as good as it gets for a village pub.

Meals	Bar meals £2.85–£12.
	Lunch £3.95–£19.95.
	Sunday roast £13.95.
Closed	Open all day.

Barry Lawlor
The Bull's Head,
Mill Lane, Mobberley,
Knutsford WA16 7HX
Tel   +44 (0)1829 720300
Web www.thebullsheadpub.co.uk

Entry 81 Map 8

The Church Inn
Mobberley

Tim Bird and Mary McLaughlin's mini-pub empire continues to thrive and grow with the addition of this 18th-century Church Inn. Sister pub to the Bull's Head, also in Mobberley, it has been fully restored and refurbished, retaining the small intimate dining rooms with their wood and tiled floors, exposed brick and beams, soft lamplight, and glowing candles. On a wild winter's day it's hard to leave, with four craft ales on tap and decent wines to quaff and some great food: sautéed lamb's kidneys followed by grilled hake with tarragon and white wine sauce, then a sticky date bread and butter pud. Or try lighter lunch/afternoon dishes like smoked haddock tart or a sirloin steak sandwich with roast tomatoes and chips. Summer terraces give views of the church or across rolling fields. A village gem.

The Three Greyhounds Inn
Allostock

The bright, many-bottled bar winks and glows as you enter, while host James has a welcome for all. Fat purple cushions soften wooden benches around a huge dual-facing fireplace; reach for the 'Brandy Bible' and settle in. The clever layout makes the space cosy and intimate, with snugs around every corner — four with firesides — and nooks and crannies aplenty. James is proud of the atmosphere, and rightly so. Families nibble and natter with relish, while walkers and couples take their time over delicious smoked haddock and leek tart or pan-fried lamb's kidneys. During annual Cheshire Game Week you can tuck into dishes such as pheasant breast with sautéed white pudding and red leg partridge croquette... Deep in the Cheshire countryside, this well-restored pub is conveniently close to the M6.

Meals	Light lunch from £6.50. Lunch & dinner from £11.95. Sunday lunch £14.50.
Closed	Open all day.

Meals	Bar meals from £5.95. Lunch & dinner from £10.50. Not 25 Dec.
Closed	Open all day.

Simon Umpleby
The Church Inn,
Church Lane, Mobberley,
Knutsford WA16 7RD
Tel   +44 (0)1565 873178
Web   www.churchinnmobberley.co.uk

Entry 82 Map 8

James Griffiths
The Three Greyhounds Inn,
Holmes Chapel Road, Allostock,
Knutsford WA16 9JY
Tel   +44 (0)1565 723455
Web   www.thethreegreyhoundsinn.co.uk

Entry 83 Map 8

Cheshire

The Duke of Portland
Lach Dennis

A recent refurbishment has created something of a style journey at the Duke. Wander between a 1920s Parisian bistro, an arty club lounge – worn leather sofas, a futuristic stone fire – and Victorian formality... before pulling up in front of a glorious carved oak bar to order a pint of Jenning's Cocker Hoop or Ringwood Best. Menus are hearty and inventive and the provenance is impeccable. Start with naturally smoked mackerel pâté flavoured with whisky, parsley and double cream before moving on to Glyn Arthur lamb, its gravy infused with tomato, basil and slow roasted garlic, its accompaniment Cheshire potatoes and spring greens. A solid wine list complements it all and there's freshly ground Illy coffee. Under the lofty dining roof is a village pub with a great sense of style and hospitality.

Meals	Lunch & dinner £9.95-£18.95.
Closed	3pm-5pm Mon-Wed.

Mike Massey
The Duke of Portland,
Penny's Lane, Lach Dennis,
Northwich CW9 7SY
Tel   +44 (0)1606 46264
Web www.dukeofportland.com

Entry 84 Map 8

Cheshire

Bhurtpore Inn
Aston

The extended Cheshire-brick village farmhouse trumpets real ales, countless bottled continental beers, one hundred malts and farmhouse ciders and perry. Whatever you choose, you can soak it up with something excellent from an ever-changing menu. The pub was named after an Indian city besieged by a local army commander: maps, paintings and ephemera spread through the warren of rooms vividly recall this deed. Low beams bow beneath water jugs and open fires crackle in the cosy lounge, where a haphazard mix of furniture and settles, a longcase clock and local bric-a-brac add tremendous character. The home-cooked food is tasty, with local produce at the fore, the portions are generous, the choice is vast, and there are curries galore! A little corker.

Meals	Lunch & bar meals from £5.50. Dinner from £8.50. Sunday lunch, 3 courses, £18. Not Friday 2pm-6.30pm.
Closed	2.30pm-6.30pm. Open all day Fri-Sun.

Simon & Nicky George
Bhurtpore Inn,
Wrenbury Road, Aston,
Nantwich CW5 8DQ
Tel   +44 (0)1270 780917
Web www.bhurtpore.co.uk

Entry 85 Map 7

Cheshire

The Fox & Barrel
Cotebrook

Legend has it that a kind former landlord allowed a pursued fox to escape to the cellar – hence the name. This busy roadside pub buzzes with drinkers and diners in equal measure, as life centres on a large bar ringed by terracotta tiles; beyond, acres of oak boards are dotted with Indian rugs. The brick fire is stacked with logs, pictures and prints fill the walls and there are plenty of snug corners in which to try a Deuchars IPA or a Weetwood cask ale. Convivial Gary chooses a mean wine list with monthly favourites on the board. Generous, crowd-pleasing menus include a fish pie of smoked haddock, salmon and prawns, and Cumberland sausage with bubble and squeak mash and onion gravy; there are hearty sandwiches too. There's a smart new York stone terrace at the front, and pub benches on lawns with pleasant rural views.

Meals	Lunch & dinner £7.95–£16.95.
	Sunday roast from £12.95.
Closed	Open all day.

Gary Kidd & Richard Cotterill
The Fox & Barrel,
Forest Road, Cotebrook,
Tarporley CW6 9DZ

| Tel | +44 (0)1829 760529 |
| Web | www.thefoxandbarrel.com |

Entry 86 Map 7

Cheshire

The Dysart Arms
Bunbury

One of those rare places – all things to all people. And, with separate spaces clustered around a central bar, it feels open and cosy at the same time. The 18th-century building has a listed interior of scrubbed floorboards, solid tables and chairs, pictures, plants, and French windows opening to terrace and garden. There's an inglenook packed with logs, a dining area in a library, and superb beers and wines. They're proud of their food too, rightly so: pan-fried pheasant wrapped in bacon, crab cakes with shredded mouli and chilli jam, roasted aubergine, goat's cheese and red pepper lasagne, toasted bara brith with caramelised bananas and cinnamon ice cream. The cheeses are taken as seriously as the cask ales (try the local Weetwood or Purple Moose) and the wines are thoughtfully chosen. Warm, intimate, friendly, and running on well-oiled wheels.

Meals	Bar meals £4.50–£10.25.
	Lunch from £4.50.
	Dinner £7.95–£16.95.
Closed	Open all day.

Kate John
The Dysart Arms,
Bowes Gate Road, Bunbury,
Tarporley CW6 9PH

| Tel | +44 (0)1829 260183 |
| Web | www.dysartarms-bunbury.co.uk |

Entry 87 Map 7

Cheshire

The Fishpool Inn
Delamere

A vast renovation, a huge investment, the doors have opened and the results are impressive: this is a thriving gastropub that delivers consistently good food to 3,000 diners a week. The cosy, traditional feel of the original front rooms has been recreated using natural or reclaimed materials (oak beams, Victorian tiles, original sandstone), and the dining room extension has been gorgeously crafted and designed. The attention to detail throughout is extraordinary. It's still very much a pub; expect up to eight local ales on tap and a mix of pub classics and modern British dishes on the menu, which is eclectic, with homemade pizzas and pies, oxtail suet puddings, and platefuls of hot haddock and chips delivered from the open (and very organised) kitchen. Posh loos, afternoon teas, and a super terrace overlooking the fields complete the civilised picture.

Meals	Light lunch from £5.95.
	Mains £9.95–£22.95.
Closed	Open all day.

Andrew & Lucy Nelson
The Fishpool Inn,
Fishpool Road, Delamere,
Chester CW8 2HP
Tel   +44 (0)1606 883277
Web   www.thefishpoolinn.co.uk

♿ ☂ ⚑ ☕ ▯ 🔊

Entry 88 Map 7

Cheshire

The Yew Tree
Spurstow

Enthusiastic owners Jon and Lindsay have identified a need for their talents in this pretty corner of Cheshire. Step in to find a fresh interior with an eclectic mix of old and new and several quirky touches – including a wall and ceiling papered in tartan and dedicated to the Queen. There are several areas for eating and drinking including handsome snugs, and the children's menu is typical of the level of care: not just sausages and mash but roasted vegetable pasta too – and Eton mess for pud. Very well-kept ales (Merlin's Gold, Stone House Station Bitter) and ten wines by the glass accompany some skilled cooking – the smoked haddock and salmon pie was spot on, and the sourcing is impeccable. There's a private paddock for marquee events and an annual Easter Beer Festival.

Meals	Lunch & bar meals from £5.95.
	Dinner from £9.50.
	Not Christmas Day.
Closed	Open all day.

Jon & Lindsay Cox
The Yew Tree,
Long Lane, Spurstow,
Bunbury CW6 9RD
Tel   +44 (0)1829 260274
Web   www.theyewtreebunbury.com

♿ ☂ ⚑ ☕ ▯ 🔊

Entry 89 Map 7

Cheshire

The Grosvenor Arms
Aldford

Pretty Aldford — all cottages and farms with barleysugar-twist chimneys and chequerboard brickwork. Not far from the old church and castle is an imposing Victorian brick and timber local rejuvenated by Brunning & Price; this is their flagship pub. Find something for everyone in this relaxing and classy pastiche: a traditional taproom and snug with a log fire, a tiled floor, dozing dogs and a old photo of the village stocks; an imposing part-panelled Library Room; a verdant conservatory. There are rustic kitchen tables on tiles and rugs, mismatched chairs, heaps of books and a dark-wood bar with hand pumps for local ale. The menu carries something for everyone, from game pie to Thai red seafood curry. In summer, you eat on huge tree-shaded lawns by the cricket pitch. Lovely!

Meals	Lunch & dinner £7.95–£22.50.
Closed	Open all day.

Tracey Owen
The Grosvenor Arms,
Chester Road, Aldford,
Chester CH3 6HJ
Tel   +44 (0)1244 620228
Web   www.grosvenorarms-aldford.co.uk

Entry 90 Map 7

Cheshire

The Architect
Chester

Built in classical villa style by architect Thomas Harrison in 1820, this imposing building boasts a massive paved terrace with prime viewing for the racecourse across the road. Inside, there's enough alcohol to float a battleship, with ales from Titanic, Weetwood and Wincle, interesting wines, champagne for the winners and a wide range of top-end, and unusual spirits. From the kitchen, under the eagle eye of Timothy Watts, flows modern British food with global influences, and several true pub classics. Try seared cured pigeon breast with sweet and sour cranberries and Jerusalem artichokes, or Vietnamese king prawn and rice noodle salad with a mint, coriander, chilli and lime dressing. There are sandwiches, charcuterie, cheeses, Cheshire ice cream and superb coffee and liqueurs.

Meals	Starters £4.95–£9.95. Charcuterie platter £17.95. Main from £10.95.
Closed	Open all day.

Jonathon Astle-Rowe
The Architect,
54 Nicholas Street,
Chester CH1 2NX
Tel   +44 (0)1244 353070
Web   www.architect-chester.co.uk

Entry 91 Map 7

The Old Coastguard
Mousehole

The Old Coastguard hugs the coast and gazes east towards St Michael's Mount and the Lizard peninsula. The lush palm-filled garden has lawns that run down to the harbour wall and just offshore lies St Clement's Isle, former home to an ancient hermit. But things are far from spartan here now and Charles and Edmund are bringing their unique style and experience to this large Victorian building. Views flood in to bar and restaurant via floor to ceiling glass windows and there's an effortless informality to the airy interiors. You can expect food of the highest and freshest calibre: scallops with courgette and basil butter, chorizo and almond crusted hake, or white bean and garlic stew, then pistachio cake with crème fraîche sorbet and fennel. A well-chosen wine list, plus local ales, ciders and much more. Upstairs are fifteen uncluttered, light and stylish bedrooms of great variety and all with views of sea or Mousehole and its boat-filled harbour: many have balconies for that first al fresco sortie in the morning to watch the sunrise. The Penwith peninsular beckons so head west for the Minack theatre, then north to Zennor and St Ives. Wonderful.

Rooms	10 doubles, 3 twin/doubles: £130–£220. 1 suite for 2: £185–£235. 1 family room for 4: £170–£200. Dinner, B&B £90 per person per night.
Meals	Lunch from £6. Dinner, 3 courses, from £30. Sunday roast from £12.50. Vegetarian options available.
Closed	One week in early January.

Charles & Edmund Inkin
The Old Coastguard,
The Parade, Mousehole,
Penzance TR19 6PR

Tel   +44 (0)1736 731222
Web   www.oldcoastguardhotel.co.uk

Cornwall

The Coldstreamer
Gulval

The Coldstreamer dates from 1895 and stands in the middle of the village opposite the church. It has one foot in the country and one foot in town – Penzance is a short drive or a good walk. There's a terrace at the front where you can catch the morning sun, a wood-burner in the bar for winter nights. Inside, the colour is red in honour of the Coldstream guards. You can order a pint of Betty Stoggs at the bar, grab the daily papers, browse a fine collection of Penzance photographs, try your hand at bagatelle. Excellent food – as important as the beer – waits in the snug restaurant (low ceilings, smart colours, exposed stone walls). Meat is from Cornwall, fish landed at Newlyn, vegetables from a local farm shop, so dig into cauliflower soup with truffle oil, seared venison with juniper, fish stew with saffron mash, tarte tatin with bay leaf ice cream. Rooms above have a warm feel – smart carpets, crisp linen, comfy beds, excellent bathrooms – and the English breakfast is superb. St Michael's Mount, St Ives, The Lizard and the coast all wait; the heliport for the Scillies is tantalisingly close.

Rooms	2 doubles, 1 twin/double: £70-£85. Dinner, B&B £50-£60 per person per night.
Meals	Lunch from £8. Dinner from £11. Sunday lunch, 3 courses, £17.
Closed	25-26 December.

Richard Tubb
The Coldstreamer,
Gulval, Penzance TR18 3BB

Tel   +44 (0)1736 362072
Web   www.coldstreamer-penzance.co.uk

The Gurnard's Head
Zennor

The coastline is magical and the hike to St Ives hard to beat. Secret beaches appear at low tide, cliffs tumble down to the water and wild flowers streak the land pink in summer. As for the pub, you couldn't hope for a better base. It's earthy, warm, stylish and friendly, with airy interiors, colourwashed walls, stripped wooden floors and log fires at both ends of the bar. Maps and local art hang on the walls, books fill every shelf; if you can't finish one, take it home and post it back. Rooms are warm and cosy, simple and spotless, with superb mattresses, throws over armchairs, Roberts radios and, in the suite, a lovely big tub. Downstairs, super food, all homemade, can be eaten wherever you want: in the bar, in the restaurant or out in the garden in good weather. Snack on rustic delights – confit duck, grilled figs – or tuck into more substantial treats: white crab salad, pear and avocado; cod with orange endive, cauliflower purée and curried apricot, chased by dark chocolate tart or popcorn ice cream. Picnics are easily arranged, there's bluegrass folk music in the bar most Mondays, and the St Ives-Penzance bus runs right outside – a huge plus.

Rooms	3 doubles, 4 twin/doubles: £110-£175. Dinner, B&B £80 per person per night.
Meals	Lunch from £12. Dinner, 3 courses, £25-£35. Sunday roast from £13.
Closed	Christmas.

Charles & Edmund Inkin
The Gurnard's Head,
Zennor, St Ives TR26 3DE
Tel   +44 (0)1736 796928
Web   www.gurnardshead.co.uk

The Plume of Feathers
Mitchell

It was an inspired move to transform the 16th-century coaching inn where John Wesley once preached into a warm and stylish pub-restaurant. Imaginative cooking draws an appreciative crowd and in summer food is available all day. Low, stripped beams, half-panelled walls hung with modern art, fresh flowers, candle-studded pine tables and soothing lighting make this place a pleasure to walk into; it's novel and it's fun. Delightful staff serve freshly cooked local produce at sensible prices – take Cornish fishcakes with sweet chilli sauce and dressed leaves, or grilled Dover sole with lemon butter. There are thick bacon sandwiches at lunch and delicious puddings – the sticky toffee pudding is a huge favourite. The central bar is lively with TV, piped music and Sharp's Doom Bar on tap. Best of all, there are seven elegant, calm and comfortable country-style bedrooms, all on the ground floor. The biggest have squishy sofas, and all have sparkling bathrooms with indulgent soaps and treats.

Rooms	4 doubles: £120.
	2 suites for 4: £145–£175.
	1 family room for 4: £140–£155.
Meals	Lunch & bar meals from £10.
	Dinner from £15.
	Sunday lunch, 3 courses, £21.
Closed	Open all day.

Daniel Trotter
The Plume of Feathers,
Mitchell,
Newquay TR8 5AX

Tel   +44 (0)1637 870129
Web   www.theplumemitchell.co.uk

The Old Custom House
Padstow

You can't miss it: the big square Custom House opposite the car park, right on Padstow's quay. It is sturdy, delightful and has weathered many a storm. Inside: a large bar on two levels with planked floors and timbered ceiling, background music and a big screen for sport. There's a coffee shop on the ground floor and a hairdresser's above. The place buzzes with trippers, locals, children and dogs. If you fancy pushing the boat out book into the modern and stylish restaurant, with its muted colours and views down over the harbour. The menu is fish-led – of course – and there's a daily changing specials board: they follow the seasons here. Try crispy fried camembert with chilli jam; cassoulet with roasted tomatoes; fish pie with creamy saffron sauce. Then catch the ferry to Rock, and tiny St Enodoc Church where John Betjeman is buried. If you wish to linger, the bedrooms are very good, with their cream patterned carpets, heated towel rails, iPod docks and relaxed seaside décor. Splash out on one with a harbour or estuary view – corner rooms have both! The most peaceful are at the top.

Rooms	19 doubles, 4 twins: £115–£230.
Meals	Lunch & dinner £8.95–£13.95.
Closed	Open all day.

Old Custom House
The Old Custom House,
South Quay,
Padstow PL28 8BL
Tel   +44 (0)1841 532359
Web   www.oldcustomhousepadstow.co.uk

Entry 96 Map 1

The Mill House Inn
Trebarwith

Coast down the steep winding lane to a 1760s mill house in a woodland setting. Trebarwith's spectacular beach – all surf and sand – is a ten-minute walk away. It's quite a spot. Back at the inn, the bar combines the best of Cornish old and Cornish new: big flagged floor, wooden tables, chapel chairs, two leather sofas by a wood-burning stove. The swanky dining room overlooking the burbling mill stream is light, elegant and very modern. Settle down to some rather good food: fish chowder; rib-eye steak with wild mushroom and pink peppercorn fricassée; rose, jasmine and orchid panna cotta. Bar meals are more traditional, they do great barbecues in summer and a band often plays at the weekend. In keeping with the seaside setting, bedrooms are simple and uncluttered, comfortable and characterful, with good shower rooms in the smaller standard rooms. Coastal trails lead to Tintagel, official home of the Arthurian legends, there's biking, surfing, crabbing… you couldn't possibly be bored.

Rooms	7 doubles: £75–£130.
	1 family room for 4: £75–£130.
	Singles £56–£97.
	Extra bed/sofabed available £20 per person per night.
	Dinner, B&B £60–£90 per person per night.
Meals	Lunch from £7.50. Dinner from £12.
	Sunday lunch, 3 courses, £17.85.
Closed	Open all day.

Mark & Kep Forbes
The Mill House Inn,
Trebarwith,
Tintagel PL34 0HD
Tel   +44 (0)1840 770200
Web   www.themillhouseinn.co.uk

Cornwall

St Tudy Inn
St Tudy

Holiday walkers and cyclists from Padstow have long loved this little pub off the beaten track, with its new slate floors and its crackling fire, its Doom Bar and Tawny on tap. But it's the food that's been the biggest draw; it still is. Chef-patron Emily sailed in in 2015 with exciting plans, a friendly team and a rustic, seasonal menu. There are four cosy dining areas including the public bar and a terrace at the back, and the rooms are charming and countrified — a battered leather chair, a basket full of logs, a fine old settle. Emily heads the kitchen and creates disarmingly simple food from the best Cornish produce: lamb tagine with apricots; squash and fennel lasagne; lemon sole with new potatoes; treacle tart with clotted cream Our sole goujons with citrus mayonnaise and a glass of white from Sicily totally hit the spot.

Meals	Lunch & bar meals from £8.95.
	Dinner from £10.95.
Closed	Sun evenings & all day Mon.

Emily Scott
St Tudy Inn,
St Tudy,
Bodmin PL30 3NN
Tel +44 (0)1208 850656
Web www.sttudyinn.com

Entry 98 Map 1

Cornwall

St Kew Inn
St Kew

Lost down a maze of lanes in a secluded wooded valley, the St Kew is a grand old inn originally built in the 15th-century for the masons working on the church. It's an irresistibly friendly place with a huge range and a warming fire, a dark slate floor, winged settles and a terrific unspoilt atmosphere — no pub paraphernalia here but look out for the resident ghost who's been spotted in the past. Pewter tankards hang over the bar where local St Austell ales are dispensed, and soup and baguettes revive weary walkers. Elsewhere the food is bang up to date. Try cured salmon with beetroot and dill yogurt, chicken breast with smoked hog's pudding, sauté potatoes and Provençal sauce, marmalade pudding and custard. In summer, the big streamside garden is the place to be.

Meals	Lunch & bar meals from £5.50.
	Dinner from £9.50.
	Sunday lunch, 3 courses, £19.50.
Closed	3pm-6pm.

Sarah Allen
St Kew Inn,
St Kew,
Bodmin PL30 3HB
Tel +44 (0)1208 841259
Web www.stkewinn.co.uk

Entry 99 Map 1

Cornwall

St Mabyn Inn & Restaurant
St Mabyn

St Mabyn is a sweet, tucked away village with an ancient church and a much-loved pub by its side. It's sturdy and handsome, with weathered Cornish stone under a slate roof, and flower baskets tumbling and bright. Locals sup in the bar, families arrive with dogs in tow (or spill into the enclosed garden) and holidaymakers come for the upmarket modern food. Sandwiches and toasted ciabattas, cherry tomato risotto, 'fish and chips with prosecco', moules marinières, and the popular Pie 'n' Pint of the Day. You can eat in the big, open-fire'd, split-level bar (upbeat stripy carpet, metal vintage ads, accent walls) or in the lower bar with its log-burner, or in the restaurant – light, airy, contemporary and vaulted. Wherever you are, all feels cheerful and inviting, and you're within striking distance of the sea.

Meals	Starters from £5.
	Dinner from £10.
	Sunday roast from £9.
Closed	Please check before you visit.

Ollie Yates, Richard Ashton
& Ivan Crowle
St Mabyn Inn, St Mabyn,
Churchtown, Bodmin PL30 3BA
Tel   +44 (0)1208 841266
Web   www.facebook.com/StMabynInn

Entry 100 Map 1

Cornwall

The Ship Inn
Wadebridge

Afloat after a superb refurbishment, one of the oldest pubs in town honours its maritime history in gilt-framed pictures on white stone walls. Padded banquettes blend with wooden stools, chairs and tables to create an intimate bar area in which to sip a pint of Doom Bar or an ale from Padstow Brewing Company. There are books to read, board games to play, wood-burners and gentle music. Two dining areas, one a glorious open-raftered room with brass ship lights and a captain's table, are pleasant spaces in which to enjoy Darren Hardy's modern-traditional pub dishes; we loved the spiced mackerel with tomato and red onion salad, and the braised oxtail with horseradish mash. Little shipmates get menus, even your pooch can eat. There are bar snacks, Sunday roasts, great music nights – even Backgammon Club.

| Meals | Lunch & dinner £5-£18.95. |
| Closed | 3pm-5pm, Mon-Sat. |

Rupert & Sarah Wilson
The Ship Inn,
Gonvena Hill,
Wadebridge PL27 6DF
Tel   +44 (0)1208 813845
Web   www.shipinnwadebridge.co.uk

Entry 101 Map 1

The Mariners
Rock

Park in posh Rock's 'pay and display', or hop on the ferry from Padstow – what better than to arrive by boat! This big modern airy pub with sliding glass windows and bustling terrace is impossible to leave on a sunny day; the staff are trendy-friendly and the views are gorgeous. It's a major port of call for holiday makers, sailors, second-homers and all who love their food, and dogs and families are welcomed too. Inside are slate floors, stylish tables, an open-to-view kitchen and a small first-floor balcony for the privileged few (arrive early!). You can have bacon baps for breakfast, Porthilly oysters for lunch, and Sharp's beers (Doom Bar, Atlantic) all day. The menu is unashamedly fish-led and our cod fillet with salsa verde and lentils was super-fresh. We hear the steaks and roasts are rather good too.

The Cornish Arms
St Merryn

It could be the blueprint for how a good country inn should be. It's unpretentious and authentic, there's a buzzy atmosphere with locals rubbing shoulders with walkers and holiday makers, and the food, as expected when Rick Stein is involved, doesn't miss a beat. We're not talking gastropub or fine dining but good honest dishes cooked well – scampi in the basket, rump steak and chips, treacle tart and custard. The atmospheric bar is where the locals down pints of Tribute – the pub is owned by the St Austell Brewery. There's a family room too, and a pool table and a wood-burner and a big garden for sunny days. The much missed canine star of Rick's TV shows would have loved a trip here, and no doubt have been thrilled by two of the beers on offer – Chalky's Bark and Chalky's Bite.

Meals	Starters from £2.80.
	Dinner from £10.50.
Closed	Open from 11am every day.

Meals	Lunch & dinner £8.95-£14.95.
	Sunday roast £12.95 (winter only).
Closed	Open all day.

Nathan Outlaw & Paul Ripley
The Mariners,
Rock PL27 6LD
Tel +44 (0)1208 863 679
Web www.themarinersrock.com

Rick & Jill Stein
The Cornish Arms,
Churchtown, St Merryn,
Padstow PL28 8ND
Tel +44 (0)1841 532700
Web www.rickstein.com

Entry 102 Map 1

Entry 103 Map 1

Cornwall

Lewinnick Lodge
Newquay

Poised above the cliff edge to a backdrop of rolling fields and hikers' trails (an inspiring setting for platefuls of St Austell mussels and Fowey oysters) this glass-fronted edifice overlooks the Atlantic; a mighty setting in all weathers. Polar opposite of the 'quaint local', Lewinnick Lodge is large and luminous with a friendly modern vibe. Be wowed by a wall of glass, a sweep of oak, a sparkling bar, an open fire; efficient staff make everyone welcome and that includes your dog. You can eat in or out and they specialise in fish, cooked 'à point' just as it should be; our haddock with ratatouille and pan-fried gnocchi burst with flavour. They're open for breakfast and the coffee is fabulous – courtesy of a Cornish coffee roaster!

Meals	Breakfast from £3.50.
	Lunch & bar meals from £5.50.
	Dinner from £11.
	Sunday roast £10.50.
Closed	Open all day.

Daniel Trotter
Lewinnick Lodge,
Pentire Headland, Newquay TR7 1QD
Tel   +44 (0)1637 870129
Web   www.hospitalitycornwall.com/
        lewinnicklodge

Entry 104 Map 1

Cornwall

The Queen's Hotel
St Ives

A smart foodie pub set back from the harbour of St Ives, hung with flowers in season. Perch on a red bar stool at the impressive white marble-topped bar and choose from St Austell's fine ales – HSD will see you reeling – or some good old Cornish Rattler cider. Head to a well-scrubbed candlelit table, or a tartan bench seat by the fireplace; if you're lucky enough to land on a Friday evening there could be live music! Matt Perry's menus are constantly evolving and have big flavours based on rustic French and Italian recipes alongside sturdy old-fashioned English offerings: try lamb faggot with crispy belly pork, carrot purée, cabbage and bacon, and onion gravy; finish with orange posset, marmalade ice cream and shortbread. Then stride south, along some of the finest coastline in Cornwall.

Meals	Lunch & bar meals from £5.
	Dinner from £8.
	Sunday roast £9.50.
	Not Monday eves (Nov-Feb).
Closed	Open all day.

Neythan Hayes
The Queen's Hotel,
High Street,
St Ives TR26 1RR
Tel   +44 (0)1736 796468
Web   www.queenshotelstives.com

Entry 105 Map 1

Cornwall

Halsetown Inn
Halsetown

Built by a Victorian philanthropist in 1831 this inn has impeccable eco credentials and has won awards for its efforts. Inside, murals and bold art mix with an old range and eclectic wooden furniture, candles on tables, fresh flowers and cool jazz in the background. Head chef Ange Baxter likes to innovate and be brave with her flavours, so elaborate dishes such as sticky soy pork belly with Japanese potato and cabbage pancake, samphire, pickled ginger, mayo and toasted sesame seeds are listed along with excellent burgers, cider-baked ham and super-fresh line-caught fish. You can walk from St Ives if the spirit moves you, then sit at the bistro style bar with a pint of Doom Bar or Skinner's ale or even a Cornish gin or a pastis! A pub with huge soul and great character.

Meals	Lunch & dinner £11.50-£20.
Closed	Sun 6pm-11pm.
	Mon-Sat 3pm-6pm.

Lisa Taylor, Sally Cuckson & Marie Dixon
Halsetown Inn,
Halsetown, St Ives TR26 3NA
Tel   +44 (0)1736 795583
Web   www.halsetowninn.co.uk

Entry 106 Map 1

Cornwall

Tinner's Arms
Zennor

Under landlords Grahame and Richard, one of Cornwall's most historic pubs thrives in the wilds of West Penwith. Close to the church in the coastal hamlet of Zennor, the 13th-century inn is pretty unspoilt with its flagstone floors, whitewashed walls and fabulously long, well-stocked bar. The food and drink have moved sharply up a gear, with lunch and evening menus changing daily: sweet potato and puy lentil curry, hake with red pepper sauce, treacle tart and clotted cream to follow. Ales come courtesy of St Austell and Sharp's. The Tinner's Arms, bursting with character and open log fires, will always be a popular stop for walkers heading for the nearby coastal paths. It's packed in summer, so spill out in the lovely large garden overlooking the sea; off-season, it could be you and the dog alone in the bar. Worth the walk from St Ives.

Meals	Lunch £5.50-£9.75.
	Dinner £9.50-£18.50.
Closed	Open all day.

Grahame Edwards & Richard Motley
Tinner's Arms,
Zennor, St Ives TR26 3BY
Tel   +44 (0)1736 796927
Web   www.tinnersarms.co.uk

Entry 107 Map 1

Cornwall

The Star Inn
St Just

Entrenched in the wild landscape close to Land's End is the "last proper pub in Cornwall". This 18th-century beauty, owned by the ex-mayor of St Just and its oldest and most authentic inn, proudly shirks the trappings of tourism and remains a drinkers' den. Bands of locals sink pints of Tinners Ale in the low-beamed, spick-and-span bar, old pub games thrive and the place is the hub of the local folk scene, with live music at least ten nights a month; singalongs and joke-telling are part of the Monday evening entertainment. The dim-lit bar is jam-packed with interest and walls are littered with seafaring and mining artefacts; coals glow in the grate on wild winter days. Come for St Austell ale and the 'craic'. There's a free juke box, mulled wine in winter and that pub rarity, a great family room.

Meals	No food served.
Closed	Open all day.

Johnny McFadden
The Star Inn,
1 Fore Street, St Just,
Penzance TR19 7LL
Tel   +44 (0)1736 788767
Web   www.thestarinn-stjust.co.uk

Entry 108 Map 1

Cornwall

The Tolcarne Inn
Newlyn

What might one expect on the menu at a pub in Newlyn, home to the Cornwall's biggest fish market? Ben Tunnicliffe, former chef at the Scarlet Hotel and the Abbey in Penzance (where he bagged a Michelin star) has set foodie hearts aflutter with his first solo venture. Fish, whatever's in season, is his thing – perfectly cooked and beautifully presented: roasted monkfish with linguine; wild mushrooms and truffle oil; fillet of brill with salsify; fish soup with rouille and crostini… it's great value too. This is a traditional fisherman's pub, simple, whitewashed and cosy and thankfully the locals are still coming. The pub is next to the sea wall and plans are afoot to raise the level of the terrace to take in the views over the bay. Bag a table outside and enjoy some of the best food in Cornwall.

Meals	Lunch & dinner from £9.50.
Closed	3pm-6pm.

Ben Tunnicliffe
The Tolcarne Inn,
Newlyn,
Penzance TR18 5PR
Tel   +44 (0)1736 363074
Web   www.tolcarneinn.co.uk

Entry 109 Map 1

Cornwall

The Victoria Inn
Perranuthnoe

With glorious Mount's Bay (beach and coastal path) down the lane, this striking pink-washed village inn draws the crowds. Arrive early and bag a seat in the stone-walled bar by the log-burner, or in the sunny sunken garden. Chef-landlord Stewart is making waves locally, using the best Cornish ingredients for bang-up-to-date food. For ale-lovers there's Doom Bar on tap, a perfect match for a lunchtime crab sandwich or haddock and chips. Cooking moves up a gear in the evenings, so try pork and peppercorn pâté with port jelly, Provençal fish stew with aïoli, wild mushroom and local greens risotto with Old Winchester cheese, orange brûlée with poached plums. Built originally to house the masons extending the church in the 12th century, this very old pub is one happy ship.

Cornwall

New Entry

The Ship
Porthleven

Imagine a weather-beaten pub hewn out of the rock on Cornwall's most southerly fishing harbour (thrilling on a stormy night). An ale-lovers' pub with a young and fun vibe, popular with salty sea dogs too, it's deluged with visitors in high summer, drawn to its position and its character. There's a cider festival in August and real ales all year round, from Surf Bum and Bal Maiden to Sharp's Coaster and Doom Bar. Inside, find granite walls, planked floors, church pews and an open fire. Drinks are drunk, songs are sung, and outside is a three-tier terrace — lower deck, bridge and crow's nest. You can have sandwiches, fish platters and spicy chicken wings, or fill up on crab cakes, lasagne, Thai curry, rump steak, battered hake with salad and fries. It's lovely grub, freshly homemade, and the fish comes straight from the sea.

Meals	Lunch & dinner £8.95–£16.75.
Closed	Sun evenings.
	Mon (November–March).

Meals	Starters from £4.95.
	Dinner from £8.95.
Closed	Open all day.

Stewart & Anna Eddy
The Victoria Inn,
Perranuthnoe,
Penzance TR20 9NP
Tel   +44 (0)1736 710309
Web   www.victoriainn-penzance.co.uk

Kate Preston
The Ship,
Mount Pleasant Road, Porthleven,
Helston TR13 9JS
Tel   +44 (0)1326 564204
Web   www.theshipinncornwall.co.uk

Entry 110 Map 1

Entry 111 Map 1

Cornwall

Trengilly Wartha Inn
Constantine

Well tucked down steep and twisting lanes, in the verdant heaven that is the Helford estuary, is this friendly Cornish inn. Choose a pint of Skinner's Trengilly Gold or St Austell HSD and enjoy a stroll in the six acres of old orchard with pond – and a gravelled pergola with ingenious underfloor heating. The main bar is a cracker with a wealth of mini-snugs formed by mid-height wooden settles, beer mats tacked to beams, cricketing memorabilia, local black and white photos, local paintings, and a display of some of the 150 wines on offer; there are 40 malts too. Chef Nick Tyler has 20 years under his belt here and keeps it fresh, local and seasonal; a shame not to try the Falmouth river mussels with onion, white wine and cream, or the crab thermidor with homemade granary bread.

Meals	Lunch from £4.80.
	Dinner & bar meals from £7.20.
	Sunday lunch, 3 courses, £20.
Closed	3pm–6pm.

Lisa & William Lea
Trengilly Wartha Inn,
Constantine,
Falmouth TR11 5RP
Tel   +44 (0)1326 340332
Web   www.trengilly.co.uk

Entry 112 Map 1

Cornwall

The Shipwright's Arms
Helford

Drop off the car, then enjoy the walk through Helford village to this 17th-century thatched pub in one of the best waterside spots in Cornwall. The main bar is a narrow space where you'll get chatting to the locals as you queue for a pint of Harbour ale or – as befits a sailors' hangout – a choice of rums (there are many). There's a snug wood-panelled banquette at one end, a marine-themed dining area with estuary views, and a part-covered eating space presided over by two magnificent ship's figure heads. Catch live bands – jazz on Sundays. Terraces tumble down to the shoreline where you may see the day's catch being unloaded. Menus are short and change daily, and deliver dishes such as roast sea bass and crab risotto, and monkfish linguine with rosemary cream, pancetta, red peppers and mangetout. A totally jolly, glorious Cornish pub – hop aboard!

Meals	Lunch & dinner £6.50–£22.
Closed	Open all day.

Hairy & Vicky Harford
The Shipwright's Arms,
Helford,
Helston TR12 6JX
Tel   +44 (0)1326 231235
Web   www.shipwrightshelford.co.uk

Entry 113 Map 1

Cornwall

The Ferryboat Inn
Helford Passage

The position is unbeatable – bang on the water with boats to hire or the ferry to whisk you across the Helford river. It's one of those rare spots that has resisted the urge to enter the 21st century, and is all the more popular for it. Inside are rugs on slate floors, a fire that burns every day, a smart restaurant tucked into the corner and an oyster bar that hums in summer (the pub is owned by oyster farmers). Outside, the allure of a watery view draws a happy crowd to the terrace, and live music entertains during the summer. St Austell ales are on tap for your pleasure, there's a good selection of wines by the glass and local nourishment to fortify walkers and boatmen alike: French onion soup, fish pie, West Country cheeses. Come for Sunday lunch with pub games, or a game of pool with a pint.

Cornwall

The Pandora Inn
Mylor Bridge

Yachtsmen moor at the end of the pontoon that reaches into the creek. The building is special: thatched, 13th-century and rebuilt following a devastating fire. The pub is named in memory of the *Pandora*, a naval ship sent to Tahiti to capture the mutineers of Captain Bligh's *Bounty*. It keeps its traditional layout on several levels, along with panelled walls, polished flags, snug alcoves, log fires, maritime mementoes, and amazingly low wooden ceilings. The award-winning menu has something to please everyone, with fresh seafood dominating the specials board, and an indulgently long wine list. Arrive early in summer – by car or by boat; park nearby and walk (the car park isn't huge). On winter weekdays it's blissfully peaceful; the postprandial walking along wooded creekside paths is a delight.

Meals	Lunch & dinner from £8.50.
Closed	Sun evenings.
	All day Mon (in winter).

Meals	Lunch & dinner £6-£19.
Closed	Open all day.

Ben Wright & Robin Hancock
The Ferryboat Inn,
Helford Passage,
Falmouth TR11 5LB
Tel   +44 (0)1326 250625
Web   www.wrightbros.eu.com/ferryboatinn

Entry 114 Map 1

John Milan & Steve Bellman
The Pandora Inn,
Restronguet, Mylor Bridge,
Falmouth TR11 5ST
Tel   +44 (0)1326 372678
Web   www.pandorainn.com

Entry 115 Map 1

Cornwall

The Roseland Inn
Philleigh

Beside a peaceful parish church, two miles from the King Harry Ferry, a cob-built Cornish treasure with its own microbrewery (their Roseland Gullable is award winning). The front courtyard is bright with blossom in spring and climbing roses in summer. Indoors: old settles with scatter cushions, worn slate floors, low black beams and winter log fires. Local photographs, gig-racing memorabilia and a corner dedicated to rugby trophies scatter the walls. Spotlessly kept, it attracts locals and visitors in search of good food, such as local farm meats and fish landed at St Mawes. Dishes range from decent sandwiches to scallops with belly pork and white onion sauce, and roast duck with raspberry jus. Staff are full of smiles – even when the pub doubles as the Roseland Rugby Club clubhouse on winter Saturday nights.

Meals	Lunch & dinner £8.50-£13.95. Sunday roast £9.95.
Closed	3pm-6pm. Open all day weekends & in summer.

Phil Heslip
The Roseland Inn,
Philleigh,
Truro TR2 5NB
Tel +44 (0)1872 580254
Web www.roselandinn.co.uk

Entry 116 Map 1

Cornwall

The Kings Head
Ruan Lanihorne

A pub with a heart, and award-winner. Niki and Andrew are warm, friendly and love what they do. Come for pine-backed stools, a comfy sofa and real fire, a lawned garden with views. An impressive collection of tea cups hangs from the ceiling, a window sparkles with coloured bottles and all is quirky and fun. The dining rooms sport hunting prints and a wood-burner, gleaming tables and Windsor chairs. Ales are from Skinners in Truro, fish from St Mawes, so tuck into scallops with bacon and garlic, venison casserole with parsley mash, the famous Ruan slow-roasted duck with pepper sauce, and a Sunday Cornish sirloin of beef with tip-top Yorkshire pudding. The quiet little village has a church with a Norman font and a creek that is a haven for waders and waterfowl… behind is the Roseland countryside. Perfect for walkers and watersporters.

Meals	Lunch from £5.15. Dinner from £9.95. Sunday lunch, 3 courses, £21.60.
Closed	2.30pm-6pm. Sun evenings & Mon all day in winter.

Andrew & Niki Law
The Kings Head,
Ruan Lanihorne, Ruan High Lanes,
Truro TR2 5NX
Tel +44 (0)1872 501263
Web www.kingsheadruan.co.uk

Entry 117 Map 1

Cornwall

The Rising Sun Inn
Altarnun

Beginning life as a farm on the edge of Bodmin Moor in the 1600s, the property later became a 'hole in the wall'. The main bar is all no-nonsense Delabole flagstones and oak floors surrounded by wall settles with long padded cushions; add guns and prints, beams, plenty of woodchip and delicately tobacco tinged paint tones. Things are all very local hereabouts, the barman brews the Penpont Ale a mile away and there's also Skinner's Spriggan or Betty Stoggs. Next door in the old cattle shed is a more contemporary dining area, its exposed stone walls hung with local art. After a blow on the moors, our pork belly hash with sauté potatoes and red chard was really delicious, followed by a good crème brûlée. The specials here change weekly and the staff are great.

Cornwall

The Springer Spaniel
Treburley

Anton Piotrowski's food is modern and exciting with punchy rich flavours. This is a brilliant roadside stop for travellers from Exeter to Cornwall, and for local foodies too; it was abuzz on a Thursday lunchtime. In the bar are a log-burner and bookcases full of books; in the dining room, simple colours and a medley of wooden furniture; the most romantic table is in the inglenook. The staff are wonderful, cheerful and knowledgeable, while muddy booted walkers and their dogs, in for a pint of Tribute, Proper Job or Cornish Rattler, are as welcome as the rest. Anton is passionate about local and seasonal: note the 'What Dad Got From the Garden' soup, the burgers made from 21-day aged beef with red onion marmalade, and the beautiful lemon sole with brown shrimp and caper butter. Delightful.

Meals	Lunch £4–£14.
	Bar meals £4–£10.
	Dinner £4–£20.
	Sunday lunch, 3 courses, £20.
Closed	2pm–6pm.
	Open all day Sat, Sun & Bank Holidays.

Meals	Bar meals from £4.
	Mains from £10.
Closed	Open all day.

Andy Mason
The Rising Sun Inn,
Altarnun PL15 7SN
Tel +44 (0)1566 86636
Web www.therisingsuninn.co.uk

Entry 118 Map 1

Anton & Clare Piotrowski
The Springer Spaniel,
Treburley,
Launceston PL15 9NS
Tel +44 (0)1579 370424
Web www.thespringerspaniel.org.uk

Entry 119 Map 2

The Samson Inn
Gilsland

On the Northumberland/Cumbria border, this Victorian pub, in a terrace of cottages, is named after one of the first steam engines on the old Carlisle-Newcastle line. Red carpeting runs throughout, there are cushioned pews in corners, tub chairs around easy tables and a couple of log stoves, while the more intimate dining room, with polished floors and dressed tables, is the backdrop to some refreshingly creative cooking. With the family farm certified organic, the emphasis is firmly on quality; our terrine of game with spiced fig compote was full of flavour and beautifully balanced. Brampton Bitter would be a nice accompaniment for sausages and mash, the wines are well considered, you might choose roast steak of hake in a bean and chickpea casserole, or a luscious chocolate torte. Finish with a whisky by the fire, surrounded by chat and good humour, before repairing to one of four warm, cosy, uncluttered rooms off the landing. Floors are insulated and everything is top quality – carpeting, mattresses, showers. Two rooms have the original cast-iron fireplaces.

Rooms	3 doubles: £70-£80.
	1 triple: £95.
Meals	Lunch from £5.
	Dinner, £10-£15.
	Packed lunch £6.
Closed	Mid-November-February.

Liam McNulty & Lauren Harrison
The Samson Inn,
Gilsland,
Brampton CA8 7DR

Tel	+44 (0)1697 747880
Web	www.thesamson.co.uk

ﾠ夫 ﾠ

George and Dragon
Clifton

Charles Lowther has found a chef who does justice to the slow-grow breeds of beef, pork and lamb produced on the Lowther Estate – and lovely wines to match, 16 by the glass. Ales and cheeses are local, berries and mushrooms are foraged, vegetables are home-grown... and his signature starter, twice-baked cheese soufflé with a hint of spinach, is divine. As for the long low coaching inn, it's been beautifully restored by craftsmen using wood, slate and stone, and painted in colours in tune with the period. Bare wooden tables, comfy sofas, intimate alcoves and crackling fires make this a delightful place to dine and unwind; old prints and archive images tell stories of the ancient estate's history. Outside is plenty of seating and a lawned play area beneath fruit trees. Upstairs are 11 bedrooms of varying sizes (some small, some large, some above the bar), perfectly decorated in classic country style. Carpeting is Cumbrian wool, beds are new, ornaments come with Lowther history, showers are walk-in, baths (just two) are roll top, and breakfasts are fresh and delicious.

Rooms	11 twin/doubles: £95–£155. Singles £79.
Meals	Lunch from £7.95. Dinner from £12.95. Sunday roast from £12.95.
Closed	Boxing Day.

Charlie Lowther
George and Dragon,
Clifton,
Penrith CA10 2ER
Tel   +44 (0)1768 865381
Web   www.georgeanddragonclifton.co.uk

Cumbria

The Royal Oak at Keswick
Keswick

Step off a pedestrianised high street, into a cosily traditional haunt. This much-loved inn beside Keswick's old Moot Hall, with its dark quarry tiles, long narrow bar and super new makeover (swish wallpapers, comfy seating) attracts a diverse crowd: walkers, holiday makers, families, suits. Now it's pulling in diners too, with accessible menus and local supplies. The grilled chicken strips are delicious for kids, the cakes and biscuits are baked in-house, and the roast cod on pea risotto could not be fresher. Arrive early and pick a seat by a fire, then order Fellside Lamb hotpot (winter doesn't get cosier than this). Most of Thwaites' cask ales are available, and well-kept. The wines are good, the landlord is interested, the staff are obliging, and there's always a water bowl for a walker's dog. There are delightful bedrooms too: the dog-friendly ones have wood laminate floors while the rest are warmly carpeted in tartan tweed, and the largest are fabulous for families. They even have parking passes for further up the street – a boon in popular Keswick.

Rooms	19 doubles: £70-£140.
Meals	Starters from £4.95. Dinner from £8.95.
Closed	Open all day.

Mark McKeown
The Royal Oak at Keswick,
Main Street,
Keswick CA12 5HZ
Tel +44 (0)1768 774584
Web www.royaloakkeswick.co.uk

The Punch Bowl Inn
Crosthwaite

In the hills above Windermere in a pretty village encircled by lanes that defeat most tourists. It's a lovely spot, deeply rural, with ten-mile views down the valley and a church next door; bell ringers practise on Friday mornings, the occasional bride glides out in summer. Yet while the Punch Bowl sits lost to the world, it is actually a deliciously funky inn. Rescued from neglect and renovated in great style, it now sparkles with a stylish mix of old and new. Outside, honeysuckle and roses ramble on stone walls. Inside, a clipped elegance runs throughout, with Farrow & Ball colours, rugs on wood floors and sofas in front of the wood-burner. Scott Fairweather's ambrosial food is a big draw, perhaps Lancashire cheese soufflé, loin of rabbit with crayfish mousse, pear soufflé and pecan ice cream. Chic bedrooms are lovely, too, all with beautiful linen, pretty fabrics and Roberts radios, while fabulous bathrooms have double-ended baths, separate showers and white robes. Four have the view, the suite is enormous, weekday prices are tempting. There's a terrace for lunch in the sun, too.

Rooms	5 doubles, 1 twin/double, 2 four-posters: £105-£235. 1 suite for 2: £180-£305. Singles from £80.
Meals	Lunch from £5. Dinner, 3 courses, £30-£35.
Closed	Open all day.

Lorraine Stanton
The Punch Bowl Inn,
Crosthwaite,
Kendal LA8 8HR
Tel   +44 (0)15395 68237
Web   www.the-punchbowl.co.uk

The Plough
Lupton

This rambling 19th-century roadside inn goes from strength to strength with an enthusiastic team in charge. Outside is a pleasant paved patio with chunky furniture for lunch on a good day; inside is a vast open space full of comfortable corners, with open fires and stove. Expect nicely battered vintage furniture, polished oak floors and colourful rugs. For lunch, tuck into terrific sandwiches or grilled mackerel fillet with dill, caper and red onion salsa, washed down with a well-kept pint of local bitter. Or go for a Fisherman's or Ploughman's Board, both with generous portions and locally sourced. Main menu dishes are fantastic and puddings a treat; try vanilla panna cotta, Lyth Valley damson compote and a jammy dodger shortbread. Wines from Kendal expert Frank Stainton, with plenty by the glass, boost a well-stocked bar. Upstairs, five big, glamorous bedrooms are dressed with pale carpets, fat mattresses, crisp linen; many have lovely views over the fells. Bathrooms have claw-foot roll tops; the spectacular 'Torsin' comes with a double monsoon shower. An irresistible addition to special places to stay in the Lakes.

Rooms	3 doubles: £115–£165.
	2 suites for 2: £165–£195.
Meals	Bar meals from £5.95.
	Lunch from £8.95.
	Dinner from £10.50.
Closed	Open all day.

Holly Duffy & Suzannah Harris
The Plough,
Cow Brow, Lupton,
Kirkby Lonsdale LA6 1PJ

| Tel | +44 (0)15395 67700 |
| Web | www.theploughatlupton.co.uk |

The Sun Inn
Kirkby Lonsdale

This lovely old inn sits between the Dales and the Lakes in an ancient market town, one of the prettiest in the north. It backs onto St Mary's churchyard, where wild flowers flourish, and on the far side you'll find 'the fairest view in England,' to quote John Ruskin. Herons fish the river Lune, lambs graze the fells, a vast sky hangs above. Turner came to paint it in 1825 and benches wait for those who want to gaze upon it. As for the Sun, it does what good inns do – looks after you in style. There's lots of pretty old stuff – stone walls, rosewood panelling, wood-burners working overtime – and it's all kept spic and span, with warm colours, fresh flowers and the daily papers on hand. You find leather banquettes, local art and chairs in the dining room from Cunard's Mauretania, so eat in style, perhaps mussels with cider, saddle of venison, Yorkshire rhubarb and ginger sponge trifle. Bedrooms upstairs are stylishly uncluttered with Cumbrian wool carpets, robes in smart bathrooms and earplugs to ward off the church bells. Car-park permits come with your room and can be used far and wide. Brilliant. *Minimum stay: 2 nights at weekends.*

Rooms	8 doubles, 2 twin/doubles: £108-£178. 1 family room for 4: £148-£178. Singles £78-£158. Extra bed/sofabed £20 per person per night. Dinner, B&B £79-£117 per person per night.
Meals	Bar snacks & lunch from £5.95. Dinner, 4 courses, £32.95. Sunday lunch, 3 courses, £22.95. Not Monday lunch.
Closed	Open all day.

Mark & Lucy Fuller
The Sun Inn,
6 Market Street, Kirkby Lonsdale,
Carnforth LA6 2AU
Tel +44 (0)15242 71965
Web www.sun-inn.info

Cumbria

The King's Head
Ravenstonedale

Deep in the Upper Eden Valley, Ravenstonedale has the monumental Howgill Fells as its backdrop. This smartly refurbished 16th-century listed inn is the perfect place to start – or finish – a major walk; close to the river Eden, its exterior whitewash gleams. Inside, an earthy colour scheme adds to the warmth, with checked wool at period windows and on old settles; furniture is mismatched in the best way, and dotted with newspapers and fresh flowers. Beams abound, and canine chums are welcome too. The menu changes regularly; there might be farmhouse cheese and onion soufflé or wood pigeon tart to start, followed by rump of Cumbrian lamb and braised red cabbage. Hobgoblin from the Wychwood Brewery and Jennings Cumberland are in top form on tap. Six stylish bedrooms await. Look forward to huge beds, perfect mattresses, deep baths… and soft colours in wool throws, tall padded headboards and pale carpets – and one or two nice vintage pieces: a table here, some china there. As for beams – they're everywhere!

Rooms	4 doubles, 2 twins: £80-£98.
Meals	Lunch from £3.95.
	Dinner from £10.50, 3 courses, £22.
Closed	Open all day.

Beverly Fothergill
The King's Head,
Ravenstonedale,
Kirkby Stephen CA17 4NH
Tel   +44 (0)15396 23050
Web   www.kings-head.com

Entry 126 Map 12

Cumbria

The Black Swan
Ravenstonedale

Duck under hanging baskets to find a good mix of people in the busy main bar, cosy with red plush stools, exposed stone and soft lighting. Or nip through to the public bar with TV, games of scrabble and newspapers to read. A small lounge is quieter, with comfy seating at bay windows and an open fire. Wherever you land you are looked after by energetic, efficient staff; choose from simple sandwiches to a three-course blow out: pan-fried pheasant breast, smoked haddock and dill fishcake, slow-cooked belly of Texel lamb, and sourdough bread to dunk. Meat comes from known local farms, the eggs are home-laid, the vegetables are fresh from Kirkby Stephen; visit the thriving village shop and take home some local produce. You are deep in the Eden valley – it would be a crime not to explore it!

Meals	Lunch from £4.50.
	Dinner, 3 courses, £25–£30.
Closed	Open all day.

Alan & Louise Dinnes
The Black Swan,
Ravenstonedale,
Kirkby Stephen CA17 4NG
Tel   +44 (0)15396 23204
Web   www.blackswanhotel.com

Entry 127 Map 12

Cumbria

Strickland Arms
Sizergh

Beside the gates to Sizergh Castle, this old pub, once desperate for attention, is now jointly run by Martin Ainscough and the National Trust. Behind the stark stone exterior find two civilised rooms decked in best NT style: earthy colours, rugs on slate and wooden floors, an eclectic mix of antiques. Order a pint of Cumbrian Legendary Loweswater Gold or Bowness Bay Swan Blonde... pick a seat by a glowing coal fire, browse through the papers while you wait and tuck into food that bears no resemblance to normal pub fare. From local and organic ingredients come potted Morecambe Bay shrimps, lamb hotpot with red cabbage and crusty bread, lemon sole with rosemary and chive butter – all delicious. There's live music once a month, and a lovely flagged front terrace with pretty views.

Meals	Lunch & dinner £10.95–£15.95.
	Bar meals £5.50–£10.95
	(lunchtime only).
	Lunch, 2 courses, £10 (Mon-Thurs).
Closed	3pm-5.30pm.
	Open all day Sat & Sun and
	May-September.

Helen & Martin Ainscough
Strickland Arms,
Sizergh,
Kendal LA8 8DZ
Tel   +44 (0)15394 42536
Web   www.thestricklandarms.com

Entry 128 Map 11

Cumbria

The Wheatsheaf
Brigsteer

An excellently refurbished village inn lost in the Lyth Valley. Whitewashed outside, golden within, it's the latest offering from Martin Clarkson, whose Midas touch knows no bounds... there's oodles of style, lovely staff, tasty food, good prices. You'll find the odd stone wall, open fires, a games' room for dominoes, perhaps low-hanging lamps or a line of decanters running along a shelf. There's great art, the daily papers, plates of cakes and a wall of clocks. Hawkshead bitter, Last Wolf from Unsworth and a couple of Wainwright ales wait at the bar, as does a collection of gin and lots of good wine. Dig into sharing plates, fabulous pizzas, perhaps a fish pie or braised beef with creamy mash, leaving room for sticky toffee pudding.

Meals	Starters from £4.25.
	Dinner from £9.95.
Closed	Open all day.

Nicki Higgs
The Wheatsheaf,
Brigsteer,
Kendal LA8 8AN
Tel   +44 (0)15395 68938
Web   www.thewheatsheafbrigsteer.co.uk

🏃 📶

Entry 129 Map 11

Cumbria

The Hare & Hounds
Bowland Bridge

Immerse yourself in the glorious Winster Valley to find a 17th-century coaching inn delightfully restored. Kerry Parsons and her team have worked miracles, unearthing stone flagged floors, beams, and cosy fireplaces. Eat in one of the comfortable bars or the elegant private dining room; enjoy a pint of Hare of the Dog while you choose what to have for lunch. The seasonal menu might include a sweet chilli pork and black pudding terrine, followed by homemade beef and ale pie and steamed vegetables, then sticky chocolate parfait (just as well this is hearty walking country). Ingredients come from the farm around the corner or elsewhere in the valley. There are pretty outside eating areas with long views over the fells, and you are a short drive from the shores of Lake Windermere and bustling Bowness.

Meals	Bar meals from £5.
	Lunch, 2 courses, £10.
	Dinner from £10.25.
	Sunday lunch, 2 courses, £12.95.
Closed	Open all day.

Kerry Parsons
The Hare & Hounds,
Bowland Bridge LA11 6NN
Tel   +44 (0)15395 68333
Web   www.hareandhounds
        bowlandbridge.co.uk

🏃 📶

Entry 130 Map 11

Cumbria

The Derby Arms
Witherslack

Step into a welcoming series of candlelit rooms with rug-strewn floors, cream and red walls, polished period furniture, old stone fireplaces, some rather grand paintings and dogs and booted walkers. The central bar heaves with hand pumps dispensing Cumbrian microbrewery ales (including Dent Aviator), hand-pressed juices from Witherslack, and many wines by the glass. Bag a seat by the fire and settle in for supper; the changing menu announces a crowd-pleasing selection of pub dishes, much prepared from fresh local produce. Start with roasted tomato and goat's cheese tart, follow with Galloway beef and ale pie with chips and in-season vegetables, or whole-tail battered scampi. It's super civilised yet nicely laid-back.

Meals	Lunch & dinner £8.95-£15.25.
Closed	3pm-5.30pm.
	Open all day Fri-Sun.

James Tucker
The Derby Arms,
Witherslack,
Grange-over-Sands LA11 6RN
Tel   +44 (0)15395 52207
Web   www.ainscoughs.co.uk

Entry 131 Map 11

Cumbria

The Swan Hotel & Spa
Newby Bridge

This rather pretty hotel stands on the river Leven, a wide sweep of water that pours out of Windermere on its way south to Morecambe Bay. It's a fabulous spot and the Swan makes the most of it. The recent refurbishment breathed new life into the old bones of this 17th-century monastic farmhouse, with its stone terrace running along to an ancient packhorse bridge. Inside, airy interiors, a couple of sitting rooms, open fires, the daily papers, a lively bar and a good restaurant to keep you going. Dig into tasty food in the bar or brasserie, perhaps beer battered fish and chips or spicy chicken burger with homemade garlic mayo. And vegetarians are not forgotten: we enjoyed our roasted aubergine with raisin and pinenut quinoa. You'll be spoilt for choice with desserts like strawberry Eton mess cheesecake and sticky toffee pudding with butterscotch sauce and ice cream.

Meals	Bar meals from £9.95.
	Lunch from £5.95.
	Dinner, 3 courses, £25-£35.
	Sunday roast from £13.95.
Closed	Open all day.

Sarah Gibbs
The Swan Hotel & Spa,
Newby Bridge LA12 8NB
Tel   +44 (0)15395 31681
Web   www.swanhotel.com

Entry 132 Map 11

Cumbria

White Hart Inn
Booth

They stand four deep at the bar in summer, the promise of delicious food and local ales too good to miss. And it is too good to miss. The White Hart is a strand of English DNA, a traditional Lakeland pub in an untouched village. Outside, stone cottages abut fields that stretch across to the fells. Inside, traditional interiors have lots of charm with flagged floors, low ceilings, sofas in front of wood-burners, then an eccentric array of objects pinned to whitewashed walls: old hayforks, clay pipes, the odd stuffed fox. Beams drip with hops, brass shines brightly, hand pumps wait for pints of Hawkshead or Laughing Gravy. As for the food, it's delicious stuff, perhaps Morecambe Bay shrimps, haunch of venison, a plate of Cumberland cheeses. Fine walking starts from the front door. Peerless.

Cumbria

General Burgoyne
Great Urswick

In a little-known part of the Lake District, this handsome 17th-century inn was a real old boozer, complete with flagged floors, open fires and beams. Not so long ago it had a spruce-up, though they kept the best bits. Craig has worked in Michelin star restaurants in Cumbria and brings his skills to a menu that promises more than standard pub grub. You'll love the fish pie and homemade burgers but you can also treat yourself to a tasty roulade – of smoked salmon, perhaps, with a citrus salad. Or roast rump of Duddon Valley lamb with dauphinoise potatoes and rosemary gravy. Or just peanuts and a pint. Follow with Chocolate Tom jelly, vanilla panna cotta, or salted caramel and peanut parfait... then plan a big walk over the fells and down to the coast. A good find.

Meals	Lunch & dinner £10.75-£15.75.
Closed	Open all day.

Meals	Lunch from £4.95.
	Dinner £9.95-£20.
	Sunday lunch, 2 courses, £12.95.
Closed	Mon all day.

Nigel & Kath Barton
White Hart Inn,
Booth,
Ulverston LA12 8JB
Tel   +44 (0)1229 861229
Web   www.whitehart-lakedistrict.co.uk

🚶 🐾 🍺 🍷

Entry 133 Map 11

Craig & Louise Sherrington
General Burgoyne,
Church Road, Great Urswick,
Ulverston LA12 0SZ
Tel   +44 (0)1229 586394
Web   www.generalburgoyne.com

🚶 🐾 🍺 🍷 🔊

Entry 134 Map 11

Cumbria

Blacksmiths Arms
Broughton Mills

In the land of rugged hills and wooded valleys, you approach down a winding lane between high hedges; once round the final bend, the low-slung farmhouse-inn comes into view. Welcome to an utterly unspoilt little local. Inside: four small slate-floored rooms with beams and low ceilings, long settles and log fires, and a bar that is strictly for drinking – there's little room for anything else. Find three cask ales (two local, one guest) and traditional cider in summer. Across the passage: a room serving proper fresh food – snacks or full meals – and two dining rooms sparkling with glass and cutlery. The blackboard advertises dishes with a contemporary slant, and beef and Herdwick lamb reared in the valley. The food is so good it gets busy; in summer you can wander onto a flowery terrace.

Meals	Bar meals from £3.95.
	Lunch & dinner £8.50-£13.95.
Closed	2.30pm-5pm Tues-Fri & Mon lunch
	(except Bank Holidays).
	Open all day Sat & Sun.

Michael & Sophie Lane
Blacksmiths Arms,
Broughton Mills,
Broughton-in-Furness LA20 6AX
Tel   +44 (0)1229 716824
Web   www.theblacksmithsarms.com

Entry 135 Map 11

Cumbria

Tower Bank Arms
Near Sawrey

Just across from the ferry, next to Hilltop – Beatrix Potter's farm – is Jemima Puddleduck's inn. (She may not have caroused here, but she did waddle by.) Surrounded by glorious National Trust acres, whitewashed buildings make up the legendary village of Sawrey; a courteous staff handles the summer crowds. Enter a slate-flagged bar with a grand open range that throws out the heat on chilly days; further in it is carpeted and cosy. Flowers and shining bits and bobs make the place homely; the oak-floored dining room is set with white linen napkins and polished cutlery. Five local ales accompany dishes to please walkers: beef casseroled in ale, Woodall's Cumberland sausages and Cumbrian lamb. The puddings are scrumptious and the cheeses reflect Cumbria's producers. Special.

Meals	Lunch from £5.
	Dinner from £11.50.
	Sunday lunch, 3 courses, £18.95.
Closed	3pm-5pm (in winter).
	Open all day Sat, Sun & in
	summer.

Anthony Hutton
Tower Bank Arms,
Near Sawrey,
Ambleside LA22 0LF
Tel   +44 (0)15394 36334
Web   www.towerbankarms.co.uk

Entry 136 Map 11

Cumbria

Masons Arms
Cartmel Fell

A perfect Lakeland inn tucked two miles inland from Lake Windermere, on the side of a hill with huge views across lush fields to distant Scout Scar. In summer, pub life decants onto a spectacular terrace – a sitting room in the sun – where window boxes and flower beds tumble with colour. The inn dates from the 16th century and is impossibly pretty and the bar is deeply traditional with roaring fires, flagged floors, wavy beams, a cosy snug… and a menu of 70 bottled beers to quench thirst. Rustic elegance upstairs comes courtesy of stripped floors, country rugs and muted walls in the first-floor dining room – so grab a window seat for fabulous views and order delicious food, anything from a sandwich to Cumbrian duck.

Meals	Breakfast hampers £15–£25. Lunch from £4.95. Bar meals from £9.95. Dinner, 3 courses, £25–£30.
Closed	Open all day.

John & Diane Taylor
Masons Arms,
Cartmel Fell,
Grange-over-Sands LA11 6NW

Tel   +44 (0)15395 68486
Web   www.masonsarmsstrawberrybank.co.uk

Entry 137 Map 11

Cumbria

The Beer Hall at Hawkshead Brewery
Staveley

Alex, an erstwhile BBC foreign correspondent, started his brewery in 2002 with little idea of the success he would find. But demand surged, and as Hawkshead Bitter established itself as one of the best pints in the Lakes, the need for greater space prompted a move across the lake to Mill Yard in Staveley (a micro-industrial park in the village). Then Alex developed The Beer Hall, adding food to the menu and now you can sup his ales and enjoy a hearty down-to-earth meal. You'll find the whole Hawkshead range at the bar and a menu that changes daily: stout and oxtail soup, wild local hare stew with dumplings, goat's cheese soufflé, omelette Arnold Bennett – and always, Brewers Lunch: a feast for carnivores. Tours of the brewery are available, and if you like what you drink, you can take some home.

Meals	Snacks from £2.50. Dinner from £9.50.
Closed	Open all day.

Chris Ramwell
The Beer Hall at Hawkshead Brewery,
Mill Yard, Staveley,
Kendal LA8 9LR

Tel   +44 (0)1539 825260
Web   www.hawksheadbrewery.co.uk

Entry 138 Map 11

Cumbria

The Yanwath Gate Inn
Yanwath

It was built as a toll gate in 1683 – hence the name. Known to locals as the Yat, the old pub has gained a reputation for its food, locally sourced and served in hearty portions. The place is immaculate, the young staff are attentive and the new landlord remains loyal to the pub's roots, so you may eat anywhere, including the sunny patio at the back. Enter a characterful, dim-lit bar, all cosy corners and crackling fire, with background music and happy chatter. Beyond is an airy, raftered dining room. The menu depends on fresh deliveries every day including Cumbrian meat and plenty of fish, there's the Yat's tapas bar, and homemade food for children, from pizza to smoked haddock and fishcakes. The 60 wines come from an excellent merchant's in Kendal and the three cask ales are Cumbrian and very well kept.

Meals	Lunch & dinner £12–£25.
Closed	Open all day.

David Gordon
The Yanwath Gate Inn,
Yanwath,
Penrith CA10 2LF
Tel   +44 (0)1768 862386
Web   www.yanwathgate.com

Entry 139 Map 11

Cumbria

Highland Drove
Great Salkeld

Yards from the Norman church with its keep-like tower (protection against marauding Scots), the old wooden front door leads to a flagged bar – cosy, warm and civilised. There's a bar-dining area with easy leather chairs and pine tables, and a popular games room with pool. With open log fires, tartan fabrics, brick and timber, this is a spruce 21st-century inn aimed at drinkers, diners and walkers. Named after the rugged cattle that were brought down from Scotland by drovers to market, the unique dining room has a Highland lodge feel, its great windows gazing to the Pennines. Tuck into wild game terrine; Lakeland venison Wellington with red wine jus; steak and ale pie, sticky toffee pudding. Beers are from the cask, wines are well-chosen. Or keep things simple with a fresh baguette in the bar.

Meals	Lunch & dinner £7.95–£18.95. Sunday roast £9.95.
Closed	2.30pm–6pm & Mon lunch (except Bank Holidays). Open all day Sat & Sun.

Donald & Paul Newton
Highland Drove,
Great Salkeld,
Penrith CA11 9NA
Tel   +44 (0)1768 898349
Web   www.highland-drove.co.uk

Entry 140 Map 11

Cumbria

Old Crown
Hesket Newmarket

In a dreamy village and porter on tap! The old pub is owned by a cooperative of 147 souls and is run by Keith and Edna. Its tiny front room with bar, settles, glowing coals, thumbed books, pictures and folk music squeezes in a dozen; a second room houses darts and pool; a third and fourth are dining rooms. This is the only pub where you can sample all of Hesket Newmarket's beers brewed in the barn at the back (ask about tours) and it is the focal point of the community, even supporting the post office whose postmistress repays in puddings and pies. Known also for its fine curries and Sunday roasts, its authenticity draws people from miles around. Prince Charles dropped by (twice) to launch the *Saving Your Village Pub* guide, walkers come for the Caldbeck Fells.

Meals	Lunch & dinner £6-£13.
	Bar meals £2.50-£6.50.
Closed	2.30pm-5.30pm, Fri-Sun.
	Open from 5.30pm Mon-Thurs.

Stephen & Beverley Bennett
Old Crown,
Hesket Newmarket,
Wigton CA7 8JG
Tel   +44 (0)1697 478288
Web   www.theoldcrownpub.co.uk

Entry 141 Map 11

Cumbria

Kirkstile Inn
Loweswater

Hard to imagine a more glorious setting than that of the Kirkstile Inn, tucked among the fells, next to an old church and a stream, a half mile from the lakes of Loweswater and Crummock. The whole place is authentic, traditional, well looked after: whitewashed walls, low beams, solid polished tables, cushioned settles, a well-stoked fire, plants, flowers and the odd horse harness to remind you of the past. Come for afternoon tea, or settle down with an unforgettable pint of Loweswater Gold or Melbreak Bitter or one of the other Cumbrian Legendary Ales, brewed by Roger in Esthwaite Water near Hawkshead. Expect local produce and unfussy traditional dishes such as steak and ale pie, chicken breast stuffed with Cumberland sausage, sticky toffee pudding, a plate of local cheeses.

Meals	Bar meals from £5.95.
	Lunch & dinner £8.95-£18.95.
	Sunday lunch, 3 courses, £18.
Closed	Open all day.

Roger Humphreys
Kirkstile Inn,
Loweswater,
Cockermouth,CA13 0RU
Tel   +44 (0)1900 85219
Web   www.kirkstile.com

Entry 142 Map 11

The Old Hall Inn
Whitehough

Welcome to a glorious stone built 16th-century coaching inn and Elizabethan manor house, family run and country-pub in character with reclaimed flagstones, chunky wooden furniture, padded pews, stools, real fires and local maps, blueprints and archive photos. Find a staggering ten cask ales on tap from local brewers Thornbridge and Bollington amongst others, and let helpful staff guide you through a multitude of bottled European and US craft beers, lagers and ciders, great wines, malts and cognacs. Food ranges from pub classics to more gourmet choices, provenance is impeccable; try locally shot game pie with braised red cabbage and handmade chips. The cheese board is special too. Eat in the main bar area or for a treat head next door to the old hall and dine beneath the beamed minstrels' gallery. You can stay here or at the charming sister pub, the Old Paper Mill, a stone's throw across the garden: all rooms have a modern country style with super patchwork quilts in some, oak furniture, wooden and brass beds and big colour photographs of gorgeous Derbyshire. *Minimum stay: 2 nights in high season.*

Rooms	8 doubles: £79-£115.
Meals	Lunch from £5.50. Bar meals & dinner from £8. Sunday lunch, 3 courses, £18.50.
Closed	Open all day.

Daniel Capper
The Old Hall Inn,
Whitehough, Chinley,
High Peak SK23 6EJ
Tel   +44 (0)1663 750529
Web   www.old-hall-inn.co.uk

The Devonshire Arms at Pilsley
Pilsley

A stroll from the Chatsworth Farm Shop and the mansion, this is the second estate-owned pub to have been spruced up by the late Duchess. Loved by estate-workers, Chatsworth visitors, well-heeled locals and the odd walker, the eye-catching interiors combine traditional wood and stone with bright richly upholstered wall benches, bold wall coverings and quirky lamps, though the bar is not made for lingering in. Making use of farm shop produce and estate-reared meats, the classic pub menu announces ham hock terrine and homemade chutney, steak and kidney pudding, farm-shop faggots with autumn vegetables, a roast-of-the-day, and new takes on old-fashioned puds — all well-priced and nicely washed down with a home-brew of Chatsworth Gold. The Duchess's eye for detail is also on display in the warm, cosy, contemporary bedrooms, with big beds, feather down duvets, delightful fabrics and throws, coffee and chocolate making facilities, country mags and terrific bathrooms. Beautiful walks start from the village; Pilsley is stunning.

Rooms	7 doubles: £79–£139.
Meals	Lunch, bar meals & dinner from £4.95.
Closed	Open all day.

Alan Hill
The Devonshire Arms at Pilsley,
High Street, Pilsley,
Bakewell DE45 1UL
Tel   +44 (0)1756 718111
Web   www.devonshirepilsley.co.uk

Entry 144 Map 8

The Devonshire Arms at Beeley
Beeley

Classic Peak District scenery surrounds Beeley's stone cottages and this public house, converted from three cottages into a coaching inn in 1747, and once visited by Edward VII. It is popular now for its proximity to great Chatsworth House; ever a civilised lunch spot for well-heeled locals, it verges on the opulent. Alongside the beams, the log fires and the settles are candy-stripe tub chairs in vibrant hues and cushions tucked into cosy crannies – irresistible. In a room where floor-to-ceiling windows overlook the beck are snazzy bar stools, a glass-fronted wine store and more enticing colours. Friendly staff in the bar and brasserie serve traditional and modern food with meat from the estate; our lamb rump with parsley pesto, spinach and rocket jus was delicious. In a stone-flagged tap room, walkers are refreshed with expertly kept ales, and the wine list is worth exploring. Bedrooms are equally stylish and smart – some upstairs, larger ones in Brookside House, others in Dove Cottage across the road.

Rooms	11 doubles, 2 twin/doubles: £109–£219. 1 suite for 2: £159–£189.
Meals	Lunch & bar meals from £9.95. Dinner, 3 courses, about £25.
Closed	Open all day.

Alan Hill
The Devonshire Arms at Beeley,
Beeley,
Matlock DE4 2NR
Tel   +44 (0)1756 718111
Web   www.devonshirebeeley.co.uk

Derbyshire

The Devonshire Arms
Middle Handley

Straddling Yorkshire and Derbyshire, the handsome 'Dev' sits back off a leafy lane, surrounded by rolling fields. A smart pale grey makeover draws you in, though there's seating by the front door if you fancy a Kelham Island pint in the sunshine. Inside: a light, contemporary space full of interest and quirk – original art on the walls, squashy leather sofas, a pair of thrones... In the stone-floored snug, a wood stove adds cheer on a chill day. The airy dining area has artfully mismatched furniture, some vintage, a couple of church pews and one long canteen-like table big enough for a full family. The short, rustic menu includes the likes of braised ox cheek, shoulder of Derbyshire lamb, ham hock fritter and a tasty monster of a hot pork and apple sandwich; wash it down with a glass of wine from nearby Renishaw Hall, the Sitwell family seat.

Derbyshire

The Devonshire Arms
Baslow

For years, the 'Dev' as it's known was a run-of-the-mill kind of place – well positioned in the centre of pretty Baslow and a stone's throw from Chatsworth House – but not particularly inviting. All that has changed. Gone are the cavernous, echoey rooms and flock wallpaper – instead, chunky oak tables and tartan wool check padded benches, funky lighting and more vintage finds than an emporium; it's kitsch but very comfortable. A crowd-pleasing menu promises to be 'unpretentious: no balancing carrots!' and includes the likes of warm black pudding salad, burgers, beef and ale pie, and celeriac risotto. Kick back in front of the wood stove in the cosy bar with a pint of Peak Ales Bakewell Best and 'Full Works and Chips' before striking out across the glorious Derbyshire Peaks.

Meals	Starters from £5. Dinner from £10.
Closed	Mon all day.

Meals	Lunch & dinner £3.25–£18.50.
Closed	Open all day.

Jill Swift
The Devonshire Arms,
Lightwood Lane, Middle Handley,
Sheffield S21 5RN
Tel   +44 (0)1246 434800
Web   www.devonshirearmsmiddlehandley.com

Gary Hodgkisson
The Devonshire Arms,
Nether End, Baslow,
Bakewell DE45 1SR
Tel   +44 (0)1246 582551
Web   www.devonshirearmsbaslow.co.uk

Entry 146 Map

Entry 147 Map 8

Derbyshire

Three Stags Heads
Wardlow

As you weave your way across the limestone plateau, don't miss this Derbyshire longhouse, modest home to a pottery and a pub. The pub is a gem and couldn't be plainer: two flagstone rooms, one warmed by a fire, the other by a coal-burning kitchen range. Settle in to a pint of Abbeydale's Black Lurcher, the house bitter with an 8% ABV; it was named in memory of one of the dogs. The menu really is a case of what is available from the surrounding area, it changes with the week and the season, and features lots of game (it has been known for squirrel to have gone into the pot). Opening times are restricted depending on whether you're here for pottery or a pint – or a plate of something hearty and wholesome from the blackboard. Soaked in history and authenticity but no museum – the hosts and the dogs see to that!

Derbyshire

The Plough
Hathersage

It's a great spot for walkers, this 16th-century former corn mill on the banks of the river, and the moment you enter you know you're in the right place. The sweeping tartan carpeting is cheering, the fires are crackling, the staff are chatty and engaging. Owner Bob, a lovely Dales man, continues to manage a brilliant team and that includes the chefs. Everything we tasted was well-presented and delicious, from the breast of duck with confit duck leg and celeriac wellington to the cheese platter and the apple crumble. The wine list is similarly good. A recent refurb sees warm red walls, scarlet-padded banquettes, and a baby grand at one end. You're on a main road but the large sloping gardens are safe for romping children, and are as gorgeous as the valley views.

Meals	Lunch & dinner £7.50–£12.50.
Closed	Mon–Thurs all day & Fri until 7pm. Open all day weekends & Bank Holidays.

Meals	Lunch & dinner £12.95–£19.95.
Closed	Open all day.

Geoff & Pat Fuller
Three Stags Heads,
Wardlow,
Buxton SK17 8RW
Tel +44 (0)1298 872268

Entry 148 Map 8

Bob & Cynthia Emery
The Plough, Leadmill, Hathersage,
Hope Valley S32 1BA
Tel +44 (0)1433 650319
Web www.theploughinn-
hathersage.co.uk

Entry 149 Map 8

Derbyshire

The Samuel Fox Country Inn
Bradwell

Chef James Duckett has swapped a thriving Devon restaurant for a chance to reconnect with his north-country roots. His new project is a welcoming Hope Valley inn, its airy open-plan interior with splendid views, warmed by wood-burners and – now that word has got around – filled with booted walkers, day-trippers and locals. The chalkboard menu suggests modern, imaginatively prepared pub dishes made with fresh local produce: there could be hake with clam casserole, pot roast guinea fowl with roasted vegetables, sage and cider, and lemon posset for pudding. Extras like home-baked bread are beyond reproach. You'd be forgiven for thinking that this is more of a restaurant than a country pub, but drinkers are always welcome; there are two real ales from local microbreweries on tap and 14 wines by the glass.

Meals	Lunch & bar meals from £10. Dinner from £13.50. Sunday lunch, 2 courses, £19–£24.
Closed	Mon & Tues.

James Duckett
The Samuel Fox Country Inn,
Stretfield Road, Bradwell,
Hope Valley S33 9JT
Tel +44 (0)1433 621562
Web www.samuelfox.co.uk

Entry 150 Map 8

Derbyshire

The Red Lion
Litton

Stunning walks start and end at this village pub, standing on the oak-studded green. The interiors are charming too, all stone floors, roaring fires and wood panelled rooms. The staff are lovely, the food is homely (and good value), and the beer is great – it's better than it's ever been. Absolution from Sheffield's Abbeydale Brewery is a favourite, as is Oakwells Barnsley Bitter. Pub classics include fish and chips and ham and eggs; puds range from treacle sponge and custard to a historic sticky toffee pudding. This is pub as hub, a happy ship full of locals and walkers. There are summer carnivals, winter fairs and a weekly fund-raising quiz that's so popular you must arrive early if you fancy a seat by the fire. In the spring, a million daffodils fringe the green – enjoy a convivial pint before striking out again.

Meals	Lunch & dinner £5.95–£9.95.
Closed	Open all day.

Andrew & Louise Holland
The Red Lion,
Litton,
Tideswell SK17 8QU
Tel +44 (0)1298 871458
Web www.theredlionlitton.co.uk

Entry 151 Map 8

The White Lion
Great Longstone

Greg and Libby Robinson have saved this handsome old village pub from a sorry end, lavishing love (and not a small amount of hard graft) into the very fabric of it. There are a handful of contemporary touches (splashy wallpaper, banquettes) but the beams, wood floors and open fire make it feel like a comfy nook to relax with a pint. The menu's pretty modern too; expect the likes of smoked chicken, chorizo and red pepper tian or gilt head bream with parsnip couscous alongside robust pub grub classics. Robinson's Dizzy Blonde is nicely kept; you can enjoy a pint in the cosy tap room with your canine chum, and a plate of bangers and mash. What's more, Sunday lunch is legendary! Just as well you're deep in the Derbyshire Dales, with super walks from the door.

Meals	Lunch & dinner from £11.95. Sunday roast from £10.75.
Closed	3pm-6pm, Mon-Fri. Sat from 9pm. Sun from 8pm.

Libby & Greg Robinson
The White Lion,
Main Street, Great Longstone,
Bakewell DE45 1TA
Tel +44 (0)1629 640252
Web www.whiteliongreatlongstone.co.uk

Entry 152 Map 8

The Royal Oak
Hurdlow

This old boozer has been rescued and tenderly returned to award-winning life. In the old bar are beams, open fires, exposed stone walls and comfortable seating; there's an extra room, too, with scrubbed wooden tables and views over fields. Honest, straightforward pub grub flows from a spanking new kitchen, and everything's homemade and wholesome. Expect hand-raised pork and chicken pie; lamb chops with leek mash; goat's cheese and red onion tart. Local beers include Hartingtons, Wincles and the award-winning Thornbridge ales. There's a campsite and bunk barn on site and the stunning Tissington Trail is on the doorstep – just as well if you're going the whole hog and choose apple crumble and custard to finish.

Meals	Breakfast from £5.95. Lunch & dinner from £8.95. Sunday lunch, 2 courses, £15.25.
Closed	Open all day.

Paul White & Justin Heslop
The Royal Oak,
Hurdlow,
Buxton SK17 9QJ
Tel +44 (0)1298 83288
Web www.peakpub.co.uk

Entry 153 Map 8

Derbyshire

The Flying Childers Inn
Stanton-in-Peak

Standing proudly on a hill in pretty Stanton, in the Peak District National Park, this handsome, stone-built, 18th-century pub was once a row of farm labourers' cottages. Owned by the village aristocrats, it gets its name from a champion racehorse owned by the 4th Duke of Devonshire, reputedly unbeaten! Walk into the snug and a cosy fire greets you; slide into a corner and clock cricket team photos going back decades, slightly skew-whiff on wonky woodchip walls. Furniture is battered, nothing matches and pot tankards hang on blackened beams. The simple menu features homemade soup and game casseroles and ham-filled cobs with chunky chutney. Well-kept Wells Bombardier is permanently on tap, plus a couple of rotating guest ales.

Meals	Bar meals £2-£5.
Closed	2pm-7pm Wed-Fri. 3pm-7pm Sat & Sun. Mon & Tues lunch.

Stuart Redfern
The Flying Childers Inn,
Stanton-in-Peak,
Matlock DE4 2LW
Tel   +44 (0)1629 636333
Web   www.flyingchilders.com

Entry 154 Map 8

Derbyshire

The Druid Inn
Birchover

A strangely enticing countryside of tors, crags, wooded knolls and stone circle-strewn moors erupts high above Matlock. In its midst stands the Druid, behind whose sober exterior lies a worn and well-loved bar, and a restaurant in which the food does the talking. You're greeted by an array of ales in tip-top condition – then a small stone fireplace to the right, padded stools and eclectic art. The dining area with its lush purple wall is a light modern backdrop for innovative takes on traditional dishes; tuck into the likes of Druid smoky fish pie with cheddar mash and greens, or halibut rarebit. Rob and chef John are passionate about food and some items are named to keep guests guessing – what are Dixie's Three Little Piggies? Outside bench-tables deliver village views, ramblers rub shoulders with epicures, and a beer garden is planned for 2015.

Meals	Lunch & dinner £9-£21.
Closed	Open all day.

Rob Innes & Joyce Simpson
The Druid Inn,
Main Street,
Birchover DE4 2BL
Tel   +44 (0)1629 653836
Web   www.druidinnbirchover.co.uk

Entry 155 Map

Derbyshire

Ye Olde Gate Inn
Brassington

One of the most exquisite pubs in Derbyshire, built from timber salvaged from the Armada. Furnishings are plain: ancient settles, rush-seated chairs, gleaming copper, a clamorous clock, a collection of pewter. Mullioned windows look onto a sheltered back garden, perfect for warm summer evenings. In winter, a fire blazes in the blackened range that dominates the quarry-tiled bar; in the dim yet atmospheric snug are a glowing range and flickering candlelight. There's a daily specials board and traditional tucker: baguettes, steak and Guinness pie, liver and onions, beer-battered fish and chips, homemade bread and butter pudding. Come too for superbly kept Marston's Pedigree on hand pump and a number of malts.

Derbyshire

Saracen's Head
Shirley

A pearl of a pub in unsung South Derbyshire. Renowned chef Robin Hunter and wife Terri have brought bags of gastropub style to the historic village, while cleverly holding on to an authentic pub feel. Slate floors give way to carpeting, light wood chairs are cushioned, an open roof space is stylishly decorated and fires crackle in cast-iron surrounds at either end. Greene King ales greet you at the bar and there's a good wine list. Linger over the menus as the smell of freshly baked breads wafts from the kitchen: modern English food and the best ingredients hold sway, and you can bring your own produce in to barter! There's rack of lamb with chorizo mash and olive and garlic jus, and lemon meringue roulade with vanilla bean ice cream – fit for Saladin himself.

Meals	Bar meals from £4.25.
	Lunch from £7.95.
	Dinner from £8.95.
	Sunday lunch, 2 courses, from £12.75.
	Not Sunday eve.
Closed	2.30pm-6pm (7pm Sun).
	Mon (except Bank Holidays)
	& Tues lunch.

Meals	Lunch & dinner from £9.25.
Closed	3pm-6pm (Mon-Sat).
	Open all day Sun.

Peter Scragg
Ye Olde Gate Inn,
Well Street, Brassington,
Matlock DE4 4HJ

Tel   +44 (0)1629 540448
Web   www.oldgateinnbrassington.co.uk

Entry 156 Map 8

Robin & Terri Hunter
Saracen's Head,
Church Lane, Shirley,
Ashbourne DE6 3AS

Tel   +44 (0)1335 360330
Web   www.saracens-head-shirley.co.uk

Entry 157 Map 8

Derbyshire

The Bulls Head
Repton

Once a derelict shell, the Bulls Head has been transformed by its owners, and the best of its old features brought to the fore. The downstairs is a jumble of connected rooms with wooden floors, stone flags, stripped timbers, chairs upholstered in cow hide, bulls heads made from bicycles, driftwood sculptures, steel pillars and, in the restaurant, 1930s gilt mirrors flanking a log-effect fire – amazing! Energetic staff flit hither and thither ferrying mouthwatering steaks and wood-fired pizzas and serious dinners: Indonesian fishcakes and seafood chowders; cannon of lamb with tomato and black olive salsa; apple, pear and blueberry crumble. There's a good kids' menu, too. It's hugely popular and the parking isn't easy, but it's one of the most exciting places in Derbyshire.

Meals	Lunch & dinner £8.95–£22.95. Sunday roast £8.95.
Closed	Open all day.

Richard & Loren Pope
The Bulls Head,
84 High Street, Repton,
Derby DE65 6GF
Tel   +44 (0)1283 704422
Web   www.thebullsheadrepton.co.uk

Entry 158 Map 8

Derbyshire

Three Horseshoes
Breedon on the Hill

Opposite the old 'village lock up', a listed village inn. Ian Davison and Jenny Ison have revitalised the old place and introduced a modern feel with a menu to match. Expect painted brickwork, seagrass matting, antique tables, Windsor chairs, eclectic pictures and masses of space. Smaller rooms include a simple quarry-tiled bar and an intimate red dining room with three tables; pride of place goes to a Victorian bar counter picked up years ago – now it displays chocolates and wine. Dishes are chalked up on boards in the bar and the award-winning formula includes such dishes as monkfish with capers and spinach, and pork and cider casserole. Marston's Pedigree on hand pump should satisfy those in for a swift half, while foodies can check out the farm shop – and the chocolate workshop across the yard.

Meals	Bar meals £4.95–£10.95. Lunch & dinner £8.95–£26.50.
Closed	Mon all day. Sun from 3pm.

Ian Davison & Jenny Ison
Three Horseshoes,
44-46 Main St, Breedon on the Hill,
Derby DE73 8AN
Tel   +44 (0)1332 695129
Web   www.thehorseshoes.com

Entry 159 Map 8

Three Crowns
Chagford

St Austell Brewery spent 19 months and oodles of cash restoring this eye-catching, 13th-century stone and thatch village beauty. Dominating Chagford, it now matches its more illustrious hotel neighbours for comfort, but realistic pricing and a relaxing informality make this swish flagship inn a popular Dartmoor bolthole. Mullioned windows, massive beams and a vast inglenook in the original bar blend with a spanking new atrium-conservatory dining room that opens to a sheltered courtyard. Wonky walls and floors upstairs lead to bedrooms in sympathy with the age and charm, with rich fabrics, contemporary wall papers, cosy bathrooms in cleverly designed spaces and every modern comfort: iPod docks, flat-screens, phones, fresh coffee, leaf tea. Book the suite for churchyard views – and a cute little sitting room perched above the old front porch. New rooms in smart new-build wings are equally good. Pop downstairs for pub classics, potted Brixham crab, Devon beef, plaice with parsley butter, and dark chocolate and orange tart. Moorland walks wait outside the door.

Rooms	20 twin/doubles: £95–£145. 1 suite for 2: £150–£190.
Meals	Lunch & dinner £8.95–£19.50.
Closed	Rarely.

Matthew & Sally Perkins
Three Crowns,
High Street,
Chagford TQ13 8AJ
Tel   +44 (0)1647 433444
Web   www.threecrowns-chagford.co.uk

Entry 160 Map 2

The Elephant's Nest Inn
Mary Tavy

The main bar puts a smile on your face, all dark beams, flagstone floors and crackling fires... you almost imagine a distant Baskerville hound baying. This is an atmospheric inn that serves delicious home-cooked food – local, seasonal and British with a twist. Tuck into antipasto of pastrami, rosette saucisson and Black Forest ham; South Devon sirloin with mushrooms, vine tomatoes and French fries; and Mrs Cook's fabulous lemon posset with blueberry compote. When suitably sated, slip off to the annexe and a nest of your own in one of three peaceful, very comfortable rooms, with gleaming oak floors heated underfoot; one room has its own private patio. Wake to a pretty garden with views to Brentor church and the moor, an exceptional breakfast and perhaps a cricket match to watch: the pub has its own ground and club. Settle back to the thwack of willow on leather with a pint of Palmer's IPA. There's Doom Bar too, Jail Ale from Princetown, and guest ales from Otter, Cotleigh, Teignworthy, Butcombe. The pub is a dog-friendly zone – check out their website for photos of the residents.

Rooms	3 twin/doubles: £88.
Meals	Lunch & dinner £8.95–£19.95.
Closed	Rarely.

Hugh & Denise Cook
The Elephant's Nest Inn,
Horndon, Mary Tavy,
Tavistock PL19 9NQ
Tel   +44 (0)1822 810273
Web   www.elephantsnest.co.uk

Tradesmans Arms
Stokenham

A little cracker of a pub, 14th-century, part-thatched and two miles from the sea. Prop up the bar, bring the dogs, tuck into the fabulous food; head chef Kris Jury and his team are making a splash in remotest Devon, using fresh local produce, making seasonal changes to the menu. Formerly a brewhouse with three cottages, the pub stands in a sleepy village near Slapton Sands and takes its name from the tradesmen who trekked the coastal bridle path. Dark-beamed, slate-floored and charmingly rustic, the oldest part has a log-burner, antique tables and inviting bar stools, while the more hushed, more modern and slightly elevated dining room is red pattern-carpeted and dotted with gilt framed pictures. Outside: a beer garden with lush countryside views. Reasons to be here: superior malt whiskies, Otter and Tribute ales, top-notch breakfasts, an extensive wine list to suit all pockets, and a homemade pie with a beautiful glaze on its puff pastry lid. They also have a children's menu, and do a great vegetarian option. The Sanders have now introduced four bedrooms with super bathrooms upstairs, the two at the front the biggest and the best.

Rooms	4 doubles: £85-£100.
Meals	Starters from £5.45.
	Dinner from £10.50.
Closed	Rarely.

Catherine Sanders
Tradesmans Arms,
Stokenham,
Kingsbridge TQ7 2SZ
Tel   +44 (0)1548 580996
Web   www.thetradesmansarms.com

Entry 162 Map 2

Devon

Nobody Inn
Doddiscombsleigh

Thankfully, little has changed since the current owners arrived in 2008; they run a happy ship. The wine and whisky lists remains over 200-strong, and the Devon cheese board continues to draw rural winers and diners from afar. Settles and tables are crammed into every corner, horse brasses brighten low beams, there's a cosy inglenook glowing with logs and part of the bar dates from Tudor times. Start with a bowl of Teign mussels, move on to rack of lamb with redcurrant and rosemary jus, finish with treacle tart: the food is beautiful, imaginative and locally sourced. Or try something traditional from the bar menu. To wash all this down: Nobody Bitter served in old pint glasses. A rare dram of Islay malt might be an excellent nightcap before retiring to one of five refurbished rooms upstairs, colour-themed according to name: Violet, Rose, Bluebell, Lily and Primrose. Quirky, fun, variously sized and extremely comfortable, they have soft carpets, super beds and decanters of sherry; bathrooms, smallish, are, bar one, en suite. The village is buried down a maze of lanes but is certainly worth the detour.

Rooms	3 doubles, 1 twin/double; 1 double with separate shower: £60–£95. Singles £45–£70.
Meals	Lunch & bar meals from £9.95. Dinner from £14.95. Sunday roast from £9.95.
Closed	New Year's Day.

Sue Burdge
Nobody Inn,
Doddiscombsleigh,
Exeter EX6 7PS
Tel   +44 (0)1647 252394
Web   www.nobodyinn.co.uk

Entry 163 Map 2

The Globe
Topsham

Expansion west away from their Cornish heartland has seen St Austell Brewery snap up some stunning Devon inns and the Globe, a substantial 17th-century building close to the Exe estuary in pretty Topsham, has already proved to be a shrewd acquisition. Locals and visitors to Exeter (four miles away) love the place. The atmosphere is relaxed and the revamped interior cleverly combines old and new, with traditional features, rich fabrics and colours. Choose to eat in the lively modern bar or the cosy dining room in the Jacobean part of the inn with its terracotta painted ceiling and old Topsham photographs. Classic bar snacks vie for attention with river Exe mussels, monkfish and tiger prawn curry, or plaice with caper and herb butter; the set lunch menu is great value. Galleried courtyard rooms are cosy, warm and full of contemporary touches — muted hues, crisp linen and thick down on superbly comfortable beds. Take the train into Exeter (15 minutes), a boat trip down the Exe to see the avocets, or explore Topsham's old port and its individual shops.

Rooms	19 twin/doubles: £65–£110.
Meals	Lunch from £4.75.
	Dinner from £9.50.
Closed	Rarely.

The Globe Team
The Globe,
Fore Street,
Topsham EX3 0HR

Tel	+44 (0)1392 873471
Web	www.theglobetopsham.co.uk

Entry 164 Map 2

Devon

Masons Arms
Branscombe

Lose yourself in tiny lanes, follow them down towards the sea, pass the Norman church, roll up at the Masons Arms. It stands in a village half a mile back from the pebble beach surrounded by glorious country, with a stone terrace at the front from which to gaze upon lush hills. It dates back to 1350 – a cider house turned country pub – and the men who cut the stone for Exeter Cathedral drank here, hence the name. Inside, simple, authentic interiors are just the thing: timber frames, low beamed ceilings, pine cladding, whitewashed walls and a roaring fire over which the spit roast is cooked on Sundays. Some bedrooms are above the inn, others are behind on the hill. Those in the pub are small and cosy (warm yellows, check fabrics, leather bedheads, super bathrooms); those behind are bigger, quieter and more traditional; they overlook a garden and share a private terrace with valley views that tumble down to the sea. Footpaths lead out – over hills, along the coast – so follow your nose, then return for super food: seared scallops, lamb cutlets, saffron and honey crème brûlée. *Minimum stay: 2 nights at weekends & in high season.*

Rooms	8 doubles, 6 twin/doubles, 6 four-posters: £80-£180. 1 family room for 4: £165-£195.
Meals	Bar meals from £9.95. Lunch from £7.50. Dinner, 3 courses, £20-£25. Sunday roast from £9.95.
Closed	Rarely.

Alison Ede
Masons Arms,
Branscombe,
Seaton EX12 3DJ
Tel   +44 (0)1297 680300
Web   www.masonsarms.co.uk

Entry 165 Map 2

Devon

The Fountain Head
Branscombe

With an ale festival in June, they take their beer seriously here: local and top brew; the food is good too. There's not much to say about the history, except that the dining room was once a forge, but there is an authentic feel: big flagstones, wood-clad walls, dim-lit corners and a tap room that used to be the cellar. No TV screens, no fruit machines, just local babble and possibly a snoozing dog. (It's great walking country.) The restaurant is dominated by a central chimney and grate; tables are candlelit and horseshoes hang from beams, along with the landlord's boots. Locals and visitors tuck into honest pub food and plenty of it – half a pint of prawns, beef and Branoc Ale pie, curry of the day, barbecues on summer Sundays. Beers are brewed in the village, ciders are Green Valley and the staff are great.

Meals	Bar meals £3.95-£5.95. Lunch & dinner £7.50-£12.
Closed	3pm-6pm.

Jon Woodley & Teresa Hoare
The Fountain Head,
Branscombe,
Seaton EX12 3BG
Tel +44 (0)1297 680359
Web www.fountainheadinn.com

Entry 166 Map 2

Devon

The Holt
Honiton

So named (a holt = the lair of an otter) because the McCaigs own the Otter Brewery in the Blackdown Hills. Joe and chef Angus run the pub, and Otter brews come from the underground eco cellar: Bitter, Ale, Bright and Head. But the spruced-up boozer on Honiton's high street is much more than the brewery 'tap'. The vibrant bar and contemporary dining room upstairs play host to live music and film nights when food is off the menu. Angus delivers modern pub food from an open-plan kitchen, the emphasis being on local produce – farm meats, estate-shot game, and smoked meats and fish from the on-site smokehouse. On seasonal menus are beefburgers, confit duck leg and sandwiches for lunch; for dinner, bream with crab and coriander cream sauce, lamb shank with herb dumplings, chocolate brownies. A superb A30 pit-stop.

Meals	Lunch from £5.50. Dinner from £12.50.
Closed	3pm-5.30pm & all day Sun & Mon.

Joe & Angus McCaig
The Holt,
178 High Street,
Honiton EX14 1LA
Tel +44 (0)1404 47707
Web www.theholt-honiton.com

Entry 167 Map 2

Devon

The Railway
Honiton

A gem of a pub, tucked just off the High Street in a vibrant market town. Built by GWR workers en route to Cornwall it has seen plenty of action; now a calmer vibe rules. The bar area is lounge style with long bench seats, Indian flagstones and café tables. The dining area beyond is upbeat and quirky with painted pulley wheels and lots of local art. Gorgeous food and an engaging atmosphere mix with a bistro-brasserie style, courtesy of vivacious Jean Sancey who serves a wide-ranging menu: zucchini fritti, pressed ham hock terrine of local pedigree pork, fragrant chicken Vietnamese salad, traditional Louisiana jambalaya, pan-seared scallops, 'bucatini puttanesca' – dazzling. Drinkers have Branscombe Branoc and Dragon Tears cider to discover.

Meals	Bar meals from £9.95. Lunch from £5.95. Dinner from £12.95.
Closed	Open all day.

Jean Sancey
The Railway,
Queen Street,
Honiton EX14 1HE
Tel   +44 (0)1404 47976
Web   www.therailwayhoniton.co.uk

Entry 168 Map 2

Devon

The Five Bells
Clyst Hydon

When the local vicar objected to the pub next to his church it was moved half a mile – to an 16th-century farmhouse. And here it still stands, with a tongue-in-cheek name to mock him. Now the call is answered by all those in search of a civilised watering hole where chef Ian Webber (of Gidleigh Park fame) produces subtle, seasonal dishes of great flavour, alongside pub favourites. Try loin of cod with lentil stew, saffron and River Exe mussels, or pan-fried lamb's liver with parsnip mash and pickled butternut squash. There's a novel 'Stammtisch' (a regulars') table, a private games room with WiFi to keep the kids happy, and an attractive, peaceful garden with far-reaching views in which to step out with a pint of Otter, Butcombe or a chilled pinot grigio. Charming staff keep it all humming along splendidly.

Meals	Lunch & dinner £9.50-£22.50. Sunday lunch & dinner, 2-3 courses, £18.50-£22.50.
Closed	3pm-6pm Mon-Sat. Open all day Sun. Please check website for seasonal opening hours.

Chris Charles
The Five Bells,
Clyst Hydon,
Cullompton EX15 2NT
Tel   +44 (0)1884 277288
Web   www.fivebells.uk.com

Entry 169 Map 2

Devon

The Jack in the Green
Rockbeare

Bustle and buzz in the light oak bar, with its flagstone floor, upholstered leather chairs and local brews on tap – Otter Ale, Butcombe Bitter. But this is more restaurant than pub: "For those who live to eat," reads the sign. In a series of sumptuous plum-carpeted rooms, Matthew Mason's menu goes in for modern and mouthwatering variations of tried and trusted favourites: Scotch egg with mustard, fish and chips in real ale batter, homemade chicken liver parfait. More ambition is on display in the bright airy restaurant, where boned and rolled pork belly with black pudding and apple sauce or fillet of Cornish cod with saffron and river Exe mussels would make succulent choices. Note too the superb-value Totally Devon menu. Paul Parnell has been at the helm for nearly 25 years and this is one happy ship.

Meals	Lunch & dinner £11.50–£19.50. Bar meals from £4.95.
Closed	3pm–5.30pm (6pm Sat). Open all day Sun.

Paul Parnell
The Jack in the Green,
Rockbeare,
Exeter EX5 2EE
Tel +44 (0)1404 822240
Web www.jackinthegreen.uk.com

Entry 170 Map 2

Devon

The Bridge Inn
Topsham

Unchanged for most of the century – and in the family for as long – the 16th-century Bridge is for ale connoisseurs. And for all who love a pub furnished in the old-style: high-back settles, ancient floors, a simple hatch. Years ago it was a brewery and malthouse, Caroline's great-grandfather was the last publican to brew his own here and the Queen chose the Bridge for her first official visit to a pub. This is beer-drinker heaven, with up to ten real ales served by gravity from the cask. There's cider and gooseberry wine, too. Cradle your pint to the background din of local chatter in the Inner Sanctum, or out in the garden by the steep river bank. Bread baked at the local farm, home-cooked hams, homemade chutneys, Devon cheeses: the Bridge's sandwiches, pork pies and ploughman's are first-class.

Meals	Bar meals £3.20–£7. Lunch from £3.20.
Closed	2pm–6pm (7pm Sun).

Caroline Cheffers-Heard
The Bridge Inn,
Bridge Hill, Topsham,
Exeter EX3 0QQ
Tel +44 (0)1392 873862
Web www.cheffers.co.uk

Entry 171 Map 2

Devon

Bickley Mill Inn
Stoneycombe

A stylish inn full of good things that sits in a peaceful valley beyond the tourist trail: you're in the lush Stoneycombe valley with Dartmouth, Dartmoor and the south Devon coast all close. Three fires burn in winter and everywhere you look something delightful catches the eye, be it a huge sofa covered with cushions, or a decked terrace and garden for a pint in the summer sun. There are lovely staff, local ales and loads to eat. Our pie of the day had the perfect shortcrust and a juicy, meaty filling, and the vegetable side dish was spot on. Try pan-fried tiger prawns, lamb shank and minted pea purée, orange and cointreau bread and butter pudding, and real food for children (fish goujons, homemade soup). A generous place for foodies, with plenty of corners for those in for a pint.

Devon

The Church House Inn
Marldon

The old village pub is a civilised place, popular with retired locals and ladies that lunch. Others come for a pint of well-kept Dartmoor Best and a chat by the fire – it's a proper all-rounder. The feel is one of a well-crafted, rustic elegance – stonework and beams, original strawberry gothic windows, crisp table settings and smiling service. The central bar has been partitioned into three areas, plus one four-tabled candlelit snug, perfect for a party, and there's a lovely sloping garden for summer. Food is modern British and locally sourced: baked hake with butterbean and chorizo ragout, Dartmouth smoked fish platter, bramble Bakewell tart with blackberry compote. The pub originally housed the artisans who worked on Marldon Church; its ancient tower overlooks the hedged garden.

Meals	Lunch from £4.50. Dinner from £8.95.
Closed	Open all day.

Meals	Lunch & dinner £9–£19.95. Sunday roast £11.95.
Closed	2.30pm–5pm (3pm–5.30pm Sun).

James & Vanessa Woodleigh-Smith
Bickley Mill Inn,
Stoneycombe,
Newton Abbot TQ12 5LN
Tel   +44 (0)1803 873201
Web   www.bickleymill.co.uk

Entry 172 Map 2

Julian Cook
The Church House Inn,
Marldon,
Paignton TQ3 1SL
Tel   +44 (0)1803 558279
Web   www.churchhousemarldon.com

Entry 173 Map 2

Devon

Turtley Corn Mill
Avonwick

The mill has six acres sloping down to the lake and space for a multitude of picnic tables: order your hampers in advance. There are ducks too, and boules, croquet, Jenga and a ginormous chess set. Inside has been transformed to create a series of spacious interconnected areas: a bar with dark slate floors and doors to the garden; a wooden-floored 'library' lined with books; a mill room (turning wheel right outside) with a wood-burner, prints on white walls, oriental rugs and newspapers to read. The food is traditional and homemade, be it local game terrine, braised beef in red wine or sea bass with minted pea sauce. There's Princetown Jail Ale on tap and a raft of wines by the glass. The South Hams are close, as are the Dartmoor tors – and it's the perfect A38 stopover!

Meals	Breakfast from £4.
	Lunch & dinner £7.50-£17.95.
Closed	Open all day.

Samantha & Scott Colton
Turtley Corn Mill,
Avonwick,
South Brent TQ10 9ES
Tel   +44 (0)1364 646100
Web   www.turtleycornmill.com

Entry 174 Map 2

Devon

Steam Packet Inn
Totnes

This family-run inn overlooks the river Dart in charming, free-thinking Totnes. On sunny days the two-tier terrace is packed with a merry throng, while inside is warm, relaxed, atmospheric, a modern space of brick walls, planked floors, black panelling and an open fire. Arrive early and nab the leather sofa. There's bench seating under the window, plentiful books, background music, old nautical paintings, and some peaceful spots for dining; there's also a big bright conservatory restaurant overlooking the river. Pub grub is what they do here and they do it very well: tomato and oregano soup with chunky bread; fresh battered cod and chips with homemade tartare sauce; West Country rump steak; lovely roasts on Sundays. There's an ale and cider festival in May, hearty sandwiches for walkers and the staff could not be nicer.

Meals	Starters from £5.50.
	Dinner from £10.95.
Closed	Open all day.

Zoe Murless
Steam Packet Inn,
St Peter's Quay,
Totnes TQ9 5EW
Tel   +44 (0)1803 863880
Web   www.steampacketinn.co.uk

Entry 175 Map 2

Devon

The Tower Inn
Slapton

Standing beside the ivy-clad ruins of a chantry tower, a flower-bedecked classic, a southern belle, loved by all who visit. Despite the hidden access and tricky parking, this 14th-century inn attracts not just locals but families from Slapton Sands. As for the low-beamed and stone-walled interior – all rustic dark-wood tables, old pews and fine stone fireplaces – it is hugely atmospheric by night, thanks to flickering candles and fires. Accompany golden, bitter-sweet St Austell Brewery Proper Job from the handpump with a plateful of sea bass with braised fennel and crab dumplings or a trio of duck, rabbit and chorizo pie; and do book at weekends. A lovely, sleepy-village pub with a super landscaped garden at the back.

Devon

Pig's Nose Inn
East Prawle

Winding lanes with skyscraper hedges weave from the main road to the edge of the world. There are an awful lot of porcine references round these parts (South Hams, Gammon Head, Piglet Stores) and the Pig's Nose is Devon's most southerly pub. Filled with character, a wood-burner and quirky ephemera, it has an atmosphere all of its own. A pie, pint and a paper at lunchtime can give way at night to the entire pub joining in a singalong; Peter's connections entice legendary acts to play in the adjacent hall. Innovations include a flurry of fur 'smoking jackets' hanging in the porch and random pots of knitting inviting punters to 'do a line'. A one-off in a sea-view village that has barely changed since the thirties.

Meals	Lunch from £5.
	Dinner from £10.
	Sunday lunch, 3 courses, £22.
	Not Sunday eve in winter.
Closed	3pm-6pm.
	Sun evenings in winter.

Meals	Lunch & dinner £6.50–£12.50.
Closed	2.30pm-6pm (7pm in winter).
	Sun evenings & Mon all day
	in winter.

Thea Butler, Dan Cheshire
& Kevin Tweddell
The Tower Inn,
Slapton, Kingsbridge TQ7 2PN
Tel   +44 (0)1548 580216
Web   www.thetowerinn.com

Peter & Lesley Webber
Pig's Nose Inn,
East Prawle,
Kingsbridge TQ7 2BY
Tel   +44 (0)1548 511209
Web   www.pigsnoseinn.co.uk

Entry 176 Map 2

Entry 177 Map 2

The Millbrook Inn
South Pool

Arrive before the boats do – they drop anchor a step away and their first port of call is this inn. The atmosphere is charming, the food is quite something, and perfect ingredients are worshipped in best seasonal style. Tuck into Start Bay crab, confit of duck leg with chorizo cassoulet, and rhubarb and apple crumble; and look out for popular 'guest chef' nights. In winter, a log fire warms the immediate bar area while padded settles and wheelback chairs cluster comfortably around tables in snugs. The stream-side terrace is tiny but assures entertainment in summer once the ducks are at play, so sit back and watch with a pint of Red Rock IPA. The owners have ambition and integrity and succeed in delivering some of the best bounty in the area; visit the Veg Shed and stock up on produce from local allotments.

The Journey's End Inn
Ringmore

Down innumerable lanes where you can sniff the sea air is this: a 13th-century pub in a pretty thatched village. Four fires keep the original monks' mews snug and cosy, and each of the main areas has a different feel: a dark, rustic and flagged drinkers' bar – with a leather sofa-filled snug off it; a panelled room with a hatch bar; and a conservatory. Take your pick from many Devon ales, straight from the barrel, or Devonian cider; or choose from a great selection of whiskies and wines. Chef Conor has cooked in Thailand and at the Burgh Island Hotel, favours a refined simplicity, and menus change daily. When we were there on a cold February's day we were tempted by the slow-roast pork cheek with Bramley apple mash and buttered Savoy cabbage; and the charred beef rib-eye with a merlot reduction and a green peppercorn aïoli.

Meals	Lunch from £5.50.
	Dinner from £10.
Closed	Open all day.

Meals	Bar meals £2–£6.50.
	Lunch from £6.
	Dinner £11.50–£19.95.
	Sunday roast £11.50–£13.75.
Closed	Mon all day.

Ian Dent & Diana Hunt
The Millbrook Inn,
South Pool,
Kingsbridge TQ7 2RW
Tel   +44 (0)1548 531581
Web   www.millbrookinnsouthpool.co.uk

Entry 178 Map 2

Conor Heneghan & Tracy Brand
The Journey's End Inn,
Ringmore,
Kingsbridge TQ7 4HL
Tel   +44 (0)1548 810205
Web   www.thejourneysendinn.co.uk

Entry 179 Map 2

Devon

The Ship Inn
Noss Mayo

The Ship is gorgeous, so lovely it's almost unfair. It stands at the head of a tidal inlet, a 16th-century pub with majestic views over the water. Outside, a terrace flanked by olive trees and lavender draws a crowd in summer, but country-house interiors are just as good. You'll find wooden floors, country rugs, roaring fires and lovely art, with nautical curios scattered attractively throughout. Upstairs, the Library doubles as a private dining room, while the Bridge has weather-proofed views... not a bad spot for a good lunch, perhaps king prawns with sweet chilli sauce, seared scallops on saffron risotto, chocolate torte with vanilla ice cream. Local ales are downstairs, Jail Ale, Weather Station, or a pint of Tribute. The coast is on your doorstep, so bring your walking boots. One of the best.

Devon

The Treby Arms
Sparkwell

Behind the unremarkable exterior is a gastropub of surprises, a place of celebrity status. Anton Piotrowski, a joint Master Chef winner, heads a happy team. The cooking is tip top, of the moment and stunning to look at. There's pigeon en croûte with bubble and squeak; 'What Dad Got From the Garden' soup; gorgonzola with confit pear sorbet... these are just the starters. Step into a small dog-friendly bar for a pint of Tribute or one of many wines, then into the dining area where a young, happy and helpful staff ferry elegant plates to wooden tables. Or upstairs to the 45-cover restaurant; they're packed out every week. Pheasant, oxtail and black pudding terrine, roast sea trout with a crab bisque, Anton's famous carrot cake – our set lunch didn't miss a beat.

Meals	Lunch & dinner £10.50–£18.95. Bar meals £4.75–£11.95. Sunday lunch, 3 courses, £20.
Closed	Open all day.

Meals	Lunch £20. Sunday roast £25. Taster menu, 6 courses, £55.
Closed	Mon all day.

Charles & Lisa Bullock
The Ship Inn,
Noss Mayo,
Plymouth PL8 1EW

Tel +44 (0)1752 872387
Web www.nossmayo.com

Entry 180 Map 2

Anton & Clare Piotrowski
The Treby Arms,
Sparkwell,
Plymouth PL7 5DD

Tel +44 (0)1752 837363
Web www.thetrebyarms.co.uk

Entry 181 Map 2

Devon

The Cornish Arms
Tavistock

After a day out on the Moors you can't do better than head to the centre of town and try out some of John Hooker's great food. A stylish refurb has transformed the old coaching inn into a modern yet reassuringly traditional place, with painted stone walls, sleek oak floors and comfortable seating. At the bar, well-kept St Austell ales dominate, accompanied by an excellent wine list and unfussy menus announcing the best of local produce. Choose from luscious Devon ham with eggs and chips; glazed pork cheek, hogs pudding and aged parmesan risotto; roast rump of lamb with broccoli purée, broad beans and mint sauce. The courtyard patio behind is a sun trap in summer and a great spot for music evenings. Explore Tavistock if you have time; it's an interesting old tin-mine town.

Meals	Lunch & dinner £9–£19.50.
Closed	Open all day.

John & Emma Hooker
The Cornish Arms,
15 West Street,
Tavistock PL19 8AN
Tel   +44 (0)1822 612145
Web   www.thecornisharmstavistock.co.uk

Entry 182 Map 2

Devon

The Peter Tavy Inn
Peter Tavy

Tough and sturdy, it's survived many a Dartmoor winter, this 15th-century inn at the end of a lane in little Peter Tavy. Inside is a pub of three rooms, with slate floors and log burners in wide granite fireplaces, and a hotch-potch of wooden chairs and tables. Find a cosy corner and contemplate your next hike over a refreshing pint – all is pleasingly rustic. They always have local ales alongside beer from Dartmoor Brewery; our halves of Jail Ale slipped down nicely. This is no gastropub but the food is homemade and hearty and comes in generous portions, from lamb cobbler to fishcakes to sizzling fajitas. There are lots of locals and everyone's friendly, families are welcome and so is your dog. For summer there's a charming beer garden out the back, with weathered picnic tables and white parasols.

Meals	Lunch from £5.75.
	Dinner from £8.95.
Closed	2.30pm–6pm (3pm Sat & Sun).

Chris & Jo Wordingham
The Peter Tavy Inn,
Peter Tavy,
Tavistock PL19 9NN
Tel   +44 (0)1822 810348
Web   www.petertavyinn.com

Entry 183 Map 2

The Royal Oak Inn
Meavy

A lovely old-fashioned community-run Dartmoor pub, on the village green (still with its 'royal oak'), where ponies trot by in summer and beauty and birdsong surround you. It's often busy with locals and walkers but if you're lucky you'll find a pew in the ancient slab-floored bar, warm and cosy with red banquettes and an open fire. Ales — including a monthly guest — are local and cask-conditioned; they even have their own Meavy Oak Ale, brewed by Dartmoor Brewery in Princetown; there's scrumpy aplenty and ten wines by the glass. The food is the best of pub grub: Wednesday night is Pie Night, Friday is Fish and Chips Night, beef and lamb comes from Dartmoor farms and the tartare sauce is homemade. Piped music and cribbage, muddy boots and muddy paws... a seriously good bolthole for families and hikers.

Meals	Bar meals from £6.95.
	Lunch from £5.
	Dinner from £8.95.
	Sunday lunch, 2 courses, £15–£18.
Closed	Open all day.

Stephen & Julie Earp
The Royal Oak Inn,
Meavy,
Yelverton PL20 6PJ

Tel   +44 (0)1822 852944
Web   www.royaloakinn.org.uk

Entry 184 Map 2

Devon

Rugglestone Inn
Widecombe in the Moor

Beside open moorland, within walking distance of the village, is a 200-year-old stone pub whose two tiny rooms lead off a stone-floored passageway; few of the daytrippers who descend on this idyllic village make it to the Rugglestone Inn. Low beams fill an old-fashioned parlour with simple furnishings and a deep-country feel. Both rooms are free of modern intrusions, the locals preferring cribbage, euchre and dominoes. The tiny bar serves local farm cider, while Teignworthy Moor Beer and Dartmoor Brewery Legend are tapped from the cask. From the kitchen comes proper home cooking — ploughman's lunches and soups, lamb shanks, fresh fish; across the babbling brook is a lawn with benches and peaceful moorland views. A modest slice of heaven.

Meals	Lunch & dinner £6.95–£10.95.
Closed	3pm-6pm Mon-Thurs
	(3pm-5pm Fri).
	Open all day Sat & Sun.

Richard & Vicki Palmer
Rugglestone Inn,
Widecombe in the Moor,
Newton Abbot TQ13 7TF

Tel   +44 (0)1364 621327
Web   www.rugglestoneinn.co.uk

Entry 185 Map 2

Devon

The Rock Inn
Haytor Vale

Originally an ale house for quarrymen and miners, the 300-year-old Rock Inn stands in a tiny village in a sheltered vale on Dartmoor's slopes. Run by the same family for 30 years, this civilised haven oozes Dickensian character; dark polished antique tables and settles on several levels, a grandfather clock and fresh flowers, cosy corners and at least two fires. Charming staff ensure it all ticks along very smoothly. Settle down in the compact carpeted bar and study a supper menu that highlights local, often organic, produce. All that fresh Dartmoor air will make you hungry, so tuck into Devon rump steak with garlic butter and chunky chips, and caramelised lemon tart with ginger ice cream. Lunchtime meals range from soup and sandwiches to local sausages in onion gravy. There's a pretty beer garden, too.

Devon

The Cleave Public House
Lustleigh

It's too pretty for words, this 15th-century longhouse on the edge of Dartmoor National Park. The main bar is classic to the core, with a granite fireplace, leather armchairs and Windsor chairs forming cosy huddles on red and gold carpeting, and a no-nonsense planked bar dispensing Otter Ales and local guests such as Yellowhammer. The head chef brings passion to the kitchen so menus are blessed with regional, seasonal produce. Bar meals don't get much better than the Dartmouth crab turnovers, or the double baked ham and gruyère soufflé, river Teign mussels and croque monsieur. There are homebaked baguettes for walkers, and good wines poured by cheerful staff. Plenty of dining tables at the back, but arrive early in summer: seats are like gold dust outside at the front.

Meals	Lunch & dinner £7.50–£18.
Closed	Open all day.

Meals	Lunch & dinner £7.50–£15. Sun lunch £9.95–£15.95.
Closed	Open all day.

Christopher & Susan Graves
The Rock Inn,
Haytor Vale,
Newton Abbot TQ13 9XP
Tel   +44 (0)1364 661305
Web   www.rock-inn.co.uk

Entry 186 Map 2

Ben & John Whitton
The Cleave Public House,
Lustleigh,
Exeter TQ13 9TJ
Tel   +44 (0)1647 277223
Web   www.thecleavelustleigh.com

Entry 187 Map 2

Devon

Ring of Bells
North Bovey

You'd be hard pressed to find a better inn on Dartmoor. First there's the village, lost in green hills. Then there's the pub, set back a bit, with a sun-trapping terrace that greets you. The place has been given a smart lick of paint but the feel remains traditional — as befits an old hostelry. Inside you get a little time travel — timber frames, ancient walls, original flagstones — as you weave through cosy rooms, ducking to avoid beams, sliding past fires that burn brightly. Order a pint of Teignworthy Gold and head back onto the terrace, or seek out the dining room and browse the daily-changing menu. Suppliers are listed on the back, meat comes from the fields around you, and fish fresh from the nearby ports. Cream teas and toasted tea cakes are served from 3pm, and brilliant walking waits — dogs are welcome.

Devon

The Horse
Moretonhampstead

The back room doubles as an art gallery, folk bands play once a month, a fabulous courtyard catches the sun. The Horse is all things to all men: friendly community centre, great little restaurant, the sort of local you'd move to the village for. And there's a deli offering homemade delights, from smoked charcuterie to bread. The front bar has charm — stripped boards, painted panelling, old settles, a wood-burner; follow the flagstones south past the open kitchen to the lofty dining room. You can spoil yourself variously with strong coffee, sparkling wine, local ale and a crispy pizza. Nigel and Malene escaped London for the country and have transformed the old biker's boozer into a foodie's joy. The welcome is second to none.

Meals	Bar meals from £6.50.
	Lunch & dinner from £8.95.
	Sunday lunch, 2 courses, from £15.
Closed	Open all day.

Meals	Breakfast & lunch from £4.95.
	Dinner from £11.95.
Closed	Sun & Mon midday–5pm.

Di Phillips
Ring of Bells,
The Village, North Bovey,
Newton Abbot TQ13 8RB
Tel   +44 (0)1647 440375
Web www.ringofbells.net

🤸 🐾 🐕 🍷

Entry 188 Map 2

Nigel Hoyle & Malene Graulund
The Horse,
George Street, Moretonhampstead,
Newton Abbot TQ13 8PG
Tel   +44 (0)1647 440242
Web www.thehorsedartmoor.co.uk

♿ 🤸 🐕 🍷 📶

Entry 189 Map 2

Chagford Inn
Chagford

In the pretty town of Chagford, enfolded by the lush hills of the National Park, is a small simple inn painted soft blue, with a black door and sparkling windows. Inside is warm and homely, friendly and quirky, and after a long walk up the Teign Valley the menu is a welcome sight. Art on the walls, logs in the burner... settle in and make yourself cosy. They bake their own bread, cure their own bresaola, buy local whenever it is possible, and bring fish in daily from the coast. The food is exciting and modern. Chef Russ, classically trained, is making big waves in Devon and his ethos is nose-to-tail, so there are pork croquettes with tarragon aïoli, roast ballotine of rabbit with a shallot ragù, and perfect rare roast beef ciabatta. The beers are local, the wine list is balanced, and everyone feels at home.

Meals	Starters from £5.50.
	Dinner from £10.50.
Closed	Open all day.

John Freeman
Chagford Inn,
7 Mill Street,
Chagford TQ13 8AW
Tel   +44 (0)1647 433109
Web   www.thechagfordinn.com/index.html

Entry 190 Map 2

Tom Cobley Tavern
Spreyton

They come by the hundreds to drink the ales at this shrine to the hop, and the front room — 1930s trapped in aspic — must qualify as one of the finest spots in the land to sample intoxicating potions. Roger treats his ales the way most of us treat our children, nurturing them with love before sending them out into the world. You'll find 14 waiting, most from the south west, with Tamar Black from Holsworthy, Legend, Jail Ale and Dragon's Breath from Dartmoor Brewery and Gun Dog from Teignworthy Brewery. Fishermen, hash runners and shooting parties drop by for a meal and dig into excellent, warming homemade pies and stews — the no-nonsense cooking goes down a treat. There's a big garden, and a thatched porch. As for Tom Cobley, he set off for Widecombe Fair from this very building.

Meals	Lunch & dinner £7.95–£15.95.
Closed	Mon all day.
	Midday-3pm Tues-Sun.

Roger & Carol Cudlip
Tom Cobley Tavern,
Spreyton,
Crediton EX17 5AL
Tel   +44 (0)1647 231314
Web   www.tomcobleytavern.co.uk

Entry 191 Map 2

Devon

Duke of York
Iddesleigh

One small room, one big fire. This is the pub that defines the phrase 'defiantly uninterested in prevailing fashions'. It stands next to the church in a tiny village marooned in Devon's glorious hinterland, as fine a spot as any in the country. Outside, a couple of benches catch the afternoon sun and locals bring their sheep to the door and stop for a pint. Inside, an inherent scruffiness is part of the Duke's DNA; it's 1960s rustic and the food is the heartiest: tureens of homemade soup; steak and kidney pudding; lamb chops with rosemary and garlic gravy. The locals treat the bar as their sitting room and they come and go, followed by their dogs. Walls are hung with old photos of village life, the ale is mostly local. Not for the faint-hearted.

Devon

The Grove Inn
Kings Nympton

The pub is in the heart of old Kings Nympton, a 'natural sacred grove' – raise a glass to your good fortune in being here. There are paintings of Devon countryside, a picture gallery of faces past and present, beams hung with bookmarks, stone walls, a slate floor, a wood-burner. Old and new combine with understated ease. Robert is the perfect host, Deborah uses the freshest produce to create her menus. Try roast May's Farm beef or Brewers Farm lamb for Sunday lunch, smoked trout with horseradish sauce, wild rabbit stew with mash, fish pie, and white chocolate cheesecake with Patrick's blackcurrants. Ales are from local breweries, ciders are Sam's Dry and Poundhouse, wine and champagnes come by the glass, and there are over 65 single malts.

Meals	Bar meals £4.50–£14.
Closed	Open all day.

Meals	Lunch & dinner £7–£17. Sunday lunch, 3 courses, £16.40. Not Sunday eve.
Closed	3pm–6pm. Mon lunch (except Bank Holidays). Sun evenings.

John Pittam
Duke of York,
Iddesleigh,
Winkleigh EX19 8BG
Tel   +44 (0)1837 810253
Web   www.dukeofyorkdevon.co.uk

Entry 192 Map 2

Deborah & Robert Smallbone
The Grove Inn,
Kings Nympton EX37 9ST
Tel   +44 (0)1769 580406
Web   www.thegroveinn.co.uk

Entry 193 Map 2

Devon

Red Lion Hotel
Chulmleigh

In a lively village, a short drive from the Taw valley, the Red Lion has welcomed man, horse and coach since the 17th century. It's the sort of place you can march into from a gale and not worry about your wellies dripping on the slate flags. Plenty of blazing log fires to roast in front of too, preferably with a pint of local cider or a local Tribute ale. In the bar, take your pick from rustic wooden settles to well-worn leather wingbacks; the TV is for big sporting events only. In the kitchen: an Italian twist, with pasta specials and handmade pizzas cooked in a stone-based oven. There are pub classics too – burgers with hand-cut chips, rump steak with all the trimmings, heavenly puddings with clotted cream. The restaurant is stylishly utilitarian, with spot-lit wooden tables and painted stone walls.

Meals	Lunch & bar meals from £5. Dinner from £7.50. Dinner, 2 courses, £12.50. Not Tuesday lunch.
Closed	Open all day.

Josie Russell
Red Lion Hotel,
East Street,
Chulmleigh EX18 7DD

Tel   +44 (0)1769 580384
Web www.theredlionchulmleigh.co.uk

Entry 194 Map 2

Devon

The Masons Arms
Knowstone

Thatched on the outside, with a beamed, flagged and inglenooked bar inside, is a classic Devon pub, the sort of place where farmers set the world to rights over pints of Cotleigh's Tawny Owl. Who would imagine, down a few worn steps, a smart light-filled extension and food from the former chef of the Waterside Inn? Mark Dodson's inspired cooking has made the Masons Arms a foodie haven. Michelin-starred menus revel in the region's fishermen, farmers and producers, so you could find roulade of pork belly with apple compote; fillet of brill with potato crust and salmon mousse; puff pastry of wild mushrooms with poached egg and pimento cream (rich, earthy and delicate all at the same time). Staff go to great lengths to make you feel at home, and if you are just here to drink, the garden is gorgeous.

Meals	Set lunch £20-£25. Dinner from £18.50. Sunday lunch, 3 courses, £36.
Closed	3pm-6pm. Sun evenings & Mon all day. Two weeks in January. August Bank Holiday & following 10 days.

Sarah Dodson
The Masons Arms,
Knowstone,
South Molton EX36 4RY

Tel   +44 (0)1398 341231
Web www.masonsarmsdevon.co.uk

Entry 195 Map 2

Devon

The Cadeleigh Arms
Cadeleigh

The villagers of Cadeleigh did not want to lose their local, so they stumped up the money and bought it! It's worth the drive down any number of lanes to get here. In the bar: ancient flagstones, high-backed benches, assorted scrubbed tables and a burner stocked with logs. In the dining room: orange carpeting, pale walls, rolling green views. There's a hillside beer garden, a skittle alley loved by kids, a room with a pool table, and ideal new landlords. They run a deli in Tiverton and keep a good house: find 16 good wines by the glass; Sam's Medium Devon Cider; and Tribute, Dartmoor Best and Legend on tap. There are juicy steaks too, and crab cakes (crispy outside, succulent within), and fabulous nut burgers for vegans. Our lamb koftas were a triumph… and the sticky toffee pudding comes with clotted cream.

Devon

The Lamb Inn
Sandford

Animal paintings brighten the bar, the chef is passionate about provenance and Bob and Tiny wag tails in delight. The old posting inn is the hub of the village. There are three open fires in winter, carpeting for cosiness, stubby candles on plain tables, tankards filled with roses and, upstairs, a window seat that looks onto the village below. (Skittles and darts too, a free cinema for films and sporting events, and a brilliant open mic night once a month.) The simple décor is matched by a blackboard menu free of affectation, the award-winning dishes ranging from a platter of West Country cheeses to slow poached salmon with pea purée and horseradish foam or haunch of venison with roasted celeriac. Round it all off with spiced poached pear and salted caramel mousse. All is locally sourced and made from scratch.

Meals	Lunch & dinner from £8.95.
Closed	Sun evenings & all day Mon.

Meals	Lunch from £9.
	Dinner, 3 courses, £20–£30.
	Sunday roast from £8.90.
Closed	Open all day.

Jac & Jane Copeland
The Cadeleigh Arms,
Cadeleigh,
Tiverton EX16 8HP
Tel   +44 (0)1884 855238
Web   www.thecadeleigharms.co.uk

Entry 196 Map 2

Mark Hildyard
& Katharine Lightfoot
The Lamb Inn,
Sandford, Crediton EX17 4LW
Tel   +44 (0)1363 773676
Web   www.lambinnsandford.co.uk

Entry 197 Map 2

The Lazy Toad Inn
Brampford Speke

Stroll the banks of the river Exe, wind up at this listed inn. Slate tiles polished to a pewter hue gleam on floors around the bar where ales from Otter, Exe Valley and St Austell vie for attention, farming implements dot one wall, bistro style art another, and a mix of tables and chairs add pizzazz. Settle down by the fire and study head chef Craig Beacham's menus, featuring locally sourced and home produced food they change every day. How about pan fried hake, buttered spinach and mussel chowder, or loin of pork with a Jerusalem artichoke purée and salt baked celeriac? There's a great little menu for kids, too, a lovely walled cobbled courtyard outside, and more garden at the back. *All ages welcome to dine.*

The Rusty Bike
Exeter

It has been said that boldness has genius in it – and here you have it, in a glorious reincarnation of a former backstreet boozer. The large open-plan space is a vintage mash-up with thought-provoking art everywhere and a splendid central bar of carved wood from which ales (and cider) from their own Fat Pig brewery flow into the cups of students, professors and all. Head Chef Darren Jory is a committed nose-to-tail man who grows the vegetables, and is often out in a boat with colourful owner Hamish. Start with a goose, clementine and smoked bacon rillette before moving on to blade of ruby red beef with parsley and garlic mash; finish with honey iced parfait with plums. And there are Devon cheese boards and tasting menus for those who want it all.

Meals	Bar snacks from £3.00.
	Lunch from £5.35.
	Dinner from £12.50.
	Sunday lunch, 3 courses, £25.
Closed	Last 3 weeks in January.

Meals	Lunch & dinner £7.50–£18.
Closed	Open all day Sun, from 5pm
	Mon–Fri & from 4pm Sat.

Harriet & Mike Daly
The Lazy Toad Inn,
Brampford Speke,
Exeter EX5 5DP
Tel +44 (0)1392 841591
Web www.thelazytoadinn.co.uk

Entry 198 Map 2

Hamish Lothian
The Rusty Bike,
67 Howell Road,
Exeter EX4 4LZ
Tel +44 (0)1392 214440
Web www.rustybike-exeter.co.uk

Entry 199 Map 2

The Bull Hotel
Bridport

Urban-chic meets rural simplicity at Richard and Nikki's Regency-style coaching inn. Funky and fun sums up this vibrant place; you feel good the moment you step through the door. Escape Bridport's bustle, kick off your shoes, plonk yourself down on a squashy sofa with a pint of Otter Bitter. The bar is open all day, for hearty English breakfasts, cappuccino and cake, for lunchtime sandwiches and high tea. For seriously good food, there's a candlelit restaurant; for summer lunches, a Victorian courtyard. Enjoy live music in the Hayloft, take a turn in the ballroom, order a cocktail in the sumptuous lounge. Daily menus are contemporary and work with the seasons and organic ingredients are locally sourced: fish is a specialty, mostly caught in Lyme Bay, and there's stone-baked pizza, vanilla rice pudding, handmade cheeses... As for the bedrooms... classic period features mix with modern pieces and antiques, there are Designer Guild fabrics, Milo sofas, big beds, Tivoli radios, waffle robes, roll top tubs and Neal's Yard delights. A boon for arty Bridport — and the fantastic Jurassic coast is a mile away. *Minimum stay: 2 nights at weekends.*

Rooms	10 doubles, 1 twin, 3 four-posters: £100-£200.
	1 suites for 2: £235-£265.
	3 family rooms for 4: £180-£200.
	1 single: £90-£115.
Meals	Lunch, 2 courses, from £12.
	Dinner, 3 courses, around £35.
	Sunday roast £19.
Closed	Rarely.

Ali Pember
The Bull Hotel,
34 East Street,
Bridport DT6 3LF

Tel   +44 (0)1308 422878
Web   www.thebullhotel.co.uk

The Anchor Inn
Seatown

You're in a perfect spot here, smack-bang on the coastal path below Golden Cap; the Anchor is a thriving, lively inn that knows exactly how to make the most of its location. The big sun terrace and gardens overlook the pebbly beach; interiors evoke driftwood and nautical cosiness, with open fires around which you can enjoy a pint of Palmers and a fresh crab sandwich, or a bowl of super fresh shellfish washed down with an excellent wine. If you've built up an appetite (there are walks from the doorstep) head chef, Samuel Hill, who grew up in Dorset and has travelled widely, will tempt you with hearty menus that hint at the East while making splendid use of locally sourced produce. Fish and lobsters direct from the beach make for the freshest of fresh dishes. Three bedrooms with deeply comfortable king-size beds are chic (a rusty tap as a coat hook, rope buoys, trunks turned into tables) with captivating sea views; you'll think you've stepped aboard an 18th-century schooner. Bathrooms have roll-top baths, walk-in showers, the fluffiest of white towels and glorious tiling, with top-notch oils and soaps. Terrific. *Minimum stay: 2 nights.*

Rooms	3 doubles: £90–£150. Singles £75–£115.
Meals	Lunch from £6.95. Dinner from £9.95.
Closed	Rarely.

2015/16
Sawday's
PUB AWARD

Pub with rooms

Paul Wiscombe
The Anchor Inn,
Seatown, Chideock,
Bridport DT6 6JU
Tel +44 (0)1297 489215
Web www.theanchorinnseatown.co.uk

Dorset

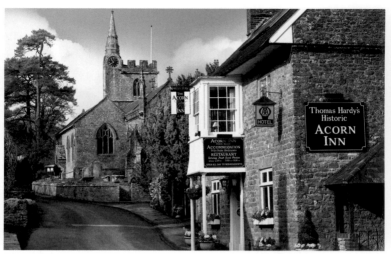

The Acorn Inn
Evershot

Perfect Evershot and rolling countryside lie at the door of this 400-year-old inn in Thomas Hardy country. Hardy called the inn the Sow and Acorn and let Tess rest a night here; had he visited today he might have let her stay longer. Red Carnation Hotels, under the guidance of Alex and chef Jack, are reviving its fortunes. It's very much a traditional inn; locals sup pints of Otter Ale in the long flagstoned bar and guests sample good food sourced within 25 miles. In the dining room, the atmosphere changes to rural country house with smartly laid tables, terracotta tiles, soft lighting and elegant fireplaces. Good gastropub fare is taken seriously, be it a roast beef and horseradish sandwich or a twice-baked cheese soufflé followed by grilled spatchcock and warm treacle tart. The service is helpful and friendly. Bedrooms creak with age and style; there are antiques and fabric wall-coverings, super little bathrooms, perhaps a wonky floor or a lovely four-poster. It's worth splashing out on a larger room if you want space.

Rooms	3 doubles, 3 twins, 3 four-posters: £99–£160. 1 suite for 2: £160–£205. Singles £89–£205. Extra bed/sofabed £20 p.p. per night. Dinner, B&B £80–£133 p.p. per night.
Meals	Bar meals from £4.95. Lunch & dinner £5.25–£22.95.
Closed	Rarely.

Jack & Alexandra Mackenzie
The Acorn Inn,
Evershot,
Dorchester DT2 0JW
Tel   +44 (0)1935 83228
Web   www.acorn-inn.co.uk

Entry 202 Map 3

The Chetnole Inn

Chetnole

This sweet little inn has the lot: a great position in a pretty village; lovely interiors that mix old and new; super food that draws a crowd, and three excellent, affordable bedrooms. Flagged floors, low ceilings and wood-burners keep things cosy inside, and you can eat in the dog-friendly bar or in the lively restaurant, even in the breakfast room if things get busy. The food is just what you want after a day in the hills, perhaps rabbit & pork rillette with a pear & squash chutney, steak and ale pie with thick-cut chips, warm apple & 'Kingston black' crumble. Tea is served with homemade coconut ice, and the ales are locally sourced and constantly changing; try the Copper Hopper Gold Rush, brewed just three miles away. Spotless bedrooms upstairs fit the mood perfectly. All are big and come with comfy beds, pretty sofas, sparkling shower rooms with robes and lovely lotions. Sherborne's to the north, the coast to the south, and the Cerne Abbas giant's in between. Brilliant.

Rooms	2 doubles, 1 twin/double: £95. Singles £70.
Meals	Bar meals from £5. Lunch & dinner £9.85-£21. Sunday roast from £10.50.
Closed	Rarely.

Simon & Maria Hudson
The Chetnole Inn,
Village Street, Chetnole,
Sherborne DT9 6NU
Tel +44 (0)1935 872337
Web www.thechetnoleinn.co.uk

The Plantation
Poole

In a peaceful conservation area on the outskirts of Poole, within strolling distance of sweeping sands and sea, is this quick getaway from London. Come for the night, or stay the weekend. The Edwardian building with its gothicky turret has become a smart new dining venue with a colonial décor and a delightful young team. Beyond the suave banquettes, the pale wood tables and the bar stocked with Upham's ales and Orchard Pig cider is a large new conservatory with a decorative tiled floor and wrought iron chairs painted tasteful green. Nothing is too much trouble for the staff who ferry good-looking dishes to happy punters: roasted bass with Dorset cured ham; quinoa with creamed celeriac; beef burgers with bacon jam; clementine custard tart with coconut sorbet. Outside is a leafy garden with a hut for spoiled smokers; upstairs are nine snazzy, well-insulated rooms. Look forward to a deep soak or a waterfall shower, bathrobes, slippers and Ren toiletries, big comfy beds and perhaps the odd sofa. Breakfast is excellent: the full English, eggs any way you want them, homemade butter, yogurts and jams.

Rooms	2 doubles, 2 twin/doubles: £130–£170.
Meals	Lunch & dinner £12–£25.
Closed	Open all day.

Jo Rogers
The Plantation,
53 Cliff Drive, Canford Cliffs,
Poole BH13 7JF
Tel   +44 (0)1202 701531
Web   www.the-plantation.co.uk

The Inn at Cranborne
Cranborne

Aussie Jane's passion for the great English inn runs deep; she waved goodbye to her jet-setting career to take on the faded Fleur de Lys in the heart of pretty Cranborne. Now the Hall & Woodhouse-owned inn glows. In the cosy bar – all panelled walls, rugs on woodblock or flagstone floors, warm heritage hues – say hello to Mike, Jane's characterful Jack Russell, then bag the smartly upholstered pew bench by the blazing wood-burner and peruse Edward Cracknell's inviting seasonal menus. In autumn, tuck into a hearty mushroom and bacon soup, then lamb rump with roast root vegetables and rosemary jus, leaving room for sticky toffee and date pudding. Look to the bar menu for sandwiches and pub classics like steak and mushroom pie. Fancy staying the night? Upstairs, rooms have a classy contemporary feel, with cord carpets, fat radiators, painted furniture, and goose down duvets with Welsh blankets on big comfortable beds. Smart tiled bathrooms (some have roll top baths) with posh Bramley toiletries have village views. Cranborne Chase and the New Forest (for walking and cycling), Salisbury and the Jurassic Coast are close.

Rooms	8 twin/doubles: £95–£120.
Meals	Lunch & dinner, 3 courses, £20–£30.
Closed	Open all day.

Jane Gould
The Inn at Cranborne,
5 Wimborne Street, Cranborne,
Wimborne BH21 5PP

Tel	+44 (0)1725 551249
Web	www.theinnatcranborne.cc.uk

Dorset

The Museum Inn
Farnham

In a village with roses round every door is one of the finest inns in England, built by the father of modern archaeology (whose museum, the Pitt Rivers, is in Oxford). Today, Heather keeps the atmosphere warm and happy. Bedrooms – big in the main house, smaller in the stables, all super-smart – have cool colours, crisp linen, fancy bathrooms (and hi-tech gadgetry in most), while the self-contained Moles Cottage is aimed at families in summer and shooters in season. The big 17th-century bar has a period feel: flagstones, inglenook, fresh flowers and a fashionable mismatch of tables and chairs. There are cosy alcoves to hide in, a book-filled drawing room to browse and a smart white-raftered dining room. The head chef's dishes range from pork belly served with red cabbage and mustard mash to roasted local-estate venison with butternut squash and sour cherry jus, cooked, of course, using the best ingredients; apple and cinnamon tarte tatin comes with iced apple parfait. Popular with the barbour-and-dog set, the Museum Inn is quietest out of season but a treat all round.

Rooms	5 doubles, 2 twin/doubles, 1 four-poster: £90–£160. 1 cottage for 8: £800–£1,200 per week.
Meals	Mains from £11.95.
Closed	Rarely.

Heather Kirk
The Museum Inn,
Farnham,
Blandford Forum DT11 8DE
Tel   +44 (0)1725 516261
Web   www.museuminn.co.uk

The King John Inn
Tollard Royal

You're on the Dorset/Wiltshire border, lost in blissful country, with paths that lead up into glorious hills. Tumble back down to this super inn, where every square inch has been refurbished, making the place shine. Expect airy interiors, a sober country feel, a sun-trapping terrace and a fire that crackles in winter. Originally a foundry, it opened as a brewery in 1859 and, when beer proved more popular than horseshoes, the inn was born. You'll find three local ales on tap but great wines too – Alex loves the stuff and has opened his own shop across the courtyard; take a bottle home if you like what you drink. As for the food, it's as local as can be – Portland crab on toast; Rushmore Estate sika venison salad with beets, carrots and bacon; banana soufflé with butterscotch sauce. Contemporary country bedrooms, three in the Coach House, are the final treat. Some are bigger than others but all come with modern fabrics, padded headboards, crisp linen and super bathrooms (one has a slipper bath). A terraced lawn gives views over a couple of rooftops onto the woods. Altogether a perfect spot.

Rooms	5 doubles, 2 interconnecting twin/doubles: £90–£140.: 1 suite for 2: £150–£170.
Meals	Bar meals from £8.95. Lunch from £12.95. Dinner from £13.95.
Closed	Rarely.

Adam Wilson
The King John Inn,
Tollard Royal,
Salisbury SP5 5PS
Tel   +44 (0)1725 516207
Web   www.kingjohninn.co.uk

Dorset

Stapleton Arms
Buckhorn Weston

An inn with a big heart. No pretensions here, just kind, knowledgeable staff committed to running the place with informal panache. A facelift has brought a touch of glamour back to this old coaching inn, and there's a delightful garden at the back. Downstairs are sofas by the fire, a piano in the bar and a restaurant in Georgian blue, with shuttered windows and candles in the fireplace. You can eat wherever you want. Pork pies (to eat in or take out), serrano ham and scotch eggs all wait at the bar, and if you want a three-course feast you must book – it's popular. There are salmon and crab fishcakes, home-baked Dorset ham, banana tarte tatin, and a beer menu: ale matters here. On Sundays groups can order their own joint of meat, and there's a menu for kids. Bedrooms above are soundproofed to ensure a good night's sleep – comfy-chic with fresh flowers, happy colours, crisp linen, a claw-foot bath. Also: maps and picnics, wellies if you want to walk, games for children, DVDs for all ages. Wincanton is close for the races.

Rooms	4 doubles: £90–£120. Singles from £72.
Meals	Lunch & bar meals from £7. Dinner, 3 courses, about £30.
Closed	Rarely.

Richard Smith
Stapleton Arms,
Church Hill, Buckhorn Weston,
Gillingham SP8 5HS

Tel   +44 (0)1963 370396
Web   www.thestapletonarms.com

Entry 208 Map 3

Dorset

The Fontmell
Fontmell Magna

The former Crown opened up shop in 2011 — with a change of name and a stylish new feel. Colourful cushions and striped bar stools, striking red and blue walls, deep leather sofas and a table laden with magazines and games combine to create a super-cosy feel. Quaff Keystone Brewery's Mallyshag Bitter and mussels and chips at scrubbed tables — or follow glass-enclosed corridors across babbling Collier's Brook to the dining room, furnished in relaxed country-house style. Jazzy rugs, old tables, a wall of shelves stacked with wine bottles and books create an easy mood, so settle down and enjoy chef Tom Shaw's imaginative cooking. Dishes include treats such as chargrilled tandoori monkfish with tiger prawn biriyani, and pork belly with roasted fillet, langoustines and cauliflower and cumin purée. Delve into the wines — the list is eclectic.

Meals	Lunch, bar meals & dinner from £9.50. Sunday lunch, 2-3 courses, £17-£23.
Closed	Open all day.

Tom Shaw
The Fontmell,
Fontmell Magna,
Shaftesbury SP7 0PA
Tel   +44 (0)1747 811441
Web   www.thefontmell.com

Entry 209 Map 3

Dorset

The Bull
Wimborne St Giles

In sleepy Wimborne St Giles, in the heart of the Cranborne Chase, and overlooking a serene river valley, stands the beautifully refurbished Bull. The open-plan bar-dining room is kitted out with old dining tables, decorative ceiling lights and paintings, along with leather armchairs and an old chesterfield by the log fire; consider the papers over a pint. Booking is advisable if you hope to eat: the food is the main draw, and the chefs are on display in the open kitchen. Choose from such delights as Thai-style crab ravioli, and beef wellington with root vegetables and madeira jus. Pudding lovers should leave room for chocolate brownie with hot chocolate sauce! Wash it all down with a local ale or a well-chosen wine by the glass. There's also a peaceful rambling garden for simple summer drinking, just the thing after a great downland walk.

Meals	Lunch from £6.50. Dinner, 3 courses, £25-£30.
Closed	Mon all day. Sun from 4pm.

Ross Nicholls
The Bull,
Wimborne St Giles,
Wimborne BH21 5NF
Tel   +44 (0)1725 517300
Web   www.bullinnwsg.com

Entry 210 Map 3

Dorset

The Square & Compass
Worth Matravers

The name honours those who cut stone from the nearby quarries. This splendid old pub has been in the family for generations and remains unchanged; a narrow, rare, drinking corridor leads to two hatches from where Palmer's Copper Ale and guest ales come from the cask. With a pint of home produced cider and a homemade pasty, you can chat in the flagged corridor or settle in the parlour; there are painted wooden panels, wall seats, local prints and cartoons, and a wood-burner to warm you on wild nights. The stone-walled main room has live music; there's cribbage and shove ha'penny and a fossil museum (the family's) next door. Gazing out across fields to the sea this pub and its sunny front terrace – occasionally dotted with roaming hens – is a popular stop for coastal path hikers. A national treasure!

Dorset

The Red Lion
Weymouth

Just a buoy's throw away from Weymouth's off-shore lifeboat, this little pub has fed and watered lifeboat crews for nearly 150 years. Behind the central bar, locals and visiting seafarers quaff pints of Otter Bitter Lifeboat Ale whilst sharing plates of fresh seafood, surrounded by nautical ropes and Morse Code flags. In winter, cosy corners panelled with old rum barrels are a great place for warming dishes such as steak and ale pie served with minted 'not so mushy peas', and warm toffee apple cake with vanilla ice cream. Outside in summer, wooden tables with lanterns are perfect for al fresco eating in the square. Rain or shine, the bar with its collection of lifeboat memorabilia is still a focal point. Even if you can't decipher the flags you can toast the crews, with a tot of one of the pub's 80 rums.

Meals	Bar snacks from £3.50.	Meals	Lunch & dinner £3.95–£14.95.
Closed	3pm-6pm. Open all day Fri-Sun & all day every day July-September.	Closed	Open all day.

	Charlie Newman & Kevin Hunt		Brian McLaughlin
	The Square & Compass,		The Red Lion,
	Worth Matravers,		Hope Square,
	Swanage BH19 3LF		Weymouth DT4 8TR
Tel	+44 (0)1929 439229	Tel	+44 (0)1305 786940
Web	www.squareandcompasspub.co.uk	Web	www.theredlionweymouth.co.uk

Entry 211 Map 3

Entry 212 Map 3

Dorset

The New Inn Cerne Abbas
Cerne Abbas

The New Inn is most certainly new; it may date to the 16th century, but Jeremy has recently refurbished and now it shines. Gone are the swirly green carpets; in their place, local slate has been laid in the bar. Lots of lovely old stuff remains – timber frames, mullioned windows, the odd settle – but the feel is fresh with warm colours, oak floors and a smart bar area in which to sup a pint of Dorset Gold or a glass of good wine. Food is top notch and locally sourced, so dig into wood pigeon and chorizo salad; hake, tomato and calamari stew; or salt beef braised in Guinness with champ mash… and leave room for dark chocolate fondant with poached apricots. Don't miss the Cerne Abbas Giant.

Meals	Lunch & dinner £5–£35.
Closed	Christmas Day.

Jeremy & Vanessa Lee
The New Inn Cerne Abbas,
14 Long Street,
Cerne Abbas DT2 7JF
Tel +44 (0)1300 341274
Web www.thenewinncerneabbas.co.uk

Entry 213 Map 3

Dorset

The Half Moon
Bridport

We loved the look of the menus – Scotch quail egg with Welsh rarebit and salad; baked hake with fennel and chorizo; rabbit fricassée with potato dumplings. And no vegetarian could turn down a plateful of rigatoni, artichoke hearts, wild mushrooms, pine nuts, parmesan and white truffle. The old, mellow, thatched Half Moon, sandwiched between two bends on the Bridport to Beaminster road, has been taken over by chef Karl, who is keen to welcome all: farmers, families, foodies and walkers. It's a Palmers Brewery pub so there are beers on tap – IPA and Copper – alongside some respectable wines. Inside are three rooms, airy and traditional: low ceilings, patterned carpeting, a mishmash of tables, a central open fire. At the peaceful back is a garden, fenced and pretty with far-reaching views.

Meals	Lunch & dinner £10–£16.50. Not Sunday eve or Monday.
Closed	Sun evenings & all day Mon.

Karl Bashford & Zuzana Prekopova
The Half Moon,
Melplash,
Bridport DT6 3UD
Tel +44 (0)1308 488321
Web www.thehalfmoonmelplash.com

Entry 214 Map 33

Durham

Lord Crewe Arms at Blanchland
Blanchland

Originally the abbot's lodge and kitchens (and its garden the cloisters), the Lord Crewe Arms has become a Grade II*-listed inn. The village, in a sheep-clad valley on the moors' edge, was built with stone from the abbey's ruins. Inside: ancient flags, inglenook fireplaces, fortress walls and a classy country décor. Public areas range from lofty to intimate and the atmospheric bar is in the vaulted crypt. With a head chef from Mark Hix's 'stable', the robust modern British menu includes steaks, chops and spit-roasted meats, fresh crab salad and ruby beets. Puddings hark back to ancient times: sea buckthorn posset, rhubarb fumble. Wines include great burgundies and clarets, ales range from Allendale's Golden Plover to Nel's Best from High House Farm, and there are water bowls for dogs in the garden. If you stay, you're in for a treat. Most rooms are divided between The Angel, a simple, beautiful, listed ex-inn across the way, and in the former tied cottages. Some bedrooms have exposed stone walls and real fires, all have soft carpets, fine fabrics, divine beds and deep baths.

Rooms	19 doubles: £106–£170.
	1 suite for 2: £135–£180.
	1 family room for 4: £165–£220.
Meals	Starters from £4.95.
	Dinner from £10.45.
	Sunday lunch, 2 courses, £21.
Closed	Rarely.

Pub with rooms

Tommy Mark
Lord Crewe Arms at Blanchland,
Blanchland,
Consett DH8 9SP
Tel   +44 (0)1666 891243
Web   www.lordcrewearms.blogspot.co.uk

Entry 215 Map 12

Durham

The Victoria Inn
Durham

An old-school drinking bar in the middle of Durham: no music, no fruit machines, just original Victorian interiors trapped in aspic. There's a roaring fire, ancient wallpaper, pints of Big Lamp and lots of local banter. In the old days, shawled ladies would pop in to retrieve an errant husband. These days it's students, bar-room philosophers and beers lovers who drop by. It's not to everyone's taste – if you want boutique interiors and impeccable service, look elsewhere – but those who like to quaff a pint or two with the odd portrait of Queen Victoria hanging on the wall will love it. Bedrooms upstairs aren't huge, but have honest prices and are a good base for exploring the city. Most have been partially refurbished in the last two years and come with lots of colour and good bathrooms. Some have brass beds, others Fleur de Lys wallpaper; the family room up in the eaves is large and airy with a contemporary style. Big breakfasts wait downstairs, Durham starts at the front door: cobbled streets, riverside walks, university and cathedral. Good restaurants wait nearby, Hadrian's Wall is close.

Rooms	4 doubles, 1 twin: £75-£80. 1 family room for 4: £85. Singles £55-£80.
Meals	Lunch from £1.50.
Closed	Rarely.

Michael Webster
The Victoria Inn,
86 Hallgarth Street,
Durham DH1 3AS

Tel   +44 (0)1913 865269
Web   www.victoriainn-durhamcity.co.uk

Entry 216 Map 12

Durham

Rose & Crown
Romaldkirk

An idyllic village of mellow stone where little has changed in 200 years. The Rose and Crown dates from 1733 and stands on the green, next to the Saxon church. Roses ramble above the door in summer, so pick up a pint and search out the sun on the gravelled forecourt. Inside is just as good. You can sit at settles in the bar and roast away in front of the fire as you rifle through the *Teesdale Mercury*, or seek out sofas in the peaceful sitting room and tuck into afternoon tea. Bedrooms are lovely. Those in the converted barn are all cool grey and muted blue hues; those in the main house come with stylish furnishings and vibrant colours; all have Bose sound systems, quietly fancy bathrooms and lots of other extras. Delicious food can be eaten informally in the bar, or in the restaurant. Try braised ox cheek with sautéed greens and triple cooked chips, followed by peanut butter mousse with caramel popcorn and maple glazed bacon. High Force waterfall and Barnard Castle are close – and you can take your wet togs to the drying room.

Rooms	8 doubles, 3 twins: £115–£160. 3 suites for 2: £180–£200. Singles £95. Dinner, B&B from £79 p.p. per night.
Meals	Lunch from £10.50. Dinner, 3 courses, from £27. Sunday roast £19.50.
Closed	23-27 December & one week in January.

	Thomas & Cheryl Robinson Rose & Crown, Romaldkirk, Barnard Castle DL12 9EB
Tel	+44 (0)1833 650213
Web	www.rose-and-crown.co.uk

Entry 217 Map 12

Durham

The Crown
Mickleton

A cute little local in a small country village that sits between the Yorkshire Dales and the High Pennines; the river Tees passes close by, High Force waterfall waits up the road, fabulous walking is all around. Inside, coolly refurbished interiors mix old-world charm with contemporary flair. You find stripped boards, cool country art, leather armchairs by the wood-burner, a pint of Cumberland ale waiting at the bar. You eat at mismatching wood tables that are scattered about, with lots of dishes available as starters or mains, perhaps Shetland mussels, homemade sausages, local goose or fillet of North Sea hake. There's haunch of venison for Sunday lunch, a pop-up farm shop, a mini beer festival and the odd hog roast. Andrew and Mandy love what they do and their enthusiasm is infectious.

Meals	Lunch & dinner £6.75–£16.95.
Closed	Open all day.

Andrew Rowbotham
The Crown,
Main Street, Mickleton,
Barnard Castle DL12 0JZ
Tel   +44 (0)1833 640381
Web   www.thecrownatmickleton.co.uk

Entry 218 Map 12

Durham

Black Bull Inn
Frosterley

Ten paces from the atmospheric Weardale Railway solid tables and cushioned settles, stone flags, ticking clocks, glowing ranges and a happy buzz. No lager in sight, just coffee and scones from 10.30am, cider from the cask and beers from a few villages away. The hop is treated with reverence – dark malty porter from Wylam Brewery, bitter from Allendale – and the good value food is a joy. Rather than devising a menu then searching for suppliers, Diane and Duncan source the produce first: local if possible, and in tune with the seasons. A rare rib of beef with lashings of homemade gravy, and crispy salmon on parsley with crushed new potatoes and chive cream is the sort of thing they do brilliantly here; and the sticky date pudding is unmissable. Regular classical, folk and jazz sessions, too… they even have their own peal of bells!

Meals	Lunch £7.95–£12.95.
	Dinner £11.95–£18.95.
	Sunday roast from £9.95.
Closed	All day Mon-Wed.

Duncan & Diane Davis
Black Bull Inn,
Bridge End, Frosterley,
Bishop Auckland DL13 2SL
Tel   +44 (0)1388 527784
Web   www.blackbullfrosterley.com

Entry 219 Map 12

Durham

Durham

Bridgewater Arms
Winston

Out in beautiful Teesdale, a lovely pub with some very good food. Once the village school, it played host to a legendary performance of Jack and the Beanstalk in 1957, though these days the stars are more likely to pop in for a slap-up dinner or a pint of Keeper's Gold. Paul looks after things with an easy style, stopping to chat or talk you through the boarded menus. You'll find beautiful old windows, a vaulted ceiling, rich colours and the odd wall of books. As for the food, it's delicious stuff, the sort you crave after a morning on the fells, perhaps langoustine in garlic butter, rack of local lamb, saffron poached pears and ginger ice cream; there's a dining terrace for summer, too. Don't miss the exceptional Bowes Museum up the road in Barnard Castle – you'll find Goya, El Greco and Canaletto on the walls.

The Fox Hole
Piercebridge

An 'old' stone-flagged bar at one end, a country-sleek restaurant at the other: the second you enter you unwind. This 'pub and kitchen' on the edge of Piercebridge was a hit the day it opened: the staff are delightful, the food is modern, and our roast fig and goat's cheese salad was fabulous. The drinks are of note too: ales on hand pump, organic wines, and a host of zippy new gins. Ellie Richmond is chef and naturally keen on provenance. The fish comes daily from Hartlepool, the bread is baked in Crook, the coffee is roasted 15 miles away and the lamb is from the other side of the road. You could have escabeche of beetroot with chorizo mayonnaise, rib-eye steak with béarnaise sauce, and lemon and thyme panna cotta. Sun streams into the restaurant, good dogs (on leads) relax by the fire, toddlers play on the fresh clipped grass.

Meals	Lunch & dinner £10–£20.
Closed	2.30pm–6pm.
	Sun & Mon.

Meals	Starters from £5.25.
	Dinner from £7.50.
	Sunday roast £12.95.
Closed	Open all day.

	Paul Grundy
	Bridgewater Arms,
	Winston,
	Darlington DL2 3RN
Tel	+44 (0)1325 730302
Web	www.thebridgewaterarms.com

	Jack Bowles & Ellie Richmond
	The Fox Hole,
	Piercebridge,
	Darlington DL2 3SJ
Tel	+44 (0)1325 374286
Web	www.the-foxhole.co.uk

Entry 220 Map 12

Entry 221 Map 12

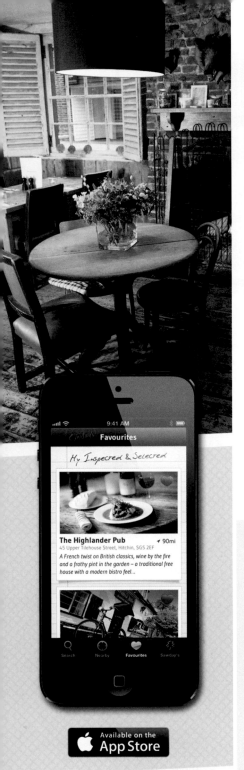

Durham

The Bay Horse
Hurworth

The pretty, bow-fronted building, painted cream under red pantiles, sits happily at the end of a terrace with open countryside beyond. Inside is nicely pubby: comforting button-back wall seating, polished oak floor boards, local prints and soft wall lamps, quiet background jazz. At least two good cask ales are served (in dimpled tankards), and stunning food from chef Marcus Bennett is brought to you by friendly folk in crisp aprons; you eat in a dining room with antique tables and proper linen napkins. Try wild duck and pistachio terrine with fig chutney, smoked bacon, scrambled egg and toasted mushroom and onion brioche – the eggs come in a shell with a soldier! Puddings are irresistible – try caramelised rice pudding with spiced autumn berries. Even the bread is home baked, and there are private dining rooms upstairs.

Meals	Bar meals from £6.95.
	Lunch from £12.95.
	Dinner from £13.95.
	Sunday lunch, 3 courses, £21.95.
Closed	Open all day.

Marcus Bennett & Jonathan Hall
The Bay Horse,
45 The Green, Hurworth,
Darlington, DL2 2AA

Tel	+44 (0)1325 720663
Web	www.thebayhorsehurworth.com

Entry 222 Map 12

Essex

The Bell Hotel
Horndon-on-the-Hill

A 600-year-old timber-framed coaching inn, as full of contented locals today as it was when pilgrims stopped on their way to Canterbury. Everything is a delight: hanging lanterns in the courtyard, stripped boards in the bar, superb staff in the restaurant, copious window boxes bursting with colour. It's a proper inn, warmly welcoming, with thick beams, country rugs, panelled walls and open fires. Stop for a pint of cask ale in the lively bar, then potter into the restaurant for top food, perhaps seared scallops with confit venison, grilled Dover sole, cherry parfait with chocolate brownie Alaska and popping candy. Christine grew up here, John joined her years ago; both are respected in the trade, as is Joanne, Master Sommelier and manager of many years. An infectious warmth runs through this ever-popular inn. As for the bedrooms, go for the suites above – or a new room in the grand Georgian property up the high street: cosily inviting, individual, quite funky. In the morning, breakfast with the papers at elegant Hill House, where further bedrooms, snazzily refurbished, lie. Then head north into Constable country.

Rooms	15 doubles, 3 twins: £50-£90. 9 suites for 2: £120-£145. Singles £45-£140. Extra bed/sofabed available £20 per person per night.
Meals	Bar meals from £8.95. Lunch from £11.95. Dinner, à la carte, £27. Not Bank Holidays.
Closed	Christmas Day & Boxing Day.

Christine & John Vereker
The Bell Hotel,
High Road, Horndon-on-the-Hill,
Stanford-le-Hope SS17 8LD
Tel   +44 (0)1375 642463
Web   www.bell-inn.co.uk

Entry 223 Map 5

The Lion Inn
Boreham

On the A12, in need of sustenance and a comfortable bed? Look no further than the Lion. Money has been lavished on the old roadside pub, now dwarfed by its restaurant and B&B extensions, rolling back to a decked terrace and a secluded herb garden. It may look big and brash but the tardis-like interior has been cleverly kitted out in eclectic style. Expect the unexpected: a long bar with gleaming beer fonts, old signs and a distinctly French feel, a bustling open-plan kitchen, a vast dining area filled with old tables, leather armchairs and standard lamps; a floor-to-ceiling wine rack covers one wall. Beyond, in the original pub, are cosy beamed dining rooms and a new conservatory. Modern menus list sharing platters and pasta meals alongside classic grills and specials like Irish stew and fish pie. Smart air-conditioned bedrooms, named after French villages are adorned with old French prints, dark repro antiques, big down-topped beds, fresh coffee; bathrooms sport rain showers, Damana lotions and the odd splash of marble. A super-duper bolthole in Essex's heart. *Open for pre-booked tables only on: Valentines Day, Mothers Day, Christmas Day, New Year's Eve.*

Rooms	17 doubles, 5 twins: £95–£175. Bridal suite: £250.
Meals	Bar meals from £6.25. Lunch from £7.95. Dinner from £9.95. Sunday lunch, 2–3 courses, £17–£22.
Closed	Boxing Day.

Clive Thomson
The Lion Inn,
Main Road, Boreham,
Chelmsford CM3 3JA
Tel   +44 (0)1245 394900
Web   www.lioninnhotel.co.uk

The Mistley Thorn
Mistley

In Constable land: a perfect coastal village where Georgian cottages gather around a river estuary with wide, light views of water, bobbing boats and green hills beyond. David and Sherri (who have a cookery school next door) run the place beautifully: staff are young, and good, there are plenty of locals tossed into the mix and a smattering of children. The mood is laid-back city wine bar rather than roadside country pub. Colours are soft and easy, the tables are of various shapes, candles flicker, modern art rubs along well with the odd antique and food is taken seriously but without reverence. There's lots of robust local fish and seafood – squid with chilli, crab cakes with mayonnaise, gurnard with black olive tapenade, brilliant chips – and a pudding list that includes cheesecake from Californian Sherri's mum. Bedrooms are calm with cream carpets, big beds and pale green paintwork; ask for a room with a view over the river. Bathrooms have a Turkish feel with tiny beige and cream tiles, spotless white baths and overhead showers. It's all entirely charming.

Rooms	5 doubles, 3 twin/doubles: £110–£125. Singles from £90. Dinner, B&B from £75 p.p. per night.
Meals	Lunch from £4.95. Set lunch, 2 courses £12.50; 3 courses £15. Dinner, 3 courses, from £30.
Closed	Rarely.

David McKay & Sherri Singleton
The Mistley Thorn,
High Street, Mistley,
Manningtree CO11 1HE
Tel   +44 (0)1206 392821
Web   www.mistleythorn.co.uk

Entry 225 Map 10

Essex

Essex

The Sun Inn
Dedham

Order a picnic at the inn, float down the Stour, tie up on the bank for lunch al fresco. You're in Constable country, in an idyllic village made rich by mills in the 16th century, and you couldn't hope to wash up in a better place. Step in to find log fires in grand grates, board games on old tables, stripped floors, an easy elegance. A panelled lounge comes with sofas and armchairs, the bar is made from a slab of local elm and the dining room is beamed and airy. Delicious food is inspired by Italy: celeriac and black cabbage soup; pasta with red mullet, tomatoes, olives, chilli and thyme; baked hake with tomatoes, fennel and parsley; pork chop with cannellini beans and salsa verde. The cheeses are local and children can have small portions of whatever they fancy.

The Pheasant
Gestingthorpe

On the Essex/Suffolk border, with serene views over the Stour valley, the Pheasant thrives under James (former garden designer) and his wife Diana. Once a run-down boozer, it is now a food-led community pub. Two cosy countrified bars draw village folk in for quiz nights, wine tastings, bonfire nights, monthly supper clubs, and the 'Thirsty Thursday Club', while well-informed foodies help swell the numbers, attracted by James's seasonal monthly menus. Enjoy potted crab followed by lamb and smoked mushroom pie; finish with apple, pear and quince crumble. James also finds time to smoke fish, seafood and cheeses, and maintain his award-winning Chelsea show garden from which most of the fruit and vegetables flow.

Meals	Lunch from £10.95. Dinner from £16.95. Not Monday lunch.
Closed	Christmas.

Meals	Dinner from £10. Bar meals from £5.95. Sunday lunch, 3 courses, £18.50.
Closed	Christmas.

Piers Baker
The Sun Inn,
High Street, Dedham,
Colchester CO7 6DF

| Tel | +44 (0)1206 323351 |
| Web | www.thesuninndedham.com |

Entry 226 Map 10

James & Diana Donoghue
The Pheasant,
Gestingthorpe,
Halstead CO9 3AU

| Tel | +44 (0)1787 461196 |
| Web | www.thepheasant.net |

Entry 227 Map 10

Essex

The Compasses at Pattiswick
Pattiswick

Slick and sophisticated bars mix flagstones with floorboards, modern furniture and soft lights with creams and sages. At heart it remains a local, with plenty of space for drinkers in for a pint of Woodforde's Wherry or Abbot Ale, yet the food is the major draw, served in the bar or the big elegant restaurant. Old favourites such as bangers with mash and onion gravy and ham, egg and chips are founded on a network of small local suppliers. More modern dishes might include smoked pigeon and pickled mushroom salad, roast cod with shellfish bisque and confit tomato, and duck with fig and port jus; and who can resist pear and almond tart with champagne sorbet? Children are very welcome; there's an adventure play area, a magician on Sunday lunchtimes, and family fun days in May and August.

Meals	Lunch from £6.75.
	Dinner from £11.95.
	Sunday roast from £12.95.
	Not Sunday eve.
Closed	Open all day.

Jono & Jane Clark
The Compasses at Pattiswick,
19 Compasses Road, Pattiswick,
Braintree CM77 8BG

Tel   +44 (0)1376 561322
Web   www.thegreatpubcompany.co.uk

Entry 228 Map 10

Essex

The Square & Compasses
Fairstead

What's not to love? A country pub with wines by the glass and ales from the cask, modern British cooking that's delicious and well-priced, and a landlord who's knowledgeable and welcoming. This popular pub is owner-run and it shows. What's more, it's in a beautiful spot, overlooking the Essex Way. Walkers with dogs beat a path to its door, and so do lucky locals. Inside are black beams and log burners, crisp napkins on old wooden tables, a bookcase of antique tomes, and snugs with dark green walls. Our pigeon with black pudding served on a bed of red cabbage, washed down with a pint of Fire Fox was full of flavour; the kitchen is known for its quality meats, and some of the vegetables are supplied by the villagers. All the pub classics are prepared from scratch too.

Meals	Starters from £4.50.
	Dinner from £10.95.
Closed	Open all day.

Victor Roome
The Square & Compasses,
Fuller Street,
Fairstead CM3 2BB

Tel   +44 (0)1245 361477
Web   www.thesquareandcompasses.co.uk

Entry 229 Map 9

Essex

Essex

The Compasses Inn
Littley Green

In a little hamlet tucked away from civilisation is The Compasses, a simple pub with a loyal following. The building is red brick and Victorian, the bar is plain (stone floors, wood tables, roaring fire: little has changed in 50 years) and it started life as the closest pub to the Ridley Brewery. Heritage is key; the family that run it have beer flowing through their veins and the Bishops Nick Arise went down a treat! Off the bar is a dining room where freshly made food – chilli con carne, filled baked potatoes, ham, egg and chips – is chalked up on the board. The meat is local and the 'huffers' (traditional triangular baps) are huge, and stuffed with a choice of fillings. Ramblers, cyclists and the local shoots drop by, and if you come with children there's a garden with picnic tables at the back.

The Eight Bells
Saffron Walden

Leanne's first 'Cosy Pub' is a beautifully restored 16th-century wool merchant's house tucked away on a street lined with wonky timbered and painted houses, an easy stroll from the town centre. Find bowed beams, old wall timbers, crackling logs in a big brick fireplace, polished wooden floors, Farrow & Ball colours and chesterfield armchairs in cosy corners; the relaxing bars are perfect for quaffing pints of Taylor's Landlord and sharing a charcuterie grazing board. Arrive early to bag a table in the historic barn at the back, replete with vaulted ceiling and painted timbers. With two wood-burners keeping things toasty, tuck into baked camembert with rustic breads, lamb shank with redcurrant and rosemary jus, and blackberry Eton mess; or come on Sunday for a classic roast. Outside is a swish summer terrace.

Meals	Lunch & dinner from £5.
Closed	Open all day.

Meals	Lunch & bar meals from £10.
	Dinner from £20.
	Sunday lunch, 2 courses, £13.50.
Closed	Open all day.

Jocelyn Ridley
The Compasses Inn,
Littley Green,
Chelmsford CM3 1BU
Tel   +44 (0)1245 362308
Web   www.compasseslittleygreen.co.uk

Entry 230 Map 9

Leanne Langman
The Eight Bells,
18 Bridge Street,
Saffron Walden CB10 1BU
Tel   +44 (0)1799 522790
Web   www.8bells-pub.co.uk

Entry 231 Map 9

Essex

The Cricketers Arms
Rickling Green

Having snapped up the Cricketers in 2011, Leanne Langman is working her magic and restoring the fortunes of this striking 200-year-old red-brick inn. The setting is tranquil and gorgeous, overlooking a vast village green and cricket pitch; arrive early on a summer Sunday to bag a bench and watch an innings or two with a pint of Wherry. Rickling Green became *the* venue for London society cricket matches in the 1880s and it's still taken seriously. There's a contemporary feel to the rambling bar and dining areas – old beams and timbers, wood and stone floors, chunky tables, colourful cushions on banquettes, sofas and easy chairs in front of a crackling log fire. Hungry? Tuck into grazing boards, risottos, fishcakes, lamb and mint pies, dry-aged steaks and sticky toffee puddings – out on the terrace on warm days.

Meals	Lunch & dinner £9.50–£16.95.
Closed	Open all day.

Leanne Langman
The Cricketers Arms,
Rickling Green,
Saffron Walden CB11 3YG
Tel   +44 (0)1799 543210
Web www.thecricketersarmsricklinggreen.co.uk

Entry 232 Map 9

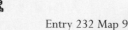

Ebrington Arms
Ebrington

The glorious gardens at Hidcote Manor and Kiftsgate Court are a ramble across fields from the Ebrington Arms. This is a relaxed and rustic Cotswold stone pub that has been restored and revived by Claire and Jim. Little has changed in the 17th-century bar, hub of the community, cosy with low beams and roaring fires. Bag a seat on the settle and share pints of Stroud Budding with the regulars, or seek out the fur dining room next door. Worn stone floors, fresh flowers and a delightful mishmash of tables set the scene for some terrific pub food cooked from mostly local produce. Dishes are simple yet full of flavour, so dive in to scallops with celeriac purée and black pudding; calves' liver with garlic mash and caramelised onions; and apple, strawberry and ginger crumble. No need to negotiate the route home when you can bed down here; bedrooms (up steepish stairs) are full of charm, with chunky wooden beds, colourful throws, plump pillows, smart bathrooms and deep window seats with village or country views. A properly unpretentious inn, run by the nicest people. One of the best. *Minimum stay: 2 nights at weekends.*

Rooms	5 doubles: £120–£125.
Meals	Lunch & dinner £9–£17.50.
	Limited menu Sunday eve.
Closed	Rarely.

Claire & Jim Alexander
Ebrington Arms,
Ebrington,
Chipping Campden GL55 6NH
Tel   +44 (0)1386 593223
Web   www.theebringtonarms.co.uk

Gloucestershire

Seagrave Arms
Weston Subedge

Locked and unloved for nearly two years, this classic Cotswold coaching inn has been restored to its former Georgian glory. Worn flagstones draw you into the cosy, wood-floored bar, where leather armchairs by the inglenook provide the perfect spot to cradle a pint of local ale, or to ponder chef and landlord Newstead Sawyer's mouthwatering, seasonal menu. Served at old dining tables in two warm and inviting candlelit rooms is delicious food: monkfish with beetroot, turnip, parsnip and pear cider sauce; partridge with smoked bacon, chestnut and salsify; crème brûlée and rhubarb; a slate of cheeses with damson jelly. Meat and game are sourced from local farms and shoots; everything – breads, chutneys, lunchtime burgers – is freshly prepared. Immaculate, well-designed bedrooms are the icing on the cake, the ground-floor ones in the annexe, the quietest at the back. Look forward to top-notch linen, handmade hot water bottles for a chilly night, fresh milk in the morning, and high-spec bathrooms with walk-in showers. You're 20 minutes from Stratford-upon-Avon, and strolling distance from Chipping Campden and the Cotswold Way.

Rooms	7 doubles: £80–£135.
	1 suite for 3: £135–£165.
Meals	Light lunch from £5.50.
	Dinner, 3 courses, around £30.
Closed	Rarely.

Hannah Brown
Seagrave Arms,
Friday Street, Weston Subedge,
Chipping Campden GL55 6QH
Tel   +44 (0)1386 840192
Web   www.seagravearms.com

The Lion Inn
Winchcombe

Annie's determination to restore an old inn's charms has been a joyous success. Push open the heavy oak door to reveal a beautiful main bar: rugs on pale-painted floors, candles at mullioned windows, rough stone walls, and a log fire crackling in a 15th-century inglenook. Jugs of fresh flowers, battered leather armchairs and grand gilt-framed paintings enhance the authentic feel. Review the papers over a pint of real ale, play scrabble, cards or one of the selection of games. Order from the seasonal menu: perhaps slowly braised brisket of Wagyu beef with mashed potato, followed by plum pudding with Earl Grey & armagnac prunes with a cassis sorbet. Country-chic rooms upstairs – one with its own small balcony, three with private staircases, one above the noisy snug bar – are toasty-warm and TV-free, with inviting beds and soothing colours, upholstered armchairs and antique furniture. Bathrooms are just as good, with Bramley products and en-suite showers. Winchcombe is on the Cotswold Way; Chipping Campden, Broadway and Cheltenham are a short drive.

Rooms	5 doubles: £110–£160. 2 suites for 3: £150–£185. Extra bed/sofabed £25 per person per night.
Meals	Lunch & dinner £9.50–£24.50.
Closed	Rarely.

Annie Fox-Hamilton
The Lion Inn,
North Street, Winchcombe
Cheltenham GL54 5PS
Tel   +44 (0)1242 603300
Web   www.thelionwinchcombe.co.uk

Gloucestershire

Horse & Groom
Bourton-on-the-Hill

You're at the top of the hill, so grab the window seats for views that pour over the Cotswolds. This is a hive of youthful endeavour, with brothers at the helm; Will cooks, Tom pours the ales, and a cheery conviviality flows. Refurbished interiors mix the old (open fires, stone walls, beamed ceilings) with the new (halogen lighting, coir matting, a cool marble bar), making this a very fine place to hole up in for a night or two. There are settles and boarded menus in the bar, stripped wooden floors and old rugs in the dining room. Food goes way beyond the pub norm, so tuck into fillet of Loch Duart salmon baked in pastry with currants, ginger and hollandaise; Cornish mackerel; Longhorn steak. Sit back in summer under the shade of damson trees with a mellow pint of Goff's Jouster and watch the chefs raid the kitchen garden – for raspberries, strawberries, broad beans, herbs and more. Bedrooms are nicely plush, smart but uncluttered; those at the front are soundproofed to minimise noise from the road. The deluxe room is huge and comes with a king-sized bed, the garden room has doors that open onto the terrace. *Minimum stay: 2 nights at weekends.*

Rooms	5 doubles: £120–£170. Singles from £80.
Meals	Lunch from £4.75. Dinner, 3 courses, £25–£30. Not Sunday night.
Closed	Christmas Day & New Year's Eve.

Tom & Will Greenstock
Horse & Groom,
Bourton-on-the-Hill,
Moreton-in-Marsh GL56 9AQ
Tel   +44 (0)1386 700413
Web   www.horseandgroom.info

Entry 236 Map 8

The White Hart Royal
Moreton-in-Marsh

Charles I reputedly sheltered at this mellow stone inn following the Battle of Marston Moor in 1644. Now beautifully restored it's the Cotswolds' outpost for Kevin Charity's thriving Bulldog Hotels, a haven for modern day travellers. A bustling bar with a blazing fire in the inglenook and Hooky ale on tap, lounges filled with period furniture, antiques and paintings, and 21st-century comforts in cosy bedrooms. The fabulous Garden and Stable Rooms are the biggest and best of the bunch: the Hayloft with exposed roof beams, the Old Stable with contemporary fabrics and vast glass-walled wet room with bath and walk-in shower, or the seductive Le Noir with a bath for two in the bedroom. Traditional pub classics vie for attention with modern British dishes on the menu, perhaps scallops with black pudding purée, smoked bacon and pea shoots, home-made beef burger with pickles and chips, cod with samphire and crab bisque, and apple and cinnamon crumble. Stunning walks, gorgeous villages and Chipping Campden are on the doorstep.

Rooms	18 doubles, 5 twins, 3 four-posters: £95-£175. 1 suite for 2, 1 family room for 4: £145-£185.
Meals	Lunch & dinner £4-£20.
Closed	Rarely.

Kevin Charity
The White Hart Royal,
High Street,
Moreton-in-Marsh GL56 0BA

Tel	+44 (0)1608 650731
Web	www.whitehartroyal.com

Entry 237 Map 8

The Five Alls
Filkins

The Snows have swapped the Swan at Southrop for a handsome 18th-century pub in postcard-pretty Filkins. The faded old coaching inn is back on track, once again full of warmth and personality. The bar throngs with locals and foaming pints of Brakspear, there are 15 wines by the glass and proper bar food: devilled kidneys on toast, hearty soups, fish and chips. Bright cotton cushions on cosy leather sofas front the inglenook, candles glow in lanterns and soft music plays; arrive early if you fancy a pre-dinner drink. Then it's into the dining room for Italian inspired British dishes – potted shrimps; roast lamb with beans, mash and salsa verde; drunken panna cotta with raspberries – served at old dining tables. Heaps of charm too, thanks to rugs on stone floors, modern art on stone walls and jugs of fresh flowers. Lovely bedrooms upstairs come with crisp linen and duck down on big comfortable beds, fat lamps, the odd wing chair and feature fireplace, local art and artefacts, and compact gorgeous bathrooms with walk-in showers and Bramley products. Burford, Thames Path walks and Buscot Park are close.

Rooms	9 doubles: £95–£140.
Meals	Lunch & dinner from £12. Set lunch £15 & £19. Sunday roast £16.
Closed	Christmas Day.

Sebastian & Lana Snow
The Five Alls,
Filkins,
Lechlade GL7 3JQ
Tel   +44 (0)1367 860875
Web   www.thefiveallsfilkins.co.uk

Entry 238 Map 8

The New Inn at Coln
Coln St Aldwyns

The New Inn is old – 1632 to be exact – but well-named nonetheless. The pub stands in a handsome Cotswold village with ivy roaming on original stone walls and a sun-trapping terrace where roses bloom in summer. Airy interiors have low ceilings, painted beams, flagged floors and fires that roar – perfect for supping pints of real ale with roast beef and horseradish sandwiches, or lingering over seared scallops, pan-roasted duck and baked lemon tart, served in red-walled dining rooms by thoroughly delightful staff. Bedrooms are a treat, all warmly elegant with soft carpets, swish bed throws, perfect white linen in good little bathrooms (a couple with claw-foot baths). There are wonky floors and the odd beam in the main house, while those in the Dovecote come in bold colours and have views across water meadows to the river; walks start from the door. Bibury, Burford and Stow are all close, so spread your wings.

Rooms	14 doubles: £110–£160.
Meals	Lunch from £5.
	Dinner, 3 courses, £20.
	Sunday roast from £11.
Closed	Rarely.

Mark Henriques
The New Inn at Coln,
Main Street, Coln St Aldwyns,
Cirencester GL7 5AN
Tel   +44 (0)1285 750651
Web   www.new-inn.co.uk

Entry 239 Map 8

The Village Pub
Barnsley

An old favourite of locals and faithfuls from far and wide, this civilised Cotswold bolthole has been given a gentle facelift by Calcot Health & Leisure — owners of Barnsley House, the country-house hotel across the road. Expect seasonal food based on the best local produce, good-quality Hook Norton ale and decent wines. There's even a service hatch to the heated patio at the back, so you can savour the sauvignon until the sun goes down. Cotswold stone and ancient flags sing the country theme; past bar and open fires, quiet alcoves provide a snug setting that entices you to stay. If you do, tuck into crab and leek tart, rib-eye steak with béarnaise sauce, or whole plaice with crab and parsley butter; sweet tooths will love the warm ginger cake with rum and raisin ice cream. Classy, spruced-up rooms are equally cosy and inviting, with soothing colours, stylish fabrics, plasma screens and iPod docks. Two stunning four-poster rooms have big bathrooms with claw-foot baths, walk-in showers, posh toiletries. Roman Cirencester and gorgeous Bibury are close by; this is classic Cotswold country.

Rooms	4 twin/doubles, 2 four-posters: £140–£165.
Meals	Lunch & bar meals from £6. Dinner from £12.50. Sunday lunch, 3 courses, £28.
Closed	Rarely.

Michele Mella
The Village Pub,
Barnsley,
Cirencester GL7 5EF
Tel   +44 (0)1285 740421
Web   www.thevillagepub.co.uk

The Catherine Wheel
Bibury

The 15th-century Catherine Wheel is the only pub in its perfect honeypot location, offering excellent food in a friendly atmosphere. Three small rooms circle the bar, so you can tuck into a private corner, while a larger dining area overlooks the orchard beer garden with trees for climbing (and apples that find their way into puddings when the harvest is good). The affordable menu is packed with those comforting classics we all love: steak and red wine pie, fish and chips, Gloucester Old Spot sausage and mash, as well as some seriously good vegetarian dishes (beetroot bourguignon with crispy confit parsnips took our fancy) and of course the local Bibury trout, here served with olive and caper mash, creamed greens and truffle oil. Chef-owner Jeremy has twenty years' experience and real passion for what he does; you'll eat well. The menu changes daily – all washed down with real ales or wines from an excellent list. Across the car park: four neatly unpretentious bedrooms with spotless shower rooms. The best treat is the setting; William Morris called Bibury 'the most beautiful village in England'. You'll have no trouble seeing why.

Rooms	8 twin/doubles: £65–£110.
Meals	Lunch & dinner £5–£14.
	Sunday roast £16–£19.50.
Closed	Rarely.

Carole White
The Catherine Wheel,
Arlington, Bibury,
Cirencester GL7 5ND
Tel   +44 (0)1285 740250
Web   www.catherinewheel-bibury.co.uk

Gloucestershire

The Wheatsheaf
Northleach

A well-kept Cotswold secret, this small former wool market town is tucked between pretty hills on a crossroads of the Roman Fosse Way. Big smiles from a young staff greet you and a pint of fresh local bitter will be in your hand before you know it. The wonderfully worn flagstones in the very well-stocked bar separate two well-proportioned and coordinated dining areas, aglow with wooden floors, striking Asian rugs and armchairs fronting crackling fires. Expect a mix of traditional English fare of unpretentious goodness and impeccable provenance, from steak frites and garlic butter to cod with roast Jerusalem artichoke, chorizo and crayfish. Wine from the best of the old world has been carefully chosen to suit all budgets. Retire to rooms in contemporary-retro style, some newly refurbished and each one a treat, with huge beds, eclectic paintings, calm colours, wall coverings. Swish bathrooms too, with roll top baths or storm showers and dressing gowns to wrap up in. A brilliant little bolthole to return to after a day out exploring the High Wold countryside and villages, with a youthful buzz.

Rooms	14 doubles: £120–£180. Extra bed £25 child, £50 adult.
Meals	Continental breakfast included; cooked extras £5–£12. Lunch from £9. Dinner, 3 courses, about £30.
Closed	Rarely.

James Parn
The Wheatsheaf,
West End, Northleach,
Cheltenham GL54 3EZ
Tel   +44 (0)1451 860244
Web   www.cotswoldswheatsheaf.com

The Fleece at Cirencester
Cirencester

Charles II once stayed at this pretty coaching inn, posing as a manservant, the story goes. Now it's had a refurb in classic English style, and bar, lounge and restaurant glow. Open all day, the Fleece has quite a buzz. Drop by for a wake-up coffee and eggs on toast; choose a deli board at lunchtime and a pint of Thwaites. There are daily specials and Sunday roasts; our steak and chips was delicious. As for the staff, they're charming, well-trained, smartly turned out. Set off into the Cotswolds for a hike with the dog, browse the antique shops and the chic little delis, then come back to the Fleece for the night (ask about parking before you arrive). The more spacious 'Character' rooms, with their beamy, up-in-the-roof feeling – lots of stairs – are the best, but all are top-notch, with plush carpets and dark boards, beds antique and new, coordinated cushions, modish wallpapers, plump pillows... face the famous market square and watch the world go by, or settle more quietly into a room at the back. The Fleece is a crowd-pleaser from start to finish.

Rooms	18 doubles, 4 twin/doubles: £85–£125.
	5 suites for 2: £115–£150.
	1 family room for 4: £75–£150.
Meals	Bar meals from £4.95.
	Lunch from £6.95.
	Dinner from £8.95.
	Sunday lunch, 2 courses, £11.95.
Closed	Rarely.

Paul Hodgkinson
The Fleece at Cirencester,
Market Place,
Cirencester GL7 2NZ
Tel   +44 (0)1285 658507
Web   www.thefleececirencester.co.uk

Entry 243 Map 8

The Royal Oak Tetbury
Tetbury

Resplendent after a full refurbishment this 17th-century coaching inn is abuzz with enthusiasm. Inside, reclaimed floorboards have been artfully fitted together, a salvaged carved oak bar has its own little 'Groucho snug' at one end. Exposed stone and a real fire co-exist with a pretty Art Deco piano whose ivories are often tinkled. Cheery staff will pull you a pint of Uley or Stroud ale – or perhaps an Orchard Pig cider – and on certain days you can even mix your own Bloody Mary. Treats in store on the menu from head chef Richard Simms feature pub classics with a twist: sharing or small plates, hearty salads, 'oak pots' with a veggie or meat option served with crusty bread or brown rice and plenty of choice for vegans. Up in the roof beneath massive beams is a more formal restaurant with a spacious, calm atmosphere. Across the cobbled yard are six bedrooms – three are dog-friendly – with a restful elegance, dreamy beds and bathrooms to linger in. And if a special occasion is the reason for your visit then the Oak Lodge room will not fail to get things off to a very good start. *Minimum stay: 2 nights at weekends & in high season.*

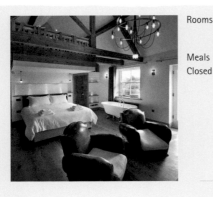

Rooms	6 doubles: £75–£160. Extra bed/sofabed £20 per person per night.
Meals	Lunch & dinner £5–£13.
Closed	Rarely.

Kate Lewis
The Royal Oak Tetbury,
1 Cirencester Road,
Tetbury GL8 8EY
Tel   +44 (0)1666 500021
Web   www.theroyaloaktetbury.co.uk

The King's Arms
Didmarton

Next to the main road in Didmarton, close to Tetbury and the Badminton Estate, is this recently refurbished inn – a perfect place in the Cotswolds. Expect beams and stone-flagged floors, inviting dark green walls adorned with antlers, fat candles on dining tables, lovely painted settles, and photos showcasing local history. There's a big old fireplace for winter, darts and dominoes in the bar, a lovely walled garden with a boules pitch and a new pizza oven that's doing brisk business. Blackboard menus on the walls are chalked up daily. Pop in for a charcuterie platter with olives and grilled breads, the King's burger with truffle mayonnaise, or pan fried bream with garlic mash, Sweet Cicely and lemon dressing – you won't go home disappointed. Wash down with a fine wine or a local tipple – Bath Gem, Uley Bitter, perhaps one of their guest beers. If you fancy staying over, rooms upstairs are cosy and stylish, with comfy beds, crisp linen, down duvets and spotless shower rooms. A couple of cottages suitable for larger groups await in the coaching stable.

Rooms	4 doubles, 1 twin/double: £95–£110. 1 single: £60–£65. 1 cottage for 4, 2 cottages for 4-6: £120–£220 per night.
Meals	Light lunch from £5.95. Mains from £12.50. Wood-fired pizzas from £8.95.
Closed	Rarely.

Mark Birchall
The King's Arms,
The Street, Didmarton,
Badminton GL9 1DT

Tel	+44 (0)1454 238 245
Web	www.kingsarmsdidmarton.co.uk

Gloucestershire

The Royal Oak
Leighterton

In a Cotswold gem of a village, a superb refurbishment of a mullion-window'd pub. Inside all is light-filled and spacious with a country-contemporary feel. There's a raised log fire, an oriental rug on old parquet, stunning oak trusses in a lofty dining room, and French windows to a big walled patio. Ales from Wadworth's, Bath and Uley, a cider from Sherston and well-chosen wines cover all tastes, while food comes with a philosophy of 'doing simple things very well'. Daily changing specials include game casserole with juniper berry dumplings and devils on horseback; pan-fried chicken with sweet braised red cabbage and anchovy and spring onion mash. The burgers are great, the Sunday roasts fabulous, and the Monarch's Way runs outside – walk to Westonbirt!

Gloucestershire

The Ostrich Inn
Newland

In the village of Newland the Ostrich is where the beer drinkers go, to sample eight changing ales. Across from All Saints Church, that 'Cathedral of the Forest', you mix with all sorts before a log fire. Walkers and trail bikers pile in for massive portions of delicious food, from Newland bread and cheese platter to rump of Welsh spring lamb with rich orange and cardamom sauce, spicy Merguez sausages and crisp diced potato. The nicotine-brown ceiling that looks in danger of imminent collapse is supported by a massive oak pillar in front of the bar where the locals chatter and jazz CDs keep the place swinging. The weekly menu, served throughout the pub, takes a step up in class, and is excellent value. Energetic Kathryn and her team, including Alfie the pub dog, encourage the buzz. To the back is a walled garden – and the loos.

Meals	Set lunch £13.95–£17.95.
	Dinner £11.95–£24.95.
	Sunday roast £14.
Closed	3pm–6pm, Mon–Fri.

Meals	Bar meals £5.50–£10.50.
	Lunch & dinner £12.50–£18.50.
Closed	3pm–6.30pm (6pm Sat).

Paul & Antonia Whitbread
The Royal Oak,
The Street, Leighterton,
Tetbury GL8 8UN
Tel   +44 (0)1666 890250
Web   www.royaloakleighterton.co.uk

Entry 246 Map 3

Kathryn Horton
The Ostrich Inn,
Newland,
Coleford GL16 8NP
Tel   +44 (0)1594 833260
Web   www.theostrichinn.com

Entry 247 Map 7

Gloucestershire

The Old Spot
Dursley

Nudged by a car park and Dursley's bus station is the charming Old Spot. Built in 1776 as a farm cottage, the pub has since gained national recognition among those who make pilgrimages to sample the brews. Indeed, the Old Spot has become something of a showcase for the beers of Uley Brewery, including Pig's Ear and Old Ric, the latter named after a former landlord. Real ciders include Weston's and Ashton Press. No surprise, for a pub named after a rare-breed pig, that there are porcine figurines and pictures dotted around, alongside old prints and posters. New head chef Patrick is moving the menu up a notch and lunch sandwiches are terrific; try roast topside of beef with caramelised onions and horseradish mayonnaise. Friendly, no-nonsense, traditional and on the Cotswold Way. For ale-lovers – a joy.

Gloucestershire

The Old Lodge
Minchinhampton

Lording it on an ancient piece of common ground is this former hunting lodge to Henry VIII. The cattle roam free; you too can wander – and gaze on the five valleys view. Expect bold art, classical columns, smooth oak and honey-coloured stone walls. Sofas sprawl around coffee tables, fireplaces crackle, the conversation is lively. With a pub feel, albeit an up-to-the-minute one, the bar serves Budding from Stroud Brewery alongside Abbotts, IPA and Otter. In the restaurant, with floor-to-ceiling windows for the view: an eco-chic bar made from reclaimed wine barrels and locally sourced delights on daily menus: pan-fried fillet of seabass, asparagus and oyster mushrooms with new potatoes; chargrilled lamb cutlets with spring pea, broccoli and spring onion bubble and squeak; spicy pear and plum crumble.

Meals	Bar meals £3.45–£9.25. Lunch only.	Meals	Lunch & dinner £10.95–£17.95. Sunday roast £13.95.
Closed	Open all day.	Closed	Open all day.

2015/16
Sawday's
PUB AWARD

Authentic pub

	Ellie Sainty		Daniel Wood
	The Old Spot,		The Old Lodge,
	2 Hill Road,		Minchinhampton,
	Dursley GL11 4JQ		Stroud GL6 9AQ
Tel	+44 (0)1453 542870	Tel	+44 (0)1453 832047
Web	www.oldspotinn.co.uk	Web	www.food-club.com

Entry 248 Map 8

Entry 249 Map 8

Gloucestershire

The Ragged Cot
Minchinhampton

The handsome old stone coaching inn stands alongside 600 acres of National Trust common land close to Gatcombe Park – ideal for walking off a fabulous lunch. The Cot's been on this spot since the 17th century so expect exposed stone walls, lovely low windows, thoughtful modern touches and a light-filled dining room overlooking the big garden. Inside, you are blissfully snug, tucked into a corner by the log fire. You can pop in for a perfect cup of coffee (all too rare in many pubs, but not at the Cot), and it's hard to resist the lunch and dinner menus. Try roasted breast of chicken in thyme butter with crushed sweet potato, followed by apple and winter berry crumble with spiced topping and fresh custard. Wellies, dogs and children are all made welcome.

Meals	Starters from £4.50.
	Dinner from £10.50.
Closed	Open all day.

Stuart Hanson
The Ragged Cot,
Cirencester Road, Minchinhampton,
Stroud GL6 8PE
Tel +44 (0)1453 884643
Web www.theraggedcot.co.uk

Entry 250 Map 8

Gloucestershire

The Tunnel House Inn
Coates

Emerge via the portico tunnel of the Severn & Thames Canal to find a gracious stone house in the clearing. It was built in the 1780s for the canal workers, and its latest conversion has been well considered. There's lots to like: laid-back hospitality, beef and horseradish sandwiches, Uley Bitter and Hook Norton, Black Dragon and Bee Sting cider, and a quirky décor. Scrubbed tables and huge faded sofas stand in front of the fire, there's a cacophony of bric-a-brac in the bar (most on the ceiling!), and an Ogygian juke box with decent tunes. In the dining room, a seasonal menu: Old Spot sausages with mash and red onion marmalade, roast belly pork with mustard-crushed new potatoes. Outside, a rather smart terrace, a big garden with open-field views – great for kids – and wild camping in Hailey Wood.

| Meals | Lunch & dinner £9.50–£15.95. |
| Closed | Open all day. |

Phil Thompson
The Tunnel House Inn,
Coates,
Cirencester GL7 6PW
Tel +44 (0)1285 770280
Web www.tunnelhouse.com

Entry 251 Map 8

Gloucestershire

The Bell at Sapperton
Sapperton

This elegant pub attracts wine lovers, foodies, ramblers and riders. Inside is a spacious but intimate décor that spreads itself across several levels — stripped beams and wood-burners, modern art on stone walls, old settles and church chairs, fresh flowers and newspapers. Sup on local Uley Old Spot or Otter Amber Bitter, dine on fresh local produce and rare-breed meats. Specials are chalked up above the fireplace and the food is generous in its range: pan-fried Madgett's Farm duck breast, lamb from Butts Farm, apple crumble crème brûlée with blackberry ice cream, and a goat's cheese called Rachel. Not a typical family pub but Sunday roasts are hugely popular and the wine list is considered, to match the clientele. Summer eating is on the well-tended terrace and spills into a 'Mediterranean' courtyard.

Meals	Bar meals from £4.95.
	Lunch from £9.95.
	Dinner from £10.95.
	Sunday lunch, 3 courses, £29.
Closed	2.30pm-6.30pm (3pm-7pm Sun).
	Open all day Sat (& Sun in summer).

Andrew & Natasha Edwards
The Bell at Sapperton,
Sapperton,
Cirencester GL7 6LE
Tel   +44 (0)1285 760298
Web   www.foodatthebell.co.uk

Entry 252 Map 8

Gloucestershire

The Woolpack Inn
Slad

If you walk through the Slad Valley one midsummer morning be sure to stop off here and raise a glass of well-kept Stroud or Uley to Laurie Lee, whose image adorns the walls a century after his birth. Unashamedly authentic, this tiny, lively, community focused pub packs them in and serves up great entertainment and fresh, local food with a no-nonsense approach to constantly changing small menus. Munch on bacon sandwiches or char-grilled local rib-eye steak with roast field mushrooms and chips, or fat, juicy mussels in a cider, cream and parsley sauce - delicious! In summer the terrace is packed with those eager for the idyllic valley views and impromptu ukulele-themed jam nights are not unheard of either. Pizza on Mondays and live music Wednesdays.

Meals	Lunch & dinner £8.95-£16.50.
	Sunday roast from £8.95.
Closed	Open all day.

Hannah Thompson
The Woolpack Inn,
Slad Road,
Slad,
Stroud GL6 7QA
Tel   +44 (0)1452 813429

Entry 253 Map 8

Gloucestershire

Old Badger Inn
Springhill

From unloved boozer to village hub – that's some journey. The Old Badger's success is down to its owners who, friendly and laid back, have brought real beer to the village. Ellie has run pubs for over 20 years and knows her trade so everyone – farmers, office workers, walkers, old, young – goes home happy. Inside are stone and wood floors, a mishmash of tables, gleaming pumps at the bar and – of course – beer mats on the ceiling. There's a log burner for winter, a big garden and a heated patio, and a separate drinking/dining room that welcomes families. If you're here for the beer, and many are, they offer Butcombe and a wide-ranging choice of ever-changing ales, mostly local. (There's wine if you must! Twelve by the glass.) On the menu? Hearty pub grub, freshly cooked including the Pie of the Day, and lovely roasts on Sundays.

Meals	Starters from £5.85. Dinner from £9.95.
Closed	Open all day.

Ellie Sainty
Old Badger Inn,
Alkerton Road, Springhill,
Eastington GL10 3AT
Tel +44 (0)1453 542870
Web www.oldbadgerinn.co.uk

Entry 254 Map 8

Gloucestershire

The Butcher's Arms
Sheepscombe

Tracking down this local involves an "are you sure this is the right road?"adventure down narrow winding lanes – to Sheepscombe, one of Laurie Lee's favourite places. If the weather's fine, and you haven't had one too many of Otter Bitter, find the most level spot you can in the garden and enjoy the views. Inside: flowery curtains at small windows, beams, brasses and bentwood chairs. Grab a perch by the wood-burning stove or a table in the little dining room and tuck into flavoursome food made from local ingredients – a roast rib of Beech Farm beef, a homemade pie. At weekends you rub shoulders with walkers, cyclists and locals. Inside or out, a place to savour. No plans for trendification, just a friendly down-to-earth place doing the thing it does best.

Meals	Lunch, bar meals & dinner from £7.95. Sunday lunch, 3 courses, £19.
Closed	3pm–6pm. Open all day Sat & Sun.

Mark & Sharon Tallents
The Butcher's Arms,
Sheepscombe,
Stroud GL6 7RH
Tel +44 (0)1452 812113
Web www.butchers-arms.co.uk

Entry 255 Map 8

Gloucestershire

The Green Dragon
Cowley

Festooned with hanging baskets, down a sleepy lane yet close to the A435, is an idyllic corner of Gloucestershire. A cider house three centuries ago, this old pub is warm, woody and atmospheric inside with a stone-flagged bar, glowing candles, crackling logs and carved mice everywhere, from bar stools to panelling – look for the delightful 'Mouseman' Thompson trademark. There are beers from Butcombe, wines from around the globe, steaks "to die for" and tasty chipolatas from Gloucester Old Spot pigs. Whether you choose a steak and kidney pudding or salmon in a creamy wine sauce you'll find the food comforting and delicious. Being on the Cotswold Way, this a good pub for walkers, and dogs are welcome on leads in the bar.

Meals	Lunch & dinner £7.50–£18.95.
Closed	Open all day.

Simon & Nicky Haly
The Green Dragon,
Cockleford, Cowley,
Cheltenham GL53 9NW
Tel   +44 (0)1242 870271
Web   www.green-dragon-inn.co.uk

Entry 256 Map 8

Gloucestershire

Yew Tree Inn
Clifford Mesne

Stride the grasslands and pine forests of May Hill before heading to this centuries-old cider press with a 'modern' façade. The cosy bar, all stone and beer mat-festooned beams, has local ales, cider from Three Choirs and a wine list that they source themselves from little-known vineyards. There is also a wine shop in a new room at the back, so buy a bottle or take a case. The small dining area is elegant yet informal with padded wooden chairs and a carved stone fireplace, while menus are seasonal and local... try steamed mussels in saffron and cider, follow with roast guinea fowl breast and confit thigh, braised cabbage and quince jus. The smart terrace has views that broaden away over trees and a very child-friendly play area just below. Charming and unpretentious.

Meals	Bar meals from £12.
	Lunch from £8.
	Dinner, 2-3 courses, £18–£23.
	Sunday lunch, 2-3 courses, £14–£17.
Closed	Sun evenings.
	Mon & Tues lunch.

Philip Todd
Yew Tree Inn,
Clifford Mesne,
Newent GL18 1JS
Tel   +44 (0)1531 820719
Web   www.yewtreeinn.com

Entry 257 Map 8

Gloucestershire

The Tavern
Cheltenham

From breakfasts of boiled eggs and soldiers to slow roast Sunday lunches and scrumptious Butts Farm burgers with slaw and fries, the menus say it all: this is a modern no-frills place with food to match. Bang in the middle of Cheltenham, it is a sister pub to the Cotswolds' Wheatsheaf Inn and attracts an urban crowd in search of cocktails and a plate or two to share; the food is modern American and British, with splashes of Asian and Mediterranean. The lower bar where you enter has high-legged metal chairs at reclaimed wooden tables and a warehousey brick wall; the more peaceful upstairs is a loft-like place with chunky trestle tables for sociable groups and an open kitchen so you can see the chefs perform. DJs on Saturdays, their own popcorn machine... this tavern is young and fun.

Meals	Bar meals from £8.
Closed	Sun all day.

The Manager
The Tavern,
5 Royal Well Place,
Cheltenham GL50 3DN
Tel   +44 (0)1242 221212
Web   www.thetaverncheltenham.com

🏃 📖 🍸

Entry 258 Map 8

Gloucestershire

The Royal Oak
Gretton

A handsome devil of a pub and no mistake! It sits beneath an oak tree on a hill looking north to Bredon Hill and the Vale of Evesham, and those in the know head for the conservatory to grab the views. The interior is a perfect blend of traditional and contemporary: worn flagstone floors, exposed stone, painted panelling and arty antlers. In summer grab a pint of Wye Valley or Brakspear ale and head outside where a game of tennis might be under way (court for hire). You may even spot a steam train at the bottom of the gently sloping garden. There's a modern pub menu plus lots of daily specials on a large blackboard; burgers and stews are hugely popular as are the char-grilled steaks. Every wine on the extensive list is available by the glass. A great pit-stop before Prescott.

Meals	Starters from £5.
	Dinner from £10.
Closed	Open all day.

Matthew & Wendy Brown
The Royal Oak,
Gretton,
Winchcombe GL54 5EP
Tel   +44 (0)1242 604999
Web   www.royaloakgretton.co.uk

♿ 🏃 🐾 📖 🍸 📶

Entry 259 Map 8

Gloucestershire

The Kings Arms
Mickleton

Everyone loves the Kings Arms – thanks to landlord Mike! It's a mellow old building in a mellow Cotswolds' village, cosy and personable inside, with a nice array of old tables and candles in bottles, and a big stone fireplace with a blazing fire. In winter locals drop by for a pint of Loose Cannon, Hook Norton or a whisky or two; in summer, visitors from Hidcote and Kiftsgate come for the picnic tables and barbecues; the garden is fabulous. On Sundays, everyone books in for the roasts, served until late for hikers and late risers. Scrumptious British food, from pan-seared scallops to slow-cooked belly pork to Mickleton Mess, is accompanied by excellent wines. Delicious pies, farmhouse butter, home-baked bread… no wonder it was buzzing on a Tuesday evening in March.

Meals	Starters from £6.50. Dinner from £12.95. Childrens menu £6.95.
Closed	Open 11am–late every day.

Mike Tayara
The Kings Arms,
High Street, Mickleton GL55 6RT
Tel   +44 (0)1386 438257
Web   www.kingsarmsmickleton.co.uk/
index.html

Entry 260 Map 8

Gloucestershire

The Fox Inn
Lower Oddington

One of our all-time favourites has just got better. Close to the grandeur of Cotswold country houses, the Fox evokes a sense of times past, all low ceilings, worn flagstones, log fire in winter and exciting, imaginative food. The bar has scrubbed pine tables topped with fresh flowers and candles, newspapers, magazines and ales on tap, and rag-washed ochre walls that date back years. Eat here or the elegant, rose-red dining room, or on the terrace (heated on cool nights) of the cottage garden. We enjoyed a delicious, subtly spiced Imam bayildi; cassoulet de luxe, a classic with a twist; a flavourful roasted red pepper tart; dark chocolate torte… and there are 60 wines to match. Before you leave, explore the honeystone village and 11th-century church, known for its fascinating frescos.

Meals	Lunch & dinner £9.50–£19.50.
Closed	3.30pm–6pm. 5pm–7pm Sun.

Peter & Louise Robinson
The Fox Inn,
Lower Oddington,
Moreton-in-Marsh GL56 0UR
Tel   +44 (0)1451 870555
Web   www.foxinn.net

Entry 261 Map 8

Gloucestershire

The Horse & Groom Village Inn
Upper Oddington

Cotswold stone, hanging baskets, hefty beams and flagstone floors, and logs around the double fireplace… is this a pub from central casting? It's 500 years old and Simon and Sally have rejuvenated without losing the charm. There's a good selection of guest ales, some from local microbreweries: choose from Wye Valley Best, Prescott Hill Climb, Chuffin Ale. Cider and lager, including Cotswold Premium, come from the Cotswold Brewing Co. nearby. The menu takes a tour of Europe, and there's traditional English too: shin of beef and root vegetable casserole; fillet of haddock topped with a chorizo, lime and parmesan crust; game from the Adlestrop Estate. Produce is organic whenever possible, breads and puddings are homemade, and there are 25 wines by the glass.

Gloucestershire

The Victoria Inn
Eastleach Turville

The golden-stoned Victoria pulls in the locals – whatever their age, whatever the weather – propping up the bar, with dogs, without dogs, or tucking into home cooking by the log fire. A simple village hostelry on the outside, it's deceptively spacious inside, and the Richardsons, in spite of opening up the interior, have kept the character and cosiness intact. The low-ceilinged and flagstoned bar offers darts, conversation and pints of Arkells 3B, while the L-shaped dining room is the backdrop for tasty platefuls of fresh food: perhaps salmon fishcakes; pork and leek sausages; slow-roasted lamb shank with garlic potatoes and red wine sauce. There are picnic tables out at the front, from where you can look down onto the stone cottages of two pretty villages. A very charming spot for a country stroll.

Meals	Bar meals from £4.50. Lunch & dinner from £12.50. Sunday roast from £15.
Closed	3pm-5.30pm.

Meals	Lunch & dinner £7.95-£14.75.
Closed	3pm-7pm.

Simon & Sally Jackson
The Horse & Groom Village Inn,
Upper Oddington,
Moreton-in-Marsh GL56 0XH
Tel   +44 (0)1451 830584
Web   www.horseandgroom.uk.com

Entry 262 Map 8

Stephen & Susan Richardson
The Victoria Inn,
Eastleach Turville,
Cirencester GL7 3NQ
Tel   +44 (0)1367 850277
Web   www.victoriainneastleach.co.uk

Entry 263 Map 8

Gloucestershire

The Swan at Southrop
Southrop

Welcome to a village inn on a village green with fires in the grate, dogs in the bar, and a potted pheasant so rich and gamey you'll find yourself asking for the recipe (our inspector did). Here on the Southrop Estate they keep their own chickens, grow their own salads and vegetables, bake their own bread, and employ a chef, Matt Wardman, who is brilliant at creating gutsy flavours from abundant local produce. Sip a pint of Doom Bar on the benches out front (note, two walled garden areas are being planned for 2015) then retire to the big, elegant, log-fired dining room for a slap-up meal; there's a kids' menu, too. The bar, full of quaffing locals on a Friday night, is similarly affable, and if you fancy a simple sandwich you know it will be first class.

Meals	Lunch & dinner £12.50–£17.
Closed	2.30pm-7pm.
	3pm-7pm Sat & Sun.
	Closed from 10pm every day.

Gemma Wall
The Swan at Southrop,
Southrop,
Lechlade GL7 3NU
Tel   +44 (0)1367 850205
Web www.theswanatsouthrop.co.uk

Entry 264 Map 8

Gloucestershire

The Keepers Arms
Quenington

It is sturdy, 18th century, refreshingly authentic and recently restored. Inside: a log-burner in a stone fireplace, earthy colours on the walls, pub furniture and one lovely large oak table. Landlord Jon has a sense of humour and loves his ale (Otter, Butcombe, Timothy Taylors…); Denzil the border terrier is an instant friend. You'll find yourself rubbing shoulders with locals sampling the pints, and enjoying straightforward, rib-stickin', filling good food. You might have a pint of prawns with Marie Rose dressing, or battered fish and chips with peas, or roast beef with all the trimmings, and find space for banoffee pie. Nine miles from Cirencester, the pub is in the centre of a charming village, with views over the Coln Valley to be enjoyed from the small stone terrace at the front.

Meals	Lunch & dinner £10.95–£16.50.
Closed	3pm-6pm Wed-Sat.
	4pm-7pm Sun.
	Open from 7pm Mon-Tues.

Jon & Michelle Gardiner
The Keepers Arms,
Church Road, Quenington,
Cirencester GL7 5BL
Tel   +44 (0)1285 750349
Web www.thekeepersarms.co.uk

Entry 265 Map 8

The Bourne Valley Inn
St Mary Bourne

A rambling brick inn close to the chalk stream in the beautiful Bourne Valley; just outside the village of St Mary Bourne in glorious downland walking country. The recent makeover is finding favour with locals and visiting shooting and fishing folk. Expect wood floors, big cushions on leather wall benches, local photographs and blazing winter fires in the deli-cum-bar. The open-to-the-rafters barn extension is a well worked dining space, with movable shelves made from painted crates, and patio doors to the garden; perfect for private parties and functions. The deli counter opens from 9am for breakfast and displays local goodies like organic meats and mozzarella from Laverstoke Farm, and fish cured and smoked on site. Tuck into mackerel ceviche with marinated beetroot and horseradish, duck breast with confit leg croquette and pancetta, and Cambridge burnt cream with chocolate truffle and pistachio crumble. Contemporary cottage-style rooms come with printed wallpaper, soft muted hues, quality linen and down on big beds, fresh coffee, and tiled bathrooms; ground floor rooms are dog friendly.

Rooms	8 doubles, 1 twin: £85–£120.
Meals	Light lunch from £5.95.
	Dinner, 3 courses, around £30.
Closed	Rarely.

Billy & Ryan
The Bourne Valley Inn,
St Mary Bourne,
Andover SP11 6BT
Tel   +44 (0)1264 738 361
Web   www.bournevalleyinn.com

Entry 266 Map 3

The Peat Spade
Longstock

Hampshire is as lovely as any county in England, deeply rural with lanes that snake through verdant countryside. As if to prove the point, the Peat Spade serves up a menu of boundless simplicity and elegance. First there's this dreamy thatched village in the Test valley, then there's the inn itself, always packed to the gunnels with lip-licking locals. Behind the lozenge-paned windows a Roberts radio on the bar brings news of English cricket, gilt mirrors sparkle above smouldering fires, candles illuminate chunky tables, and fishing rods hang from the ceiling; fishing packages can be arranged with local ghillies. There's a horseshoe bar, two private dining rooms, a roof terrace for summer breakfasts and the food is fabulous — mussels with cider and bacon, stone bass with chilli and crab risotto; sirloin steak with triple-cooked chips and peppercorn sauce. Lovely rooms above the bar and in the Peat House next door, come in Fired Earth colours with sisal matting, big wooden beds, top mattresses, crisp white linen — the works. Stroll the Test Valley Way, visit Stockbridge, Salisbury and Winchester, all are close.

Rooms	6 doubles, 2 twin/doubles: £100–£130.
Meals	Lunch & dinner £5–£25.
Closed	Christmas.

Nikki Swulinska
The Peat Spade,
Village Street, Longstock,
Stockbridge SO20 6DR
Tel   +44 (0)1264 810612
Web   www.peatspadeinn.co.uk

Entry 267 Map 3

Hampshire

The King's Head
Hursley

The King's Head dates back to 1810 and stands opposite Hursley's ancient church. The pub was once a coaching inn linking London to the New Forest. These days the feel is half country pub, half country house. You find armchairs in front of roaring fires, shuttered windows in a Georgian dining room and, in the bar, excellent ales on tap. Elegant bedrooms are a treat. Two have slipper baths, all have warm colours, fancy bathrooms, soft carpeting and comfy beds. Some are smaller, as is reflected in the price; a couple have space for sofas. Downstairs, delicious rustic fare awaits in bar and restaurant alike, perhaps duck leg with confit fondant potato and red cabbage, or lamb rump with champ mash and woodland mushrooms; puds include sticky toffee pudding with toffee sauce and caramel ice cream. You get film nights, book clubs, skittles every now and then, and wine tastings in a vaulted cellar. Richard Cromwell, Oliver's son, lived in the village.

Rooms	4 doubles, 2 twin/doubles: £110-£140. 1 suite for 2: £130-£140. 1 single: £85.
Meals	Light lunch from £5.95. Mains from £12.95.
Closed	Rarely.

Mark & Penny Thornhill
The King's Head,
Main Road, Hursley,
Winchester SO21 2JW
Tel   +44 (0)1962 775208
Web   www.kingsheadhursley.co.uk

Entry 268 Map 3

The East End Arms
East End

A good little local hidden down New Forest lanes, winningly unpretentious and owned by John Illsley of Dire Straits. Walkers, wax jackets and locals congregate in the small, rustic Foresters Bar with its chatty community vibe, and walls come lined with the famous. The carpeted-cosy dining room, all cottagey furniture and roaring log fire, cocks a snook at gastropub remodelling, but the menus change twice daily – a rare treat – and make the best of seasonal produce. Try saddle of venison, whole baked seabass or locally caught Lymington crab. A paved terrace invites al fresco drinking, while bedrooms on the back add va-va-voom. Fresh, clean-lined and cosy, in fashionably neutral tones that bring the forest indoors, they sport roman blinds and Mulberry fabrics. Stylish bathrooms and paintings by John Illsley himself add warmth and class; fine breakfasts are the cherry on the cake. A great little find for anyone who loves the New Forest – neither new nor a forest, but fine open heathland nonetheless and excellent hiking terrain.

Rooms	5 twin/doubles: £99–£120.
Meals	Lunch from £5.50.
	Dinner from £10.50.
	Not Sunday eve.
Closed	Rarely.

John Illsley
The East End Arms,
Lymington Road, East End,
Lymington SO41 5SY
Tel   +44 (0)1590 626223
Web   www.eastendarms.co.uk

The Running Horse
Littleton

The Upham pubs are known and admired for the age of their buildings and their retro-country makeovers. This one is no exception. Built in the 1850s and painted a stylish grey, the Running Horse, set back from the road into the village and with fields behind, is wonderfully close to Winchester. Enter to find a spacious interior of wooden floors and buttonback banquettes, mahogany bar stools with red leather tops, and smartly restored 1930s furniture. Chirpy staff serve well-kept Upham's ales, decently priced wines, malt whiskies, cocktails, real ciders, fancy sandwiches (focaccia, ciabatta or doorstep) and tasty pub food. You could choose prawn and chorizo pasta in a tomato sauce, or steak and ale pie with seasonal veg, and children have their own menu. Smokers are spoiled with a stylish, cushioned, heated hut. At the back lie nine peaceful, ground-floor bedrooms in a V-shaped annexe by the beer garden. Designer-decorated in simple rustic style, they come with brightly striped pillow cases and blinds, cafetières, Freeview TV, and spotless modern bathrooms.

Rooms	6 doubles, 2 twins: £105.
	1 family room for 4: £135.
Meals	Mains from £12.95.
	Dinner, 3 courses, £30.
Closed	Rarely.

Anita Peel
The Running Horse,
88 Main Road, Littleton,
Winchester SO22 6QS
Tel   +44 (0)1962 880218
Web   www.runninghorseinn.co.uk

Entry 270 Map 4

The Old Vine
Winchester

In a small square overlooking the cathedral and mature trees, this red-bricked Georgian building has sash windows and hanging baskets – all tickety-boo and smart. Walk straight into the bustling bar with its beamed ceiling, upright timbers, open fires and a partly covered outdoor terrace for sunny days where a cheerful team serve Ringwood Best and three guest ales on rotation; the wine list has helpful comments to accompany the specials board. If you get peckish after all the quaffing, you can have anything from a hearty sandwich (Hampshire pork sausages and red onion relish) to Scottish salmon fillet with Hampshire watercress & crème fraîche sauce, then homemade butterscotch & treacle sponge pudding and custard or some excellent local cheese. Stumble upstairs to rather posh bedrooms, with a mix of antique-looking and contemporary furniture. Colour schemes are muted with dashes of bold on throws and cushions, mahogany sleigh beds are deep and comfortable and you can splash about in bathrooms flaunting fluffy towels and gleaming taps.

Rooms	4 doubles, 1 twin/double: £130–£220. 1 annexe for 3: £160–£190. Singles £120–£140. Extra bed/sofabed £40 per person per night.
Meals	Lunch & dinner £10.90–£18.50.
Closed	Rarely.

Ashton Gray
The Old Vine,
8 Great Minster Street,
Winchester SO23 9HA

Tel	+44 (0)1962 854616
Web	www.oldvinewinchester.com

Entry 271 Map 4

Hampshire

The Woolpack Inn
Totford

It's hard to fault this lovely little inn, deep in the Candover Valley. Its brick and flint exterior dates to 1880, views shoot across fields to a distant church, and there are terraces to the front and the side. Dogs doze by the fire, walkers and cyclists quench their thirst with pints of Woolpack, and shooting parties drop in seasonally. New landlord Megs has refurbished in style, so expect striped banquettes and high-backed leather chairs in the dining room and a nice woody feel in the bar. Head chef Ryan's seasonal menu has a broad appeal, ranging from pub classics like burgers with smoked cheddar and Heineken-battered fish to more modish dishes like confit pork belly with potato gratin, and – of course! – game sourced within five miles. Sunday lunch is madly popular – don't forget to book. Hike, bike, visit Winchester Cathedral just over the hill, then return to cosy bedrooms named after game birds with brick and flint walls, big firm beds, gun cupboards and dark leather furnishings, storm showers and natural toiletries; those on the ground floor are ideal for dog owners.

Rooms	6 doubles: £95–£120.
	1 suite for 4: £170.
Meals	Light lunch from £8.50.
	Mains from £11.50.
Closed	Rarely.

Andrew (Megs) Cooper
The Woolpack Inn,
Totford, Northington,
Alresford SO24 9TJ
Tel   +44 (0)1962 734184
Web   www.thewoolpackinn.co.uk

The Anchor Inn
Lower Froyle

This smart country dining pub has a lovely style. The house is Edwardian with 14th-century roots and its treasure-trove interiors are full of beautiful things: timber frames, wavy beams, oils by the score, trumpets and a piano in the bar. Old photographs of Charterhouse School cover the walls, there are sofas by the fire in the panelled bar and busts on plinths in the airy restaurant, where you dine on proper English food: devilled kidneys, lemon sole, treacle tart with clotted cream. Doors open onto a lawned garden with country views, so come in summer for lunch in the sun. Bedrooms upstairs are seriously indulging, with beautifully upholstered armchairs, seagrass matting, fine linen on comfy beds, flat-screen TVs. There are power showers, huge towels and bathrobes, too. One room is open to the rafters and comes with Nelson and friends framed on the wall; another has an enormous window that opens onto a private balcony. Don't come looking for a gastropub; do come looking for good ales, sublime food and old-world interiors. A treat.

Rooms	4 doubles: £90–£150. 1 suite for 2: £140–£170.
Meals	Light lunch from £7. Mains from £13.
Closed	Rarely.

Alexandra Rooke
The Anchor Inn,
Lower Froyle,
Alton GU34 4NA

Tel   +44 (0)1420 23261
Web   www.anchorinnatlowerfroyle.co.uk

The Wellington Arms
Baughurst

Lost down a web of lanes, the 'Welly' draws foodies from miles around. Cosy, relaxed and decorated in style – old dining tables, crystal decanters, terracotta floor – the newly extended bar-dining room fills quickly, so make sure you book to sample Jason's inventive modern cooking. Boards are chalked up daily and the produce mainly home-grown or organic. Kick off with home-grown courgette flowers stuffed with ricotta, parmesan and lemon zest, follow with rack of home-reared lamb with root vegetable mash and crab apple jelly, finish with elderflower jelly, strawberry and raspberry sorbet. Migrate to the huge garden for summer meals and views of the pub's small holding: handfuls of pigs and sheep, bees, and hens of all sorts; buy the eggs at the bar. Stay over and get cosy in either one of the three rooms, housed in the former wine store and pig shed. Expect exposed brick and beams, vast Benchmark beds topped with goose down duvets, fresh flowers, coffee machines, mini-fridges, and slate tiled bathrooms with underfloor heating and walk-in rain showers. Breakfast too is a treat.

Rooms	3 doubles: £95–£200.
Meals	Set lunch £15.75–£18.75.
	Dinner £11–£21.
Closed	Rarely.

Jason King & Simon Page
The Wellington Arms,
Baughurst Road,
Baughurst RG26 5LP
Tel   +44 (0)118 982 0110
Web   www.thewellingtonarms.com

Yew Tree Inn
Highclere

The attractive brick Yew Tree stands beside the A343 south of the village and is perfect for visiting Highclere Castle (of Downton Abbey fame). A contemporary makeover stitches a rambling dining room into the old fabric of this 16th-century building, all inglenooks, timbers and uncluttered walls. Expect an elegant air, cracking log fires, rugs on red and black tiled floors, glowing candles on old dining tables, leather wall benches and wing chairs. From the beautiful copper-topped bar order great coffee or a pint of Upham ale and peruse the papers in a cosy corner. The best of British food is championed here: carpaccio of Trinley Estate White Park beef; cumin-spiced Faccombe partridge with turmeric and coriander rice, Brixham plaice with lemon brown butter; baked plum and mulled apple crumble. Cottagey rooms are compact and come with beams, statement William Morris wallpaper, tartan blankets, the finest linen and down, and fresh bathrooms with storm showers and bathrobes; ground floor rooms have dog beds and water bowls.

Rooms	8 doubles: £95–£120.
Meals	Lunch & dinner £8.50–£25.
	Sunday roast £17.50–£19.95.
Closed	Rarely.

Simon Davis
Yew Tree Inn,
Hollington Cross, Andover Road,
Highclere, Newbury RG20 9SE
Tel   +44 (0)1635 253360
Web   www.theyewtree.co.uk

Entry 275 Map 4

Hampshire

The Plough Inn
Longparish

A high-rolling dining pub in a delightful Test Valley village: the Plough has pedigree galore. Owner James Durrant (former head chef at London's Michelin-starred Maze) fronts the kitchen, while on-the-ball service is warm and genuine; there's no fine-dining flashiness here. James prefers to keep things simple yet sophisticated, his cooking driven by top-quality produce and flavour: haddock in Ringwood Best batter with triple cooked chips and mushy peas; pot-roasted pig's tongue and cheek with grilled gem and mustard mash. As for the refurbished old pub, it blends dark beams, exposed bricks and log-burners with fresh white walls and modern flourishes, while the dinky bar comes with a snug. Outside is a smart sweep of decking; ales, exciting wines and bar-menu classics add further appeal.

Hampshire

The Greyhound on the Test
Stockbridge

Civilised, one-street Stockbridge is England's fly-fishing capital, and the colour-washed Greyhound reels in fishing folk and foodies. The 15th-century coaching inn is a dapper, food-and-wine-centred affair run with charm and panache by Lucy Townsend, while chef Alan produces modern dishes based on skill and impeccable produce. Try Dorset crab on toast; braised cod cheeks with linguine and curried saffron sauce; hake with lemon butter; rabbit cassoulet; chocolate fondant. In the bar are low dark beams and a big inglenook. In the open-plan dining area, wooden floors, more beams, and high stools at a walnut-topped bar: graze on oysters or potted shrimps. A garden at the back overlooks the Test; rest awhile with a glass of chablis – or cast a line.

Meals	Lunch & bar meals from £5.50. Dinner from £12.50. Not Sunday eve.
Closed	Sun from 6pm.

Meals	Lunch & dinner £16.50–£20. Not Sunday eve.
Closed	Open all day.

James & Louise Durrant
The Plough Inn,
Longparish,
Andover SP11 6PB
Tel   +44 (0)1264 720358
Web   www.theploughinn.info

Entry 276 Map 3

Lucy Townsend
The Greyhound on the Test,
31 High Street,
Stockbridge SO20 6EY
Tel   +44 (0)1264 810833
Web   www.thegreyhoundonthetest.co.uk

Entry 277 Map 3

The Rose & Thistle
Rockbourne

Rockbourne is the kind of village where you might find Miss Marple trimming a rose bush. The pub is dreamy too, and started life as two thatched cottages; the two fireplaces should come as no surprise. It's a great mix of oak beams and timbers, carved benches and flagstones, country-style fabrics and tables strewn with magazines – an enchanting place to return to after visiting Rockbourne's Roman villa. Chris Chester-Sterne makes use of fresh local produce: estate game in season; pork with champ, black pudding and cider; veal with béarnaise sauce. In summer you can dine in the garden, perhaps smoked trout and scrambled eggs or steak and kidney pud. The changing chalkboard menu favours Cornish fish.

The Royal Oak
Fritham

Small, ancient, thatched and secluded is this ale-lover's retreat. No fruit machines, but lots of bonhomie. Locals chat around the bar; ramblers and dogs drop by. Huge fires crackle through the winter, demanding you linger. Neil and Pauline McCulloch believe in local produce and deliver honest, unpretentious pub lunches: ploughman's with homemade pâté, French-dressed local crab, sausages from a local butcher, no chips. Though rustically simple, the three small rooms are perfect, with pale boards, solid tables and spindleback chairs, darts, dominoes and cribbage. Five local beers are drawn from the cask, including Hop Back Summer Lightning and Royal Oak by Bowman ales. There's more: a large garden for barbecues and a beer and food festival in September. Pub heaven?

Meals	Bar meals from £5.
	Lunch & dinner £9.50-£19.50.
Closed	3pm-6pm.
	Sun from 8pm November-March.

Meals	Lunch & dinner £4.50-£9.
Closed	3pm-5.30pm.
	Open all day Sat & Sun.
	Open all day July-September.

Chris Chester-Sterne
The Rose & Thistle,
Rockbourne,
Fordingbridge SP6 3NL
Tel   +44 (0)1725 518236
Web   www.roseandthistle.co.uk

Entry 278 Map 3

Neil & Pauline McCulloch
The Royal Oak,
Fritham,
Lyndhurst SO43 7HJ
Tel   +44 (0)2380 812606

Entry 279 Map 3

Hampshire

The Oak Inn
Bank

Aptly named (among the forest oaks), this 18th-century pub, with a double-bay frontage and a red phone box by the door, is a friendly and traditional little place. It's loved not just by locals but walkers and cyclists who pour in at weekends for "classic British pub food with a modern twist" – and much of the produce has been reared or caught within the New Forest (note the symbols on the menu). Others drop in for a pint of Gales Seafarers in the low-beamed bar, or the little garden sheltered by a big yew. Blackboard specials might include whole baked John Dory or local venison sausages; doorstep sandwiches and homemade steak and ale pie catch the eye of the walkers. Come for dark red walls and winter fires, cottagey furniture and old-fashioned comfort.

Meals	Lunch & dinner £8.95–£16.95.
Closed	3.30pm–6pm.
	Open all day Sat & Sun.

Martin Sliva & Zuzana Slivova
The Oak Inn,
Pinkney Lane, Bank,
Lyndhurst SO43 7FE
Tel   +44 (0)2380 282350
Web   www.oakinnlyndhurst.co.uk

Entry 280 Map 3

Hampshire

The Green Man
Winchester

From outside, this Victorian pub – opposite the city's dinky cinema – looks much like any other. But the savvy Winchester set know it could win an Oscar for its gorgeous, idiosyncratic interiors. An imaginative makeover delivers a successful marriage of original features with stylish frills, bold colours in upholstery and seating, clever lighting and interesting objects. Upstairs the dining room has a romantic, shabby-chic vibe with chandeliers, candlesticks and Roman blinds. Real ales line up alongside well-chosen wines and a menu for all appetites gives you slow-cooked pig's cheek and lentil casserole, and lamb loin fillet and braised shoulder with potato croquettes, peas, wild nettles and lemon thyme. There are artisan cheeses and west country ice cream.

Meals	Lunch & dinner from £10.95.
	Set dinner from £24.95.
	Platters from £8.95.
Closed	Open all day.

Jayne Gillin
The Green Man,
53 Southgate Street,
Winchester SO23 9EH
Tel   +44 (0)1962 866809
Web   www.greenmanwinchester.co.uk

Entry 281 Map 4

Hampshire

The Wykeham Arms
Winchester

The old Wykeham is English to the core, full of its own traditions and hidden away between the cathedral and the city's famous school. Ceilings drip with memorabilia and bow-tied regulars, pints in hand, chat. It's grand, a throwback to the past and brimming with warm colours and atmosphere. There are small red-shaded lamps on graffiti-etched desks (ex-Winchester College), three roaring fires and two dining rooms. Food is not cheap, but certainly reliable, from posh sandwiches and cottage pie at lunch to daily-changing evening dishes, perhaps juniper infused venison saddle or aged Hampshire rib-eye steak with béarnaise sauce. The Fuller's Gales ales are good, the wine list is interesting (20 by the glass), and the staff are young and laid-back.

Hampshire

Chestnut Horse
Easton

In the beautiful Itchen valley, this rather smart 16th-century dining pub is in the capable hands of Karen Wells. A decked terrace leads to a warren of snug rooms around a central bar, warmed by log fires, and at night it is cosy and candlelit. Eat in the low beamed 'red' room, with cushioned settles, a mix of dining tables and a wood-burning stove, or in the panelled and memorabilia-filled 'green' room. Try the two-course menu (smoked mackerel pâté, sea bream with pesto dressing, apple and walnut pie) – great value. Or tuck into beer-battered fish and chips, vegetable potato cake with dressed leaves, or wild boar casserole with apple cobbler. There are great local ales, decent wines and champagne by the glass. A relaxed and civilised pub.

Meals	Bar meals £7-£10.
	Lunch £7-£15.
	Dinner £15-£24.
	Sunday lunch, 3 courses, £23.
Closed	Open all day.

Meals	Lunch & dinner £10-£18;
	2 courses, £12.
	Sunday roast £12.
Closed	4pm-5.30pm Mon-Thurs.
	Open all day Fri-Sun.

Jon Howard
The Wykeham Arms,
75 Kingsgate Street,
Winchester SO23 9PE
Tel   +44 (0)1962 853834
Web   www.wykehamarmswinchester.co.uk

Entry 282 Map 4

Karen Wells
Chestnut Horse,
Easton,
Winchester SO21 1EG
Tel   +44 (0)1962 779257
Web   www.thechestnuthorse.com

Entry 283 Map 4

Hampshire

Bush Inn
Ovington

Down a meandering lane alongside the clear-running waters of the Itchen, a 17th-century jewel in Hampshire's crown. In winter, the bar is dark and atmospheric: a roaring log fire, candles on tables, walls gas lamp-lit. In summer, what nicer, in the words of a visitor, than to sit on the bridge with a pint, the evening sun filtering through the trees, the trout hiding in the reeds below. The garden is lovely in summer, and you can stroll along the river. Cottage furniture and high-backed pews fill a series of small buffed-up rooms off the bar, where walls are hung with fishing and country paraphernalia, and the kitchen is contemporary: tiger prawn and rocket linguine; Stornoway black pudding salad; sausages with chilli and garlic. City dwellers come for the cosy atmosphere and the sophisticated food.

Hampshire

The English Partridge
Bighton

The name gives a clue to the Partridge's countryside credentials, though not to its tucked-away village setting in Hampshire's huntin', shootin' and fishin' quarter. It's had a stylish revamp, but the modest property still retains the timeless air and charm of a proper local. Discover a cosy snug, a huge inglenook in the main bar, good solid furniture and sporting prints on the walls. A lighter and airier new extension has a dining vibe, but nevertheless fulfils the pukka country brief. Good British food is a strength here; try traditional classics like seared liver, bacon and mash or be more adventurous with fillet of cod, brown shrimp, samphire and new potatoes. Good ales abound and it is excellent value.

Meals	Sandwiches from £6.75.
	Lunch & dinner £10–£18.50.
	Weekday set menus £15–£17.50.
Closed	3pm–6pm.
	Open all day Sat & Sun.

Meals	Lunch & dinner £10–£18.
Closed	3pm–5pm Mon–Fri.
	Sun evenings.

Matthew & Imogen Lee
Bush Inn,
Ovington,
Alresford SO24 0RE
Tel   +44 (0)1962 732764
Web   www.thebushinn.co.uk

Entry 284 Map 4

Ryan Healey
The English Partridge,
Bighton,
Alresford SO24 9RE
Tel   +44 (0)1962 732859
Web   www.englishpartridge.co.uk

Entry 285 Map 4

Hampshire

The Flower Pots Inn
Cheriton

Ramblers and beer enthusiasts beat a path to Paul and Patricia's door, where a ward-winning pints of Flowerpots Bitter and Gooden's Gold are brewed in the brewhouse across the car park. Open fires burn in two bars: one a wallpapered parlour, the other a quarry-tiled public bar with scrubbed pine and an illuminated, glass-topped well. Ales are tapped from casks behind a counter hung with hops, and drunk to the accompaniment of happy chat; no music or electronic wizardry here. In keeping with the simplicity of the place, the menu is short and straightforward: baps with home-cooked ham, sandwiches toasted or plain, home-cooked hotpots, spicy chilli with garlic bread, hearty winter soups – all served with a smile from a happy staff.

Hampshire

The Thomas Lord
West Meon

Named after the founder of Lord's Cricket Ground, the Thomas Lord is much loved and hard to fault. And, in spite of remodelling raising the gastro credentials, it keeps its endearing community vibe. Join locals (and dogs) over a trio of local Upham ales at the bar, or settle into leather armchairs around winter fires. Associated cricketing prints and paraphernalia still decorate the walls (old bats, balls, caps, shoes) while the darkly beamed bar's weathered wooden furniture gives way to a duo of preened, dedicated dining areas. Menus are rammed with local produce (including pickings from the pub's potager) and foodies relish it all, from the beef burgers and the cottage pies to the more sophisticated dishes such as gurnard fillet with bacon and onion sauté potatoes, cauliflower purée and smoked mussels.

Meals	Lunch & dinner £5–£10. Not Sunday or bank holiday eves.
Closed	2.30pm–6pm. 3pm–7pm Sun.

Meals	Lunch from £15. Dinner from £22.
Closed	Open all day.

Paul Tickner & Patricia Bartlett
The Flower Pots Inn,
Cheriton,
Alresford SO24 0QQ

Tel   +44 (0)1962 771318
Web   www.flowerpots-inn.co.uk

Entry 286 Map 4

Clare Winterbottom
The Thomas Lord,
West Meon,
Petersfield GU32 1LN

Tel   +44 (0)1730 829244
Web   www.thethomaslord.co.uk

Entry 287 Map 4

White Star Tavern & Dining Rooms
Southampton

Large etched windows carry the White Star logo, while a cluster of lounges at the front come decked with funky seating and retro chesterfields. The place is stocked with a modish mix of real ales, continental lagers, premium spirits and cocktails. Around the big bar, to a backdrop of original wood panelling, is crescent-shaped seating for casual dining; wide floorboards and original chandeliers add to the cosmopolitan vibe. The more formal dining area comes with a softer approach: stylish wallpaper and sophisticated lighting. The cooking hits all the fashionable notes, with an all-day selection of 'small plates' as well as à la carte. Dishes include ham hock and leek soup, and lamb rump with shallot confit and black olive tapenade. Young and fun.

The Bugle
Hamble

Hamble's famous pub, celebrated by yachtsmen the world over, was saved by those behind Southampton's White Star Tavern. Using traditional materials and methods they have remodelled the Bugle's 16th-century heart; find new-and-old oak beams and standing timbers, stripped-back brick fireplaces and open fires, new flagstone floors and polished boards. The atmosphere is relaxed, the bar throngs on sailing days, there's a simply adorned dining area for escaping the bustle and a private room upstairs. A wide-ranging clientele informs the style of the food. Sit at the bar with a pint of Bowmans Swift One and a choice of tapas or go the whole hog and order mussels and chips or pork belly with bubble and squeak and cider gravy. Slip off to the super front terrace for views of bobbing boats on the Hamble.

Meals	Bar meals £4.50–£11.
	Lunch & dinner £9.50–£19.
Closed	Christmas & Boxing Day.

Meals	Bar meals from £10.50.
	Lunch from £5.50.
	Dinner from £10.50.
	Sunday lunch, 3 courses, £19.
Closed	Open all day.

Matthew Boyle
White Star Tavern & Dining Rooms,
28 Oxford Street,
Southampton SO14 3DJ

Tel   +44 (0)2380 821990
Web   www.whitestartavern.co.uk

Entry 288 Map 4

Matthew Boyle
The Bugle,
High Street, Hamble,
Southampton SO31 4HA

Tel   +44 (0)2380 453000
Web   www.buglehamble.co.uk

Entry 289 Map 4

The Bakers Arms
Droxford

Set in the attractive Meon Valley, this small village pub is a bit of a find for lovers of modern British cooking. For locals, there's the added plus of Droxford's Bowman Ales — and the post office and village stores parked on the side. Inside has a relaxed, traditional charm and a winter fire. The L-shaped, opened-up space is light and cheery, the customary miscellany of old wooden furniture and a few bar stools offset by a cosy dining room vibe. The kitchen's chalkboard menu pleases all with its use of prime local produce and seasonal dishes with punchy flavours and, in this rolling countryside, the local meats are a forte; organic Hyden Farm pork belly with smoked eel from the river Test, local sausages with mash and shallot gravy. An excellent meeting place for a civilised crowd.

The Old Drum
Petersfield

This remodelled, 16th-century Petersfield inn now has the locals beating a path to its door: not a hint remains of the sticky-carpeted old boozer! The light and airy bar's pastel shades are buoyed by sunny-natured service, while the leather armchairs and trendy retro furniture are softened by warm textiles and flower displays. Exposed brick and winter fires add character; local ales, well-chosen wines and good coffee encourage visitors to linger. In the cosy beamed restaurant is a darker, more traditional look. The kitchen turns out some enjoyable modern British cooking, from the blackboard bar specials like shin of beef and Sussex ale stew to a scrumptious rendition of cod loin with purple sprouting broccoli and wild mushroom gratin.

Meals	Lunch & dinner £10.95–£17.95.
Closed	Sun eves.
	Monday all day.

Meals	Lunch from £6.20.
	Dinner from £10.
Closed	3pm–5pm, Mon-Fri.

Adam & Anna Cordery
The Bakers Arms,
High Street, Droxford,
Southampton SO32 3PA
Tel   +44 (0)1489 877533
Web   www.thebakersarmsdroxford.com

Entry 290 Map 4

Simon Hawkins
The Old Drum,
Chapel Street,
Petersfield GU32 3DP
Tel   +44 (0)1730 300544
Web   www.theolddrum.co.uk

Entry 291 Map 4

Hampshire

Harrow Inn
Steep

The 16th-century Harrow is a gem. Unspoilt, brick-and-tiled, it hides down a country lane that dwindles into a footpath by a stream (not easy to find!). It has been in Claire and Nisa McCutcheon's family since 1929 and they keep it as it must always have been. Where nicer to drink a pint than within these two small rooms with timbered walls, scrubbed elm tables and brick inglenook, lit in winter? Behind a hatch-like serving counter, barrels of local ale rest on racks, bundles of drying hops hang above. There's a small wild orchard garden; only the hum of the hidden A3 disturbs the calm. Food is limited to generously filled sandwiches, fresh soups, homemade quiches, a ploughman's platter, treacle tart, all served with a smile. Loos are a quick dash across the lane.

Meals	Bar meals £4.50-£14.
Closed	2.30pm-6pm Mon-Fri. 3pm-6pm Sat & 3pm-7pm Sun. Sun evenings October-May.

Claire & Nisa McCutcheon
Harrow Inn,
Steep,
Petersfield GU32 2DA
Tel   +44 (0)1730 262685
Web   www.harrow-inn.co.uk

Entry 292 Map 4

Hampshire

The Sun Inn
Bentworth

Timothy Taylor's Landlord, Hog's Back Tea, Andwell's Resolute, Ringwood Best, Fuller's London Pride… a parade of hand pumps pulls you in. There's charm, too, in this flower-decked local, once two 17th-century cottages. Little has changed. On ancient bricks and bare boards is a rustic mix of scrubbed pine tables, oak benches and settles; beams are hung with brasses, walls heaped with prints and plates; there are fresh flowers, candlelight and newspapers. Log-fired inglenooks warm interlinking rooms and food is mostly perfect English: steak and ale pie, calves' liver and bacon, Sunday roasts, warming puddings. Hidden down a tiny lane on the edge of a village in Hampshire, the Sun could scarcely be more rural. Footpaths radiate from the door.

Meals	Lunch & dinner £8.95-£15.95. Sunday roast £10.95.
Closed	3pm-6pm. Open all day Sun.

Mary Holmes
The Sun Inn,
Bentworth,
Alton GU34 5JT
Tel   +44 (0)1420 562338
Web   www.thesuninnbentworth.co.uk

Entry 293 Map 4

The Purefoy Arms
Preston Candover

The owners of this foodie venue in the lovely Candover Valley know a thing or two about running an inn. Their previous venture was in Mayfair but they've taken to village life with this gentle remodelling of a 19th-century building, warm, light and contemporary with its framework intact. Hand-written menus tick the requisite local-and-seasonal boxes and draw a loyal band. Expect big-hearted dishes like venison and mushroom pie with kale and onions, or veal Holstein with frites and watercress, ultra-comforting desserts like apple crumble and ginger parkin, and exquisite chocs! The separate rare-breed steak menu includes Chateaubriand for two, with a wine list to match. Hand-pump ales at the bar keep the traditionalist happy; for sunny days there's a well-kept terrace and garden at the back.

Hoddington Arms
Upton Grey

At the heart of pretty, upmarket Upton Grey (just along from the village pond), the 'Hodd' is a real find. Warmth and good cheer abound, with winter fires, exposed brick walls and pale-wood beams and timbers softened by lamps, scatter cushions and fabrics. The bar itself has a wine bar vibe, but armchairs, pouffes and a sofa add restful touches. Find leather banquettes and stripped floorboards in the dining area where you feast on classical British cuisine with a modern twist, perhaps steak tartare with bone marrow gratin, oyster mayo and a caper, shallot and parsley salad. The pub is at the heart of village life, hosting the local beer and cider festivals, so enjoy a pint of the specially brewed 'Hodd' ale. You can spill out into the lovely garden in summer.

Meals	Bar meals from £3. Lunch from £6.50. Dinner from £10. Sunday roast £13.95.
Closed	Sun evenings & all day Mon.

Meals	Lunch & dinner £5-£25. Sunday roast £12-£14.
Closed	Open all day.

Andres & Marie-Louise Alemany
The Purefoy Arms,
Preston Candover,
Alresford RG25 2EJ

Tel	+44 (0)1256 389777
Web	www.thepurefoyarms.co.uk

Entry 294 Map 4

Alex & Greg Ewart
Hoddington Arms,
Bidden Road, Upton Grey,
Basingstoke RG25 2RL

Tel	+44 (0)1256 862371
Web	www.hoddingtonarms.co.uk

Entry 295 Map 4

The Bridge Inn
Michaelchurch Escley

In the wilds of Herefordshire, getting here is half the fun (though it could be tricky in the dark). In a pretty spot down by the river, beneath the Black Hill of Bruce Chatwin fame, the 16th-century Bridge started life as a house, achingly lovely on its river side with willows weeping down the footbridge. Walkers descend, as do local farmers and shooting parties, and Glyn is the nicest host. Inside, hops hang from dark beams and the wood-burner belts out heat, there are solid wooden pews, scrubbed pine tables and small bar stools on the other side. It's properly pubby and perfect for out here. Eat in one of two dining areas with contemporary colours on the walls; our pints of Butty Bach slipped down nicely and our food — hake with seafood stew, and barbecue brisket — was very, very good. Stay the night? We would! There are super country bedrooms in the farmhouse a minute away; find antiques, flagstone floors and a dark panelled sitting room below. Breakfast back at the pub — full English spiced up with chorizo — is outstanding.

Rooms	1 double, 2 twin/doubles: £95. Hay Festival price for 2 per night: £165.
Meals	Lunch £8-£22. Dinner £12-£22.
Closed	Rarely.

2015/16
Sawday's
PUB AWARD

Favourite newcomer

Glyn Bufton & Gisela Vargas
The Bridge Inn,
Michaelchurch Escley,
Hereford HR2 0JW

| Tel | +44 (0)1981 510646 |
| Web | www.thebridgeinnmichaelchurch.co.uk |

Entry 296 Map 7

The Saracens Head
Symonds Yat

The inn dates from the 16th century and became a pub in the 18th but has a 21st-century buzz now, thanks to its friendly young staff and its big choice of dining tables. Dishes are chalked up on the blackboard by the bar – exotic sandwiches, pheasant terrine, wild boar with chive mash, Welsh goat's cheese panna cotta, crème brûlée – all so delicious that people travel from far. The terraces by the water attract a crowd in summer and lend a seaside-holiday feel, so sit back with your Wye Valley Ale and watch the canoeists float by. In winter, the public bar is a warm haven; you can roast by the wood-burner as you watch the trippers come for Symonds Yat. A shame not to stay: upstairs and in the Boathouse next door are a flurry of bedrooms, light, airy and contemporary, some oak-floored, others carpeted, all with smart bathrooms. Ask for a room with a view up and down the river. The bar staff still, obligingly, run the old hand-cranked ferry across the lovely limpid water. Breakfast, by the way, is one of the best.

Rooms	8 doubles, 2 twins: £89–£138. Singles from £59.
Meals	Bar meals £4.95–£16.95. Lunch & dinner £9.50–£19.95. Sunday roast £9.95–£15.
Closed	Christmas Day.

Chris & Peter Rollinson
The Saracens Head,
Symonds Yat,
Ross-on-Wye HR9 6JL
Tel +44 (0)1600 890435
Web www.saracensheadinn.co.uk

Herefordshire

The Mill Race
Walford

As the 'ecclesiastical' door swings open, prepare yourself for a stylish place. A stainless steel kitchen glistens behind a granite-topped bar, there are counter-style bar tables and leather armchairs, a wood-burner divides the eating areas and a food provenance blackboard shows how seriously food is taken here. The kitchen team choose the meat and the game from their 1,000 acre farm and estate and help dig the vegetables; they'll even catch the trout for the table. Linger long over roast leg of red partridge with mash, bread sauce and watercress salad, or roast Gower pollock with crushed potatoes, wild mushrooms and parsley oil. A new carbon-neutral wood fired pizza oven, lit on certain days only, sits on the rear terrace. Look across the Wye to the ruins of Goodrich Castle, sip ales from the same valley. Fabulous.

Meals	Lunch & bar meals from £5. Dinner from £9.50. Sunday roast £15–£18.
Closed	3pm–5pm. Open all day Sat & Sun.

Luke Freeman
The Mill Race,
Walford,
Ross-on-Wye HR9 5QS
Tel +44 (0)1989 562891
Web www.millrace.info

Entry 298 Map 7

Herefordshire

The Oak Inn
Staplow

Just west of the Malvern Hills – a freehouse dating from the 1600s, sympathetically refurbished. Farmhouse tables and chairs stand on polished flagstones, hops hang from beams and wood-burners crackle in exposed brick hearths – it's country pub to the core. There are ales from Bathams and Wye Valley and good ciders like Robinson's Flagon and Weston's Stowford Press. Traditional home-cooked dishes with a modern twist are the order of the day; try local free-range pork belly with 'boozy' mustard mash or braised venison casserole with spiced red cabbage. Lighter options include deli boards with home-cured meats, sandwiches and homemade golden beetroot soup with horseradish cream. The pretty garden is backed by orchards, while the fires and candles in the bar, two snugs and dining area are kept glowing by a bright and attentive team. A super little pub.

Meals	Starters & light meals from £5.50. Lunch & dinner from £12.50.
Closed	3pm–5.30pm Mon–Sat. 3pm–7pm Sun.

Hylton Haylett & Julie Woollard
The Oak Inn,
Bromyard Road, Staplow,
Ledbury HR8 1NP
Tel +44 (0)1531 640954
Web www.oakinnstaplow.co.uk

Entry 299 Map 8

The Butchers Arms
Woolhope

Chef Stephen Bull was one of the architects of the modern British food revolution in the 1980s, and he continues to draw foodies to The Butchers Arms. A splendid 16th-century half-timbered pub tucked down a winding lane in walking country, it is noted for its low beams and smouldering log fires. Bull is in the kitchen as much as he is behind the bar, proffering top-notch Wye Valley ale, local ciders and perries, and well-chosen wines. The ingredients-driven seasonal menu reads like a 'greatest hits' from his London restaurant days and makes delectable use of local produce: the signature dish of twice-baked cheese soufflé; pork chop with apples, sage and calvados; warm ginger cake with treacle toffee ice cream. In the summer, enjoy the peace of the sheltered garden with its babbling stream.

Meals	Lunch & dinner £9.50-£16.
Closed	3pm-6pm.
	Sun evenings & Mon all day.

Stephen Bull
The Butchers Arms,
Woolhope,
Hereford HR1 4RF
Tel   +44 (0)1432 860281
Web   www.butchersarmswoolhope.com

Entry 300 Map 7

The Kilpeck Inn
Kilpeck

Kilpeck — known for its Norman church — has a second string to its bow: a super little country inn with a facelift. It stands on the edge of the village overlooking beautiful fields, ten miles south of Hereford. Outside, smart white walls sparkle in the sun. Inside: old stone, slate floors and a warm contemporary feel. Find darts in the locals' bar, alongside the daily papers and a smouldering fire, and original beams, candle lanterns and painted panelling in the airy restaurant. Dig into the sort of food you'd hope to find in a country inn: river Exe mussels in a cider and sage cream sauce with hand cut chips; shepherd's pie with green beans, redcurrant and red wine jus. It's as local as possible and seriously green, what with low food miles, hi-spec insulation and a rainwater tank. Walkers rejoice: the Black Mountains and Offa's Dyke are close.

Meals	Lunch & bar meals from £5.95.
	Dinner £9.95-£17.95.
	Sunday lunch, 3 courses, £15.95.
	Not Sunday eve.
Closed	2.30pm-5.30pm Mon-Sat.

Zoe Ainge
The Kilpeck Inn,
Kilpeck,
Hereford HR2 9DN
Tel   +44 (0)1981 570464
Web   www.kilpeckinn.com

Entry 301 Map 7

Herefordshire

Carpenter's Arms
Walterstone

A little chapel-side pub in the middle of nowhere, hard to find but perfect in every way. Vera has been dispensing Wadworth 6X and Breconshire Golden Valley from the hatch for years and everyone gets a welcome: locals, walkers, families, babies. Through an ancient oak doorway is a tiny bar with a log-fired range and a dining area to the side. Floors are Welsh slate, settles polished oak, tables cast iron, walls open stone; it's as cared for as can be. On the menu: beef and Guinness pie, faggots and mash, bread and butter pudding – honest homemade food, some organic, at great prices. Beer is served from the drum, cider and perry from the flagon. Spill into the grassy garden and gaze up at the Skirrid, or pull on your hiking boots and climb it.

Meals	Lunch & dinner £10.95–£14.95. Bar meals from £5.
Closed	Open all day.

Vera Watkins
Carpenter's Arms,
Walterstone, Hereford HR2 0DX
Tel +44 (0)1873 890353
Web www.thecarpentersarms
walterstone.com

Entry 302 Map 7

Herefordshire

The Pandy Inn
Dorstone

Built in 1185, this half-timbered Herefordshire delight is a contender for 'oldest pub in the land'. Heavy beams, worn flagged floors, smoke-smudged stone and a vast oak lintel over the old log grate. This is the country of Golden Valley and Butty Bach ales and 'cloudy' scrumpy – no wonder there's a buzz. On the menus are organic Hereford beef steaks and delicious seasonal specials: choose from hearty baguettes, walkers' soups with superb bread, homemade fish pie, and Welsh lamb shank with redcurrant and red wine sauce. Families and dogs are welcome here and children spin into the garden with picnic tables and play area in summer. You are in the 'Golden Valley' so follow lunch with a visit to Abbey Dore and Arthur's Stone, or bookish Hay-on-Wye, a short drive. Special place, special people.

Meals	Lunch from £4.95. Dinner from £10.95. Sunday roast £10.95.
Closed	Open all day.

Bill & Magdalena Gannon
The Pandy Inn,
Dorstone,
Hereford HR3 6AN
Tel +44 (0)1981 550273
Web www.pandyinn.co.uk

Entry 303 Map 7

Herefordshire

The New Inn
Pembridge

Perfect for English heritage lovers with big appetites. The food is generously portioned, the building is as old as can be (1311), and Pembridge is a remarkable survivor; its market hall, where you can sup a pint in summer, could be in deepest France. It is a simple but great pleasure to amble into this ancient inn, order a drink and squeeze into the curved back settle in the flagstoned bar; in winter the logs are lit. This is the most timeless of old locals, with photos of village shenanigans up on the wall and a dart board put to good use. Upstairs has floral carpets, books and sofa – a reassuring spot in which to tuck into the comforting likes of smoked chicken and avocado salad, steak and ale pie, and seafood stew. Jane Melvin is happy doing what she does best.

Meals	Bar meals £5.95–£8.50.
	Lunch & dinner £6.95–£12.
	Dinner from £15.
	Sunday lunch, 3 courses, £16.
Closed	3pm–6pm.

Jane Melvin
The New Inn,
Market Square,
Pembridge,
Leominster HR6 9DZ
Tel   +44 (0)1544 388427

Entry 304 Map 7

Herefordshire

The Stagg Inn
Titley

Deep in the wild Welsh borderlands lies the first British pub to have been awarded a Michelin star, back in 2001. Gavroche-trained Steve Reynolds defying all odds, ended up a Herefordshire food hero. As for provenance: the only thing you're not told is the name of the bird from which your pigeon breast (perfectly served on herb risotto) came. Most of the produce is very local, some is organic, with fresh fruit and vegetables from the kitchen garden. Seductive and restorative is the exceptional food: goat's cheese and fennel tart, saddle of venison with horseradish gnocchi and kümmel, bread and butter pudding with clotted cream, a cheese trolley resplendent with 15 regional beauties. The intimate bar is perfect and dog-friendly, there's beer from Wye Valley Brewery, cider from Dunkerton's and some very classy wines.

Meals	Bar meals £9.80.
	Lunch & dinner from £25.
	Sunday lunch, 3 courses, £19.30.
Closed	Mon & Tues.

Steve & Nicola Reynolds
The Stagg Inn,
Titley,
Kington HR5 3RL
Tel   +44 (0)1544 230221
Web   www.thestagg.co.uk

Entry 305 Map 7

Hertfordshire

The Jolly Waggoner
Ardeley

Not often is a pub run by a farm and this isn't the only unusual thing about the Jolly Waggoner. Church Farm also provides rare-breed meat and 'heritage' fruit and veg for the pub's menu. Nurse a pint of Buntingford Highwayman in an armchair by the fire, or tuck into produce from 'over the road': hidden corners of the bar or smarter restaurant are perfect for enjoying seasonal soup with 'kitchen garden' vegetables, and slow-roasted rare-breed pork belly with mustard mash, crispy crackling and greens. On farm tours, you can walk off a final plate of apple crumble served with warm crème anglais. Summertime brings beer lovers to the pretty garden and annual beer festival, and don't be surprised to find the vicar behind the bar. With 'guest landlord evenings' there's no knowing who might be pulling your pints!

Hertfordshire

The Fox
Willian

Cliff and James's village pub has a fresh modern feel and a menu that showcases British ingredients, including seafood from the Norfolk coast and local farm meats. It could beat many neighbourhood restaurants into a cocked hat but part of its charm is that it's a place where beer drinkers are most definitely welcome – try a pint of Brancaster ale from the Nye family brewery. A cool, formal dining room sits astride a relaxed bar where Brancaster oysters in sesame tempura add glamour to a menu that includes beef and pork burgers with sweet onion and chilli relish. The restaurant is a mix of French bistro and British pub: braised beef cheeks with creamy garlic mash and red wine sauce, a couple of roasts on Sundays, chocolate orange fondant. This Fox is one you'd do well to hunt down.

Meals	Lunch & dinner £10.50-£19.95.
Closed	Open all day.

Meals	Lunch & bar meals from £9.95. Dinner from £12.25. Sunday lunch, 3 courses, £26.40. Not Sunday eve.
Closed	Open all day.

Tim Waygood
The Jolly Waggoner,
Church Farm, Ardeley,
Stevenage SG2 7AH
Tel   +44 (0)1438 861350
Web www.jollywaggoner.co.uk

Entry 306 Map 9

Cliff & James Nye
The Fox,
Willian,
Letchworth SG6 2AE
Tel   +44 (0)1462 480233
Web www.foxatwillian.co.uk

Entry 307 Map 9

Hertfordshire

The Radcliffe
Hitchin

This Victorian town pub, unremarkable on the outside, understated within, is worth seeking out for anyone inspired by ingredient-led cooking backed by solid technique. The beef braised in red wine, served in its own cast-iron pot, was meltingly tender and tasty, as was chicken cooled 'en sous vide' with gnocchi and baby beets. Sweet tooths may be tempted by sticky carrot cake with stem ginger and mascarpone, or raspberry crème brûlée. A three-sided bar stands in the centre of an airy main room but the rest of the place — polished wooden floors, blue-green panelling — is given over to dining. The lunch menu and the specials change daily, the staff are unfailingly friendly, ales come from Buntingford Brewery, lagers are of note and the broad-price wine list, with its fun tasting notes, is marvellously approachable and accessible.

Meals	Lunch & dinner £15-£21.
	Set lunch £12-£15 (Mon-Fri).
Closed	Open all day.

Tanya Kayson
The Radcliffe,
31 Walsworth Road,
Hitchin SG4 9ST
Tel   +44 (0)1462 456111
Web   www.radcliffearms.com

Entry 308 Map 9

Hertfordshire

Hermitage Rd
Hitchin

What a surprise: a former ballroom and nightclub in the heart of Hitchin; Anglian Country Inns opened its fourth dining venue in 2011. From the street and the coffee bar (all-day cakes, pasties, sandwiches) stairs lead up to a cavernous bar and dining room, funkily stripped back in New York loft style, with exposed brick walls, acres of oak floor, subtle lighting, arched floor-to-ceiling windows and open-to-view kitchen. Chill out with a cocktail or a pint of Brancaster brew, share a charcuterie board at high tables, or watch the food being cooked from the dining table — steaming Brancaster mussels; rack of sticky pork ribs; beetroot, mint and spinach risotto; sirloin steak from the grill; roast cod with clam, bacon and potato chowder. Everyone is beating a path to Hermitage Rd — make sure you book!

Meals	Lunch, bar meals & dinner
	from £9.50.
	Sunday lunch, 2 courses, £18.
Closed	Open all day.

Howard Nye
Hermitage Rd,
20-21 Hermitage Road,
Hitchin SG5 1BT
Tel   +44 (0)1462 433603
Web   www.hermitagerd.co.uk

Entry 309 Map 9

Hertfordshire

The Highlander Pub
Hitchin

The Prutton family have been running this wonderful pub for over 30 years. Now the new generation – the Anglo-French partnership of Charlotte and Eric, back from several years in the Alps – add youthful energy and culinary skill to the family provenance. Their passion shines through. This is an unpretentious local that moves with the times and there's an informal Gallic bistro feel to the place. Stand over your pint at the bar, or settle back into one of the settles; read the papers, scan the menu. Behind the immaculate bar, all aubergine and white, wines are enticingly displayed, local art hangs on the walls. Eric's delicious food fuses the best traditions of France and England, from tasty ploughman's to duck leg confit with sarladaise potatoes and red wine jus – and Sunday lunches worth missing breakfast for.

Meals	Lunch from £4.10.
	Dinner from £5.65.
Closed	2.30pm-6pm (7pm Sun).
	Open all day Fri & Sat.

**Charlotte Prutton
& Eric Ransinangue**
The Highlander Pub, 45 Upper
Tilehouse Street, Hitchin SG5 2EF
Tel   +44 (0)1462 454612
Web www.highlanderpubhitchin.co.uk

Entry 310 Map 9

Hertfordshire

The White Horse
Hatching Green

This is a very pretty pub whose frontage changes height three times; the original bar is split-level, the area to the left was once the stable, and there's a newish extension out the back. Welcome to one of Peach Pubs' latest enterprises, a consummately professional operation. It's a pub with a broad appeal: ladies pop in for fresh roasted coffee, gents read the papers by the bar, families drop by for lunch. Choose between sandwiches, deli board and daily roast, or from the modern semi-seasonal menu: perhaps slow-roast lamb shank with rosemary gravy, or warm gruyère polenta with tomato fondue. The bar area is cosy and comfy with rustic walls and open fire, the extension is stylish, with sparkling wooden floors and neat banquettes, and there's a whopping dining terrace for summer.

Meals	Deli board £12.
	Lunch & dinner £11–£19.50.
Closed	Open all day.

Jordan Marr
The White Horse,
Redbourn Lane, Hatching Green,
Harpenden AL5 2JP
Tel   +44 (0)1582 469290
Web www.thewhitehorseharpenden.co.uk

Entry 311 Map 9

Hertfordshire

The Verulam Arms
St Albans

Sloe gin martini, elderflower champagne, woodruff and apple armagnac, horseradish schnapps: take your pick! The foragers who run the Verulam, a cosy corner pub in the heart of St Albans, make beautiful booze from the Hertfordshire hedgerows. They run foraging walks and wild tapas feasts, the meat and game come from a network of hunters and on Sundays they put their spin on the Great British Roast (foraged vegetables, wild herb seasonings). Enter a traditional interior of sage green and cream walls and plain tables, blackboards chalked up with seasonal menus, and, behind the bar, biodynamic wines, Tring and Adnams and their own 'wild' beers. From a tiny kitchen flow flower fritters and wild watercress gnocchi, venison burgers in brioche buns, rumps of local lamb with champ mash, and a wonderful sticky toffee pudding.

Meals	Starters from £7. Dinner from £15.50. Sunday roast from £13.50.
Closed	Open all day.

**George Fredenham
& Gerald Waldeck**
The Verulam Arms, 41 Lower
Dagnall Street, St Albans AL3 4QE

Tel   +44 (0)1727 836004
Web www.the-foragers.com/the-verulam-arms

Entry 312 Map 9

Hertfordshire

The Alford Arms
Frithsden

It isn't easy to find, so come armed with precise directions before you set out! In a hamlet enfolded by acres of National Trust common land, David and Becky Salisbury's gastropub is worth any number of missed turns. Inside are two interlinked rooms, bright and airy, with soft colours, scrubbed pine tables, wooden and tile floors. Food is taken seriously and ingredients are as organic, free-range and delicious as can be. On a menu that divides dishes into small plates and main meals, find warm confit rabbit and wild mushroom tart, baked smoked haddock and prawn pancake, pan-roasted Buckinghamshire venison haunch with sticky red cabbage, whole baked sea bass, homemade ice cream. Wine drinkers have the choice of 22 by the glass; service is informed and friendly. Arrive early on a warm day to take your pick of the teak tables on the sun-trapping front terrace.

Meals	Lunch, bar meals & dinner £11.75-£19.75.
Closed	Open all day.

David & Becky Salisbury
The Alford Arms,
Frithsden,
Hemel Hempstead HP1 3DD

Tel   +44 (0)1442 864480
Web www.alfordarmsfrithsden.co.uk

Entry 313 Map 9

Hertfordshire

The Bricklayers Arms
Flaunden

Tucked away at a remote crossroads in the exotically named Hogpits Bottom ('hog' being local dialect for shale) is a pretty, ivy-strewn 18th-century building with low beams, blazing fires and timbered walls. Once a row of cottages and shops, and an ale house since 1832, this listed building is rammed with diners daily and Alvin's staff are run off their feet. French chef Claude Pallait turns out local rare breed fillets of pork with apple compote and cider jus; Little Missenden lamb with a pea flan; home-smoked fish; good old steak and kidney pie. All are delicious, all are prepared from locally sourced or organic ingredients where possible. There's an excellent range of ales, and 140 wines, ports and armagnacs. While away summer days in the garden, or watch the world go by from the benches out front.

Meals	Bar meals from £8.95.
	Lunch & dinner £9.95–£24.95.
Closed	Open all day.

Alvin Michaels
The Bricklayers Arms,
Hogpits Bottom, Flaunden,
Hemel Hempstead HP3 0PH
Tel   +44 (0)1494 862200
Web   www.bricklayersarms.com

Entry 314 Map 9

Hertfordshire

The Sun at Northaw
Northaw

The 16th-century pub overlooking Northaw's pretty green shines in this north-of-London culinary desert. Passionate about food provenance, Oliver ensures his menus bristle with fabulous produce and, as the menu food map shows, most of it is from Hertfordshire and neighbouring Essex. Find biodynamic, organic, outdoor-reared and artisan goodies, all delicious. There's 'rose' (welfare-friendly) veal chop with celeriac and crab apple mash; local wood pigeon with brussel sprout tops, bacon and salsify; a classic beer-battered haddock with chips and mushy peas. Kids are looked after with organic, guilt-free portions of their own. The rustic-chic interior oozes charm and atmosphere: soothing green hues, cottage-style fireplaces, board and stone floors, smart antique tables. Gorgeous.

Meals	Lunch & dinner £9.50–£19.50.
	Sunday lunch, 3 courses, £16.50.
Closed	Sun evenings from 7pm
	& all day Mon.

Oliver Smith & Sarah Doyle
The Sun at Northaw,
1 Judges Hill, Northaw,
Potters Bar EN6 4NL
Tel   +44 (0)1707 655507
Web   www.thesunatnorthaw.co.uk

Entry 315 Map 9

Hertfordshire

The Fox & Hounds
Hunsdon

London chefs quitting fabulous establishments to transform country boozers may be two a penny, but few have managed it with the aplomb of James Rix. In the comfy laid-back bar: a log fire, the daily papers, local ales on tap and a menu that changes twice daily. Things step up a gear in the smart country-house-on-a-shoestring dining room, with its cosy log-burner, polished old tables and crystal chandelier: a funky backdrop to black pudding from Normandy, wild mushrooms with a fried duck egg or squid and chermoula, followed by whole grilled back bream, pepperonata, monks beard and salsa verde. Puddings include salted caramel ice cream and biscotti. Even the focaccia is homemade. A recent refurb added a Josper charcoal oven, to the delight of diners. It's a treat to see an old pub in the right hands, and booking is recommended.

Hertfordshire

The Bull
Watton-at-Stone

The timbered Bull is a wonderful time-warp gem of a village pub, oozing 15th-century charm. Its warren of rooms is filled with fresh flowers, glowing candles, and old dining tables on bare boards or slate-tiled floors. Menus champion seasonal British and rustic European dishes; classic pub favourites like fish and chips and pork belly with fennel and cider sauce vie for attention alongside tapas-style deli dishes (salt and pepper squid, crab beignets) and sun-dried tomato and garlic polenta. Leave room for Sicilian glazed lemon tart and wash a satisfying meal down with a pint of Wherry or Doom Bar. Open from 9.30am for perusing the papers over coffee and pastries, it is well worth the short trek from Stevenage, Welwyn or Ware. Don't miss nearby Knebworth House.

Meals	Bar meals £4.95–£16.50. Lunch & dinner £9–£22. Sunday lunch, 3 courses, £29.50. Not Sunday eve or Monday.
Closed	4pm–6pm, Sun evenings & Mon (except Bank Holidays).

Meals	Light lunches from £7.50. Mains £9.95–£18.95.
Closed	Open all day.

	James Rix The Fox & Hounds, 2 High Street, Hunsdon, Ware SG12 8NH
Tel	+44 (0)1279 843999
Web	www.foxandhounds-hunsdon.co.uk

Entry 316 Map 9

	Alastair & Anna Bramley The Bull, High Street, Watton-at-Stone, Stevenage SG14 3SB
Tel	+44 (0)1920 831032
Web	www.thebullwatton.co.uk

Entry 317 Map 9

Hertfordshire

The Dukes Head
Hatfield Broad Oak

In the centre of Hatfield Broad Oak is a local loved not only for its great ales but also its food. Inside in the bar, cosy with cottage windows and wood-burning stoves, ales (Doom Bar, Adnam's Ghost Ship) are on tap. At scrubbed wood tables you can tuck into Chef Justin Flodman's hearty menus: chicken liver pâté with fig jam and hazelnut brioche; Barnston steak and kidney pudding with celeriac purée and 'House of Parliament' gravy. One law that should be made here is to leave space for pudding. Justin's pastry-training produces treats such as an elaborate honeycomb parfait with chocolate 'soil', toffee pudding slice and popcorn, accompanied by an extensive pudding wine list. There's also a conservatory dining room for larger groups and a lovely garden in summer, where the chickens cluck as contentedly as the guests.

Hertfordshire

Water Lane Bar & Restaurant
Bishops Stortford

Anglian Country Inns opened their second urban outpost in 2014, following the roaring success of their first – Hermitage Road, Hitchin. This casual dining venue occupies the old Hawkes Brewery site and, once again, the refurbishment is striking. Downstairs, in an awesomely proportioned, stone-vaulted cellar bar, you can order cocktails, craft beers and spirits, and graze on tasty bar snacks. Then find a table in an industrial-look dining room with stripped-back brick walls, exposed pipe work and copper lamps suspended from high ceilings. On the all-day menu are wild mushrooms with charred campagrain, bourbon-glazed belly ribs, hake with langoustine and butter bean cassoulet and, joy of joys, ginger snaps with vanilla Cambridge cream. Burger Buddy Tuesdays, lazy Sunday roasts, live Friday music... all is possible here.

Meals	Starters from £5.
	Dinner from £11.25.
	Sunday roast from £13.
Closed	Open all day.

Meals	Lunch from £6.
	Dinner from £12.
Closed	Mon all day.

	Liz & Justin Flodman
	The Dukes Head,
	High Street, Hatfield Broad Oak,
	Bishops Stortford CM22 7HH
Tel	+44 (0)1279 718598
Web	www.thedukeshead.co.uk

Entry 318 Map 9

	The Manager
	Water Lane Bar & Restaurant,
	31 Water Lane,
	Bishops Stortford CM23 2JZ
Tel	+44 (0)1279 211888
Web	www.waterlane.co

Entry 319 Map 9

The Pilot Boat Inn
Bembridge

This amphibious-looking Bembridge Harbour landmark s ship-shape in more ways than one. Behind the nautical portholes and narrow Mackintosh windows of its Art Deco ship, award-winning landlord George has assembled friendly staff, good booze and generous plates of simple, fresh and often fishy pub cuisine. Snatch sea views from the side garden, savouring a speciality crab sandwich. Whether a dog walker, child-festooned parent or beachcomber with sand-tingled toes, warm welcomes await. Bar décor is eclectic, occasionally opulent. Floors and furnishings are dark wood, red walls frame vintage prints. Sofa seating is kitsch and comfy, board games beckon, bright fish somersault in tanks. Try an Island Brewery Yachtsman's Ale, something from the wine list (decent mid-range options) or a draft Stowford Press, Grolsch or Guinness. The ranks of banter-fuelled islanders swell in summer with yachty types and holidaymakers – but why stray, with five compact and contemporary rooms upstairs? You'll find maritime flavours, reassuringly expensive mattresses, compact Art Deco en suites. A happy harbourside base.

Rooms	3 doubles, 2 twin/doubles: £90.
Meals	Lunch & dinner £8–£20.
Closed	Rarely.

George & Juliet Bristow
The Pilot Boat Inn,
Station Road,
Bembridge PO35 5NN
Tel   +44 (0)1983 872077
Web   www.thepilotboatinn.com

Entry 320 Map 4

Isle of Wight

The Boathouse
Seaview

Walking up from Ryde, sit on a bench facing the sea with a pint of Ringwood Best and watch the fishing boats roll in with the day's catch; some of it may land on your plate. On the fringe of pretty Seaview village, this rambling Victorian seafront pub has long been part of the isle's defensive history, with a group of Dad's Army garden figurines a charming remnant of its previous incarnation. Inside, stretch back on one of the sofas and admire the little oddities: Art Nouveau touches in chair shapes and fireplace, an ornate gilt mirror, metal sail structures… and a varnished dinghy propped against a wall. It's a civilised backdrop for your lobster thermidor. Otherwise, the turf's as local as the surf, with Isle of Wight steaks and a trio of sausages and mash among the most popular dishes, together with the island's very own ploughman's.

Meals	Bar meals from £10.25.
	Lunch from £5.50.
	Dinner, 2 courses from £18.50.
Closed	Open all day.

	Andrew McArthur
	The Boathouse,
	Springvale Road,
	Seaview PO34 5AW
Tel	+44 (0)1983 810616
Web	www.theboathouseiow.co.uk

Entry 321 Map 4

Isle of Wight

The Fishbourne Inn
Fishbourne

Behind the bar are racked wines and gleaming pumps of Stowford Press and Stella Artois. In the dining room: crisp white menus and leather-look chairs. The mock Tudor pub on the leafy residential road has had a smart modern refurb. Find shiny new floors, large sofas, neutral colours and a wide-ranging clientele, thanks to the Portmouth-bound ferry: it's next door. Business travellers mix with tourists and Isle of Wighters on trips round the island, all in need of a tasty breakfast, lunch or dinner. There's no shortage of choice: menus range from 'Seafood Specialities' and 'Pub Favourites' to 'For the Smaller Appetite' and 'Deli Boards for Two to Share', and roasts on Sundays. Terraces and pub benches cosily set amongst well-tended shrubs fill up fast on warm days. Staff are friendly and professional.

Meals	Lunch & dinner £5–£19.
Closed	Open all day.

	Martin Bullock
	The Fishbourne Inn,
	Fishbourne,
	Ryde PO33 4EU
Tel	+44 (0)1983 882823
Web	www.thefishbourne.co.uk

Entry 322 Map 4

Isle of Wight

Isle of Wight

The New Inn
Shalfleet

Built in 1746, the former fishermen's haunt is worth more than a passing nod – especially if you are on the 65-mile coastal path trail. (Arrive by boat and moor at Shalfleet Quay.) The place draws a cheery mix of tourists, walkers and sailors to a spick-and-span bar with 900-year-old flagstones, beams and old fireplaces, and pine-tabled dining rooms decked with nautical bits and bobs. Refreshment includes pints of island-brewed ales and fresh seafood chalked up on a daily-changing board. The huge fish platter is a treat; other choices might include sea bass, locally sourced shellfish or a simple grilled plaice. The crab sandwiches are memorable and carnivores are not forgotten; tuck into prime steak and game in season. And there's a decked garden for summer supping.

The Taverners
Godshill

A pub for all seasons: in summer take your pint (Taverners Own or a good guest beer) into a pretty rear garden with boules, picnic tables, vegetable beds and roaming chickens. In winter, hunker down by the front bar fire amid flagstone floors and wooden tables. There are a couple of sofas too for after lunch snoozers. Food is straightforward, fresh and local, skilfully cooked by Roger who used to head the kitchen at London's Haymarket Hotel; the family room has been converted into a shop selling home-baked goodies and island foodstuffs. Lovely to see hand-raised free-range pork pie, homemade pickles and 'my Nan's lemon meringue pie' on the simple menu; the wine list is short but well-chosen, there's freshly squeezed orange juice, and proper hot chocolate too.

Meals	Bar meals from £9.25. Lunch from £6.75.
Closed	Open all day.

Meals	Lunch & dinner £8–£13.50.
Closed	Sun evenings from 5pm (except Bank Holidays & school holidays).

Daniel Witherwick
The New Inn,
Main Road, Shalfleet,
Newport PO30 4NS
Tel +44 (0)1983 531314
Web www.thenew-inn.co.uk

Entry 323 Map 3

Roger Serjent
The Taverners,
High Street, Godshill,
Ventnor PO38 3HZ
Tel +44 (0)1983 840707
Web www.thetavernersgodshill.co.uk

Entry 324 Map 4

The Bull Hotel
Wrotham

Peacefully wedged between the M20 and M26, Wrotham and its rambling old coaching inn sit on Kent's glorious North Downs, smack-bang on the Pilgrim's Way. Refurbishment of the Bull – the village hub – has been a labour of love. The final flurry has seen some lovely bedrooms come to life; oak floors, period fireplaces and ceiling timbers have been revealed. Creature comforts are plentiful: crisp linen, smart beds, deep leather sofas and old-fashioned radiators, while good bathrooms have underfloor heating, power showers and Duck Island lotions. Downstairs, in a bar once frequented by Battle of Britain pilots (note the stamps on the ceiling), you find Dark Star ales, interesting wines and good seasonal food, perhaps venison sausages, a 30-day-aged fillet steak, an orange and almond cake. It's a great country bolthole for the modern-day pilgrim and for Eurotunnel/port-bound travellers. Walks start from the front door and National Trust gems – Knole Park and Churchill's Chartwell – are close.

Rooms	8 doubles, 2 twins, 1 four-poster: £79–£129. Singles from £69.
Meals	Bar meals from £9. Lunch from £6.50. Dinner, 3 courses, £25–£35. Sunday roast from £12.
Closed	New Year's Day.

Martin Deadman
The Bull Hotel,
Bull Lane, Wrotham,
Sevenoaks TN15 7RF
Tel   +44 (0)1732 789800
Web   www.thebullhotel.com

Leicester Arms
Penshurst

Rescued from closure and refurbished with style and flair in late 2013 by Julian Leefe-Griffiths, the creeper-clad 16th-century inn stands in picture-postcard Penshurst, opposite the gates to Penshurst Place and Gardens. Expect heavy oak doors and wooden floors, wall timbers and leaded windows, glowing woodburning stoves and candles on darkwood tables – perfect for supping a pint of local Larkins Traditional. At polished tables in the purple panelled dining room, quite grand with gilt-framed family portraits and chandeliers, enjoy some classic British food – lunchtime steak sandwich with horseradish cream and chips, or ham hock with fennel pickle and mustard mayo, followed by Old Spot toad-in-the-hole with mash and kale, and sticky toffee pudding with cobnut ice cream. Bedrooms ramble across two floors, all sport heritage hues, Hypnos mattresses and the best linen on antique beds, eclectic furnishings, posh tiled Aston Matthews bathrooms, and gorgeous views to Penshurst church or across rolling countryside. Hever Castle is close; stunning estate walks start from the front door.

Rooms	6 doubles, 3 four-posters: £119–£159. 2 family rooms for 4: £159. 2 singles: £99–£119.
Meals	Continental breakfast included; full cooked £8. Lunch from £4.50. Sunday roast from £12.95. Dinner, 3 courses, £25–£30.
Closed	Rarely.

Melissa Porter
Leicester Arms,
High Street, Penshurst,
Tonbridge TN11 8BT
Tel   +44 (0)1892 871617
Web   www.theleicesterarmshotel.com

Kent

The Vineyard
Lamberhurst

Real ales, real food and real English wines – from Lamberhurst Vineyard, naturally. Martial and Natasha Chaussy, who took over in 2012, have breathed new life into the pub on the green, making the most of its 15th-century origins (low ceilings, beams, brick, flags, planked floor) and sprucing up the gorgeous interior with a smart, rustic-chic look – old rugs, leather sofas and wing chairs, colourful fabrics and fat church candles. Folk are drawn by the relaxed and friendly atmosphere, the winter fires, the local ales (from the barrel), the wines, the new dining room and the food. Menus combine pub classics with French brasserie-style dishes: baked camembert with shallot jam; a Kentish game board; sea bass with crayfish beurre blanc; pear and almond tart. Don't miss the Sunday roasts! New elegant bedrooms in four cottage-style suites added in 2013 have downstairs sitting areas and wet rooms (huge walk-in showers), with spiral staircases leading to bedrooms in the eaves. Expect low futon beds, quirky retro furnishings, leather sofas, iPod dock radios and private terraces. Close to Scotney Castle, Sissinghurst and Pashley Manor Gardens.

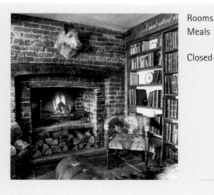

Rooms	4 suites: £100–£110.
Meals	Bar meals from £7.
	Lunch & dinner £9–£18.
Closed	Rarely.

Martial & Natasha Chaussy
The Vineyard,
Lamberhurst Down, Lamberhurst,
Tunbridge Wells TN3 8EU
Tel   +44 (0)1892 890222
Web   www.elitepubs.com

Entry 327 Map 5

The George Hotel
Cranbrook

Casual and understated, the pale woods and soft colours of the interior complement 13th-century origins; it may look like a brasserie but this is Cranbrook's favourite local. While a network of local producers has been assiduously encouraged, it is the consistently high standards that keep the place thriving. The kitchen moves deftly through a repertoire of modern dishes — rack of Park Farm lamb with mash, pancetta, kale and rosemary jus, halibut with dill cream sauce — while the old pub classic is thrown in: Spitfire beer-battered cod and chips, shepherd's pie, chargrilled rib-eye steak. And well-kept Shepherd Neame ales make a matchless accompaniment to a ham and mustard sandwich, and the wines are excellent. Climb 'one of the noblest staircases in Kent' to discover hugely stylish and individual bedrooms themed according to colour; the rooms in the old building are full of historic charm, with wonky floors and historic timbers; 'Crimson' has a superb four-poster. Sissinghurst's gardens are gloriously close.

Rooms	11 doubles, 1 twin: £85–£150.
Meals	Lunch, bar meals & dinner from £8.95.
Closed	Rarely.

Ian Huxley
The George Hotel,
Stone Street,
Cranbrook TN17 3HE

Tel	+44 (0)1795 532206
Web	www.thegeorgehotelkent.co.uk

Entry 328 Map 5

Kent

The Queen's Inn
Hawkshurst

Sharon and Sally Ann took on the run-down Queen's Inn in early 2014 having run a successful catering company for many years. Rather than deliver food to different venues across Kent, it was time to provide the venue to showcase Sally Ann's cooking and this rambling old village inn fitted the bill perfectly. Revived with panache, the wisteria-festooned Georgian façade hides a cosy, beamed 16th-century interior: a bar with wooden floor and huge fireplace, and upstairs, wonky corridors leading to quirky, hugely individual rooms. Expect a retro feel throughout with chunky dial phones, old-style radios, painted furniture and jazzy fabrics and lamps, plus goose down duvets, coffee and homemade brownies. Bathrooms are smart; room five has a free-standing tub in the room. Downstairs, rustic and modern combine in the dining room, with its ancient plank floor, brick fireplace and contemporary print wallpaper. In the bar, relax with a pint of Hophead or tuck into Moroccan spiced rack of lamb, sea bass with samphire, crab and chive sauce, Park Farm sausages and mash, baked vanilla cheesecake. NT treasures (Sissinghurst & Bodiam) and Pashley Manor Gardens are on the doorstep.

Rooms	5 doubles: £95-£180.
	1 family room for 4: £135.
	Singles £85.
Meals	Starters from £5.
	Dinner from £12.50.
Closed	Rarely.

Sharon Retmanski
The Queen's Inn,
Rye Road,
Hawkshurst TN18 4EY
Tel   +44 (0)1580 754233
Web   www.thequeensinnhawkhurst.co.uk

Entry 329 Map 5

Royal Hotel
Deal

Whether out on the decked terrace listening to the waves raking the beach, or in the lounge bar cosy with leather chairs, chesterfields and fire, you can follow in the footsteps of Lord Nelson and Emma. They stayed here in the winter of 1801. It was an inspired move by Shepherd Neame – the oldest brewery in the country – to rescue and transform this run-down seaside hotel. The bedroom look is understated and stylish, and a gentle nautical theme plays. Colours are softly modern, bathrooms immaculate and the quietest rooms are at the back – though the three most popular come with a sea-view balcony and an in-room claw-foot bath. With food available all day, the Royal has proved a hit with families drawn by the beach and the please-all menu of pub classics – yours to peruse wherever you sit. As for the deckside colonial-style bar, it makes a popular 19th hole inside and out; golfers come to play the celebrated Open Championship course, Royal St George's, as well as qualifying courses Prince's and Royal Cinque Port.

Rooms	5 doubles, 1 twin: £80–£195.
	1 family room for 4: £95–£135.
	1 single: £70–£90.
Meals	Breakfast from £4.95.
	Bar meals from £6.50.
	Dinner from £9.95.
	Sunday lunch, 3 courses, £19.
Closed	Rarely.

Glenn & Joice Wisdom
Royal Hotel,
Beach Street,
Deal CT14 6JD

Tel	+44 (0)1304 375555
Web	www.theroyalhotel.com

The Royal Albion
Broadstairs

Broadstairs – nicely old-fashioned, with character – held a special place in Charles Dickens' heart. Our English watering place he called it, and this gloriously situated Georgian hotel played host to the great man for many summers; Nicholas Nickleby was written here. Run down in recent years, it has been rescued by Shepherd Neame, who have cast their magic wand over the place. Now all sorts come, not just the Dickens Trail tourists but young families and locals, irresistibly drawn by the views of Viking Bay. Catch them from the big light-filled Ballards Lounge or the suntrap double-decked terrace. Light bites in the bar and Sunday roasts are popular, with seafood a speciality in the more formal dining room (crab and prawn risotto, fillet of bass with warm potato salad). This would be a lovely place for a beachy break, so why not stay? Obviously the sea-facing rooms are the ones to go for, but all the renovated rooms are comfortable. Colours are pale with the odd splash of colour from bolster or cushion; bathrooms are slick and modern. And the staff are the best.

Rooms	14 doubles, 3 twins: £85–£145. 3 singles: £70–£105.
Meals	Lunch & dinner £10.95–£15.95. Bar meals £6.95–£12.95.
Closed	Rarely.

Dean & Vicky Markham
The Royal Albion,
6-10 Albion Street,
Broadstairs CT10 1AN
Tel   +44 (0)1843 868071
Web   www.albionbroadstairs.co.uk

Entry 331 Map 5

The Marine Hotel
Whitstable

Perched above Tankerton's pebbly beach, just east of Whitstable, this grand-looking home was acquired in 1949 by Shepherd Neame, Britain's oldest brewery. Following a 2012 makeover, the brewery's 'unbranded' flagship inn-hotel is now a stylish north coast retreat, gleaming from top-to-toe. Step into the buzzy, nautically themed bar for a pint of Spitfire, or relax in the elegant Orangery extension – for breakfast or afternoon tea from the in-house coffee shop. Arrive early for a window seat and sea view in the bar, where the menu delivers pub classics; whitebait with lime and coriander mayonnaise; steak and ale pie; crab, prawn and chilli linguine. Look to the restaurant menu (also served in the bar) for the likes of lamb rump with rosemary and redcurrant jus, and red mullet with winter vegetable ratatouille; leave room for ginger sponge. Plush carpeted bedrooms upstairs have contemporary fabrics, big comfy beds and smart bathrooms. Splash out on a superior sea view room for a balcony, more space and cosseting extras.

Rooms	28 doubles, 2 twins: £85–£145.
Meals	Starters from £5.95.
	Dinner from £9.95.
Closed	Rarely.

The Manager
The Marine Hotel,
Marine Parade,
Whitstable CT5 2BE
Tel   +44 (0)1227 272672
Web   www.marinewhitstable.co.uk

Kent

The Sportsman
Seasalter

Brothers Steve and Phil Harris's pub is a Michelin starred haven amid marshland, beach huts and caravan sites, with the North Sea somewhere behind. The blackboard menu, short and sweet, promises everything seasonal and local; meat comes from farms within sight of the front door, Whitstable is just down the road. Order a native oyster or two to slurp while waiting for smoked mackerel with Bramley apple jelly or pork terrine. Roast chicken with bacon, sprouts and bread sauce is an old fashioned treat; apple sorbet and burnt cream makes a stunning finale. There's a tasting menu (book in advance), delicious bread, hams cured in the beer cellar, they churn their own butter and make their own salt. You eat at large chunky tables made from reclaimed wood in any of three airy rooms with marsh views. Exceptional.

Meals	Lunch & dinner £17.95–£22.95. Tasting menu £65. Not Sunday eve or Monday.
Closed	3pm–6pm.

Phil & Stephen Harris
The Sportsman,
Faversham Road, Seasalter,
Whitstable CT5 4BP
Tel +44 (0)1227 273370
Web www.thesportsmanseasalter.co.uk

Entry 333 Map 5

Kent

The Three Mariners
Oare

After a ramble across Oare marshes, welcome to a hideaway of good things. Food, mostly sourced from farms and day boats, is excellent value and it's the sort of place where you wish you could try everything that goes by. Potted crab, fish soup, and roast widgeon with red cabbage and parsnip potato cake represent contemporary pub classics, while a slow-roasted shoulder of lamb (for six to share at Sunday lunch) has a reassuringly timeless appeal. This 400-year-old pub comes with a laid-back medley of furniture and a double-sided log fire, cleverly dividing dining room from bar. It's simple and understated with an easy informality and lots of bare wood – a place to treasure; many do. There are Shepherd Neame ales and a modest and thoughtful selection of wines.

Meals	Lunch & dinner £12.50–£19. Set lunch, 3 courses, £11.95–£16.95. Set dinner, 3 courses, £16.95. Not 25 Dec.
Closed	24 December (evening).

John O'Riordan
The Three Mariners,
2 Church Road, Oare,
Faversham ME13 0QA
Tel +44 (0)1795 533633
Web www.thethreemarinersoare.co.uk

Entry 334 Map 5

The Red Lion
Stodmarsh

Down rutted lanes that wind through bluebell woods is an enchanting village and a 15th-century pub. Step into tiny bare-boarded rooms with log fires, draped hops, prints, menus, wine bottles, milk churns, trugs, baskets, candles on every table and one bossy cat. Richard and Carol took over in 2013 and have promised to maintain the quirky country appeal that everyone loves. A basket of freshly laid eggs (chickens roam the garden), chutney and a sign for the sale of locally smoked ham add to the rural feel. Greene King IPA and Old Speckled Hen are tapped from barrels behind the bar and everyone is a regular, or looks like one. Menus change with the seasons and oxtail in ale with horseradish mash or cock-a-leekie pie will arrive on big painted plates. The quality is high. It doesn't get much better than this.

The Granville
Street End

Straddling the divide between restaurant and pub, the Granville mirrors its older sibling, the Sportsman in Seasalter, admirably. The fire crackles, leather sofas fill one corner and there's a separate drinkers' bar. It's a pleasure to sit back here, downing oysters with shallot vinegar and a pint of stout or a well-chosen wine. Overseeing it all is Gabrielle Harris, aided by chef Jim Shave who heads up an open-to-view kitchen that deals in modern and delicious dishes. Chalked up on the blackboards are impeccably sourced, tried-and-trusted favourites like roast Monkshill Farm chicken breast with wild mushroom sauce or roast pork belly with crackling. There's seriously good homemade bread and sticky toffee pud for afters. Great for walkers, foodies, families – and the Channel tunnel.

Meals	Lunch & dinner £10.95–£20.95.		Meals	Lunch & dinner £11.95–£19.95.
Closed	Open all day.		Closed	3pm–5.30pm. Open all day Sun.

Richard & Carol Vale
The Red Lion,
Stodmarsh,
Canterbury CT3 4BA

Tel   +44 (0)1227 721339
Web   www.theredlionstodmarsh.com

Entry 335 Map 5

Phil & Gabrielle Harris
The Granville,
Faussett Hill, Street End,
Canterbury CT4 7AL

Tel   +44 (0)1227 700402
Web   www.thegranvillecanterbury.com

Entry 336 Map 5

Five Bells Inn
East Brabourne

Looking for somewhere that's quirky, full of character, champions local produce and has community spirit? Seek out this 15th-century village inn tucked beneath the North Downs. Alison and John revamped the building in 2011 and there's much to delight the eye: hopped beams, wood and tiled floors, exposed bricks walls, eclectic furnishings, blazing fires and individual touches – candles in upturned wine bottles, posh unisex loos. There's a local-produce shop in the bar, and the bar-cum-deli counter displays Kent ales, cider, olives, cheeses and Wye Bakery bread. Menus bristle with farm foods – Alkham beef and lamb, Potten Farm fruit and vegetables, estate game. Downland walkers and lucky locals love the place, dropping by for breakfast from 9am, acoustic music, farmers' markets, craft fairs, and harvest supper.

The Plough
Stalisfield Green

Wonderful walks, Swale estuary views, a raft of lagers, ciders and Kentish ales, and land-rustic country cooking – just a few reasons for seeking out this 15th-century hall house hidden in a hamlet high on the North Downs. Beamed bars have wooden floors, old scrubbed pine tables, green and terracotta hues and log fires. Doors in the light airy garden room open onto a peaceful patio for a pint of Hopdaemon ale or a heady Biddenden cider. Menus brim with local produce – saltmarsh lamb, rare-breed pork, delicious Angus beef from surrounding farms – while chef-patron Richard makes the bread, ice cream, pickles, sausages and home-smoked goodies. Typically, tuck into scallops with celeriac remoulade and apple caramel, lamb rump with baby beets and parsnip purée, and banana tarte tatin. It's quite a find.

Meals	Breakfast £5–£8. Lunch & dinner £10–£15.
Closed	Open all day.

Meals	Lunch & dinner £10.95–£18.95.
Closed	Open all day.

Alison Rogers
Five Bells Inn,
The Street, East Brabourne,
Ashford TN25 5LP
Tel +44 (0)1303 813334
Web www.fivebellsinnbrabourne.com

Entry 337 Map 5

Richard & Marianne Baker
The Plough,
Stalisfield Green,
Faversham ME13 0HY
Tel +44 (0)1795 890256
Web www.theploughinnstalisfield.co.uk

Entry 338 Map 5

The Dirty Habit
Hollingbourne

Crackling fires in beamed bars, enjoyable food and pints of Harvey's lure walkers and foodies to this North Downs treasure by the Pilgrim's Way; monks once offer ale and lodgings to pilgrims en route to Canterbury. Elite Pubs have refurbished beautifully, restoring Georgian wall panelling in the bar and, in the Monks Corner room, preserving a 13th-century brick floor, rafters and bread oven. Daily menus make good use of local and seasonal and combine pub classics with Mediterranean dishes. You could start with devilled lamb's kidneys, move on to crab and crayfish linguine, or partridge with bacon and chestnut sauce, and finish with apple and orange tart. Sharing deli boards, afternoon teas and Sunday roasts complete the picture, there's a landscaped terrace too, and stunning downland walks that start from the door.

Meals	Lunch & dinner £9.50–£24.50.
Closed	Open all day.

Martial & Natasha Chaussy
The Dirty Habit,
The Pilgrims Way, Upper Street,
Hollingbourne, Maidstone ME17 1UW
Tel   +44 (0)1622 880880
Web   www.elitepubs.com/the_dirtyhabit

Entry 339 Map 5

The Cricketers Inn
Meopham

Aptly named, Meopham is considered to be the birthplace of Kent cricket in 1776. This spick-and-span whitewashed pub overlooks the picture-book village green where the cricket club still play. Bag a bench on summer Sundays to watch the action with a pint of Harvey's Best and a round of tuna with horseradish mayonnaise sandwiches, or a steak and ale pie from the all day menu, or tuck into the full monty — sirloin of beef with roast duck fat potatoes and Yorkshire pud. In winter, hunker down beside the raised log fire in the bar with red-painted ceiling, wood floor and a wealth of cricketing memorabilia and dine heartily (salt and pepper squid; lamb shoulder; bread and butter pudding) in the impressive dining room extension. The posh heated terrace overlooks an early 19th-century smock mill.

Meals	Starters from £4.95. Dinner from £9.50.
Closed	Open all day.

Brian Whiting
The Cricketers Inn,
Wrotham Road, Meopham,
Gravesend DA13 0QA
Tel   +44 (0)1474 812163
Web   www.thecricketersinn.co.uk

Entry 340 Map 5

Kent

Kent

The George & Dragon
Chipstead

Ben James snapped up a failing boozer in leafy Chipstead, a 16th-century timbered gem, in 2009. Spruced up with style, minutes from Sevenoaks and the M25, it comes with log fires, timbers and beams, a classy daily menu bristling with produce from the larders of Kent and Sussex, and great wines. At lunch, accompany a pint of Westerham Grasshopper Ale with a succulent steak sandwich or share a deliboard of cured meats, cheeses and chutneys. At dinner, tuck into such delicacies as pigeon and pancetta salad; seared Chart Farm 'sika' venison; roast chicken breast with butterbeans and chorizo. Vegetarian dishes are very good: Blue Monday cheese, pear and walnut salad; wild mushroom risotto with truffle oil. Shun the motorway services – it's the best pit-stop for miles.

The Farm House
West Malling

The only village centre venue for Elite Pubs is a fine Elizabethan building on the High Street in West Malling, a busy little village west of Maidstone. The Farm House throngs with diners and drinkers, who spill out of the contemporary bar on warm days to share a charcuterie board and a bottle of Malbec at rustic tables on the terrace or in the pretty walled garden, which overlook a 15th-century barn. Escape the bar hub-bub and book a table in the smart, wood-floored dining room for scallops with pea and mint purée followed by crab linguini and apple and rhubarb crumble. All day sandwiches and pizzas, traditional afternoon teas and Kentish ales on tap complete the thriving picture.

| Meals | Lunch & dinner £9-£18.50. |
| Closed | Open all day. |

Meals	Lunch & dinner from £10.90.
	Sunday roast from £11.90.
Closed	Open all day.

Ben James
The George & Dragon,
39 High Street, Chipstead,
Sevenoaks TN13 2RW
Tel   +44 (0)1732 779019
Web   www.georgeanddragonchipstead.com

Entry 341 Map 5

Martial & Natasha Chaussy
The Farm House,
97-99 High Street,
West Malling ME19 6NA
Tel   +44 (0)1732 843257
Web   www.elitepubs.com

Entry 342 Map 5

Kent

The Swan on the Green
West Peckham

West Peckham may be the back of beyond — a well-heeled beyond — but there's nothing backward about Gordon Milligan's pub. People are drawn by its good food, and beer from the microbrewery at the back. The interior is fresh, contemporary and open-plan: blond wood, rush-seated chairs, stylish black and white photography. Under the Swan Ales label, half a dozen brews are funnelled from the central bar: Ginger Swan, Swan Mild, Trumpeter Best, Fuggles, Bewick, Cygnet. Menus are a compendium of updated pub classics: tomato and root vegetable chowder; red mullet with mussel broth; crispy duck confit with red wine jus. Gordon and his team have created a balanced mix of drinking bar and dining areas in a 16th-century pub; you can even borrow a rug and eat on the village green.

Kent

The Chaser Inn
Shipbourne

Whiting & Hammond's flagship dining pub is a striking, colonial-style building beside the parish church with serene views over the village green. Its name is associated with the Fairlawne Estate where steeplechase horses, including the Queen Mother's, were trained. From the impressive porticoed frontage enter a warren of cosy, country-smart rooms — rugs on bare boards, fat candles on old tables, bookcases groaning with books. Browse the papers with a pint of Abbot by the fire or tuck into some hearty British food, best enjoyed in the timber-vaulted dining room. From the daily menu try potted rabbit or devilled lamb's kidneys then whole plaice with caper and citrus butter; top it all with lemon tart. Come for weekend breakfasts or Sunday roasts, then walk to Ightham Mote (NT) — the Greensand Way passes the front door.

Meals	Bar meals £5.65–£12.95. Lunch & dinner £9.95–£15.95. Not Sunday or Monday eve.
Closed	3pm–6pm. Check Sun evenings in winter.

Meals	Lunch & dinner £9.95–£12.95.
Closed	Open all day.

Gordon Milligan
The Swan on the Green,
The Village Green, West Peckham,
Maidstone ME18 5JW
Tel +44 (0)1622 812271
Web www.swan-on-the-green.co.uk

Entry 343 Map 5

Paul Roser
The Chaser Inn,
Stumble Hill, Shipbourne,
Tonbridge TN11 9PE
Tel +44 (0)1732 810360
Web www.thechaser.co.uk

Entry 344 Map 5

Kent

The Kings Head
Bessels Green

Brian Whiting pushed open the doors to the stylishly remodelled Kings Head in 2014, confident that the Whiting and Hammond trademark look and feel of the spruced-up interior and innovative pub menu would wow Sevenoaks diners. Rugs on bare boards, chunky church candles on old dining tables, walls of prints and posters lined with shelves of books, all set the scene for feasts of crab and lobster ravioli or smoked bacon and pea soup, followed by sausage toad-in-the-hole or Catalan fish and shellfish stew, and sticky toffee pudding. Local Westerham ales, great coffee, a sheltered rear terrace with posh tables and brollies, and three heated garden dining huts complete the promising picture. A cracking new pit-stop close to the M25, the A21, Chartwell and Knole Park (NT), and Sevenoaks town centre.

Meals	Starters from £4.95. Dinner from £9.50.
Closed	Open all day.

Brian Whiting
The Kings Head,
2 Westerham Road, Bessels Green,
Sevenoaks TN13 2QA
Tel   +44 (0)1732 452081
Web   www.kingsheadbesselsgreen.co.uk

Entry 345 Map 5

Kent

The Little Brown Jug
Chiddingstone Causeway

Set beside a rural lane deep in the Kentish Weald, Whiting & Hammond's HQ and flagship pub makes a handy pit-stop after visiting nearby Penshurst Place, Chiddingstone Castle, or even Hever Castle; all are minutes away. Or, round off a cracking country walk with a pint of local ale in the beautiful garden. Tardis-like, the bar extends back into several inter-linked dining areas with intimate corners, book-filled shelves, old pictures and mirrors, rugs on wood floors, and old dining tables topped with candles. Seasonal daily menus, combine hearty British pub classics with specials such as braised shoulder of lamb, and traditional puds like sticky toffee pudding with vanilla ice cream. Heated garden huts with your own waiter (seating eight) are perfect for family lunches at any time of year.

Meals	Starters from £4.95. Dinner from £9.50.
Closed	Open all day.

Brian Whiting
The Little Brown Jug,
Chiddingstone Causeway,
Tonbridge TN11 8JJ
Tel   +44 (0)1892 870318
Web   www.thelittlebrownjug.co.uk

Entry 346 Map 5

Kent

Kent

The Poacher and Partridge
Tudeley

In the peaceful flatlands of Kent, a two-minute drive from Tudeley's little church (famous for Chagall's exquisite stained-glass windows) is a new addition to Elite Pubs' classy stable. Through a new-timbered entrance enter a big airy space with pristine slates on the floor and a bright contemporary décor. Bentwood chairs at plain tables contrast with attractive upbeat fabrics and theatrical pops of colour; there's a specials board above the fire, a charming pair of partridges (stuffed) by a window, and a big rustic wood-fired oven from which pizzas and steaks flow. Service is attentive and the good-looking food ranges from rabbit and prune terrine to quinoa salad to broad bean risotto, chicken supreme, fish and chips and lot of lovely puds. Outside: a big terrace with views across fields, a summer bar and grill, and a super children's playground.

The Poet at Matfield
Matfield

Not long after launching the catering company Pop Creative, James and head chef Charlie took on Matfield's run-down pub by the green. They spruced it up, renamed it The Poet after Siegfried Sassoon (born and bred in the village) and foodies have flocked ever since. A resounding thumbs up has been given to the revived 17th-century interior, and to the short imaginative menus. Arrive early for the glossy green chesterfield by the fire in the bar; graze on a deli board and a pint of Old Dairy bitter. Or settle in to the beamed and brick-floored Bakery room for seasonally led modern British food: chicken liver and foie gras parfait with date and apple crumble; sea bass with parmesan gnocchi and lobster bisque; chocolate and caramel delice. The roast lunches are wonderful and there's evening jazz on Sundays.

Meals	Dinner from £11.95.
Closed	Open all day.

Meals	Lunch & dinner £13.50–£26. Set menu (Monday-Friday) £14.95-£16.95.
Closed	Open all day.

The Manager
The Poacher and Partridge,
Hartlake Road, Tudeley,
Tonbridge TN11 0PH
Tel   +44 (0)1732 358934
Web   www.elitepubs.com/poacher_partridge

Entry 347 Map 5

James Spencer
The Poet at Matfield,
Maidstone Road, Matfield,
Tonbridge TN12 7JH
Tel   +44 (0)1892 722416
Web   www.thepoetatmatfield.co.uk

Entry 348 Map 5

George & Dragon
Speldhurst

"We buy from people not companies" says Julian Leefe-Griffiths, before launching into an exuberant description of the produce he finds in the woods and the beers that come from Chiddingstone. Meat, game and vegetables are local and often organic; artisan cheeses come mostly from Sussex. The team's breathed new life into this black and white timbered inn. It's a characterful old place, loved for its vast flagstones, heavy oak doors, enormous inglenook and carved beams. Gutsy food is the biggest treat: seared pigeon with smoked bacon and puy lentils, wild rabbit ragout with pasta, roast Chevening Estate pheasant with confit leg, dauphinoise and greens, pear tarte tatin with cinnamon ice cream, spiced cider syrup and caramel jelly. The atmosphere is easy, the staff friendly, and there's a lovely rear garden.

Meals	Bar meals £5.50–£9.50. Lunch & dinner £9.50–£15.50.
Closed	Open all day.

Julian Leefe-Griffiths
George & Dragon,
Speldhurst Hill, Speldhurst,
Tunbridge Wells TN3 0NN

Tel   +44 (0)1892 863125
Web   www.speldhurst.com

Entry 349 Map 5

The Black Pig
Tunbridge Wells

Rustic menus brimming with local organic and biodynamic foods put Julian Leefe-Griffiths's George & Dragon on the culinary map a decade ago. Keen to replicate the success in upmarket Tunbridge Wells, he's spruced up the Orson Welles and re-named it after a tasty rare-breed pig. In the bar, leather chairs, contemporary wall coverings and a chandelier; in the dining areas, earthy colours, rustic tables topped with candles, and planked floors. From the kitchen flow sausage rolls with chutney, slow-roasted Groombridge Park belly pork with apple and sage, and Three Little Pigs, a board laden with English, Italian and Spanish hams. Non-porcine dishes include lamb chops with wild garlic aïoli, saddle of rabbit with pancetta, and hake with salsa verde. Pig heaven in Tunbridge Wells.

Meals	Lunch from £7.50. Dinner from £10.50.
Closed	Open all day.

Julian Leefe-Griffiths
The Black Pig,
18 Grove Hill Road,
Tunbridge Wells TN1 1RZ

Tel   +44 (0)1892 523030
Web   www.theblackpig.net

Entry 350 Map 5

The Three Chimneys
Biddenden

Imagine tiny unspoilt rooms of stripped brick, faded paintwork, ancient timber and smouldering fires. During the Napoleonic wars French officers imprisoned nearby were allowed to wander as far as the point where the three paths meet (the 'trois chemins' – hence the name). There's farm cider and Adnams Best Bitter drawn straight from the cask, and the cooking is modern and tasty; parmesan and herb-crusted loin of lamb; chocolate and praline torte with pistachio ice cream. You can eat in the bars (though not the public one) as well as the charming restaurant with stylish conservatory extension, or on the sheltered patio. They pretty much get the balance right between pub and restaurant here, so prop up the bar for as long as you like.

Meals	Lunch & dinner £11.95–£18.95.
	Bar meals £3.95–£8.95.
Closed	3pm–5.30pm.
	3.30pm–6pm Sun.

Craig Smith
The Three Chimneys,
Hareplain Road, Biddenden,
Ashford TN27 8LW
Tel   +44 (0)1580 291472
Web   www.thethreechimneys.co.uk

Entry 351 Map 5

The Milk House
Sissinghurst

The gardens at Sissinghurst Castle were designed by Vita Sackville-West; if you stay at this cute village pub, you can stroll over after breakfast, via apple orchards and bluebell woods. As for The Milk House, Dane and Sarah have recently refurbished from top to toe, making it a great base from which to explore this deeply rural area. It's also a place for a very good meal, with food taking centre stage, seasonal and mostly sourced within 20 miles. Outside, there's a smart dining terrace, a duck pond behind, then lawns for a pint in the sun with views over open country. Airy interiors have an easy style with woven willow lampshades hanging above the bar. Dig into fabulous food, perhaps home-cured smoked salmon, free-range Park Farm beef, chocolate tart with kirsch-soaked cherries or a plate of matchless local cheese.

Meals	Lunch from £4.
	Dinner, 3 courses, from £30.
	Sunday roast from £12.95.
Closed	Open all day.

Dane & Sarah Allchorne
The Milk House,
The Street, Sissinghurst
Cranbrook TN17 2JG
Tel   +44 (0)1580 720200
Web   www.themilkhouse.co.uk

Entry 352 Map 5

The Bull
Benenden

Overlooking Benenden's large and lovely green, complete with cricket pitch and parish church, the 17th-century Bull draws an appreciative crowd, especially on match days. Behind the unusual paned windows, the appeal is obvious in this rustic-chic bar, all stripped wooden floors, fat church candles, scrubbed tables, cushioned settles, and a blazing fire in the inglenook. The dining room is equally informal and relaxed. Come for heady Biddenden cider or a cracking pint of Old Dairy Red Top, brewed along the road at Hole Park. The food is hearty and locally sourced – farm meats, Rye Bay seafood – and the menu holds such delights as scallops with sweet chilli butter, wild rabbit and bacon casserole, fish pie, treacle tart, and some rather good sandwiches. Once a month there's live music and the place heaves.

Meals	Bar meals from £9.50.
	Lunch from £6.95.
	Dinner from £10.50.
	Sunday roast £11.50.
	Not Sunday eve.
Closed	Open all day.

Mark & Lucy Barron-Reid
The Bull,
Benenden,
Cranbrook TN17 4DE
Tel   +44 (0)1580 240054
Web www.thebullatbenenden.co.uk

Entry 353 Map 5

The Great House
Gills Green

In rolling Wealden countryside, the Elizabethan weatherboard cottages – now one smart cosy pub – invite you in with an alluring mix of old beams, wood floors and eclectic furnishings. There are log fires in the rambling bar, and a Mediterranean-style terrace (stone flower urns, Italian designer chairs) off the airy Orangery dining room. Menus combine a modern British and a French brasserie feel, so nibble on air-cured ham – sliced theatre-style from a huge leg on the butcher's block – then tuck into game stew from the Aga or halibut with tarragon mash and brown shrimp butter; make space for apple and plum crumble. Alternatively, pop in for a shared deli board (Kentish game), linger over afternoon tea or book in for Sunday roasts; it's all delicious. There are pints of Harvey's and 20 wines by the glass.

| Meals | Lunch & dinner £9.50–£24.50. |
| Closed | Open all day. |

Martial & Natasha Chaussy
The Great House,
Gills Green,
Cranbrook TN18 5EJ
Tel   +44 (0)1580 753119
Web www.elitepubs.com/the_greathouse

Entry 354 Map 5

Red Pump Inn
Bashall Eaves

Down meandering lanes in the stunning Ribble valley is a handsome roadside pub with a south-facing terrace tumbled with flowers. In the bar: stone floors, an open fire, richly worn oak settles and tables, books scattered here and there, and shuttered windows with green views. Beers include Moorhouses and Timothy Taylor; pints are poured for the shoot during the season. For lunch there are two rooms to choose from: one cosy with mustard walls, the other with bare oak tables and settles by the wood-burner. In the evening, sit in the large, beamed, candlelit restaurant and tuck in to something from the chargrill. The menu is warming, hearty and rich, and meat comes from Ginger Pig. Try beef in burgundy, Fran's Irish stew, or the mushroom, nut and cranberry Wellington. Delicious! Upstairs, three white-painted bedrooms have golden silk bedspreads, luxurious linens, spic and span bathrooms with thick snowy towels. And the views! They're planning five more rooms, too. Clitheroe Castle and the Forest of Bowland are nearby.

Rooms	3 twin/doubles: £75–£115. Singles £65–£95.
Meals	Bar meals from £4.50. Lunch & dinner £9.50–£17.95.
Closed	Rarely.

Jonathan & Fran Gledhill
Red Pump Inn,
Clitheroe Road, Bashall Eaves,
Clitheroe BB7 3DA
Tel   +44 (0)1254 826227
Web   www.theredpumpinn.co.uk

Lancashire

Millstone Hotel
Mellor

Modern meets traditional – in a handsome 18th-century coaching inn in a pretty village on the edge of the Ribble valley. There's a welcoming glow in the bar, with its oak beams and panelling, richly patina'd furniture, grandfather clocks and smart carpeting. Get cosy by the roaring fire with a pint of local Thwaites Bitter and a crispy duck spring roll. Or eat in the stylish new dining room with warm wood-panelled walls. Local ingredients are carefully sourced – poultry from Goosnargh, lamb from Pendle, shrimps from Morecambe Bay. The food is wholesome and unpretentious – including a chutney that bursts with fruit from Balderstone, served with Eccles cake and crumbly cheese. Then there's Ribblesdale goats cheese and avocado salad, a nibbles board piled high with chipolata and black pudding fritters, Wainwright ales suet pudding with mushy peas, or roast venison haunch with chestnuts, horseradish dumplings and mash. Bedrooms ooze comfort: sumptuous fabrics and luxurious linen, Roberts radios and plasma TVs, high-spec bathrooms and umbrellas for wet days. No wonder it's popular.

Rooms	23 twin/doubles: £75–£125. Singles £75–£125.
Meals	Lunch & dinner £8.95–£16.95.
Closed	Rarely.

Anson Bolton
Millstone Hotel,
Church Lane, Mellor,
Blackburn BB2 7JR

Tel   +44 (0)1254 813333
Web   www.millstonehotel.co.uk

Entry 356 Map 12

The Cartford Inn
Little Eccleston

Ten miles inland from the bling of Blackpool stands a handsome 17th-century pub on the banks of the river Wyre. Once 'Dirty Annie' ruled the roost; now stylish Patrick and Julie reign. Enter the etched glass and oak door to find an airy, open-plan space filled with fabulous open fires, polished floors and the bold use of statement wallpaper. Contemporary black and white photographs, candles and huge vases of flowers add to the vibe; locally sourced ingredients shine through the menu. Try Lytham prawns in chilli, lime, garlic and coriander, or leek and creamy Lancashire cheese tartlets. Fleetwood fish pie makes the most of the catch; oxtail and beef in real ale (served with suet pudding, mashed potato, green beans and beetroot salad) is richly dense. Stunning boutiquey bedrooms have carved French beds dressed in crisp linen, signature wallpapers, sumptuous textured fabrics and little chandeliers. The penthouse suite has its own rooftop terrace with far-reaching views. Bathrooms are bronze-tiled and dramatic, with roll top baths and walk-in showers. Some place!

Rooms	10 doubles, 1 twin: £120-£130. 1 suite for 2: 200. 2 family rooms for 3-4: £140. Singles from £65.
Meals	Lunch from £8.50. Dinner, 3 courses, £25-£35. Not Monday lunch.
Closed	Christmas Day.

Patrick & Julie Beaume
The Cartford Inn,
Cartford Lane, Little Eccleston,
Preston PR3 0YP

| Tel | +44 (0)1995 670166 |
| Web | www.thecartfordinn.co.uk |

Lancashire

Penny Street Bridge
Lancaster

This grand old city pub-hotel has had a chequered past but its facelift is bound to impress. High ceilings, stained-glass windows, huge Art Deco lights (yes, the originals) and ornate plasterwork abounds. And the elegant dining room with its vintage mismatch of furniture and gleaming parquet is a pleasing space from which to ponder a varied menu; scallops with crab, apple and chilli is a typically good-looking dish. In the bar, sandwiches are packed with the likes of Lancashire cheese and chutney; for something more substantial, go for a light crispy stone-baked pizza — we're told they're going down a treat. Well-kept Thwaites cask beers await, and there's a selection of wines by the glass. Contemporary bedrooms of different shapes and sizes pick up on the period mood, and are comfortable and quiet, with drenching showers and triple-glazed windows, plasma TVs, bright white linen; one has a beautiful listed wardrobe! Breakfast is full Lancashire — the works, and delicious. In short, a lovely friendly pub-hotel, and a fine place for a spot of retail therapy, slap in the throbbing heart of historic Lancaster.

Rooms	28 doubles: £70–£105. Singles from £64.
Meals	Breakfast £8.95. Lunch from £6.95. Bar meals from £5.95. Dinner from £8.95. Sunday lunch, 2 courses, £11.95.
Closed	Rarely.

Joe Ruddock
Penny Street Bridge,
Penny Street,
Lancaster LA1 1XT
Tel   +44 (0)1524 388313
Web   www.pennystreetbridge.co.uk

Entry 358 Map 11

Lancashire

Lancashire

The Highwayman
Burrow

Hot on the heels of the Three Fishes at Mitton, the Highwayman is the second pub for Ribble Valley Inns. In this stylishly revamped old stone inn in the beautiful Lune Valley, Nigel Haworth raids the rich borderlands of Cumbria and Yorkshire in his pursuit of good produce; his heroes are showcased on menus and walls. Look forward to heather-reared lamb Lancashire hotpot, Lake District sirloin steak, warm Flookburgh shrimps, caramel sticky toffee pudding. There are a raft of classy wines by the glass and Thwaites Lancaster Bomber on tap. Knowledgeable staff add good service to a gloriously informal interior of stone and wooden floors, eclectic old tables and cosy corners with log fires. For summer: a fantastic terrace and garden.

The Fenwick Arms
Claughton

Joycleyn and her thriving Seafood Pub Company added the Fenwick Arms to the portfolio in 2013 following a contemporary spruce up of the black-and-white timbered pub. Minutes from the M6 (J34), it stands in the glorious Lune Valley and makes the perfect pit stop for sublime seafood or a well-cooked pub classic and a pint of Hetton Pale Ale. The Neve family fish merchants supply the fresh seafood daily; there could be roast hake paired with creamed artichokes, kale and sage, and delicious Malaysian seafood curry. Carnivores can tuck into smoked duck or rib-eye steak with pepper sauce. The setting is soothing, warm and cosy-smart with painted low beams and panelled walls, plank and parquet floors, logs blazing in black ranges, and old settles and dining tables. It will be hard to leave.

Meals	Lunch & dinner £9.95–£19.75. Sunday lunch, 3 courses, £19.50.
Closed	Open all day.

Meals	Lunch, 3 courses, £15. Mains £10.50–£19.50.
Closed	Open all day.

Nigel Haworth & Craig Bancroft
The Highwayman,
Burrow,
Carnforth LA6 2RJ
Tel   +44 (0)1524 273338
Web   www.highwaymaninn.co.uk

Entry 359 Map 12

Joycleyn Neve
The Fenwick Arms,
Lancaster Road, Claughton,
Lancaster LA2 9LA
Tel   +44 (0)1524 221157
Web   www.fenwickarms.co.uk

Entry 360 Map 12

The Spread Eagle
Sawley

With the river Ribble winding its winsome way along one side, and the Cistercian Sawley Abbey 100 yards down the other, the reborn Spread Eagle must be a contender for the 'loveliest location' gong. Martin Clarkson's eye for design has created a pleasing combo of old and new: reclaimed flagged floors, carved settles and antique sofas, kitschy curtains, crushed velvet, funky tartan and a bold wallpaper of books. Retro posters on Farrow & Ball walls proclaim 'Eat your greens', but there's nothing vintage about the menu. To start: air-dried ham with blue cheese panna cotta and quince paste. To follow: wild mushroom, broccoli, smoked garlic and shallot tagliolini with basil cream. We can't omit the warm parkin with treacle sauce (just walk it all off later).

Assheton Arms
Downham

Delightful Downham is owned by the Clitheroes and they keep a close eye on 'modern' developments; seems they approve of the changes wrought by the Neve family to this historic pub. Gone is the fusty old warren of rooms; now you are welcomed by linked spaces full of light and warmth with stone floors, wood stoves, cheery duck-egg blue walls and oak furniture. Seafood is central to the menu; Chris Neve is from a long line of sea dogs and as a former trawlerman knows a thing or two about fish. Expect the likes of crab Waldorf salad, king prawn and shredded pork gyoza and queenie scallops. Follow up with monkfish perhaps... meat eaters are nicely catered for too, with Goosnargh chicken pie and Gazegill lamb. With Black Sheep, Taylors and Thwaites on tap, it's the perfect place to drop into after a hike up Pendle Hill.

Meals	Lunch & bar meals from £8.95.
	Dinner from £9.95.
	Sunday roast from £14.95.
Closed	Open all day.

Meals	Lunch & dinner £8.50–£15.50.
Closed	3pm-7pm.
	Open all day Sat & Sun.

Greig & Natalie Barnes
The Spread Eagle,
Sawley,
Clitheroe BB7 4NH
Tel   +44 (0)1200 441202
Web   www.spreadeaglesawley.co.uk

Entry 361 Map 12

Joycelyn Neve
Assheton Arms,
Downham,
Clitheroe BB7 4BJ
Tel   +44 (0)1200 441227
Web   www.asshetonarms.com

Entry 362 Map 12

Lancashire

Duke of York
Grindleton

In the magnificent Ribble Valley, a roadside pub, a reformed boozer, sitting in the shadow of Pendle Hill. In the bar are oak floors, wood-burning stoves, beams, and a gloriously kitsch velvet candelabra. The place is full of quirkery; a full-length mirror above a leather banquette; designer chairs in raspberry pink chenille. Chef-patron Michael Heathcote is largely self-taught, and his touch is inspired. Black winter truffle tagliolini with chanterelle mushrooms, chargrilled fillet of beef with braised ox cheek... and chump of Gazegill organic lamb with mini shoulder pudding, confit root vegetables, braised red cabbage and lamb reduction to stir your imagination. A silky Earl Grey and cardamom panna cotta makes a fresh finish. So, a seriously talented chef in an appealing village – beat a path to his door!

Meals	Bar meals from £7.50.
	Lunch from £11.99.
	Dinner from £12.99.
	Sunday lunch, 3 courses, £18.50.
	Not Monday (except Bank Holidays).
Closed	3pm–6pm.
	Mon all day.

Michael Heathcote
Duke of York,
Grindleton,
Clitheroe BB7 4QR

Tel	+44 (0)1200 423226
Web	www.dukeofyorkgrindleton.com

Entry 363 Map 12

Lancashire

The Lower Buck
Waddington

Look for the church as you enter the village and you'll discover an 18th-century treasure tucked behind – peaceful and unspoiled. Andrew Warburton took over the stone pub in 2005 and, while gently upgrading, has preserved the layout and atmosphere beautifully. Devoid of machines and music, each of the three rooms off the slate-tiled lobby has polished rug-strewn floors, cream walls, old prints, big mirrors, ticking clocks, crackling fires, and a mix of dark wood dining tables. Banter with the locals over a pint of Bowland Hen Harrier, or order from a menu that's chock full of pub classics made from local ingredients, including meat and veg from Longridge farms. Fancy Morecambe Bay potted shrimps, Lancashire hotpot, steak and kidney pie, plum and apple crumble? Perfect after a Ribble Valley ramble.

Meals	Lunch & dinner from £9.95.
Closed	Open all day.

Andrew Warburton
The Lower Buck,
Edisford Road, Waddington,
Clitheroe BB7 3HU

Tel	+44 (0)1200 423342
Web	www.lowerbuckinn.co.uk

Entry 364 Map 12

Higher Buck Inn
Waddington

In the little village of Waddington, loved for its almshouses, brook and Coronation Gardens, is a welcoming pub in an attractive position. Rendered in off-white and sage green, it has posh patio furniture out the front and easy parking at the back. Inside are new slate floors and modern parquet, soft carpeting and a chunky wood bar, snazzy checks, cosy corners and plenty of 'distressed' wood panelling. It's relaxed, airy, comfortable and welcoming, there's background music and a wood stove at the end. Ales are Thwaites (the full range), coffee is Nespresso, and the food is really good value, from the prawn cocktails with Bloody Mary mousse to the steak puddings with Bomber Ale. The rib-eye's delicious on the grill, and the fish and (triple-cooked) chips is ten out of ten.

Meals	Starters from £4. Dinner from £11.
Closed	Open all day.

Michael Heathcote
Higher Buck Inn,
Waddington BB7 3HZ
Tel   +44 (0)1200 423226
Web   www.higherbuck.com

Entry 365 Map 12

The Inn at Whitewell
Whitewell

The old deerkeeper's lodge sits just above the river Hodder with views across parkland to rising fells. Merchants used to stop by and fill up with wine, food and song before heading north through notorious bandit country. Now barbours and muddy dogs mix with frocks and suits. You can eat in the bar but the long restaurant and the outside terrace drink in the view – which will only increase your enjoyment of Bowland lamb with cassoulet of beans and root vegetables, homemade ice cream and fine wines (including their own well-priced Vintner's). In the bar, antiques, bric-a-brac, peat fires, old copies of *The Beano*, fish and chips, warm crab cakes and local bangers. At weekends it gets packed and if you want a table, the more formal restaurant takes bookings. You'll love it.

Meals	Bar meals from £8. Dinner £25–£35.
Closed	Open all day.

Charles Bowman
The Inn at Whitewell,
Dunsop Road, Whitewell,
Clitheroe BB7 3AT
Tel   +44 (0)1200 448222
Web   www.innatwhitewell.com

Entry 366 Map 12

Lancashire

The Three Fishes
Mitton

The suppliers and growers are listed on the back of every menu – Lancashire is a hotbed of food artisans – and the 17th-century village pub in the lovely Ribble Valley has taken gastropubbery to a mouthwatering level. This long whitewashed public house has been refurbed in rustic-smart fashion and is vast: up to 130 inside, a further 60 out. Walls are pale brick, floors stone, lighting subtle, winter logs glow, and the big new wing armchairs have been upholstered in tartan – fabulous! Wines are gorgeous, local ale and real cider is served and the beer-friendly food celebrates traditional British delicacies. We loved the game terrine with pear chutney, the Lancashire hotpot with braised red cabbage, and the chocolate tart with honeycomb. The places heaves so arrive early, especially on Sunday.

Meals	Lunch & dinner £9–£17.95.
	Sunday roast £15–£19.50.
Closed	Open all day.

Nigel Haworth & Craig Bancroft
The Three Fishes,
Mitton Road, Mitton,
Clitheroe BB7 9PQ
Tel +44 (0)1254 826888
Web www.thethreefishes.com

Entry 367 Map 12

Lancashire

Freemasons at Wiswell
Wiswel

This old village pub has had a facelift; pots, plantings and a gravel drive swish it up. Inside, antique rugs on stone-flagged floors, gleaming oak furniture and beams, leather wing chairs, fires and fresh flowers. A series of rooms upstairs promise sophisticated dining at antique refectory tables set with white linen. Back down in the bar, Pride of Pendle and Blonde Witch are cask conditioned, whilst a cellar of 250 wines awaits. Local lad 'done good' (most recently at Stanley House Hotel), Steven Smith produces dishes bursting with seasonal ingredients: poached and roast wood pigeon with pressed leeks and hazelnuts; steamed game pudding; organic salmon fried in vanilla oil with Morecambe Bay mussels and fennel. Magners cider granita with hot cinnamon doughnuts rounds things off beautifully.

Meals	Lunch & dinner £10.95–£28.95.
	Seasonal set menu £13.95–£15.95.
	Tasting menu £55.
Closed	Open all day.

Steven Smith
Freemasons at Wiswell,
8 Vicarage Fold, Wiswell,
Clitheroe BB7 9DF
Tel +44 (0)1254 822218
Web www.freemasonsatwiswell.com

Entry 368 Map 12

Lancashire

The Clog and Billycock
Blackburn

Following the success of the Three Fishes and the Highwayman, another winner from Ribble Valley. Now the old boozer in the leafy village close to Blackburn has crackling fires, gleaming oak furniture and an eye-catching beamed atrium: a sensitively lit showcase for a collection of black and white photographs of the pub's esteemed growers and producers. The colour scheme is subtle and calming yet there's a great buzz to the place, as staff ferry beautiful food to cosy tables. Tuck into heather-fed lamb hotpot with pickled red cabbage, follow with jam roly poly and custard. With a great outside space, an inspiring children's menu, attentive staff and fine wines and ales, this pleasingly named pub is one to get excited about.

Lancashire

The Oyster & Otter
Feniscowles

Joycelyn Neve, daughter of one of Fleetwood's most prominent fish merchants, has lavished money on this once boarded-up community boozer. The result is a swish contemporary dining pub, all blond wood floors, chunky tables, cushioned benches and modern art; business has boomed since day one. With the pick of the day's catch (and more) just a phone call away, to create a seafood-driven gastropub was the obvious aim; the appetite locally for fresh fish and seafood has been staggering. Fish lovers flock in for Malaysian seafood curry, tikka-spiced monkfish, and classic haddock and chips (also available to take away), while carnivores tuck into Gazegill Organics slow-cooked lamb, or Pendle Hill 28-day dry-aged steak with pepper sauce. Don't miss the seafood nights with wines matched to each course – or the Sunday roast lunches.

Meals	Lunch & dinner £8.95–£19.75. Sunday lunch, 3 courses, £19.50.
Closed	Open all day.

Meals	Lunch & dinner £9.50–£22.50.
Closed	Open all day.

Nigel Haworth & Craig Bancroft
The Clog and Billycock,
Billinge End Road,
Blackburn BB2 6QB
Tel   +44 (0)1254 201163
Web   www.theclogandbillycock.com

Entry 369 Map 12

Joycelyn Neve
The Oyster & Otter,
631 Livesey Branch Road,
Feniscowles, Blackburn BB2 5DQ
Tel   +44 (0)1254 203200
Web   www.oysterandotter.co.uk

Entry 370 Map 12

Lancashire

The Eagle & Child
Ramsbottom

Glen Duckett has taken a boarded-up Thwaites pub with a bad reputation and transformed it into a thriving food-led pub. A passionate desire to do something different, and a clear vision from the start, to create a community pub with top-quality food, was key to the pub's early success. Menus focus on Lancashire's food heritage and classic local recipes and ingredients are given a modern twist. Hearty and affordable dishes include black pudding Scotch egg; braised beef shin and oxtail suet pudding; plum tart and clotted cream. Disadvantaged young local people are trained in the kitchen, and, aided by community group Incredible Edible Ramsbottom, Glen has transformed former waste ground into a beer garden – a fabulous space for education, food production, drinking and dining.

Meals	Lunch from £5.95.
	Dinner from £9.95.
	Sunday lunch, 2 courses, £13.95.
Closed	Open all day.

Glen Duckett
The Eagle & Child,
3 Whalley Road, Ramsbottom,
Bury BL0 0DL
Tel   +44 (0)1706 557181
Web   www.eagle-and-child.com

Entry 371 Map 12

Lancashire

The Rams Head Inn
Denshaw

You're on the border here and the views are glorious. High on the Saddleworth moors between Oldham and Ripponden, the Rams Head is two miles from the motorway but you'd never know. Unspoilt inside and out, there's an authentic, old-farmhouse feel. Small rooms, cosy with log fires in winter, are carpeted, half-panelled, beamed, and filled with memorabilia. With a range of cask ales and wine by the glass drinkers are made very welcome. Menus announce a heart-warming selection of tasty food: game and venison in season, seafood, great steaks, puddings like treacle tart with ice cream as well as other classic British dishes. A wonderfully isolated Lancashire outpost, staffed by people who care, and with a farm shop, a deli and a tea room to boot.

Meals	Lunch & dinner £9.50–£17.95.
	Deli snacks from £2.50.
Closed	Mon all day.

G R Haigh
The Rams Head Inn,
Ripponden Road, Denshaw,
Oldham OL3 5UN
Tel   +44 (0)1457 874802
Web   www.ramsheaddenshaw.co.uk

Entry 372 Map 12

Lancashire

The Eagle & Child
Bispham Green

An old-school pub on the village green with its own shop next door. Martin has a farm up the road, so you can sample his beef in the restaurant then buy some to take home. Inside: warm colours, rugs on flagged floors, hops hanging from old beams, logs crackling on an open fire. Hand pumps line the bar, locals gather to chew the cud (one of the brewers drinks here). You can eat wherever you want, in the bar by the fire or in a cosy room up a couple of steps. Boarded menus trumpet irresistible delights, perhaps slow-cooked rib of beef or locally-shot partridge, but simpler dishes are on tap too, perhaps Irish mussels, a Lancashire hotpot or root vegetable and lentil stew. A beer festival in May brings in a crowd, as does Sunday lunch, and there's a lovely garden at the back that comes with a bowling green.

Lancashire

Farmers Arms
Great Eccleston

The Farmers Arms shines like a beacon in the Fylde. Snapped up and refurbished by the innovative Seafood Pub Company in 2013, it is worth noting should you wish to exchange the bling of Blackpool for a stylish country pub. From street food style crab and shrimp empanadas with chimichurri, and clay pot dishes like Szechuan monkfish, the menu extends to Persian chicken, beef sirloin with pepper sauce, and chalkboard fish specials. Dine al fresco at teak tables on the sheltered terrace or take your pick of four smart dining areas, kitted out with painted panelled walls, old dining tables on polished wooden floors, feature stone fireplaces with wood-burners, and rich fabrics. Pop in for a pint of Black Sheep with the papers, then bag the table by the fire in the welcoming bar.

Meals	Lunch & dinner £10-£16.50. Bar meals £3.75-£10.
Closed	3pm-5.30pm. Open all day Sat & Sun.

Meals	Lunch from £6.95. Dinner £10.50-£23.50.
Closed	Open all day.

Helen & Martin Ainscough
The Eagle & Child,
Malt Kiln Lane, Bispham Green,
Ormskirk L40 3SG
Tel   +44 (0)15394 42536
Web   www.ainscoughs.co.uk

Entry 373 Map 11

Joycelyn Neve
Farmers Arms,
Halsalls Square, Great Eccleston,
Preston PR3 0YE
Tel   +44 (0)1995 672018
Web   www.greatecclestonpub.co.uk

Entry 374 Map 11

Leicestershire

The White Swan
Shawell

Chef/patron Rory comes with a London pedigree – his food is modern and delicious – and now runs his own place in a pretty little village in Leicestershire. Everyone gets a welcome: wax jackets and walkers, foodies and families, drinkers and dogs. Inside: chesterfield sofas and two log-burners, smart dark wood dining tables and upholstered chairs, great ales from Dow Bridge and a bank of illuminated fridges showcasing the wine on offer – a great feature. It's a tasteful backdrop for glowing white platefuls of good-looking food, from braised rabbit maltagliati (pasta to you!) topped with parmesan and parsley, to beef in red wine with soft polenta, and dark chocolate and coffee mousse. Our rib-eye steak ciabatta was gorgeous, and there's a stone terrace for summer.

Meals	Lunch & dinner £12.50–£21.50.
Closed	Open all day.

Rory Mclean & Samantha Laye
The White Swan,
Main Street, Shawell,
Lutterworth LE17 6AG
Tel   +44 (0)1788 860357
Web   www.whiteswanshawell.co.uk

Entry 375 Map 8

Leicestershire

The Hercules Revived
Sutton Cheney

Behind the charming painted façade of the 18th-century Hercules, opposite the church – you can't miss it – lies a totally refurbished pub. With its oak beams and floors, and cream walls; this place has taken a dramatic turn for the better. You can sit on a stylish tweed chair and enjoy a prosecco or espresso, or nurse a Guinness with the dog by the fire. It's neat and dandy, laid-back and friendly, and there's a rather posh restaurant upstairs. Pick an area to dine in according to your mood... all have upholstered chairs and grey carpeting, and the area to the front left has a fine view across the field to the church. We hear good reports of the food: a beautiful shin of beef, a herb-crusted cod with crayfish linguine, a refreshing lemon and lime syllabub. A lovely bunch of producers supply the goods, including Leicestershire cheeses.

Meals	Lunch & dinner £10.95–£20.95.
Closed	Open all day.

Oliver & Sian Warner
The Hercules Revived,
Main Street, Sutton Cheney,
Market Bosworth CV13 0AG
Tel   +44 (0)1455 699336
Web   www.herculesrevived.co.uk

Entry 376 Map 8

Leicestershire

The Curzon Arms
Woodhouse Eaves

In the village of Woodhouse Eaves is a pub that ticks almost every box. With four well-known real ales (Timothy Taylor's Landlord, Sharp's Doom Bar, York Guzzler and Bath Gem) and Weston's Cider, this is the place to go for a pint! It attracts a crowd – suits and locals, friends and office parties, families at weekends, horses in summer, walkers en route. Refurbished in traditional style, with leather banquette seating and heritage colours, the interiors are warm and appealing. Painted beam ceilings and prints on the walls, a chesterfield sofa, a box of toys, log-burners belting out the heat. There are a 'pie of the day' and a 'catch of the day,' too, a cheese platter with tasting notes, wines to satisfy most, and chips crisp and hot. The terrace is attractive even on a winter's day and the garden is big enough to play in.

Leicestershire

The Cow & Plough
Oadby

A one-storey pub housed in the former milking sheds of a working farm just outside Leicester. The Lounts founded it in 1989 and filled it with good beer and a hoard of brewery memorabilia: the back bars are stuffed with tin plate ads, mirrors and bottles, and there's a conservatory with piano and plants and beams decked with dried hops. It later became an outlet for their Steamin' Billy ales (named after Elizabeth's Jack Russell who 'steamed' after energetic country pursuits). In the farm's old visitor centre is the restaurant, its high beams draped with fairylights and lanterns, cosy backdrop to generous portions of pub classics and some more adventurous mains. The pub has won awards and become a place for shooting lunches; it's also popular with the Leicester rugby team supporters.

Meals	Lunch from £5.95.
	Dinner, 2-3 courses, £15.95–£18.95.
Closed	Open all day Sat & Sun.

Meals	Bar meals from £6.95.
	Lunch from £9.95.
	Dinner from £12.95.
	Sunday lunch, 3 courses, £14.95.
Closed	Open all day.

Ben Moore
The Curzon Arms,
44 Maplewell Road,
Woodhouse Eaves LE12 8QZ
Tel   +44 (0)1509 890377
Web   www.thecurzonarms.com

Entry 377 Map 8

Leighton Turner
The Cow & Plough,
Stoughton Grange Farm, Gartree
Road, Oadby, Leicester LE2 2FB
Tel   +44 (0)116 272 0852
Web   www.steamin-billy.co.uk

Entry 378 Map 8

Red Lion Inn
Stathern

Quirky stylishness and cheerful service. The rambling Red Lion feels like a home, with its books and papers, steep settles and open fires; gamekeepers frequent the flagstoned bar. A trusted network of growers and suppliers fills the kitchen with game from the Belvoir estate, cheeses from the local dairy, fruits and vegetables from nearby farms. Blackboard specials offer a choice that leaps between fashion and tradition: seared scallops with spiced yellow split pea dahl; village-made sausages with mustard mash; braised fillet of brill, mushroom fricassée; treacle tart, fruit compote, clotted cream ice cream. The set Sunday lunch is good value, the wine list is imaginative, beers include their own ale, cocktails include their own blackberries and strawberries, and children have homemade lemonade. Superb.

The Berkeley Arms
Wymondham

In the middle of the village of Wymondham is an exemplary pub. Enter a low-beamed, pine-tabled, light-filled room, with an original terracotta tiled floor and a fire at the carpeted end. It's a wonderfully intimate place to drink and eat, and if you prefer to be more formal, there's a stylish dining room too. Owners Louise and Neil met at Hambleton Hall so the food is special and the suppliers are lovingly listed. Pigeons, tomatoes and rhubarb come from Ray and Pam Elsome; mint, marrows and flowers from Ken Hill. We tried the pâté of rabbit, pork and prune; the pasta with pickled walnuts, reblochon cheese and truffle oil; the pear and ginger crumble with pear sorbet — all were exquisite. In summer you can stroll in the garden, take in the pretty views, retreat to the smokers' shelter. Staff are friendly, polite, perfect.

Meals	Bar meals from £6.50. Lunch & dinner from £9.95. Sunday lunch, 3 courses, £19.50.
Closed	3pm-6pm. Sun evenings & Mon all day. Open all day Fri & Sat.

Meals	Bar meals from £10. Lunch from £14.95. Dinner from £25. Sunday lunch, 2 courses, £17.95.
Closed	Sun evenings & all day Mon.

Ben Jones & Sean Hope
Red Lion Inn,
2 Red Lion Street, Stathern,
Melton Mowbray LE14 4HS

Tel +44 (0)1949 860868
Web www.theredlioninn.co.uk

Entry 379 Map 9

Neil & Louise Hitchen
The Berkeley Arms,
59 Main Street, Wymondham,
Melton Mowbray LE14 2AG

Tel +44 (0)1572 787587
Web www.theberkeleyarms.co.uk

Entry 380 Map 9

Lincolnshire

The Chequers Inn
Woolsthorpe

A perfect English inn with beautiful country all around and Belvoir castle looming over the fields as you drop down into the village. In summer, the cricket team play in the field behind, popping in to quench their thirst after a hard day's work. The Chequers started life as a bakery, but has been an inn for 200 years, and is now the hub of this estate village. With exposed timbers, a rug-strewn bar, Farrow & Ball colours and a flurry of open fires, it marries old-fashioned charm with rustic chic. The bar is beautifully busy with four hand-pumped ales, plenty of wines by the glass, 50 malt whiskies, and 30 gins. Food is eaten across four rooms, the robust dishes a satisfying mix of traditional and modern: quail and pigeon, rib of beef, fillet of bream with chive mash, mulled poached pear with cinnamon ice cream. Four cute bedrooms wait in the stable block. The big room at the top, recently refurbished, is coolly contemporary with a fabulous state-of-the-art wet room; find crisp white linen and accent wallpapers in those below. The vale of Belvoir and its grand castle wait.

Rooms	3 doubles: £75.
	1 family room for 4: £120.
	Singles from £50.
Meals	Lunch from £4.95.
	Dinner from £13.
	Sunday roast from £13.95
Closed	25, 26 December & 1 January afternoons.

Justin & Joanne Chad
The Chequers Inn,
Main Street, Woolsthorpe,
Grantham NG32 1LU
Tel   +44 (0)1476 870701
Web   www.chequersinn.net

Entry 381 Map 9

The Six Bells
Witham on the Hill

The latest venture from feted restaurateurs Jim and Sharon, and the trimmings in the front bar tell you everything about the place: mammoth barista machine at one end, champagne bucket beside the beer pumps, log-fired bread oven in the corner. This century-old village manor house has been made over with polished floors, wainscoting in Annie Sloan colours, and a trio of ceramic ducks flying ironically above the bar. The hipsterish staff ferry good-looking food to the table: signature steaks from butcher Owen Taylor; caramel crème brûlée with sweet and sour apples. Classy cooking for sure, but the Six Bells appeals to all: tuck in to homemade pizza for a tenner, ale from Star Brewing, and you can take home a loaf from that aromatic oven. Digest dinner by the woodburner with a complimentary tot of homemade mint vodka; it doesn't half soften the blow. Better still, retire upstairs to one of three newly primped bedrooms. Doubles are compact and tidily tailored, with carved beds and accent wallpapers, iPod docks and Nespresso makers. The star is the Hayloft suite, with original windows and village views.

Rooms	2 doubles: £80–£95. 1 suite: £120–£150.
Meals	Lunch from £7.50. Dinner, two courses, £20. Sunday roast from £13.
Closed	31 December–1 January.

Jim & Sharon Trevor
The Six Bells,
Main Street, Witham on the Hill,
Bourne PE10 0JH

Tel	+44 (0)1778 590360
Web	www.sixbellswitham.co.uk

Lincolnshire

The Bull & Swan
Stamford

A magical renovation, an ancient inn that stands a short walk from the middle of glorious Stamford, part of the Burghley estate. The Order of Little Bedlam, a 17th-century aristocratic drinking club, would surely have popped in for the odd snifter. Not that they had it this good… step inside to discover varnished wood floors, golden stone walls, fires smouldering all over the place and newspapers hanging on poles. At the bar venison Scotch eggs are impossible to resist, as are a raft of local ales and splendid wines. You eat wherever you want, here or in the dining room across the coach arch, where leather-backed settles take the strain and regal oils adorn the walls. As for beautiful bedrooms, they come in country-house style with huge beds, fabulous linen, warm colours and super-funky bathrooms. Most are big, all are delightful, two interconnect for families, and mattresses are divine. Downstairs, delicious food waits, perhaps stilton on toast, Burghley game pie, apple and blueberry crumble. And don't miss Burghley, a five-minute stroll, one of Britain's finest houses.

Rooms	5 doubles, 2 twins: £100–£140. Dinner, B&B £75–£95 per person per night.
Meals	Lunch from £5.50. Dinner from £12.95. Sunday roast from £13.95.
Closed	Rarely.

Paul Brown
The Bull & Swan,
St Martins,
Stamford PE9 2LJ

Tel	+44 (0)1780 766412
Web	www.thebullandswan.co.uk

Entry 383 Map 9

The White Hart
Ufford

Wash up at the White Hart and mix with the locals, drawn by the country atmosphere and the bar. The ales are good too: Oakham Jeffrey Hudson, Fullers London Pride, Adnam's Southwold. Farmers gather on Fridays, the cricket team drops by on Sundays; in summer life spills onto the terrace. Flags, floorboards and a log burner continue the rustic feel; railway signs, wooden pitch forks and hanging station lamps add colour. You can eat simply or more grandly, anything from a ploughman's to a three-course feast, much is seasonal and complemented by the wine list; great cheese boards, too. Walk through rooms with lovely scrubbed tables to the Orangery, a conservatory-style restaurant furnished with Lloyd Loom chairs. This forgotten slip of England — Stamford is five miles — is prettier than most imagine.

Meals	Lunch & dinner £10–£15. Bar meals £5.25–£8.75. Sunday lunch, 3 courses, £19.50. Not Sunday eve.
Closed	Open all day.

Michael Thurlby & Sue Olver
The White Hart,
Main Street, Ufford,
Stamford PE9 3BH
Tel   +44 (0)1780 740250
Web   www.whitehartufford.co.uk

Entry 384 Map 9

The Tobie Norris
Stamford

Built in 1280, remodelled in 1663 and 2006, the Tobie Norris draws you in to a warren of stunningly atmospheric rooms and takes you back to the old days — Cromwellian at least. Huge stone flags, oak settles and the smell of woodsmoke assail you as you leave the pavements behind. Between the main rooms is a staircase leading to three more, each with vast exposed timbers, little recesses and tiny doors, character and style. Find a church pew or a leather armchair and sit back with your Ufford Ales and Adnams — or a wine from a list of 21, each available by the glass. Dogs doze on bare boards, perfect staff ferry pizzas and plates of smoked salmon linguine there are rotating ales on tap and you could stay here all day.

Meals	Lunch, bar meals & dinner from £9.95. Not Sunday eve.
Closed	Open all day.

Michael Thurlby & Will Fry
The Tobie Norris,
12 St Paul's Street,
Stamford PE9 2BE
Tel   +44 (0)1780 753800
Web   www.tobienorris.com

Entry 385 Map 9

Lincolnshire

The White Horse
Baston

When a village campaign to save this 18th-century local foundered, farmer Mark Richardson rode to the rescue – and how. The stoutly rustic Spinning Wheel has become the rather slinky White Horse, enlivened by what Mark calls a "meaty, manly menu" of Baston-reared produce and a smiling welcome from its young team. The bricks in the bay window are from the Richardson family farm, the stripped-back beams have been rifled from Grandad's barn, and (best of all) a handsome slice of felled sycamore serves as a counter in the snug. Mark's real coup, though, was tempting Ben and Germaine Larter to come run the place: Ben bossing the kitchen with a chef's eye, Germaine keen as mustard that everyone has a great time. Don't miss their exemplary Sunday roasts, super value and filled with flavour.

Lincolnshire

Smith's of Bourne
Bourne

For 140 years this was John Smith's Grocers, where four generations of men in crisp white overalls dispensed sugar, butter and bacon by the pound. You feel they would approve of its immaculate reinvention as a high street alehouse, from the beautiful green-and-gold picture windows to the panelled front bar, busy with intriguing bric-a-brac. A first visit to Smith's is an adventure, its warren of sepia-lit rooms bringing surprises at every door. There's an old-fashioned cook's pantry with titanic inglenook; a hop-hung minstrel's gallery; even a room done up like stables, with horses' troughs and tin buckets for lampshades. More importantly, the victuals here still bring the townsfolk flocking: six real ales from across the nation, and hearty beef pie and pot-roast partridge sourced from local fields and served in vintage cookware.

Meals	Lunch £6.50–£9.
	Dinner £11.50–£16.50.
	Sunday lunch, 1-3 courses, £12–£18.
	Not Monday, Tuesday lunch or
	Sunday eve.
Closed	Mon & Tues lunch.

Meals	Light lunch from £5.
	Meals £11–£19.
	Platter to share £16–£22.
	Sundays noon-3pm only.
Closed	Open all day.

Ben & Germaine Larter
The White Horse,
4 Church Street, Baston,
Peterborough PE6 9PE
Tel +44 (0)1778 560923
Web www.thewhitehorsebaston.co.uk

Entry 386 Map 9

Pat & Jane Taylor
Smith's of Bourne,
25 North Street,
Bourne PE10 9AE
Tel +44 (0)1778 426819
Web www.smithsofbourne.co.uk

Entry 387 Map 9

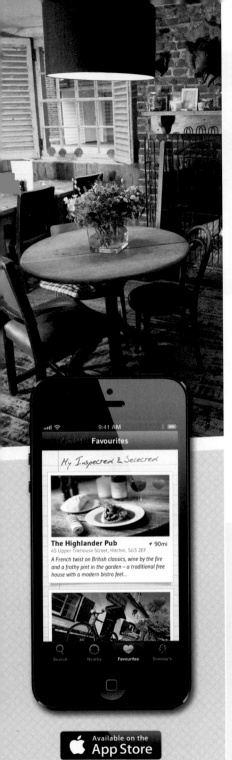

Lincolnshire

The New Inn
Grimsby

Beautifully refurbished village inn on the Brockelsby estate, built in the 16th century to welcome hungry travellers. Outside, you find a kitchen garden, a well-kept lawn and a smart terrace for lunch in the sun. Inside, a country-house feel runs through the restaurant — smart fabrics, pretty colours, art from the estate. The bar has attitude, too: grey panelling, red suede banquettes, a roaring fire and pints of hand-drawn local ales. Back in the restaurant, Ian's delicious food waits. He's worked alongside Gordon Ramsay, Raymond Blanc and Michael Caines, and much of what you eat is grown or reared on the estate, perhaps Jerusalem artichoke and truffle soup, saddle of venison with roasted root vegetables, caramelised pear with butterscotch sauce. Walk it off in the North Lincolnshire wolds; sublime, yet ignored, you'll have them all to yourself. Worth a detour.

Meals	Bar menu from £3.50. Lunch, 2 courses £15, 3 courses £18. Dinner from £14.50.
Closed	Open all day.

Ian & Lisa Matfin
The New Inn,
2 High Street, Great Limber,
Grimsby DN37 8JL
Tel   +44 (0)1469 569998
Web   www.thenewinngreatlimber.co.uk

Entry 388 Map 13

The Victoria
Richmond

In the leafy suburb of Richmond, with a church and Sheen Common as neighbours, this long-established pub has been transformed by Greg Bellamy and Paul Merret. Find wooden floors, open brickwork, and sofas to flop on as you check out the menu for long, leisurely meals in the conservatory. Here, foodies and families tuck into crisp-battered Cornish squid with tomato, mint, chilli and lime; pan-roasted guinea fowl with spiced pastilla and smoked aubergine; pecan and walnut baklava with nectarine and honey ice cream. Beef comes from a small butcher in Devon, mussels from Norfolk and there's a forager for the elderflower and mushrooms! The wine list bursts with passion and helpful notes: a shame not to allow yourself to be led. The atmosphere is friendly, purposeful and fun, so stay a while: in the back wing are seven comfortable, contemporary-style bedrooms with iPod docks and WiFi; the quietest are at the top and the breakfasts are great. You are within striking distance of a cycle ride through Richmond Park, and ten minutes from Twickenham if rugby is your passion. And there's a play garden for children.

Rooms	5 doubles, 2 twin/doubles: £120–£150. Singles £125.
Meals	Lunch & bar meals from £6. Dinner from £13. Sunday lunch £24–£28. Set menu, 2 courses, £12.50 (Monday-Thursday).
Closed	Rarely.

Bookings Team at The Victoria
The Victoria,
10 West Temple Sheen,
Richmond SW14 7RT
Tel   +44 (0)20 8876 4238
Web   www.thevictoria.net

The Orange Public House & Hotel
Belgravia

Tall sash windows, lofty ceilings and distressed furniture and floorboards give The Orange its smartly weathered good looks. The lovingly restored corner-sited Georgian building (a brewery in a past life) comes flooded by light and looks out over Orange Square, its bustling ground-floor bar delivering ales like Sussex Best, or well-chosen wines and seasonal cocktails to a well-heeled Sloaney crowd in its labyrinth of character rooms. Upstairs and downstairs this is one stylish, all-occasions affair, with a slightly more formal restaurant on the first floor and fashionable bedrooms above. Smiley, clued-up young staff ferry dishes to and fro, the modern European menu changing with the seasons; take an opener pork, fennel and manchego scotch egg (with romesco sauce), and after that, maybe one of the wood-fired pizzas (Laverstoke Farm buffalo mozzarella, tomato and basil perhaps) or mains like Anglesey mussels in a bouillabaisse sauce with pomme frites. Of the four country-chic bedrooms — all pastel beige and sage green with lightwood floors, king-sized beds and marble bathrooms — one has a bathtub and pitched-roof ceiling crossed by beams. Breakfasts are a must.

Rooms	4 doubles: £205–£240.
Meals	Bar meals from £5.
	Lunch from £6.50.
	Dinner from £10.50.
	Sunday lunch, 3 courses, £30.
Closed	Rarely.

Reservations
The Orange Public House & Hotel,
37 Pimlico Road,
Belgravia SW1W 8NE

Tel	+44 (0)20 7881 9844
Web	www.theorange.co.uk

Entry 390 Map 4

The Grazing Goat
Marylebone

Where goats once grazed, smart boutiques flourish, but you barely know you're in the heart of town. Step inside, to a stylish serene space of light oak tables, sage green walls and beige textiles – more country cool than urban glitz. Graze on eggs Benedict at breakfast; at lunch, or dinner, move onto house cocktails and well-chosen wines. Dishes might include line-caught cod fillet with crushed baby potatoes, sautéed spinach and a pickled beetroot dressing, or 28-day dried Castle of Mey fillet steak from the grill. What's good about this intimate pub (little sister to the characterful Thomas Cubitt and The Orange) is that it attracts a varied crowd, from chaps in suits to Portman village locals and tourists taking a break from Oxford Street. Ales include Doom Bar, juice is freshly squeezed, breakfasts are superb. There's a slightly more formal restaurant upstairs and eight bedrooms over a further three floors. Each comes in boutique country-house style; marble bathrooms have roll top tubs or powerful showers; cool neutral shades and sash windows keep things super-fresh.

Rooms	8 doubles: £210–£250.
Meals	Bar meals from £8.
	Lunch £9.50.
	Dinner from £15.50.
	Sunday lunch, 3 courses, £30.
Closed	Rarely.

Reservations
The Grazing Goat,
6 New Quebec Street,
Marylebone W1H 7RQ
Tel +44 (0)20 7724 7243
Web www.thegrazinggoat.co.uk

London

The Punchbowl
Mayfair

Near the higgledy-piggledy streets of Shepherds Market is the handsome Punchbowl, now spread over three floors and cunningly fusing Georgian tradition with up-to-the-minute glamour. Inside this former Court, the ground floor is a smart country-city pub, while upstairs is an art deco dining room. Up again to the Club for private parties in an opulent Victorian setting. At the bar, law-abiding Londoners sample pints of IPA Deuchars or the pub's own tipple '1750' with braised shin and bone marrow on beef dripping toast perhaps, or a hearty burger. In the dining room, you can feast on the likes of pan-fried lemon sole, or smoked Yorkshire venison loin, and there may be time to sneak in a dark chocolate and orange slice with bitter chocolate sorbet before the last cry of 'order'.

London

The Thomas Cubitt
Belgravia

As well-upholstered as Belgravia itself, the ground-floor bar has high ceilings, oak-block floors, tall windows that open to tables in the street and a bit of panelling thrown in for good measure. A cords and cashmere crowd is drawn by the classic country-house feel, the real ales, the superb wines, and the kitchen, which puts more thought into what it produces than many a full-blown restaurant. In the bar is a reassuring selection of pub favourites — organic beef burgers, grilled sausages with roasted red onion gravy and buttery mash — and the organic Sunday roasts are great. In the elegant dove-grey dining room upstairs the food is fiercely modern (take grilled tuna with red pepper and pearl barley and langoustine bisque). It's popular, and the friendliness of the staff, even under pressure, is a pleasure.

Meals	Lunch & dinner £6.50-£30.
Closed	Open all day.

Meals	Lunch from £12.
	Dinner from £13.50.
	Sunday roast from £17.
Closed	Open all day.

James Mitchell
The Punchbowl,
41 Farm Street,
Mayfair W1J 5RP
Tel +44 (0)20 7493 6841
Web www.punchbowllondon.com

Entry 392 Map 4

The Manager
The Thomas Cubitt,
44 Elizabeth St,
Belgravia SW1W 9PA
Tel +44 (0)20 7730 6060
Web www.thethomascubitt.co.uk

Entry 393 Map 4

The Pantechnicon Rooms
Belgravia

This pretty Georgian 'public house and dining room' sits in a landmark location near Sloane Street, the perfect spot for people watching. Inside: mellow walls, oval sash windows, soft jazz and a big buzz – very SW1. Take your time; this isn't somewhere to pop into; punters are here for serious drinks and canapés in the private room upstairs, or for the food which is pricey but praiseworthy, upmarket pub grub. The weekend brunches (served until 4pm) caught our eye – how about sage and sweetcorn fritters with streaky bacon, avocado and heirloom tomatoes, or an open fillet steak sandwich with spinach, fried egg and béarnaise sauce? If you stay for lunch, you can indulge in Carlingford rock oysters, or settle in for one of their famous Sunday roasts. The bar is dog-friendly, and Knightsbridge beckons.

Meals	Starters from £8.
	Dinner from £12.
	Sunday roast from £16.50.
Closed	9am–midday, Mon–Fri.

Saskia van de Wetering de Rooy
The Pantechnicon Rooms,
10 Motcombe Street,
Belgravia SW1X 8LA

Tel   +44 (0)20 7730 6074
Web www.thepantechnicon.com

Entry 394 Map 4

Admiral Codrington
Chelsea

It may be hiding down a Chelsea back street, but the savvy beat a path to The Cod. Recently remodelled, the Victorian-style central bar is rich in dark-wood panelling, floorboards, furniture, while pale green walls are hung with prints; banquettes, sofas and subtle lighting add softness. The restaurant, by contrast, is a light contemporary space with a retractable glass skylight (a wow in summer), low-slung green seats, straw coloured wall banquettes, and fishy prints to reflect the nautical name. Tuck into delicate chilli salt squid and a pint of Upham Punters on the small all-weather terrace, or a hearty Black Angus rump and ever-popular beer-battered fish and chips in the restaurant. Or how about line caught sea trout with pak choi, roast salsify and shellfish oil, and a chilled bottle of Gavi di Gavi?

Meals	Lunch from £9.95.
	Dinner, 3 courses, from £23.75.
Closed	Open all day.

Siobhain Mosley
Admiral Codrington,
17 Mossop Street,
Chelsea SW3 2LY

Tel   +44 (0)20 7581 0005
Web www.theadmiralcodrington.co.uk

Entry 395 Map 4

London

The Pig's Ear
Chelsea

Off the King's Road, a great little corner pub serving Uley Pig's Ear on tap and a zippy Bloody Mary – drinking is encouraged. In the chattering bar (this is Chelsea) are high ceilings, planked floors, big mirrors, a zinc-top bar and formica tables; upstairs, a cosy sash-windowed dining room with twinkly lights and not a touch of Victoriana. Staff are knowledgeable, casually dressed and perky in keeping with the spirit of the place. Cooking is rousingly rustic – part French, part English. The beef brisket and ox cheek casserole, topped with robust Jerusalem artichoke crisps, was deep flavoured and succulent; the orange panna cotta smooth, citrusy and decorated with a sesame tuile. There are cured herrings and rock oysters, and most nights it's rammed.

Meals	Bar meals from £5.50.
	Lunch from £8.50.
	Dinner from £14.
	Sunday lunch, 3 courses, £26.
Closed	Open all day.

Simon Cherry
The Pig's Ear,
35 Old Church Street,
Chelsea SW3 5BS

Tel +44 (0)20 7352 2908
Web www.thepigsear.info

Entry 396 Map 4

London

The Sands End
Fulham

Down a residential street off Wandsworth Bridge Road the faithful flock. One of the business partners was formerly an equerry to the Prince of Wales (sightings of the young princes are not unfounded) but its popularity is most likely down to its menu, market-based, daily-changing and surprisingly affordable. The food zings with flavour – queen scallops with spinach and smoked gubbeen; braised beef, onion and mushroom pie; chocolate brownie – and complements the urban rusticity of scrubbed tables, planked floors and displays of bottled produce. While half the place is restaurant, the rest is old-fashioned bar, serving beers, wine and slices of hand-raised pork pie. Staff are friendly and attitude-free.

Meals	Lunch & dinner £12–£18.
	Bar meals from £3.
Closed	Open all day.

Eamonn Manson & Mark Dyer
The Sands End,
135–137 Stephendale Road,
Fulham SW6 2PR

Tel +44 (0)20 7731 7823
Web www.thesandsend.co.uk

Entry 397 Map 4

London

The Harwood Arms
Fulham

A pint's throw from Fulham Broadway. There's an easy-on-the-eye modernity to this big-windowed gastropub on the corner, well-dressed with a Shaker-ish feel and a Michelin star. Menus, driven by seasonality and provenance, revel in an intelligent simplicity, with game a speciality. The chef is Barry Fitzgerald (ex Arbutus and Wild Honey) so you're in mighty good hands. Expect to book days or weeks in advance – for game 'tea' served with a venison sausage roll; pheasant Kiev with champ and turnips glazed with mead; warm Bramley apple doughnuts with spiced sugar; sweet egg custard tart with drunk raisins. Hand-pump ales, well-chosen wines, tasty bar snacks, a classy vegetarian menu and a laid-back but informed staff make this one civilised bolthole.

London

The Princess Victoria
Shepherd's Bush

Once a Georgian gin palace, then an Irish boozer, now a big, light-filled, parquet-floored pub, with a curve of bar selling cask ales and shelves stacked with wines to the ceiling. Despite this the focus of the Princess lies in the dining room beyond, a beautiful room of French elegant panelled walls and high ceilings, candelabras, mirrors, old oils (and stuffed animals – there's a country-house feel). People travel far and wide for the food and Matt Reuther likes to keep it British; they also have an on-site charcuterie. Friendly staff ferry luscious dishes to big tables, from crispy pig cheeks to rock oysters. Obviously it's more restaurant than pub, but note the blackboard of guest beers, and ongoing support of local producers like Sipsmith Gin.

Meals	Bar snacks £3-£8.
	Lunch & dinner, 2 courses,
	£25-£33.50.
Closed	Mon lunch.

Meals	Bar meals from £9.50.
	Lunch from £10.
	Dinner from £12.50.
Closed	Open all day.

Brett Graham & Mike Robinson
The Harwood Arms,
Walham Grove,
Fulham SW6 1QP
Tel   +44 (0)20 7386 1847
Web   www.harwoodarms.com

🐾 🏃 ✈ 📶

Entry 398 Map 4

James McLean
The Princess Victoria,
217 Uxbridge Road,
Shepherd's Bush W12 9DT
Tel   +44 (0)20 8749 5886
Web   www.princessvictoria.co.uk

🏃 ✈ 🐕 🍷 📶

Entry 399 Map 4

London

Havelock Tavern
Brook Green

The staff are brilliant, the owners are new, and the dedication to wonderful food has not wavered. On the corner of a residential street behind Brook Green, this is not a restaurant in an old pub: it's a pub that serves good food. The kitchen hatch is ever open and the blackboard changes twice daily, the ales are numerous, so are the wines (many by the glass) and the room is abuzz with all ages. The floor is planked, there's a mishmash of tables, the sun adds a sparkle, a small fire crackles away. Chalked up on the board at lunch time we saw borlotti bean soup with parmesan, roast duck breast with a sorrel salad, crème brûlée with pistachio biscuits, platters of British cheeses... All of it thoughtfully sourced, all of it delicious. On Saturday afternoons the Kings Cross Jazz Club comes to play.

The Hampshire Hog
Hammersmith

Opposite the likes of Kings Kebabs & Pizzas, the little painted pig flies proudly out the front of this 'pantry-pub', fighting its quirky corner. This is a beacon on the Hammersmith/Ravenscourt border, a light bright refuge to which locals are drawn, from chatty office workers to breakfasting babies; at weekends, families descend. Wooden floors have been stripped and walls painted cream, wicker chairs have sheepskin throws, chandeliers twinkle and flowers top tables. To the left of the bar is the Pantry, its walls lined with lagers, wines, chutneys, breads, coffees and jams, its tables bright with fresh organic dishes. (Our rare chargrilled beef with shaved vegetables, green papaya and pomegranate salad was delicious.) The bar fronts an open-hatch kitchen; the dining area opens to a pretty garden. One for foodies.

Meals	Starters from £5.50.
	Dinner from £11.50.
Closed	Open all day.

Meals	Bar meals from £4.50.
	Lunch & dinner £5.50–£22.
	Sunday roast £5.50–£19.
	Not Sunday eve.
Closed	Sun evenings.

	Jonny Haughton & Pete Richnell
	Havelock Tavern,
	57 Masbro Road,
	Brook Green W14 0LS
Tel	+44 (0)20 7603 5374
Web	www.havelocktavern.com

ᯤ ᚷ ᕽ ᗌ ᯤ ᕽ

Entry 400 Map 4

	Macarena Freire
	The Hampshire Hog,
	227 King Street,
	Hammersmith W6 9JT
Tel	+44 (0)20 8748 3391
Web	www.thehampshirehog.com

ᯤ ᚷ ᕽ ᯤ ᕽ

Entry 401 Map 4

The Anglesea Arms
Hammersmith

Everyone loves Hammersmith's long-running Anglesea — home to the well-heeled and the young at heart. Find an opened-up space and an endearingly shabby-chic interior, a log fire, a chesterfield, retro furniture and banquette seating. It's high octane but convivial, the bar delivering four ales and a score of wines by glass. As for the cooking, it's fabulous, ferried from an open theatre kitchen to a relaxed sky-lit dining area. Ticking all the local-and-seasonal boxes, dishes, chalked up on a daily-changing menu, are uncomplicated and flavour-driven: skate with butterbean casserole and salsa verde; panna cotta with winter berries; steamed orange pudding and custard. You can dine wherever you like, including the cordoned-off front terrace in summer. Lovely!

The Carpenter's Arms
Hammersmith

An extraordinary distillation of gastropub and local in a charming backwater between King Street and the Great West Road (aka the A4). The glorious single bar has bare boards, plain tables, a fire that glows on chilly days and doors giving onto a sheltered little garden. And it's done well for itself, being a popular spot for a discerning mix while managing (just) to hold on to its pubby feel. An ever-changing seasonal menu sees inventive dishes popping up every day: seared scallops with butterbeans, pine nuts and saffron; rib-eye steak with fries and Café de Paris butter; apple tart 'fine' with nutmeg ice cream. Service is exuberant and warm, the atmosphere is laid back. It's a satisfying place to dine.

Meals	Lunch from £10.
	Dinner from £14.
	Sunday roast from £17.
Closed	Open all day.

Meals	Lunch & dinner £8–£16.95.
Closed	Open all day.

Michael Mann
The Anglesea Arms,
35 Wingate Road,
Hammersmith W6 0UR
Tel   +44 (0)20 8749 1291
Web   www.anglesea-arms.com

Simon Cherry & Matt Jacomb
The Carpenter's Arms,
91 Black Lion Lane,
Hammersmith W6 9BG
Tel   +44 (0)20 8741 8386
Web   www.carpentersarmsw6.co.uk

Entry 402 Map 4

Entry 403 Map 4

The Brown Dog
Barnes

Set the satnav to find a small, friendly gem, hiding down the streets of pretty Barnes 'village' – great after a Richmond Park romp. Post makeover it's opened-up and pared-back. Copper lights dangle from the red ceiling over the bar, there are floorboards, banquette seats and solid-wood furniture. Not a lot of passing trade here, just regulars with their families and their dogs (pig's ears are stocked behind the bar). It's as much gastro as pub, the kitchen driven by top seasonal ingredients and a light modish touch. Try the classics – shepherd's pie – or the posh: roasted monkfish tails with baked pumpkin, curly kale and sage pesto. Local-brewery cask ales and well-selected wines up the ante, while a rear terrace keeps al fresco lovers on board.

The Ship
Wandsworth

Drinking a pint of Young's Special next to a concrete works doesn't sound enticing, but the riverside terrace by Wandsworth Bridge is a dreamy spot. Chilly evenings still draw the crowds to this super old pub, so cosy with its warm-red and sage-green walls, and to its conservatory, with a central chopping-board table and a wood-burning stove. Chef Shaun Harrington sources fresh ingredients to create his seasonal menus. Try braised pork belly with caramelised white cabbage, fondant potato and bacon and herb dumplings; parsnip, tomato and goat's cheese gratin; Jerusalem artichoke and chestnut mushroom fricassée. The Ship opens its arms to all, there are live acoustic duos, Irish music on Tuesdays, and quiz nights. Families and friends gather merrily in summer.

Meals	Lunch & dinner £8.25–£17.
Closed	Open all day.

Meals	Lunch & dinner £9.95–£19.95.
Closed	Open all day.

	Andrew Marshall
	The Brown Dog,
	28 Cross Street,
	Barnes SW13 0AP
Tel	+44 (0)20 8392 2200
Web	www.thebrowndog.co.uk

Entry 404 Map 4

	Oisin Rogers
	The Ship,
	41 Jews Row,
	Wandsworth SW18 1TB
Tel	+44 (0)20 8870 9667
Web	www.theship.co.uk

Entry 405 Map 4

The Alma
Wandsworth

Exceedingly handsome in up-and-come Wandsworth, the much-loved Alma is named after a Crimean battle. Its green tiled façade is still intact, as are its parquet floors and mahogany bar. Above, a mirrored staircase looks down on the jolly hubbub below. The staff are relaxed but attentive and you can drink whatever you like – vodka, gin, malts, wines by the glass, Young's and guest ales. The restaurant is more formal – soft blue walls, blue check tweed chairs – but it's still mostly stuffed with locals enjoying the fresh, seasonal produce and the popular homemade pies. Tuck into good old-fashioned pub grub, or savour slowly the warm mushroom salad with pomegranates, the sea bream with prawn butter, the lemon tart with thyme sorbet.

The Jolly Gardeners
Wandsworth

The pub is home to the delightful Dhruv – born in Mexico, raised in India, winner of Master Chef 2010. Now, in an unprepossessing street in Earlsfield, he is pursuing his dream. Lucky locals: the food is a mix of modern Mediterranean, classic pub and exotic oriental, and the old Victorian boozer is packed every night. It's a building of two halves: handsome L-shaped front (bare boards, high ceilings, modish colours) and, at the back, a roofed conservatory with an open kitchen hatch. Sink into the soft leather sofa with an award-winning pint (Wandle, Northcote Blond) or get stuck in to a gastronomic night. There's pork belly with carrot and cardamom purée; baked aubergine with Italian cheeses and hazelnut pesto; rhubarb and vanilla panna cotta. We chose spiced crab cakes with fennel and tamarind yoghurt and they were absolutely delicious.

Meals	Starters from £4.95.
	Dinner from £11.95.
Closed	Open all day.

Meals	Starters from £6.50.
	Lunch & dinner from £11.50.
Closed	Open all day Mon-Sat
	& midday-6pm Sun.

2015/16
Sawday's
PUB AWARD

Favourite newcomer

Sean Young
The Alma,
499 Old York Road,
Wandsworth SW18 1TF
Tel   +44 (0)20 8870 2537
Web   www.almawandsworth.com

Entry 406 Map 4

Stephen Robb
The Jolly Gardeners,
214 Garratt Lane,
Wandsworth SW18 4EA
Tel   +44 (0)20 8870 8417
Web   www.thejollygardeners.co.uk

Entry 407 Map 4

London

Canton Arms
Stockwell

In increasingly salubrious Stockwell is a high-ceilinged, screen-dominated bar, aimed at those in for a pint. Beyond: ox-red panelled walls, Edwardian mirrors, leaded windows, fat candles and diners of all ages. No bookings, it's first come first served, and you can linger as long as you like; note the teapots and the books. Trish Hilferty, "unsung heroine of the gastropub scene", heads the kitchen. The foie gras toasties are legendary and the menu changes daily with lunch smaller than dinner: three starters, three mains, big rustic flavours and a special way with meat. Imagine slow-cooked Hereford beef shoulder with roasties, and panna cotta with grappa and quince. Drinks range from Bloody Mary to Black Sheep from Yorkshire to marvellous wines. A pub driven by passion, it's superb value. Give it a whirl.

London

The Crooked Well
Camberwell

Set up by a group of friends sharing a love of great food (and a training at Le Gavroche and Hotel du Vin) this new-wave neighbourhood pub stands between vibrant Camberwell and leafy Grove Lane. The commitment is to rustic British food, with the emphasis on shared dishes (such as rabbit and bacon pie) and family-roast platters on Sundays. On Matt's menu find scallop and squid ink risotto; Torbay sole with capers and anchovy; treacle tart with orange mascarpone. Basking in natural light, the elegant bar-dining room has a laid-back feel, with comfy armchairs in one corner. In the stylish dining section, Art Deco wallpaper and candles on eclectic tables. Cocktails, wine by the carafe, jazz nights, BYO wine dinners and fish-and-chip Fridays complete this pleasing picture.

Meals	Bar meals from £2.80.
	Lunch from £8.80.
	Dinner from £14.
	Sunday roast £14.
	Not Sunday eve or Monday lunch.
Closed	Mon until 5pm.

Meals	Lunch & dinner £8.75–£17.90.
Closed	Open all day.

Trish Hilferty
Canton Arms,
177 South Lambeth Road,
Stockwell SW8 1XP
Tel +44 (0)20 7582 8710
Web www.cantonarms.com

Entry 408 Map 4

Hector Skinner & Jen Aries
The Crooked Well,
16 Grove Lane,
Camberwell SE5 8SY
Tel +44 (0)20 7252 7798
Web www.thecrookedwell.com

Entry 409 Map 4

London

Anchor & Hope
Southwark

Come for some of the plainest yet gutsiest cooking in London; chef Jonathan Jones attracts a crowd. The food is described as 'English bistro', and give or take the odd foreign exception (a chorizo broth, a melting pommes dauphinoise), it is just that. The menu is adventurous yet striking in its simplicity: warm snail and bacon salad, smoked herring with fennel and orange, slip soles with anchovy butter, rabbit with pearl barley and sherry, homemade liqueurs, blackberry meringue. The beer comes from Charles Wells, the wine list has 18 by the glass. Staff are youthful – and may be rushed. Décor is 1930s sober and the restaurant area glows by candlelight. No bookings bar Sunday lunch and a legend in the making – but arrive early (or late) and you may get a table.

Meals	Lunch & dinner £10–£20.
	Sunday lunch, 3 courses, £30.
Closed	Mon lunch & Sun evenings.
	Open all day Tues-Sat.

Robert Shaw
Anchor & Hope,
36 The Cut,
Southwark SE1 8LP
Tel   +44 (0)20 7928 9898

Entry 410 Map 4

London

The Garrison Public House
Bermondsey

The kitchen is open, staff are laid-back, decibels are high and tables are crammed. The Garrison bounces with bonhomie, more eaterie than pub. What's more, it has the confidence to be different: traditional benches and French boutique chairs, pistachio paintwork and quirky objets and the vegetables for the kitchen displayed in crates by the hatch. Earthy food reflects the décor (steak sandwich, chickpea and pumpkin tagine, Morecambe Bay potted shrimps) – classic British with a continental twist – most of it, from apricots to Orkney mussels, coming from the market down the road. Accompany a bottle of St Peter's with a rib-eye steak with watercress and roquefort butter. Arrive for breakfast, stay for dinner and a movie: there's a cinema downstairs and free screenings every Sunday.

Meals	Lunch & dinner £9.50–£15.90.
Closed	Open all day.

Clive Watson & Adam White
The Garrison Public House,
99 Bermondsey Street,
Bermondsey SE1 3XB
Tel   +44 (0)20 7089 9355
Web   www.thegarrison.co.uk

Entry 411 Map 4

London

The Old Brewery
Greenwich

A one-off on the bank of the Thames, a brewery founded in 1717 when beer was drunk in favour of water. The interior is cavernous, listed, unique, and a shrine to the world's beers: taste before choosing your pint. Beyond are the restaurant and tea room, in a brewing area with vast gleaming tanks and funky beer bottle chandeliers. All is rich to reflect the warmth of the beers: dark woods, deep reds, terracottas; they also hold classes for aspiring brewers. Staff may be passionate about the golden brew but food is taken seriously too and the best of traditional British is served: fish from Billingsgate, meat from rare breeds, cheese from Neal's Yard. There's raspberry beer for jelly terrines and the spent brewing grain is used to make the bread.

London

The Gun
Docklands

Fiendishly difficult to find, but persevere. The front room, dominated by a dark panelled bar, is hugely atmospheric – a planked floor, settles, battered leather sofas, the smell of truffles in the air. The restaurant area is pristine, and a loose nautical theme runs through the prints and paintings. Bag a table by the fire; settle in till the sun sets over the river, on a candlelit terrace. In the bar is a reassuring selection of pub favourites – fish pie, beef shin burger with fat chips – while the restaurant menu is fiercely modern: scallops with samphire, wild garlic and hot butter; roast saddle of wild rabbit with black pudding and shoulder Scotch broth. Weekend brunch from 11.30am to 1pm is too popular not to book; Portuguese barbecues employ Billingsgate fish. Wow.

Meals	Bar meals from £5.50. Lunch & dinner from £10.
Closed	Open all day.

Meals	Lunch & dinner £11.95–£18. Bar meals from £4.50.
Closed	Open all day.

Alastair Hook
The Old Brewery, The Pepys Building,
The Old Royal Naval College,
Greenwich SE10 9LW
Tel   +44 (0)20 3327 1280
Web   www.oldbrewerygreenwich.com

Entry 412 Map 4

Tom & Ed Martin
The Gun,
27 Coldharbour,
Docklands E14 9NS
Tel   +44 (0)20 7515 5222
Web   www.thegundocklands.com

Entry 413 Map 4

London

The Fox
Shoreditch

It may be tucked away from the main drag of Shoreditch but it's still filled with bright young things. Upstairs: a dining room with large windows, plain furniture, silver candlesticks, an open fire, and modern European food that makes the best of local, seasonal supplies. Try small but delicious tapas (chorizo cooked in red wine, marinated anchovies with toasted almonds) or tuck into a rare-breed 'bacon chop' with cloves, russet apples, cider and mash – followed by spiced pear and almond cake. Menus are updated monthly, the wine list is long, and ales include guests like Otter and Harvey's Best. A lovely sturdy Victorian pub with a big central bare-boarded bar that rocks for a special occasion; further up the narrow staircase is a cosy private dining room, opulent with sparkling glasses and Chinese wallpaper.

London

The Jugged Hare
Clerkenwell

An unexpected shrine in the City of London to the British countryside. The Jugged Hare, part of the old Whitbread Brewery, is not just about beer: stuffed creatures in glass cases around the bar tell of another passion. The very best of British meat is worshipped and with a kitchen supplied by rare-breed farmers and gamekeepers, there are some fabulous treats on the menu. The lively bar is ideal for sampling their own ales or Southwold Bitter, accompanied by black pudding croquettes with Guinness sauce, maybe. The pub's dining room, with its open hatch, is a fun place to fully indulge, so how about a blue cheese, dandelion, walnut and fennel salad, then roast whole legged partridge with game chips, and apple junket with spiced shortbread to follow? Before leaving, pay homage to the birds and beasts of the land and check out the chefs' daily 'meat display'.

Meals	Lunch & dinner from £9.	Meals	Lunch & dinner £6.50-£27.
Closed	Open all day Mon-Fri & from 6pm Sat. Closed from 5pm Sun.	Closed	Open all day.

	Harry Cooper		The Manager
	The Fox,		The Jugged Hare,
	28 Paul Street,		49 Chiswell Street,
	Shoreditch EC2A 4LB		Clerkenwell EC1Y 4SA
Tel	+44 (0)20 7729 5708	Tel	+44 (0)20 7614 0134
Web	www.thefoxpublichouse.co.uk	Web	www.thejuggedhare.com

The White Swan
Holborn

The old journalists' den has become a pub of note. At plain tables on unpolished boards, City traders order real ales and fine wines. Upstairs is a smart restaurant that serves some flavoursome modern food. How about loin and neck of Herdwick lamb, Jersey royal croquettes and grelot onions? Or Peterhead cod with clams, leeks and seashore vegetables? Cheese and wine lists are encyclopaedic, and regulars get lockers for unfinished spirits. The daily bar menu covers the pub classics – tuck into slow roast Gloucester Old Spot pork belly with celeriac remoulade and apple sauce, or brilliant fish and chips (the fish hand-picked daily from Billingsgate market). Leave room for apple parfait with elderflower, or chocolate delice and crème fraîche sorbet. Delicious.

Meals	Bar meals from £8-£15.
	Lunch & dinner £15-£18.
Closed	Open all day Mon-Fri.
	Private parties only Sat & Sun.

Nadia Evans
The White Swan,
108 Fetter Lane,
Holborn EC4A 1ES
Tel +44 (0)20 7242 9122
Web www.thewhiteswanlondon.com

Entry 416 Map 4

Jerusalem Tavern
Clerkenwell

There's so much atmosphere here you could bottle it up and take it home – along with one of the beers. Old Clerkenwell has reinvented itself and the tiny 1720 tavern epitomises all that is best about the place. The name is new, acquired when the St Peter's Brewery of Suffolk took it over and stocked it with their ales and fruit beers. Step in to a reincarnation of a nooked and crannied interior, candlelit at night with a winter fire; come before six if you want a table. Lunchtime food is simple and English (bangers and mash, a roast, a fine platter of cheese) with ingredients from Smithfield Market, and the pork scratchings are epic. Staff are friendly and know their beer, and the full range of St Peter's ales is all there, from the cask or the specially designed bottle.

Meals	Lunch £5-£10.
Closed	All day Sat & Sun.

Dave Hart
Jerusalem Tavern,
55 Britton Street,
Clerkenwell EC1M 5UQ
Tel +44 (0)20 7490 4281
Web www.stpetersbrewery.co.uk

Entry 417 Map 4

Coach & Horses
Clerkenwell

Gone are the days when the Edwardian pub was a corner boozer; now it fills with a media crowd. Enjoy a pint of London Pride in the small panelled bar as you check out a tempting blackboard menu. British dishes are devised with enthusiasm and ingredients burst with flavour: venison and partridge terrine with chutney; sea bream with lentils, fennel and salsa verde; quince and almond tart with clotted cream. Rare-breed meats are reared at Elwy Valley in Wales, fish is delivered daily; there's charcuterie and cheeses too. The bar specialises in malt whiskies and attentive staff lay on nibbles of toasted pumpkin seeds in keeping with the pub's logo, a pumpkin pulled by four mice. Note: most tables have a reserved sign on them on busy nights. Best book.

Meals	Lunch & dinner £10.75–£14.
	Bar meals £4–£8.
Closed	Sat lunch & Sun evenings.

Giles Webster
Coach & Horses,
26–28 Ray Street,
Clerkenwell EC1R 3DJ

| Tel | +44 (0)20 7278 8990 |
| Web | www.thecoachandhorses.com |

Entry 418 Map 4

The Easton
Clerkenwell

Home from home for the Amnesty International crowd, whose headquarters are down the street, this corner pub may look like the classic London boozer but inside is airy and modern. Bare boards, plain windows, a long bar topped with fresh flowers, funky wallpaper at the far end… drinkers and diners mingle over pints of Timothy Taylor and global house-white and wonder what to pick from the ever-changing board. The kitchen goes in for rustic portions of chargrilled lemon and thyme pork chops; roast tomato and chorizo stew; Springbok sausages with spring onion champ and braised red cabbage. It's a godsend for the area, with pub tables spilling onto the pavement and a genuinely local feel. Staff are charming, even on Fridays when the drinkers descend and hearty dishes are replaced with tapas.

| Meals | Lunch & dinner £9–£16. |
| Closed | Open all day. |

Andrew Marshall
The Easton,
22 Easton Street,
Clerkenwell WC1X 0DS

| Tel | +44 (0)20 7278 7608 |
| Web | www.theeastonpub.co.uk |

Entry 419 Map 4

The Lady Ottoline
Bloomsbury

Tucked off the Gray's Inn Road is a pretty little pub with elegant grey paintwork, huge Georgian windows and a sun-dappled pavement for seats outside. Find a sedate interior of dark wood floors, leather banquettes and panelling painted deep grey. Candles are lit on dim days, spirits gleam behind a mahogany bar, and when the barman's not serving, he's polishing the pub's doors. It's a little oasis for drinkers and dreamers (good dogs too) and a wonderful place for a celebration. Up a narrow stair is a large lofty dining room with exposed brick walls, and, alongside, "the cosiest dining room in Bloomsbury" (seats 12). They take their spirits seriously, source wines from small growers, serve several beers from the USA and glorious roasts. All the produce is traceable and sustainable, from the hand-picked Cornish crab to the Hereford Beef burgers to the Tamworth pork scotch egg.

The Duke of Cambridge
Islington

Thanks to pioneering Geetie Singh, 'organic' and 'sustainable' are the watchwords at Britain's first organic pub, and British-rustic is the style. Wines, beers, spirits are certified organic and they buy as locally as they can to cut down on food miles. Most of the beers are brewed around London, meat comes from two farms, and fish is Marine Conservation Society-approved. Impeccable produce and menus change twice a day. It's a sprawling airy space with a comfortable, easy atmosphere; you could be alone happily here. Sit back and take your fill of lentil and pancetta soup, mussels with chorizo, fennel and chives, game pie with braised red cabbage, broad bean and asparagus salad with ricotta, crusty bread, fruity olive oil, quince crumble and cream – in the lovely airy planked bar, or in the restaurant. Justifiably rammed.

Meals	Starters from £6. Mains from £12.50.
Closed	Bank Holiday Mondays.

Meals	Lunch & dinner £9-£22.
Closed	Open all day.

Hannah Bonnell
The Lady Ottoline,
11A Northington Street,
Bloomsbury WC1N 2JF
Tel +44 (0)20 7831 0008
Web www.theladyottoline.com

Entry 420 Map 4

Geetie Singh
The Duke of Cambridge,
30 St Peter's Street,
Islington N1 8JT
Tel +44 (0)20 7359 3066
Web www.dukeorganic.co.uk

Entry 421 Map 4

Charles Lamb Public House
Islington

Everyone's welcome at Camille and Hobby's small pub, hidden down a tangle of streets behind Camden Passage. It's a dear little place that keeps its pubby feel, with two unshowy bar rooms and well-kept hand-pump beer. The blackboard menu – fresh, short, ever-changing – is a surprise. Eat informally at plainly set tables in either bar, on serrano ham with celeriac remoulade, or Lancashire hotpot; Camille is French so there may be duck confit too. On Sundays: all-day roast beef and Yorkshire pudding. It's good home-cooked food and you need to get here early: tables cannot be booked. Walk it all off with a stroll along the bosky banks of the Regent's Canal; seek out the house where essayist and poet Charles Lamb lived, two streets away.

Smokehouse
Islington

Hard to imagine that behind this red brick pub lies a glorious selection of craft beers to challenge the palate, and salamis around the tiled bar for robust snacks. Scottish chef Neil Rankin knows his stuff and has great local craft beers and ales on tap. As for the food, in a dining room with simple plank tables, a 'beer blackboard' and a kitchen hatch, drinkers are lured into the gastronomic unknown. At first glance the menu follows tradition, but there are some surprising dishes too. Imagine crispy lobster frittata or foie gras with apple pie and duck egg to start, followed by roasted cod with masala cockles and clams, or peppered ox-cheek with gravy and cauliflower cheese. Then a pudding named 'Krun Chee Nut' – what can that be? The reviews are starry-eyed so visit and find out!

Meals	Lunch & dinner £9–£12. Sunday roast £10.50–£12.
Closed	Open from 4pm Mon & Tues. Open all day Wed-Sun.

Meals	Lunch & dinner £12.50–£19.
Closed	Open all day Sat & Sun. Open from 5pm Mon-Fri.

	Hobby & Camille Limon
	Charles Lamb Public House,
	16 Elia Street,
	Islington N1 8DE
Tel	+44 (0)20 7837 5040
Web	www.thecharleslambpub.com

	The Manager
	Smokehouse,
	63-69 Canonbury Road,
	Islington N1 2DG
Tel	+44 (0)20 7354 1144
Web	www.smokehouseislington.co.uk

Entry 422 Map 4

Entry 423 Map 4

London

Drapers Arms
Islington

Reborn in 2009, the pared-back, opened-up Georgian building in a residential area of charming period houses has high ceilings, bare boards and an eclectic mix of tables and chairs – expect a chilled community vibe. The kitchen, under chef James de Jung, fits the mood and ethic to a tee. Gutsy no-nonsense British dishes appear on twice-daily changing menus: grilled ox tongue with split peas and ham hock; grilled quail with braised chard and aïoli; lentils with roast shallots, roast butternut squash and goat's curd. Room should be left for the lardy cake with crème fraîche and a generous plate of British cheeses. Hand-pump ales, enterprising wines, a cooly decorative dining room upstairs and a classy courtyard garden top a super-charged act.

London

The Lansdowne
Primrose Hill

It's buzzing, laid-back, open-plan and atmospherically lit, with big wooden tables and a dark blue décor. Upstairs is an elegant charming 60-seat restaurant where a cool crowd is treated to tempting aromas from the pizza oven and the open kitchen hatch; downstairs is abuzz. Couples come for late breakfasts, young families for early roast lunch, and everyone for the in-house muffins. There's deep-fried whitebait with tahini, semolina gnocchi with roast squash and mozzarella, old-fashioned ginger pudding. On offer are two draught ales and one real cider but really this is a wine, lager and olives place; the wines are good and don't cost the earth. Outside in summer is a little oasis to which you can retreat and leave the city behind.

Meals	Bar meals from £4.50. Lunch from £9.50. Dinner from £11.50. Sunday lunch, 3 courses, £24.
Closed	Open all day.

Meals	Lunch & dinner £11.50–£16. Bar meals £5–£7.50.
Closed	Open all day.

	Nick Gibson
	Drapers Arms,
	44 Barnsbury Street,
	Islington N1 1ER
Tel	+44 (0)20 7619 0348
Web	www.thedrapersarms.com

Entry 424 Map 4

	The Manager
	The Lansdowne,
	90 Gloucester Avenue,
	Primrose Hill NW1 8HX
Tel	+44 (0)20 7483 0409
Web	www.thelansdownepub.co.uk

Entry 425 Map 4

The Grafton
Kentish Town

The once dingy old boozer has been transformed to former Victorian glory by owners Susie and Joel. It is now a sanctuary for craft beer lovers. Behind the bar, knowledgeable staff pull firm favourites such as Hogs Back TEA, but encourage you to try local brews such as Portobello Star. It's not just the array of beers that draws the crowds. Will Dee of the Fat Butcher, now the Grafton's resident chef, is passionate about doing 'interesting technical things" with meat. At scrubbed tables, cheddar and ale croquettes come with smoked ketchup, and 12-hour pork shoulder with crackling and apple sauce. Traditional apple pie and custard is another firm favourite. If you're sticking to pints, there may be some of Will's homemade salamis left to snack on; if not, spare a thought for them maturing in the cellar!

The Southampton Arms
Kentish Town

Where else in London has so many ciders (the real stuff) and ales, welcomes all comers (not just locals) and has a pub dog? You couldn't sit on your own here long without someone chatting to you. This little Victorian pub on Highgate Hill (a former Kentish Town dive) is long and thin with a table the length of the bar and a record player in the far corner that plays the blues; on sunny afternoons the sun hits the hand pumps and tankards, and there's no sign of Farrow & Ball. Along with the ever-changing ales from small breweries are sausage rolls, salami, pulled pork baps with warm crackling and vegetarian Scotch eggs, there are quiz nights on Mondays and the piano plays three times a week. They don't have a phone and don't reserve seats, tables "or any of that caper". It's perfect if you're skint. Cash only.

Meals	Lunch & dinner £8.50–£15.50.		Meals	Bar snacks from £2.
Closed	Open all day.		Closed	Open all day.

Joel Czopor & Susie Clarke
The Grafton,
20 Prince of Wales Road,
Kentish Town NW5 3LG
Tel   +44 (0)20 7482 4466
Web   www.thegraftonnw5.co.uk

Peter Holt
The Southampton Arms,
139 Highgate Road,
Kentish Town NW5 1LE
Web   www.thesouthamptonarms.co.uk

Entry 426 Map 4

Entry 427 Map 4

London

The Bull
Highgate

At Highgate's Bull, beer and food go hand in hand. In the cosy bar, homemade sausage rolls are stacked alongside pumps serving their own ales; we enjoyed our Beer Street and Highgate Winter. But that's just a hint at what goes on at the back. In the kitchen, master brewer Joanna keeps the beer flowing alongside chefs who work on the menus, many using the beers. By the open fire, locals tuck into ale-cured salmon, caper berries with Beer Street mustard dressing, and roast pork belly with artichoke purée, purple truffle potatoes and black pudding croquettes. It's worth taking a break - before you dive into your baked vanilla cheesecake with blood orange jelly – to read the bar's vast blackboard explaining the brewing process. You can also visit the kitchen to see the mash tuns churning.

London

Holly Bush
Hampstead

Down a Hampstead cul-de-sac, the stables once owned by painter George Romney have become a hugely loved pub. It's one of the most Dickensian places you could go for Sunday lunch in London: a labyrinth of corridors leading to treacle-coloured rooms, cosy corners, painted settles, tables set with board games, potted ferns on the bar. Ale rules at the Holly Bush, where the chef cooks not with wine but with beer and the aromas of beef and ale pie prove a temptation for drinkers to become diners. Guinness rarebit followed by sticky toffee pudding will educate the beer lover's palate, while Sunday roasts and scotch eggs are a hit with regulars. Upstairs in the dining room, all pistachio walls and wooden floors, the celebration of all things British continues. The staff are as happy as the punters. One of the best.

| Meals | Lunch & dinner £9.50–£23. |
| Closed | Open all day. |

Meals	Bar meals £3.50–£6.
	Lunch & dinner £8–£15.
Closed	Open all day.

Dan Fox
The Bull,
13 North Hill,
Highgate N6 4AB
Tel   +44 (0)20 8341 0510
Web   www.thebullhighgate.co.uk

Entry 428 Map 4

Hannah Borkulak
Holly Bush,
22 Holly Mount,
Hampstead NW3 6SG
Tel   +44 (0)20 7435 2892
Web   www.hollybushhampstead.co.uk

Entry 429 Map 4

London

Parlour
Kensal Rise

Taking on this run-down Regent Street pub in July 2013, maverick chef Jesse Dunford Wood set about realising his vision for a modern-day city pub with passion and innovation; and started with the quirky and apt name 'Parlour'. Open from 10am for breakfast (unlimited toast and marmite), then 'funky British' brunch, lunch and dinner, his menus brim with humour and a huge dose of nostalgia – fish soup, chicken Kiev, marshmallow Wagon Wheel. The eclectic clientele like the unusual craft keg beers too, the fine wines, fancy cocktails, great coffee, the Sunday lunch sharing platters, and the Chef's Table for seven, where surprise dishes are delivered in theatrical style. Stylish, full of personality, refreshingly different, the Parlour is a game-changer to watch.

London

Truscott Arms
Maida Vale

A place of note, its pared back lofty interiors home to wine tastings, art exhibitions, events and summer parties as well as to seriously good food. It is independently owned, dynamically run, and a Swiss-born designer was behind the restoration. The result is a light, airy, friendly space with a zinc-topped bar down one side, a Moorish tiled floor, and the subtlest, palest paintwork. Find yourself a velvet bar stool and order a craft beer (Camden Hells Lager? why not!) or sail upstairs to ceiling roses and elegant parquet. Head chef is Irish Aidan McGee (ex Launceston Place, with a passion for sustainability) and his menus are a wonder. Trealy Farm scotch quail's egg with salsa verde, 35-day aged rib-eye with girolle mushrooms, Kentish Well Pudding with russet apples and brandy ice cream. It doesn't get much better.

Meals	Lunch £4–£14.50.
	Dinner £9.50–£19.50.
Closed	Mon all day.

Meals	Breakfast available.
	Bar snacks from £8.
	Set dinner, £32–£37.
Closed	Open all day.

Jesse Dunford Wood
Parlour,
5 Regent Street,
Kensal Rise NW10 5LG
Tel   +44 (0)20 8969 2184
Web   www.parlourkensal.com

Entry 430 Map 4

Andrew & Mary Jane Fishwick
Truscott Arms,
55 Shirland Rd,
Maida Vale W9 2JD
Tel   +44 (0)20 7266 9198
Web   www.thetruscottarms.com

Entry 431 Map 4

The Berney Arms
Barton Bendish

In a peaceful estate village in open country, by a village green, is a spruced-up inn with candy-coloured tables out front. The sleek feel continues within, and there is much to love, from the the the bar areas with beautiful fires and beams, settles and leather chairs and cheeky Pirelli posters, to the bright restaurant with linen tablecloths and a stylish French-country feel. The menu is good-looking and tempting and attracts Norfolk foodies, so you can look forward to treats like local game terrine wrapped in bacon estate venison with red wine jus, and chocolate truffle torte with toffee ice cream. Friendly staff bustle efficiently, while the atmosphere tempts one to linger (as does the promise of afternoon tea). The conversion of the old stables, forge and carriage house is impressive, and is home to stylish bedrooms with some original features – the suite has a splendid brick forge. Find dark wood floors and clean lines, chunky wood and brass beds, good bathrooms and private terraces – each room has one. Off the beaten track but well worth knowing if visiting the north Norfolk coast.

Rooms	6 doubles, 1 twin: £85–£115. 1 suite for 4: £115–£130. Singles £65–£85.
Meals	Lunch & dinner £9.50–£19.95.
Closed	Rarely.

Phil & Sue Hirst
The Berney Arms,
Church Road, Barton Bendish,
King's Lynn PE33 9GF

| Tel | +44 (0)1366 347995 |
| Web | www.theberneyarms.co.uk |

The Orange Tree
Thornham

The Orange Tree knows what a modern food pub should be. From the wicker fencing fronting the garden to the sage-splashed front, the approach says it all; owners Mark and Jo have made subtle changes to this treasure off the village green. Step inside, to polished wood floors, cosy mulberry walls, log-stuffed fireplaces. Snuggle up at a cheeky table à deux in the bar, or be welcomed into one of two dining rooms. This is a fabulous area for food, the pub sources locally and well and there's something for everyone on Philip Milner's menu. Try lamb and apricot hotpot; beer-battered haddock with lemon and caper mayonnaise; salmon, chilli and crayfish cakes with ginger and soy dressing; garlic roasted halibut with passionfruit jus; enjoy the odd whacky touch. Stay the night? Money and thought has been lavished on courtyard chalet bedrooms at the back, which, though small, are cosy, comfy and contemporary, with wooden floors, Farrow & Ball colours, coffeemakers and wet rooms. Come for urban chic, divine food and a happy feel. If you're a birdwatcher, don't miss Titchwell Nature Reserve.

Rooms	5 twin/doubles, 1 family room for 4: £85.
Meals	Lunch & dinner £10-£22.
Closed	Rarely.

Mark & Jo Goode
The Orange Tree,
High Street, Thornham,
Hunstanton PE36 6LY
Tel   +44 (0)1485 512213
Web   www.theorangetreethornham.co.uk

Entry 433 Map 9

The White Horse
Brancaster Staithe

The setting is magical. Fabulous views reach across the marshes and the boat-bobbed water; dinghies sail on the evening high tide. The coastal path starts right outside this neat inn and the garden provides the perfect spot for a post-stroll pint. Inside the marine theme continues, in a modern, crisp way: seascape colours, natural materials, pictures of boats, bowls of pebbles and shells, and big windows for the views. Simple, stylish bedrooms reflect the seaside feel to a tee, and all have gleaming new bathrooms. Those upstairs capture the ever-changing light; those on the ground floor have flower-bright terraces leading to the marshes and a New England feel. A perfect place for bird-spotting, especially geese in winter – bring the binoculars. Later, dine by candlelight on mussels and oysters, mullet with bean, chorizo and tomato ragout, blade of beef with thyme jus; all of it as local and seasonal as possible and served with a great big smile. Huge sunsets, great food, and a welcome for children and dogs... what's to stop you staying the night? *Minimum stay: 2 nights at weekends.*

Rooms	11 doubles, 4 twins: £100–£230. Extra bed £30 per person per night. Cots £5. Dogs £10.
Meals	Lunch & bar meals from £9.95. Dinner from £13.95.
Closed	Rarely.

Cliff & James Nye
The White Horse,
Brancaster Staithe PE31 8BY
Tel   +44 (0)1485 210262
Web   www.whitehorsebrancaster.co.uk

The Duck Inn
Stanhoe

The Stanhoe Crown morphed into the Duck in 2010, and Ben and Sarah took on this much extended and spruced-up village local in 2013. Enter from the car park a slate-floored bar, with barrels of Elgood's ale racked behind glass, and simple tables and benches for those who appreciate a well-kept pint of Black Dog. Cosy dining rooms beyond are rustic-smart with their wood and slate floors, wood-burning stoves, candles on scrubbed tables, and really interesting local art adorning the walls. Expect to find memorable open sandwiches, seasonal dishes and fresh local fish on the menu, all beautifully prepared by Ben, perhaps scotch quail eggs with mustard and tarragon mayonnaise, baked cod with wild mushroom risotto and crispy braised ox cheek, or Norfolk beef sirloin with skinny fries. Leave room for treacle spice cake with clotted cream. Bedrooms have a contemporary feel, with thick down duvets on big comfy beds, deep sofas, plasma screens, fresh coffee, and swish bathrooms with baths and walk-in showers. You are close to trendy Burnham Market, Brancaster Beach and the famous saltmarshes.

Rooms	1 double, 1 twin: £95–£125.
Meals	Lunch from £6.95.
	Dinner from £11.25.
	Sunday roast £12.95.
Closed	Rarely.

Sarah & Ben Handley
The Duck Inn,
Burnham Road, Stanhoe,
King's Lynn PE31 8QD
Tel   +44 (0)1485 518330
Web   www.duckinn.co.uk

The Wiveton Bell
Wiveton

The pull of the great outdoors led Berni and Sandy to the Norfolk coast and a pretty pub on a village green, a church by its side. The setting may be bucolic but Wiveton is no backwater; on highdays and holidays these coastal outposts of North Norfolk can be busier than the King's Road. City escapees, with or without kids in tow, will find much to love, for a rustic-chic makeover has transformed the interiors of this charming whitewashed inn (beams, chunky tables, polished plank floors); now it's a bona fide bistro pub. The menu is seductive, ranging from treacle-cured braised blade of beef to pork belly with potato and black pudding terrine, to simple haddock and chips. It's all so lovely you'll want to stay the night – and why not? Four opulent bedrooms in shabby-chic style – three with furnished terraces – come with antique beds and goose down pillows, mini CD players, iPod docks and books; cosy bathrooms have bathrobes and top toiletries. Staff are wonderfully relaxed and fresh croissants are delivered to the door. *Minimum stay: 2 nights at weekends.*

Rooms	4 doubles: £95–£140.
Meals	Lunch from £6.95.
	Dinner, 3 courses, around £30.
Closed	Rarely.

Rosie Vickers
The Wiveton Bell,
Blakeney Road, Wiveton,
Holt NR25 7TL
Tel   +44 (0)1263 740101
Web   www.wivetonbell.com

Entry 436 Map 10

Saracens Head
Wolterton

Lost in the lanes of deepest Norfolk, an English inn that's hard to beat. Outside, Georgian red-brick walls ripple around, encircling a beautiful courtyard where you can sit for sundowners in summer before slipping into the restaurant for a good meal. Tim and Janie came back from the Alps, unable to resist the allure of this inn. A sympathetic refurbishment has brightened things up, but the spirit remains the same: this is a country-house pub with lovely staff who go the extra mile. Downstairs the bar hums with happy locals who come for Norfolk ales and good French wines, while the food in the restaurant is as good as it ever was, perhaps Morston mussels, pork belly with mustard mash, whole sea bass with ginger and spring onions, and seasonal game. Upstairs you'll find a sitting room on the landing, where windows frame country views, and six cosy bedrooms. All have smart carpets, pale wood furniture, soothing colours, comfy beds and sparkling new bathrooms. Breakfast sets you up for the day, so explore the coast at Cromer, play golf on the cliffs at Sheringham, or visit Blickling Hall, a Jacobean pile. Blissful.

Rooms	5 twin/doubles: £100–£110. 1 family room for 4: £110–£140. Singles from £70.
Meals	Lunch from £6.50. Dinner, 3 courses, £25–£35. Not Monday or Tuesday lunch Oct–June.
Closed	Christmas.

	Tim & Janie Elwes Saracens Head, Wolterton, Norwich NR11 7LZ
Tel	+44 (0)1263 768909
Web	www.saracenshead-norfolk.co.uk

Entry 437 Map 10

The Gunton Arms
Thorpe Market

Click open the latch gate and enter Gunton Park. The beautifully restored Gunton Arms overlooks one thousand acres of lush and historic parkland and the setting is stunning. Art dealer Ivor Braka has lavished money on the once faded hotel and the results are impressive... who would not love the chic hunting-lodge style? Warm red hues, wooden floors, a blazing log fire in the traditional bar (dogs welcome too), elegant lounges with pretty views of deer from every window. Quaff pints of Wherry alongside gamekeepers and gentry; tuck into rib of beef cooked over the fire in the vaulted dining room. Stuart (ex-Mark Hix) champions locally sourced ingredients, so enjoy mixed grill of estate fallow deer served with crab apple jelly; Brancaster mussels and chilli tossed in linguine; Cromer crab in summer. Irresistible bedrooms ooze country-house charm: antiques, gorgeous fabrics, Persian rugs, old prints and paintings and indulgent marble-tiled bathrooms, some with deep tubs and walk-in showers... wake to parkland views. An unusual, hospitable, richly atmospheric find.

Rooms	8 doubles: £95–£165.
Meals	Bar meals £1.50–£5.50.
	Lunch & dinner from £10.50.
Closed	25 December.

Simone Baker & Stuart Tattersall
The Gunton Arms,
Cromer Road, Thorpe Market,
Norwich NR11 8TZ
Tel   +44 (0)1263 832010
Web   www.theguntonarms.co.uk

The Dabbling Duck
Great Massingham

After a campaign by villagers to buy their local in 2006, the neglected Rose & Crown became the Dabbling Duck and the pub was revived with panache and perches prettily by the green. Business has been brisk, food is the draw and beers from the barrel – well-kept Adnams and Woodforde's. As for the mood, it is warmly endearing. The bar has been cut from a single slice of ancient Norfolk oak, there are high-backed settles by a blazing log fire, sober hues, rug-strewn floors, chunky candles on scrubbed tables, and shelves lined with books and board games. Views are to the village. There are local Brancaster Mussels, fish and chips, homemade pies. Or try Hen on her nest: malt-roasted chicken breast, baby turnips, crispy egg, and brown bread sauce. The care and attention to detail extends to gorgeous bedrooms with big brass beds, colourful cushions and throws, plasma screens, Roberts radios and wood-floored bathrooms; cookies and fresh coffee on tap. All this, 20 minutes from the beach and the bird-rich saltmarshes.

Rooms	5 twin/doubles: £85.
	1 single: £65.
	Extra bed/sofabed £15 per person per night. Dinner, B&B £65–£75 per person per night.
Meals	Bar meals from £5.
	Lunch from £5.75.
	Dinner from £10.
Closed	Rarely.

Mark Dobby
The Dabbling Duck,
11 Abbey Road, Great Massingham,
King's Lynn PE32 2HN

Tel	+44 (0)1485 520827
Web	www.thedabblingduck.co.uk

The Wildebeest Arms
Stoke Holy Cross

A rarity in the 1990s, a country inn offering top-notch pub food. The Wildebeest is still one of the most popular dining pubs in Norfolk – it may be no great shakes on the outside but inside is special. Modernised to create one long room split by a bar, there are rich yellow walls, dark oak beams, a winter fire and an African safari lodge feel. Ales include Woodforde's Wherry, there's an impressive list of wines and the food is up-to-the-minute and freshly made. Tuck into scallops with leek tart and shellfish bisque foam, or local venison with cep purée and wilted greens, and don't miss Tunisian orange cake with chocolate ice cream. Come for steaks on Wednesday, great-value lunches and proper Sunday roasts. Then head for Norwich for city bustle, or don your wellies and explore.

The Walpole Arms
Itteringham

A local farming family bought this Norfolk food pub in 2012 and the unspoilt brick-and-timber cottage in sleepy Itteringham remains a favourite for first-class modern British food. Daily menus are utterly seasonal and delight in fresh local produce – pork, beef and pheasant reared on the Harrold farm, Cromer crab, Morston mussels and venison from the Gunton Estate. Typically, there's Norfolk Dapple soufflé; chicken, ham hock and leek pie with creamy mash; vanilla rice pudding with brandy poached apricots. You can eat in the bar, with rough brick walls, beamed ceilings, standing timbers and wood-burner, or in the stylish Garden Room. East Anglian ales too, from Adnams and Woodforde's, a first-class list of wines, a glorious vine-covered terrace for summer, and great walks from the door across the Blickling Estate.

Meals	Lunch from £5.95.
	Dinner from £6.50.
	Sunday lunch, 3 courses, £19.50.
Closed	3pm-6pm.

Meals	Lunch & dinner £9.95-£17.
Closed	3pm-6pm.
	Sun evenings.

David Cappendell & Jez King
The Wildebeest Arms,
82-86 Norwich Road, Stoke Holy
Cross, Norwich NR14 8QJ
Tel   +44 (0)1508 492497
Web   www.animalinns.co.uk

Entry 440 Map 10

Oliver Harrold
The Walpole Arms,
The Common, Itteringham,
Norwich, NR11 7AR
Tel   +44 (0)1263 587258
Web   www.thewalpolearms.co.uk

Entry 441 Map 10

Norfolk

The Pigs
Edgefield

This gutsy gastropub stands for all we love. "Pig in charge" Tim Abbott, along with fellow foodie entrepreneurs, fights the corner for proudly British food locally sourced, and is ever on the look out for suppliers; barter your produce for a pint! This is the retro village pub of your dreams – decent ales, great wines and a menu that delivers tastes long forgotten. Try potted rabbit with redcurrant jelly, venison burgers on toasted muffins, slow-roast lamb shoulder with fresh thyme, caramelised rice pudding. It's brilliant for families: a new adventure play area, a playroom full of toys, and a menu for 'piglets' served with in-house lemonade. Bar 'iffits' (Norfolk tapas), homemade pork scratchings and mixed pickle pots are further enticements, as are quiz nights and pub games.

Meals	Lunch & dinner £9.95-£14.50.
Closed	Open all day.

Tim Abbott
The Pigs,
Norwich Road, Edgefield,
Melton Constable NR24 2RL
Tel   +44 (0)1263 587634
Web   www.thepigs.org.uk

Entry 442 Map 10

Norfolk

The Kings Head
Letheringsett

In family-happy gardens close to Holt and the glorious Norfolk coast, this rambling manor-like building has been revamped with panache by Pickled Inns. The mood is rustic-chic: rugs on wooden boards or terracotta, fat table lamps, bookcases crammed with books to browse, big mirrors, warm hues and feature fireplaces fronted by squashy leather; there's a civilised feel. Adnams and Woodforde's ales, decent wines and classy pub food are further enticements, as menus salute the region's fishermen, farmers and traders. Enjoy scallops with pork belly and forced rhubarb, halibut with potato and chorizo terrine and buttered kale, warm chocolate and Guinness cake, and Norfolk cheeses. There are cows in the field (theirs) and a willow maze in the garden.

Meals	Lunch from £6.95.
	Dinner from £13.95.
	Sunday roast £15.95 & £19.95.
Closed	Open all day.

Dan Hutchinson
The Kings Head,
Holt Road, Letheringsett,
Holt NR25 7AR
Tel   +44 (0)1263 712691
Web   www.kingsheadnorfolk.co.uk

Entry 443 Map 10

Norfolk

The Dun Cow
Salthouse

Seasoned Norfolk landlord Dan Goff sold up in Blakeney (The White Horse) and has headed a few miles east to the Dun Cow. Dan has now revitalised this coastal gem beside the village green. Glorious views across Cley Marshes from the spruced-up bar and beer garden draw twitchers, tourists and coastal-path walkers in their droves. Cord matting and slate tiles have replaced swirly carpet and old pine, there are painted settles, fat radiators, nautical pictures on brick and flint walls, and a glowing wood-burner; it's a delicious rustic space that few want to leave. Fresh, locally sourced food on seasonal menus (venison Scotch egg, Morston mussels, game stew, treacle tart), Adnams and Woodforde's ales on tap, and weekly quiz and music nights complete the pleasing picture. Mobbed in summer.

Meals	Bar snacks £4–£7.
	Lunch & dinner £9–£17.
Closed	Open all day.

Dan Goff
The Dun Cow,
Salthouse,
Cromer NR25 7XA
Tel   +44 (0)1263 740467
Web   www.salthouseduncow.com

Entry 444 Map 10

Norfolk

The Anchor
Morston

Taste the salty sea — Morston mussels, Thornham oysters, Blakeney crab — then wash it all down with a pint of Woodforde's Wherry. All a village pub should be is this whitewashed inn and more, ever since young Harry and Rowan took the helm in 2012. Inside is a warren of intimate and lived-in rooms, each with its own story to tell: wooden floors, coal fires, fishing photos, a random collection of tables and chairs. The former café-style dining room is now cosy smart, with its deep red walls, grand dresser, painted furniture and wood-burning stove. Around every corner are enthusiastic birders, chattering locals and happy travellers. Top-notch pub food (using best local ingredients) includes fish stew, bourguignon, bakewell tart. On a sunny day stretch out in the secluded beer garden — and book a seal trip while you sup.

| Meals | Lunch & dinner £8.95–£18.95. |
| Closed | Open all day. |

Harry Farrow & Rowan Glennie
The Anchor,
22 The Street, Morston,
Holt NR25 7AA
Tel   +44 (0)1263 741392
Web   www.morstonanchor.co.uk

Entry 445 Map 10

Norfolk

Red Lion
Stiffkey

Tucked into the side of a hill, overlooking the meadows where beef cattle graze, is an inn that's a pleasure to step into, a warren of three small rooms with bare floorboards and 17th-century quarry tiles, sunflower yellow walls, open log fires and stripped settles, old pews and scrubbed tables. The pub attracts a loyal crowd for its fresh seafood — crab from Wells boats, mussels from Mark Randall in the village, beer-battered cod — and first-rate ales from brewers such as Woodforde's and Yetmans. Locals rub shoulders with booted walkers and birdwatchers recovering from the rigours of the Norfolk Coast Path and the Stiffkey marshes. After a day on the beach the large, airy conservatory is popular with families. Dogs, too, are made welcome.

Meals	Lunch, bar meals & dinner from £9.95. Sunday lunch, 3 courses, £20.
Closed	Open all day.

Stephen Franklin
Red Lion,
44 Wells Road, Stiffkey,
Wells-next-the-Sea NR23 1AJ

| Tel | +44 (0)1328 830552 |
| Web | www.stiffkey.com |

Entry 446 Map 10

Norfolk

The Three Horseshoes
Warham

In a rural backwater, a rural treasure. This row of 18th-century cottages — now a pub — hides a mile from the coastal path and glorious salt marshes. Inside: three plain rooms that have barely changed since the thirties — gas lights, deal tables, Victorian fireplaces and a pianola that performs once in a while. Vintage entertainment includes an intriguing American Mills one-armed bandit converted for modern coins and a rare Norfolk 'twister' set into the ceiling — for village roulette, apparently. The food is in keeping, just traditional English dishes based emphatically on Norfolk produce (locally shot game, hearty casseroles, shortcrust pies) enhanced by pints of Wherry straight from the cask. Alternatively, sample local cider or homemade lemonade.

Meals	Lunch from £4.20. Bar meals & dinner from £7.80. Sunday roast £8.20.
Closed	2.30pm–6pm.

Iain Salmon
The Three Horseshoes,
69 The Street, Warham,
Wells-next-the-Sea NR23 1NL

| Tel | +44 (0)1328 710547 |
| Web | www.warhamhorseshoes.co.uk |

Entry 447 Map 10

Norfolk

Carpenter's Arms
Wighton

Carsten and Sue's country-cottage local is a real curio. Set at the foot of a somnolent hamlet within easy rambling range of Walsingham, all seems familiar enough when you approach – save for the Danish flag fluttering in the lane. Indoors, however, all bets are off: décor is hyperactive, from cherubs and fairylights to challenging modern art. Tables and chairs are in country-craft colours, there's a mess of mismatched cushions. It's not artful and it shouldn't work, but it does. The clientele is similarly eclectic: walkers with their dogs, extended families having lunch, authentic Norfolk yokels in fisherman's whiskers. Choose from homemade pies, plate-breaking roasts, and Carsten's specially imported herrings, washed down with a shot of schnapps. Don't expect gastro-dining or fine wines. Do expect a megawatt welcome and stacks of quirk.

Meals	Lunch & dinner £7.95–£12.95.
Closed	2.30pm–5.30pm.
	Open all day Sun
	(& all day Sat in summer).

Carsten & Susan Lund
Carpenter's Arms,
High Street,
Wighton,
Wells-next-the-Sea NR23 1PF
Tel +44 (0)1328 821994

Entry 448 Map 9

Norfolk

The Crown Hotel
Wells-next-the-Sea

The interior of this handsome 16th-century coaching inn has been neatly smartened up yet remains atmospheric with its open fires, bare boards and easy chairs. It's run by Chris Coubrough, an enterprising chef-landlord who knows how to cook. Order pub food at the bar and eat in the lounges or lovely modern conservatory: a hearty serving of Brancaster mussels, roast venison, or the Crown beef burger with pepper relish and a pint of Adnams Bitter. Bold colours, modern art and attractively laid tables give life to the restaurant where local ingredients are translated into global ideas: whole baked mackerel with lime and chilli butter; Ryburgh quail stuffed with chicken, sage and chestnut on beetroot risotto; raspberry and white chocolate cheesecake.

Meals	Lunch & dinner from £11.25.
	Set menu £12.95 & £15.95.
	Sunday roast £10.95.
Closed	Open all day.

Chris Coubrough
The Crown Hotel,
The Buttlands,
Wells-next-the-Sea NR23 1EX
Tel +44 (0)1328 710209
Web www.crownhotelnorfolk.co.uk

Entry 449 Map 10

Norfolk

The Jolly Sailors
Brancaster Staithe

Cliff and James Nye have revived a 200-year-old coastal treasure. 'Eat, Drink and be Jolly' says it all: not only is this a community boozer geared to locals and families but it attracts all those who flock to Brancaster's beach, which lies just across the road. In the classic bar, replete with beams, tiled floor, settles and a wood-burner pumping out the heat, dads can enjoy pints of home-brewed Brancaster ales while kids can watch the pizzas being baked in the open-to-view oven. Hearty traditional pub dishes using fresh local produce include mussels cooked in wine, onion, garlic and cream; lamb and mint pie; gammon, egg and chips; and good ol' fish and chips (delicious). It may be less classy than the Nyes' White Horse Inn down the road, but the Sailors is a great little pit-stop for families, beach bums and walkers.

Meals	Lunch & bar meals from £8.50.
	Dinner from £9.50.
	Sunday lunch, 3 courses, £20.
Closed	Open all day.

Community pub

Cliff & James Nye
The Jolly Sailors,
Brancaster Staithe,
King's Lynn PE31 8BJ
Tel   +44 (0)1485 210314
Web   www.jollysailorsbrancaster.co.uk

Entry 450 Map 10

Norfolk

The Ship Inn Hotel
Brancaster

The swanky Ship is smack on the coast road, a ten-minute walk from Brancaster beach. Once a grim boozer, this cosy coastal bolthole is now the first port of call for post-beach drinks and tucker; kids and dogs are welcome. Grab a pint of Adnams and a crab sandwich, or linger over game terrine with tomato compote... temptingly followed by venison casserole with creamy mash and kale, perhaps, then sticky toffee pudding. The bar is stylish, the food locally sourced and the dining atmosphere relaxed and informal. Be wowed by a quirky-chic décor: jute blinds, driftwood lights, slate-topped tables, striped fabrics, antique mirrors, objets d'art, and map-of-Norfolk wallpaper in the Map Room — a fun place to end a glorious day on the beach.

Meals	Lunch from £6.95.
	Dinner from £12.45.
	Sunday roast £15.95–£19.95.
Closed	Open all day.

Dan Hutchinson
The Ship Inn Hotel,
Brancaster,
King's Lynn PE31 8AP
Tel   +44 (0)1485 210333
Web   www.shiphotelnorfolk.co.uk

Entry 451 Map 9

Norfolk

The Rose & Crown
Snettisham

Roses round the door and twisting passages within – gloriously English. Good value, too. In spite of 40 wines on the list, half available by the glass, the Rose & Crown is still proud to be a pub. The village cricket team has a special corner of the Back Bar, the walled garden was once the bowling green and children have a magnificent wooden galleon to 'sail'. Inside: a warren of rooms with low ceilings and uneven floors, old beams and log fires, and a garden room for summer gatherings. They are highly regarded for local, seasonal produce, so try one of their 'classics' – Cinderella pumpkin risotto, lemongrass and chilli venison; meat eaters have prime-steak burgers with Monterey Jack cheese and French fries. For golfers, Brancaster and Hunstanton; for shoppers, Burnham Market; for birdwatchers, Snettisham and Titchwell.

Norfolk

Bedingfeld Arms
Oxborough

Local farmers Stephen and Catkin rescued this striking 18th-century coaching inn, Oxborough's only pub. Despite juggling farm life and a stone masonry business, they have worked wonders, breathing new life into the place for the locals and for visitors to Oxburgh Hall, the magnificent National Trust property that stands opposite. Expect a warm, relaxed feel throughout and a Pugin stone fireplace (naturally), flowers and lamps, fireside leather sofas and wing chairs in the wood-floored bar. Tuck into a club sandwich or chicken and mushroom pie with an Adnams ale, or settle into the country-rustic dining rooms for the house terrine with pear and grape chutney, venison with red wine and blackcurrant jus, and baked orange cheesecake with cranberry jam. A super little inn.

Meals	Bar meals from £5.50.
	Lunch from £8.50.
	Dinner from £9.50.
	Sunday roast £11.
Closed	Open all day.

Meals	Light lunch from £5.75.
	Dinner £10–£18.
Closed	Open all day.

Anthony & Jeannette Goodrich
The Rose & Crown,
Old Church Road, Snettisham,
King's Lynn PE31 7LX
Tel   +44 (0)1485 541382
Web   www.roseandcrownsnettisham.co.uk

Entry 452 Map 9

Stephen & Catkin Parker
Bedingfeld Arms,
Oxborough,
Downham Market PE33 9PS
Tel   +44 (0)1366 328300
Web   www.bedingfeldarms.co.uk

Entry 453 Map 9

Northamptonshire

The Talbot
Oundle

The splendid 17th-century Talbot, built with stones from Fotheringhay Castle, dominates this beautiful market town. In 1638, the castle's oak staircase (descended by Mary Queen of Scots on the day of her execution in 1587) was installed. Working closely with English Heritage, Kevin Charity has sympathetically revived the building, and breathed new life into the impressive interior. The bustling bar retreats into plush sitting and dining areas; a lounge whose wall-to-ceiling windows overlook a historic inner courtyard. Modern touches blend with period furnishings and fireplaces, and you can eat wherever you like. A crowd-pleasing menu offers sharing platters, cod and chips and the Talbot Burger alongside fancier fare such as venison with a juniper and red wine sauce. Pick of the bedrooms are the feature rooms and the suites (all good value), comfortable and traditional with original beams and soft carpets, period furniture and rich fabrics, beds topped with Beltrami linen and big bathrooms with claw-foot baths and walk-in showers.

Rooms	21 doubles, 4 twin/doubles, 1 four-poster: £75-£195. 5 suites for 2, 1 family room for 4: £120-£195. 2 singles: £65-£95.
Meals	Lunch & dinner £4-£20.
Closed	Rarely.

Kevin Charity
The Talbot,
New Street,
Oundle PE8 4EA
Tel   +44 (0)1832 273621
Web   www.thetalbot-oundle.com

Entry 454 Map 9

The Olde Coach House
Ashby St Ledgers

With its tidy thatched cottages and handsome church, Ashby St Ledgers is a bit of a gem. It's ancient enough to get a mention in the Domesday Book, and its Manor House was owned by one of Guy Fawkes' plotters. This is an attractive pub with a modern country interior: wooden floors, feature wallpaper, logs by the wood-burner, a squishy leather sofa. Order a pint of Bombardier in the bar, take it to the huge and lovely garden, let the children and dogs frolic. Under white painted rafters, friendly approachable staff ferry platefuls of good-looking food to pine tables: French onion soup with cheese croutons, homemade fishcakes with tartare sauce, pizzas, steaks, burgers, and perhaps sticky toffee pudding. It's a really good place for business folk to meet – and, come the weekend, friends and families. You can stay the night: four good rooms lie upstairs and a further bunch above the Coach House, tasteful, boutiquey and new. Splash out on the luxury ones for rain showers, iPod docks, pillow menus etc; Ashby is the largest. We hear excellent reports of the breakfasts.

Rooms	12 doubles, 2 twins, 1 single: £65–£95.
Meals	Lunch & dinner £6.95–£17.95.
Closed	Rarely.

Mark Butler
The Olde Coach House,
Main Street, Ashby St Ledgers,
Rugby CV23 8UN
Tel   +44 (0)1788 890349
Web   www.oldecoachhouse.co.uk

Entry 455 Map 8

Northamptonshire

The Red Lion
Culworth

Culworth has it all: thatched cottages, sweet green, grand manor – and the Red Lion, a classic old local revived by chef Justin Lefevre. The 70s décor has gone; the stone and wood floors, the timbers and the fireplaces have been rediscovered; there's a rustic-chic feel. Now diners mingle with locals, booted walkers quaff pints of Tribute in the bar, dogs doze, and, if you bring in your surplus veg, you collect points towards a free meal! In keeping, the food is unpretentious and delicious. Try garlic and thyme-roasted Moreton Pinkney mushrooms on focaccia; Buckby beef burger topped with slow-cooked pulled rib of beef and house relish; sea bream on a potato and spring onion salad; blackberry crème brûlée with blackcurrant sorbet. The garden is huge with village views.

Northamptonshire

The Queen's Head
Bulwick

A mellow old stone pub opposite the church in a lovely village – you'll wish it was your local. The simple beamed, flagstoned bar rambles into country-styled dining rooms that deliver atmosphere and charm, their thick beams and timbers and wonky walls expressing a history that goes back 600 years. New landlords took over in 2011 and intend to keep things simple. Nor do they want to lose the village pub feel – bell ringers still head across the road every Wednesday evening. There's a stone oven on the decked summer terrace, and you can expect traditional pub food with a modern twist – devilled lamb's kidneys; saddle of lamb with a sun-dried tomato and rosemary crust; apple and caramel tart. A cracking pit-stop should you find yourself thirsty on the A43.

Meals	Lunch & dinner £8.50-£16.
Closed	3pm-6pm.
	Mon all day.

Meals	Lunch & dinner £9.95-£19.95.
Closed	3pm-6pm.
	5pm-7pm Sun.
	Mon all day.

Justin Lefevre
The Red Lion,
High Street, Culworth,
Banbury OX17 2BD
Tel   +44 (0)1295 760050
Web   www.theredlionculworth.co.uk

Entry 456 Map 8

Rob Windeler
The Queen's Head,
Bulwick,
Corby NN17 3DY
Tel   +44 (0)1780 450272
Web   www.thequeensheadbulwick.co.uk

Entry 457 Map 9

The Duke of Wellington
Newton

The village inn has been transformed. Now, at the back, is a generous L-shaped space for diners: exposed stone walls and sleek wooden floors keep things rural, white paintwork, crisp curtains and immaculate furniture add style, and French windows open to a big, sheltered, south-facing terrace with views across the valley. But it's still a pub at the front, with its smart stone-flagged bar, glowing log-burner and good old English darts. As for the food, it's traditional British comfort food made using local, seasonal produce including slow-cooked pork shoulder with sage and onion boulangère potatoes, and sausages with mustard mash. People come for roast cod fillet with smoked haddock brandade; crispy parma ham and leek velouté; roast duck breast with butter roasted roots, fondant potato and wholegrain mustard; families can tuck into roast sirloin of Northumbrian beef – served pink – on Sundays. Bedrooms excel; nothing has been overlooked. Expect top beds and bed linen, beams, baths and skylights with remote controls, and scatter rugs on polished wood floors. Only the best for innkeeper Rob Harris.

Rooms	6 doubles, 1 twin: £95–£120.
Meals	Lunch & dinner from £9.95.
	Sunday roast £11.95.
Closed	Rarely.

Rob Harris
The Duke of Wellington,
Newton,
Corbridge NE43 7UL
Tel   +44 (0)1661 844446
Web   www.thedukeofwellingtoninn.co.uk

Entry 458 Map 12

Battlesteads Hotel
Wark

In the land of castles, stone circles and fortified towers is Battlesteads, an old inn given a new lease of life by owners who choose to be 'green'. The boiler burns wood chips from local sustainable forestry, a polytunnel produces the salads, all raw waste is composted; the Slades have won a bevy of awards, from 'Considerate Hotel of the Year' to a Green Tourism gold. Enter a large, cosy, low-beamed and panelled bar with a wood-burning stove and local cask ales. A step further and you find a spacious dining area: leather chairs at dark wood tables and a conservatory dining room that reaches into a sunny walled garden. The menus show a commitment to sourcing locally and the food is flavoursome. The Northumbrian fillet steak with Cumbrian blue cheese is meltingly tender and you must try Dee's award-winning bread and butter pudding! The housekeeping is exemplary; bedrooms are spotless, spacious, carpeted and comfortable, and there's wheelchair access on the ground floor. Hadrian's Wall is marvellously close.

Rooms	14 doubles, 4 twins: £95–£165.
	3 family rooms for 4: £115–£135.
	1 single: £70–£95.
Meals	Lunch from £9.75.
	Dinner from £10.75.
	Sunday lunch, 3 courses, £15.50.
Closed	Christmas, 25-26 December.

Richard & Dee Slade
Battlesteads Hotel,
Wark,
Hexham NE48 3LS
Tel   +44 (0)1434 230209
Web   www.battlesteads.com

Entry 459 Map 14

The Pheasant Inn
Stannersburn

A super little inn run with an instinctive understanding of its traditions. The stone walls carry old photos of the community: from colliery to smithy, a record of its past. The bars are wonderful: brass beer taps glow, anything wooden has been polished to perfection and the clock above the fire keeps perfect time. The house ales are expertly kept – Timothy Taylor's, Wylam Gold Tankard – and Robin cooks with relish: Kielder cheese soufflé, game and mushroom pie, and their famous slow-roasted Northumbrian lamb, all with colour from a pair of rather productive veg and fruit gardens. Bedrooms in the old hay barn are uncluttered, cosy and comfortable, and you'll get a prize breakfast the next morning – accompanied maybe by a view of the sheepdogs bringing the flock in for shearing. This is the glorious Northumberland National Park – no traffic jams, no rush – and close to the Kielder observatory, drawing astronomers and star gazers with the darkest night skies in the country. Hire bikes and cycle round the lake, or saddle a pony and take to the hills.
Minimum stay: 2 nights at weekends.

Rooms	4 doubles, 3 twins: £95–£100. 1 family room for 4: £95–£140. Singles £65–£70. Extra bed/sofabed £15 per person per night. Dinner, B&B £70–£75 per person per night.
Meals	Bar meals from £9.95. Dinner, 3 courses, £20–£30.
Closed	Christmas.

Walter, Irene & Robin Kershaw
The Pheasant Inn,
Stannersburn,
Hexham NE48 1DD

Tel	+44 (0)1434 240382
Web	www.thepheasantinn.com

Northumberland

The Tankerville Arms
Eglingham

Fancy exploring the rolling acres between Northumberland's dramatic coast and the wild Cheviot Hills? Charming Eglingham has the best inn for miles, a hospitable bolthole run by George and Mary. The long stone-built tavern, a boon for ramblers and cyclists, cheerfully mixes traditional and new. In the lounge and bar are carpeted and stone-flagged floors, blackened beams, log fires and plush seating. In the kitchen is a traditional British approach, all seasonal menus and chalkboard specials featuring local produce – game and wild mushroom terrine, steak and ale pie, aubergine and vegetable jalfrezi with mango chutney, chocolate and Bailey's cheesecake – as well as hearty sandwiches and Sunday lunchtime roasts. Drinkers can sample Northumbrian brews, or choose from a well-balanced list of wines.

Meals	Bar meals from £6.
	Lunch & dinner from £12.
Closed	Open all day.

George & Mary Elliott
The Tankerville Arms,
15 The Village, Eglingham,
Alnwick NE66 2TX
Tel   +44 (0)1665 578444
Web   www.tankervillearms.com

Entry 461 Map 14

Northumberland

The Olde Ship
Seahouses

A nautical gem – of which the Glen dynasty has been at the helm for a century, their enthusiasm ever undimmed. The coastal inn sparkles with maritime memorabilia reminding you of Seahouses' heritage and the days when Grace Darling rowed through the waves to rescue stricken souls. Settle in by a glowing fire with a decent pint (no fewer than ten ales!). In the recently refurbished Cabin Bar you are treated to hearty pub food: ham hock terrine, chicken and mushroom casserole, fish chowder and bosun's fish stew, ginger trifle... then order coffee and mints in the lounge. The whole place creaks with history. Gaze across the harbour to the Farne Islands, catch the ferry, or set off for a bracing coastal walk to Bamburgh Castle.

Meals	Lunch from £8.
	Bar meals & dinner from £10.
	Sunday lunch, 3 courses, £10.50.
Closed	Late November-mid January.

D Swan & J Glen
The Olde Ship,
7-9 Main Street,
Seahouses NE68 7RD
Tel   +44 (0)1665 720200
Web   www.seahouses.co.uk

Entry 462 Map 14

The Ship Inn
Low Newton-by-the-Sea

Film nights, folk nights, beer that's brewed ten paces from the front door, lovely staff, tasty food, and a beautiful position on the Northumbrian coast. The Ship is tiny, two wonderfully authentic rooms with stripped floors, stone walls, old settles and a wood-burner for winter. There are maps, the odd nautical touch, but mostly the happy chatter of hungry souls digging into a good lunch, perhaps a hand-picked crab sandwich or a bowl of homemade soup. Christine came north with no intention of running a pub, but as befalls most who visit, she fell under its spell; now it's a place of pilgrimage for many. The food is simple, scrumptious and as local as possible: crabs and kippers from Seahouses, free-range organic meat from the Borders. In summer, life spills onto the cobbles outside. Blissful.

The Jolly Fisherman Inn
Craster

A beautifully refurbished coastal pub that sits above the harbour at pretty Craster. The view from the dining room is hypnotic, a clean sweep out to sea and up the Northumbrian coast. It's a great spot for fresh seafood and a huge hit with the locals, who come for a bucket of Shetland mussels or the pub's famous crab sandwich. The attractive bar has wooden floors, leather banquettes, a fire that roars and old photographs on the walls. Outside, the garden looks the right way, perfect for lunch in summer. Pints of Timothy Taylor and Black Sheep wait at the bar alongside lots of good wines. Dinner is more extensive, perhaps crab soup, Northumbrian venison, meringues with black cherries and ice cream. Coastal walks start from the front door: south to Howick, north to Dunstanburgh Castle.

Meals	Lunch £2–£8.95.
	Dinner £8.95–£23.
Closed	Open all day.

Meals	Lunch from £6.95.
	Dinner from £10.50.
	Sunday roast from £10.95.
Closed	Open all day.

Christine Forsyth
The Ship Inn,
The Square, Low Newton-by-the-Sea,
Alnwick NE66 3EL

| Tel | +44 (0)1665 576262 |
| Web | www.shipinnnewton.co.uk |

  Entry 463 Map 14

David Whitehead
The Jolly Fisherman Inn,
Haven Hill, Craster,
Alnwick NE66 3TR

| Tel | +44 (0)1665 576461 |
| Web | www.thejollyfishermancraster.co.uk |

  Entry 464 Map 14

Northumberland

Barrasford Arms
Barrasford

Chef/landlord Tony Binks is slowly upgrading this substantial inn with a sheltered garden close to Hadrian's Wall. Expect a mix of locals (the marrow club meet here) and a robust atmosphere, with beers from nearby High House Farm and Allendale Breweries on hand pump. The bar has a high ceiling, deep velour upholstery, various stuffed animals and antlers, local photographs and dark varnished wood. Tony's passion for real food is evident: each week he buys a rare-breed pig locally, the shoulder for sausages and the legs for Sunday lunch (with sublime crackling) — even the pickled onions and eggs are local. Try chilli beetroot risotto with a glass of spicy Masseria dei Trullari Primitivo del Tarantino. You eat in one of three dining rooms, popular with farmers and fishermen; you are a stone's throw from the rushing north Tyne.

| Meals | Lunch, 2 courses £13; 3 courses £16 (Tuesday-Saturday). Dinner £9.50-£18. Sunday roast £15 & £17.50. Not Sunday eve. |
| Closed | Mon all day. Sun 3pm-12am. |

Tony Binks
Barrasford Arms,
Barrasford,
Hexham NE48 4AA
Tel +44 (0)1434 681237
Web www.barrasfordarms.co.uk

Entry 465 Map 14

Northumberland

Rat Inn
Anick

Tucked into the south-facing hillside, overlooking the Tyne Valley, this hard-to-find old drovers' inn has an irresistible appeal. The bar is cosy, with gleaming dark oak, flagged floor, simple tables and chairs, a roaring fire: sup a pint of something local or a good glass of wine while you toy with the idea of nibbles or a sandwich (try honey roast ham and pease pudding) to appease your rumbling tum. Those who have yomped heartily to get here may be hungrier, so look to the blackboard and its excellent, mostly regional delights: roast Northumberland rib of beef with watercress and golden chips for two is delicious, and maybe rice pudding afterwards. The sun room has grand views of the spectacular valley, and on warm days you can spill out into the little garden with its benches and pretty shrubs.

| Meals | Bar meals from £1.95. Lunch & dinner £8.95-£18.95. Sunday roast £8.95. |
| Closed | Open all day. |

Local, seasonal & organic produce

Phil Mason & Karen Errington
Rat Inn,
Anick,
Hexham NE46 4LN
Tel +44 (0)1434 602814
Web www.theratinn.com

Entry 466 Map 12

The Feathers Inn
Hedley on the Hill

Helen and Rhian have worked hard to develop the Feathers' reputation as a destination for food, yet the pub has not lost its pubby feel. What a treat, west of Newcastle, to find such an authentic little place. In the two bars are old beams, exposed stone, open fires and a simple cottagey feel; you're as much at home browsing the papers as enjoying a fireside chat. Ale is excellent, with four cask beers from local or microbreweries, and wines are taken as seriously. As for the food – grilled mackerel with grain mustard butter and crispy shallots, black pudding stuffed local rabbit with cider cream sauce, wild cherry and kirsch Bakewell tart – it is cooked with passion and skill from locally sourced produce; Rhian will even let you in to the secrets of some of his recipes. A star in the making.

The Staith House
North Shields

Former Masterchef finalist John Calton and his family team bravely took on this failing fisherman's boozer in 2013. Following a serious spruce up they haven't looked back, as the quirky interior (wood panelling with portholes, scrubbed brick, colourful chairs, maps on ceilings) and John's food soon found favour with the locals. The daily menu embraces the seasons and their relationship with Northumbrian farmers and skippers ensures only the best produce fills the fridges. Best to arrive early (it's a small place) to tuck into quay-landed fish and chips; hake with black pudding, chorizo and aïoli; and dark chocolate fondant. Or wash down a lamb and mint scotch egg with an Old Speckled Hen at the bar. Monthly wine and food tasting menus and summer barbecues overlooking the harbour complete the pleasing picture.

Meals	Lunch £9–£12.
	Dinner £11–£18.
	Sunday lunch, 3 courses, £20.
Closed	Mon lunch (except Bank Holidays).

Meals	Dinner £10.50–£28.
Closed	Open all day.

Helen Greer & Rhian Cradock
The Feathers Inn,
Hedley on the Hill,
Stocksfield NE43 7SW
Tel   +44 (0)1661 843607
Web   www.thefeathers.net

Entry 467 Map 12

John Calton
The Staith House,
57 Low Lights,
North Shields Fish Quay NE30 1JA
Tel   +44 (0)1912 70 8441
Web   www.thestaithhouse.co.uk

Entry 468 Map

Nottinghamshire

The Full Moon
Morton

The Prices took on this creeper-clad Morton landmark in 2013, and have preserved the villagey friendliness: fish-and-chip takeaways, a toy cupboard for the kids, family fun-runs and an annual scarecrow trail. As for the food, chef James Stanton takes classic British ingredients and teeters them in elegant bonsai stacks on rustic hunks of slate. Eye-catching starters include pea, ham hock and truffle oil soup, and goat's cheese fondue with parsnip crisps, pine nuts and confit garlic; you can eat more substantially from the main-course menu for under a tenner. There's a buzz in the bar, where locals hold court and the coal fire fizzes, but the trimmings are coolly contemporary: pale wood and pinstriped upholstery in tones of silver, blue and grey. A great little find – you can even get married here.

Meals	Lunch £5.50–£12.
	Dinner £11–£18.50.
	Sunday lunch, 2 courses, £16.
Closed	Open all day.

Richard & Alicia Price
The Full Moon,
Main Street, Morton,
Southwell NG25 0UT
Tel +44 (0)1636 830251
Web www.thefullmoonmorton.co.uk

Entry 469 Map 8

Nottinghamshire

Caunton Beck
Caunton

Having hatched the successful Wig & Mitre in Lincoln, the Hopes looked for a rural equivalent and found one in this pretty village, then reconstructed the skeleton of the 16th-century Hole Arms. The elongated bar, with shining brass trimmings, frosted glass, scrubbed tables, serious tableware and rosebuds in tiny vases, is a hugely popular spot for breakfast with the papers from 8am, and later, sandwiches, daily blackboard lunches and set meals. It's deliciously rich comfort food (lamb and sage faggots, roast venison) with some oriental surprises, such as wok fried sesame and chilli chicken Singapore noodles. Puddings are fabulous. The dining room is less intimate, there's a cosy fire in winter, parasol picnic sets on the small front lawn in summer, and well-managed ales on hand pump all year around.

| Meals | Lunch & dinner £9.50–£22.50. |
| Closed | Open all day. |

Gill Woolsgrove
Caunton Beck,
Main Street, Caunton,
Newark NG23 6AB
Tel +44 (0)1522 538902
Web www.wigandmitre.com

Entry 470 Map 9

Nottinghamshire

The Prince Rupert
Newark

Now sympathetically restored, this 15th-century town-centre local creaks with history and has a deliciously pubby feel. It's just the kind of place you hope to chance upon – not grand, not scruffy, just right, where locals pile in for pints of local ale and as much thought goes into the beers as the wines. The entrance opens to a series of small rooms where, among dark beams and polished wood, warmth and cosiness emanate from an open fire and a little seating spot snug enough for two. But upstairs is where the biggest treat lies: two rooms revealing the ancient building's glory, all beamed ceilings and timbered walls, and an ancient skylight exposed during the renovation. The regularly changing menu reveals further simple enticements: stone-baked pizzas; ham, eggs and sauté potatoes; beef lasagne.

Nottinghamshire

Martin's Arms
Colston Bassett

An Elizabethan farmhouse that became an ale house around 1700, and an inn 100 years later. Today it is a deeply civilised pub. The front room exudes country-house charm – scatter cushions on sofas and settles, crackling logs in Jacobean fireplaces – and you can order a splendid ploughman's with Colston Bassett stilton from the dairy up the road (do visit). In the restaurant, menus change daily, while highlights include pan-fried scallops with Stafford black pudding; locally shot game with seasonal vegetables; delicious Sunday roast beef. Polish it off with treacle sponge and butterscotch sauce with brandy butter ice cream. Behind the bar is an impressive range of well-kept real ales, cognacs and malts, with 20 wines (including sparkling and champagne) by the glass or carafe, and a further 22 by the bottle.

Meals	Lunch & dinner from £6.95.
	Not Sunday.
Closed	Open all day.

Meals	Bar meals from £7.50.
	Lunch £5.95.
	Dinner from £14.50.
	Sunday roast £18.95 & £23.95.
	No food Christmas Day.
Closed	3pm-6pm Mon-Sat.
	5pm-7pm Sun.

Tony & Heidi Yale
The Prince Rupert,
46 Stodman Street,
Newark NG24 1AW

Tel +44 (0)1636 918121
Web www.theprincerupert.co.uk

Entry 471 Map 9

Lynne Strafford Bryan
& Salvatore Inguanta
Martin's Arms, School Lane, Colston
Bassett, Nottingham NG12 3FD

Tel +44 (0)1949 81361
Web www.themartinsarms.co.uk

Entry 472 Map 9

Oxfordshire

The Three Pigeons Inn
Banbury

Close to the centre of busy Banbury town is this pretty thatched coaching inn, owned by Tina and Paul Laird. Recently refurbished with oak flooring, the original stone walls hark back to its beginnings while two attractive coal-effect gas burners (no logs allowed because of the thatch!), one snug in the old inglenook, lend warmth. At the rear of the pub is a large stone terrace with weathered oak seating for 60. The team is friendly and well-informed, serving a refreshing choice of old ales; they are also great on whiskies and wines by the glass. As for the menus, you'll find pigeon breasts with asparagus tips and wild mushrooms, Spring lamb rump with dauphinoise potatoes, and an array of super puddings including a truly indulgent white chocolate and raspberry cheesecake. Cheeses are served with homemade chutneys and port jelly. Upstairs are three very smart bedrooms, with feature wallpapers and characterful beams, swish bathrooms and superb French-style beds. All overlook the courtyard, all are perfectly peaceful. *All rooms hired as a suite (sleeps 4 adults, 2 children) £225.*

Rooms	3 doubles: £105 - £125.. Singles £105. Extra bed £30-£40 per person per night.
Meals	Lunch & dinner £12.95-£18.95.
Closed	Rarely.

Tina Laird
The Three Pigeons Inn,
3 Southam Road,
Banbury OX16 2ED
Tel   +44 (0)1295 275220
Web   www.thethreepigeons.com

Entry 473 Map 8

The White Horse Inn
Duns Tew

The White Horse has been on a roll since Michael arrived in 2014. The atmosphere is convivial, the food exceptional and the stables have been transformed. Old flagged floors, inglenooks and open fires, candles on wooden tables, a corner with a Chesterfield, a snug for a private party, guest ales behind the bar. This handsome 17th-century building, tucked away in the pretty village of Duns Tew, is all you hope a Cotswolds pub will be. Beyond is the restaurant, less rustic but still atmospheric: dark chairs and tables, old standing timbers, a log-burner at one end. Braised squid with tomatoes and white wine aïoli; leek and gruyère tart; cottage pie with greens. The menu changes daily, the fruit and veg are from North Aston Organics, the lamb is from the farm up the road (sweet, lean Zwartbles meat favoured by Rick Stein). No garden, but you can eat on the terrace in summer. In the stables there are four fresh new bedrooms, two up, two down, each stylish and delightful, with down-feather pillows and tartan wool throws. Breakfast is worth getting up for. *Pets by arrangement.*

Rooms	7 doubles, 1 twin: £71–£85.
Meals	Dinner from £11.
Closed	Rarely.

Adam Marley
The White Horse Inn,
Daisy Hill,
Duns Tew OX25 6JS
Tel   +44 (0)1869 340272
Web   www.dunstewwhitehorse.co.uk

Entry 474 Map 8

Oxfordshire

The Kingham Plough
Kingham

You don't expect to find locals clamouring for a table in a country pub on a cold Tuesday in February, but different rules apply at the Kingham Plough. Emily, once junior sous chef at the famous Fat Duck in Bray, is now doing her own thing and it would seem the locals approve. You eat in the tithe barn, now a splendid dining room, with ceilings open to ancient rafters and excellent art on the walls. Attentive staff bring sublime food. Dig into game broth with pheasant dumplings, fabulous lamb hotpot with crispy kale, and hot chocolate fondant with blood orange sorbet. Interiors elsewhere are equally pretty, all the result of a delightful refurbishment. There's a piano by the fire in the locals' bar, a terrace outside for summer dining, fruit trees, herbs and lavender in the garden. Bedrooms, three of which are small, have honest prices, super-comfy beds, flat-screen TVs, smart carpets, white linen and the odd beam; one has a claw-foot bath. Arrive by train, straight from London, to be met by a bus that delivers you to the front door. The Daylesford Organic Farm Shop/café is close. *Minimum stay: 2 nights at weekends.*

Rooms	7 twin/doubles: £90–£130. Singles from £75.
Meals	Bar meals from £5. Lunch from £15. Dinner, 3 courses, about £30. Sunday roast from £17.
Closed	Christmas Day.

Emily Watkins & Miles Lampson
The Kingham Plough,
The Green, Kingham,
Chipping Norton OX7 6YD
Tel   +44 (0)1608 658327
Web   www.thekinghamplough.co.uk

Entry 475 Map 8

The Wild Rabbit
Kingham

Lady Bamford, owner of the trendy Daylesford Organic Farm Shop, surprised everyone when she spent a mint transforming Kingham's Tollgate Inn into the Wild Rabbit, a posh pub with rooms. With her farm shop & café, cookery school and treatment rooms just down the road (or a scenic tramp across fields), it makes perfect sense. It's seriously smart, all neutral tones, stone walls and tiled floors, but it remains a proper local, welcoming dogs and muddy-booted walkers and farmers for a pint of Hooky and an ox tongue sandwich at the green-slate bar. In the lofty oak-framed dining room: an open kitchen, bread oven, laden farmhouse table and stone fireplace. Savour crab ravioli with crab bisque, Wooton estate venison with cranberry jus, steamed ginger pud. Retire to one of twelve stunning bedrooms, stripped back to reveal natural Cotswold stone, with bespoke furnishings, luxury linen on big beds (some have four-posters), mini-bars, Nespresso machines, and swish tiled bathrooms with Bamford products. A treat and good value too. *Pets by arrangement.*

Rooms	11 doubles: £135–£225.
	1 family room for 4: £225.
Meals	Starters from £7.50.
	Dinner from £13.50.
Closed	Rarely.

Graham Williams
The Wild Rabbit,
Church Street, Kingham,
Chipping Norton OX7 6YA

Tel   +44 (0)1608 658389
Web   www.thewildrabbit.co.uk

Entry 476 Map 8

Oxfordshire

The Kings Head Inn
Bledington

About as Doctor Dolittle-esque as it gets. Achingly pretty Cotswold stone cottages around a village green with quacking ducks, a pond and a perfect pub with a cobbled courtyard. Archie is young, affable and charming with locals and guests, but Nic is his greatest asset – a milliner, she has done up the bedrooms and they look fabulous. All are different, most have a stunning view, some family furniture mixed in with 'bits' she's picked up, painted wood, great colours and lush fabrics. The bar is lively – not with music but with talk – so choose rooms over the courtyard if you prefer a quiet evening. The pretty flagstoned dining room (exposed stone walls, Farrow & Ball paints, pale wood tables) is inviting, there are lovely unpompous touches like jugs of cow parsley in the loo, and you can lunch by the fire in the bar – on devilled kidneys, sausage and mash, local Dexter beef and Guinness pie. There's a brilliant new chef and they do homemade puds, serious cheeses, too, and breakfasts are huge! Loads to do round these parts: antiques in Stow, walking and riding in gorgeous countryside, and a music festival in June. *Minimum stay: 2 nights at weekends.*

Rooms	9 doubles, 3 twin/doubles: £100–£135. Singles £80–£100.
Meals	Lunch from £7.50. Dinner, 3 courses, from £30. Sunday roast £15.
Closed	Christmas, 25-27 December.

Archie & Nicola Orr-Ewing
The Kings Head Inn,
The Green, Bledington,
Chipping Norton OX7 6XQ
Tel   +44 (0)1608 658365
Web   www.kingsheadinn.net

Entry 477 Map 8

The Feathered Nest Country Inn
Nether Westcote

The village is tiny, the view is fantastic, the bar is lively, the rooms are a treat. This 300-year-old malthouse recently had a facelift and now shines. Interiors mix all the old originals – stone walls, timber frames, beamed ceilings, open fires – with a contemporary, rustic style. The net result is an extremely attractive country inn, one of the best in the south. Downstairs, one room flows into another. You get beautiful bay windows, roaring fires, saddled bar stools, green leather armchairs. Everywhere you go something lovely catches the eye, not least the view – one of the best in the Cotswolds; it will draw you to the terrace where your eyes drift off over quilted fields to a distant ridge. You get beds of lavender, swathes of lawn, a vegetable garden that serves the kitchen. Bedrooms upstairs are gorgeous. One is enormous, two have the view, beds are dressed in crisp linen. Most have power showers, one has a claw-foot bath, all have robes. There's even a Nespresso machine in every room. Super food waits downstairs: Old Spot terrine, Fairford chicken, rhubarb and champagne jelly. *Minimum stay: 2 nights at weekends.*

Rooms	3 doubles: £190–£250. Singles £160–£220.
Meals	Lunch & dinner £6.50–£30. Not Sunday eve.
Closed	Rarely.

Tony & Amanda Timmer
The Feathered Nest Country Inn,
Nether Westcote,
Chipping Norton OX7 6SD

Tel	+44 (0)1993 833030
Web	www.thefeatherednestinn.co.uk

Entry 478 Map 8

Oxfordshire

The Swan
Swinbrook

This ancient pub sits in glorious country with the river Windrush yards from the door and a cricket pitch waiting beyond. It started life as a water mill and stands on the Devonshire estate (the late Duchess advised on its restoration). Outside, wisteria wanders along stone walls and creepers blush red in the autumn sun. Interiors come laden with period charm: beautiful windows, open fires, warm colours, the odd beam. Over the years thirsty feet have worn grooves into 400-year-old flagstones, so follow in their footsteps and stop for a pint of Hook Norton at the bar, then eat from a seasonal menu that brims with local produce: deep-fried Windrush goat's cheese, Foxbury Farm chargrilled steak, rich chocolate tart with orange sorbet. Fires roar in winter while doors in the conservatory restaurant open onto a pretty garden in good weather. Bedrooms in the old forge are the most recent addition: expect 15th-century walls and 21st-century interior design. You get pastel colours to soak up the light, smart white linen on comfy beds and a pink chaise longue in the suite. Special.

Rooms	4 doubles, 1 twin: £125–£150. 1 suite for 2: £180–£195. Cottage - 5 twin/doubles: £125–£150. Singles from £70.
Meals	Lunch from £5. Dinner, 3 courses, about £30. Sunday roast from £14.95.
Closed	Christmas Day & Boxing Day.

Archie & Nicola Orr-Ewing
The Swan,
Swinbrook,
Burford OX18 4DY
Tel   +44 (0)1993 823339
Web   www.theswanswinbrook.co.uk

Entry 479 Map 8

The Angel at Burford
Burford

It's a Hook Norton house so they sell the excellent Hooky and stout, and a guest beer too. Take a pint to the sofa by the roaring log fire, or a good whisky or wine; this is what winter Sundays were made for. The Angel, listed and 16th-century, is tucked peacefully away from the broad beautiful high street. Take a look at the ever-changing blackboard menu with its focus on simplicity and quality, there's something for everyone: delicious pastrami sandwiches with French fries and dressed salad, moules marinière, rare-beef Sunday roasts, trios of cheeses and refreshing sorbets. Three big, comfortable and characterful rooms come with the requisite beams, sash windows and creaking wood floors, one overlooking the pretty courtyard and garden. Perhaps the perfect Cotswolds' pub. *One night weekend stays welcome.*

Rooms	2 doubles, 1 twin/double: £90–£120. Dinner, B&B £130–£160 per person per night.
Meals	Lunch & dinner £13.50–£21.50.
Closed	18 January to 11 February.

Gemma Finch & Terrance King
The Angel at Burford,
14 Witney Street,
Burford OX18 4SN

Tel	+44 (0)1993 822714
Web	www.theangelatburford.co.uk

Entry 480 Map 8

Old Swan & Minster Mill
Minster Lovell

Understated magic abounds at this 16th-century riverside inn, a half-timbered beauty transformed into a charming gastropub. In the rambling bar are gnarled beams and timbers, bright kilims and stone-flagged floors, and crisp checked armchairs by big beautiful fireplaces – aromatic with logs in winter. In perfect sympathy with the mood, traditional British food is cooked with a modern approach by head chef, David Mwita; ingredients are of the best quality and the vegetables are home-grown. Menus change daily; try seared king scallops, Cotswold rack of lamb, rib-eye steak with horseradish mayonnaise... and for pudding, classic caramelised lemon tart. Steep twisting stairs lead to very fine bedrooms that combine solid darkwood antiques with every modern comfort – luxurious linen and fine down, big beds, cafetières of coffee, decanters of sloe gin, bathrobes in lovely bathrooms. (There are many more rooms in the modern Minster Mill across the road, smaller but overlooking beautiful gardens.) Oxford and Burford are close
Minimum stay: 2 nights at weekends.

Rooms	57 doubles: £165–£275.
	1 suite for 2: £350.
	2 singles: £155.
Meals	Bar meals from £8.50.
	Lunch from £9.50.
	Dinner from £14.95.
	Sunday lunch, 3 courses, £30.
Closed	Rarely.

Patrick Jones
Old Swan & Minster Mill,
Old Minster Lovell, Minster Lovell,
Witney OX29 0RN
Tel   +44 (0)1993 774441
Web   www.oldswanandminstermill.com

The Maytime Inn
Asthall

The setting is gorgeous, the village is historic, and the 17th-century coaching inn has its own smithy. Set off on a circular walk and end up in the bar. A cool young team run this rather posh pub, and that includes chef Dom whose flavours and pairings are terrific: inventive but not over the top. There's wild mushroom risotto with truffle oil and pea shoots, and rose loin of veal with spiced tomato sauce – Cotswolds-sourced of course; even the butter is local. Sandwiches, rib-eye steaks, fish and chips too. As for Dom's damson gin and Katie's sponge cake – not for kids – they make a perfect pair. Indeed, there are 15 varieties of gin on offer, Dominic knows his whiskeys and wines, and there are interesting guest ales too. Dining areas are split level, a top-notch modern take on traditional, all new slate flag floors and tartan cushions, Windsor chairs and white-painted beams. Outside: a kitchen garden and a suntrap terrace. On the ground floor: handsome bedrooms with delicious beds, folding desks and all the technology. The quietest are away from the courtyard; go for a large room if you fancy a deep soak.

Rooms	6 doubles: £95–£150.
Meals	Starters from £6.50.
	Dinner from £12.50.
Closed	Rarely.

	Dominic Wood
	The Maytime Inn,
	Asthall,
	Burford OX18 4HW
Tel	+44 (0)1993 822068
Web	www.themaytime.com

Entry 482 Map 8

Oxfordshire

The Trout at Tadpole Bridge
Buckland Marsh

A 17th-century Cotswold inn on the banks of the Thames, so pick up a pint, drift into the garden and watch life float by. The Trout is a drinking fisherman's paradise, walls are busy with bendy rods, children are liked and dogs can doze in the flagstoned bars. The downstairs is open plan and timber-framed, there are gilt mirrors and logs piled high in alcoves. Gareth and Helen have cast their fairy dust into every corner: super bedrooms, fabulous modern food (fish chowder, Kelmscott pork belly, pear frangipane tart), a relaxed style. Bedrooms at the back are away from the crowd and three open onto a small courtyard – but you may prefer to stay put in your room and indulge in funky fabrics, monsoon showers (one room has a claw-foot bath), DVD players, a library of films. Sleigh beds, brass beds, upholstered armchairs... one even has a roof terrace. You can watch boats pass from the breakfast table, feast on local sausages, tuck into homemade marmalade courtesy of Helen's mum. Food is as local as possible, and there are maps for walkers to keep you fit. Bliss! *Minimum stay: 2 nights at weekends.*

Rooms	2 doubles, 3 twin/doubles: £130. 1 suite for 2: £160. Singles from £85.
Meals	Lunch from £5. Dinner, 3 courses, about £30. Sunday roast from £14.95.
Closed	Christmas Day & Boxing Day.

Gareth & Helen Pugh
The Trout at Tadpole Bridge,
Buckland Marsh,
Faringdon SN7 8RF
Tel   +44 (0)1367 870382
Web   www.trout-inn.co.uk

Entry 483 Map 8

The Lamb at Buckland
Buckland

Follow the signs through picture-perfect Buckland to the 18th-century Lamb, tucked into a green corner of this historic estate village. The combined talents and enthusiasms of Shelley and chef Richard have turned this little inn into one of the best; it's an absolute gem. Step into a simple, rustic bar to find crackling logs, low beams, fat candles, old dining tables, leather wing chairs, local ales and Cotswold gin. Beyond is the more refined dining room, where modern seasonal menus champion local suppliers (Kelmscott pork, home-grown vegetables, and local game). Beautiful food flows from the kitchen: duck balls with red cabbage; roasted fillet of pork with prunes and pancetta; butternut squash and sweet potato gallette with goat's cheese and mushroom cream sauce; warm chocolate and walnut brownies. The trio of bedrooms here is delightful: crisp cotton, down duvets, colourful throws, a mix of pine and painted furniture, iPod-radios, bathrooms fresh and simple. The Thames Path, William Morris's Kelmscott Manor and Oxford are close by.

Rooms	3 doubles: £80–£90.
Meals	Bar meals from £6.
	Lunch from £9.50.
	Dinner from £12.95.
	Sunday roast from £12.
	Not Sunday eve & Mondays.
Closed	Rarely.

Richard & Shelley Terry
The Lamb at Buckland,
Lamb Lane, Buckland,
Faringdon SN7 8QN

Tel	+44 (0)1367 870484
Web	www.lambatbuckland.co.uk

Entry 484 Map 8

Oxfordshire

The Fat Fox Inn
Watlington

A stone's throw from the big smoke yet wonderfully rural. Historic Watlington is on the edge of the Chiltern Hills, red kites wheel above beech woods and the Ridgeway runs through. The 17th-century building has been part pub, butchers, bakery and shop in its day but is now an inn to the core. The bronze buddha on the bar gazes serenely over pumps with Brakspear Bitter and Oxford Gold, the carpeted bar is cosy and simple, there's an open fire, sofas and an elegant separate dining room with oriental rugs. Consider smoked chicken and foie gras terrine, fig chutney and sourdough toast; fillet of pollock, chick pea, chorizo and sherry stew with saffron aïoli; lemon financier and thyme ice cream – just some of the delights from chef Mark Gambles and quite simply divine. Staff and owner are delightful and the whole place hums along on this team's super-friendly and engaging manner. Set well behind the bustle in several old barns are a variety of bedrooms – some with signature beds and trappings, all with antiques, beams and small neat bathrooms.

Rooms	5 doubles, 4 twins: £75–£119.
	Singles £65–£109.
	Extra bed/sofabed £20 per person per night.
Meals	Bar meals from £5.
	Lunch from £12.
	Dinner from £27.
	Sunday lunch, 2-3 courses, £20–£25.
Closed	Rarely.

John Riddell
The Fat Fox Inn,
13 Shirburn Street,
Watlington OX49 5BU

Tel	+44 (0)1491 613040
Web	www.thefatfoxinn.co.uk

Entry 485 Map 4

The Cherry Tree Inn
Stoke Row

A short drive from London (and Oxford) is a handsome old pub in Stoke Row, with food, service and bedrooms to match. It is one of three dining pubs in the Henley area run by the same operator. Throughout all is fresh, light and airy, with chunky wood tables and pale colours, and floors of stripped wood or stone; of the bars, the biggest is in the middle, warm and cosy with an open fire. You can eat where you like and the food is pub grub done well, with lots on the menu. Sunday lunches see two roasts as well as fish pie or sausages, and always a dish for vegetarians; there are tasty meals for little ones and puddings that sound suitably naughty. You could drop by for a pint of Brakspear and a platter of ham, salami, pork belly and chorizo, or tuck into tandoori chicken breast with all the trimmings, or beer-battered cod. In summer there are pig roasts in the beer garden. Crisp linen, cream walls, big beds, generous breakfasts… it's also a good weekend base for the area, with four ground-floor bedrooms in the wood-clad barn, a stagger away. Your dog can stay too.

Rooms	4 doubles: £85–£100. Singles £65–£85.
Meals	Lunch from £6.95. Sunday lunch from £12.50. À la carte dinner £20–£30. Not Sunday eve.
Closed	Rarely.

Lolly & Doug Green
The Cherry Tree Inn,
Stoke Row,
Henley-on-Thames RG9 5QA

Tel	+44 (0)1491 680430
Web	www.thecherrytreeinn.co.uk

Entry 486 Map 4

The Star Inn
Wantage

Brush up your navigation to seek out this 300-year-old dining pub lost down lanes in a sleepy hamlet. Interior designer Caron Williams bought her faded and failing local and, with talented chef Dave Watts (ex Le Manoir aux Quat'Saison), has put it firmly on Oxfordshire's culinary map. It may be a foodie destination but the spruced up bar, with its wood floors, old pine tables and hop adorned beams, has a relaxed feel – dogs, walkers and cyclists are all welcome. Peruse the papers over a pint of Hooky and a bar snack (sandwiches, burger, scotch egg), or settle in for a memorable meal, Dave's food is top notch and the set menu is a steal: crispy pig's head with salted cod, chorizo and red pepper dressing, followed by venison with quince, braised red cabbage and nut butter pan juices, and prune and armagnac rice pudding. Refurbished rooms in the converted barn are contemporary and chic with rustic charm. Calm colours, rich fabrics, fine linen on big beds and smart tiled bathrooms with top toiletries. A star in the making.

Rooms	4 twin/doubles: £95–£105. 1 suite for 2: £125. 1 family room for 4: £135. 2 singles: £75.
Meals	Starters from £5.95. Dinner from £9.
Closed	Rarely.

Caron Williams & Dave Watts
The Star Inn,
Watery Lane, Sparsholt,
Wantage OX12 9PL
Tel   +44 (0)1235 751873
Web   www.thestarsparsholt.co.uk

Oxfordshire

The Lord Nelson
Brightwell Baldwin

The back-lane setting of Brightwell Baldwin lives up to expectations: cottages tumbling down the hill, a church perched on a bank, a rambling inn festooned with flowers, flags on Trafalgar Day. The creamy façade and front veranda entice you into a civilised interior: wonky beams, logs fires, cosy corners; antiques, fine old prints and Nelson memorabilia keep the eye entertained. Most come to dine, and dine well, on game in the autumn or scallops with lime and coriander dressing; rack of lamb with red wine sauce; sea bass on crab mash with tomato and black olive tapenade. Retire to the snug (deep sofas, table lamps, a country-house feel) for coffee and a little doze. And there's more – Brakspear on tap, 20 wines by the glass, friendly, smiley service and a wonderful rear terrace for summer sipping when the lobster and crab festival is celebrated in style.

Meals	Lunch & dinner £10.50–£18.95.
	Bar meals £10.
Closed	3pm–6pm.
	Open all day Sun.

Roger & Carole Shippey
The Lord Nelson,
Brightwell Baldwin,
Watlington OX49 5NP
Tel +44 (0)1491 612497
Web www.lordnelson-inn.co.uk

Entry 488 Map 4

Oxfordshire

The Red Lion
Britwell Salome

In the hamlet of Britwell Salome is a modest little pub that deserves celebration. Foodies should absolutely seek it out, for its commitment to superb produce and in-house butchery. Walk straight into the planked, dog-friendly bar: a big squishy chesterfield, dark wooden tables, burgundy walls, an open fire, and a patio garden that opens in summer. The dining area, spread across low-ceilinged nooks where a hotch-potch of tables are set with glasses, cutlery and paper napkins, is a disarmingly simple backdrop to rousing British cooking – outstanding food from chef Andrew Hill. There are Scotch eggs made with black pudding, hot pork rillettes on toast, succulent mutton burgers, whole lemon sole with capers, and the baked strawberry custard is exquisite. It's not a dining room that happens to be a pub, it's a pub that welcomes all.

Meals	Lunch & dinner £12.50–£21.50.
	Sandwiches £4.50.
	Set lunch £15 & £19.
Closed	3pm–6pm.
	Sun evenings.

Eilidh Ferguson
The Red Lion,
Britwell Salome,
Watlington OX49 5LG
Tel +44 (0)1491 613140
Web www.theredlionbritwellsalome.co.uk

Entry 489 Map 4

Oxfordshire

The Crooked Billet
Stoke Row

Dick Turpin apparently courted the landlord's daughter and Kate Winslet held her wedding breakfast here. Pints of Brakspear are drawn direct from the cask (there is no bar!) and the rusticity of the place charms all who manage to find it: beams and inglenooks, walls lined with bottles and baskets of spent corks, old pine. In the larger room, red walls display old photographs and mirrors; shelves are stacked with books… by candlelight it's irresistible. It's more restaurant than pub, so the menu is modern, eclectic and long: salt and pepper squid with chilli jam, Moroccan spiced lamb rump, Bakewell tart and custard. The food is founded on well-sourced raw materials (allotment holders are encouraged) and bolstered by a satisfying wine list. Weekly music, too, and a big garden bordering the beech woods where children may roam.

Meals	Lunch & dinner £12.50-£20.
Closed	2.30pm-7pm.
	Open all day Sat & Sun.

Paul Clerehugh
The Crooked Billet,
Newlands Lane, Stoke Row,
Henley-on-Thames RG9 5PU
Tel   +44 (0)1491 681048
Web   www.thecrookedbillet.co.uk

Entry 490 Map 4

Oxfordshire

The Five Horseshoes
Maidensgrove

This cute pub-cottage sits on Maidensgrove Common, in a remote spot high in the Chilterns, on a lane that winds past Russell's Water near Stonor House. Arrive early for the best seat in the garden and the finest view in Oxfordshire: imagine gazing on rolling hills, pint of Brakspears to hand, red kites wheeling overhead, steaks sizzling on the chargrill. Windows in the conservatory dining room also get the view – or you can head for the rambling bars where roaring hearths warm the cockles. Find low crooked ceilings, beams, nooks, burgundy carpets, cushioned settles and tables that have been collected over years – a perfect place to tuck into fresh, plump mussels and chunks of homemade bread to mop up the juices. They make their own ginger beer and there are roasts on Sundays. Then head off into the hills.

Meals	Bar meals £5-£9.75.
	Lunch & dinner £8.50-£16.
	Sunday roast £15.75-£18.50.
Closed	Mon all day.
	Sun 6pm-11pm.

Dan & Tracey Taverner
The Five Horseshoes,
Maidensgrove,
Henley-on-Thames RG9 6EX
Tel   +44 (0)1491 641282
Web   www.thefivehorseshoes.co.uk

Entry 491 Map 4

Oxfordshire

The Plowden Arms
Shiplake

Inside has a 1920s feel; at any minute Agatha Christie might enter and order herself a gin fizz. Dark polished chairs sit on oak parquet, there's an open brick fireplace with hops above, and shining glasses on tables. And you'll find old forgotten favourites on the menu; Matthew worked at the Savoy Grill and calls himself "unashamedly old-fashioned." So tuck into herrings in oatmeal with sweet lemon salad, lamb cutlets cooked à la Reform Club in 1839, and barley cream with blackcurrant compote. The British cheeses with pear chutney are a delight (you can tell a lot from a cheeseboard) and if the slow-roast shoulder of pork is anything to go by, Matthew is a fabulous chef. Ales are in great condition, wines are mostly European, dogs are welcome, and the sloping garden next to fields is heaven on a summer's day.

Meals	Dinner, 2 courses, £14.50; 3 courses, £18.
Closed	Mon all day. 2.30pm–5pm Tues–Fri. 3pm–5pm Sat. Open midday–4pm Sun.

Matthew Woodley & Ruth Peters
The Plowden Arms,
Reading Road, Shiplake,
Henley-on-Thames RG9 4BX

| Tel | +44 (0)118 940 2794 |
| Web | www.plowdenarmsshiplake.co.uk |

Entry 492 Map 4

Oxfordshire

The Quince Tree
Stonor

In a tiny hamlet, a truffle's throw from Henley-on-Thames, surrounded by sweeping hills, is something exciting: a foodie complex of farm shop, café and restaurant built around the old pub that fronts them. Inside, all is light, cool and modern. The airy café is great for families, the deli is divine (Wyre Forest salami, local cassis, elegant macaroons), and the pub is dominated by immaculate dining tables. The overall feel is gastro, the menu changes regularly and our Farm Platter was exceptional. Try winter vegetable salad with crispy potato and truffle dressing; pork belly with homemade black pudding, creamed potato and quince chutney; warm chocolate pot with blood orange sorbet. What's more, with multiple stools at the bar, you can as easily drop by for a perfectly kept pint of Rebellion as for a wine from the short, modern list.

Meals	Bar meals £9.95–£12.95. Lunch & dinner £13–£19.
Closed	Open all day.

Amy Yardley
The Quince Tree,
Stonor,
Henley-on-Thames RG9 6HE

| Tel | +44 (0)1491 639039 |
| Web | www.thequincetree.com |

Entry 493 Map 4

Oxfordshire

The Frog
Skirmett

On the village main street, deep in the beautiful Hambledon valley, this 18th-century coaching inn is surrounded by open meadows and glorious walks. Head for the secluded garden, pint of Marlow Rebellion in hand, gaze across the valley and watch the red kites wheel. Or choose a sofa by the fire and mingle with locals and walkers. Wood floors, wall-mounted beer lists, bold mirrors and homogenous tables fill the dining areas where menus list hearty pub classics – steak, Guinness and mushroom pie, smoked haddock on champ with mustard sauce, lamb rump with port and redcurrant sauce – alongside the deli boards. Don't miss the sticky toffee pudding – or the once-a-month pub 'shop' selling Noelle's savoury pastries, cakes and chutneys.

Meals	Lunch & bar meals from £6.95. Dinner from £9.95. Not Sunday eve Nov-April.
Closed	3pm-6pm. Open all day Sun (except Sun eves in winter).

Jim Crowe & Noelle Greene
The Frog,
Skirmett,
Henley-on-Thames RG9 6TG
Tel   +44 (0)1491 638996
Web   www.thefrogatskirmett.co.uk

Entry 494 Map 4

Oxfordshire

The White Hart
Fyfield

Stone mullioned windows, huge oak timbers and a magnificent arch-braced roof form a historic backdrop for oak settles, wrought-iron candle holders, white linen napkins and delicious food cooked by Mark. The menu is modern, British and changes from day to day depending upon what is fresh, in season and from the restaurant's brimming kitchen garden (purple Shiraz mange tout, fine beans, courgettes, beetroot, Chantenay carrots, Swiss chard, cherries…). There's scallops, black pudding beignet and piccalilli sauce; venison haunch and cottage pie with creamed cabbage and girolles; buttermilk panna cotta, caramelised orange and honeycomb crumble. Suppliers are mostly local and mentioned on the menu so you can see where everything's from. Enjoy four real ales and Cheddar valley cider, served by friendly staff who are capable and knowledgeable.

Meals	Bar meals £6-£20. Lunch & dinner £13-£20. Sunday lunch, 3 courses, £26. Not Sunday eve.
Closed	3pm-5.30pm & Mon all day (except Bank Holidays). Open all day Sat & Sun.

Mark & Kay Chandler
The White Hart,
Main Road, Fyfield,
Abingdon OX13 5LW
Tel   +44 (0)1865 390585
Web   www.whitehart-fyfield.com

Entry 495 Map 8

Oxfordshire

The Mole Inn
Toot Baldon

The Mole continues to wow Oxford foodies – it's packed most days. Expect an impeccable stone exterior, topiary in the garden and a ravishing bar. There are stripped beams and chunky walls, black leather sofas, logs in the grate and a dresser that groans with rustic breads and olive jars. Chic rusticity extends into three dining areas: fat candles on blond wood tables, thick terracotta floors, the sun angling in on a delicious plate of beef casserole. Daily specials point to a modern British menu peppered with eastern inspiration: devilled kidneys on a toasted muffin with tzatziki; crab risotto with chilli, ginger and lime. The cooking is excellent; we enjoyed a mixed grill of fish with fries and lime mayonnaise, and a terrific treacle tart. Warm, friendly staff complete the picture.

Meals	Bar meals £5.95–£9.95. Lunch & dinner £12.95–£18.
Closed	Open all day.

Gary Witchalls
The Mole Inn,
Toot Baldon,
Oxford OX44 9NG
Tel   +44 (0)1865 340001
Web   www.moleinn.com

Entry 496 Map 8

Oxfordshire

The Magdalen Arms
Oxford

Suburban Oxford is not the most obvious setting for some of Britain's best pub food. But Anchor & Hope graduates Florence Fowler and Tony Abarno have created a hostelry worthy of foodie acclaim. Those fretting over another local hijacked for elaborate gastropubbery need not: half this pub's not inconsiderable space is cutlery free and, thanks to four well-kept real ales, classy cocktails and a billiards table, drinkers will find much to like; plus a chop house-chic interior of advertising posters, scuffed wooden floor, mishmash wooden tables and bright streams of bunting – the antithesis of fine dining. Equally unpretentious is the food: gutsy, produce-led fare, as affordable as it is likeable. Knuckle down to Hereford beef with duck fat potato cake and béarnaise; braised shank of wild boar with polenta; boozy cherries and buttermilk pudding.

Meals	Lunch & dinner from £13. Sunday lunch, 3 courses, £30.
Closed	Mon & Tues lunch.

Florence Fowler & Tony Abarno
The Magdalen Arms,
Iffley Road,
Oxford OX4 1SJ
Tel   +44 (0)1865 243159
Web   www.magdalenarms.com

Entry 497 Map 8

Oxfordshire

The Fishes
Oxfordshire
North Hinksey

Three acres of gardens, minutes from the A34, walking distance from the dreaming spires —The Fishes has it all. It's run by Peach Pubs, the most innovative small pub group in the land; where else can you borrow a rug for the garden, order a Pimm's and a picnic basket for two and spread out by a river? Or order a family roast beef platter for the weekend, and on Sunday sit down to it on the veranda. There's lots to enjoy: a deli board selection; starters of sautéed squid linguine with chilli, lemon and parsley; goat's cheese and spinach risotto; venison with bubble and squeak; sea bream with cider cream sauce; sausage and mash. Greene King ales, decent wines by the glass and a passion for locally sourced produce complete this happy picture. Just get there early on a fine day!

Meals	Bar meals from £5.
	Lunch from £7.
	Dinner from £10.
	Sunday roast £14.95.
Closed	Open all day.

Owain Llywd Jones
The Fishes,
North Hinksey,
Oxford OX2 0NA
Tel   +44 (0)1865 249796
Web   www.fishesoxford.co.uk

Entry 498 Map 8

Oxfordshire

The Rickety Press
Oxford

Jericho is a pretty quarter of Oxford and The Rickety Press, a big corner pub, is a quick cycle ride from the centre. It's the sort of place where you can eat bang up to date, faultless food in the restaurant or in the bar; we had pan-fried cod and chips with tartare sauce. The central bar is cool, contemporary, inviting, with antique stripped floors, background jazz and books on bold walls; the restaurant is at the back, similar but larger, with a log-burner. Staff love what they're doing and care about the details. You could have the foie gras and chicken liver pâté to start, then the deep-sea moules frites or the sharing rib from the grill. Made with love, no pretence. Note: if you bring the car, there's a Pay & Display a five-minute walk.

Meals	Lunch from £8.
	Dinner, 2 courses, from £12.50.
Closed	Open all day.

Leo Johnson & Christopher Manners
The Rickety Press,
67 Cranham Street,
Oxford OX2 6DE
Tel   +44 (0)1865 424581
Web   www.thericketypress.com

Entry 499 Map 8

Oxfordshire

The Anchor Inn
Oxford

A pint of Wadworth, an Aspalls cider, a café latte or a glass of Domaine de la Renaudie – whatever you choose, it will charm you. The Jericho district of North Oxford is home to one of the city's best food pubs, which Julian Rosser took over in late 2014. In two high-ceilinged bars of elegant simplicity – cool colours, beech tables, carved stone fireplaces – professors, professionals and canal-side walkers tuck into such delights as grilled corn-fed chicken with winter leaves and aïoli, crunchy farro with squash, radicchio, taleggio and chestnuts, and steamed marmalade pudding with custard... or simply a haggis scotch egg (ours was perfect). Young staff deliver seasonal and good-looking dishes with aplomb. Outside is a south-facing terrace, enclosed and child safe; dogs are most welcome too.

Oxfordshire

Jacobs Inn
Wolvercote

From the Oxford sausages at breakfast to the home-cured meats and the home-baked focaccia, this is the place for nose-to-tail dining – and our rabbit ballotine with wild mushroom salad and truffle oil was fabulous. It's an old Cotswolds inn in a suburb of Oxford on the footpath to Port Meadow, and if you just fancy a pint and a pot of chipolatas, you're still in for a treat: the ales change daily and the chipolatas are from the garden (they keep pigs and hens). Inside all is airy, rustic, beautiful, with old tongue-and-groove walls and wide plank floors, books to read, chesterfields to recline on, and a fair few stuffed animals on the walls (very à la mode). Dogs doze by the fire, children tuck into baby burgers, and in summer you spill into the grounds, with picnic tables, deckchairs and great big terrace.

Meals	Bar meals £4–£7.85. Lunch & dinner £9.50–£16.
Closed	Open all day.

Meals	Lunch from £3.50. Dinner from £7.
Closed	Open all day.

Local, seasonal &
organic produce

	Julian Rosser The Anchor Inn, 2 Hayfield Road, Walton Manor, Oxford OX2 6TT
Tel	+44 (0)1865 510282
Web	www.theanchoroxford.com

Entry 500 Map 8

	Damion & Johnny Jacobs Inn, 130 Godstow Road, Wolvercote OX2 8PG
Tel	+44 (0)1865 514333
Web	www.jacobs-inn.com

Entry 501 Map 8

Oxfordshire

Oxfordshire

The Rose & Crown
Shilton

Cosy, friendly, foodie, and run with great panache. The 16th-century Rose & Crown, set in an idyllic Cotswolds village, holds just two rooms: the bar itself, simple and unadorned, and a (slightly) larger extension built in 1701. There's an open fire in the inglenook, a medley of kitchen tables and chairs, well-kept beers, serious wines, and Martin, star of the show. With an impressive London pedigree behind him, he is warm, witty and passionate about food. Join a happy crowd for delicious, authentic renditions of parsnip and chestnut soup, roast partridge with blackberries, steak and mushroom pie, spotted dick and frangipane tart. Cosiness and low beams for winter, a sheltered garden for summer, warmth and conviviality all year round. A gem.

The Fleece
Witney

A half hour west of Oxford, on Witney's sweeping green, is the first outpost of what has become the hugely successful Peach Pubs. Step in to a sparkling gastropub interior — wooden floors, plum walls, squashy sofas, low tables — with continental opening hours that start with coffee and bacon sarnies at 8.30am. It's a humdinger of a place, tempting casual drinkers for pints of Greene King. Thumbs up for the regularly changing wine list at sensible prices, and for the all-day sandwiches, salads and deli-board menu. Starters of charcuterie, olive tapenade, marinated chillies, guinea fowl salad, followed by such delights as braised shoulder of lamb with roasted winter roots, or sweet potato lasagne with jalapeño pesto, all ferried to packed tables by an enthusiastic and attentive staff.

Meals	Lunch £8.50–£15.50.
	Dinner £9–£15.50.
	Sunday lunch, 3 courses, £21.
Closed	3pm–6pm.
	Open all day Fri–Sun & Bank Holidays.

Meals	Bar meals from £5.
	Lunch from £7.
	Dinner from £11.
	Sunday roast £13.50.
Closed	Christmas Day.

	Martin Coldicott
	The Rose & Crown,
	Shilton,
	Burford OX18 4AB
Tel	+44 (0)1993 842280
Web	www.roseandcrownshilton.com

	Helen Sprason
	The Fleece,
	11 Church Green,
	Witney OX28 4AZ
Tel	+44 (0)1993 892270
Web	www.fleecewitney.co.uk

Entry 502 Map 8

Entry 503 Map 8

Oxfordshire

Royal Oak
Ramsden

Winter fires, piles of magazines and well-thumbed books by the inglenook make this the perfect place for a pint of real ale, so tuck into a corner filled with plump scatter cushions, or join the band of locals at the bar. Some good food can be had in the pubby bar – open-stone walls, cream and soft green windows – as well as in the extension beyond, where glass doors open to a pretty terrace with wrought-iron chairs and outdoor heaters for chilly nights. Confit duck with puy lentils and garlic potatoes, succulent burgers, and calves' liver with Madeira should put a smile on your face; in winter, there's lots of game. Well-behaved children and dogs are welcome, the staff are delightful, the village is a stunner and the walking is wonderful. After 25 years in the business you won't hear a bad word said about this place.

Oxfordshire

New Entry

The Crown
Woodstock

In idyllic Woodstock, down the road from Blenheim Palace, is the listed, mellow old Crown. Inside? A large, light, bright, sleek, smiling place. Palest walls, orange lights, Nordic chairs, background music and a dog called Rory (belongs to the chef). There are two open fires, a sitting area with sofas and a stunning decorative sweep of Portuguese floor. Butcombe or bellini, vodka, gin, champagne by the glass: the drinks are various and classy. So is the food; there's Provençal fish stew, roast rump of lamb with spinach, salmon with brown shrimp butter, and small plates that look sensational: Jerusalem artichokes with kale; wood-roast king prawns with chilli. The wood-fired pizzas are awesome as is the blood orange posset. Outside: a little furnished courtyard.

Meals	Lunch & dinner £11-£22.95. Bar meals from £5. Sunday lunch, 3 courses, £21.95.
Closed	3pm-6.30pm. Open all day weekends.

Meals	Small plates from £6. Dinner from £9.
Closed	Open all day.

Jon Oldham
Royal Oak,
High Street, Ramsden,
Chipping Norton OX7 3AU

Tel   +44 (0)1993 868213
Web   www.royaloakramsden.com

Entry 504 Map 8

Julian Rosser
The Crown,
High Street,
Woodstock OX20 1TE

Tel   +44 (0)1865 510282
Web   www.thecrownwoodstock.com

Entry 505 Map 8

Oxfordshire

Killingworth Castle
Wootton

The family behind the Ebrington Arms has renovated this 17th-century inn to its former glory, with plans afoot for further restoration including bedrooms. Wood floors sweep from side bar to main bar to dining room, burners in brick fireplaces belt out heat and wood tables are set with white china. Smiling staff ferry Uley ales and Cotswold cider to locals, dog walkers and drinkers; the rest are here for the food: roast venison and faggot croquette with beetroot dauphinoise, kale and juniper; blackberry and frangipane tart. And the best chips in Oxfordshire! Famous for their real ales, there's a focus on small brewers; wines showcase independent makers; and there's a nifty selection of malt whiskies and brandies. Try a pint of their home-brewed Yubby Bitter in the big beer garden. It's the perfect community pub.

Meals	Lunch & dinner from £13.50.
	Monday-Friday lunch £7.
Closed	Open all day.

Claire & Jim Alexander
Killingworth Castle,
Glympton Road, Wootton,
Chipping Norton OX20 1EJ
Tel   +44 (0)1993 811401
Web   www.thekillingworthcastle.com

Entry 506 Map 8

Oxfordshire

Nut Tree Inn
Murcott

Find Michelin-starred food at this whitewashed thatched pub (idyllic!), breads and pork pies you can pre-book to take home and pigs out the back. Imogen and Mike are friendly and fun and operate their own version of 'The Good Life'; they grow loads of lovely produce. The bar is soothing, relaxing, with an open fire, stools, leather chesterfields, cookery books to peruse. Off here: a big vaulted dining room. Choose from delicious bar food (smoked Loch Duart salmon, fillet steak, artisan cheeses) or take a look at the specials: tartare of Charolais beef; tea-smoked wild goose with mango purée; roast fillet of Cornish cod with green herb risotto; hot caramel soufflé with walnut ice cream. There's real ale, draught cider, a long wine list and a pretty terrace. The Nut Tree is a happy ship that caters effortlessly for all.

Meals	Lunch & dinner £17–£27.
	Bar meals £5.50–£10.
	Sunday roast from £15.50.
	Set menu, 2 courses, £18.
	Tasting menu £55.
	Not Sunday eve or Monday.
Closed	Sun evenings & all day Mon.

Michael & Imogen North
Nut Tree Inn,
Murcott,
Kidlington OX5 2RE
Tel   +44 (0)1865 331253
Web   www.nuttreeinn.co.uk

Entry 507 Map 8

Oxfordshire

The Oxford Arms
Kirtlington

A robust 19th-century dining pub tucked down a lane in a village eight miles from Oxford. Windows are sage-green, window boxes spill geraniums in summer and the coat of arms above the door shows an ox walking through a ford. The main bar faces south, the floors are flagged and boarded, wood smoke tinges the air; decide what to eat as you sip a half of Hooky Bitter or something excellent from the wine list. To one side is a candlelit dining area with large and small tables and comfy sofas; the other side is more pubby and informal with bar stools and farmhouse chairs. Wherever you decide to eat there's the convivial rumble of chat in the background and the food is good. Try potted shrimps with toast, Salcombe crabs with artisan bread, confit duck leg, roast pork belly with black pudding.

Oxfordshire

The Muddy Duck
Hethe

In a remote but not too remote village is a handsome, honey-stoned pub. If you dropped by for a Hooky and homemade scratchings, it would be worth it just for the bar, a wonderful space with low beams and a roaring fire. The vaulted restaurant has been charmingly refurbished, with stripped wooden floors, 60 covers and an open kitchen. Friendly, knowledgeable staff ferry beautiful platefuls of (mostly local, often seasonal) food. Meat is raised to high welfare standards, fish (sustainable only) is cooked the day it's caught. You could have Cornish squid and avocado salsa to start, stuffed pork belly with roasted apples to follow, and fruits with iced crème chiboust to finish. Our Scotch egg with black pudding was brilliant. Outside: a rustically furnished stone terrace and a pizza oven.

Meals	Bar meals from £6.50. Lunch & dinner from £12. Sunday lunch, 3 courses, £26.	Meals	Lunch & dinner £11.50–£24. Not Sunday eve.
Closed	3pm–6pm. Sun evenings.	Closed	Open all day.

	Bryn Jones The Oxford Arms, Troy Lane, Kirtlington OX5 3HA		**The Manager** The Muddy Duck, Main Street, Hethe, Bicester OX27 8ES
Tel	+44 (0)1869 350208	Tel	+44 (0)1869 278099
Web	www.oxford-arms.co.uk	Web	www.themuddyduckpub.co.uk

Oxfordshire

Oxfordshire

The Chequers
Churchill

Eye-catching with an immaculate frontage, the Chequers stands smartly on the village lane. Prepare for a dramatic, airy and open-plan interior of low beams, scrubbed tables on walker-friendly boards, stone walls, roaring wood-burner and a dart board put to good use. Soaring blue-green rafters and a vast dresser racked with wine bottles create an impression in the dining extension, where a blackboard up high announces the food: simple, British-traditional, and well priced. There are devilled kidneys on toast, steak and oyster pie, grilled lemon sole with brown butter, bavette steak with fries. The roasts are delicious, the service is terrific, but most exceptional are the beers: six real ales (Yankee from Roosters, Budding from Stroud) and six local keg beers. There are also ten wines by the glass.

Falkland Arms
Great Tew

Five hundred years on and the logs still glow in the stone-flagged bar under a low-slung timbered ceiling that drips with tankards and jugs. Tradition runs deep: the hop is treated with reverence, ales are changed weekly, old pump clips hang from the bar and they stock tins of snuff with names like Irish High Toast and Crumbs of Comfort. In summer Morris Men jingle in the lane outside and life spills out onto the terrace at the front and the lovely big garden behind. Dig into a homemade burger and ploughman's in front of the fire or hop next door to the tiny beamed dining room for such home-cooked delights as Guinness-baked ham hock with leek and sweetcorn champ. Perfect pub, perfect village, and blissfully short on modern trappings.

Meals	Lunch & dinner £4–£16.50.
Closed	Open all day.

Meals	Bar meals from £4.95.
	Lunch from £7.95.
	Dinner from £8.95.
	Sunday lunch, 3 courses, £17.95.
Closed	Open all day.

Sam Pearman
The Chequers,
Church Road, Churchill,
Chipping Norton OX7 6NJ
Tel +44 (0)1608 659393
Web www.thechequerschurchill.com

Entry 510 Map 8

Kathryn Partridge
& Richard Bennett
Falkland Arms, 19-21 The Green,
Great Tew, Chipping Norton OX7 4DB
Tel +44 (0)1608 683653
Web www.falklandarms.co.uk

Entry 511 Map 8

The Castle at Edgehill
Edgehill

The food ranges from indulgent sea bream with saffron potatoes to baby rump burgers for children to dog biscuits by the bar – and the Hooky goes down a treat. This former folly, built in 1742, stands in a peerless position 700 feet above sea level; on a clear day you can see the Malvern Hills. The Hook Norton brewery took over in 1922, and new landlords swept in in 2014; the place glows. A once dingy bar ushers you in to an open stone fireplace, earthy colours and lovely wines by the glass. Then a library with leather chesterfields and wood-panelled walls, a restaurant with patterned carpeting and a purple feature wall, and an elevated conservatory with floor-to-ceiling windows – book a table with a ringside view. In summer you can spill into the garden for picnic tables, views and a sparkling Kir Royal.

Wykham Arms
Sibford Gower

Another beautifully presented little pub in a Cotswolds village. You'd expect cushions and chintz, instead you get creams and deep reds, flag floors, two fires and a homely farmhouse feel. Life revolves around the central bar, and the menu, served through a warren of connected rooms, spills over with local seasonal produce, "with one foot firmly in the past". Tuck into Cornish scallops with celeriac remoulade; salmon with beetroot and artichoke salad; wild boar and apple sausages with beer mustard mash – flavours are strong, clean and uncomplicated. The fish is native to UK waters and there are lots of wines by the glass, excellent and affordable. Families and dogs are very welcome; for summer there's a big patio and a wooded garden.

Meals	Starters from £6.50.
	Dinner from £13.
	Breakfast available.
Closed	Mon-Sat 11pm.
	Sun 9pm.

Meals	Bar meals from £8.50.
	Lunch from £10.
	Dinner £10–£18.50.
	Sunday lunch, 3 courses, £20.
	Not Sunday eve.
Closed	3pm-6pm.
	Mon all day.

Claire Higgs
The Castle at Edgehill,
Edgehill,
Banbury OX15 6DJ
Tel   +44 (0)1295 670 255
Web www.castleatedgehill.co.uk

Entry 512 Map 8

Damian & Deborah Bradley
Wykham Arms,
Temple Mill Road, Sibford Gower,
Banbury OX15 5RX
Tel   +44 (0)1295 788808
Web www.wykhamarms.co.uk

Entry 513 Map 8

Rutland

The Olive Branch
Clipsham

A lovely pub in a sleepy Rutland village, where bridle paths lead out across peaceful fields. The inn dates to the 17th century and is built of Clipsham stone. Inside, a warm, informal rustic chic hits the spot perfectly; come for open fires, old beams, exposed stone walls and choir stalls in the bar. Chalk boards on tables in the restaurant reveal the names of the evening's diners, while the food – seared scallops with black pudding fritter, slow-roast pork belly with creamed leeks and apple sauce – elates. As do the hampers that you can whisk away for picnics in the countryside. Bedrooms in Beech House across the lane are impeccable. Three have terraces, one has a free-standing bath, all come with crisp linen, pretty beds, Roberts radios, real coffee. Super breakfasts – smoothies, boiled eggs and soldiers, the full cooked works – are served in a smartly renovated barn, with flames leaping in the wood-burner. The front garden fills in summer, the sloe gin comes from local berries, and Newark is close for the biggest antiques market in Europe. A total gem.

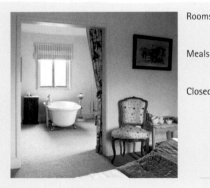

Rooms	5 doubles: £115–£195.
	1 family room for 4: £115–£195.
	Singles from £97.50.
Meals	Lunch from £6.25.
	Dinner, 3 courses, £25–£35.
	Sunday roast from £4.95.
Closed	Rarely.

Ben Jones & Sean Hope
The Olive Branch,
Main Street, Clipsham,
Oakham LE15 7SH

Tel   +44 (0)1780 410355
Web   www.theolivebranchpub.com

Entry 514 Map 9

Rutland

Rutland

The Lord Nelson
Oakham

Tucked into the corner of the market square, this 17th-century boozer comes with masses of atmosphere, cheery quaffers and good conversation. London Pride and Castle Rock's Harvest Pale, among others, provide the lubrication, there's Aspall cider and an impressive wine list. Pick one of the varied seats on offer, up or down stairs, and settle in for lunch or dinner. Food ranges from pub classics to modern European plus an Asian twist or two. There's antipasto, deli options and speciality stone-baked pizzas as well as nibbles and breads. No chips, no table reservations, no children under four years and none at all after 8pm! A courtyard patio at the back is heated and snug. Full of character and fun in an almost Dickensian manner.

Marquess of Exeter
Lyddington

Pevsner loved this area of market towns and 'unforgettable villages', and the pub, in honey-coloured stone and topped with thatch, is a perfect example. Three log fires wait to warm you and there are plenty of comfy armchairs and sofas to sink into with a pint of Brakspear Bitter or a glass of well-selected wine. Chef and owner Brian designs menus that showcase unfussy home-cooked dishes with modern twists, strong on flavours and with a touch of finesse: crispy salt and chilli squid with lime and bean sprouts followed by grilled sea bass fillet; roast butternut squash with red onion, walnuts and a lemon dressing. The sharing dishes are also hugely popular. Rutland Water is just up the road — come and discover this gem of a county.

| Meals | Lunch from £5.95.
Dinner from £10.95. |
| Closed | 25 December. |

| Meals | Lunch & dinner £12.95–£18.50. |
| Closed | Open all day. |

Michael Thurlby
The Lord Nelson,
11 Market Place,
Oakham LE15 6DT
Tel +44 (0)1572 868340
Web www.thelordnelsonoakham.com

Entry 515 Map 9

Brian Baker
Marquess of Exeter,
52 Main Street, Lyddington,
Uppingham LE15 9LT
Tel +44 (0)1572 822477
Web www.marquessexeter.co.uk

Entry 516 Map 9

Charlton Arms
Ludford

Cedric Bosi (ex-Hibiscus) has returned to Ludlow to take on a poshed-up old inn slap on the bridge over the Teme with decked riverside terraces and gorgeous Ludlow views. If you love the sound of running water, this is for you. Great for families and large groups, too; at weekends, wedding parties drop by. There's a cosy little hop-strung bar and a seat by the fire, a larger seating area up behind, and big sweeping dining rooms with high-backed chairs and light pouring in through bay windows. There's no garden as such – but a canopied terrace with an artificial grass deck is planned. As for the food, it's top-notch pub fare with families' needs taken care of, delicious roasts on Sundays and a menu that changes daily. Wines are from Bibendum, ales include Ludlow Gold and ciders Robinson's Flagon. Bedrooms above, some with fancy spa baths, all with padded headboards and super thick carpets, have been recently refurbished. Tempest, Hamlet and Montague have the best river views; Othello has a hot tub on its own huge terrace.

Rooms	9 doubles: £90–£120.
Meals	Lunch and dinner from £11.50.
	Sunday roasts from £12.50.
Closed	Rarely.

Cedric & Amy Bosi
Charlton Arms,
Ludford,
Ludlow SY8 1PJ
Tel   +44 (0)1584 872813
Web   www.thecharltonarms.co.uk

Entry 517 Map 7

Baron at Bucknell
Bucknell

A stone's throw from Ludlow yet in the midst of the Shropshire Hills, the Baron sits at the base of Bucknell Mynd in a tranquil village by the Teme Valley. Peace reigns supreme and a flurry of super walks lead from the door: guides are behind the bar. Phil and Debbie have worked wonders on the bedrooms; all five are well-groomed and tasteful with oak furniture, contemporary wallpaper, stylish lighting and fat mattresses to induce deep sleep; one has a Juliet balcony, all have country views. Bathrooms are modern and white, one with a double-ended whirlpool bath. Ales from Hobson and Wye Valley await in the simple bar with its traditional carpet and wooden seating. Homemade pub food is the mantra here, uncomplicated and cooked to order. Start with glazed goat's cheese and beetroot salad with rocket, pine nuts and crusty bread, move on to slow-braised lamb shank with a fruity minty couscous. Eat in the restaurant beside a large millstone and grinding wheel and a huge wooden cider press dated 1770, or in the conservatory that overlooks the garden with boules pitches. You can camp, too!

Rooms	3 doubles, 2 twin/doubles: £90–£130.
Meals	Lunch & dinner £10.95–£16.50.
Closed	Rarely.

Phil & Debbie Wright
Baron at Bucknell,
Bucknell,
Ludlow SY7 0AH
Tel   +44 (0)1547 530549
Web   www.baronatbucknell.co.uk

Entry 518 Map 7

Shropshire

Riverside Inn
Cound

There's a great buzz in this big comfortable huntin', shootin' and fishin' inn, standing on a magnificent bend of the Severn, looking out to the Wrekin and beyond. It's worth seeking out for its roaring wood-burner in winter and its dining conservatory – with views – all year round. In summer there's a pretty garden smartly furnished, from which you can fish from the bank for salmon and trout. The seasonal monthly menu might start with a winter vegetable and lentil broth, and move on to roast pork belly with an apricot and sage sauce, or a beef and Guinness shortcrust pie. There's port to accompany the cheese, and lovely Salopian beers and homemade puddings; we enjoyed the raspberry and thyme crème brûlée. It's all good value and reassuringly traditional; the service is both friendly and efficient. And there's no need to hurry home: upstairs are seven well-proportioned and comfortable Georgian bedrooms, with extras like chocs on the pillow. The 'executive' rooms have river views from sash windows, but all are in excellent order.

Rooms	6 doubles, 1 twin: £65–£75. Singles £50.
Meals	Lunch & dinner £7.75–£14.
Closed	Christmas Day.

Peter Stanford-Davis
Riverside Inn,
Cound,
Shrewsbury SY5 6AF
Tel   +44 (0)1952 510900
Web   www.theriversideinn.net

Entry 519 Map 7

The Hundred House Hotel
Norton

The Phillips family has been at the helm for 25 years and Henry is an innkeeper with humour. As for the inn, having begun its life in the 14th century, it rambles charmingly inside as well as out. Enter a world of blazing log fires, soft brick walls, oak panelling and quarry-tiled floors. Dried flowers hang from beams, herbs sit in vases, and blackboard menus trumpet Hundred House fish pie, roast rack of Shropshire lamb and double chocolate mousse with orange anglaise. You are surrounded by Sylvia's wild and wonderful collage art hanging on the walls, and the fun continues in riotously patterned and floral bedrooms upstairs. Just go easy on the ale before you open the door: some have a swing hanging from the oak beams with a vibrant velvet seat. Lounge on antique beds – large, comfortable and wrapped in lavender-scented sheets. Wander out with a pint of Ironbridge Brewery and share a quiet moment with a few stone lions in the beautiful garden, a flight of fancy full of herbaceous plants and over a hundred herbs – a summer treat. You can tie the knot in the restored Tithe Barn.

Rooms	8 doubles, 1 twin/double: £79-£140. Singles from £55.
Meals	Lunch from £4.95. Dinner & bar meals from £8.95. Sunday lunch, 2 courses, £16.95.
Closed	Rarely.

The Phillips Family
The Hundred House Hotel,
Bridgnorth Road, Norton,
Shifnal TF11 9EE

Tel   +44 (0)1952 580240
Web   www.hundredhouse.co.uk

The Woodbridge
Coalbridge

In the birthplace of the industrial revolution is this handsome pub, built in 1785 along with a wooden bridge to Coalport. It surveys the river Severn, and the cast-iron bridge that now spans it. A vast open-plan interior comes with plenty of cosy corners and the new garden room flows along the river bank. The abundance of cask ales would quench a furnace with Bishop's Castle, Hobson's, Tunfield and Phoenix Breweries well represented; there's Aspall Suffolk Cyder and a great wine list too. Daily changing menus feature modern British and pub classics, from a confit duck leg, bacon, butter bean and pearl barley cassoulet to steak and kidney suet pudding with English mustard mash, and a sweet potato, carrot and rocket quiche. A raised terrace and masses of seating strung out along the river is the icing on the cake.

All Nations
Madeley

The old Victorian pub, spruce and white, could be an extension of the Victorian open air museum t'other side of the bridge. Step across the threshold and you're into timeworn-tavern territory — cast-iron tables, leatherette benches, coal fire at one end, log fire at the other. Old photographs of Ironbridge strew the walls, secondhand paperbacks ask to be taken home (donations to charity), spotless loos await outside, and dogs doze. It's a chatty, friendly, ex-miners' ale house and some of the locals could have been here forever. Drink is own-brew, well-kept, low-cost Dabley from the hatch plus three others and a cider, while the menu encompasses several sorts of roll — black pudding perhaps, or cheese and onion, with tomato on request. Catch it before it's gone.

Meals	Lunch & dinner £10.75-£25.95.
Closed	Open all day.

Meals	Filled rolls £1.90-£3.
Closed	Open all day.

	Vrata Krist
	The Woodbridge,
	Coalbridge TF8 7JF
Tel	+44 (0)1952 882054
Web	www.brunningandprice.co.uk/
	woodbridge

Entry 521 Map 8

	Jim Birtwistle
	All Nations,
	20 Coalport Road,
	Madeley,
	Telford TF7 5DP
Tel	+44 (0)1952 585747

Entry 522 Map 8

New Inn
Baschurch

Outside, jolly hanging baskets and a whitewashed frontage. Inside, a sympathetic stripping back of old brick and beams and an open fire, comfortable sofas at one end, contemporary oak dining tables at the other and a big bar in between. In spite of the 48 covers, a well-placed wall and brick fireplace give the dining areas a certain intimacy. There are five ales on the pump, and house wines served by Jenny Bean and her charming staff. In the kitchen, Marcus cooks up a storm: ham hock and parsley terrine with cheese scone and spiced apple chutney; roast duck breast with sweet plum and star anise jus; white chocolate and mascarpone cheesecake. It's delicious. In summer you spill out to sun shades and decking.

The Boathouse
Shrewsbury

Recently snapped up by the owners of the Lion & Pheasant in the centre of town and linked by a glorious riverside path, this huge historic pub stands on the banks of the Severn overlooking Quarry Park. Swamped in summer (and during very wet winters!), the smart decked terrace and big riverside garden now draw the crowds for cool drinks, pretty views, and top-notch bar food from the new Garden Bar and Kitchen. On cool days, arrive early to bag a fireside table or a river view in the spruced-up inside. Scandinavian colours, a rustic wooden floor, dark beams and cushioned benches set the scene for pints of Shropshire Gold and hearty plates of food — potted ham hock with red onion marmalade; charcoal-grilled steaks; towering burgers with chips and coleslaw served on wooden boards. With excellent service, it's great for events and private dinners, too.

Meals	Bar meals £4.95-£8.50.
	Lunch & dinner £9.50–£16.95.
	Sunday roast £14 & £17.
	Not Sunday eve.
Closed	3pm-6pm.
	Open all day Sat & Sun.

Meals	Bar snacks from £4.
	Lunch from £6.50.
	Dinner from £11.
Closed	Open all day.

Marcus & Jenny Bean
New Inn,
Church Road, Baschurch,
Shrewsbury SY4 2EF

Tel +44 (0)1939 260335
Web www.thenewinnbaschurch.co.uk

Entry 523 Map 7

Jim Littler
The Boathouse,
New Street,
Shrewsbury SY3 8JQ

Tel +44 (0)1743 770345
Web www.boathouseshrewsbury.co.uk

Entry 524 Map 7

Shropshire

The Lion & Pheasant
Shrewsbury

Old meets new in this stunning transformation of a town centre inn, with exposed beams, delicious log fire and a pale Scandinavian décor with rustic touches. Have a crack at Wood Shropshire Lad or Salopian Shropshire Gold while you peek at the menu, created by chef Matthew Strefford. Roast chestnut and thyme soup; crispy pork cheek terrine; roast hake, mussels, chickpeas and chorizo; British roast veal, onion soubise, sage and walnut pesto; this is food to linger over. The wine list is long and includes a dazzling array of dessert wines, port and different fizzes; the cocktails are works of art. Staff are young, friendly and deeply efficient. Packed with character and atmosphere; decibels can be high.

Shropshire

White Horse Inn
Pulverbatch

The drive to get here is a treat, across the secret hills of Shropshire. This is a very old pub, with a restaurant built on at the back (scrubbed pine tables, oatmeal carpet, good art) but the old main bar is the most seductive, with wonky floors, a chesterfield here, a settle there, and a hint of woodsmoke from the big old grate. Walkers and cyclists, on their way to the Long Mynd, can recuperate with a trio of local-farm sausages on wholegrain mustard mash, or a casserole of Shropshire lamb. Steve's passion for food comes over strongly. Menus change monthly to reflect the best of each season, they rear their own pigs and lamb, and everything is made in-house from the bread to the ice cream. There's no garden, but smart new parasoled tables at the front, and you're surrounded by beautiful countryside.

Meals	Bar meals from £6.50. Lunch & dinner £4.95–£17.95.
Closed	Open all day.

Meals	Lunch & dinner £7.25–£14.95.
Closed	2pm-6.30pm & Mon lunch. Open all day Sat & Sun.

Jim Littler
The Lion & Pheasant,
50 Wyle Cop,
Shrewsbury SY1 1XJ
Tel   +44 (0)1743 770345
Web www.lionandpheasant.co.uk

Entry 525 Map 7

Steve & Vikki Nash
White Horse Inn,
Pulverbatch, Shrewsbury SY5 8DS
Tel   +44 (0)1743 718247
Web www.thewhitehorseinn
pulverbatch.co.uk

Entry 526 Map 7

Shropshire

The Bridges
Ratlinghope

Beer drinkers are in heaven here – the Bridges is tap house for the Three Tuns Brewery in Bishops Castle. Their craft beers have quite a pedigree and their Shropshire brewhouse is the oldest licensed in Britain (hence their signature bitter '1642': nutty, spicy, with a long-lingering finish). Pumps crowd the newly extended bar – nine beers were on tap when we visited. Ask the helpful staff to get you started, and stick to 'thirds' to get you further through the list! The cosy bar is propped up by a gaggle of locals; the dining room is rustic, simple, with a brick fireplace and terracotta floor. Walkers and cyclists drop in to refuel. Food, like everything here, is fuss-free and honest – try the local ham, egg and chips. Drinkers spill out across the lane in summer, to picnic benches made from old beer barrels, as kids roll up trouser legs and paddle in the stream.

The Three Tuns
Bishops Castle

There's been a licensed brewery next door since 1642 (the oldest brewing license in the UK). Pub and brewery are now under separate ownership but the pub still sells up to four of their beers at any one time, and very good they are too. The place has an unassuming air, like the rest of this time-warp town. The separate snug, public bar and lounge are simply decorated with pale green paintwork, scrubbed tables, leather booths and old oak flooring. (In contrast are some impressive marble loos.) Or dine in the oak-framed, conservatory room, on grilled hake, chorizo, roasted pepper sauce with new potatoes and green beans, and, they say, the best rib-eye steaks in Shropshire. There's a great mix of regulars, from suits to bohemians, a real fire in the stone fireplace, and live music at weekends.

Meals	Bar meals & lunch from £5.95. Dinner from £10.95. Sunday roast £12.95. Not Sun/Mon eves in Nov-Feb.	Meals	Lunch from £5.75. Dinner from £10.50. Sunday roast £10.25. Not Sunday eve.
Closed	Open all day.	Closed	Open all day.

	John Russell The Bridges, Ratlinghope, Church Stretton SY5 0ST		Tim & Catherine Curtis-Evans The Three Tuns, Salop Street, Bishops Castle SY9 5BW
Tel	+44 (0)1588 650260	Tel	+44 (0)1588 638797
Web	www.thebridgespub.co.uk	Web	www.thethreetunsinn.co.uk

Entry 527 Map 7

Entry 528 Map 7

Shropshire

The Crown Country Inn
Munslow

Richard and Jane Arnold bought this listed Tudor inn in a parlous state. A courtroom, a doctor's surgery and a jail in previous lives, it is now a happy place. While locals gather for a chat and a pint of Corvedale Golden Dale at dark polished tables in the log-stoved bar, the secret of the inn's success is revealed on its walls, adorned with food awards and a map of suppliers. Proprietor and chef Richard is passionate about local produce and the menu is stuffed with it. Try crostini ('little toasts') of local black pudding with Wenlock Edge Farm bacon; lamb tagine; roast smoked chicken with mustard creamed leeks. As for the cheese board, it's a treat of lesser-known British cheeses, including the hop-rolled Hereford Hop. There's a sun-trap terrace for summer drinking.

Shropshire

The Sun Inn
Leintwardine

The Sun shines into the 21st century with a great eco extension at the back; yet this authentic old pub remains true to the spirit of former landlady Flossie. Carry a pint of Hobson's or a Marcher Man cider to one of two front parlour bars and raise your glass to your good fortune – you have landed in a timeless old gem! Menus are short and simple: a daily homemade soup and stew, local pork pies, a ploughman's – and they're generous enough to let you slip next door for a plate of fish and chips to bring back and devour. There's a pretty garden for summer, good walks along the river and always plenty of action, from winter wassailing (yes, it's making a comeback) to St George's Day celebrations. Gary will see that you're brilliantly looked after.

Meals	Lunch & dinner £11.95–£16.95. Bar meals £4.95–£11.50.
Closed	2.30pm-6.45pm. Sun from 3pm & Mon all day.

Meals	Bar meals from £3.
Closed	Open all day Tues-Sun & Mon 5.30pm-11pm.

Richard & Jane Arnold
The Crown Country Inn,
Munslow,
Craven Arms SY7 9ET
Tel   +44 (0)1584 841205
Web   www.crowncountryinn.co.uk

Entry 529 Map 7

Andy Price
The Sun Inn,
Rosemary Lane, Leintwardine,
Craven Arms SY7 0LP
Tel   +44 (0)1547 540705
Web   www.suninn-leintwardine.co.uk

Entry 530 Map 7

Farmers Arms
West Hatch

You don't often trek into deepest Somerset and wash up at a deeply groovy inn, but that's what you get at the Farmer's, so brave the narrow country lanes and head to the top of the hill. All the country treats are on hand. Outside, cows in the fields, cockerels crowing and long clean views; inside, friendly people, open fires and a timber-framed bar. It's all the result of a total renovation, and one airy room now rolls into another giving a sense of colour and comfort, space and light. Imagine terracotta-tiled floors and beamed ceilings, yellow tongue-and-groove panelling, old pine dining tables dressed with pots of rosemary and logs piled high in the alcoves. Stay the night in off-beat but elegant and big rooms with distinctive beds (all antique) and expansive, gleaming wooden floors. There are power showers and claw-foot baths, one room has a daybed, others have sofas, another a courtyard. Super food flies from the kitchen – grilled sardines, rib-eye steak, chocolate and mint mousse – and you can eat on the terrace in summer. The pub is also on a new circular bridle path funded by English Heritage.

Rooms	4 doubles, 1 twin/double: £75-£125. Singles from £75.
Meals	Lunch & dinner £5-£35.
Closed	Rarely.

Dionne Walsh
Farmers Arms,
West Hatch,
Taunton TA3 5RS
Tel   +44 (0)1823 480980
Web   www.farmersarmssomerset.co.uk

Entry 531 Map 2

Lord Poulett Arms
Hinton St George

In a ravishing village, a ravishing inn, French at heart and quietly groovy. Part pub, part country house, with walls painted in reds and greens and old rugs covering flagged floors, it fuses classical design with earthy rusticity. A fire burns on both sides of the chimney in the dining room; on one side you can sink into leather armchairs, on the other you can eat under beams at antique oak tables while candles flicker. Take refuge with the daily papers on the sofa in the locals' bar or head past a pile of logs at the back door and discover an informal French garden of box and bay trees, with a piste for boules, a creeper-shaded terrace, a hammock. Bedrooms upstairs come in funky country-house style, with fancy flock wallpaper, perhaps crushed velvet curtains, a small chandelier or a carved-wood bed. Two rooms have slipper baths behind screens in the room; two have claw-foot baths in bathrooms one step across the landing; Roberts radios add to the fun. Brilliant food includes summer barbecues, Sunday roasts and the full works at breakfast. Great value and friendly to all – dogs included.

Rooms	2 doubles;
	2 doubles with separate bath: £85-£95.
	Singles from £60.
Meals	Lunch from £5.
	Dinner, 3 courses, £20-£35.
Closed	Rarely.

Steve & Michelle Hill
Lord Poulett Arms,
High Street,
Hinton St George TA17 8SE

Tel   +44 (0)1460 73149
Web   www.lordpoulettarms.com

Entry 532 Map 3

The Queens Arms
Corton Denham

Stride across rolling fields, feast on Corton Denham lamb, retire to a perfect room. Buried down several Dorset/Somerset borders lanes, Gordon and Jeanette Reid's 18th-century stone pub has an elegant exterior – more country gentleman's house than pub. The bar, with its rug-strewn flagstones and bare boards, pew benches, deep sofas and crackling fire, is most charming. In the light, bright dining room that doubles up as a cinema on week nights, and on the terrace in summer, robust British dishes are distinguished by fresh ingredients from local suppliers. Try pheasant, pigeon and black pudding terrine, follow with monkfish with chive velouté, make room for a comforting crumble. Bedrooms are beautifully designed in soothing colours, and all have lovely views over the village and surrounding hills. New coach house rooms are super, too: underfloor heating, down duvets, brass and sleigh beds, iPod docks and immaculate wet rooms. Expect Gyle59 on tap, homemade pork pies on the bar, Gloucester Old Spot bacon at breakfast and enjoy stunning walks from the door. *Dogs welcome in ground-floor bedroom.*

Rooms	6 doubles, 2 twin/doubles: £110-£190. Family room: £200. Singles £85-£120.
Meals	Starters from £6.25. Dinner from £10.50.
Closed	Rarely.

Local, seasonal &
organic produce

	Gordon & Jeanette Reid The Queens Arms, Corton Denham, Sherborne DT9 4LR
Tel	+44 (0)1963 220317
Web	www.thequeensarms.com

Entry 533 Map 3

The White Hart
Somerton

Cool inns with lovely rooms in interesting parts of the land are a big hit with lots of us – we like the easy style, the local food, the good prices and the happy staff. The White Hart is a case in point, a beautifully refurbished inn. It sits on Somerton's ancient market square, 16th-century bricks and mortar, 21st-century lipstick and pearls. Inside, old and new mix beautifully: stone walls and parquet flooring, lovely sofas in front of the fire, funky lamps hanging above the bar. There are soft colours, padded window seats, country rugs, antler chandeliers. A cute booth in a stone turret, then cathedral ceilings in the airy restaurant, where lovely food waits, perhaps a chargrilled steak, smoked mackerel fishcakes, a pizza cooked in the wood-fired oven. In summer, you spill onto a smart courtyard or into the garden for views of open country. Upstairs, fabulous bedrooms await. You might find timber frames, a claw-foot bath, a wall of paper or stripped boards. All have super beds, flat-screen TVs, lovely bathrooms and a nice price. Beautiful Somerset is all around, don't miss it.

Rooms	8 doubles: £85–£130.
Meals	Lunch from £6.
	Dinner, 3 courses, £25–£30.
	Sunday roast from £15.
Closed	Rarely.

Natalie Patrick
The White Hart,
Market Place,
Somerton TA11 7LX
Tel   +44 (0)1458 272273
Web   www.whitehartsomerton.com

Entry 534 Map 3

The Swan
Wedmore

The Swan is gorgeous, a contemporary take on a village local. It's part of a new wave of cool little pubs that open all day and do so much more than serve a good pint. Locals come for breakfast, pop in to buy a loaf of bread, then return for afternoon tea and raid the cake stands. It's set back from the road, with a sprinkling of tables and chairs on the pavement in French-café style. Interiors mix old and new brilliantly. You get Farrow & Ball colours and cool lamps hanging above the bar, then lovely old rugs on boarded floors and a wood-burner to keep things toasty. Push inland and find an airy restaurant open to the rafters that overlooks the garden. Here you dig into Tom Blake's fabulous food (he's ex-River Cottage), anything from a Cornish crab sandwich with lemon mayo to a three-course feast, maybe Wye valley asparagus, Wedmore lamb chops, bitter chocolate mousse with chocolate cookies. Bedrooms are lovely. Two have fancy roll top tubs in the rooms themselves, you get vintage French furniture, iPod docks, colourful throws and walk-in power showers. Glastonbury is close, as are the Mendips.

Rooms	4 doubles, 2 twin/doubles: £85–£120. Extra bed £20 per person per night. Cots available.
Meals	Lunch from £5. Dinner, 3 courses, from £25. Sunday roast from £14. Bar meals only Sunday night.
Closed	Rarely.

Jen Edwards
The Swan,
Cheddar Road,
Wedmore BS28 4EQ
Tel   +44 (0)1934 710337
Web   www.theswanwedmore.com

Entry 535 Map 3

Somerset

The Talbot Inn at Mells
Mells

A timeless feudal village (church, manor house, unspoilt stone cottages) is the setting for Matt, Charlie and Dan's beautifully restored Talbot Inn. Huge oak doors open to a cobbled courtyard and tithe-barn sitting room on one side (big sofas, a Sunday cinema), and bar and dining rooms on the other. Inside, a warren of passageways, low doorways, nooks, crannies and beams – all you'd hope for from a 15th-century inn. Rugs on stone or wood floors, flickering candles on old dining tables, crackling log fires and Farrow & Ball hues draw you in for local ales, fine wines and lovely pub food. Tuck into roast beef sandwiches with horseradish, rocket and chips; sea bream with white beans, chorizo, fennel and salsa verde; leg of lamb with roasted garlic; vanilla rice pudding. At weekends, eat simply grilled meat and fish at shared tables in the Coach House Grill, a finely renovated barn. Bedrooms, two across the cobbles, six up ancient stone steps, are the best, some cosy small, some huge with claw-foot baths beside modern four-posters. The effortless hospitality is a big plus. Bring your boots: this is walking country.

Rooms	8 doubles: £95–£150.
Meals	Lunch & dinner £5–£30.
	Sunday lunch, 2 courses, £15.
Closed	Rarely.

Matt Greenlees
The Talbot Inn at Mells,
Selwood Street, Mells,
Frome BA11 3PN

Tel   +44 (0)1373 812254
Web   www.talbotinn.com

Entry 536 Map 3

Archangel
Frome

In lovely old Frome: a coaching inn that opened its doors in 1311. Its recent renovation is exceptional; the old bones of the building brought back to life, then dressed gracefully with 21st-century design. The bar and dining areas are magnificent, ancient walls embrace a floating glass mezzanine cube while French windows open to a courtyard in summer, and beds of lavender give the feel of Provence. Exposed stone mixes with deep purples, there are cowhide rugs, a zinc-topped bar, and vast Renaissance murals. You can sink into sofas for cocktails or appreciate some seriously good food. Perhaps fish and chips with home-made tartare sauce and mushy peas; game pie with buttery greens and mash; chocolate brownie with Amaretto ice cream and honeycomb. Bedrooms are a steal. Some are open to the rafters, most have zinc bathtubs in the room, all come with golden beds, crisp linen, and speakers in bathroom ceilings. Bath, Longleat and Stonehenge are within striking distance, but you may just choose to linger.

Rooms	9 doubles: £80–£150. 1 single: £70–£80.
Meals	Light lunch from £6.50. Mains from £9.50.
Closed	Rarely.

	Ross Nichol Archangel, 1 King Street, Frome BA11 1BH
Tel	+44 (0)1373 456111
Web	www.archangelfrome.com

Entry 537 Map 3

Ring O Bells
Compton Martin

Listed in the Domesday Book and rescued from decline by energetic quartet, Miles, Luca, Matt and Fiona, this lovely pub is now the local not only for Compton Martin but neighbouring Ubley, whose villagers have their own bar, complete with one of Somerset's biggest inglenooks. A second bar serves locals who want a quiet quaff while the main dining area is abuzz with families, especially at weekends when the roast lunches do a roaring trade. Rightly so, since the food here is something special – Harlequin squash soup, Cornish sardines, smokey cheese burger with chilli jam – children are encouraged to order small portions from the main menu, great for little gourmets who can romp it off in the big gardens at the back. Two nicely simple bedrooms overlook the car park, thick-walled for peace and quiet with comfy beds and spotless shower-rooms. Your room key comes with its own cow bell, so you ring sweetly as you retire after sampling the pub's terrific range of single malts. Miles, music guru, may persuade a famous artist or two to perform (Kylie Minogue did) while lovely Luca welcomes locals and visitors alike. A gem.

Rooms	2 doubles: £90.
Meals	Bar snacks from £4. Lunch, 2 courses, £12. Dinner £10–£17.
Closed	Rarely.

The Manager
Ring O Bells,
The Street,
Compton Martin BS40 6JE
Tel +44 (0)1761 221 284
Web www.ringobellscomptonmartin.co.uk

Entry 538 Map 3

The Hunters Rest Inn
Clutton

Astride Clutton Hill with fine views over the Cam valley the inn began life in the 1750s — as a hunting lodge. Later it became a smallholding and tavern. It's a big place, rambling around a large central bar, part wood, part stone, its bar topped with copper. There's plenty of jostling space so get ready to order from the Butcombe, Otter and guest ales and the Original Broad Oak and Pheasant Plucker ciders. Get cosy among the old oak and pine settles, the red carpeting and the tables to fit all sizes, the quirky wine-label wallpaper, the horse and country paraphernalia, the fires crackling away. Food is hale and hearty: shepherd's pie, pickled beetroot, crusty bread, wild mushroom risotto. Children are well looked after and there's a play area in the garden. The fun continues upstairs with rooms that range from traditional four-poster with antiques to contemporary chic. All are distinctive, all have views, several look south to the Mendips; others have private terraces. Stylish bathrooms have bold tiles, roll top baths and thick towels. A most enjoyable 'sprack and spry' hideaway.

Rooms	4 doubles, 1 twin: £95–£130. Singles £67.50–£77.50.
Meals	Lunch & dinner £8.25–£17.95.
Closed	Rarely.

Paul Thomas
The Hunters Rest Inn,
King Lane, Clutton Hill,
Clutton BS39 5QL

Tel	+44 (0)1761 452303
Web	www.huntersrest.co.uk

Somerset

The George at Backwell
Backwell

A smart and stylish inn that's an athletic stone's throw from Bristol with a relaxed modern country feel. Enter via the pretty paved courtyard garden, through doors that throw open in summer. Inside new flagstones and wooden floorboards, tartan chairs and leather stools, a large double-sided wood-burner belts out heat and high tables add a bistro feel. There's Butcombe and Bath ales at the bar alongside Thatcher's Dry cider and a wine list that covers old and new world. Menus of traditional pub classics with a twist feature grills, burgers, salads, and pizzas from their own oven with novel toppings – pulled pork, pastrami, dill pickle or Monterey Jack cheese. The dining room is laid back with painted beams and plenty of natural light. But if The George has a rabbit to pull out of a hat it has to be the bedrooms and bathrooms upstairs. Seven 'George' themed rooms with masses of fun and style await: Hypnos beds, designer furniture, arty touches and a super high comfort factor. Are you a Clooney, a Best or a VII?

Rooms	5 doubles, 2 twin/doubles: £79–£119.
Meals	Lunch & dinner from £11.95.
Closed	Rarely.

Mary Gould
The George at Backwell,
125 Farleigh Road,
Backwell BS48 3PG
Tel +44 (0)1275 462770
Web www.thegeorgeatbackwell.com

Entry 540 Map 3

The Battleaxes
Wraxall

Originally a meeting place for workers on the Tyntesfield estate, this lovely inn now basks in a playful Victorian country-house style. Tasselled lampshades hang above the bar, the odd stately bust wears a flat cap, pot plants rise next to leather sofas. The painted bar, imaginatively stocked, features the inn's own Flatcappers Ale as well as other local brews, while The Club Room – once the village hall – is a lively dining room… though this is an informal place and you can eat wherever you want. The food is excellent, lovely pub classics that are hard to resist, perhaps local gammon, free-range eggs and hand-cut chips or shepherd's pie with a white wine gravy and pickled red cabbage. Upstairs, a clutch of beautiful rooms wait. All come grandly adorned: lovely big beds, fat leather armchairs, fantastic walk-in showers. You get period wallpapers and lots of colour; one has a free-standing bath and a shower for two. Pick up the papers and sink into a sofa or spin across the road and walk on the Tyntesfield estate. The coast at Clevedon is close. Brilliant.

Rooms	6 doubles: £90–£140.
Meals	Lunch & dinner from £8.95.
	Sunday lunch, 3 courses, £19.95.
Closed	Rarely.

Sarah Davidson
The Battleaxes,
Wraxall BS48 1LQ

Tel	+44 (0)1275 857473
Web	www.flatcappers.co.uk/the-battleaxes

Entry 541 Map 3

Bristol

The Bird in Hand
Long Ashton

Yes, it's a Sawday's favourite local, an unassuming little pub on Long Ashton's high street. Enter the bar, sparkling and new, for a pint of Gem or the guest ale of the week; turn right for plain tables and deep blue-grey walls. Owner Toby Gritten is as excited about foraged ingredients as he is about "heritage vegetables, forgotten cuts and wild fish," and his sentiments are echoed by those of chef Jake. Elegant dishes are served on white plates by friendly staff – baked egg with woodland mushrooms and brioche; roast belly of Old Spot with scrumpy and apple sauce; quince and almond crumble. Come on Sunday for champagne rhubarb fizz and a choice of two roasts, or gnocchi with artichokes and salsify. The food is satisfying, unshowy and steeped in flavour.

Meals	Lunch & dinner from £9.
	Sunday roast from £12.50.
Closed	Open all day.

Jake Platt
The Bird in Hand,
17 Weston Road,
Long Ashton BS41 9LA
Tel   +44 (0)1275 395222
Web   www.bird-in-hand.co.uk

Entry 542 Map 3

Somerset

The Black Horse
Clapton-in-Gordano

The Snug Bar once doubled as the village lock-up and, if it weren't for the electric lighting, you'd be hard pushed to remember you were in the 21st century. With flagstones and dark moody wood, the main room bears the scuffs of centuries of drinking. Settles and old tables sit around the walls; cottage windows with wobbly shutters let a little of the outside in. The fire roars in its vast hearth beneath a fine set of antique guns – pull off your muddy boots and settle in. Sepia prints of parish cricket teams and steam tractors clutter the walls and cask ales pour from the stone ledge behind the hatch bar. The food is unfancy bar fodder, with daily specials. Ale takes pride of place; beneath the chalkboard, six jacketed casks squat above drip pans. There are fine wines too, and plenty of garden.

Meals	Lunch & dinner £3.50–£7.95.
Closed	Open all day.

Nicholas Evans
The Black Horse,
Clevedon Lane, Clapton-in-Gordano,
Bristol BS20 7RH
Tel   +44 (0)1275 842105
Web   www.thekicker.co.uk

Entry 543 Map 3

Somerset

The Plough Inn
Wrington

If once the Plough languished, now it's been reborn, as a friendly village pub serving excellent local food. On the second Friday of every month, the terrace hosts a farmers' market, while quiz nights, steak nights and long Sunday lunches are part of its DNA. Warm colours, a smouldering fire and low ceilings give a traditional feel, while the restaurant at the back – complete with wood-burner in the middle of the room – is a stylish addition with walls of glass that open to the garden. A great place for some lovely food, anything from a steak ciabatta to a fillet of cod stuffed with a herb and lemon mousse. Wash it all down with your favourite tipple: a glass of red, a pint of Butcombe, a dram of whisky, a soupçon of Taylor's vintage port. John Locke the philosopher was born in the village and lies in the churchyard.

Somerset

The Pony & Trap
Knowle Hill

Just outside pretty Chew Magna, a short drive from Bristol and Bath, is one of the best little gastropubs in the country. Josh Eggleton, who earned his spurs in France, Sicily and America, has won his first Michelin star. Provenance is all; from the blue cheese panna cotta to the fillet of pork with celeriac purée, almost every ingredient has travelled only a few miles to the plate. Deer is bought from a local marksman, eggs are from the chickens in the garden, berries from the hedges and perfect spears of asparagus straight from the patch. As for the views, they're stunning, and both the conservatory-style dining room and the large sloping garden – dine out on a summer's day – have them. For winter the bar is the place to be – super-cosy with wood panelling, old cider flagons and a cast-iron range.

Meals	Lunch from £4.95.
	Dinner from £9.50.
	Sunday roast from £10.50.
Closed	Closed 3pm-5pm Mon-Thurs.
	Open all day Fri-Sun.

Meals	Lunch from £9.50.
	Dinner £18-£23.
	Sunday lunch, 2 courses, £26;
	3 courses £30.
Closed	Open all day.

	Jason Read
	The Plough Inn,
	High Street, Wrington,
	Congresbury BS40 5QA
Tel	+44 (0)1934 862871
Web	www.theploughatwrington.co.uk

Entry 544 Map 3

	Josh Eggleton
	The Pony & Trap,
	Knowle Hill,
	Chew Magna BS40 8TQ
Tel	+44 (0)1275 332627
Web	www.theponyandtrap.co.uk

Entry 545 Map 3

Somerset

The Crown
Churchill

Once a coaching stop between Bristol and Exeter, then the village grocer's, now an unspoilt pub. Modern makeovers have passed it by and beer reigns supreme, with up to ten ales tapped from the barrel. For years this little gem has resisted piped music and electronic games; who needs them in these beamed and flagstoned bars? The rustic surroundings and the jolly atmosphere draw both locals and walkers treading the Mendip hills. Find a seat by the log fire, cradle a pint of Butcombe or RCH PG Steam bitter, be lulled by the hum of regulars at the bar. If you're here at lunchtime you'll find a short, traditional, blackboard menu: warming bowls of soup, thick-cut rare roast beef sandwiches, winter casseroles, treacle pud. Evenings are reserved for the serious art of ale drinking, and it's packed at weekends.

Somerset

The George
Wedmore

Wedmore's striking 15th-century coaching inn was lost in another century until Gordon Stevens took over. His vision for the vast stone building has breathed new life into a labyrinth of rooms that ooze character and charm. Wooden floors, half-panelled walls, stone fireplaces, old prints, warm greens and terracottas, wax-encrusted candlesticks on scrubbed dining tables... such is the setting for pints of Potholer and Orchard Pig cider. Food is hearty and locally sourced, and the menu ranges from crab sandwiches and afternoon teacakes with jam (yes!) to rack of Mendip lamb, beef and vegetable stew, and spicy pork curry. There's a cracking locals' bar, and a curry restaurant next door (in the bit that dates from 1760).

Meals	Lunch & bar meals from £4.85.
	No food in evenings.
Closed	Open all day.

Meals	Bar meals £5.
	Lunch from £7.
	Dinner from £12.
	Sunday lunch, 2 courses, £18.
	Not Sunday eve.
Closed	Open all day.

	Brian Clements
	The Crown,
	The Batch, Churchill,
	Congresbury BS25 5PP
Tel	+44 (0)1934 852995

Entry 546 Map 3

	Gordon Stevens
	The George,
	Church Street, Wedmore,
	Cheddar BS28 4AB
Tel	+44 (0)1934 712124
Web	www.thegeorgewedmore.co.uk

Entry 547 Map 3

Somerset

The Sheppey Inn
Lower Godney

A funky country pub, one of the best in the west. Its exterior gives no hint of the wonders within – part cider house, part cool hotel. Low beamed ceilings in the bar, high white walls in the barn. There are cute booths, David Hockney prints, 50s retro furniture, the odd guitar waiting to be played. Music matters here: fantastic jazz, blues and funk bubbles away nicely, while a small stage hosts the odd travelling band. Local ales, scrumptious ciders, Belgian beers and lovely wines all wait, as does super food. Try French onion soup, a splendid fish stew or Somerset beef with Yorkshire pudding and red wine gravy. In summer, life decants onto a small terrace that hangs above a tiny river; otters pass, fields stretch out beyond. Glastonbury and the Somerset Levels wait. Out of this world.

Somerset

The Three Horseshoes Inn
Batcombe

A magnificent spot, England at its best. You get the full works here: a beautiful valley lost to the world, an English village impeccably preserved, a great little inn that sits in the shade of an ancient church tower. Inside, fires burn at both ends of the bar, there are low ceilings, window seats and a warm mix of traditional and contemporary. Rustic food hits the spot perfectly. Westcombe Cheddar sandwiches come with a real ale chutney, and if you want something more substantial, you can have it: pan-fried quail with ginger purée, tiger prawns in an Asian broth, Dorset mussels with lemongrass and chilli. In summer you slip outside and take your choice from a pretty courtyard where walls are clad in wisteria, and a lush lawn, where you can sip your pint as church bells chime. Great walks start from the front door.

Meals	Lunch from £5.95.	Meals	Lunch from £6.
	Dinner from £8.95.		Dinner, 3 courses, £25–£30.
	Sunday roast from £10.50.		Sunday roast from £11.50.
Closed	3pm–5pm, Tues–Fri.	Closed	Open all day.

2015/16
Sawday's
PUB AWARD

Community pub

	Mark Hey & Liz Chamberlain		Kaveh Javvi
	The Sheppey Inn,		The Three Horseshoes Inn,
	Lower Godney,		Batcombe,
	Glastonbury BA5 1RZ		Frome BA4 6HE
Tel	+44 (0)1458 831594	Tel	+44 (0)1749 850359
Web	www.thesheppey.co.uk	Web	www.thethreehorseshoesinn.com

Entry 548 Map 3 — Entry 549 Map 3

Somerset

The Montague Inn
Shepton Montague

The O'Callaghans' 17th-century public house has been a stables, livery, grocery; now it is an inn in the true sense of the word. All remains beautiful, with Bath Ales and regional guests that may come from Butcombe and Blindman's Brewery, two wood-burners in the bar, candles on stripped pine tables and delicious produce from organic neighbouring farms. Chef Matt Dean's food is simple yet imaginative: chunky lunchtime ploughman's of local cheeses, and daily specials such as a hot pot on Tuesdays and fresh fish and chips on Fridays. Try the grilled local goat's cheese in a celery, apple and walnut salad, or seared fillet of local beef with garlic cream mash, bacon and lentil jus – all of it's brilliant. The restaurant and rear terrace have bosky views to Redlynch and Alfred's Tower.

Somerset

Kings Arms
Charlton Horethorne

A brilliantly run pub near Sherborne. With three dining pubs and a thriving food company behind them, Tony and Sarah are stars in the west country pub world, and the Kings Arms, with its bell ringers' lunches and local ciders and beers, has status as a proper local. The striking old façade opens to a contemporary-chic décor of wood and stone floors, good art, bold walls, vintage dining tables, cheery wood-burner, and squashy leather sofas. The restaurant has a coir-matted floor, arched mirrors – and outside is a terrace with views. On Sarah's daily-changing, local-produce menus, you find roasted pork belly with apple terrine; lamb rump with rosemary jus with butternut squash; ricotta ravioli with marjoram butter sauce; apple and calvados trifle. Delicious food for children too.

Meals	Bar meals & lunches from £4.95. Dinner from £11.95. Sunday lunch, 3 courses, £21.50. Not Sunday eve.
Closed	3pm-6pm Mon-Sat. Sun 4pm-12am.

Meals	Lunch & dinner £8.95–£16.50. Sunday roast £11.50.
Closed	Open all day.

Sean & Suzy O'Callaghan
The Montague Inn,
Shepton Montague,
Wincanton BA9 8JW
Tel   +44 (0)1749 813213
Web   www.themontagueinn.co.uk

Entry 550 Map 3

Tony & Sarah Lethbridge
Kings Arms,
Charlton Horethorne,
Sherborne DT9 4NL
Tel   +44 (0)1963 220281
Web   www.thekingsarms.co.uk

Entry 551 Map 3

Somerset

The Red Lion Inn
Babcary

The Red Lion's transformation into a stylish inn in sleepy Babcary, is now complete. Clare and Charles's passion for this thatched local ensures it combines the best of pub tradition — a cosy rustic feel, local ales — with top-notch food, a café on the terrace, and bedrooms in a converted barn. Hair-cord carpets, sofas and a blazing fire in the cast-iron stove welcome you to the bar/lounge, while a dozen well-spaced country dining tables fill the beamed and flagstoned dining room. Daily menus offer pub classics like beef burger with homemade chutney; confit chicken and black pudding terrine; roast partridge with parsnip purée, cabbage and bacon; hot chocolate fondant. The best A303 stopover for miles.

Somerset

The Devonshire Arms
Long Sutton

A lively English village with a well-kept green. The inn, 400 years old, was once a hunting lodge for the Dukes of Devonshire; a rather smart pillared porch survives at the front. These days open-plan interiors are warmly contemporary with high ceilings, blond floorboards and fresh flowers everywhere. Hop onto brown leather stools at the bar and order a pint of Moor Revival, or sink into sofas in front of the fire and crack open a bottle of wine. In summer, life spills onto the terrace at the front, the courtyard at the back and the lawned garden beyond. The hosts are engaging and the food's a joy; choose from ploughman's with homemade chutney or game burger and chips, linger over lamb rump with roast vegetables and puy lentils, dive into dark chocolate fondant. Then walk off your indulgence in style.

Meals	Bar meals from £5.95.
	Lunch from £6.80.
	Dinner from £8.50.
	Sunday lunch, 3 courses, £22.50.
Closed	Open all day.

Meals	Lunch from £5.95.
	Dinner, 3 courses, from £30.
	Sunday roast from £12.95.
Closed	25th/26th December.

Clare & Charles Garrard
The Red Lion Inn,
Babcary,
Somerton TA11 7ED
Tel   +44 (0)1458 223230
Web   www.redlionbabcary.co.uk

Entry 552 Map 3

Philip & Sheila Mepham
The Devonshire Arms,
Long Sutton,
Langport TA10 9LP
Tel   +44 (0)1458 241271
Web   www.thedevonshirearms.com

Entry 553 Map 3

Somerset

Halfway House
Pitney Hill

First and foremost, the beer is second to none. As many as ten cask ales and ciders are lovingly nurtured by happy staff for grateful locals who love this pub. Inside, simple bricks and mortar require no embellishment: low ceilings, flagged floors, three smouldering fires and the constant flow of happy chatter. The food is as good as the beer. At lunch you dig into simple delights, perhaps deep-fried whitebait or a French onion tart, while at dinner you can try one of the pub's revered curries, washed down with a pint of Summer Lightning. Elsewhere, maps for walkers, the daily papers, a community notice board and a chesterfield by the fire. Children and dogs are very welcome. Simply wonderful.

Meals	Lunch & dinner £4.50–£10.95. Not Sunday eve.
Closed	3pm–5.30pm. Open all day Sun.

Mark Phillips
Halfway House,
Pitney Hill,
Langport TA10 9AB
Tel   +44 (0)1458 252513
Web   www.thehalfwayhouse.co.uk

Entry 554 Map 3

Somerset

Rose & Crown Inn (Eli's)
Huish Episcopi

Quirky, unspoilt and in the family for over 140 years. The layout has evolved, gradually taking over the family home. There's no bar as such; you choose from the casks. Walk in and you step back to the 1930s; even the loos are historic. The cider and the beer (Glastonbury Mystery Tor) are tasty, the locals are lovely, the landlady is perfect; there are worn flagstones and aged panelling in four low parlours radiating off a central tap room, and an (almost modern) pool and juke box room. They do folk music nights and occasional quiz nights and Morris dancers drop by in summer. The food is brilliant value: creamy winter vegetable soup, a tasty pork, apple and cider cobbler, steak and ale pie, bread and butter pudding. Everyone's happy and children like the little play area outside.

Meals	Lunch & dinner £6.95–£7.95.
Closed	2.30pm–5.30pm, Mon–Thurs. Open all day Fri–Sun.

Steve & Maureen Pittard & Patricia O'Malley
Rose & Crown Inn (Eli's),
Huish Episcopi,
Langport TA10 9QT
Tel   +44 (0)1458 250494

Entry 555 Map 3

The Helyar Arms
East Coker

Mathieu Eke's gastropub is worth leaving the A30 for – for the atmosphere, the food (lots from local suppliers) and the handsome village it lives in. Daily boards of tasty dishes express the enterprising style: scallops with black pudding and chive beurre blanc, roast rump of Coker lamb with fondant potato, baby leeks and redcurrant jus, sticky toffee pudding. Real ales, Somerset cider and global wines are well priced. For ploughman's there might be local cheeses, such as Montgomery cheddar served with homemade chutney. Low beams, sofas by the log fire, pictures crowding the walls, flickering candles on old tables, daily papers and board games in the bar, a raftered restaurant in the apple loft, a garden and skittles… this is a great all-round village pub!

The White Horse
Haselbury Plucknett

In Haselbury Plucknett (the first part means Hazel Grove) in rural Somerset, owners Richard and Rebecca have brought culinary panache and first-class hospitality to this traditional pub. Expect flagstone floors, and, quite possibly, in front of the open fireplace, a slumbering dog. There are ales from Teignworthy and Butcombe, feisty local scrumpy at the bar, and menus that feature pub classics as well as dishes with a Gallic twist. Snack on homemade focaccia; try saltmarsh lamb rump with pomme purée and spiced aubergine, tomato and tapenade sauce, or 38 day-hung Hereford steak; finish with chocolate terrine and pistachio ice cream. Or choose from a great selection of cheeses. A comprehensive wine list accompanies it all, there's a pretty garden with a re-opened well, and super friendly staff.

Meals	Lunch & dinner £8.50–£16.
	Sunday roast from £9.
Closed	3pm-6pm.

Meals	Bar meals from £5.
	Lunch from £10.
	Dinner £10-£25.
Closed	Sun evenings & all day Mon.

Mathieu Eke
The Helyar Arms,
Moor Lane, East Coker,
Yeovil BA22 9JR
Tel   +44 (0)1935 862332
Web   www.helyar-arms.co.uk

Rebecca Robinson
The White Horse,
North Street, Haselbury Plucknett,
Yeovil TA18 7RJ
Tel   +44 (0)1460 78873
Web   www.thewhitehorsehaselbury.com

Entry 556 Map 3

Entry 557 Map 3

The Candlelight Inn
Bishopswood

Aptly named, this 17th-century flint built pub shines in the heart of the Blackdown Hills. Inside and out are polished woods of all hues, exposed stonework and brick with timber framing, a cold-smoker out the back and two wood-burners in. Stone flags border the bar where you can choose from four real ales, as well as guest beers lovingly tended by Tom. Sheppy's Farmhouse cider too, and Bolhayes Perry, a perfect accompaniment to the sandwiches. Chef Vincent's specials include whole grilled Torbay sole and grilled rump steak with his own herb butter; in winter, there's takeaway fish and chips on Wednesday evenings. It's all homemade, including the ice cream. The lovely light dining area frames views to the pretty garden; its fishpond and covered barbecue look over the river Yarty.

The Blagdon Inn
Blagdon Hill

Alongside a resurgence of interest in artisanal produce is the desire of a number of kitchens to raise their own livestock and grow their own veg. And so it is at this village pub just outside Taunton, where a very special chef heads the kitchen and the service is warm, knowledgeable and attentive. Bar areas are simple, cosy, charming, contemporary, with new stone flags and a duck egg blue bar, dark country furniture and a real fire, and lots of nooks and crannies. Families, foodies, walkers, dogs, all find a welcome here, along with platefuls of linguine with wild mushroom sauce, and sea bass from Lyme Bay (ours was fabulous). Puddings are naughty or fancy, beers are local, wines are global, and if you order pork belly croquette with apple mash, kale, sesame and cider gravy you know most of it came from their patch.

Meals	Bar meals from £4.
	Lunch from £9.50.
	Dinner from £12.
	Set lunch £14–£18.
	Sunday roast £11–£20.
Closed	Mon all day.

Meals	Bar meals & starters from £5.75.
	Mains from £9.95.
Closed	Mon all day.

	Debbie Lush
	The Candlelight Inn,
	Bishopswood,
	Chard TA20 3RS
Tel	+44 (0)1460 234476
Web	www.candlelight-inn.co.uk

	Nigel Capel
	The Blagdon Inn,
	Honiton Road, Blagdon Hill,
	Taunton TA3 7SG
Tel	+44 (0)1823 421296
Web	www.blagdoninn.co.uk

Entry 558 Map 2

Entry 559 Map

Somerset

Somerset

The Rising Sun Inn
Bagborough

The Sun shines more brightly than ever in the hands of the ambitious Brinkmans. In sleepy West Bagborough on the flanks of the Quantock Hills, it has been constructed around 16th-century cob walls and a magnificent door, its post-fire reincarnation bold and craftsman-led, with 80 tons of solid oak timbers and windows and a slate-floored bar. Add Art Nouveau features, spotlighting and swagged drapery and you find one very smart pub. There's Exmoor, Proper Job and Butcombe to sample and, high in the rafters, a dining room with views that unfurl to Exmoor. It's an impressive setting for impressive food: goat's cheese on a walnut and plum salad; fillet of beef with peppercorn sauce; lemon sole with crayfish tails; bread and butter pudding. Worth walking down the hill for.

Woods Bar & Dining Room
Dulverton

A warm and cosy place in a lively Exmoor village, replete with antlers and country paraphernalia, to the delight of wine-quaffing farmers and gentry. Foodies too have much to be grateful for. Find daily-changing modern menus and an emphasis on seasonal sourcing... perhaps roast tomato soup with serrano ham; roast Exmoor lamb with confit garlic and rosemary sauce; rich chocolate brownies. Or pop in for a stilton and onion marmalade baguette. A stable-like partition divides the space into two intimate seating areas, beyond which is a smart, soft-lit and deeply cosy bar: two wood-burners, lots of pine, a few barrel tables, exposed stone. Ales include Dartmoor Best and Devon Coast IPA but the wines are the thing, many by the glass. Friendly landlords Sally and Paddy welcome families and dogs.

Meals	Bar meals from £5.95.
	Lunch from £9.50.
	Dinner from £11.
Closed	3pm-6pm.

Meals	Bar meals from £5.
	Lunch & dinner £8.50-£16.50.
Closed	3pm-6pm (7pm Sun).

	Jon & Christine Brinkman
	The Rising Sun Inn,
	Bagborough,
	Taunton TA4 3EF
Tel	+44 (0)1823 432575
Web	www.risingsuninn.info

Entry 560 Map 2

	Sally & Paddy Groves
	Woods Bar & Dining Room,
	4 Bank Square,
	Dulverton TA22 9BU
Tel	+44 (0)1398 324007
Web	www.woodsdulverton.co.uk

Entry 561 Map 2

Somerset

Tarr Farm Inn
Tarr Steps

No traffic lights, no mobile signals, peace for miles. Tucked into the Barle valley, a hop from the clapper bridge at Tarr Steps, this well-established 16th-century inn is surrounded by woodland above the hauntingly high spaces of Exmoor. The garden views are sublime – where better to test the best West Country cheeses followed by the perfect coffee? Inside, the blue-carpeted, low-beamed main bar has comfy window seats and gleaming black leather sofas, and Exmoor Ale and Magner's cider flow as easily as the conversation. To fill the gap after a bracing walk the menu draws on local game (hunting and shooting are big here) so tuck into venison and rabbit casserole or pan-roasted partridge – partnered by a hundred French and New World wines.

Meals	Lunch £4.50–£14.95. Dinner £5.50–£21. Sunday roast £4.50–£14.95.
Closed	Open all day.

Hilary Lester
Tarr Farm Inn,
Tarr Steps,
Dulverton TA22 9PY
Tel   +44 (0)1643 851507
Web   www.tarrfarm.co.uk

🥩 🍷 🔊

Entry 562 Map 2

Staffordshire

The Duncombe Arms
Ellastone

The bar is sleek and stylishly laid out, with rustic nooks to settle into, the music plays discreetly and the food is absolutely beautiful. Diners include many regulars and returning Londoners, even though this is Staffordshire. James is passionate about making the Duncombe excel, and excel it does: the staff are on the ball and there's a top team in the kitchen, headed by Matt Wadsley. Platefuls of flavoursome food, modern British with touches of rusticity, are delivered to inviting tables in dining areas cosy, lofty, private, airy or al fresco; take you pick. Our sea bass with crushed new potatoes and slow-cooked cherry tomatoes was faultless. There are wines from Bibendum, 13 top malts, Duncombe Ale on tap, and in summer you can spill into a huge garden with views across the Dove Valley.

Meals	Bar snacks £6-£7.
	Lunch & dinner from £12.
Closed	Open all day.

Favourite newcomer

	James Oddy	
	The Duncombe Arms,	
	Ellastone,	
	Ashbourne DE6 2GZ	
Tel	+44 (0)1335.324275	
Web	www.duncombearms.co.uk	

Entry 563 Map 8

Staffordshire

The George
Alstonefield

A green sward ripples endlessly in this remote limestone village, perched on a plateau between the remarkable gorges of the rivers Dove and Manifold. Set amidst this verdant Eden, the handsome George is an ultra-reliable local, in the family for four decades and lovingly managed by Emily. As you walk into small, timeless rooms of old beams, gleaming quarry tiles and crackling log fire, you know you're in safe hands. It's an unhurried place, where everyone knows everyone else (or soon will), ramblers cram the benches out front and time passes slowly. The 18th-century coaching house is perfect for private parties. The welcome is warm, the beer's on song and the food is fab. Young chefs are creative with seasonal produce, so there's Devon crab, steak and real ale pie, and treacle tart.

Meals	Bar meals £5.50-£16.
	Lunch & dinner £12-£24.
Closed	3pm-6pm.
	Open all day Fri-Sun.

	Emily Brighton	
	The George,	
	Alstonefield,	
	Ashbourne DE6 2FX	
Tel	+44 (0)1335 310205	
Web	www.thegeorgeatalstonefield.com	

Entry 564 Map 8

Suffolk

The Bell Inn
Walberswick

The road ends at this tiny summer-soft, winter-bleak fishing village. Swim, sail, walk the beach to Dunwich or seek refuge in the Bell, a 600-year-old inn by the green, unspoilt, with old beams and flagstones, curved wooden settles and crackling log fires. Time has also given it a few nooks and crannies in which to hide with a pint of Adnams Broadside. Since he arrived in 2010, Nick Atfield has poured energy and delight into revitalising this seaside gem. The menu mixes hearty bar food with imaginative modern dishes, making good use of local pork and lamb and daily deliveries of Lowestoft fish; on the menu you may find cider-braised sausages, confit duck leg, Cromer crab salad, and walnut brownies. Small, charming bedrooms have been refurbished with a classic seaside feel, all full of comfort and some with blissful river Blyth views. Outside, soak up the sun in the big garden and gaze on beach huts, dunes and sea. An absolute treat for families, dogs and East Anglian architecture buffs.

Rooms	4 doubles, 1 twin: £90–£100.
	1 family room for 4: £130–£150.
Meals	Lunch & dinner £5.95–£15.
Closed	Rarely.

Nick Atfield
The Bell Inn,
Ferry Road, Walberswick,
Southwold IP18 6TN
Tel   +44 (0)1502 723109
Web   www.bellinnwalberswick.co.uk

Entry 565 Map 10

The Anchor
Walberswick

Beer guru Mark and wife Sophie are doing wonders at this well-loved pub. To the sound of the sea crashing on the beach beyond, the vast lawn hosts summer soirées and barbecues. Inside, sand, stone and aqua tones are redolent of the ocean and open skies and add a contemporary touch, while Sophie's menus overflow with produce sourced from a rich vein of organic farms and top local butchers. Fresh food is definitely on the menu (ask about food safaris) and the allotment at the back has doubled in size. Their "Extra Special" wine list is very impressive and seasonal food is matched to beer and wine: try game terrine with Flying Dog IPA, or roast cod, lentils and chorizo, with a glass of pouilly fumé. Tempura rock oysters with a draught wheat beer are a summer treat, out on the sun terrace overlooking allotments, beach huts and distant sea. Verdant borders festooned with beach-loving plants front the six spruced up chalet rooms. Now cedar-clad, they have smart new bathrooms, comfortable beds and soft Farrow & Ball hues; three have terraces for savouring the sunrise. Dogs are welcome too.

Rooms	9 doubles, 1 single/double: £95–£150.
Meals	Lunch from £5.25.
	Sunday lunch, 2 courses, £20.
	Dinner, 3 courses, about £30.
Closed	Christmas Day.

Mark & Sophie Dorber
The Anchor,
Main Street, Walberswick,
Southwold IP18 6UA
Tel   +44 (0)1502 722112
Web   www.anchoratwalberswick.com

Entry 566 Map 10

The Ship
Dunwich

Once a great port, Dunwich is now a tiny (but famous) village, gradually sinking into the sea. Its well-loved smugglers' inn, almost on the beach, overlooks the salt marsh and sea and pulls in wind-blown walkers and birdwatchers from the Minsmere Reserve. In the old-fashioned bar – nautical bric-a-brac, flagged floors, simple furnishings and a stove that belts out the heat – you can tuck into legendary hake and chips washed down with a pint of Adnams. There's also a more modern dining room where hearty food combines with traditional dishes: glorious big platefuls of ham, egg and chips, Blythburgh pork belly and ham hock terrine, and lamb cutlets served with an individual shepherd's pie. Up the fine Victorian staircase are spruced up bedrooms – simple, uncluttered – with period features, cord carpets, brass beds, old pine, little shower rooms. Rooms at the front have glorious salt marsh views, two new rooms overlook the garden, courtyard rooms are cosy with pine, and the family room under the eaves is fabulous: single beds, a big futon-style bean bag, and a flat-screen for the kids. *Special midweek rates off season.*

Rooms	11 doubles, 1 twin: £112–£135.
	3 family rooms for 4: £130–£135.
Meals	Bar meals from £9.75.
	Lunch from £6.95.
	Dinner from £9.95.
	Sunday roast £11.95.
Closed	Rarely.

Matt Goodwin
The Ship,
St James's Street, Dunwich,
Saxmundham IP17 3DT
Tel   +44 (0)1728 648219
Web   www.shipatdunwich.co.uk

Entry 567 Map 10

Sibton White Horse
Sibton

Step through the door of an unassuming pub and prepare for a surprise. The heart of this thriving village local is 16th-century and the bar is steeped in character: old pews, huge inglenook, horsebrasses on blackened beams, wonky walls, a fire in winter. (Take a peek through the window panel into the cellar to see a reclaimed Roman floor.) Ale drinkers will note the gleaming brass beer engines on the old oak servery and settle in for pints of Adnams and Woodforde's, or a weekly guest beer. Food is seasonal, with local game, meat from the next village and veg from the kitchen garden. There's chicken, tomato and herb terrine with tomato chutney; roast breast and confit leg of duck with wild mushroom jus; sticky toffee pudding. The bread is homemade, it's all delicious, and on sunny days you can spill onto the lawns. Thoroughly modern annexe bedrooms are furnished in old and new pine; beds are comfy; bathrooms fresh; views are to open countryside. You are 20 minutes from Aldeburgh and charming Southwold: enjoy beach cricket, a pint of prawns, a dip in the North Sea.

Rooms	5 twin/doubles: £80–£90.
Meals	Lunch from £6.50.
	Dinner from £10.50.
	Sunday roast £12.95.
Closed	Rarely.

Neil & Gill Mason
Sibton White Horse,
Halesworth Road, Sibton,
Saxmundham IP17 2JJ

Tel	+44 (0)1728 660337
Web	www.sibtonwhitehorseinn.co.uk

The Crown at Woodbridge
Woodbridge

Everyone loves Woodbridge's Crown, from its pastel façade to its cool laid-back interiors and humorous touches: beneath a sloping glass roof an immaculate wooden skiff is suspended. Welcome to a 400-year-old pub with great food and a long granite-topped bar, urbane bedrooms and a cosmopolitan air. In intimate dining rooms, chef-patron Stephen David's menu trawls Europe for inspiration and draws as much as it can on Suffolk's natural larder. Look forward to hearty dishes full of flavour and some amazing taste combinations: lamb sweetbreads with celeriac purée and minted apple crème fraîche; chilli fried squid, spaghetti, lime tomato dressing and spinach; Pimm's jelly. Wash it all down with Adnams or Meantime beers or delve into the impressive list of wines. Cosseting bedrooms decorated in chic, Nantucket style and themed in white and grey are a further attraction. There are big beds, quirky touches and a host of extras, from fruit, fresh coffee and homemade shortbread to soft bathrobes and heated bathroom floors. As for the staff, nothing is too much trouble for them. A welcoming Suffolk bolthole – unmissable!

Rooms	8 twin/doubles: £100–£160.
	2 family rooms for 4: £120–£160.
	Singles from £95.
Meals	Lunch & dinner £6–£30.
	Sunday roast from £12.50.
Closed	Rarely.

Garth Wray
The Crown at Woodbridge,
Thoroughfare,
Woodbridge IP12 1AD
Tel   +44 (0)1394 384242
Web   www.thecrownatwoodbridge.co.uk

Entry 569 Map 10

The Crown
Stoke-by-Nayland

In pretty Stoke-by-Nayland, is this rather relaxing pub. Enter to find low-ceilinged, rambling rooms decked in muted colours, and space to prop up the bar and down a pint from Adnams. The mood is warm, appealing and refreshingly music-free, and the seasonal menu is a sympathetic combination of traditional and contemporary. To shining tables chefs dispatch exuberant renditions of wild Norfolk mussels with bacon and parsley on toast, and locally shot pheasant served with bacon, prunes and leeks; sticky quince and ginger puddings and platters British cheeses. From an outstanding wine list, wines are matched to the food, and you can take a case home from the pub shop. Stay a while: in a smart new-build behind, rather posh bedrooms lie, with brass beds and elegant wallpapers, top mattresses and bathrooms with storm showers and heated towel rails. Three rooms have French windows leading to a terrace, all have thick carpets and toasty warm floors. Head to the terrace on sunny days: the views are fabulous too.

Rooms	10 doubles: £135–£225.
	1 suite for 2: £195–£245.
	Singles £95–£150.
	Extra bed/sofabed £10–£30 per
	person per night.
Meals	Lunch & dinner £5–£25.
Closed	Rarely.

Richard Sunderland
The Crown,
Park Street, Stoke-by-Nayland,
Colchester CO6 4SE

Tel	+44 (0)1206 262001
Web	www.crowninn.net

Entry 570 Map 10

Long Melford Swan
Long Melford

Long Melford – home to TV's Lovejoy – is as achingly pretty as a Suffolk village can be, and the Swan is in the middle of it. Enter the airy bar, with blond oak beams and pale blue palette, an open fire, background music, original art, the odd dozing dog. In the restaurant: cool tartan carpeting and bold feature walls, shining glasses and upholstered chairs. As for the food, it's modern, Suffolk-local and executed with flair, from the eggs cocotte at breakfast to the small plates for gourmets (the cockle popcorn with crab mayonnaise is fabulous) to a full-blown herb-crusted rack of lamb for two to share, with confit shallots and château potatoes. Parents can relax in the terraced, parasol'd garden; drinkers can choose whatever they fancy: a peachy bellini, an espresso Martini, a Sancerre rosé, a pint of Green King IPA. Stay the night? Yes please. Next door is Melford House with four luxy bedrooms, two up, two down, each better than the last. Say wow to sumptuous headboards, gilt framed mirrors, subtle colours, atmospheric lighting and bathrooms with Noble Isle toiletries. You could hardly be more spoiled!

Rooms	4 doubles: £90–£175.
Meals	Lunch from £7.50.
	Dinner from £14.
	Sunday roast from £14.
Closed	Rarely.

Lorna Pissarro
Long Melford Swan,
Hall Street,
Long Melford CO10 9JQ
Tel   +44 (0)1787 464545
Web   www.longmelfordswan.co.uk

Entry 571 Map 10

Suffolk

The Packhorse Inn
Moulton

The rise of the cool country inn continues apace and the most recent member to join the club is the Packhorse, a beautifully renovated country pub that was rescued from abject neglect. These days it's a small-scale pleasure dome – striking interiors and ambrosial food that elate – yet it remains a village local with a lovely bar that welcomes all. The bar and dining room are open plan with a fire that burns on two sides and the odd armchair to take the strain. You'll find varnished floorboards, beautiful art, low-hanging lamps at the cool little bar. Irresistible food waits, maybe truffled goat's cheese with quince and figs, Suffolk venison and kidney pudding, plum tarte tatin with fruit-cake ice cream. There's a terrace for good weather and a private dining room turns into a very cool meeting room.

Suffolk

The White Horse
Whepstead

Built in 1640, with a 19th-century addition, this rural beauty is worth more than a passing nod. Gary and Di Kingshott are continuing the modus operandi that made the Beehive at Horringer such a favourite with the local country lifers. Stock in trade are real ales from Adnams, a reasonably priced wine list, cosy fires, and a chatty, informal beamed bar. Comfortable dining areas are decorated in fresh, contemporary colours – one doubles as an art gallery – while a blackboard menu promises unpretentious dishes strong on flavour: fried duck egg on toast with a sauté of wild mushrooms; beef bourguignon; treacle tart. Fun, friendly and charismatic: it's hard to believe that this grand cru of a pub was picked up in a distress sale.

Meals	Lunch from £6.
	Dinner, 3 courses, from £35.
Closed	Open all day.

Meals	Bar meals from £8.95.
	Lunch & dinner from £9.95.
	Sunday lunch, 3 courses, £24.45.
Closed	Sun evenings.

	Philip Turner
	The Packhorse Inn,
	Bridge Street, Moulton,
	Newmarket CB8 8SP
Tel	+44 (0)1638 751818
Web	www.thepackhorseinn.com

Entry 572 Map 9

	Gary & Diane Kingshott
	The White Horse,
	Rede Road, Whepstead,
	Bury St Edmunds IP29 4SS
Tel	+44 (0)1284 735760
Web	www.whitehorsewhepstead.co.uk

Entry 573 Map 10

Suffolk

The Angel Hotel
Lavenham

Little Lavenham, built on wool, is Suffolk's most celebrated town, with 340 listed buildings of limewashed timber and ochre, each one a gem, and enough tea shops to satisfy the nations's thirst. Welcome to the Angel, standing proud on the corner of Market Square since 1420. In 2014 Cosy Pubs gave it the sympathetic makeover it deserved: dark-grey woodwork, off-white render. Inside it shines. There's spruce wood in the bar, brown leather chesterfields around the inglenook, leather club armchairs in the snug, and a window seat in the bay. The tourists flock and the locals are returning, for the warm service and the no-nonsense food: rare-breed pork sausages with silky mash, coq au vin with pearl onions, rump steak from the grill. The set lunches are good value and there's a sizeable garden at the rear.

Meals	Dinner from £12.
Closed	Open all day.

Alex Burgess
The Angel Hotel,
Market Place,
Lavenham CO10 9QZ
Tel   +44 (0)1787 247 388
Web   www.theangellavenham.co.uk

Entry 574 Map 10

Suffolk

The Hadleigh Ram
Hadleigh

In the market town of Hadleigh is a very good pub, country-classy and contemporary yet intimate and friendly: almost impossible to fault. The lighting is inviting, the bar is free-flowing, there's tongue and groove panelling and very helpful young staff. As for the food, it is serious, delicious and more beautiful with every course. They bake their own bread so the sandwiches are special, and they are passionate about seasonality and provenance. Set lunch is a steal: pheasant boudin with bacon crumb and endive perhaps, then pressed skate with mash and cockle cream, followed by ginger and lemon poached pear with coconut bavarois. Dogs are allowed in the enclosed courtyard and the bar; later they can romp on the banks of the Brett. It's a Greene King pub – but you may prefer a cocktail!

Meals	Set lunch, 2 courses, £15.95; 3 courses, £17.95.
Closed	Open all day.

Lorna Pissarro & Oliver Macmillan
The Hadleigh Ram,
5 Market Place,
Hadleigh IP7 5DL
Tel   +44 (0)1473 822880
Web   www.thehadleighram.co.uk

Entry 575 Map 10

Suffolk

The Angel Inn
Stoke-by-Nayland

Soft lamplight glows in the windows of this 16th-century inn deep in 'Constable country'. Spruced up by Exclusive Inns, the bar divides into two. Find carved beams, open brickwork, log fires, polished wood tables, chesterfields and wing chairs, fresh flowers and candles, fine prints and paintings, and a few antique pieces to add to the appeal. The Angel fills early and menus include a good value lunchtime 'classics' choice – sausages with mash and onion gravy; battered haddock – and an imaginative carte. Tuck into Denham Estate venison scotch egg; pork belly with Madeira broth; treacle tart with white chocolate ice cream. Eat in the bar, the galleried restaurant (once a brewhouse) or at laid tables on the terrace at the back on warm summer evenings.

Suffolk

The Swan
Stratford St Mary

Mark and Sophie Dorber's super Dedham Vale outpost (see The Anchor in Walberswick, Suffolk) is maturing apace. For beer buffs: tip-top hand-pulled ales and a global array of draught and bottled craft beers – a rare treat in Britain; wine lovers enjoy a stimulating esoteric list. Stephen Miles's food will not disappoint; try pig's head croquette; whole plaice with clams, bacon and celeriac chowder; bitter chocolate and salted caramel tart. The 16th-century charm of this creaky old inn survives in its intimate rooms, sagging black beams, brick-parquet floors and requisite comforts of fat radiators and log fires; the gorgeous dining rooms come with obligatory wall timbers, antique tables and church candles. Exciting plans include a microbrewery and bedrooms plus regular tastings and feasting in the grounds.

Meals	Lunch £13.95–£15.95.
	Dinner £14.50–£22.50.
	Sunday lunch, 2 courses, £16.95.
Closed	Open all day.

Meals	Bar meals from £2.
	Lunch from £5.
	Dinner from £13.
Closed	Open all day.

Bartholomew Bizbal
The Angel Inn,
Polstead Street, Stoke-by-Nayland,
Colchester CO6 4SA

Tel	+44 (0)1206 263245
Web	www.angelinnsuffolk.co.uk

Entry 576 Map 10

Mark Dorber
The Swan,
Lower Street, Stratford St Mary,
Ipswich CO7 6JR

Tel	+44 (0)1206 321244
Web	www.stratfordswan.com

Entry 577 Map 10

Suffolk

The Ramsholt Arms
Ramsholt

In a setting that is all location, location, location (at the end of a lane, right beside a tidal beach overlooking the river Deben), this former farmhouse, ferryman's cottage and smugglers' inn is the place to be on a warm summer's evening. Watch the sun setting over the water and listen to the plaintive call of the curlew over the marshes, while you sup a pint of Adnams ale on the terrace, accompanied by a pulled pork bap from the barbecue. On wild winter days settle into the cosy atmosphere of the simply spruced up bar, with its big picture windows and watery views, and tuck into local estate game, braised shin of beef or sea bass with pea purée, followed by cherry and almond tart. Max and Polly are doing a grand job at this waterside gem. Rewarding riverside walks complete the picture.

Meals	Starters £4.50–£7.
	Dinner £10–£16.
Closed	Open all day.

Max & Polly Durrant
The Ramsholt Arms,
Ramsholt,
Woodbridge IP12 3AB
Tel   +44 (0)1394 411209
Web   www.theramsholtarms.com

Entry 578 Map 10

Suffolk

The Ufford Crown
Ufford

Having successfully run pubs in London for 12 years, Max Durrant, wife Polly and her chef-brother Will Hardiman returned to Suffolk to take on the Ufford Crown. The new-look Crown and Will's innovative cooking and seasonal menus proved an instant hit with the locals of Woodbridge. Old dining tables on polished wood or parquet floors in the cosy bar or dining area set the scene for Will's pork rillettes with dill pickles, or butternut squash, sweet potato and chilli soup. You could try sea bass with spinach, pea and lemon risotto; Dingley Dell pork belly with apple sauce; rice pudding with orange compote. Lighter lunchtime dishes include ham, duck egg and chips and a steak sandwich with remoulade, best washed down with a pint of Earl Soham Gold. A foodie haven for famished A12 travellers.

Meals	Starters £4.50–£9.
	Dinner £10–£17.
Closed	Tues.
	3pm–5pm Mon, Wed–Fri.

Max & Polly Durrant
The Ufford Crown,
High Street, Ufford,
Woodbridge IP13 6EL
Tel   +44 (0)1394 461030
Web   www.theuffordcrown.com

Entry 579 Map 10

Suffolk

The Greyhound Inn
Pettistree

Stewart and Louise are reinventing one of the oldest boozers in Suffolk, and all who discover it, love it. It's a warm and friendly place to be, unspoilt and wood-floored, with a log-burner in the brick fireplace and a dining room with grey-panelled walls. Stewart – a Scot – knows his ales and his whiskies, and oversees a few Scottish gins too, while Louise cooks imaginative and seasonal food, including venison from her parents' estate. She cures her own salmon, then serves it with dill cream; whisks up homemade basil gnocchi and beautiful hake fishcakes on creamed leeks; offers curry nights on Thursdays and themed nights once a month. Families will be happy with small portions for kids and a safely fenced garden – and the elderflower panna cotta with poached gooseberries is to die for.

Suffolk

The Froize
Chillesford

Impassioned by local produce before it became fashionable, David Grimwood lives in chef's whites or shooting tweeds – a Suffolk countryman too chivalrous to accept his reputation as East Anglia's best game cook. Off the beaten track, the path to these once charmingly remote 18th-century keepers' cottages is well worn by regulars. Blythburgh pork, Orford and Lowestoft fish, bags of local game (much of it retrieved by the landlord's black labs) combined with retro rustic cooking reflect the 'field, forest and foreshore' landscape. A perfect roast joint always stands alongside reworked classics such as devilled kidneys, stuffed skate wing or cider-braised rabbit and prunes, and the homemade puddings are legendary. Ales are the county's best, mostly Adnams. There's Aspall's cider, too.

Meals	Starters from £5.95.
	Dinner from £10.95.
Closed	Mon.

Meals	Lunch & dinner from £13.50.
Closed	Mon (except Bank Holidays).

Louise & Stewart McKenzie
The Greyhound Inn,
The Street, Pettistree,
Woodbridge IP13 0HP
Tel +44 (0)1728 746451
Web www.greyhoundinnpettistree.co.uk

Entry 580 Map 10

David Grimwood
The Froize,
The Street, Chillesford,
Woodbridge IP12 3PU
Tel +44 (0)1394 450282
Web www.froize.co.uk

Entry 581 Map 10

Suffolk

Station Hotel
Framlingham

The railway disappeared long ago. Now the former buildings are business units, but the Station Hotel continues to thrive. Cask ales (a classic Victorian bitter, a sweet, wintry porter) are perfect accompaniments for the gutsy cooking. Chalked up on the board are a roast squash, chilli and ginger soup; confit duck leg; whole sea bass with chorizo, pepper and spinach casserole; lemongrass and ginger crème brûlée... all very good. Lunch is quiet but it bustles at night, helped along by chef Mike Jones and a friendly team. The building is shabby-boho, the interior is charming. Expect blackened stripped boards, cream papered walls, a wood-fired oven, and bone-handled knives partnering paper serviettes. Outside: a terrace sprinkled with tables under the tree.

Suffolk

The King's Head
Laxfield

Known locally as the Low House because it lies in a dip below the churchyard, the 600-year-old pub is one of Suffolk's treasures. Little has changed in the last 100 years and its four rooms creak with character – expect narrow passageways, low ceilings, wood panelling and tiny fires for chilly eves. The simple parlour is dominated by a three-sided, high-backed settle and there's no bar – far too new-fangled a concept for this place. Instead, Adnams ales are served from barrels in the tap room. In keeping with the authenticity, the food is rustic, hearty and homemade, the short blackboard menu listing soup, sandwiches, hot dishes and puds. It's the sort of place where folk music starts up spontaneously and summer brings Morris men. The garden overlooking the brook at the back was once a bowling green – lovely.

Meals	Bar meals £3.25-£11.	
	Lunch & dinner £4-£15.75.	
Closed	Open all day.	

Meals	Bar meals £4.25-£6.	
	Lunch & dinner £6.50-£9.50.	
Closed	3pm-6pm.	
	Open all day in summer.	

	Mike Jones
	Station Hotel,
	Station Road, Framlingham,
	Woodbridge IP13 9EE
Tel	+44 (0)1728 723455
Web	www.thestationhotel.net

Entry 582 Map 10

	Robert Wilson
	The King's Head,
	Gorams Mill Lane, Laxfield,
	Woodbridge IP13 8DW
Tel	+44 (0)1986 798395
Web	www.laxfieldkingshead.co.uk

Entry 583 Map 10

Suffolk

The Dolphin Inn
Thorpeness

Thorpeness is a one-off, the turn-of-the-century brainchild of G S Ogilvie, who set out to create a holiday resort free of piers and promenades and entirely safe for children. The Dolphin, in the middle of the village, is a great little inn. There are two lively bars, open fires and wooden floors in the dining room and, outside, a terrace and lawn for barbecues and al fresco dinners. No-nonsense food hits the spot, perhaps grilled sardines with basil pesto, chargrilled steak with chunky chips, a plate of local cheeses. Stay a while – you're spoiled for things to do: a great golf course, an unspoilt sand and pebble beach, and a 64-acre lake, the Meare, which is never more than three-feet deep and was inspired by the creator of Peter Pan; children can row, canoe up creeks and discover islands.

Suffolk

Eels Foot Inn
East Bridge

The sign depicts an eel wriggling out of an old boot. This plain-looking, oddly named backwater village pub lives up to its slightly eccentric reputation. It's a twitchers' pub where you find watchers and wardens from Minsmere RSPB Reserve swapping stories with visitors – walkers, cyclists, holidaymakers. All are drawn by the full-range of Adnams ales and the hearty food (beer battered cod, steak and ale pie, treacle tart), served in a cosy wood-floored bar with a log fire and simple furnishings; there's a homely upper dining area, too. Don't miss the craic on music nights – every Thursday is Squit Night (a folk, country and blues jamming session); the last Sunday of the month is folk night. The place is mobbed in summer... and there are new beer gardens to enjoy.

Meals	Lunch & dinner £10.50-£19.50.
Closed	Mon in January, February & March.

Meals	Lunch & dinner £5-£13.
Closed	3pm-6pm. Open all day Sat & Sun.

David James
The Dolphin Inn,
Peace Place,
Thorpeness IP16 4FE
Tel   +44 (0)1728 454994
Web   www.thorpenessdolphin.com

Entry 584 Map 10

Julian Wallis
Eels Foot Inn,
East Bridge,
Leiston IP16 4SN
Tel   +44 (0)1728 830154
Web   www.theeelsfootinn.co.uk

Entry 585 Map 10

Suffolk

Suffolk

The Westleton Crown
Westleton

One of England's oldest coaching inns, with 800 years of continuous service under its belt, in a village two miles from the sea. Aldeburgh and Southwold are close, Minsmere is a walk away. Inside, Farrow & Ball colours and leather sofas join panelled walls, stripped floors, ancient beams and spindle-back chairs. Weave around and find nooks and crannies in which to hide, flames flickering in open fires, a huge map on the wall for walkers. You can eat wherever you want – including the restaurant that opens onto charming terraced gardens and tasty barbecues. Enjoy marsh-fed sirloin of beef with hand-cut chips, pan-fried halibut with clementine butter sauce, blackberry crème brûlée... the fish comes off the boats at Lowestoft, and the fish and chips are fabulous.

The Crown
Southwold

Well-heeled weekenders flock to Southwold most of the year; outside the season it's a gem. The Crown, stalwart of the dining pub world, oozes metro chic. Ceilings are elegantly beamed, walls are colourwashed and uncluttered, the bar is large and laid-back. Adnams is on home turf – you would struggle to find a smarter brewery tap. The wood-panelled rear snug is the province of traditionalists, the brasserie wine bar at the front is beloved of the urban crowd. As for the produce, it's fresh, local and seasonal, perhaps roast Gressingham duck breast with kumquats and a winter spice liqueur glaze, or slow-cooked pork belly and seared scallops with thyme marinated apples. And then a banoffee pain perdu: cinnamon roll, caramelised banana, candied almonds, toffee sauce. The wine list is oenophiles' heaven.

Meals	Lunch & bar meals from £5.50. Dinner from £11.95. Sunday roast from £14.95.
Closed	Open all day.

Meals	Lunch from £8.95. Dinner from £12.95. Sunday lunch, 3 courses, £18.95.
Closed	3pm-6.30pm Mon-Fri in winter. Open all day in summer.

	Gareth Clarke The Westleton Crown, The Street, Westleton, Saxmundham IP17 3AD
Tel	+44 (0)1728 648777
Web	www.westletoncrown.co.uk

Entry 586 Map 10

	Lukas Juszczak The Crown, 90 High Street, Southwold IP18 6DP
Tel	+44 (0)1502 722275
Web	www.adnams.co.uk/hotels

Entry 587 Map 10

Suffolk

Harbour Inn
Southwold

Cracking ales from Adnams up the road and the best fish and chips for miles – two good reasons to visit this old waterside pub. Hidden away down by the boats beside the river Blyth, its elevated dining room and back terrace offer views across the marshes and the common to Southwold. On wild winter days hunker down with a pint of Ghost Ship by the blazing wood-burner in the panelled and beamed top and bottom bars, both topped with nautical bric-a-brac: old ensigns dress the ceiling, sea charts and harbour and fishing photos line the walls. Worn tiled floors, pine settles and scrubbed tables complete the unspoilt scene, so order a steaming bowl of Brancaster mussels and settle in. Or fish stew, Dover sole with brown shrimp butter, rib-eye steak with all the trimmings.

Meals	Lunch & dinner £9.50–£16.
Closed	Open all day.

Nick Atfield
Harbour Inn,
Blackshore Quay,
Southwold IP18 6TA
Tel   +44 (0)1502 722381
Web   www.harbourinnsouthwold.co.uk

Entry 588 Map 10

Suffolk

The Swan House
Beccles

This bar-cum-restaurant-cum-boutique inn stands in the shadow of the church tower, in an atmospheric market town on the edge of the Broads. Run with effortless charm by owners Roland and Carmela for 20 years, the old Swan House occupies several buildings woven together; one is Jacobean, all wonky beams and oak floors. The Swan House opens first for coffee, then drinks in the bar, then lunch and dinner. Sink into a sofa by the fire and check out seasonal menus promising local delights: pea, apple and ginger soup; pork belly with prune jus; Italian bread and butter pudding. You eat at rustic pine tables in a beamed, red-walled room or in a smaller, more contemporary dining room; drinkers and diners can spill onto pavement tables on summer days. A rare find.

Meals	Lunch from £6.
	Dinner £14–£17.50.
	Sunday roast from £14.
Closed	Open all day.

Roland Blunk & Carmela Sabatini
The Swan House,
By the tower,
Beccles NR34 9HE
Tel   +44 (0)1502 713474
Web   www.swan-house.com

Entry 589 Map 10

The Merry Harriers
Hambledon

Leafy countryside rolls away on all sides from a historic pub that has dispensed ale and fare since 1710. Inside, a huge inglenook warms wine racks with grapes from every corner of the globe – including a Château Y'quem (a delicious chilled dessert wine) while blackboards list specials and local events. There's wood galore in the bar, painted, scrubbed and polished, and Pilgrim's Progress and Surrey Hills Shere Drop on tap. The dining area is slightly more formal, but the relaxed atmosphere reaches everywhere. Traditional menus come with a Mediterranean twist and local provenance; their own smoked trout is a speciality. Enjoy tuna niçoise and Tuscan bean cassoulet, sausage and mash and ham hash cakes; great sandwiches too. The pretty garden will keep children happy with its swings and slides, watched over by the owners' nine llamas – organise a trek if the spirit takes you! In a converted barn to one side of the garden are three compact and excellently presented bedrooms with oak and painted wooden furniture and fine linen; in summer, breakfast hampers come to you.

Rooms	3 doubles: £85–£110.
Meals	Bar meals from £6.
	Lunch £6–£22.
	Dinner £12.50–£22.
Closed	Rarely.

Colin Stoneley
The Merry Harriers,
Hambledon Road, Hambledon,
Godalming GU8 4DR
Tel   +44 (0)1428 682883
Web   www.merryharriers.com

Entry 590 Map 4

The Swan Inn
Chiddingfold

After 20 years at Knightsbridge's revered Swag & Tails, Annemaria and Stuart escaped to the country to revive an old Surrey bolthole. What you find now are sparkling dining areas and a cool bar, wooden floors, blazing log fires, chunky tables and bags of style. It may be more classy eatery than traditional pub, but there's artisan ale from Surrey Hills Brewery, big smiles from attentive staff, and proper homemade burgers for those in for a bite. And more: beer-battered haddock with fries and pea purée, chargrilled rib-eye steak with caramelised shallots and béarnaise sauce, scallops with black pudding and smoked bacon risotto cake, braised beef cheeks with horseradish mash and curly kale – unpretentious dishes that juggle popular with modern. If you're staying, contemporary bedrooms are warm and cosy, with excellent linen and downy duvets, big beds and flat-screen TVs, sofas in spacious suites, and trendy bathrooms with power showers and toiletries. Outside: a super landscaped garden for summer socialising. In short, the Swan represents a relaxed revival of an old inn in a rather fetching village. *High chairs available. All rooms are air conditioned.*

Rooms	8 doubles: £100-£135.
	1 suite for 2: £150-£180.
	1 family room for 4: £140-£165.
Meals	Bar meals from £7.50.
	Lunch & dinner £7.50-19.95.
	Sunday lunch, 3 courses, £26-£28.
Closed	Rarely.

Annemaria & Stuart Boomer-Davies
The Swan Inn,
Petworth Road, Chiddingfold,
Godalming GU8 4TY

Tel	+44 (0)1428 684688
Web	www.theswaninnchiddingfold.com

Entry 591 Map 4

The Crown Inn
Chiddingfold

Beautifully restored, the Crown is a contender (one of many) for the oldest hostelry in the country. Thirteenth-century bowed brick walls, warped weathered timbers, plaster ceilings and lattice windows; welcome to the world of the highwaymen. The bar's stained-glass leaded lights – for which Chiddingfold was once famous – tell of 'the Lion and the Unicorn's fight for the Crown', while the pattern-carpeted main bar has a beautiful stone fireplace from 1619 and a crackling winter fire. It's a fascinating place so, pint of Sharp's Doom in hand, take a wander and a gander at the small glass case of coins that date back to 1558. The menu lists straightforward classic dishes – coq au vin, game pie, fish and chips, apple and rhubarb crumble – prepared from excellent ingredients.

Meals	Lunch & dinner £10-£20.
Closed	Open all day.

Marcus Tapping
The Crown Inn,
The Green, Chiddingfold,
Godalming GU8 4TX
Tel   +44 (0)1428 682255
Web   www.thecrownchiddingfold.com

Entry 592 Map 4

Dog & Pheasant
Brook

Safe in the hands of the two Davids, this popular roadside inn is full of bonhomie. The food may be the driving force, but the small bar heaves with locals in for a pint of Broadside or a glass of pinot noir. Smart and cosy it is, with black wood ceiling beams, striking wall timbers and warming winter fires. Service is friendly and upbeat. Chef Joseph Wright's lengthy repertoire should please all with classic and modern dishes, lots of fish (eg pan-fried fillet of rainbow trout with curly kale and roasted garlic sauce) and blackboard specials to complement the menu. Wednesday 'Grill Night' is not to be missed and sees Joseph cooking all the meats in the central inglenook fireplace. There's a terrace, a big garden and a private dining room upstairs.

Meals	Lunch & dinner £8-£17.
Closed	Open all day.

David Gough & David Hall
Dog & Pheasant,
Haslemere Road, Brook,
Godalming GU8 5UJ
Tel   +44 (0)1428 682763
Web   www.dogandpheasant.com

Entry 593 Map 4

The Three Horseshoes
Thursley

Be sure to pack your boots as the walking is divine, especially when the leaves turn. Then slake your thirst with a pint from the Hog's Back or Surrey Hill's Breweries, or one of many wines by the glass. Gloriously old-fashioned and rambling – beams, brick fireplace, woodchip wallpaper hung with archive photos – it is run by a gregarious team who keep an often busy throng happy. Daily changing menus are unfussy and big on flavour. Favourites include pan-fried calves' liver with Wiltshire bacon, mashed potato and chantenay carrots; salmon and smoked haddock fishcakes with mixed salad and dill mayonnaise. There are hearty sandwiches, good desserts and British and French cheese boards with wines and ports to match. The large grassed garden has fine views, and there's a rather smart terrace.

The Stag on the River
Eashing

Through Eashing, to a small bridge with a warning that heavy loads might lead to its demise; this pretty stone structure built by 13th-century monks forms an essential link to the Stag on the River. With a lease dating back to 1771, the pub is the place to discover home cooking, real ales and a happy buzz. Produce is fresh and local and includes the new standard of local beef, 'Surrey Beef'. Try pork belly with apple and gooseberry sauce or fish pie with parmesan mash; finish with dark chocolate and hazelnut terrine. In spring and summer the terrace by the water makes a languorous spot for supping a pint of Surrey Hills Shere Drop; in winter you can seek out a cosy corner in one of several rambling rooms, where open fires warm the stylishly upholstered wingback chairs.

Meals	Lunch & dinner £9.50–£21.
	Sunday roast £14.50–£18.
Closed	3pm-5.30pm Mon-Fri.
	Sun from 7pm.

| Meals | Lunch & dinner £10.75–£22.95. |
| Closed | Open all day. |

David Alders & Sandra Proni
The Three Horseshoes,
Dye House Road, Thursley,
Godalming GU8 6QD
Tel   +44 (0)1252 703268
Web   www.threehorseshoesthursley.com

Entry 594 Map 4

Mark Robson
The Stag on the River,
Lower Eashing Lane, Eashing,
Godalming GU7 2QG
Tel   +44 (0)1483 421568
Web   www.stagontherivereashing.co.uk

Entry 595 Map 4

Surrey

The Richard Onslow
Cranleigh

A spruced-up Surrey outpost for innovative Peach Pubs. Since John Taylor revamped the old tile-hung inn, named after the Onslows of Clandon Park, it has become the hub of Cranleigh. Period features – fireplaces, ancient beams and low doorways – blend beautifully with contemporary touches to create a super-relaxed backdrop for monthly quiz and movie nights and enjoyable dining. Call in for breakfast from 7.30am; share a deli board heaped with cheeses and cold cuts; tuck into a daily roast. There's linguine with squid, clams, cockles, lemon and parsley, and lamb shank with tomato ragout, available at lunch and dinner. Choose between the laid-back bars or the retro dining room, a high-ceilinged space with huge mirrors and lampshades, upholstered banquettes and old tables.

Surrey

The Hare & Hounds
Lingfield

Eric and Tracy Payet have changed little since taking over this striking pub close to Lingfield Racecourse. It's still an idiosyncratic place where quirky collectables and bold paintings fill every corner and wall. Bar bustle can be surveyed from old cinema seats or one of a pair of throne-like chairs; cushion-laden banquettes make a cosy spot from which to view Eric's (ex-Club Gascon, London) menus. Look to the chalkboard for daily dishes: rabbit stew with mustard sauce; roast hake with confit fennel. On the printed menu find parmesan and pea risotto; honey-glazed pork chop with black pudding and caramelised apple; roast pear clafoutis. Diners are as happy among the hop garlands of the main bar as beneath the artwork in the lovely dining room. Nurse a summer pint of Abbot Ale in the partly decked garden.

Meals	Bar meals from £5.
	Lunch from £7.
	Dinner from £11.
	Sunday roast £13.50.
Closed	Christmas Day.

| Meals | Lunch & dinner £7.95–£18.95. |
| Closed | Sun from 7pm. |

John Taylor
The Richard Onslow,
113-117 High Street,
Cranleigh GU6 8AU
Tel   +44 (0)1483 274922
Web   www.therichardonslow.co.uk

Entry 596 Map 4

Eric & Tracy Payet
The Hare & Hounds,
Common Road,
Lingfield RH7 6BZ
Tel   +44 (0)1342 832351
Web   www.hareandhoundspublichouse.co.uk

Entry 597 Map 4

Surrey

The Parrot
Forest Green

Having left a mini-empire of London pubs for a livestock farm in the Surrey hills, Linda Gotto finds time for her lovely, rambling, 17th-century pub overlooking the village green. She is passionate about food, its provenance and quality, and the Parrot showcases produce reared and grown on the farm – Shorthorn veal, Middlewhite pork, mutton from Dorset crosses, eggs from Copper Morans. Find them on the short imaginative menu in the form of game pie; lamb rump with minted pea purée; roast belly pork with mash and braised cabbage – or in the farm shop next door. Elsewhere, beams, flagstones and lovely bits and bobs, old settles and blazing fires, London Pride on tap and 16 wines by the glass; they do weddings, too. The value is outstanding.

Meals	Bar meals from £5.50.
	Lunch & dinner £9.50–£18.
	Sunday lunch, 3 courses, £25.
	Not Sunday eve.
Closed	Open all day.

Linda Gotto
The Parrot,
Forest Green,
Dorking RH5 5RZ
Tel +44 (0)1306 621339
Web www.theparrot.co.uk

Entry 598 Map 4

Surrey

The Anchor
Ripley

The clued-up Ripley set will know the Anchor is related to renowned restaurant Drake's just across the High Street. Though its Michelin-starred patron Steve Drake moved his head chef (Mike Wall-Palmer) over to run the pub kitchen, the Anchor isn't all flashy dining pretension, rather a relaxed, inviting place turning out simple, creative food alongside good ales and interesting wines. This listed pub (once almshouses) has been spruced up; find comfy armchairs round a log-burner, fashionable dark wood furniture, slate floors and original features in interlinked areas. Enjoy innovative snacks such as puffed pork skin with apple sauce, or opt for something heartier like slow-cooked duck leg, savoy cabbage, mash potato and liquorice sauce.

Meals	Lunch, 2 courses, £15;
	3 courses, £19 (Tuesday-Saturday).
	Dinner £12-£24.
	Sunday roast from £15.
Closed	Mon all day.
	Sun 6pm-12am.

Iain McArthur
The Anchor,
High Street, Ripley,
Woking GU23 6AE
Tel +44 (0)1483 211866
Web www.ripleyanchor.co.uk

Entry 599 Map 4

The Inn @ West End
West End

Wine importer Gerry Price pulls the punters in from all over Surrey – the wine shop glows with 500 wines. Stylishly revamped dining areas are light and modern with wooden floors and fine fabrics, and the atmosphere is relaxed and friendly – quiz nights, film club, barbecues, boules. The homely bar has hand-pumped ale from Fuller's and Young's along with local beers and that list of wines is enticing, with a nod to Portuguese shores. Monthly menus have modern British choices – perhaps hearty kedgeree or pot-roasted pork with cabbage and dauphinoise potatoes; in winter there's partridge, pheasant, woodcock and teal. A pastry chef masterminds the desserts, the cheeses are farmhouse best, there are good-value set lunches, lunchtime wine tastings, popular wine dinners – and a summer wood oven!

The Canbury Arms
Kingston upon Thames

Much has changed since Michael and Charlotte bought the dilapidated Canbury Arms a decade ago – then they could only feed guests grilled chorizo ciabattas. Now, visitors can enjoy real ales, good wines and delicious treats. Built in the late 1800s to feed and water Victorian white collar workers, this handsome corner pub has remained popular with locals who pop in for pints of Twickenham's Naked Ladies and ox cheek croquettes with horseradish aïoli. You can eat in the main bar or garden room; there's a pretty terrace in summer for hog roasts and pints as the sun goes down. Try roast baby back ribs and sweet potatoes in the Canbury's own marinade, or pan-fried salmon with baby prawn and crab linguine. The railway workers may have gone, but the breakfasts are now popular with locals – from full English to a latte with warm croissants served with homemade preserves.

Meals	Lunch & dinner £5.25–£32.50. Sunday lunch, 2 courses, £24.95. Not 25 & 26 December.
Closed	3pm–5pm. Open all day Sat & Sun.

Meals	Bar meals £5. Lunch & dinner £12–£18. Sunday roast from £15.
Closed	Open all day.

Gerry & Ann Price
The Inn @ West End,
42 Guildford Road, West End,
Woking GU24 9PW
Tel   +44 (0)1276 858652
Web   www.the-inn.co.uk

The Manager
The Canbury Arms,
49 Canbury Park Road,
Kingston upon Thames KT2 6LQ
Tel   +44 (0)20 8255 9129
Web   www.thecanburyarms.com

Entry 600 Map 4

Entry 601 Map 4

The Blacksmiths
Chichester

A beautiful little pub, freshly painted and as spruce as can be, run by the nicest people. There are crackling fires, pale floors, seating upholstered in charcoal leather and benches topped with sheepskins and throws: very modern and Nordic. It's the sort of place where you might come for a business lunch – or, equally, tip up with the kids and the dogs on the way to the Witterings; in summer the garden is fabulous. There are long Sussex views, a raised fire pit for tasty morsels, and two patios, one with a sail-like awning. Overlooking the garden is the restaurant, slightly more formal but equally stylish. Based around fresh local ingredients, the menu ranges from huge open sandwiches to venison sausages to warm chocolate brownies, and there are mini homemade burgers (with Birds Eye peas!) for the children. Up a teensy stair are the lovely bedrooms, Skylark, Lapwing and Barn Owl, each with exquisite bird-traced wallpapers and pale wood furniture. You'll love them all: the crisp white linen, the light-filled bathrooms, the Cowshed lotions, the grey-painted boards, and the soothing views of endless green fields.

Rooms	3 doubles: £120-£150.
Meals	Starters from £5.50.
	Dinner from £10.95.
	Sunday roast from £12.50.
Closed	Christmas & New Year.

The Manager
The Blacksmiths,
Selsey Road,
Chichester PO20 7PR
Tel   +44 (0)1243 785578
Web   www.the-blacksmiths.co.uk

The White Horse
Chilgrove

Beautiful Sussex downland provides a backcloth to this very English inn close to Chichester. Long, low and whitewashed, it dates from 1768 and was once a staging post; now it's the perfect place for foodies and wine buffs to be fed and watered in style. The relaxing timbered bar and dining room combines contemporary-smart with traditional charm: blazing wood-burners, heritage hues, fat candles on scrubbed tables, rugs on upholstered benches. There are serious wines (flick through the 'Red Book') and a delicious monthly menu – fishfinger sandwiches, oxtail linguini, venison and mustard ragù, whole lemon sole, rhubarb and almond crumble. A secluded courtyard and spacious garden rooms blend rustic-chic with modern design, featuring steamer trunks, architectural four-poster beds, striking wall coverings, posh linen, sheepskin rugs and iconic retro furnishings. Bathrooms are swish; two have hot tubs on private patios. Glorious Goodwood draws the racing set, while stunning downland rambles radiate from the front door.

Rooms	12 doubles, 1 twin: £90–£175. 2 suites for 2 (2 doubles, each with hot tub): £140–£190.
Meals	Light lunch from £5.50. Dinner from £12.95
Closed	Rarely.

Niki Burr
The White Horse,
High Street, Chilgrove,
Chichester PO18 9HX
Tel   +44 (0)1243 519 444
Web   www.thewhitehorse.co.uk

Entry 603 Map 4

The White Hart
South Harting

Inside this rural pub all feels cosy and welcoming, with antlers above the fireplace, logs stacked by the burner and a happy mix of tables, lamps and chairs: the pub manager is a self-confessed rummager! As they lie somewhat in the middle of nowhere they stock food essentials as well as all the good things behind the bar: local ales, unusual spirits, nice wines, great coffee. Walkers drop by for sandwiches, locals for pints, builders for pies (crisp, delicious ones) and everyone loves the garden in summer. In the kitchen the focus is on high quality pub food, from house pâté with chutney to pork chops on sweet potato mash to fruit crumbles with ice cream or custard; children get small portions and much is vegetarian. Dogs are welcome and the garden's great, with 30 bird boxes and feeders, and tea lights hanging from the spreading magnolia. One of the bedrooms, perfect for a family stopover, has its own private entrance and is bedecked in checks, stripes and antlers. Great views, and great coffee in the morning. Marvellous.

Rooms	5 doubles, 1 twin: £90–£110.
Meals	Bar meals from £5–£16.
	Lunch from £4.
	Dinner from £12.50.
Closed	Rarely.

The Manager
The White Hart,
The Street,
South Harting GU31 5QB

Tel	+44 (0)1730 825124
Web	www.the-whitehart.co.uk

The Horse Guards Inn
Tillington

After a visit to Petworth House, head for the pub on the park's western edge. Up from the tiny lane, views sweep towards the South Downs from the pub's hammock'd garden. Inside: a series of rambling and intimate rooms furnished with quirky pieces, fresh flowers, wonky beams, brick floors, painted panelling, old pine tables and four log fires – one in an old back range. Sam and Misa love this pub and their passion is reflected in the homemade treats on sale by the door and the chalkboards championing the producers (the latest a goat farmer with a dairy). Beautiful dishes include summer soup of local berries with mint and crème fraîche, gazpacho of heritage tomatoes, potted rabbit, a rich fish pie. Our hot beef sandwich, served with homemade horseradish sauce, was delicious. Each of the three bedrooms is simple, characterful and contemporary, from the smallish brass-bedded double with a sloping floor and a view of the church to the wonderfully romantic cottage. Hand-made chocolates are on the house; bathrooms stock local treats. A very happy place in a sleepy Sussex village.

Rooms	2 twin/doubles: £85–£120.
	1 cottage suite: £105–£140.
Meals	Bar meals from £6.
	Lunch & dinner from £10.
Closed	Christmas Day.

Sam & Misha Beard
The Horse Guards Inn,
Tillington,
Petworth GU28 9AF
Tel   +44 (0)1798 342332
Web   www.thehorseguardsinn.co.uk

Entry 605 Map 4

The Old House Inn
Copthorne

The wonky tiled roof and the black-and-white timbered façade draw the eye to this former farmworker's cottage – and entice one in. It stands beside a B-road that services Crawley and Gatwick, so step inside and leave the modern day behind. The 16th-century Old House is heaped with charm, in latticed windows, bowed oak beams, wonky walls, sloping floors, and cosy nooks and alcoves. This is now a stunning modern inn with a new bar and dining area, transformed from a former faded French restaurant. We love the warm textured fabrics and comfy banquettes, the chunky leather armchairs by log burners, the fat candles on old dining tables, and the retro pub artefacts. Equally up-to-date is the menu, a modern British choice with pub classics (wild boar sausages with red onion marmalade) alongside such dishes as pan-fried hake with smoked bacon and cockle cream, or honey-glazed duck with spiced red cabbage. Rooms in the converted barn are named after local woods and sport earthy hues, big wooden beds, the best linen and down. Bathrooms are spoiling, two with claw-foot baths.

Rooms	5 doubles, 1 twin/double: £110–£130. Extra bed/sofabed £15 per person per night.
Meals	Set lunch, 2 courses £13; 3 courses £16. Mains from £11.50. Dinner, 3 courses, £27–£30.
Closed	Rarely.

Stephen Godsave
The Old House Inn,
Effingham Road, Copthorne,
Crawley RH10 3JB
Tel   +44 (0)1342 718529
Web   www.theoldhouseinn.co.uk

Entry 606 Map 4

Sussex

The Cat
West Hoathly

Owner Andrew swapped grand Gravetye Manor for the buzzy, pubby atmosphere of The Cat in 2009; he hasn't looked back. The 16th-century building, a fine medieval hall house with a Victorian extension, has been comfortably modernised without losing its character. Inside are beamed ceilings and panelling, planked floors, splendid inglenooks, and an airy room that leads to a garden at the back, furnished with teak and posh brollies. Harvey's Ale and some top-notch pub food, passionately put together from fresh local ingredients by chef Max Leonard, attract a solid, old-fashioned crowd: retired locals, foodies and walkers. Tuck into rare roast beef and horseradish sandwiches, Rye Bay sea bass with brown shrimp and caper butter, South Downs lamb chops with dauphinoise (and leave room for treacle tart!). The setting is idyllic, in a pretty village opposite a 12th-century church – best viewed from two of four bright and comfortable bedrooms. Crisp linen on big beds, rich fabrics, fawn carpets, fresh bathrooms and antique touches illustrate the style. A sweet retreat in a charming village backwater.

Rooms	4 doubles: £110–£150. Singles £90–£110. Extra bed/sofabed £20 per person per night.
Meals	Bar meals from £6. Lunch & dinner from £12. Sunday lunch, 3 courses, £26.
Closed	Rarely.

Andrew Russell
The Cat,
Queen's Square, West Hoathly,
East Grinstead RH19 4PP

Tel +44 (0)1342 810369
Web www.catinn.co.uk

Entry 607 Map 4

The Griffin Inn
Fletching

A proper inn, one of the best, a community local that draws a well-heeled and devoted crowd. The occasional touch of scruffiness makes it almost perfect; lovers of fancy design need not apply. The Pullan family run it with huge passion. You get cosy open fires, 400-year-old beams, oak panelling, settles, red carpets, prints on the walls… it's aged well. There's a lively bar, a small club room for racing on Saturdays and two cricket teams play in summer. Bedrooms are tremendous value for money and full of uncluttered country-inn elegance: uneven floors above the bar, lovely old furniture, soft coloured walls, free-standing Victorian baths, huge shower heads, crisp linen, fluffy bathrobes, handmade soaps. Rooms in the coach house are quieter, those in next-door Griffin House quieter still. Smart menus based on the finest seasonal produce include fresh fish from Rye and Fletching lamb; both food and beers are as local as can be. There's a wood oven on the terrace and, on summer Sundays, a spit-roast barbecue – accompanied by ten-mile views stretching across Sheffield Park to the South Downs. *Minimum stay: 2 nights on bank holiday weekends.*

Rooms	6 doubles, 7 four-posters: £85-£145. Singles £70-£80 (Sun-Thur).
Meals	Bar meals from £6.50. Dinner, 3 courses, £30-£40.
Closed	Christmas Day.

Nigel & James Pullan
The Griffin Inn,
Fletching,
Uckfield TN22 3SS

Tel	+44 (0)1825 722890
Web	www.thegriffininn.co.uk

Entry 608 Map 4

The Bull
Ditchling

In a picturesque village, a pretty inn, dark and cosy and warmed by cheery fires and candlelight. The rambling and atmospheric bar hasn't changed for years, there are four ales on tap including Dark Star, and the other areas have been stylishly transformed, with pine and parquet and modern art on mellow walls. And there's some rather upmarket food to match, like filo-encrusted cannon of lamb stuffed with apricots and cumin. The ciabattas are filled with locally smoked salmon and horseradish cream and all of the produce can be traced back to local farms; game comes from the Balcombe estate. Similar treats can be found on the children's menu, and you can eat or drink wherever you like, including the snug at the back (and for as long as you wish). Bring wellies or bikes and try out the high-level trails on the South Downs, return to bedrooms where new and old blend successfully. Expect rain showers, comfortable beds, crisp linen and a bit of noise from below until closing time. This year, there's a new kitchen, an extended restaurant and big new rooms in the converted barn out back too. *Minimum stay: 2 nights at weekends.*

Rooms	3 doubles, 1 twin/double: £100–£160.
Meals	Lunch from £5.
	Dinner, 3 courses, £25–£35.
Closed	Rarely.

Dominic Worrall
The Bull,
2 High Street, Ditchling,
Hassocks BN6 8TA
Tel   +44 (0)1273 843147
Web   www.thebullditchling.com

Entry 609 Map 4

The Ram Inn
Firle

The road runs out once it reaches Firle village nestling beneath the South Downs... hard to believe now, but this quiet backwater was once a staging post. Built of brick and flint, the inn reveals a fascinating history – the Georgian part was once a courthouse and the kitchen goes back 500 years. Rescued from closure in 2006, the Ram Inn is once again thriving. Its three rooms have been decorated in rustic-chic style – bare boards and parquet, coal fires in old brick fireplaces, chunky candles on darkwood tables. Walkers stomp in from the Downs for pints of Harveys Sussex and hot steak sandwiches; foodies flock after dark for great fresh food, perhaps ham and pea broth, rump of Hankham Farm organic lamb with red wine jus, and sticky toffee pudding. Retire upstairs to quirky, individual rooms with bold colours, exposed beams, super comfortable beds, fluffy bathrobes in tiled bathrooms, and dreamy village or South Downs views. And there's a splendid flint-walled garden for peaceful summer supping. Handy for Charleston Farmhouse, country home to the Bloomsbury set.

Rooms	2 doubles, 2 twin/doubles: £90–£145. Singles £80–£100. Extra bed/sofabed £40 per person per night.
Meals	Lunch & dinner £9.95–£16.95. Sunday roast £11.95.
Closed	Rarely.

Hayley Bayes
The Ram Inn,
The Street, Firle,
Lewes BN8 6NS

Tel	+44 (0)1273 858222
Web	www.raminn.co.uk

Entry 610 Map 4

Sussex

The Tiger Inn
East Dean

Beside a sloping village green in a fold of the South Downs, the award-winning Tiger is one classy inn. After a blustery walk on Beachy Head – or a stride up the tiny 'Hobbs Eares' valley to old Friston Church – how delightful to duck your head and enter an atmospheric main bar, all low beams, stone floors, ancient settles, intriguing antiques, cosy corners and a big crackling fire. The Tiger Inn is a supporter of the community so you'll find estate-brewed ales like Legless Rambler and organic meat from estate farms. From a revamped kitchen flow traditional sandwiches, ploughman's and stews; come evening, hot platters of sausage and mash, and salmon and spicy chorizo cassoulet. Desserts include steamed pudding of the day – see the blackboard. No reason not to stay the night: bolthole bedrooms above ooze luxury and style: calming colours, feather down bedding, an eclectic mix of pretty old pine and antique furnishings, fine beds, fresh bathrooms. Book 'Minnie' for views of the green and the Downs. Mobbed in summer, the old Tiger is a refuge in winter.

Rooms	4 doubles, 1 twin: £110–£120.
Meals	Lunch & dinner from £8.95.
	Sunday lunch, 3 courses, around £20.
Closed	Rarely.

Janice Avis
The Tiger Inn,
The Green, East Dean,
Eastbourne BN20 0DA
Tel   +44 (0)1323 423209
Web   www.beachyhead.org.uk

The Ship Inn
Rye

The 16th-century smuggler's warehouse stands by the quay at the bottom of cobbled Mermaid Street. Climb the church tower for stunning coast and marsh views, then retreat to the laid-back warmth of the Ship's rustic bars. Cosy nooks, ancient timbers, blazing fires and a quirkily delicious décor characterise this place; there are battered leather sofas, simple café-style chairs, old pine tables and good paintings and prints. Quaff a pint of Harvey's Sussex or local farm cider, leaf through the daily papers, play one of the board games – there are heaps. Lunch and dinner menus are short and imaginative and make good use of local ingredients, so tuck into confit duck with grilled aubergine and saffron yoghurt, roast sea bream with buttered samphire, warm salad of squid, fennel and chorizo, and fresh Rye Bay fish. The relaxed funky feel extends to bright and beachy bedrooms upstairs, with their painted wooden floors, jazzy wall coverings, comfortable beds and splashes of colour. Extras include Roberts radios, sticks of rock, and rubber ducks in simple bathrooms. And they love dogs.

Rooms	10 doubles: £80–£110.
Meals	Lunch & dinner £11.75–£18.50.
Closed	Rarely.

Karen Northcote
The Ship Inn,
The Strand,
Rye TN31 7DB
Tel   +44 (0)1797 222233
Web   www.theshipinnrye.co.uk

Entry 612 Map 5

Sussex

The George in Rye
Rye

Ancient Rye has a history. It's a reclaimed island, a wealthy cinque port which once had its own army yet often fell into French hands. Henry James lived here, and the oldest working church clock in England chimes at the top of the hill. As for The George, it stands serenely on the cobbled high street. It was built in 1575 from reclaimed ships' timbers and its exposed beams and joists remain on display to this day. A contemporary revamp in classical style trumpets airy interiors, stripped floors, panelled walls and open fires – Jane Austen in the 21st century. There's a huge leather sofa in the bar by the fire, screen prints of the Beatles on the walls in reception, voile curtains and parquet floors in the restaurant. Divine bedrooms, including ten recent additions, come in all shapes and sizes, but fabulous fabrics, Frette linen, flat-screen TVs and Vi-Spring mattresses are standard, as are Ren potions by the bath and cashmere covers on hot water bottles. Superb food in the smart new Grill restaurant – Rye Bay lobster, Romney Marsh lamb – can be washed down by local English wines.

Rooms	8 doubles, 21 twin/doubles: £135-£195.
	5 suites for 2: £295-£325.
	Singles from £95.
Meals	Lunch & dinner £6-£35.
Closed	Open all day.

Alex & Katie Clarke
The George in Rye,
98 High Street,
Rye TN31 7JT
Tel   +44 (0)1797 222114
Web   www.thegeorgeinrye.com

The George Inn
Robertsbridge

This handsome old inn in pretty Robertsbridge has a warm welcome for all. The bare-boarded, earthy-hued bar/dining area is the perfect setting for richly textured fabrics, wool and leather chairs and sofas, painted tables and beautiful period pieces. Family portraits gaze serenely down as you enjoy a pint of Rother Valley Level Best and get cosy by the brick inglenook – famously favoured by Hilaire Belloc. If you're peckish, look to the chalkboards for the day's local and seasonal dishes: locally landed lemon sole, Rye Bay scallops, slow-roasted pork belly with Bramley apple spiced compote, chargrilled lamb rump with minted rösti. Or opt for a chargrilled rib eye steak, cut to size and order. Leave room for lovely puddings, especially the chocolatey ones. Upstairs, money has been lavished on four gorgeous luxury-steeped rooms with superb Hypnos beds, signature wallpapers, rich fabrics, antique furniture and beautiful en suite shower rooms. Perfect for visiting nearby Battle, Bodiam Castle, Pashley Manor Gardens and more besides.

Rooms	4 twin/doubles: £95-£130. Singles £80-£100.
Meals	Bar meals from £9.75. Lunch from £5. Dinner from £10. Sunday roast £10.75. Not Sunday eve or Monday.
Closed	Rarely.

John & Jane Turner
The George Inn,
High Street, Robertsbridge,
Battle TN32 5AW
Tel   +44 (0)1580 880315
Web   www.thegeorgerobertsbridge.co.uk

Sussex

The Bell
Ticehurst

Rescued, restored and reinvented, the old Bell is back: a community hub, a dining pub and a fabulous, fun place to stay. Enter to find oodles of 16th-century charm – rugs on bare boards, gilt-framed paintings on red walls, bowed beams, crackling logs in a brick inglenook. In the gorgeous bar-dining room and the cosy snug are innumerable and original design details: top-hat lampshades, spilling piles of floor-to-ceiling books, French Horn urinals in the gents, witty anecdotes on walls in antique scripts, a stuffed squirrel on a rocking chair. The rustic-chic bedrooms too will make you smile, each with a huge Somnus bed gorgeously dressed, a silver birch trunk rising from a planked floor, rich fabrics, fat radiators, perhaps a sparkling chandelier. Bathrooms are in jazzy, funky fashion, some with claw-foot baths. Back in the bar, enjoy Harveys ales and delicious pub dishes on modern seasonal menus – Rye Bay scallops, lamb chops with bubble and squeak, Cambridge burnt cream. The 'stable with the table' hosts table talks (debates), wine tastings and supplier dinners. One amazing community inn.

Rooms	5 doubles, 2 twin/doubles: £90–£155.
Meals	Lunch & dinner £6.50–£21.50.
Closed	Rarely.

Jhonnie de Oliveira
The Bell,
High Street,
Ticehurst TN5 7AS
Tel   +44 (0)1580 200234
Web   www.thebellinticehurst.com

Entry 615 Map 5

The Globe Inn Marsh
Rye

Expect the unexpected at this quirky clapboard-covered boozer on the edge of Rye. Bought to life by the Rogers family (who also run the Five Bells at Brabourne) there's much to catch the eye inside from corrugated iron walls, hanging buoys and glowing oil lamps to wine bottle candelabras and lobster pot lampshades. You won't find a 'proper' bar, instead a line of pumps dispensing top-notch Sussex and Kent ales. Menus are hand-scribbled, but don't let that deceive you — food is taken seriously here. Come for brunch or lunch with friends, order a pizza from the wood-fired oven, or choose one of the 'Daily Doings', handsome local offerings that change as regularly as the sun rises — Rye Bay scallops, Dungeness sea bass, Romney salt marsh lamb. Three blazing winter log fires and a super side terrace for summer drinking add to the year-round appeal.

The Crown
Hastings

Just a short stroll up from the beach and the newly-opened Jerwood Gallery, this old corner boozer oozes artful charm and hipster-cool. Décor is shabby-chic, the mood is laid-back, and the craft beer list is curated by an expert palate. Taken over by Tess and her team in 2014, the Crown celebrates fantastic local produce. Menus bristle with local artisan producers; there's coffee from Rye Bay, ice cream from Bodiam, and mugs from Gopsall Pottery in Winchelsea. Sit back and enjoy a pint of Old Dairy Red Top, lunch on local-ale rarebit with chutney, or go the whole hog and tuck into beach-landed skate with caper, lemon and parsley butter. Community spirit rings throughout and everyone is welcome, including the kids and the dog. Anything goes, from live music, weekly quizzes and pub games to Sunday morning storytelling and monthly craft markets.

Meals	Lunch from £6.50.
	Dinner from £11.
Closed	3pm-6pm Mon-Thurs.
	Open all day Fri-Sun.

Meals	Bar snacks from £2.
	Lunch from £4.50.
	Dinner from £10.
Closed	Open all day.

The Owner
The Globe Inn Marsh,
10 Military Rd, Rye,
East Sussex TN31 7NX
Tel   +44 (0)1797 225220
Web   www.globeinnmarshrye.com

Entry 616 Map 5

Tess Eaton & Andrew Swan
The Crown,
64–66 All Saints Street,
Hastings TN34 3BN
Tel   +44 (0)1424 465100
Web   www.thecrownhastings.co.uk

Entry 617 Map 5

Sussex

The Mark Cross Inn
Mark Cross

Set back from the A267 south of Tunbridge Wells, this whitewashed old inn makes the most of its lofty location in Mark Cross. On warm summer days arrive early to bag a table in the garden and savour the glorious rolling views across the Sussex Weald, best enjoyed with a pint of Harvey's Sussex in hand. Retreat inside in winter to find rambling rooms with old tables on rug-strewn wood floors and every inch of wall space filled with old paintings and prints and shelves groaning with books. The atmosphere is relaxed, the staff happy, and diners, children and dogs will all feel pampered. Daily menus run the gamut of pub classics and modern gastropub dishes – ham, egg and chips, moules and chips, confit pork belly with bubble and squeak, thyme and smoked garlic sauce, and sea bass with crab and crayfish risotto.

Meals	Starters from £4.95. Dinner from £10.95.
Closed	Open all day.

Brian Whiting
The Mark Cross Inn,
Mark Cross,
Crowborough TN6 3NP
Tel +44 (0)1892 852423
Web www.themarkcross.co.uk

Entry 618 Map 5

Sussex

The Dorset Arms
Withyam

Set back from the road, the striking façade of the Dorset Arms oozes history and charm. Inside find thick beams, wall studs, an ancient Sussex oak floor, and an enormous log fire in the bar. An ale house since 1735, its fortunes have been revived by the current Lord De La Warr, who bought the pub back from Harvey's of Lewes in 2013. Locals love the candles on old tables, colourful cushions on wall benches, the odd cosy wing chair in a corner, and family paintings and photos. There's ale from local Larkins, Tonbridge and Black Cat micro-breweries and a changing menu with produce from the Buckhurst Estate. Try potted crab on toast, or Scotch egg with mustard mayonnaise, then venison steak, stilton mash and redcurrant jus, and rice pudding with blackberry compote. Or go for the locally famous Buckhurst Park sausages, made to the Lord's own recipe.

Meals	Starters from £4. Dinner from £10. Sunday roast from £14.
Closed	Open all day.

Charlie Blundell
The Dorset Arms,
Buckhurst Park,
Withyam TN7 4BD
Tel +44 (0)1892 770278
Web www.dorset-arms.co.uk

Entry 619 Map 5

Sussex

The Star Inn
Old Heathfield

Built as an inn for pilgrims in the 14th century, with a rough honey-stone façade, The Star has gained a few creepers over the centuries and its atmospheric interior has mellowed nicely. Low-beamed ceilings, wall settles and panelling, huge log-fuelled inglenook — it's cosy, candlelit and inviting. The appeal in summer is the peaceful award-winning garden, bright with flowers, quirky with hand-crafted furniture; the long view to the South Downs coast was once painted by Turner. The chalkboard lists game pie, venison from Heathfield Park, shoulder of lamb with garlic potatoes, fish and chips, warm treacle tart. To drink, try Harveys Sussex Bitter from Lewes. And visit the impressive church with its fine early-English tower — it's right next door.

Meals	Lunch & dinner £9.50–£17.35.
Closed	Open all day.

Mike & Sue Chappell
The Star Inn,
Church Street, Old Heathfield,
Heathfield TN21 9AH
Tel   +44 (0)1435 863570
Web   www.starinnoldheathfield.co.uk

Entry 620 Map 5

Sussex

The Gun
Gun Hill

Winding lanes lead to a 16th-century farmhouse with glorious views across rolling countryside. Its name originates from the cannon foundries that were located at Gun Hill. Expect a neat open-plan interior with comfortably furnished alcoves, several log fires and an Aga in the cosy main bar. Plank floors, thick candles on scrubbed tables, fresh flowers and bold artwork create a civilised feel, menus champion local produce and every dish is freshly prepared. Kick off with a game terrine with red onion compote, follow with pan-fried halibut with tarragon sauce, finish with a warm chocolate fondant. Worth hunting down in all seasons, it has a terrace and lawn for summer days. Pick up the 'Gun Walk' leaflet and explore the surrounding footpaths.

Meals	Bar meals from £5.60.
	Lunch from £8.95.
	Dinner from £11.50.
Closed	3pm–6pm in winter.
	Open all day Sat, Sun & in summer.

Alex Tudor
The Gun,
Gun Hill,
Heathfield TN21 0JU
Tel   +44 (0)1825 872361
Web   www.thegunhouse.co.uk

Entry 621 Map 5

Farm @ Friday Street
Langney

The imposing 17th-century building and its name are the sole reminders that it was a fully functioning farm until the early 1980s. Houses have replaced the fields and Langney has morphed into a suburb of Eastbourne, yet the old farmhouse continues to thrive as a pub serving good food to hungry residents. Beams and timbers abound, log fires blaze in brick fireplaces and fat candles flicker in the rambling and atmospheric old rooms. The dining extension, with soaring rafters and tables on two levels, has a private dining room and an open kitchen, delivering sausages and mash with onion gravy, battered cod with chunky chips, confit pork belly with garlic mash and mustard sauce, and sticky toffee pud. All day sandwiches (such as steak and red onion marmalade) – best washed down with a pint of Landlord – complete the picture.

George Inn
Alfriston

You can't miss the ancient façade as you stroll down Alfriston's high street. Step inside the creaky old inn, first licensed in 1397, where things are historic still, to find worn planked floors, head-cracking beams, thick standing timbers, and a huge inglenook crackling with logs in winter. Hop bines are strewn above the bar: the cosiest possible setting for tasty pub fare and a foaming pint of Greene King. Share a rustic board for two laden with seafood and roasted garlic, bread and warm olive oil, or tuck into old-style ham, egg and chips and sticky toffee pudding. There are hearty steaks, daily risottos, and, in the evening, big dishes like venison casserole and pork belly. Munch in the flint-walled garden, explore the village, hike the South Downs Way.

Meals	Starters from £5.95.
	Dinner from £9.95.
Closed	Open all day.

Meals	Lunch & bar meals from £4.95.
	Dinner from £10.95.
	Sunday lunch, 3 courses, £21.
Closed	Open all day.

Brian Whiting
Farm @ Friday Street,
15 Friday Street, Langney,
Eastbourne BN23 8AP
Tel   +44 (0)1323 766049
Web   www.farmfridaystreet.com

Entry 622 Map 5

Roland & Cate Couch
George Inn,
High Street, Alfriston,
Polegate BN26 5SY
Tel   +44 (0)1323 870319
Web   www.thegeorge-alfriston.com

Entry 623 Map 5

Sussex

The Sussex Ox
Polegate

Just below the South Downs, the Sussex Ox is a popular retreat with ramblers and A27 escapees – time it right and you'll catch a sunset from the garden. David and Suzanne have invested well in refurbishing the rambling old place, and now there's a clean and civilised feel: cream walls, wonky timbers, wood or worn-brick floors, painted panelling, vases overflowing with lilies. Find a cushioned pew at a scrubbed pine table in the Garden Room for the best of the sweeping views. Daily printed menus list hearty, locally sourced choices – lunchtime sandwiches and soups, ale-battered pollock, lamb shank with redcurrant and thyme jus, white chocolate cheesecake, artisan cheeses. Ales come from the Dark Star and Harveys breweries, best enjoyed in summer on the decked terrace.

Meals	Lunch & dinner £8.75–£15.
Closed	3pm–6pm.

David & Suzanne Pritchard
The Sussex Ox,
Milton Street,
Polegate BN26 5RL
Tel   +44 (0)1323 870840
Web   www.thesussexox.co.uk

Entry 624 Map 5

Sussex

The Snowdrop Inn
Lewes

The former Victorian bargeman's pub is tucked away down a dead-end lane on the edge of town, semi-derelict with a rough reputation when Tony and Dominic took over in 2009. Now it's the heart of the community, a colourful local that appeals to all, welcoming families and dogs, ale aficionados and music lovers. The quirky barge theme to the décor creates a warm and cosy atmosphere, there's a passion for craft beers and Sussex ales, and the cooking is a big surprise. Daily menus offer good value fresh food prepared from local and organic ingredients – sweet potato and ginger soup, home-reared pork, Hophead ale sausages, Irish stew, apple crumble and custard. It's the base for the South Street Bonfire Society and they organise a brilliant beer festival as part of Lewes's Octoberfeast.

Meals	Lunch, dinner & Sunday roast from £10.50.
Closed	Open all day.

Tony Leonard & Dominic McCartan
The Snowdrop Inn,
119 South Street,
Lewes BN7 2BU
Tel   +44 (0)1273 471018
Web   www.thesnowdropinn.com

Entry 625 Map 4

Sussex

Stanmer House
Brighton

Whiting & Hammond's grandest and most unique venue is a stunning 18th-century mansion set in 5,000 acres of glorious parkland north of Brighton. It's a pub, restaurant, tea room and conference/wedding venue all rolled into one. The relaxed approach has been key to its success, opening from 9am for breakfast, with food served all day and traditional afternoon teas a big draw. Ramblers, dog walkers and city escapees pile in for eggs Benedict, coffee and cake, deli-board sandwiches (pastrami with pickles and mustard mayonnaise), beef and Guinness hotpot, and rib-eye steak with béarnaise, served throughout impressive high-ceilinged rooms. Find a bar serving three real ales; two lovely lounges with sofas and log fires; grand dining rooms with chandeliers, rugs on wood floors, and garden views.

Meals	Starters from £5.95. Dinner from £9.95.
Closed	Open all day.

Brian Whiting
Stanmer House,
Stanmer Park,
Brighton BN1 9QA
Tel +44 (0)1273 680400
Web www.stanmerhouse.co.uk

Entry 626 Map 4

Sussex

The Coach & Horses
Danehill

With ale on tap from Harveys in Lewes, fresh fish from Seaford and lamb from the field opposite, this is one special pub. The central bar is its throbbing hub, wooden panelling and open fires the backdrop for jugs of mulled wine in winter-cosy rooms. During the rest of the year the big raised garden comes into its own; spread yourselves on the freshly rebuilt adults-only terrace under the boughs of the spreading maple. Whatever the weather, the food attracts folk from far and wide. In the stable block restaurant a changing seasonal menu from chef Dan Hockaday places the emphasis on quality rather than quantity, in butterbean and garlic soup, spicy crab and saffron risotto, roast pork belly with salsa verde. Pub classics include chicken and leek pie and lamb stew. Delicious! A lovely rural pub, a true local.

Meals	Lunch & dinner £10.50–£19.95. Bar meals £6.75–£10.50 (lunchtime only).
Closed	3pm–5.30pm Mon to Fri. Open all day Sat & Sun.

Ian & Catherine Philpots
The Coach & Horses,
Coach & Horses Lane, Danehill,
Haywards Heath RH17 7JF
Tel +44 (0)1825 740369
Web www.coachandhorses.danehill.biz

Entry 627 Map 4

Sussex

The Crabtree
Lower Beeding

Welcome to a former haunt of Hilaire Belloc, who'd sit in the garden munching bread and Sussex cheese. You can do the same, on benches topped with fleeces. This country pub has it all: a vast inglenook stacked with logs, lots of cosy flagstone'd corners, a daily menu that supports local producers, and a rather stylish wine list. Pop in for a pint and a pie, a scrumptious snack (Scotch egg and curried mayo, red pepper hummus with spiced flatbread) or a beautifully presented three courses. There are great Sunday lunches too, and a kids' menu that will delight. Get chatty in the open bar, filled with light from the big sash window; find a wicker chair in the sunshiney Garden Room, where a dresser overflows with biscotti and crabapple jellies. There are local events on Fridays, sweet Sussex views and the staff are totally on the ball.

Meals	Lunch from £10.
	Dinner from £12.
	Sunday lunch, 2 courses, £16.
Closed	Open all day.

Simon Hope
The Crabtree,
Brighton Road, Lower Beeding,
Horsham RH13 6PT
Tel   +44 (0)1403 892666
Web www.crabtreesussex.co.uk

Entry 628 Map 4

Sussex

Royal Oak
Wineham

The part-tiled, part-timbered cottage — almost lost down a country road — is six centuries old and has been refreshing locals for two. In the charming bar and tiny rear room are brick and boarded floors, a huge log-fired inglenook, sturdy rustic furniture, and antique corkscrews, pottery jugs and aged artefacts hanging from low-slung beams. Michael and Sharon Bailey have changed little since taking over in 2007, drawing Harveys Best straight from the cask (no pumps) and, in keeping with ale house tradition, delivering a menu of freshly made pub food using locally sourced produce. Expect an updated full menu as well as a light lunch: sandwiches, ploughman's, hearty soups. No music or electronic hubbub, just traditional pub games, makes this heart-warmer a rural survivor.

Meals	Lunch & dinner £8.95-£15.95.
Closed	2.30pm-5.30pm
	(3.30pm-6pm Sat, 4pm-7pm Sun).

Michael & Sharon Bailey
Royal Oak,
Wineham Lane,
Wineham,
Henfield BN5 9AY
Tel   +44 (0)1444 881252

Entry 629 Map 4

The Ginger Fox
Albourne

This country pub looks splendidly traditional, its thatch crowned by a fox stalking a pheasant. The second of Ben McKeller's Sussex Gingerman pubs, it has a contemporary zing. Both its aim (to create modern British dishes from the finest produce) and its look (armchairs, banquettes, stone floors, open fires) are close to the Hove original – a cool uncluttered style that blends with the old. Chalked-up menus are short and to the point: roast breast of pheasant with braised-leg cottage pie; sea bass with confit shallot potatoes and salsify; tomato risotto with parmesan crisps and pea shoots. There's Welsh rarebit as an alternative to chocolate jaffa brûlée; it teams nicely with a pint of Harveys Sussex Best. Service is friendly and well-dressed.

The George at Burpham
Burpham

Tucked away in a sleepy South Downs village, this wonderful little pub that dates from the 1700s was facing extinction – until the locals bought it. Now it's back, run by locals, supplied by locals, and refurbished by locals too. By the welcoming fire, with a pint of the pub's own beer and homemade pork scratchings, it's easy to see why this was once a haunt for smugglers. Now folk enjoy simple and delicious dishes in the cosy bar or the cottagey dining areas; try game terrine with cranberry compote, and house beef burger with Welsh rarebit topping. The pub's motto may be 'by the locals, for the locals, of the locals' but visitors are extremely welcome. Which is just as well – if not, the treacle sponge with salted caramel ice cream would have to be smuggled out!

| Meals | Lunch & dinner £10.50–£16.50. |
| Closed | Open all day. |

| Meals | Lunch & dinner £9.75–£23.95. |
| Closed | 3pm-6pm Mon-Fri. |

Ben McKeller
The Ginger Fox,
Muddleswood Road, Albourne,
Hassocks BN6 9EA
Tel +44 (0)1273 857888
Web www.gingermanrestaurants.com

Entry 630 Map 4

Martin Bear
The George at Burpham,
Main Street, Burpham,
Arundel BN18 9RR
Tel +44 (0)1903 883131
Web www.georgeatburpham.co.uk

Entry 631 Map 4

The George
Eartham

Tucked away in the South Downs is a very English cosy pub. It's not just the Cath Kidston country kitchen bar and the Saint George references that wave the British flag; behind the bar are artisan beers, stouts, meads, cordials, and British and Commonwealth wines. Well-kept beers such as Goodwood Organic Sussex Ale make a fine accompaniment to the locally sourced dishes: Sussex rarebit on artisan bread; pork chops with butternut squash mash, leeks and apple and ale gravy; seasonal fruit crumbles. In summer there's a pretty garden for barbecues and James's annual beer festival. What's more, you're so near the glorious South Downs (they know all the routes) that there's every excuse for a spot of Sussex cheese board indulgence before striding uphill.

Anglesey Arms at Halnaker
Halnaker

Laid back, relaxed, free of airs and graces, a Georgian brick pub in charming West Sussex. This cracking local is lovingly run by George and Jools Jackson, both committed to keeping it charming and old-fashioned. Expect varnished and stripped pine, flagstones, beams and panelling, crackling log fires, locals at the bar, and a cosier, smarter dining room. Guest ales are local and food is fresh and home-cooked using great local produce – crab and lobster from Selsey, or traceable meats in hearty pies: organic South Downs lamb and pork, well-hung beef from the Goodwood estate, venison and game from local shoots. Even the ciders, wines and spirits are organic. A great little local, with inter-pub cricket, golf and quizzes and regular 'moules and boules' events in the two-acre garden. Perfect for lazy summer afternoons.

Meals	Lunch & dinner £9.50-£17.95.
Closed	Open all day.

Meals	Lunch from £8.50.
	Dinner from £10.50.
	Sunday roast £13.
Closed	3pm-5.30pm.
	Open all day Sun.

James Anthony Thompson
The George,
Eartham,
Chichester PO18 0LT
Tel   +44 (0)1243 814340
Web   www.thegeorgeeartham.com

Entry 632 Map 4

George & Jools Jackson
Anglesey Arms at Halnaker,
Halnaker,
Chichester PO18 0NQ
Tel   +44 (0)1243 773474
Web   www.angleseyarms.co.uk

Entry 633 Map 4

The Fox Goes Free
Charlton

King William III may have stopped off to refresh his hunting parties. Now this 400-year-old flint pub, secreted away in the South Downs, is home to fine ales from local breweries. Settle down by a blazing fire under beamed ceilings for a pint of Ballards Best and the pub's own Fox Goes Free; in summer you have a garden with farmland views. The traditional bar food suits the surroundings, with scrubbed tables and choir chairs. Everything from the chips to the ice cream is homemade; tuck into Cumberland sausages with bubble and squeak and onion marmalade, or whole baked camembert, confit garlic and toasted fingers. Main courses are tempting too, with locally reared Tamworth pork or roasted monkfish. Goodwood racecourse is up the hill, downland walks start from the door.

Meals	Lunch & dinner £10.95–£17.50.
	Bar meals £10.95–£12.50.
	Sunday roast £10.50–£15.95.
Closed	26 December & 1 January (evenings).

David Coxon
The Fox Goes Free,
Charlton,
Chichester PO18 0HU
Tel   +44 (0)1243 811461
Web www.thefoxgoesfree.com

Entry 634 Map 4

The Royal Oak Inn
East Lavant

There's a cheery wine-bar feel to the Royal Oak; locals and young professionals come with their children and it's as countrified as can be. Inside, a modern-rustic look with traditional touches prevails: stripped floors, exposed brickwork, dark leather sofas, open fires and racing pictures on the walls: this was once part of the Goodwood estate. The dining area is big, light and airy, with a conservatory from which you can amble out onto a terrace that's warmed by outdoor lamps on summer nights. At scrubbed-top tables you can tuck into delicious trio of Barbary duck, seared scallops on pumpkin purée, fig tart with pistachio ice cream. Staff are attentive, a secret garden looks over cornfields, and you're well-placed for Chichester Theatre and the boats at pretty Bosham.

Meals	Lunch from £7.95.
	Dinner, 3 courses, about £35.
	Sunday roast from £25–£29.
Closed	Open all day.

Charles Ullmann
The Royal Oak Inn,
Pook Lane, East Lavant,
Chichester PO18 0AX
Tel   +44 (0)1243 527434
Web www.royaloakeastlavant.co.uk

Entry 635 Map 4

The Earl of March
Lavant

Having been taken over by ex-Ritz chef Giles Thompson, this is one snappy performer. It's a clean-lined, fashionable space with a cosmopolitan vibe: modern leather seating in the bar area, high-backed suede chairs in the dining room, and sepia prints of racing cars and aircraft on the walls. Bolstered by specials, the up-tempo dining roster delivers game in season and wonderful fresh seafood. On the summer Champagne & Seafood menu are dressed Selsey crab salad, king prawns with mayonnaise, whole smoked mackerel with saffron rouille. There's a bar and terrace menu, too (Sussex ham and eggs, beer-battered haddock) and great South Downs views from the terrace and dining area. Faultless service, gorgeous food, and it's child friendly.

The Crab & Lobster
Sidlesham

Backing directly onto Pagham Harbour and the bird-rich marshes, the gentle Crab flaunts an inglenook fireplace and ancient flagstones that blend effortlessly with dark leather banquettes, ornate mirrors and vintage photos. This sparkling pub is managed by Sam but is often driven by the locals; Burns Night and wine evenings are big events. Windows offer endless sea views and there's a fishy focus to the menu, as you might expect – crab and lobster ravioli, organic sea trout with niçoise salad, Cornish sardines with black olive butter. Carnivores can tuck into lamb cutlets with roasted garlic and thyme jus, and all is served on stylish white plates. Enjoy a pint of local Sussex and choose a seat on the back terrace for views of sheep-grazed meadows and marshes.

Meals	Bar meals from £10.50. Lunch from £12.50. Dinner from £18.50. Sunday lunch, 3 courses, £21.50.	Meals	Bar meals from £6.50. Lunch from £11.95. Dinner, 3 courses, £35. Sunday lunch, 2 courses, £26.
Closed	Open all day.	Closed	Open all day.

Giles Thompson
The Earl of March,
Lavant,
Chichester PO18 0BQ
Tel   +44 (0)1243 533993
Web   www.theearlofmarch.com

Entry 636 Map 4

Sam Bakose
The Crab & Lobster,
Mill Lane, Sidlesham,
Chichester PO20 7NB
Tel   +44 (0)1243 641233
Web   www.crab-lobster.co.uk

Entry 637 Map 4

Sussex

The Lamb Inn
West Wittering

Many head to West Wittering for sailing in summer and beach walks in winter. Now there's another reason to visit – The Lamb. New owners have breathed life into this lovely little pub and created a refreshingly unpretentious watering hole. Under low ceilings, by cottage windows, enjoy pints of Badgers and share mixed plates of 'grilled sausage' with fresh bread. In the small sunny dining room, sailors and regulars tuck into local produce – pan-fried scallops and sea bass with lemon grass sauce; lamb hotpot with sweet potato and roast vegetables; homemade fruit crumble. This little building was once a farm cottage until the owner bought a barrel of beer to share with his friends. The rest is history but the hospitality lives on, extended to all who pass – with a tot of Sailor Jerry's rum ever ready, for sailors heading further afield.

Meals	Lunch & dinner £5-£22.
Closed	Open all day.

Dave Skinner & Jim Robertson
The Lamb Inn,
Chichester Road, West Wittering,
Chichester PO20 8QA
Tel +44 (0)1243 511 105
Web www.thelambwittering.co.uk

🚶 🐕 🍺

Entry 638 Map 4

Sussex

Richmond Arms
West Ashling

This little beauty may hide away in an idyllic red-roofed village, but it's barely ten minutes from Chichester. The Jacks' conversion is warm, modern and hugely appealing, thanks to mellow pastel colours, a real fire in winter and chunky oak tables. There are local ales at the pint-sized central bar, and a feature wine rack to one side that announces the dining credentials; most come here to eat. The bar blackboard bubbles with fashionable grazing plates, from chorizo and lemon-crumbed sprats to Thai-spiced fish tempura, and all is produced with imagination and skill. Enjoy Sussex saltmarsh rib-eye (cooked over charcoal) with beef-dripping chips and béarnaise sauce, and peanut butter and chocolate fondant. Marvellous.

Meals	Bar meals from £4.95.
	Lunch from £6.95.
	Dinner from £15.95.
	Sunday lunch, 2 courses £22.90;
	3 courses £29.65.
Closed	Sun evenings & all day Mon & Tues.
	Christmas & New Year
	(until mid–January).

William & Emma Jack
Richmond Arms,
Mill Road, West Ashling,
Chichester PO18 8EA
Tel +44 (0)1243 572046
Web www.therichmondarms.co.uk

♿ 🚶 🐕 🍷 📶

Entry 639 Map 4

Sussex

The Star & Garter
East Dean

If fresh fish takes your fancy then follow the winding lanes to this 18th-century pub. Hidden in the folds of the South Downs, with miles of breezy walks from the front door, the old ale house now draws the well-shod. Seafood platters spill over with whole Selsey lobster and crabs, scallops, wild salmon, crevettes and prawns. Along with the big bowls of mussels and the whole baked bass, there's venison pie and a mouthwatering game grill — partridge from West Dean, pigeon from East Dean, local wild boar sausages. Drink Sussex ales straight from the cellar in an open-plan room where hops decorate stripped beams, old village photographs line bare-brick walls and the daily papers fill the rack by the door. In summer, head for the sun-trap patio or lawned gardens.

Meals	Lunch & dinner £11–£21. Bar meals £7.50–£9.50. Sunday roast £12.
Closed	3pm–6pm. Open all day Sat & Sun.

Michael Harris
The Star & Garter,
East Dean,
Chichester PO18 0JG
Tel   +44 (0)1243 811318
Web   www.thestarandgarter.co.uk

Entry 640 Map 4

Sussex

The Three Horseshoes
Elsted

Low beams, latched doors, brick floors, high settles, cream bowed walls, big log fires and home-cooked food: all that you'd hope for, and more. Built in 1540 as a drovers' ale house, it has no cellar, so staff pull ales from the barrel instead. The lower bar was formerly a butcher's shop and still has the ceiling hooks. Local seafood, meat and game appear on a tempting country menu and are served in snug rooms — Selsey sea bass, cottage pie, venison goulash, steak and kidney Guinness pie. The main dining room is smarter and less rustic and also comes with its wood-burning stove. In summer, sit in the glorious garden, with golden pints and cracking views over the South Downs. Landlady Sue looks after you well.

Meals	Bar meals £6.95–£9.95. Lunch & dinner £8.95–£17.95.
Closed	2.30pm–6pm. 3pm–7pm Sun.

Sue Beavis & Michael Newton
The Three Horseshoes,
Elsted,
Midhurst GU29 0JY
Tel   +44 (0)1730 825746

Entry 641 Map 4

Noah's Ark
Lurgashall

In an idyllic setting – beside village pond and churchyard, overlooking a cricket green – the Ark restores faith in the future of the English country pub. In this couple's hands, the old village boozer has become a place of charm; no more darts, but a surprise at every turn. From bar to cosy dining areas – and one barn-like room – are beams, floorboards, open fires, traditional country furniture and a sprinkling of modern leather. The kitchen's insistence on good-quality (local, seasonal) produce results in a roll-call of British dishes; come evening, the simple bar menu is bolstered by such dishes as pan-fried wood pigeon breast with sautéed savoy cabbage and crispy pancetta. A cottagey garden to the side and picnic tables out front complete the very pleasing package.

Halfway Bridge Inn
Petworth

Fancy visiting Petworth House or a walk on Wittering Beach? Sam Bakose has put his magic to work on this mellow old coaching inn deep in polo country, just back from the A272. A series of spruced-up rooms comes with cosy corners and split levels, the bar with a modern look, the rest more traditional: scrubbed tables, crackling fires, fat candles. Thirsts are quenched by local Langham and Long Man beers and 25 wines by the glass, and the food is a satisfying mix of traditional and modern British, the menus evolving with the seasons. Tuck into moules and chips at the bar or pork belly and black pudding terrine, or baked bream with clam and caper butter – and leave room for prune and armagnac tart! For summer there's a sheltered patio with posh tables and brollies.

Meals	Lunch & dinner £10.95–£18.95. Bar meals from £6. Sunday lunch, 3 courses, £23.
Closed	3.45pm–5.30pm. Sun evenings.

Meals	Bar meals £6.50–£12.50. Lunch & dinner £14.50–£28.
Closed	Open all day.

Henry Coghlan & Amy Whitmore
Noah's Ark,
Lurgashall,
Petworth GU28 9ET
Tel   +44 (0)1428 707346
Web   www.noahsarkinn.co.uk

Entry 642 Map 4

Sam Bakose
Halfway Bridge Inn,
Halfway Bridge,
Petworth GU28 9BP
Tel   +44 (0)1798 861281
Web   www.halfwaybridge.co.uk

Entry 643 Map 4

Sussex

The Duke of Cumberland Arms
Henley

In the spring the Duke looks divine, its cottage walls engulfed by flowering wisteria. Beyond is the tiered garden, with babbling pools and huge Weald views. Latch doors lead to two tiny bars that creak with character — painted tongue-and-groove walls, low ceilings, scrubbed tables, log fires in the grate. Choose a pint of Hip Hop or Goodwood Organic Blonde from the cask. Rescued from closure by a local a few years back, the Duke has Simon Goodman as chef-landlord (2010 Pub Chef of the Year), the new dining room, a light, modern, country confection with a big fire, is a show-stopper, and there's a terrace with a marvellous view. Daily menus rely on fresh local produce, including Goodwood organic rib-eye steak, estate venison and South Downs lamb; Sunday roasts are brought as a joint to the table. A treasure.

Sussex

The Stag
Petworth

The quintessential Sussex pub — some might say (and often do), the best pub in the world. Beneath 16th-century beams by a crackling fire — or out in the garden in summer — riders, walkers and locals enjoy a natter over well-kept Badger and Sussex Bitter. Wholesome home-cooked food is another draw, the traditional suet puddings and jam roly polys being the biggest temptation; note too a fine mutton and pearl barley broth. A sweet shop in a former life, this little inn still pulls the children in; today there's a room in which they may play undisturbed. Lots for adults too: a darts team, jazz nights in summer, the Mummers at Christmas. Find a 17th-century stone-floored bar, a large old clock that ticks above the inglenook, a dining room carpeted and cosy, and a tethering post should you drop by with your horse.

Meals	Lunch £7.25–£17.95.
	Dinner £14.95–£21.95.
Closed	3pm–5pm (in winter).
	Open all day in summer.

Meals	Bar meals £6–£18.
	Lunch & dinner £7.50–£18.
	Not Sun or Mon eves.
Closed	3pm–6pm Mon–Fri.
	Open all day Sat & Sun.

	Simon Goodman
	The Duke of Cumberland Arms,
	Henley,
	Haslemere GU27 3HQ
Tel	+44 (0)1428 652280
Web	www.dukeofcumberland.com

Entry 644 Map 4

	Erika Godsland
	The Stag,
	Balls Cross,
	Petworth GU28 9JP
Tel	+44 (0)1403 820241
Web	www.staginn-ballscross.co.uk

Entry 645 Map 4

The Bell Alderminster
Alderminster

Big changes have been rung at this 600-year-old coaching inn where you're spoilt for choice when it comes to finding a perch: leather armchairs by the fire, country divans, reading room, conservatory? The walls display vintage sepia canvases of the Alscot Estate – they own the pub and provide some of the produce – while Wye Valley HPA backs up the Alscot ale. For those in a hurry, the grazing boards, sandwiches and baguettes are ideal but for those with time, the full works are worth lingering over. You could start with smoked chicken and pancetta salad with a dolcelatte dressing, move on to confit duck with sweet and sour sauce and crushed new potatoes, and finish with white chocolate crunch cheesecake with blueberry-vodka soaked apricots: you'll leave happy and well fed. The wine list has grapes to suit all, charming staff see that it ticks along nicely and if you think downstairs is good, upstairs is even better. Four rooms await, each different, each fabulous, from the proudly patriotic to the boldly opulent. Bathrooms are utterly spoiling. A stylish summer garden makes this special from start to finish.

Rooms	5 doubles, 2 twins: £95–£140. 2 suites for 2: £145–£165. Singles from £70 (Sun-Thur).
Meals	Bar meals from £7. Lunch, 2 courses, from £14.50 (Mon-Fri). Dinner, 3 courses, from £18 (Mon-Thurs). Sunday lunch, 3 courses, £25.
Closed	Rarely.

Chris Swain
The Bell Alderminster,
Shipston Road, Alderminster,
Stratford-upon-Avon CV37 8NY
Tel   +44 (0)1789 450414
Web   www.thebellald.co.uk

Entry 646 Map 8

The Howard Arms
Ilmington

The Howard buzzes with good-humoured babble as well-kept beer flows from the flagstoned bar. Logs crackle contentedly in a vast open fire; a blackboard menu scales the wall above; a dining room at the far end has unexpected elegance, with great swathes of bold colour and some noble paintings. Gorgeous bedrooms are set discreetly apart from the joyful throng, a mix of period style and modern luxury beautifully: one with a painted antique headboard and bleached beams, another more folksy, while the newer rooms in the annexe come in more contemporary style with fancy bathrooms. All are individual, all huge by pub standards. The village is a surprise, too, literally tucked under a lone hill, with an unusual church surrounded by orchards and an extended village green. Round off an idyllic walk amid buzzing bees and wild flowers with a meal at the inn, perhaps salmon trio with celeriac remoulade and orange dressing, then beef, ale and mustard pie, then spiced pear and apple flapjack crumble. From a menu with seasonal local produce, the food is inventive and upmarket.

Rooms	5 doubles, 3 twin/doubles: £95-£145. Singles from £85.
Meals	Lunch from £4.50. Dinner from £10.50
Closed	Rarely.

Grant Owen
The Howard Arms,
Lower Green, Ilmington,
Shipston-on-Stour CV36 4LT
Tel   +44 (0)1608 682226
Web   www.howardarms.com

Entry 647 Map 8

The Fuzzy Duck
Armscote

Nestled in rolling folds of Cotswold countryside, close to Stratford-upon-Avon, is this 18th-century coaching inn, polished to perfection by Tania, Adrian and their team. Beautiful fireplaces and gleaming tables, fine china and big sprays of wildflowers tell a tale of comfort and luxury, while the smiling staff are rightly proud of this gem of a pub. You dine like kings and queens in the sparkling bar, or in the clever conversion at the back, overlooking grounds that are part-orchard, part-walled-garden. Try Cotswold chicken breast with slow-cooked chorizo and white bean stew, or a splendid ploughman's with warm scotch quail's egg. For pudding, try the zingy lemon posset, or treacle tart with orange scented milk ice. If you over-indulge, borrow wellies in your size for a bracing walk then back to your beautiful bed above the bar; rooms are sound-proofed and two have double loft beds (up very vertical ladders) for families. Best of all, the generous team has provided indulgent treats: lovely slippers; a nightcap tipple – come prepared to be spoiled.

Rooms	2 doubles: £110–£140.
	2 family rooms for 4: £180–£200.
Meals	Lunch, 2 courses, £15; 3 courses, £18.
	Dinner from £12.95.
Closed	Rarely.

The Manager
The Fuzzy Duck,
Ilmington Road, Armscote,
Stratford-upon-Avon CV37 8DD
Tel   +44 (0)1608 682 635
Web   www.fuzzyduckarmscote.com

Entry 648 Map 8

The Red Lion
Long Compton

Dogs are welcome in this ancient warren of a pub where canine sketches adorn the walls; 'the Landlady' – the pub's own chocolate lab – is often around. Enter to a mouthwatering aroma of imaginative dishes from chef/co-patron Sarah Keightley. Crispy-battered cod and chips with caper berries and mushy peas are served on *The Red Lion Times*, and pork tenderloin comes wrapped in pancetta with apple purée and black pudding. A meltingly warm pear and ginger pudding with toffee sauce rounds it all off nicely. Easy to find, this characterful pub has benefited from a wonderful refurb and there's space for everyone, from the pool room to the restaurant to the beautiful flagged bar with fire and wood-burning stove. There are five bedrooms too, the quietest at the back, which reflect the unfussy approach: natural colours and crisp ginghams; comfort and attention to quality make up for their size, though the King Room has an ante chamber should anyone snore! It is cheerful, hospitable, and breakfasts are worth waking up for.

Rooms	2 doubles, 1 twin, 1 family room for 4: £90-£140. 1 single: £60.
Meals	Lunch & dinner £11.95-£18.95.
Closed	Rarely.

Lisa Phipps & Sarah Keightley
The Red Lion,
Main Street, Long Compton,
Shipston-on-Stour CV36 5JS

Tel	+44 (0)1608 684221
Web	www.redlion-longcompton.co.uk

Entry 649 Map 8

Warwickshire

The Inn at Farnborough
Farnborough

Anthony and Jo's mellow ironstone pub dates from the 16th century and is the hub of picture-book Farnborough, within walking distance of Farnborough Hall (National Trust). Transformed into a smart gastropub a decade ago, it successfully embraces the traditional with modern British seasonal menus using the best local suppliers. Find warm hues, subtle lighting, open fires, rustic stone floors and fresh flowers throughout a maze of interconnecting rooms with cosy corners. The food is gorgeous: posh bar nibbles (fishcakes with lemon mayo), pub classics, duck and orange parfait; Moroccan spiced pheasant and vegetable tagine with coriander and pistachio quinoa; chocolate bread and butter pudding. Colour spills from tubs and borders in the landscaped gardens, perfect for summer sipping – try a pint of Purity Ale.

Meals	Bar meals £5-£12.
	Lunch & dinner £8.95-£19.95.
Closed	3pm-6pm.
	Open all day Fri-Sun.

Anthony Robinson
The Inn at Farnborough,
Farnborough,
Banbury OX17 1DZ
Tel   +44 (0)1295 690615
Web   www.innatfarnborough.co.uk

Entry 650 Map 8

Warwickshire

The Bell Inn
Ladbroke

A pub with a pleasing front and a respectable air, and a pub that's easy to find. It stands opposite a lovely Tudor thatch house and its young owners attract a diverse crowd: tweedy checkshirts, comfortable couples, young mums with their laptops. The aim is to cook the best seasonal produce and to keep it simple, and the service is quick, attentive and cheerful – perfect. Huw knows his food and is attuned to the talents of his chef, Steve. Our fillet of plaice with dill sauce couldn't have been fresher, and the berry-and-apple crumble came with a delicious jug of just-made custard. There's a bistro pub feel, nothing too heavy or too shiny, with open fires in the bar in winter and a dining area that leads seamlessly to the back. The garden potters to a small stream – enjoy a pint of Boon Doggle, but keep little ones on leads!

Meals	Lunch & dinner £13.50-£16.50.
Closed	Mon all day.

Ruth & Huw Griffiths
The Bell Inn,
Banbury Road,
Ladbroke CV47 2BY
Tel   +44 (0)1926 811224
Web   www.thebellinnladbroke.co.uk

Entry 651 Map 8

Warwickshire

The Chequers Inn
Ettington

New life has been breathed into this north Cotswold pub by Kirstin and James – and how! A bold style of classic British meets country French thanks to rich tapestries, gilt mirrors, padded chairs, round tables and aged wooden flooring throughout. There is a proper glowing wood bar with St Austell Tribute and London Pride on tap; plus Stowford Press cider, an impressive wine selection and several varieties of fizz for special occasions. The calm, elegant Provençal dining area at the back overlooks a well-planted and sheltered garden which hides the chef's veg patch. Start with honey-glazed crispy duck salad with hoisin dressing and cashew nuts, move on to brill with buttered mash and gremolata. The puds will also tempt, and then there's freshly ground coffee. Different, slightly decadent, and definitely worth a visit.

Warwickshire

The One Elm
Stratford-upon-Avon

Stratford has a reputation for great pubs and theatre, and was the birthplace of the first Slug and Lettuce. In the narrow building that The Slug once occupied stands The One Elm, now owned by Peach Pubs. The wood-floored bar is light, lofty and airy, the décor is chic – comfy chairs and sofas, a log-burner, a youthful feel – and the tree-shaded courtyard has a great vibe. In the bar are good beers and great wines; at the back, the restaurant, with a private and secluded dining area on the mezzanine and a short but mouthwatering menu. There's a chargrill section, a 'roast of the day' and a variety of deli boards available all day. Being slightly off the tourist trail this attracts a local crowd. The friendly staff are on tap from breakfast until closing time.

Meals	Lunch & bar meals from £4.50. Dinner £9.50-£16.95. Sunday lunch, 3 courses, £23.45.
Closed	3pm-5pm. Sun evenings & Mon.

Meals	Lunch & bar meals from £4. Dinner from £9. Sunday roast from £11.50.
Closed	Christmas Day.

James & Kirstin Viggers
The Chequers Inn,
91 Banbury Road, Ettington,
Stratford-upon-Avon CV37 7SR
Tel +44 (0)1789 740387
Web www.the-chequers-ettington.co.uk

Entry 652 Map 8

Julie Crump
The One Elm,
1 Guild Street,
Stratford-upon-Avon CV37 6QZ
Tel +44 (0)1789 404919
Web www.oneelmstratford.co.uk

Entry 653 Map 8

Warwickshire

Bell Inn
Welford-on-Avon

If things Shakespearian inspire you, then the timbered high street's 17th-century Bell will not disappoint. There is a richness about the natural oak beams and settles, the stone floors strewn with Persian rugs, the dog-grates cradling glowing embers. This is a historic village inn that serves top-quality, locally sourced food, be it simple pub favourites such as pork loin with sausage and bean cassoulet or a more Gallic beef bourguignon served with mash. Don't miss the Indian-inspired Fridays, or the excellent wine list. If you're into food provenance, every supplier is listed on the back of the menu and they are almost all small independents. Staff are happy, attentive and long-serving. Cask ales, kids' portions – a wonderful traditional English pub.

Warwickshire

The Crabmill
Preston Bagot

The lovely, rambling building, with tiny leaded windows and wonky beams, once contained a cider press. Later a pub, now it's a gastro haven with a dining room for every mood – one stone and scented with lilies, another brown, its walls hung with risqué drawings; the third is a candlelit mushroom-cream. There's a steely bar with sandblasted glass panels, great flagstones and a winter fire. At the back, a split-level lounge with wooden floors, elegant tub chairs and a garden that heads off into open countryside; there's also a stylish paved area outside. The food is popular and the dishes imaginative and colourful, from simple soup to ploughman's with pork pie and pickles to roast pork belly with black pudding.

Meals	Bar meals from £5.
	Lunch & dinner £9.95–£18.50.
	Sunday roast £12.95–£13.75.
Closed	3pm–6pm.
	Open all day Sat & Sun.

Meals	Lunch & dinner £5.95–£18.95.
	Sunday roast £12.75.
Closed	Sun evenings from 6pm.

Colin & Teresa Ombler
Bell Inn,
Binton Road, Welford-on-Avon,
Stratford-upon-Avon CV37 8EB
Tel   +44 (0)1789 750353
Web   www.thebellwelford.co.uk

Entry 654 Map 8

Sally Coll
The Crabmill,
Preston Bagot,
Henley-in-Arden B95 5EE
Tel   +44 (0)1926 843342
Web   www.thecrabmill.co.uk

Entry 655 Map 8

The Rose & Crown
Warwick

Peach Pubs' flagship Rose & Crown opens for breakfast bacon sarnies and stays open all day. Enter the cheery front bar with its red and white walls, big leather sofas and crackling winter fire. To the back is the bustling eating area and a private room for parties. The food is scrummy and children enjoy downsized versions from the main menu. The tapas-style portions of cheeses, hams, mixed olives and rustic breads slip down easily with a pint of Purity Gold or a glass of pinot, while hot dishes are modern British with a Mediterranean slant. Try roast cod with pea purée, smoked haddock and prawn pie with winter greens, or Cornish lamb casserole with creamy mash. Young, fun and conveniently central for Warwick, which has history in spades.

Meals	Bar meals £5.
	Lunch from £7.
	Dinner from £11.
	Sunday roast £13.50.
Closed	Christmas Day.

Suzie Ayling
The Rose & Crown,
30 Market Place,
Warwick CV34 4SH

Tel	+44 (0)1926 411117
Web	www.roseandcrownwarwick.co.uk

Entry 656 Map 8

The Star & Garter
Leamington Spa

A gorgeous Leamington pub in the heartland of Warwickshire. Find a fun, light and airy bar on two levels, with wooden floors, upholstered wall benches, colourful quirky leather easy chairs, red walls in window-seat snugs, bold silver stars, a warming log fire, and big windows with street views. There's a dining area beyond with an open kitchen, and an enticing private dining room with a terrace upstairs – ideal for family gatherings. Using free range meats from Aubrey Allen, menus offer daily roasts, deli boards served all day, devilled lamb's kidneys, tempura monkfish cheeks, sticky toffee pudding. Don't miss the Sunday jazz brunches, or Monday night's Burger & Blues.

Meals	Lunch & dinner £11.50–£18.75.
Closed	Open all day.

Jeremy Kynaston
The Star & Garter,
4-6 Warwick Street,
Leamington Spa CV32 5LL

Tel	+44 (0)1926 359960
Web	www.starandgarterleamington.co.uk

Entry 657 Map 8

Warwickshire

The Case is Altered
Hatton

No food, no mobiles and a Sopwith Pup propeller suspended from the ceiling – a Warwickshire treasure. There's even a vintage bar billiards machine, operated by sixpences from behind the bar. In the main room are terracotta tiles, leather-covered settles and walls covered in yellowing posters offering beverages at a penny a pint. Jackie does not open her arms to children or dogs: this is a place for liquid refreshment only – and devotees travel some distance for the homemade pork scratchings and the expertly kept beer. The sign used to show lawyers arguing but the name has nothing to do with the law; once it was, simply, 'The Case', and so small that it was not eligible for a spirit licence. Later it was made larger, the name was changed, and everyone was happy. They've been that way ever since.

Warwickshire

The Bluebell
Henley-in-Arden

Leigh and Duncan Taylor went to town updating this 500-year-old coaching inn – one of the most distinctive bistro pubs in the country. A clever combination of country casual and urban chic means atmosphere and style are delivered in spades: bold colours and striking furniture meet ancient beams, flagstones and a big fireplace. Real ales, wines and an irresistible menu draw keen diners from far and near, ingredients are sourced with care, vegetables are grown on the owners' allotment. The menu combines colourful modern dishes – dill-cured Loch Duart salmon, Salcombe crab fritter, and Jimmy Butler's free-range pork for two (loin, belly, cheeks, crackling). Beer-battered haddock with hand-cooked chips are a favourite. Lunch on the decked area is sublime.

Meals	No food served.
Closed	2.30pm–6pm. 2.15pm–7pm Sun.

Meals	Lunch & dinner £13–£19. Set menu £15 & £18. Sunday roast £13.95. Afternoon tea £15. Not Monday & Sunday eve.
Closed	Mon (except Bank Holidays).

Jackie & Charlie Willacy
The Case is Altered,
Case Lane, Five Ways,
Hatton,
Warwick CV35 7JD
Tel   +44 (0)1926 484206

Entry 658 Map 8

Duncan & Leigh Taylor
The Bluebell,
93 High Street,
Henley-in-Arden B95 5AT
Tel   +44 (0)1564 793049
Web   www.bluebellhenley.co.uk

Entry 659 Map 8

Warwickshire

The Orange Tree
Chadwick End

The flagship pub of Classic Country Pubs has a striking interior. You'll love the earthy colours, the low limewashed beams, the log fires, big lamps, deep sofas around low tables and the airy dining rooms. This tastefully rustic décor, Mediterranean with oriental touches, is matched by an ambitious, Italian-inspired menu – note the gorgeous Italian-style deli counter showing off breads, cheeses and vintage oils. Food-lovers descend in droves for authentic fired pizzas and full-flavoured meat dishes cooked on the on-view rotisserie spit. There's homemade pasta, delicious warm salads, fish specials. All this plus great wines by the bottle or glass, real ales, a heated patio dotted with teak tables and all-day opening hours.

Meals	Lunch & bar meals from £5.95.
	Dinner £7.95–£25.95.
	Sunday roast from £12.95.
	Not Sunday eve.
Closed	Open all day.

Paul Hales
The Orange Tree,
Warwick Road, Chadwick End,
Solihull B93 0BN
Tel   +44 (0)1564 785364
Web   www.theorangetreepub.co.uk

🏃 🐕 🍸 📶

Entry 660 Map 8

Warwickshire

The Almanack
Kenilworth

Clever Peach Pubs continues to reinvent the gastropub. This, their tenth venture, is a swish new-build beneath apartments in Kenilworth town centre. It opened in 2009 and business has boomed since. Although more trendy bar-restaurant than pub, there's a vast island bar, lots of spacious informal seating and local Purity ales on tap. Expect a cool retro feel, with vintage 60s and 70s armchairs and sofas and a colourfully eclectic décor throughout. Pop in for breakfast or coffee and cake and settle down to free WiFi – or graze from a modern pub menu. In the all-day, open-to-view kitchen, corned beef hash and BLT sandwiches are created, along with substantial lunches and suppers: a daily roast, coq au vin with creamy mash, a fish deli-board, duck with redcurrant jus. Young and fun.

Meals	Bar meals from £5.
	Lunch from £6.75.
	Dinner from £11.
	Sunday roast £13.95.
Closed	Open all day.

Jonathan Carter
The Almanack,
Abbey End North,
Kenilworth CV8 1QJ
Tel   +44 (0)1926 353637
Web   www.thealmanack-kenilworth.co.uk

♿ 🏃 🐕 🍸 📶

Entry 661 Map 8

Warwickshire

The Malt Shovel at Barston
Barston

A smart, bright, food-driven place that knows its market and caters to it well. Whether you're ensconced in the powder-blue and cream bar (with a fire in the grate at the far end), on the trellis-shaded terrace in summer, or in the country restaurant, the food is to savour, and the Tribute and Old Speckled Hen are matched by decent wines. The menu covers international as well as pubby treats (Aberdeenshire rump steak; crayfish and cress breaded scampi with lemon and lavender dressing; sticky toffee pudding with clotted cream ice cream) and executes both with aplomb. The culinary innovation extends to the vegetarian options, perhaps a filo tart of crushed carrot topped with a poached egg, courgette strips and rocket pesto. A slick operation out in the country, warm, friendly and relaxed.

Meals	Lunch & dinner £11.95–£21.50. Not Sunday eve.
Closed	Open all day.

Helen Somerfield
The Malt Shovel at Barston,
Barston Lane, Barston,
Solihull B92 0JP
Tel   +44 (0)1675 443223
Web   www.themaltshovelatbarston.com

    点 戈 ⿰ ⛄ 🠶

Entry 662 Map 8

Warwickshire

The Boot Inn
Lapworth

The Boot was here long before the canal that runs past the back garden. With its exposed timbers, quarry floors, open fires and daily papers it combines old-fashioned charm with rustic chic. Under the guidance of Paul Salisbury and James Elliot, the once down-at-heel boozer became one of the first gastropubs of the Midlands. Menus have a distinct touch of Mediterranean and Pacific rim: fresh tian of spiced crab, Asian five-spice duck breast, dukkah-spiced rack of lamb, great Greek sharing plates topped with olives. Ingredients are as fresh as can be and seafood dishes are a speciality. Eat in the lounge or in the stylishly revamped dining room upstairs. In summer, go al fresco: there's a lovely terrace to the side.

Meals	Lunch from £6. Dinner from £9. Sunday roast £12.95.
Closed	Open all day.

Paul Salisbury & James Elliot
The Boot Inn,
Old Warwick Road, Lapworth,
Solihull B94 6JU
Tel   +44 (0)1564 782464
Web   www.lovelypubs.co.uk

    点 戈 ⿰ ⛄

Entry 663 Map 8

Warwickshire

The Punchbowl
Lapworth

The Punchbowl comes with a big pubby fire and a friendly bar dispensing Timothy Taylor's Landlord. But the building is new; the original burnt down a few years ago. James Feeney has a flair for design and from simple materials has created contemporary opulence: candelabra on long tables, ornate mirrors on brick walls, and windows swept by crushed velvet. And the food is really delicious – we chose a sharing platter of seared scallops with dressed crab, grilled prawns and fishcakes. Beef Wellington comes with wilted spinach and smoked potato purée, Gressingham duck breast with potato rösti, maple and black pepper. Thatcher's Gold cider washes it all down beautifully, there's a vegetarian dish of the day and the glassed-in patio has a conservatory feel.

Meals	Lunch from £5.95.
	Dinner from £9.95.
Closed	Open all day.

James Feeney
The Punchbowl,
Mill Lane, Lapworth,
Solihull B94 6HR
Tel   +44 (0)1564 784564
Web   www.thepunchbowllapworth.com

Entry 664 Map 8

Wiltshire

The Beckford Arms
Tisbury

You arrive in style: a fine sweep though the Fonthill estate and under the Triumphal Arch. Wash up at this country-house inn and expect to be seduced; after a severe fire it has risen, phoenix-like, from the ashes. Outside, a half-acre garden is ridiculously pretty – hammocks in the trees, parasols on the terrace, church spire soaring to the heavens – and this Georgian house is equally sublime, an inn for all seasons. Inside: a drawing room where facing sofas are warmed by a roaring fire; a restaurant with a wall of glass that opens onto the terrace; a bar with parquet flooring for an excellent local pint. Follow your nose and chance upon the odd chandelier, roaming wisteria, logs piled high inside and out and a rather grand mahogany table in the private dining room. Bedrooms are small but perfectly formed with prices to match: white walls, the best linen, sisal matting, super bathrooms. As for the food, there's much to please, perhaps marrow fritters with lemon mayo, local partridge with bread sauce, chocolate bread and butter pudding. There are film nights most Sundays; the cricket team comes to celebrate.

Rooms	7 doubles, 1 twin/double: £95–£120.
	2 pavilions for 2: £175–£195.
Meals	Dinner from £30.
Closed	Rarely.

Charlie Luxton
The Beckford Arms,
Fonthill Gifford, Tisbury,
Salisbury SP3 6PX

Tel   +44 (0)1747 870385
Web   www.beckfordarms.com

Entry 665 Map 3

The Castle Inn
Bradford-on-Avon

On top of the hill that dips down to the mellow heart of Bradford-on-Avon, this heart-warming renovation of a neglected Bath stone inn is the work of Flatcappers, who, in their first foray into the world of real pubs, have struck gold. Enter a warren of planked rooms – one large, three small – in muted greys, reds and greens, lovingly and imaginatively restored. Imagine solid stone walls and little log fires, recycled chairs and long farmhouse tables, a leather sofa to sink into, books on the shelves, prints on the walls and a youthful vibe. Six ales from local breweries dominate the bar as locals pop in for a pint and the papers, and muted jazz plays. An Anglo-Saxon take on tapas stands alongside British pub classics, the specials are special (rabbit ragout with handmade pappardelle) and our Sunday sirloin with Yorkshire pud was heaven. Above, four equally characterful bedrooms have modish wallpapers and stylish hues, wonky door frames and period fireplaces, stunning walk-in bathrooms and wide-reaching views of the church, or the White Horse on the Wiltshire hills. And breakfast lasts until 12!

Rooms	3 doubles, 1 family room for 4: £100–£140.
Meals	Lunch & dinner £7.95–£18.95.
Closed	Christmas Day & Boxing Day.

Ben Paxton
The Castle Inn,
Mount Pleasant,
Bradford-on-Avon BA15 1SJ
Tel   +44 (0)1225 865657
Web   www.flatcappers.co.uk

The Northey
Box

The former Box Station Hotel owes its architecture to Brunel. The glory for its refurbishment rests on the shoulders of Sally Warburton – an undeniable modernity now sashays down the corridors. Where Noël Coward once entertained with a song there is cool jazz from Ella or Frank so settle into the leather lounge area with a 6X or one of the many excellent wines on offer and get in the swing. 'Bib Gourmand' approved menus specialise in fish and offer hearty pub food, and sandwiches, ciabatta, salads and snacks. Eat in the large boldly lit dining area at chunky wooden tables, in the cosier bar or, in summer, out in the pretty garden beneath a pair of giant pines. Those staying the night will be royally spoilt as slick bedrooms sport pieces of one-off furniture and sculpture – and beds are super comfortable with dazzling white linen and thick mattresses. One room has a decked balcony, all have coffee-machines, while gorgeous bathrooms are a tribute to slate, stone and pale travertine – spaces to wallow in with thick robes and towels and Molton Brown toiletries. Prepare to pamper!

Rooms	5 doubles: £89–£145.
Meals	Lunch & bar meals from £6. Dinner from £11.
Closed	Rarely.

Mark Warburton
The Northey,
Bath Road, Box,
Corsham SN13 8AE
Tel   +44 (0)1225 742333
Web   www.ohhcompany.co.uk

The Old House at Home
Burton

If you're headed for Castle Combe or the Badminton Horse Trials, why not drop by the Old House at Home, a great little place for dinner and a bed? This traditional ivy-clad pub is no more than a five-minute drive away. The Warburton family have been at its helm for 28 years, with Mark and Matthew now driving the family business (which includes The Northey at Box) with passion and verve. Each of the six bedrooms, built from local stone in the hillside garden at the back, is named after a different wine from around the world and, although compact, are cosy and stylishly kitted out. Find wooden floors, rich fabrics, fashionable wallpapers, opulent throws, top-notch beds, coffee machines, plasma screens and fancy wet rooms. In contrast, tradition reigns supreme in the old pub, distinguished by ancient beams, old dining tables and crackling logs in a lovely open fireplace. Expect Wadworth 6X on tap and a wide-ranging menu that combines classics like ham, egg and chips with... tiger prawn and monkfish linguine, beef fillet flamed in cognac, infused with garlic, mushrooms and red wine, and orange and lime tart.

Rooms	5 doubles, 1 twin: £89-£140.
Meals	Lunch & bar meals from £6.
	Dinner from £11.
	Sunday lunch, 3 courses, £16.
Closed	Rarely.

Mark Warburton
The Old House at Home,
Burton,
Chippenham SN14 7LT
Tel   +44 (0)1454 218227
Web   www.ohhcompany.co.uk

Entry 668 Map 3

Wiltshire

Methuen Arms Hotel
Corsham

Built around the remains of a 14th-century nunnery, converted into a brewery and coaching inn in 1608, and with an impressive Georgian façade, the Methuen has history in spades. Restyled as a boutique inn following a sympathetic restoration, its doors swung open in 2010 to reveal a stunning interior. From a grand tiled hallway a sweeping staircase leads to ultra-stylish bedrooms, those in the former nunnery oozing character with wonky beams and other fascinating features. All have colourful headboards on big beds, wonderfully upholstered armchairs, funky colourful rugs and some rather swish bathrooms, the best with roll top tubs and walk-in showers. Back downstairs are rugs on stone and wood floors, crackling logs in old stone fireplaces, glowing candles on tables and vintage photos of Corsham; the traditional bar and informal dining rooms are truly inviting. A seasonal modern British menu is a further enticement, so tuck into pasta with game ragout; fish pie; lamb marinated in oregano and garlic. This grand, almost Tardis-like, inn promises more rooms in the future.

Rooms	11 doubles, 2 twin/doubles: £140-£175. 1 family room for 4: £150-£220. Singles from £90.
Meals	Lunch from £5.95. Early supper £18.50-£21.50. Sunday roast from £18.50. Dinner, 3 courses, from £30.
Closed	Rarely.

Martin & Debbie Still
Methuen Arms Hotel,
2 High Street,
Corsham SN13 0HB
Tel   +44 (0)1249 717060
Web   www.themethuenarms.com

Entry 669 Map 3

Sign of the Angel
Lacock

You might find the cast of Downton Abbey staying at this 15th-century coaching inn — and for method actors, it must be a dream. Occupying centre-stage in one the prettiest of all English villages, the Sign of the Angel is a genuine period piece: all chalky whitewash and wonky beams, artful oak furniture and flagstoned passageways. The inn was taken over by energetic young brothers Tom and Jack last year, and has been impeccably renovated to trumpet its age. The owners are from farming stock, and it shows in head chef Jon's menu: everything from the bread to the sorbets are locally sourced and homemade: warm mackerel rarebit, brioche and heritage tomato salad; baked tenderloin in local bacon stuffed with pear and Bath cheese; Bramley crumble with toffee apple ice cream. Upstairs, the bedrooms let the antique architecture do the talking: pretty box windows and wainscotting; beams that extend into the bathrooms as well as the bedrooms. The duck-feather bed linen is a narcoleptic's nightmare, and the chef's home-made cookies are waiting on your tea tray.

Rooms	5 doubles: £120–£140.
Meals	Lunch from £5.50.
	Dinner from £16.
	Sunday lunch, 2 courses £19;
	3 courses £22.
	Cream teas from £7.50.
Closed	Rarely.

Tom Nicholas
Sign of the Angel,
6 Church Street,
Lacock SN15 2LB
Tel   +44 (0)1249 730230
Web   www.signoftheangel.co.uk

Wiltshire

The George & Dragon
Rowde

Behind the whitewashed exterior hides a low-ceilinged bar, its stone fireplace ablaze in winter, its half-panelled walls lined with old paintings, its antique clock ticking away the hours. Furnishings are authentically period, there are wooden boards in the dining room, painted walls and plenty of dark timber. The kitchen's chutneys and preserves are for sale, international bottled beers and organic ciders line the shelves and hand-pumped Butcombe Bitter announces itself on the bar. Experienced owners are maintaining the pub's reputation for fish delivered fresh from Cornwall – with the odd concession to meat eaters. There are puddings to diet for, and specials such as delectable chargrilled scallops with black pudding brochettes or whole grilled mackerel with anchovy butter. Rooms are charming and individual – Country, Classic or Funky – with wall timbers and wonky floors, contemporary wall coverings, White Company duvets and linen on wooden or brass beds; bathrooms are the business; the complimentary breakfast is continental. Great value, and a treat to come back to after a long walk along the Kennet & Avon Canal.

Rooms	2 twin/doubles, 1 family room for 2: £55–£115.
Meals	Lunch & dinner £9.95–£18.50. Sunday roast £19.50.
Closed	Rarely.

Chris Day & Michelle & Philip Hale
The George & Dragon,
High Street, Rowde,
Devizes SN10 2PN
Tel +44 (0)1380 723053
Web www.thegeorgeanddragonrowde.co.uk

Entry 671 Map 3

Red Lion Freehouse & Troutbeck Guest House
East Chisenbury

Unless you found yourself lost on Salisbury Plain, chances are you wouldn't stumble upon the Red Lion. You'd be missing much: this smart thatched village inn is a local serving ale from Wiltshire microbreweries, a restaurant drawing food lovers from far and wide, and, since December 2012, a glorious place to stay, with the addition of ultra cosy rooms in a spruced up property (Troutbeck) just down the lane. Having worked under Thomas Keller at the breathtaking Per Se restaurant in New York, owner-chefs Guy and Brittany Manning apply cutting-edge cookery techniques to simple rustic dishes and the results are very special. The Michelin-starred menu offers the likes of chicken liver pâté with Madeira jelly, braised ox cheek with mash, bacon, and red wine, and caramel poached apples with candied walnuts and sage ice cream. Indulge yourself and then retire to one of the five very individual rooms; all have luxury Somnus beds, the finest cotton and down, Bang & Olufsen flatscreens, fluffy bathrobes and organic smellies in natural stone bathrooms, and a private deck with serene rural views across the Avon chalk stream. Exceptional.

Rooms	5 doubles: £130–£230.
Meals	Bar meals from £7.
	Lunch & dinner £15–£20.
	Sunday lunch, 2 courses, £20.
Closed	Rarely.

Guy & Brittany Manning
Red Lion Freehouse
& Troutbeck Guest House,
East Chisenbury, Pewsey SN9 6AQ
Tel   +44 (0)1980 671124
Web   www.redlionfreehouse.com

Wiltshire

The Bell at Ramsbury
Ramsbury

New owners snapped up The Bell, creating a classy new-wave inn and one that showcases Ramsbury Estate produce. Come for Ramsbury beers, kitchen garden fruit and veg, and seasonal game. Completing this pleasing picture are nine stunning bedrooms named after game birds and fish. Cosy lodgings for fishermen, and for those exploring the glorious Marlborough Downs, they come with soothing Farrow & Ball colours, rich fabrics, down duvets, big beds, vintage books, and super bathrooms with rain showers, White Company lotions and heated slate floors. Back downstairs, accompany your fish and chips with a pint of Gold in the smart, hop-adorned bar, or bag the sofa in the library-style lounge and entertain yourself with a copy of *The Field*. Or pop into the stylish restaurant for assiette of spring lamb, followed by lemon ice mousse perhaps. There's also a wonderful little café (Café Bella) at the back, serving teas, coffee and cakes during the day. As for the village, it's really pretty, and the pub, standing neatly just off the main square, is 100 yards from the river bank.

Rooms	7 doubles, 2 twins: £110–£150.
Meals	Bar meals £7–£17.
	Lunch £20–£25.
	Dinner £30–£45.
	Sunday lunch, 2 courses, £19.50.
Closed	Rarely.

Ramsbury Estates
The Bell at Ramsbury,
The Square, Ramsbury,
Marlborough SN8 2PE
Tel   +44 (0)1672 520230
Web   www.thebellramsbury.com

The Red Lion Inn
Cricklade

A stroll from the ancient North Meadow, famous for its spring show of wild fritillaries, the rambling old coaching inn lies off the Thames path. Specialising in seasonal, locally sourced and often organic food, it combines contemporary features with a charming 16th-century fabric and extends its welcome to all (and that includes your dog). In the red-carpeted bar, all low beams, stone walls, ancient settles and log fires, treat yourself to a pint of ale; the choice is mind-boggling, from Arbor Motueka to Butcombe Bitter. Lunches involve the best of English classics: real burgers with triple-cooked chips; chicken and locally foraged wild mushroom pie; delicious homemade bread and a beer to match each dish. Evening dishes, served at reclaimed wooden tables in the elegant restaurant, include tea-smoked salmon, roast local pork with crispy potatoes, black pudding and sprouting broccoli, rhubarb and ginger crumble. The pick of the bedrooms are the two in the old stables with their stone walls and tiled floors, chunky, hand-crafted beds, crisp linen, and bathrooms that sparkle.

Rooms	3 doubles, 2 twin/doubles: £80–£90. Extra bed/sofabed £20 per person per night.
Meals	Lunch & bar meals from £6. Dinner from £9. Sunday lunch, 3 courses, £19.95.
Closed	Rarely.

	Tom Gee
	The Red Lion Inn,
	74 High Street,
	Cricklade SN6 6DD
Tel	+44 (0)1793 750776
Web	www.theredlioncricklade.co.uk

Wiltshire

The Potting Shed Pub
Crudwell

Jonathan and Julian, owners of the Rectory Hotel across the road, have transformed the village inn. Open fireplaces and kilim sofas fat with cushions make you feel at home, while door handles fashioned from trowels, hand pumps from fork handles and old butchers' block tables will have you smiling. Eat in the big airy dining room with mix 'n' match antiques, or in one of the cosy corners around the bar. The food is exuberantly British, from game boudin to turkey stuffed with parmesan. Two acres and an apple orchard at the back have been turned into an organic vegetable patch, while local ales, and dog treats on the bar, reflect the focus on real-pub values. There's an excellent children's menu and puds to warm your heart; try the egg custard tart with clove honey.

Meals	Lunch from £5.50.
	Dinner from £11.95.
Closed	Open all day.

Jonathan Barry & Julian Muggridge
The Potting Shed Pub,
Crudwell,
Malmesbury SN16 9EW
Tel   +44 (0)1666 577833
Web www.thepottingshedpub.com

Entry 675 Map 3

Wiltshire

The Vine Tree
Norton

With a fine store of ales and over 40 wines by the glass the former watermill is a watering hole in every sense. It may be hidden away but the faithful return for the food and the beer. On Sundays, memorable roast sirloin of beef from the neighbour's farm is served with all the trimmings. There's plenty of fresh fish, too, local game in season, sautéed scallops with wild mushroom risotto, and a very pretty niçoise salad. Cheeses are local and delicious. Service is young and friendly and surroundings are inviting: deep red walls, candlelight and beams, a wood-burning stove. Tables in the minuscule upstairs room are super-cosy; in summer, eat and chat on the big immaculate terrace. This Vine Tree has a rich harvest for guests (and their dogs) to reap, and the walking is lovely.

Meals	Bar meals from £4.95.
	Lunch from £8.95.
	Dinner from £13.95.
	Not Sun eve in winter.
Closed	2.30pm-7pm Mon-Sat.
	Open midday-3.15pm Sun.

Charles Walker & Tiggi Wood
The Vine Tree,
Foxley Road, Norton,
Malmesbury SN16 0JP
Tel   +44 (0)1666 837654
Web www.thevinetree.co.uk

Entry 676 Map 3

Wiltshire

The Rattlebone Inn
Sherston

Built in the late 17th century and named after Saxon warrior John Rattlebone, this village pub is all flagstones and low beams, and friendly Rob distributing Young's Bitter and St Austell Tribute. There are numerous nooks and crannies from which you can delve into the menus: perhaps Gloucester Old Spot belly of pork with bubble and squeak and cider gravy, or potted smoked haddock with a poached egg. There are interesting wines too, and good cheeses and desserts like white chocolate and pistachio cheesecake with salted caramel. A wood-burner keeps things toasty in winter while outside, just off Sherston's high street, are two patio areas, a pair of boules pistes and a skittle alley. On certain days you can try Mangold hurling – an old West Country sport.

Meals	Lunch from £5.95.
	Dinner from £11.50.
	Sunday roast from £10.50.
Closed	3pm-5pm.
	Open all day Sat & Sun.

Jason Read
The Rattlebone Inn,
Church Street, Sherston,
Malmesbury SN16 0LR

Tel +44 (0)1666 840871
Web www.therattlebone.co.uk

Entry 677 Map 3

Wiltshire

The White Horse Inn
Compton Bassett

Whitewashed walls echo the chalk horse that gave its name to this very handsome village inn. Inside all is as neat as a new pin. Lovingly polished parquet glows beneath scrubbed wooden tables, while padded bar stools and assorted chairs – some antique and carved – are well spaced around the reclaimed oak bar. Having been a grocer's shop, a bakery and an inn during its long life the pub now focuses on what it does best: providing great food and drink to villagers and visitors. Eat by the sturdy wood-burner in the bar or in the elegant terracotta dining area with its beams and mullioned windows. Lunches are relaxed affairs of sandwiches and pub classics (homemade sausages and creamy mash, dried smoked bacon and red wine shallot jus). Dinner lists pork and game from the pub's own farm in season, and children are well looked after.

Meals	Bar meals from £5.95.
	Lunch from £9.95.
	Dinner from £11.95.
	Sunday roast from £10.95.
Closed	Open all day.

Danny & Tara Adams
The White Horse Inn,
Compton Bassett,
Calne SN11 8RG

Tel +44 (0)1249 813118
Web www.whitehorse-comptonbassett.co.uk

Entry 678 Map 3

Wiltshire

The Barbury Inn
Broad Hinton

Discover ancient and mysterious chalk downland scenery all around with horses both real and carved onto hillsides. This late 18th-century inn sits beside the road to Avebury and has been given a kind makeover with a plush-rustic mix of exposed brick, scrubbed pine and painted furniture, rattan chairs and pews — it's all super-civilised. Take your pick from St Austell or Prescott ale or peruse the extensive wine list. Chef Roger Hawkshaw believes in letting the produce do the talking, seasonal menus feature his own salted beef and tongue, terrines, pickles and sauces, and bread. There's fillet of Loch Duart salmon, olive mustard potatoes, roasted peppers and basil pesto too, as well as pub classics and great desserts. After a blast along The Ridgeway, a mile away, this is the perfect post-walk treat.

Meals	Lunch & dinner £10.75–£19.75.
Closed	Open all day.

Charles Walker & Tiggi Wood
The Barbury Inn,
Broad Hinton,
Swindon SN4 9PF
Tel   +44 (0)1793 731510
Web   www.thebarburyinn.co.uk

Entry 679 Map 3

Wiltshire

The Royal Oak
Bishopstone

Passionately organic, delightfully unpreachy. In 2005 the simple pub in the idyllic village was taken on by farmer Helen Browning and has been flying the flag ever since. There's food bartering with locals, a wild garden with barbecues (they provide the produce, you do the rest) and open days with hay bales for kids to romp on. The planked, beamed open-plan bar has a roaring fire and the staff are friendly, but best of all is the menu that changes twice daily: crayfish from the Thames served with Bishopstone watercress, home-cured bacon from home-reared pigs, asparagus from Lotmead down the road, fish from the boats out of Newlyn, gooseberries from the garden. Perfect ingredients, perfect food, beer from Arkells and six wines by the glass.

Meals	Bar meals £3.95–£6.50.
	Lunch & dinner £8–£20.
	Sunday roast from £12.50.
Closed	3pm–6pm.
	Open all day Sat & Sun.

Helen & Tim Browning Finney
The Royal Oak,
Easterbrook Farm, Bishopstone,
Swindon SN6 8PP
Tel   +44 (0)1793 790481
Web   www.royaloakbishopstone.co.uk

Entry 680 Map 3

Wiltshire

The Three Tuns
Great Bedwyn

Drive through woodland from Marlborough to arrive at a pretty village and this late 18th-century pub, in the capable hands of a young husband and wife team. James has gained experience in London, Seattle and Italy and places a very homemade emphasis on his modern classic pub dishes. Begin with seared scallops, deep fried ham hock ballotine and cauliflower purée before a wild venison burger with bacon and onion jam and chips, then perhaps toffee apple crème brûlée and cinnamon shortbread. The bar has a well-loved traditional feel with a glorious brick fireplace, old floorboards and panelling, beams and rustic signage. A lovely place to raise a pint of Butcombe or Ramsbury ale, poured by smiley Ashley. Plus a small garden with a boules pitch, and Savernake Forest nearby.

Wiltshire

The Malet Arms
Newton Tony

Formerly a bakehouse for a long-lost manor, the old flintstone pub draws walkers from miles. Expect cracking local ales, country cooking and a cheerful welcome from the Cardews. The low-beamed bar, all rustic furnishings, log fires, old pictures and interesting bits and pieces, would be a cosy spot for a pint of Stonehenge Heel Stone. Hearty food, listed on boards above the fireplaces, reflects the rural setting, with local game (shot by Noel) a winter favourite. Fill your boots with a rich stew of pheasant and pigeon in Guinness, proper fish and chips or a local beefburger, and follow with Annie's speciality: an old English pudding (try the walnut and date tart). The pub cricket team play on the field opposite and there's a summer music festival in the paddock. A true community pub.

Meals	Starters £6–£9.
	Lunch & dinner £12–£22.
Closed	Mon.

Meals	Lunch & dinner £9.50–£15.
Closed	3pm-6pm.
	3pm-7pm Sun.

Ashley & James Wilsey
The Three Tuns,
1 High Street, Great Bedwyn,
Marlborough SN8 3NU
Tel +44 (0)1672 870280
Web www.threetunsbedwyn.co.uk

Entry 681 Map 3

Noel & Annie Cardew
The Malet Arms,
Newton Tony,
Salisbury SP4 0HF
Tel +44 (0)1980 629279
Web www.maletarms.com

Entry 682 Map 3

Wiltshire

The Horseshoe Inn
Ebbesbourne Wake

The Ebble Valley and Ebbesbourne Wake appear to have escaped the modern age. A bucolic charm pervades this village inn, dozing down tiny lanes close to the Dorset border and run as a "proper country pub" by the Bath family for 30 years. Climbing roses cling to the 17th-century brick façade, while the traditional layout – two bars around a central servery – survives. Old farming implements and country bygones fill every available cranny and a mix of furniture is arranged around the crackling winter fire. Beer is tapped straight from the cask and food is hearty and wholesome, prepared by Pat Bath using local meat and veg, and game from the shoots. Tuck into steak and kidney pie, fresh fish bake, nursery puddings and three roasts on Sundays (do book). Benches and flowers fill the garden.

Wiltshire

The Forester Inn
Donhead St Andrew

Tiny lanes frothing with cowparsley twist down to this wonderful little pub in Donhead St Andrew. The revitalised 600-year-old inn has rustic walls and low dark beams, logs in the inglenook and planked floors; colours are muted, there's not an ounce of flounce and locals still prop up the bar of a late weekday lunchtime. People travel some way for Andrew Kilburn's cooking: a trio of lamb chops with bubble and squeak, a goat's cheese omelette, a pudding cooked to order; the food is seriously good. Andrew uses local Rushmore venison, Old Spot pork and specialises in fresh Cornish seafood – brill with shellfish bisque and mussels, skate wing with brown butter and capers. Lucky dogs get delicious gravy bones, the garden terrace has views, there are three ales on tap, Westons Organic cider and ten gorgeous wines by the glass.

Meals	Bar meals £4.95–£12.95. Lunch & dinner £9.95–£17. Sunday roast from £9.50. Tuesday eve 'Simple Supper' £10.
Closed	3pm–6.30pm. Sun from 4pm & Mon until 7pm.

Meals	Bar meals from £7. Lunch from £7.50. Dinner from £12.50. Sunday lunch, 3 courses, £25.50. Not Sunday eve.
Closed	3pm–6.30pm. Sun from 4pm.

2015/16
Sawday's
PUB AWARD

Authentic pub

Anthony & Patricia Bath
The Horseshoe Inn,
The Cross,
Ebbesbourne Wake,
Salisbury SP5 5JF
Tel   +44 (0)1722 780474

Entry 683 Map 3

Chris & Lizzie Matthews
The Forester Inn,
Lower Street, Donhead St Andrew,
Shaftesbury SP7 9EE
Tel   +44 (0)1747 828038
Web   www.theforesterdonheadstandrew.co.uk

Entry 684 Map 3

Wiltshire

Fox & Hounds
East Knoyle

Beech trees and high ridges: make time for a walk with views over the vale, then land at the 17th-century thatched pub on the green. Inside are two areas: one bright and conservatory-like, with a great view, the other older and cosier, its fireplace flanked by small red leather sofas. There are warming ales from Palmers and Butcombe, and Hop Back's inimitable Summer Lightning, and a well-presented wine card that tells you exactly what you'll get. No-nonsense New Zealander Murray cooks in an eclectic, untypical gastro style. Tuck into a chorizo, bean and red pepper casserole in red wine with belly pork, or a sweet onion, ricotta and parmesan tart, and follow with melting chocolate fondant and mascarpone cream; no need to feel sinful. Then stay till the pub closes.

Meals	Lunch & dinner £9-£17.
Closed	3pm-5.30pm.

Murray Seator
Fox & Hounds, The Green,
East Knoyle, Salisbury SP3 6BN
Tel   +44 (0)1747 830573
Web   www.foxandhounds-
eastknoyle.co.uk

Entry 685 Map 3

Wiltshire

The Bath Arms at Longleat
Horningsham

A 17th-century coaching inn on the Longleat estate in a small village lost in the country; geese swim in the river, cows laze in the fields and lush woodland wraps around you. Inside find flagstones and boarded floors, Farrow & Ball paints; outside, two large stone terraces, separated by beds of lavender, (you can eat out here in good weather). The restaurant takes food and drink seriously and there is a commitment to very local, very fresh ingredients and traditional preserving methods: smoking, curing, potting and pickling – try the game and ale pie with homemade pastry. The wine list is comprehensive and a good selection of draught beer includes Pride and Golden Apostle from Wessex Brewery. Bring the children (and the pooch); the staff are super friendly. Longleat is at the bottom of the hill – the walk down is majestic.

Meals	Lunch from £5.
	Dinner, 2 courses, £25.
	Set lunch £12.50 & £15.
Closed	Open all day.

Tommy Whitty
The Bath Arms at Longleat,
Horningsham,
Warminster BA12 7LY
Tel   +44 (0)1985 844308
Web   www.batharms.co.uk

Entry 686 Map 3

Wiltshire

The Boot
Berwick St James

In the pretty village of Berwick St James in the Till valley sits this 'real British inn' where Giles and Cathy are working their quiet magic. The striking building – 17th-century and listed, with flint and limestone bands – was once owned by Lord Malmesbury and was later home to a boot and shoemaker who gave it its name. Inside, it's richly atmospheric, and very welcoming. You can sit snugly at the fireside with a ploughman's and a pint, or bring the family for Sunday lunch. Lush gardens, great Wadworth beers and pub food cooked with passion draws visitors and walkers. Tuck into lavender and cider roast ham with eggs and home-cut wedges, or Barnsley chop with bubble and squeak; for the more adventurous, there's a crab, whisky and sweetcorn risotto. Dogs and children welcome.

Meals	Light lunches from £6.50.
	Mains from £10.
Closed	Mon (except Bank Holidays).

Giles & Cathy Dickinson
The Boot,
High Street, Berwick St James,
Salisbury SP3 4TN

Tel	+44 (0)1722 790243
Web	www.theboot.pub

Entry 687 Map 3

Wiltshire

The Woolpack
Sutton Veny

You can't judge a book by its cover and the interior of this traditional 1930s pub was magically transformed when Tim and Abbie swept in. A log fire crackles in the fireplace warming the polished oak floorboards and the seats closest to it. Vibrant artwork on the walls, exposed brickwork, jazzy fabrics and gentle background music all create an upbeat feel and, whilst not huge, there is a distinct drinking and eating area. You'll be instantly welcomed from behind the light modern bar where Ringwood and other local ales hold court and there are well-chosen wines to suit all. Large blackboards display freshly cooked dishes such as warm salad of scallops with crispy pancetta or carved duck breast, seasonal veggies and creamed potato; finish with a brioche and butter pudding. A fun stop.

Meals	Lunch & dinner £10.95–£21.95.
Closed	3pm–5.30pm Tues–Sat.
	Open from 5.30pm Mon and
	midday–3pm Sun.

Tim and Abbie Smith
The Woolpack,
High Street, Sutton Veny,
Warminster BA12 7AW

Tel	+44 (0)1985 840 834
Web	www.woolpackpub.co.uk

Entry 688 Map 3

Wiltshire

The Prince Leopold Inn
Upton Lovell

Named after Queen Victoria's youngest son 'The Leo' has, over the 150 years of its existence, been many things but has now perhaps reached its apogee. Step in to find a craftsman-built bar with super stylish bar stools; so down a pint of London Pride or Otter ale. A Victorian snug and some cosy parlour rooms lead off here; at the back is a contemporary dining room with views across the river Wyle to water meadows. Here – and in the bar – you can sample mezze style plates available as starters, mains or to share: perhaps grilled figs and halloumi cheese on a bed of leaves with a balsamic glaze, or oven-baked sardines with chilli, lemon and garlic. From pub classics to fine dining, from sandwiches to puddings, it's good news all the way.

Meals	Lunch & dinner £10.50–£19.
Closed	Open all day.

Liza Kearney
The Prince Leopold Inn,
Upton Lovell,
Warminster BA12 0JP
Tel   +44 (0)1985 850460
Web   www.princeleopold.co.uk

Entry 689 Map 3

Wiltshire

The Three Daggers
Edington

Superb pub, sparkling brewery, and first-class farm shop across the yard. Restored, renamed and rejuvenated, the Three Daggers thrives as a village local, and a stop-off for conscientious foodies. Find stripped beams, slate tiles, church candles on old dining tables, chapel chairs, cushioned benches, a blazing log fire and a new conservatory for dining. Flick through the papers with a pint of Stonehenge or tuck straight into Adrian's food. A sharing board laden with game goodies, a lamb shank shepherd's pie, a plate of pork belly with a cider and thyme sauce – it's all delicious, and so is the sticky toffee pudding. Sample their wares on brewery nights, every Thursday. Check out the farm shop before you go, magnificent inside and out; and don't miss Edington's church.

Meals	Bar meals from £6.50.
	Lunch from £9.50.
	Dinner from £12.
Closed	3pm-5pm.
	Open all day Sat & Sun.
	Open all day every day April-Sept.

Robin Brown
The Three Daggers,
Westbury Road, Edington,
Westbury BA13 4PG
Tel   +44 (0)1380 830940
Web   www.threedaggers.co.uk

Entry 690 Map 3

Wiltshire

The Muddy Duck
Bradford-on-Avon

In 1125 Cluniac monks founded a monastery in the village; this venerable building was their sleeping quarters. It became an alehouse in the 19th century to satisfy the miners who dug Bath stone from under these hills. Now it's a gorgeous old inn with an ancient wisteria gracing the stone courtyard at the front, then a smart terraced garden with views across open farmland behind. Inside, old and new mix gracefully: wooden floors, the odd beam and half-panelled walls, red leather bar stools, armchairs in front of the fire and low-hanging lamps in the restaurant. The bar plays host to a colourful cast of dog-walkers, farmers and shoot parties, who come for a pint of Butcombe. Don't miss the food, perhaps grilled sardines, rib-eye steak, local duck, honey panna cotta. Bath is close.

Wiltshire

The Fox
Broughton Gifford

You are in good hands here, along with the wire fox in the window. An amphitheatre of leather sofas and armchairs is the backdrop to a dazzling array of beverages: Gem, Otter and Butcombe ales, ciders from Bounders and Ashton Press, a score of malts, numerous high end spirits and some seriously good wines. But eat you must and the best is yet to come. Alex and his team are passionate about using seasonal, regional produce, and raise their own pigs to produce sausages, charcuterie, air- and wet-cured hams, and bacon – a smoke house is planned. As for the pork chops, they're the stuff of legend, and much of the bread is home-baked; you'll be joining the queue at the door. Behind is a garden flanked by pines and willows, tubs of herbs and vegetables; further back are the pigs and the hens. Prepare to unwind!

Meals	Lunch from £4.95.
	Dinner, 3 courses, from £30.
Closed	Open all day.

Meals	Lunch & bar meals from £8.50.
	Dinner from £11.95.
	Sunday lunch, 3 courses, £27.95.
	Not Sunday eve or Monday lunch.
Closed	Open all day.

Joe Holden
The Muddy Duck,
Monkton Farleigh,
Bath BA15 2QH
Tel   +44 (0)1225 858705
Web   www.themuddyduckbath.co.uk

Entry 691 Map 3

Alex Geneen
The Fox,
The Street, Broughton Gifford,
Melksham SN12 8PN
Tel   +44 (0)1225 782949
Web   www.thefox-broughtongifford.co.uk

Entry 692 Map 3

Talbot Inn
Newnham Bridge

This fine 19th-century red brick coaching inn once welcomed hop and apple pickers to the Teme Valley for a season's work. Now, after a meticulous renovation, it caters for weary travellers' needs in the best possible manner. Grab an armchair by the fire with a pint of Wye Valley or Hobson's Ale, and admire photos of local rural heritage. Menus operate from a specials board and have a rustic-contemporary appeal: start with goat's cheese on brioche, beetroot carpaccio and toasted pine nuts, before sea bass fillet, white bean mash, baby spinach and a citrus butter sauce. The beef wellington is a favourite, as is the pheasant in season. There's a peaceful lounge, a panelled dining room and charming staff and owners will see that your stay is just right. Bedrooms are calm, uncluttered and stylish with soft carpets, bespoke headboards and one-off pieces of furniture: bathrooms are equally sleek, with limestone tiling and White Company toiletries. All are a good size, have super-thick curtains to absorb a small amount of road noise, and beds for the sweetest of dreams.

Rooms	7 doubles: £85–£105.
Meals	Lunch & dinner £9.95–£14.95. Sunday roast £16.50 & £19.95.
Closed	Rarely.

Ian Dowling
Talbot Inn,
Newnham Bridge,
Tenbury Wells WR15 8JF

Tel   +44 (0)1584 781941
Web   www.talbotinnnewnhambridge.co.uk

Entry 693 Map 8

Worcestershire

Bell & Cross Inn
Clent

No cavernous interior but a network of small cosy rooms that reveal the roots of this 19th-century pub — and the determination of its owners to maintain its integrity. These cosy rooms decked in smart modern hues are usually filled with happy eaters, here for grilled sea bass with prawns and rocket, or a lightly tweaked pub classic such as faggots with cheese mash. Owner Roger Narbett — busy now at his other pub, The Chequers — was chef to the England football team and footie memorabilia lines the corridors. Wife Jo runs a brisk yet friendly service; co-owner Paul Mohan is a classically trained chef. It's still a place for the locals though, as they crowd into the snug bar with four real ales and an open fire. You're at the foot of the Clent hills yet close to Birmingham — and there's a nice big garden, too.

Worcestershire

The Chequers
Cutnall Green

The Chequers was rebuilt in the 1930s on the site of an ancient coaching inn. You'd never know: its open fires, comfy sofas and snug little booths have evolved as smoothly as its menu. While the thirsty gather round the church-panel bar with pints of Timothy Taylor's, the hungry head for the dining room, cosy and candlelit with cranberry walls, blond beams and a huge display of wines. Make the most of a vibrant 'mod Brit' menu from award-winning chef Roger Narbett: the food bursts with flavour. There's chicken liver parfait with plum compote, pot-roasted belly pork with crackling and duck-fat potatoes, and apple tarte tatin. And if the liqueur coffees catch your fancy, slip off and savour one in the Players' Lounge, a small room that has photos of Roger's Football Chef days.

Meals	Lunch & dinner £8.50–£15.50. Sunday roast £13.50.
Closed	3pm–6pm. Open all day Sun.

Meals	Bar meals £4.95–£11.95. Lunch & dinner £9.25–£16.25.
Closed	3pm–6pm (Mon–Sat). Open all day Sun.

	Roger & Jo Narbett Bell & Cross Inn, Bromsgrove Road, Clent, Stourbridge DY9 9QL
Tel	+44 (0)1562 730319
Web	www.bellandcrossclent.co.uk

Entry 694 Map 8

	Roger & Jo Narbett The Chequers, Kidderminster Road, Cutnall Green, Droitwich WR9 0PJ
Tel	+44 (0)1299 851292
Web	www.chequerscutnallgreen.co.uk

Entry 695 Map 8

Worcestershire

The Fleece Inn
Bretforton

"No potato crisps to be sold in the bar". So ordered Lola Taplin when The Fleece was bequeathed to the National Trust after 500 years in her family. It's the sort of tradition that thrives at this quintessential English pub where you pitch up for fresh local food, ales from Uley and their home-brewed cider. Local sausages with red onion marmalade the red wine gravy, Tewkesbury mustard mash vegetables and orchard apple crumble may tempt you but there is more. The Asparagus Festival commences in the courtyard, with an auction on the last Sunday in May, and summer festivals twirl with Morris dancers. The medieval barn, the perfect setting for weddings, is stuffed with historical artefacts, stone flagged floors, big log fires, ancient beams and a wonderful collection of pewter.

Meals	Bar meals from £5.25. Lunch & dinner from £8.75.
Closed	3pm-6pm Mon & Tues (September-May).

Nigel Smith
The Fleece Inn,
The Cross, Bretforton,
Evesham WR11 7JE
Tel   +44 (0)1386 831173
Web   www.thefleeceinn.co.uk

Entry 696 Map 8

Worcestershire

Butcher's Arms
Eldersfield

A 16th-century pub for Slow Foodies – with a lovely big garden where you can relax and enjoy the surroundings. The Butcher's is a place for regulars popping in for pints of Wye Valley Bitter from the cask and Herefordshire cider; now there's a Michelin star. Elizabeth does friendly front of house, James has a hands-on philosophy and cooks single-handedly for just 18 covers. His gutsy British dishes use local produce from named suppliers, so you can swoon over aged fillet of Hereford beef with oxtail in pastry, girolle mushrooms and fondant potato, or that old English delicacy Bath chap, served with potato scone and grain mustard. The finale? Seville orange marmalade pudding with Drambuie custard, should you fancy. A marvellous little place for some 'nose to tail' dining.

Meals	Lunch & dinner £16-£24. Bookings only at lunch. Not Sunday eve or Monday. Not Bank Holidays.
Closed	2.30pm-7pm. Sun evenings & Mon all day. 10 days in August & January.

James & Elizabeth Winter
Butcher's Arms,
Lime Street, Eldersfield,
Gloucester GL19 4NX
Tel   +44 (0)1452 840381
Web   www.thebutchersarms.net

Entry 697 Map 8

Worcestershire

The Inn at Welland
Welland

David and Gillian have created a 'contemporary traditional' style that effortlessly flows. Those who just want to sup their Butty Bach or Otter bitter, can – but the main sweep has gorgeous limestone tile flooring and a mix of tables and chairs. A bleached wooden sideboard dispenses Provençal olives and artisan breads and beside it a stack of wine cases is filled with bin end bottles – for later perhaps? The kitchen team (now with a dedicated pastry chef) serve up a proper gastro medley, including ice creams, sorbets and petit fours. Enjoy pan fried Cornish scallops with a pea mint purée, crisp lardons and tomato oil followed by crisp belly pork, garlic mash, pak choi, orange and ginger jus. There are log fires and, in the garden, one of the terraces has a glass veranda with a wood-burner.

Meals	Lunch & dinner from £11.
	Bar meals from £6.50.
	Sunday roast £21.50 & £26.
Closed	Mon & Sun evenings.

David & Gillian Pinchbeck
The Inn at Welland,
Drake Street, Welland,
Malvern WR13 6LN
Tel   +44 (0)1684 592317
Web   www.theinnatwelland.co.uk

Entry 698 Map 8

Worcestershire

Nag's Head
Malvern

It's easily passed by, but this low-slung white pub, converted from what was a row of cottages, is worth hunting down. Tucked away down the side streets of lovely Malvern it's a paradise for fans of whisky and real ale; lovers of either may have to be stretcher'd off. There are 25 single malts on offer and 15 beers on tap, three of which are made at the pub's brewery at Callow End. No wonder the artefact-crammed bar, almost Dickensian in character, gets packed. Stick to the timber-clad dining room (once a boxing gym) for food – hearty homemade fare (ham hock terrine, cajun monkfish) is what you'll find – and let the serious ale buffs monopolise the bar. A pub's pub managed by helpful, chatty staff. A great find.

Meals	Lunch & dinner £10.50–£17.50.
Closed	Open all day.

Claire Keane
Nag's Head,
Bank Street,
Malvern WR14 2JG
Tel   +44 (0)1684 574373
Web   www.nagsheadmalvern.co.uk

Entry 699 Map 8

The Horseshoe Inn
Levisham

This handsome old stone built, pantile roofed pub takes pride of place at the head of stunning, broad-laned Levisham, a magnet for train enthusiasts – the North Yorks Moors railway runs through the bottom of the valley a mile down the road. You're guaranteed the warmest of welcomes in the Horseshoe with its oak-floored, beamed bar, and a pleasing pub grub menu promises the likes of Whitby haddock with chunky chips, and venison pie. Well-kept Theakstons and Yorkshire Moors from the local Cropton Brewery keeps the real ale lovers happy – park yourself in front of a roaring open fire with a pint and the paper after a stroll through nearby Dalby Forest. There's so much to do and see locally you should make a night or two of it; opt for one of the luxurious, contemporary 'garden rooms' with big beds, fat mattresses and spanking new bathrooms. If you fancy a fabulous view down the village, take a cosy, spotless room above the pub. Either way, this is the ideal base for some serious yomping (terrific walks start from the door), or a trip down memory lane on the steam train.

Rooms	4 doubles, 3 twin/doubles: £80–£90.
	2 singles: £40.
Meals	Bar meals from £5.95.
	Lunch from £4.95.
	Dinner from £10.50.
	Sunday lunch, 3 courses, £20.
Closed	Rarely.

Charles & Toby Wood
The Horseshoe Inn,
Main Street, Levisham,
Pickering YO18 7NL

| Tel | +44 (0)1751 460240 |
| Web | www.horseshoelevisham.co.uk |

Entry 700 Map 13

The Fox & Hounds
Sinnington

The 18th-century coaching inn sits handsomely on the main street in sleepy Sinnington, on the edge of the North Yorkshire moors; the mounting block by the front door hints at its past. You feel embraced by the place the moment you walk in: Andrew and Catherine have been welcoming folk for many years and have hospitality down to a fine art. The feel is utterly traditional, all oak settles, open fires, prints on dark green walls and hops hanging from beams; relax with a pint of Copper Dragon or a seasonal brew from the Black Sheep brewery while choosing your lunch. Seared King scallops with saffron and fennel risotto makes a mouthwatering starter; follow with roast Gressingham duck breast in a red wine jus or the seafood platter. If you can find room – portions are generous – the assiette of puddings is perfect for sharing: chocolate and honeycomb torte, crème caramel, treacle tart and blackberry cheesecake with homemade ice cream. There are ten comfy, homely, spotless bedrooms, four of them on the ground floor, all with crisp linen, most with modern bathrooms. Lovely. *Minimum stay: 2 nights at weekends.*

Rooms	8 doubles, 2 twins: £70–£170. Singles £59–£94.
Meals	Light lunch from £9.95. Dinner £11.50–£23.75. Sunday lunch, 3 courses, £22.
Closed	25-27 December.

Andrew & Catherine Stephens
The Fox & Hounds,
Main Street, Sinnington,
York YO62 6SQ

Tel	+44 (0)1751 431577
Web	www.thefoxandhoundsinn.co.uk

Judge's Lodging
York

Across Museum Gardens, in the centre of York, is this handsome Georgian townhouse with a strikingly luxurious interior. In the cellar: vaulted rooms, cool tunes, stone floors, Farrow & Ball colours, quirky mismatched furniture. Upstairs: three dining rooms, grand, elegant and eye-catching. Vintage grey-blue panelling, tall sash windows, semi-circular sofas, illuminated sculptures. All is cosy but classy, and the service is informal but attentive. If our butter bean stew with confit duck on chorizo was anything to go by, the food is impressive too, and the double pork chop, dominating a chunky wooden platter, was packed with flavour. The wines are wide-ranging and the beers are Thwaites, delivered in perfect condition from a giant copper tank. Join the punters on the galleried decked terrace and unwind, then treat yourself to a stay in a top-notch room with feature wallpapers and fabulous beds. The quietest are away from the courtyard, and the grandest and most graceful at the top of the house, one with an original marble fireplace and a York Minster view. Breakfasts are sumptuous.

Rooms	21 doubles: £100–£125.
Meals	Lunch from £4.95.
	Dinner from £9.
Closed	Rarely.

Rachel Mayes
Judge's Lodging,
9 Lendal,
York YO1 8AQ
Tel   +44 (0)1904 639312
Web   www.judgeslodgingyork.co.uk

Entry 702 Map 13

The Durham Ox
Crayke

At the picturesque top of the Grand Old Duke of York's hill is an L-shaped bar of flagstones and rose walls, worn leather armchairs, carved panelling and big fires. There are two more bars to either side, a new wood floored extension with exposed brickwork and a dapper wine-themed restaurant that draws all and sundry. Chalkboards above the stone fireplace and seasonal menus list game terrine with homemade chutney, prime Yorkshire rib-eye steak, frites with béarnaise sauce and rich sunken chocolate tart. The Bar Bites menu and the Sunday roasts are inevitably popular. There's a coffee shop serving homemade truffles, and a garden with a marquee for frivolity. No need to drive home: the delightfully quirky rooms in the old farmworkers' cottages have been renovated in contemporary, country-house style. Expect original quarry-tile floors, warmly painted walls, beams and revamped bathrooms, and a new room in the pub, The Studio, reached via its own outside staircase. The long views across the valley are stunning; in summer, flowers burst from stone troughs. Peacefulness 20 minutes outside York.

Rooms	1 cottage for 4, 4 cottages for 2: £120-£180 per night. 1 studio for 2: £150 per night. Singles £100-£150. Extra bed/sofabed £30 per person per night.
Meals	Bar meals from £6.95. Lunch & dinner £8.95-£26.95. Sunday roast from £14.95.
Closed	Rarely.

Michael Ibbotson
The Durham Ox,
Westway, Crayke,
York YO61 4TE
Tel   +44 (0)1347 821506
Web   www.thedurhamox.com

The Carpenters Arms
Felixkirk

Peace has returned to sleepy Felixkirk following a dramatic transformation by Provenance Inns. Michael and Sasha Ibbotson have worked hard to create one rather stylish country inn, keeping period detail in the traditional bar whilst adding a modern garden room, a decked terrace and eight garden rooms. Built into the hillside below the church, set around a landscaped garden, these stunningly swish rooms have private patios and picture windows for a view that stretches across the Vale of Mowbray to the Dales. Inside are sweeping floors, gas fires and honesty bars, big beds topped with duckdown and bathrooms with toasty floors. Back in the pub, stone floors, wonky beams, open fires, scarlet walls and comfy old furniture – an inviting backdrop for tasty food. Try scallops with garlic and parsley butter; pork fillet wrapped in Serrano ham with apple mash and mustard sauce; rib-eye steak with dauphinoise potatoes and Madeira jus. There's a cracking wine list, an intimate private dining room, and the staff are local and lovely. Fabulous moorland walking, too; bring the boots.

Rooms	8 doubles, 2 twin/doubles: £120-£185. Singles from £100.
Meals	Lunch & dinner £10.95-£19.95. Bar meals £3.95-£8.95. Sunday roast from £13.95.
Closed	Rarely.

Michael Ibbotson
The Carpenters Arms,
Felixkirk,
Thirsk YO7 2DP
Tel   +44 (0)1845 537369
Web   www.thecarpentersarmsfelixkirk.com

Entry 704 Map 12

The Oak Tree Inn
Helperby

Helperby is a historic spot and this new village pub is the jewel in its crown. The mellow brick exterior has scrubbed up nicely and a big paved area at the back is a great place to eat out on a sunny day. Inside, the old snug remains, complete with its open fire, oak floors and beams. Two bright and airy dining spaces, one by the rather sophisticated bar, strike a more clubby note: tartan check wool on wing chairs, ruby-red walls, dark elegant tables. An impressive line of brews beckon, including Timothy Taylor and Theakstons, so enjoy a pint by the fire while you choose your food. Souped-up pub classics are chalked on boards: home-cured salmon with capers, shallots and lemon dressing perhaps, followed by local venison with sautéed wild mushrooms and red wine sauce. Upstairs, soak any aches and pains away in a deep bath bubbling with L'Occitane treats. The six sumptuous bedrooms have funky wine-glass chandeliers, huge beds and fine linen, generously padded headboards and monster mirrors. After a spot of retail therapy in nearby Thirsk, Knaresborough or York, the Oak Tree is a pleasure to come home to.

Rooms	5 doubles, 1 twin/double: £120–£150.
Meals	Lunch from £7.
	Dinner from £14.95.
	Sunday lunch, 2 courses £14.95,
	3 courses, £17.95.
Closed	Rarely.

Michael Ibbotson
The Oak Tree Inn,
Raskelf Road, Helperby,
York YO61 2PH
Tel   +44 (0)1423 789189
Web   www.theoaktreehelperby.com

The General Tarleton
Ferrensby

John and Claire run this old coaching inn with easy charm. It's a community hub, a default destination for locals in search of good food and drink. The stylish low-beamed brasserie-bar mixes rough stone walls with leather chairs, period colours and a roaring fire. You'll find a pint of hand-pumped Black Sheep, then a dozen well-chosen wines by the glass. Good food with Yorkshire roots ranges from pub classics to posh nosh, anything from cheese soufflé to warm rabbit terrine, fish pie to haunch of venison, dark chocolate fondant with Horlicks ice cream to mascarpone panna cotta. There's a beautiful sitting room with comfy sofas and a log burner or a stone terrace in summer for lunch in the sun. Expect a good buzz and delightful staff. If you're tempted to stay, comfortable, well-equipped bedrooms in a purpose-built extension have recently been refurbished in elegant style: smart colours, crisp linen and homemade biscuits, with Molton Brown oils in good bathrooms. But the food is the thing – it's fabulous – as are the breakfasts. York, Harrogate, the Dales and the Moors wait.

Rooms	11 doubles, 2 twins: £129.
Meals	Lunch from £7.50.
	Dinner from £13.50.
	Sunday roast £22–£26.
Closed	Rarely.

John Topham
The General Tarleton,
Boroughbridge Road, Ferrensby,
Knaresborough HG5 0PZ
Tel   +44 (0)1423 340284
Web   www.generaltarleton.co.uk

Entry 706 Map 12

The Crescent Inn
Ilkley

The handsome Victorian building wrapped round a corner on the high street in Ilkley has been restored to its former glory – and it feels as though it's always been this way. Smooth walls are a vibrant blue, reflected in upholstered settles and checked wool curtains at tall windows; floors are in old oak and a glorious fire at the end of the comfortable bar belts out the heat. Choose from an impressive list of speciality beers and ciders, seven cask ales and wines by the glass. The value-for-money menu includes a gourmet British beef burger with skinny fries and a ploughman's platter that positively groans under the weight of local pork pie, ham off the bone and scrumptious Yorkshire cheeses. Pub classics are chalked up on boards, so tuck in to steak, ale and mushroom pie or fish and chips. At the top of an elegant curved staircase 11 peaceful, high-ceilinged, boutiquey bedrooms await, some in French country style, all with sumptuous linen, fat mattresses and sleek state of the art bathrooms. In short, the perfect spot in which to relax after a bracing yomp on the moors (or round Ilkley's fabulous shops!).

Rooms	11 doubles: £75–£145.
Meals	Bar meals from £5.95.
	Lunch from £9.95.
	Dinner from £13.90.
	Sunday roast £11.95–£13.95.
Closed	Rarely.

Richard Paterson
The Crescent Inn,
Brook Street,
Ilkley LS29 8DG

Tel   +44 (0)1943 811250
Web   www.thecrescentinn.co.uk

The Shibden Mill Inn
Shibden

The rambling and beautifully renovated old corn mill is hidden in a tranquil wooded valley overlooking Red Beck, just minutes from the hustle and bustle of Halifax; at night, the peaceful stream-side terrace is floodlit and heated, for idyllic summer drinking. An unstuffy integrity lies at the heart of Simon Heaton's welcoming inn, from the front-of-house warmth to the pubby bar where locals gather for a natter over a pint of Shibden Bitter. From the modern British kitchen innovative dishes flow: potted pork with pickled quail eggs, sorrel and mushroom ketchup; lamb rump and kidney gratin with butternut squash; mallard and curried pigeon Wellington; banana soufflé with toffee ice cream. There are beams and timbers, roaring log fires and stone-flagged floors, deep sofas and soothing colours in the cosy, candlelit bar and dining rooms, and the wine list is impressive. Refurbished bedrooms are comfortable, individual and decorated with warmth and style, with big beds, bold colours, Roberts radios and smart tiled bathrooms.

Rooms	10 doubles: £95–£149. 1 suite for 2: £165–£195. Singles £95–£125.
Meals	Lunch & dinner £11.50–£19. Sunday roast £12.95.
Closed	Rarely.

Pub with rooms

Simon Heaton
The Shibden Mill Inn,
Shibden Mill Fold, Shibden,
Halifax HX3 7UL
Tel +44 (0)1422 365840
Web www.shibdenmillinn.com

Entry 708 Map 12

The Lister Arms at Malham
Malham

You'll be hard pushed to find a finer looking pub in a more gorgeous village. The National Trust's Malham is a favourite with potholers (this part of Yorkshire is rich with caverns) but there are many surface pleasures to be had. Sitting on the edge of the village green, the 17th-century coaching inn was once home to the first Lord of Ribblesdale and very grand it looks too. But don't stand on ceremony: inside are flagged floors, wood-burning stoves and well-kept local ales. Rachel puts an interesting menu together using mostly local produce. You could start with warm pigeon salad… and move onto slow-braised pork belly with mash and dijon mustard sauce; if you have room, finish with rhubarb and ginger crème brûlée. Staying the night? Choose a contemporary new room in the refurbished cottage, or head upstairs to one of the comfy bedrooms with calm colours, lovely linen and pristine bathrooms; many have views over the village green to the hills beyond. A perfect place to park yourself for a few days above ground.

Rooms	5 doubles, 1 twin, 3 family rooms for 4: £80–£130. Singles £80–£130.
Meals	Bar meals from £6.95. Lunch & dinner from £10.50. Sunday lunch, 3 courses, £15.50.
Closed	Rarely.

Darren Dunn
The Lister Arms at Malham,
Malham,
Skipton BD23 4DB
Tel   +44 (0)1729 830330
Web   www.listerarms.co.uk

The Angel Inn
Hetton

The old drovers' inn remains staunchly, reassuringly traditional – but comes with wines that have come, over the years, to rival the hand-pumped Yorkshire ales. There's even a 'cave' for functions and private-party tastings. Expect nooks, crannies, beams and crackling fires, and a stylish restaurant. Thought has gone into every detail, from the antique furniture in the timbered rooms (one with a marvellous oak-panelled bar) to the fabrics and the colours. Menus change with each season and include dishes ranging from filo 'moneybags' of seafood in lobster sauce – the fish comes fresh from Fleetwood – to their own Yorkshire twist on tapas ('Yapas'!). Vegetarians are looked after and the sticky toffee pudding is legendary. Exquisite bedrooms, split between the converted barn and adjacent Sycamore House, are all different; perhaps a French armoire, a brass bed, a claw-foot bath, a private garden. All have top-quality fabrics, pretty colours, cosy bathrooms, and, in the newer rooms, a contemporary feel. The glorious up-hill-and-down-dale drive to get here is part of the charm.

Rooms	9 doubles: £150–£175. 5 suites for 2: £175–£200. Singles from £125.
Meals	Bar meals from £15.95. Lunch from £12.95. Dinner £15.95–£38.50. Sunday roast £24.50.
Closed	Christmas Day & 1 week in January.

Juliet Watkins
The Angel Inn,
Hetton,
Skipton BD23 6LT
Tel +44 (0)1756 730263
Web www.angelhetton.co.uk

Entry 710 Map 12

Queens Arms
Litton

It's a good day when a rural pub re-opens. This one sits in Litton, one of the most remote villages in this corner of the Dales and as pretty as it gets, with a smattering of handsome, thick-walled 17th-century houses, wildflower meadows and the river Skirfare burbling through. The Queens Arms, long, low and freshly whitewashed, is a fabulous find after a lovely walk. A lick of paint has smartened the inside without routing tradition; flagged floors, open fire, beams and stone walls remain. There's a new regime in the tiny kitchen, and a short and appealing menu. Seared Littondale mallard breast with homemade carrot and ginger chutney is a substantial starter, while pot roast wild rabbit with prunes will set you up nicely for that stroll – particularly if you finish with treacle sponge. Upstairs: six bedrooms in calming colours with crisp white linen, fat wool headboards and long views from the low windows. As you'd expect in a building this age, no wall is straight, but the wobbliness just adds to the charm, along with some lovely antique pieces. Spotless shower rooms complete the picture.

Rooms	3 doubles, 2 twin/doubles: £88-£160. 1 family room for 4: £105-£160. Singles £65-£73.
Meals	Lunch & dinner £4.95-£12.95.
Closed	Rarely.

John Younger
Queens Arms,
Litton,
Skipton BD23 5QJ
Tel   +44 (0)1756 770096
Web   www.queensarmslitton.co.uk

Entry 711 Map 12

The Lion at Settle
Settle

Generations of travellers have enjoyed the welcome at this grand 17th-century coaching inn; following a recent renovation its doors are open to all. Original features have been saved, including smooth oak floors, a fabulous inglenook fireplace in the grand entrance hall and the graceful sweeping staircase; comfortable sofas and chairs are upholstered in checked tartan wool. Locally sourced ingredients dominate a menu which places its emphasis on comfort: try Settle Pudding (tender braised beef with a suet lid) and homemade Scotch egg with thick-cut chips, and, if you can find room, the sticky toffee pudding is a must. The elegant but cosy dining room with its pleasingly mismatched furniture, panelled walls and old photos, buzzes with friendly chat. If you're a Three Peaks bagger, a devotee of the stunning Settle to Carlisle railway or simply want to get away from it all you can stay in characterful bedrooms with five-star mattresses, white cotton bed linen, immaculate bathrooms, plasma screens and fresh milk for your morning cuppa. The historic town is worth exploring: lose yourself in its cobbled alleyways.

Rooms	14 twin/doubles: £75–£130. Family room from £100.
Meals	Bar meals from £5.95. Lunch from £6.95. Dinner from £8.95.
Closed	Rarely.

Louise Van Delft
The Lion at Settle,
Duke Street,
Settle BD24 9DU
Tel   +44 (0)1729 822203
Web   www.thelionsettle.co.uk

The Kings Head
Kettlewell

It's worth dropping by for the fireplace alone – irresistible, monumental and smouldering on 18th-century flags. You could have a pint of Hetton Pale Ale, a Montrachet by the glass, a proper espresso... and pigeon breast salad with black pudding bon bons; the black pudding as light as a feather. Owner Michael Pighill has 20 years' cheffing under his belt and his short inspired menu, chalked up on a board, changes every two days. Local fishermen bring trout to the door and the meat is from Jacksons of Cracoe. There are rare beef sandwiches, heritage potatoes and delicious Goosnargh chicken with Wensleydale cheese. If you can't bear to leave then you must stay, in one of five white-and-grey bedrooms above, two overlooking a stream. Colours are muted, beds are wide, bathrooms are snazzy, there are flat screens, books, homemade biscuits and wonky walls. The pub, in one of the cutest villages in the Dales, sits on a lane opposite the church. The parking may be difficult but the setting is idyllic, and the Tour de France passed right by in 2014.

Rooms	4 doubles, 1 twin: £90.
Meals	Lunch & dinner £12–£20.
Closed	Rarely.

Michael & Jenny Pighills
The Kings Head,
The Green, Kettlewell,
Skipton BD23 5RD
Tel +44 (0)1756 761600
Web www.thekingsheadkettlewell.co.uk

Entry 713 Map 12

The Punch Bowl Inn
Low Row

The hamlet of Low Row clings to the hillside high above the Swale. The parasol'd front is a sun-trap, the views to the moors are superb and Gunnerside, Muker and Keld are a walk away. Inside, a contemporary-cum-traditional style is the order of the day for food and décor. Plain walls have the odd picture or cream panelling; pine tables are married with matching chairs. There's a unique bar crafted by 'Mouseman' Thompson (spot the mouse carving), the place is spotless, tasteful and cosy on wild winter nights when the fires are lit. Real ales and good wines flow, but the food is the draw, with the evening menu written on the mirror; try Asian spiced beef with couscous and sweet chilli sauce, braised pork belly with mash, crackling and cider jus, chocolate brownie with chocolate sauce and ice cream to finish. Other favourites include braised beef casserole and Cogden Hall Farm steaks – perfect for walkers and shooters. Upstairs, individual rooms ramble over two floors; some have chunky wooden beds and bold wall coverings; all have fresh, modern bathrooms and stunning views.

Rooms	9 doubles, 2 twins: £99–£110.
Meals	Bar meals & lunch from £8.95.
	Dinner from £13.95.
	Sunday roast £10.50.
Closed	Rarely.

Charles Cody
The Punch Bowl Inn,
Low Row,
Richmond DL11 6PF

Tel	+44 (0)1748 884567
Web	www.pbinn.co.uk

Entry 714 Map 12

Yorkshire

Charles Bathurst Inn
Arkengarthdale

Retreat after a bracing walk to the Codys' wonderful whitewashed inn high up Arkengarthdale, a moorland spot above glorious Swaledale; it's the wild and remote location that sets this place apart. Spruced up and extended over the years, it retains a classic 'inn' feel, period features blending effortlessly with blazing winter fires in the rustic bar and rambling dining rooms. Charles and Stacy rely almost exclusively on local staff and suppliers, with Black Sheep beers from Masham, locally-shot grouse, Swaledale lamb, and fish from Hartlepool. Bag a table, look to the mirror menu and tuck into smoked haddock chowder or scotch egg with homemade piccalilli, followed by shank and neck of lamb with carrot and swede mash, dauphinoise potatoes and lamb jus, leaving room for steamed chocolate pudding with chocolate sauce. Retreat upstairs for a peaceful night's sleep, and wake to a stunning view. Individual rooms, some simple and traditional, others more grand, come with bold colours, cast iron or big wooden beds, and modern tiled bathrooms. Famous walks in some of Britain's most beautiful countryside are on the doorstep.

Rooms	14 doubles, 5 twins: £99–£110.
Meals	Starters from £4.50. Dinner from £10.
Closed	Rarely.

Charles Cody
Charles Bathurst Inn,
Arkengarthdale,
Richmond DL11 6EN
Tel   +44 (0)1748 884567
Web   www.cbinn.co.uk

Entry 715 Map 12

Sandpiper Inn
Leyburn

Leyburn is lovely, a fine old market town on the edge of the Yorkshire Dales, one of the most beautiful places in England. As for the Sandpiper, this 17th-century stone inn sits peacefully on the square. Inside, cosy interiors have low ceilings, the odd beam and the best food in town. Jonathan, a Roux scholar, has cooked for presidents and prime ministers, robust food that elates. In the bar, locals put the world to rights over pints of Black Sheep while contemplating irresistible menus: salted squid or roasted chorizo if you fancy Yorkshire tapas; battered haddock or omelette Arnold Bennett if you want to explore the bar menu; or the full works in an attractive dining room, perhaps cheese soufflé, Swinton venison, dark chocolate marquise with white chocolate ice cream. Whisky lovers will appreciate the large collection of malts behind the bar. Upstairs, two simple bedrooms have a warm country feel with robes and good showers in the bathrooms. And don't miss the roast rib of beef for Sunday lunch or the market in the square on Fridays.

Rooms	2 doubles: £95–£110.
Meals	Bar meals from £5.
	Lunch from £8.50.
	Dinner from £10.95.
	Sunday lunch, 3 courses, £25.20.
Closed	Rarely.

Jonathan & Janine Harrison
Sandpiper Inn,
Railway Street,
Leyburn DL8 5AT
Tel   +44 (0)1969 622206
Web   www.sandpiperinn.co.uk

The White Bear Five Star Country Inn
Masham

Minutes from the bustle of an ancient market square stands the Theakston family's face-lifted flagship inn. In the handsome public bar, an open fire throws golden light on old oak floors, whilst gleaming brass platters jostle for space with newspapers, local magazines and great jugs of fresh flowers. Sit with a pint of Theakston's Best Bitter in the cosy tap room complete with dart board and cribbage, or wander through to the elegant dining room, where local and seasonal produce has prominence. Try steak and ale pie, or rolled fillet of plaice with cream dill sauce, then banana butterscotch pancakes — beautiful fuel for an afternoon tramp up into the heart of Wensleydale. On your return, 14 luxurious bedrooms await across the yard in what was the Lightfoot brewery, but don't expect nostalgia; the style is contemporary, with warm tones and splashes of colour, sumptuous textiles, great big beds and cutting edge bathrooms, and some lovely views across town. As a special treat, book the penthouse suite with a raftered ceiling and a swish bathroom — it's vast.

Rooms	13 twin/doubles: £120.
	1 suite for 2: £200–£220.
Meals	Lunch from £4.95.
	Dinner, 3 courses, from £30.
Closed	Rarely.

Sue Thomas
The White Bear Five Star Country Inn,
Wellgarth, Masham,
Ripon HG4 4EN

Tel	+44 (0)1765 689319
Web	www.thewhitebearhotel.co.uk

Black Horse Inn
Northallerton

A quirky village inn with lots of style and humour, where the notion of blandness has been banished in perpetuity. Outside, a couple of mannequins sit on the terrace chewing the cud; inside an original Space Invaders machine waits in a corner. Low ceilings, big colours and cool tunes in the flagstoned bar make you feel at home, so grab a pint of Black Sheep, then toast away in front of a fire. You can eat here or up in the restaurant with candles flickering at night. The food is delicious, anything from hot roast beef sandwiches to confit of local rabbit, shepherd's pie with honey-glazed carrots, tarte tatin with crème anglaise. As for the bedrooms, some are smaller, others bigger, but all offer comfort and style in equal measure with earthy colours, crisp linen and robes in good bathrooms (two have claw-foot baths in the room). One opens onto a private terrace, the family room has two rooms with twin beds for children. All are named after racehorses (there are five race courses close by). You can eat outside in good weather. Sunday lunch is popular, so book early.

Rooms	5 doubles, 1 twin: £75–£160.
	1 family room for 2–4: £95–£180.
Meals	Starters from £5.50.
	Mains from £11.50.
	Sunday lunch from £12.
Closed	Rarely.

Jackie Gardner
Black Horse Inn,
7 Lumley Lane, Kirkby Fleetham,
Northallerton DL7 0SH

Tel   +44 (0)1609 749010
Web   www.blackhorsekirkbyfleetham.com

Entry 718 Map 12

The Buck Inn
Maunby

It's always pleasing when a run-down village pub is rescued, even more so when the rescuers are a young couple with tons of energy, passion and a plan. Matthew Roath and his partner Sammy Clark — only in their mid-20s — have turned this sorry old boozer around. It might not be the most inviting exterior but any qualms are dispelled as you walk in; find open fires, beams, slouchy leather sofas in the big but cosy bar and the warmest of welcomes. Matthew's appealing, value-for-money menu features the likes of locally shot rabbit, rare-breed pork cheek and East Coast hake fillet (or steak suet pudding and a pint of Theakstons if you prefer) all cooked and presented with flair and care. Coupled with Sammy's front of house skills, The Buck is a classic in the making.

The Hare
Scawton

You're on the brink of spectacular Sutton Bank here and it's pretty lofty, though the pretty pub with its freshly whitewashed front and cheery pantile roof nestles into the hillside. It's thought to date back to the 13th century and monks, knights, pilgrims and marauding Scots are said to have enjoyed its hospitality; enjoy a welcome today from owners Paul and Liz Jackson. Wood stoves, rich red walls and beams signal a traditional, rural pub but there's a surprise in store. Paul's skills in the kitchen produce fine tasting menus along the lines of scallop with smoked eel, apple and celeriac. You don't have to dress to the nines though; call by after a walk round nearby Rievaulx Abbey and settle down to a leisurely lunch; start with the Sutton Bank Dexter with watercress, macadmia, smoked oil and bone marrow. A classic in the making.

Meals	Lunch & dinner from £8.95.
	Sunday roast from £9.95.
	Not Sunday eve.
Closed	Mon all day.
	3pm-5pm Tues-Thurs.

Meals	Lunch tasting menu, £25, £25 & £55.
	Dinner tasting menu £25, £45 & £65.
Closed	3pm-6pm.
	Sun evenings & Mon all day.

Matthew Roath & Sammy Clark
The Buck Inn,
Maunby,
Thirsk YO7 4HD
Tel   +44 (0)1845 587777
Web   www.thebuckinnmaunby.co.uk

Entry 719 Map 12

Paul & Liz Jackson
The Hare,
Scawton,
Thirsk YO7 2HG
Tel   +44 (0)1845 597769
Web   www.thehare-inn.com

Entry 720 Map 12

Yorkshire

The Star Inn
Harome

You know you've hit the jackpot as soon as you step into the 14th-century Star – low ceilings, flagged floors, gleaming oak, flickering fire. Andrew's food is rooted in Yorkshire tradition, refined with French flair and written in plain English on ever-changing menus that brim with local produce. Swoon over the likes of white onion and smoked salmon soup with chestnut chantilly; risotto of partridge with black trumpet mushrooms; mutton and caper suet pudding; dark chocolate and satsuma tart; cheeses of the week. There's a bar with a Sunday papers-and-pint feel, a coffee loft in the eaves, their deli across the road, and now a new dining room with acres of white linen and lovely French windows to the garden. Even the schnapps is homemade.

Meals	Lunch & dinner £16–£24.
Closed	Mon lunch.

Andrew Pern
The Star Inn,
High Street, Harome,
Helmsley YO62 5JE
Tel +44 (0)1439 770397
Web www.thestaratharome.co.uk

Entry 721 Map 13

Yorkshire

The Royal Oak
Nunnington

In a distractingly pretty village is a handsome stone pub, once neglected, now revived, and loved by all who visit. Jill and Abbi (Italophiles both) are introducing Italy to North Yorks. No surprise that families are given a big welcome, and fish and chips join arms with the 'menu al giorno' (there's Yorkshire rarebit, gammon and pineapple, sticky toffee pudding and Sunday roasts, too). Plates of Tuscan deliciousness are ferried from the kitchen to the dining bar, which is shambolic in the nicest way. Tartan wool carpets, standing timbers, scrubbed tables, old mirrors, fresh flowers, tons of books, a wall of old keys, an eclectic mix of music on the stereo – seems like they've been here for years! There's a games room with bar billiards, a patio at the back and cosy fires for dogs. Cask ales, wines, local craft beers, espresso… marvellous.

Meals	Starters from £4.50.
	Dinner from £9.50.
Closed	Mon & Tues.

Jill & Abbi Greetham
The Royal Oak,
Church Street, Nunnington,
York YO62 5US
Tel +44 (0)1439 748271
Web www.nunningtonroyaloak.co.uk

Entry 722 Map 13

Yorkshire

The Grapes Inn
Slingsby

Sometimes you walk into a pub and know it's a classic in the making. Locals Leigh and Catharine Spooner, a couple with no previous experience in the trade but a ton of enthusiasm took a chance and bought this handsome but run-down Georgian village boozer and have transformed it. All the good bits remain – stone floors, period windows, open fires – and they've filled it full of fabulous antique furniture of the period, plus a smattering of kitsch vintage finds. With jugs of fresh flowers, light jazz in the background and a short homely menu chalked on a board (the steak pie with herb suet crust is a winner) it's a fabulous spot to sit with a pint of Timothy Taylor's Landlord before a tour round nearby Castle Howard.

Yorkshire

The Blacksmith's Arms
Lastingham

Low black beams, glowing fires, antique saddles, a ghost called Ella and a pint of Copper Dragon. You almost slide down to the lovely little village, so deeply is it sunk into the valley. This low, rambling, dimly-lit pub has provided shelter and comfort to monks and shepherds since 1693; now it is visited by gamekeepers, walkers and church enthusiasts: ancient St Mary's sits next door and a secret tunnel runs between the two. Once an impoverished priest with 13 children ran both the pub and church; the current landlord is approved by all. The little dining rooms are not quite as atmospheric as the bar with its lit range, but this is a great place for a gossip and a pint – and a proper Yorkshire portion of game casserole or lamb and mint pie. Delicious.

Meals	Lunch £5.50.
	Starters £4.95.
	Dinner from £9.95.
	Not Sun eve.
Closed	Mon all day.
	2.30-5.30pm Wed-Fri.

Meals	Lunch & dinner £8.95-£14.95.
Closed	Tues lunch.

Leigh & Catharine Spooner
The Grapes Inn,
Railway Street,
Slingsby YO62 4AL
Tel   +44 (0)1653 628076
Web   www.thegrapesinn-slingsby.co.uk

Entry 723 Map 13

Peter & Hilary Trafford
The Blacksmith's Arms,
Front Street, Lastingham,
York YO62 6TL
Tel   +44 (0)1751 417247
Web   www.blacksmithslastingham.co.uk

Entry 724 Map 13

Yorkshire

The Wheatsheaf Inn
Egton

Unlike many pubs in the Whitby area, the family-run Wheatsheaf has avoided expansion and held on to its soul. Indeed, it sits so modestly back from the village's wide main street you could pass it by. The first entrance brings you into the main bar, all low beams and cushioned settles, but the biggest treat is the bar with its old Yorkshire range – aglow most of the year. This drinkers' den takes 16 at a push and is a favourite of walkers, fishermen and dogs; the river Esk at the foot of the steep hill is famous for fly fishing, hence the angling memorabilia. A range of cask ales ensures the chat flows, while the food sustains walkers: finnan haddock kedgeree, oxtail soup, local partridge in season, steaks from local farmers.

Yorkshire

The Birch Hall
Beck Hole

Two small bars with a shop in between, unaltered for 70 years. Wooded hillsides and a stone bridge straddling the rushing river and, inside, a glimpse of life before World War II. The Big Bar has been beautifully repapered and has a little open fire, dominoes, darts and service from a hatch; benches come from the station waiting room at Beck Hole. The shop (postcards, traditional sweets) has its original fittings, as does the Little Bar with its handpumps for three cask ales. The original 19th-century enamel sign hangs above the door. Food is simple and authentic: local pies, baked stotties, homemade scones, delicious beer cake. Steep steps take you to the terraced garden that looks over the inn and across the valley. Parking is scarce so show patience and courtesy in this old-fashioned place.

Meals	Bar meals from £8.50. Lunch & dinner £8.50–£17.95. Sunday roast £15.
Closed	2.30pm–5.30pm & Mon lunch. Open all day Sat & Sun.

Meals	Bar snacks from £1.90.
Closed	3pm–7.30pm. Mon evenings & all day Tues in winter. Open all day in summer.

Nigel & Elaine Pulling
The Wheatsheaf Inn,
High Street, Egton,
Whitby YO21 1TZ
Tel   +44 (0)1947 895271
Web   www.wheatsheafegton.com

Entry 725 Map 13

Glenys & Neil Crampton
The Birch Hall,
Beck Hole,
Whitby YO22 5LE
Tel   +44 (0)1947 896245
Web   www.beckhole.info

Entry 726 Map 13

Yorkshire

The White Swan Inn
Pickering

Victor swapped the City for the North Yorkshire Moors and this old coaching inn; the place oozes comfort and style. Duck in through the front door to a tiny, cosy, panelled tap room serving real Yorkshire ales, with smart country furniture, fine wines and eager young staff. In the dining room, find heaven on a plate as you dig into supper. Try seared hand-dived king scallops with air-dried ham, Levisham mutton with Irish cabbage, poached rhubarb on toasted brioche and homemade ice cream. Menus change monthly and 80% of the ingredients are locally sourced, with meat coming from the legendary Ginger Pig. Don't miss the beamed club room for a roaring fire, board games and an honesty bar. Castle Howard is nearby, the moors are wild, the steam railway is fun.

Meals	Lunch from £5.25.
	Dinner £13.95–£27.95.
	Sunday roast from £12.95.
Closed	Open all day.

Victor & Marion Buchanan
The White Swan Inn,
Market Place,
Pickering YO18 7AA
Tel   +44 (0)1751 472288
Web   www.white-swan.co.uk

Entry 727 Map 13

Yorkshire

The Anvil Inn
Sawdon

The fact that this village is not on a bus route suggests you are in the back of beyond — but we urge you to beat a path to its very cosy door. The Anvil was a working forge until the mid 1980s, the building is over 200 years old and the lofty, all-stone workshop has become a bar — an unusual centrepiece to a great little pub. Partner-chefs Mark and Alexandra have pulled the place up by its bootstraps and created an environment to linger long in. Settle into an old oak pew, lounge by the wood-burner in a leather tub chair, order a pint — Daleside, Wold Top — and scan the menu. Invention without pretension is the philosophy here, and thoughtfully executed, locally sourced food flows from the kitchen. A classic in the making.

Meals	Lunch & dinner from £9.50–£15.45.
	Sunday roast £11.50.
Closed	2.30pm–6.30pm
	& all day Mon & Tues.

Mark Wilson & Alexandra Warricker
The Anvil Inn,
Main Street, Sawdon,
Scarborough YO13 9DY
Tel   +44 (0)1723 859896
Web   www.theanvilinnsawdon.co.uk

Entry 728 Map 13

Yorkshire

Yorkshire

The Crown & Cushion
Welburn

Provenance Inns go from strength to strength. The latest addition to the stable bears all their trademarks (good beer, many wines by the glass, a pleasing value for money menu and a big welcome) but this nicely spruced-up old village pub, just a mile from the roaring A64, feels subtly different. Maybe it's the moss green palette, the coal fires, or the tap room? Whatever; it's a very pleasant spot for a pint of Black Sheep Bitter and a plate of local beef carpaccio, or the cracking Crown & Cushion pie. Gird your loins with treacle sponge and custard if you've planned to take advantage of one of the wonderful walks from the door. Outside, the flagged, be-shrubbed garden is lovely place to sit out on a good day, with long views across the rolling Howardian Hills.

The White Horse Inn (Nellie's)
Beverley

You could pass the White Horse by: its brick front and old pub sign do not stand out on busy Hengate. Inside, step back 200 years. Known as 'Nellie's', this is a wonderfully atmospheric little place, and your eyes will take a while to become accustomed, so dim are the gas-lit passages. Little has changed in these small rooms with their old quarry tiles, bare boards, smoke-stained walls and open fires. Furniture is a mix of high-backed settles, padded benches, marble-topped tables and a gas-lit, pulley-controlled chandelier. Food is straightforward and good value: sandwiches, bangers and mash, steak and ale pie, spotted dick with custard. Just one concession to the modern age: a games room at the back with pool tables, juke box and darts.

| Meals | Starters from £5.95. Dinner from £11.95. |
| Closed | Open all day. |

| Meals | Lunch & dinner from £4. |
| Closed | Open all day. |

Michael Ibbotson
The Crown & Cushion,
Welburn,
York YO60 7DZ
Tel +44 (0)1347 821506
Web www.thecrownandcushionwelburn.com

Entry 729 Map 13

The Landlord
The White Horse Inn (Nellie's),
22 Hengate,
Beverley HU17 8BN
Tel +44 (0)1482 861973
Web www.nellies.co.uk

Entry 730 Map 13

Yorkshire

The Star at Sancton
Sancton

There was a time when every farming village in the Yorkshire Wolds had a pub that was the beating heart of the community. By the time Ben and Lindsey Cox bought the 800-year-old building its heart had stopped. But youth and enthusiasm prevailed, and now the welcome is warm, the fires are lit and the comfortable, laid-back vibe gives barely a nod to the pub's sorry past. It's still very much a place for locals to pop in for a pint – beer is from the Copper Dragon and Wold Top breweries – but you must stay to eat. Ben is making a name for himself and the menu is tempting. Try Ben's Yorkshire pudding with confit oxtail and onion gravy (after all, he is the Yorkshire Pudding champion for the second year running) or Anna's Happy Trotter belly pork, braised kale and bacon with black pudding, Harrogate Blue bonbon and cyder reduction. Much of the produce comes from their allotment and orchard – a real treat.

| Meals | Bar meals £4.95–£11.95. Lunch & dinner £13.95–£21.95. Set lunch £16.95–£18.95. |
| Closed | Mon all day. |

Ben & Lindsey Cox
The Star at Sancton,
Sancton,
Market Weighton YO43 4QP
Tel +44 (0)1430 827269
Web www.thestaratsancton.co.uk

Entry 731 Map 13

Yorkshire

The Goodmanham Arms
Goodmanham

In the middle of a village of whitewashed cottages, in yet-to-be-discovered 'Hockneyshire', is a simple red brick pub. Built in the 1800s it's handsome enough, with a pantile roof and a beer garden at the back. Inside is another story! Enter a wood-clad wonder of old settles and wheel-back chairs, ticking clocks and roaring fires, brasses, baskets, books and candles, and All Hallows ales behind the bar: Abbie and Vito have a craft brewery out the back (Dark Mild, Gold and Porter). They're CAMRA award-winners too, so there's Ragged Robin and Old Peculier and guest beers that rotate weekly. In one of three linking rooms (one housing Vito's motorbikes), is a magnificent range on which they do the cooking. Arrive early if you want a table; the Gypsy Pot, tender beef cooked in ale, is sublime. Old-fashioned, timeless, and with a welcome second to none.

| Meals | Lunch & dinner from £8.95. |
| Closed | Open all day. |

Authentic pub

Vito Logozzi
The Goodmanham Arms,
Main Street, Goodmanham,
Market Weighton YO43 3JA
Tel +44 (0)1430 873849
Web www.goodmanhamarms.co.uk

Entry 732 Map 13

Yorkshire

The Blue Bell
York

Unlike most city pubs, this one is as it's always been – a mecca for real ale fans. Its narrow brick frontage on Fossgate, not far from The Shambles, is easy to miss. Find it and you enter a corridor that leads to the back. On the right, a tiny bar with red-tiled floor and high ceilings, a cast-iron and tiled fireplace and Edwardian stained glass, settle seating on two sides and iron-leg tables. 'Ladies only' were confined to the narrow back lounge; now the red carpet is trodden by all. Polished panelling, interesting old pictures, ticking clocks and general clutter… all this and a terrific range of cask beers – at least seven – and wines too. No hot food but you can get a hearty lunchtime sandwich. And don't miss the annual beer festival in November!

Meals	Sandwiches from £2.
Closed	Open all day.

Jim Hardie
The Blue Bell,
53 Fossgate,
York YO1 9TF
Tel +44 (0)1904 654904

Entry 733 Map 13

Yorkshire

Dawnay Arms
Newton on Ouse

The script on the lintel reads 1778. This stately building in a very pretty village has been rescued by Kerry and Martel, who have taken a step sideways from their Leeds brasserie. Now the old boozer is a shrine to modernity. Stone flagged floors and massive fireplaces have been kept, and church pews and chunky tables (constructed from timber pilfered from a Durham post office) sit stylishly to a pale backdrop enlivened by bright funky cushions and modern art in rococo frames. Faultless food scrupulously sourced flows from a kitchen run by maestro Martel – steak and kidney pudding with root vegetables and ale sauce; treacle tart with butterscotch ice cream. There's a glorious riverside garden for lazy summer days.

Meals	Lunch from £7.95.
	Dinner from £9.95.
	Sunday lunch, 3 courses, £17.95.
Closed	3pm–6pm. Mon.
	Open all day Sat & Sun.

Kerry Smith
Dawnay Arms,
Newton on Ouse,
York YO30 2BR
Tel +44 (0)1347 848345
Web www.thedawnayatnewton.co.uk

Entry 734 Map 12

The Alice Hawthorn
Nun Monkton

It's a picture-book setting — a cul-de-sac village with a pond on the green, ducks wobbling about, the tallest maypole in the land, then a country pub serving ambrosial food. It's all the work of Josh Overington, his second venture since opening Le Cochon Aveugle in York, an intimate restaurant that's making a big splash. Now he's cooking up great food in the country, too, his skills honed in two of England's finest Michelin-starred pubs: the Hand and Flowers in Marlow and the Pipe and Glass in South Dalton. Inside, the back bar has a lovely feel, a blend of modern and traditional, with stripped boards, cool colours and a wood-burner to pump out the heat. Then there's the elegant restaurant where you dig into scrumptious food, perhaps devilled whitebait, local game, ginger parkin with pear and damson ice cream. Don't miss it.

Meals	Lunch & dinner from £8.95.
	Sunday roast from £8.95.
Closed	Mon all day.

Josh Overington
The Alice Hawthorn,
Nun Monkton,
York YO26 8EW
Tel +44 (0)1423 330303
Web www.thealicehawthorn.com

Entry 735 Map 12

The Punch Bowl Inn
Marton

The good people of Marton have got back their lovely local, thanks to the care and skill of Sasha and Michael Ibbotson. A gleaming coat of whitewash invites you in and the light lofty bar with its stunning cruck-barn ceiling tells of 16th-century origins. There's a very pleasing mix of oak settles and smart velvet chairs, open fires, polished wood floors and ruby-red walls. Tuck into twice-baked blue cheese soufflé with cauliflower purée or more substantially, confit shoulder of lamb. Veggies are well-served: try autumn field mushroom risotto or roast cherry vine tomato and sweet basil penne. Puds are a treat — bitter lemon posset with chantilly cream; apple and berry crumble with proper custard. In summer, a stylish courtyard at the back is a suntrap — a fab spot for a glass of something chilled.

Meals	Lunch from £7.95.
	Dinner from £12.75.
Closed	Open all day.

Michael Ibbotson
The Punch Bowl Inn, Marton,
Marton–cum-Grafton, York YO51 9QY
Tel +44 (0)1423 322519
Web www.thepunchbowlmarton
cumgrafton.com

Entry 736 Map 12

Yorkshire

The Shoulder of Mutton
Kirkby Overblow

A handsome old inn between Harrogate and Harewood House with views rolling south over green hills to Wharfe Valley. Warm, stylish interiors mix old and new to great effect – original stone walls and low ceilings, then contemporary fabrics and a wall or two of paper. There's an open fire at one end, a wood burner at the other, stone flags and oak floors in between. As for the chattering band of happy locals, they flock in for fine Yorkshire ales, a glass of good wine and a tasty plate of comfort cooking, perhaps goat's cheese en croûte, shoulder of Masham lamb, lemon drizzle cake with raspberry sauce. In summer, you decant into a child-friendly garden and eat in the shade of ancient trees. Sunday lunch is a feast – local walks help you atone – while homemade chutneys and pickles are available to take home. A treat.

Meals	Lunch & dinner £9.95-£19.50. Sunday lunch, 3 courses, £18.95.
Closed	3pm-6pm. Mon.

Kate Deacon
The Shoulder of Mutton,
Main Street, Kirkby Overblow,
Harrogate HG3 1HD
Tel   +44 (0)1423 871205
Web   www.shoulderofmuttonharrogate.co.uk

Entry 737 Map 12

Yorkshire

New Entry

Friends of Ham
Leeds

Beers, cheeses, charcuterie: that's all they do, but boy they do it well! Off the narrow dusty approach to the main train station is a big airy bar of scrubbed 'school' tables, designer chairs, funky swine prints and a fabulous buzz. Downstairs: a long, low, atmospheric room with benched tables, sofa-ed corners, bookshelf wallpapers and warm lighting; it's hipster-friendly and extremely inviting. We had hot-smoked Bath chaps (pigs' cheeks), Ibérico de Bellota (the king of Spanish ham), Jésus du Pays Basque (French salami with rum), and Vacherin, Comté and Stichelton cheeses. All were delightful. Beers are draught and bottled and global, from chocolate stouts to floral ales; wines are from interesting vineyards. Freshen up with a spring green salad, or round off your indulgence with chocolate panettone – served with crème pâtissière and rhubarb purée.

Meals	Small plates from £5.50. Sharing boards from £12.50.
Closed	Open all day.

Claire & Anthony Kitching
Friends of Ham,
4 New Station Street,
Leeds LS1 5DL
Tel   +44 (0)113 242 0275
Web   www.friendsofham.com

Entry 738 Map 12

The Chequers Inn
Ledsham

Fires glow, horse brasses gleam... this honey-stone village inn could be in the Dales. In fact, you're a couple of miles from the A1. Panelled, carpeted rooms radiating off the central bar are cosy with log fires and plush red upholstery; faded photographs are a reminder of an earlier age. Rare hand-pumped ales from the Brown Cow Brewery at Selby do justice to good English food of Yorkshire proportions: steaming platefuls of loin of venison and red cabbage, wild boar with onion confit and sweet potato mash... just when you think you're replete, along comes chocolate torte with cream. The pub has been welcoming travellers since the 18th century and still closes on Sundays: in 1832 the lady of Ledsham Hall, confronting a drunken farmer on her way to church, insisted they close on the Sabbath!

Broadfield Ale House
Sheffield

Not too long ago, this gnarly old city pub was a sticky-carpeted, nicotine-drenched dive, but the forward-thinking team from the Sheffield-based Forum group have completely turned it around. Lots of period features remain; stunning stained and etched glass, oak floors and open fires in all three rooms and they've added great beer and a simple but very inviting menu. Featuring prominently are homemade sausages and pies – ham, leek and cider, or beef, ale and mushroom – served with fat chips and of course mushy peas. Elsewhere, the likes of maple-glazed ham hock and slow beer-braised brisket will delight – all this and nicely kept pints of Abbeydale Moonshine and Bradfield's Farmers Pale Ale among half a dozen others. It's good to see the Broadfield has got its mojo back.

Meals	Lunch & dinner £5.50–£19.95.
Closed	Sun.

Meals	Lunch & dinner £7.50–£10.
Closed	Open all day.

Chris Wraith
The Chequers Inn,
Claypit Lane, Ledsham,
Leeds LS25 5LP
Tel   +44 (0)1977 683135
Web   www.thechequersinn.com

Entry 739 Map 12

Mark Simcox
Broadfield Ale House,
452 Abbeydale Road,
Sheffield S7 1FR
Tel   +44 (0)114 255 0200
Web   www.thebroadfield.co.uk

Entry 740 Map 12

Yorkshire

The Inn at Troway
Troway

High on a hill with rolling country views sits a 1930s mock Tudor pub with an arms-open-to-all approach. Inside, polished wood and terracotta sweep you towards a bar primed with Thornbridge's Wild Swan and Jaipur alongside Black Sheep and Cocker Hoop ales. On either side are open-plan areas with red leather sofas, padded bench seats, period fireplaces and modern cartoon prints on walls. Enthusiastic staff settle you in and blackboards list the great meal offers for families, from grills, fish and chips and sandwiches to modern pub classics – perhaps Yorkshire pheasant with parsnip purée and buttered vegetables. Great homemade desserts as well, and pork crackling with apple sauce (the real deal!). There's a separate games room, lots of fresh flowers and treats for children on arrival.

Meals	Bar meals from £2.
	Lunch & dinner from £8.
	Sunday roast from £10.
Closed	Open all day.

Richard Smith
The Inn at Troway,
Snowdon Lane, Troway,
Sheffield S21 5RU

Tel   +44 (0)1246 290751
Web   www.relaxeatanddrink.com

Entry 741 Map 8

Yorkshire

The Cricket Inn
Totley

'Children, dogs, muddy boots welcome!' says this old stone pub, next to the cricket pitch in a leafy Sheffield suburb; the feel is rural. After a walk in the woods, put up your feet by the fire and pick up a pint of specially brewed Jaipur. Or take a ringside seat by the pitch in summer. Local restaurateurs Richard and Victoria Smith have joined forces with Thornbridge Brewery to create a laid-back, welcoming dining pub with stone floors, tongue-and-groove walls and open fires. They have a Portuguese chef now and their own smoker, so you can enjoy smoked beef brisket, smoked haddock risotto, smoked chicken... or mini Scotch eggs, beef jerky with black garlic aïoli, Portuguese fish stew. The food is pricey but praiseworthy, the service is warm and there's a great vibe.

Meals	Bar meals from £5.
	Lunch & dinner £12–£20.
	Sunday roast from £13.50.
Closed	Open all day.

Richard Smith
The Cricket Inn,
Penny Lane, Totley,
Sheffield S17 3AZ

Tel   +44 (0)1246 417666
Web   www.relaxeatanddrink.com

Entry 742 Map 8

Yorkshire

The Old Bridge Inn
Ripponden

An ancient packhorse bridge and a little low inn... such is the setting. Family involvement over decades has resulted in a thoroughly civilised, unspoilt little local. Three carpeted, oak-panelled, split-level rooms – dimly lit – are furnished with old oak settles and rush-seated chairs. The small green-walled snug at the top is atmospheric; the bar has a lofty ceiling with exposed timbers and a huge fireplace with a log-burning stove; the lower room is good for dining. Buffet lunches are as popular as ever, and the evening menu reveals sound English cooking (ham hock terrine with piccalilli; Bury black pudding, bacon and poached egg salad; Hubberton steak, ale and mushroom pie; Yorkshire cheeses) with a modern slant. The bar is well used by locals who come for Timothy Taylor's Best Bitter, Landlord and Golden Best. The wines are good, too.

Meals	Lunch £4.50–£14.50. Dinner from £9. No food Sunday eve.
Closed	3pm–5.30pm. Open all day Fri–Sun.

Tim & Lindsay Eaton Walker
The Old Bridge Inn,
Priest Lane,
Ripponden HX6 4DF
Tel   +44 (0)1422 822595
Web   www.theoldbridgeinn.co.uk

Entry 743 Map 12

Yorkshire

The Wheatley Arms
Ben Rhydding

New life has been breathed into this vast old stone inn – and how! Oak floors, open fires, a dog-friendly bar... it feels as if it's been like this for years. A labyrinth of rooms are linked by a vivid décor; bold textiles, original prints, clusters of mini-collections – something interesting at every turn. A wide range of well-kept ale will please beer lovers, whilst a confident menu should please the rest. Potted meat with homemade pickle perhaps followed by pan-fried lamb's liver with bacon and mash; roast Yorkshire venison; scampi in a basket (it's back!). And puddings are impossible to resist; the apricot and cinnamon beignets with lemon and pine nut parfait are divine. Refreshingly unpompous, friendly and on the ball – prepare to be wowed.

Meals	Lunch & dinner from £10.95. Sunday lunch, 3 courses, from £19.95. Not Sunday eves.
Closed	Open all day.

Kate Peil
The Wheatley Arms,
Wheatley Lane, Ben Rhydding,
Ilkley LS29 8PP
Tel   +44 (0)1943 816496
Web   www.wheatleyarms.co.uk

Entry 744 Map 12

Ilkley Moor Vaults
Ilkley

A stone's throw from the centre of genteel, elegant, bustling Ilkley town is an establishment known for years as 'the Taps'. Though Jo and the loyal team have spruced it up you can still whet your whistle with a good pint of local ale, but there's so much more to enjoy. Joining the stone flagged floors, the scrubbed pine tables and the crackling fires are kitschy standard lamps with tasselled shades and a menu that promises robust dishes with a twist – and delivers. Out back is a smoker and kitchen garden, so air miles don't exist. You could happily take root here all day. When hunger hits, tuck into the likes of beef and ale pie, wild mushroom and spinach omelette, Vaults rarebit and tomato chutney, or a whole pheasant pie to share. The vibe is young but completely inclusive. Don't hesitate, just go.

Fountaine Inn
Linton

Linton, a heartbeat from the fleshpots of Grassington, has the whole caboodle, including Vanbrugh's stunning Fountaine Hospital and almshouses. Here is a village green complete with ducks and tiny humpback bridge; on its edge sits the historic Fountaine Inn. Inside, a warren of attractive rooms includes a chic snug with comfortable high-backed banquettes, beams and a cracking open fire. Theakstons, Thwaites and John Smiths are on tap while the crowd-pleasing menu features smoked haddock rarebit, Kilney smoked trout niçoise and pot roast poussin with leeks. In the winter, beef braised in Fountaine Pale Ale is a rib-sticking winner. This is perhaps the 'pubbiest' of the Clarksons' Skipton-based group – the kind of place you want on your doorstep.

Meals	Bar meals from £4.95.
	Lunch from £5.95.
	Dinner from £9.95.
	Sunday roast £10.95.
Closed	3pm-5pm. Mon.
	Open all day Sat & Sun.

Meals	Lunch & dinner £7.50–£14.
	Set menu £9.95.
Closed	Open all day.

	Jo		Chris Gregson
	Ilkley Moor Vaults,		Fountaine Inn,
	Stockeld Road,		Linton,
	Ilkley LS29 9HD		Skipton BD23 5HJ
Tel	+44 (0)1943 607012	Tel	+44 (0)1756 752210
Web	www.ilkleymoorvaults.co.uk	Web	www.fountaineinnatlinton.co.uk

Entry 745 Map 12   Entry 746 Map 12

Yorkshire

Craven Arms
Appletreewick

Authentically restored, this ancient rustic, creeper-clad pub (built in 1548) stands among gorgeous hills overlooking Wharfedale. It's a favourite with walkers so you could end up wagging a chin with them by the glowing cast-iron range in the stone-flagged bar. Just plain settles, panelled walls, thick beams, nothing more; beyond, a snug with simple benches and valley views, and a homely dining room. The final treat are the Wharfedale ales – Folly Gold, Executioner. Head out back to the loo to take a peek at the amazing function room housed in a replica medieval barn. Back in the bar, free of music and flashing games, find hot sandwiches and a legendary slow-roasted and minted lamb shoulder. Just the job after a blustery hike or cycle ride across the moors.

Meals	Bar meals £7.50–£10.50.
	Lunch & dinner £8.95–£15.25.
Closed	Open all day.

Mark Cooper
Craven Arms,
Appletreewick,
Skipton BD23 6DA
Tel +44 (0)1756 720270
Web www.craven-cruckbarn.co.uk

Entry 747 Map 12

Yorkshire

The Bull
Broughton

Off the main road to Skipton is this handsome, sprawling, mellow stone pub, with a big attractive patio at the back. The Bull is a great 'celebration' pub, and tops for Sunday lunch too. Being part of the Ribble Valley Inns group, it shares the same plush-but-relaxed décor that draws a crowd (smart flagged floors, chunky wood tables, open fires) and the same passion for local artisan producers, whose commissioned photos hang on the walls. Attentive young staff deliver good-looking dishes that are packed with flavour, including duck and black pudding hash cakes, and chargrilled rump burgers with homemade piccalilli. There are ten wines by the glass and cask ales too – local, of course.

Meals	Dinner, 2 courses, £12.50;
	3 courses £15.
	Sunday lunch, 2 courses, £17.50,
	3 courses £21.
Closed	Open all day.

Dan McCarthy
The Bull,
Broughton,
Skipton BD23 3AE
Tel +44 (0)1756 792065
Web www.thebullatbroughton.com

Entry 748 Map 12

Yorkshire

The Tempest Arms
Elslack

A 16th-century ale house with great prices, friendly staff and an easy style on the fringe of the pretty hamlet of Elslack. Inside you find stone walls and old beams, settles and plump cushions, Yorkshire ales on tap and a smart beamed restaurant. An airy open-plan feel runs throughout with sofas and armchairs strategically placed in front of a fire that burns on both sides. Delicious traditional food is a big draw – the inn was packed for lunch on a Tuesday in April. You can eat wherever you want, so grab a seat and dig into twice-cooked belly pork with sage stuffing and Yorkshire pud, slow-braised lamb shoulder roast with roots, cream mash and mint gravy. Finish off with Yorkshire parkin, rhubarb ice cream and a caramel sauce. It's great for a private party, and walkers and dogs pile in: the Dales are on the doorstep.

Yorkshire

The Falcon Inn
Arncliffe

The Falcon is tucked onto the village green of Arncliffe in Littondale, one of the most remote of Yorkshire's dales. Several generations of Millers have been licensees here, preserving a way of life almost lost. The fine bay-windowed building looks more private house than village local; inside find few frills and old-fashioned hospitality. The entrance passageway leads to a small hallway at the foot of the stairs, there's a tiny bar counter facing you, and a small simple lounge, a log fire and haphazard pictures. The sunny back room looks across the garden to open fells and the loos are out the back. Timothy Taylor's Boltmaker is served straight from the cask in a jug, then dispensed into pint glasses at the bar, and at lunchtime you can order pie and peas, sandwiches and ploughman's. Deeply traditional. A Yorkshire gem.

Meals	Lunch & bar meals from £8.95. Dinner from £14.95.
Closed	Open all day.

Meals	Bar meals £2.50–£6. Lunch only.
Closed	3pm–7pm. Reduced winter opening times, phone to check.

Martin & Veronica Clarkson
The Tempest Arms,
Elslack,
Skipton BD23 3AY
Tel   +44 (0)1282 842450
Web   www.tempestarms.co.uk

Entry 749 Map 12

Joanne & Steven Hodgson
The Falcon Inn,
Arncliffe,
Skipton BD23 5QE
Tel   +44 (0)1756 770205
Web   www.thefalconinn.com

Entry 750 Map 12

Yorkshire

The Oak Tree Inn
Hutton Magna

A tiny Dales' cottage at the end of a row, masquerading as a pub, the Oak Tree was discovered by the Rosses. Alastair trained at The Savoy, together they have created a relaxed and welcoming gem. The front bar has its original panelling and whitewashed stone, a medley of tables, squishy leather sofas, newspapers, fresh flowers, an open fire. The dark green dining area at the back is cosily lit, its tables separated by pews. Locally shot game appears on the menu in season and the produce is as fresh as can be. Try prosecco-poached shellfish with cucumber and crab mayonnaise; herb-crusted saddle of lamb with garlic and rosemary potatoes, sweet peppers, aubergine and fennel; hot chocolate fondant with delice and pistachio ice cream. The food is always a joy.

Yorkshire

The Black Bull
Richmond

The Black Bull – a famous old name in Yorkshire dining – is the latest addition to Provenance Inns and its collection of fine hostelries. It's received the trademark makeover to bring it into the 21st century, the most notable addition being a smart restaurant, where walls of glass open onto a terrace for lunch in good weather. Inside, there's a panelled bar with armchairs in front of a wood-burner where you can sink a pint of Black Sheep (brewed down the road). Then there's the excellent food. Menus are extensive, a smörgåsbord of fresh, local produce, with fish and chips and a good burger sitting alongside East Coast lobster and charcoaled steaks. You'll find Côte de Boeuf and Chateaubriand, too, and an excellent wine list to help wash them down. Smart bedrooms are on the way, there's live jazz on Sunday nights, even the odd Murder Mystery evening.

Meals	Starters from £5.50. Dinner, 3 courses, from £33.	Meals	Lunch from £4.95. Dinner from £12.95.
Closed	Tues–Sun lunch & all day Mon.	Closed	Open all day.

	Alastair & Claire Ross The Oak Tree Inn, Hutton Magna, Richmond DL11 7HH		Fred Truman The Black Bull, Moulton, Richmond DL10 6QJ
Tel	+44 (0)1833 627371	Tel	+44 (0)1325 377556
		Web	www.theblackbullmoulton.com

Entry 751 Map 12

Entry 752 Map 12

The Blue Lion
East Witton

The front bar at the Blue Lion is one of the best in the land – little has changed since it was built at the end of the 18th century. It's a delightful mix of flagged floors, open fires, beautiful old settles, newspapers on poles, polished beer taps for Yorkshire ale, bunches of dried flowers hanging from beams. It's a bustling place that serves delicious food and no one seems in a hurry to leave. The two restaurants have boarded floors and shuttered Georgian windows, log fires and candles everywhere. Food is hearty and deliciously English, perhaps potted partridge with red onion marmalade, whole roast grouse with bread sauce, apple crumble with toffee custard. There's an excellent wine list, too, and a garden at the back for Pimm's in summer. Jervaulx Abbey is a mile away, and you can follow the river up to Middleham with stepping stones to help you cross.

Black Sheep Brewery
Masham

Masham is a hugely appealing market town in Wensleydale, and has the added attraction of being home to the Black Sheep. The visitor centre and bistro are integral at this handsome stone shrine to good ale. The guided tour is fascinating, and you may whet your appetite with a glass or two of bitter before settling down to lunch in the restaurant. Food is straightforward and tasty, perhaps pork medallions with black pudding, sausages and mash or braised lamb shank with root vegetables in beer. The coffee and snacks are delicious and there's a 'pub', of course, with old oak floors and all those great Black Sheep beers on tap. The dining area on its spacious mezzanine has far-reaching views over the town to the hills beyond – fabulous.

Meals	Lunch from £13.50.
	Dinner from £27.50.
Closed	Open all day.

Meals	Lunch from £4.95.
	Dinner from £10.95.
	Sunday lunch, 3 courses, £17.50.
Closed	Sun-Wed evenings.

	Paul & Helen Klein
	The Blue Lion,
	East Witton,
	Leyburn DL8 4SN
Tel	+44 (0)1969 624273
Web	www.thebluelion.co.uk

Entry 753 Map 12

	Ellie Best
	Black Sheep Brewery,
	Wellgarth, Masham,
	Ripon HG4 4EN
Tel	+44 (0)1765 689227
Web	www.blacksheepbrewery.co.uk

Entry 754 Map 12

Wales

The Black Lion Inn
Holyhead

The lion roars again thanks to the hard work of owners Mari and Leigh who have transformed this once derelict late 18th-century country inn into an award-winning local champion. Contemporary slate tiles wrap round a modern bar, lime rendered walls host modern pictures – one a fabulous collage of the menu's provenance. French windows open to a paved patio with views across the car park to fields, one of which will soon grow vegetables and herbs for the kitchen. Ales from Marstons and local Welsh breweries and interesting wines set you up for modern British dishes. Try fresh-as-can-be local pan-fried scallops with black pudding on a bed of wilted lettuce topped with butter sauce, or beef from Mari's father's own Hereford herd. Upstairs are two hugely comfortable rooms with open rafters, thick carpets and handmade oak furniture: the mattresses are top of the range, the bathrooms gleam with white tiles, mosaic inlay and sleek chrome. You are beside a road but thick walls and small windows ensure blissful calm, while eco-energy keeps you snug. Glorious Anglesey awaits.

Rooms	1 double: £115.
	1 family room for 4: £140.
	Single £90.
Meals	Lunch & dinner £6–£19.
Closed	Rarely.

Leigh & Mari Faulkner
The Black Lion Inn,
Llanfaethlu,
Holyhead LL65 4NL
Tel   +44 (0)1407 730718
Web   www.blacklionanglesey.com

Anglesey

Ship Inn
Red Wharf Bay

The boatmen still walk across from the estuary with their catch. Inside the Ship, fires roar in several fireplaces and bars share nautical bits and bobs. There are pews and benches and bare stone walls, and big blackboards where the daily specials change almost by the hour. At night, the menu proffers Welsh seafood based on the best the boats have brought in: grilled turbot served with lemon and seasonal vegetables; dressed crab. But the old Ship is so much more – a family-friendly public house where, for 30 years, regulars and visitors have enjoyed great ales and freshly prepared food, from 'brechdanau' (sandwiches) to 'pwdin' (bread pudding). Fine Welsh cheeses, too. These lovely people are as proud of their hospitality as they are of their language, and the vast sea and sand views from the terraces are inspiring.

Meals	Lunch & dinner £11.50–£16.95.
Closed	Open all day.

Neil Kenneally
Ship Inn,
Red Wharf Bay,
Pentraeth LL75 8RJ
Tel +44 (0)1248 852568
Web www.shipinnredwharfbay.co.uk

Entry 756 Map 6

Anglesey

Ye Olde Bulls Head Inn
Beaumaris

The former haunt of Johnson and Dickens now attracts drinkers and foodies like bees to clover. In the rambling, snug-alcoved bar there's draught Bass on offer; in the modern brasserie in the stables are ten wines by the glass – and tasty food to go with it, perhaps Moroccan fish stew or confit duck leg. Upstairs sees a sophisticated remodelling, in the intimate Loft Restaurant – along with pieces of ancient weaponry and an antique ducking stool. Welsh dishes are designed around seafood from the Menai Strait, and as much beef, lamb and game as the chefs can source on the island. The results: lamb loin rolled in thyme and garlic with coriander jus; wild turbot with braised pig's cheeks, fondant potato and glazed vegetables… seasoned as required with Anglesey sea salt. Service comes with warmth and charm.

Meals	Lunch & dinner in brasserie £5–£30. Dinner in restaurant, 3 courses, £45 (Tues-Sat, evenings only).
Closed	Open all day.

David Robertson
Ye Olde Bulls Head Inn,
Castle Street,
Beaumaris LL58 8AP
Tel +44 (0)1248 810329
Web www.bullsheadinn.co.uk

Entry 757 Map 6

The Dolaucothi Arms
Llanwrda

Tucked away in the heart of the Carmarthenshire countryside, this gem of a pub shines bright. Lovely Esther and Dave have brought the Dolaucothi back to life – you'll notice little touches like Esther's floral reupholstering on the mix-and-match dining chairs, and friendly clutches of blooms in jugs and antique bottles. Dave's gorgeous gardens flank the walk up the little path; as you come in, there's a happy buzz in the air and the tempting scent of fresh home cooking; some ingredients are foraged from the surroundings by the chef. The dining room and bar are all in warm neutrals, with terracotta tiles and wood-burners. Sink into the velvety green chesterfield in the snug with a bottle of local brew or a glass of wine – Esther and Dave can advise. Foodwise, try the pork and elderflower sausages or homemade pie; both are local and delicious. Hop up the little staircase, and you'll find two quiet bedrooms with garden views in soft tones of olive or wild rose. Snuggle up with the cosy woollen throws, and spoil yourself in the brilliant bathrooms. There's even a little tipple on the chest of drawers for a nightcap!

Rooms	2 doubles: £75-£80. Singles £55. Extra bed/sofabed £20 per person per night.
Meals	Lunch from £5. Dinner, 3 courses, £20. Sunday roast from £9.
Closed	26 December, 2 January.

David Joy & Esther Hubert
The Dolaucothi Arms,
Pumpsaint,
Llanwrda SA19 8UW
Tel   +44 (0)1558 650237
Web   www.thedolaucothiarms.co.uk

Entry 758 Map 6

Carmarthenshire

Y Polyn
Nantgaredig

The pub sits by a fork in the roads, one leading to Aberglasney, the other to the National Botanic Garden of Wales. This lot know their onions and Susan was head chef at the Worshipful Company of Innholders, The interior, sporting warm colours, herringbone mats, local art, candles and fresh flowers introduces a contemporary shabby chic. A wicker sofa and armchairs by the fire encourage you to lounge, the restaurant has a happy mix of tables and chairs, and the menu is pleasingly simple, with fresh local ingredients well put together. Start with pork rillettes with pickled root vegetable, move onto duck confit with braised puy lentils or red mullet with saffron, potato and leek broth, finish with egg custard tart with honey roast plums. You are equally welcome to just pop in for a drink.

Meals	Lunch & dinner £10–£29.50. Sunday lunch, 2 courses, £18.50.
Closed	4pm-7pm, Sun evenings & Mon.

Mark & Susan Manson
Y Polyn,
Nantgaredig,
Carmarthen SA32 7LH

Tel   +44 (0)1267 290000
Web   www.ypolynrestaurant.co.uk

Entry 759 Map 6

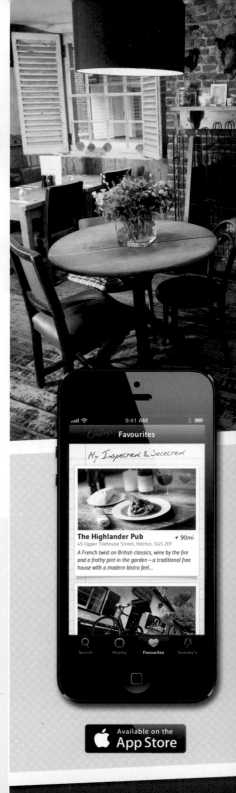

Y Talbot
Tregaron

In the centre of tiny Tregaron, the crisply Georgian frontage of Y Talbot makes a big impression, part modern-rustic drovers inn and part old-fashioned hotel. Inside the inn: an enormous inglenook with bread oven, slate floors, thick walls gleaming with hanging brass and copper. You dine in what was once the stable, with oak furniture and soapstone sculptures, where everything is light and bright. The hotel is all white corridors and glass doors, its curved wooden staircase leading to rooms which are cool and white and comfortable, with big smart bathrooms. The rooms on the top floor are cosiest, with low windows to views over the square. Two new airy rooms at the rear of the pub are big enough for families. Friendly Mick and Nia will point you towards the best walks while head chef Dafydd Watkin (who worked under Marco Pierre White) does a mean Cambrian lamb shoulder, and works wonders with the day's fresh fish catch. All this and local tipples such as Purple Moose, Gwynt y Ddraig cider and Mantle from the latest micro brewery on the block.

Rooms	8 twin/doubles: £80–£120.
	3 family rooms for 4: £110–£160.
	2 singles: £50–£70.
	Extra bed/sofabed £15–£30 per person per night.
	Dinner, B&B £80–£100 per person per night.
Meals	Starters from £4.75.
	Dinner £9–£18.
Closed	Christmas Day.

Mick Taylor
Y Talbot,
Tregaron SY25 6JL
Tel   +44 (0)1974 298208
Web   www.ytalbot.com

Entry 760 Map 6

Ceredigion

Harbourmaster
Aberaeron

Lobster boats at lunch, twinkling harbour lights at dinner, real ale, well-chosen wines, dazzling service. The old harbourmaster's residence has become decidedly chic with an inspirational restaurant and bar. Step in to find a space that's cosy but cool: soft shades, blocked-oak tables. In the celebrated bistro, daily menus are studded with the best local produce and the dishes delight: Carlingford oysters; hake with squash risotto and a basil beurre blanc; confit duck leg with redcurrant jus; bakewell tart with almond ice cream. In the bar (open for breakfast from 8am) tuck into local crab and parsley risotto, Welsh rib-eye steak or a stone-baked pizza. The Heulyns' dedication to all that is best about Wales shines forth. Cycle tracks spin off into the hills, coastal paths lead north and south.

Ceredigion

Y Ffarmers
Llanfihangel y Creuddyn

The drive to this pretty village, once a silver and lead mining community, is well worth it. Previously a farm and tax collector's office, Y Ffarmers has found its true calling under the delightful stewardship of chef Rhodri and wife Esther. You can walk into the quarry-tiled bar with mud on your boots and not an eyelid will be batted; enjoy a pint of Evan Evans or Felinfoel. The dining rooms next door have polished oak flooring, an assortment of tables, books on Wales, and terrific local art on walls, with regular choral or harp evenings adding a real Welsh flavour. Everything is made from scratch, from bread and rolls to relishes and puddings. Menus range from Penlan gammon, egg and chips to lamb tagine with Medjool dates, and a pomegranate and mint couscous too.

Meals	Lunch & bar meals from £6. Dinner, 3 courses, about £30. Sunday roast £25.
Closed	Open all day.

Meals	Lunch & dinner £5–£18.50. Sunday roast £16–£19.50.
Closed	Mon all day (except school summer holidays).

Glyn & Menna Heulyn
Harbourmaster,
Pen Cei,
Aberaeron SA46 0BT
Tel   +44 (0)1545 570755
Web   www.harbour-master.com

Entry 761 Map 6

Esther Prytherch
Y Ffarmers,
Llanfihangel y Creuddyn,
Aberystwyth SY23 4LA
Tel   +44 (0)1974 261275
Web   www.yffarmers.co.uk

Entry 762 Map 7

The Queen's Head
Glanwydden

The old wheelwright's cottage has gone up in the world. Now, under low beams, are polished tables, smart tartan carpeting, walls strewn with maps and a roaring fire in the bar. The food is good, the portions generous and you can see the cooks at work through the open hatch. This is home-cooked pub food with a modern twist; in summer there'll be fresh Conwy crab and Great Orme lobster. Friendly, smartly turned-out staff serve starters of crispy duck leg or Conwy fish soup, then salmon and coriander fishcakes, then Welsh rump steaks with garlic butter... desserts might include raspberry and amaretto trifle. Robert and Sally Cureton have been here for over 30 years, nurturing a country local that puts those of Llandudno to shame. Complete the treat by booking a night in the old parish storehouse across the road, a sweet retreat for two and recently revamped. A gallery bedroom under white-painted eaves, a bathroom lavishly tiled, a small private garden for breakfast coffee and fresh croissants... perfect for a romantic break.

Rooms	1 cottage for 2 (self-catering option also available): £90–£150 per night.
Meals	Lunch & dinner £9.95–£21.95. Sunday roast £10.95.
Closed	Rarely.

Robert & Sally Cureton
The Queen's Head,
Glanwydden,
Llandudno Junction LL31 9JP
Tel   +44 (0)1492 546570
Web   www.queensheadglanwydden.co.uk

Conwy

The Albion
Conwy

For lovers of real ale and lively chat no visit to Conwy would be complete without raising a glass here. Tucked just beside the ancient town walls by one of the narrow stone gateways is an unassuming pub. Inside is spacious with roaring fires and comfy interiors: Tiffany style lamps and chandeliers, an antique banquette, dark polished wood floorboards and Art Deco touches. Run as a joint venture by the Conwy, Great Orme, Nant and Purple Moose Breweries the real ale on offer is outstanding and there's no fine dining to interfere with the flow, just handmade pork pies and pickled eggs. There's a neat central courtyard for warmer days and it's super dog-friendly too. The Albion buzzes with humanity and good cheer, and staff know their beer-led business.

| Meals | Bar snacks only. |
| Closed | Open all day. |

Stuart Chapman-Edwards
The Albion,
Upper Gate Street, Conwy LL32 8RF
Tel   +44 (0)1492 582484
Web   www.conwybrewery.co.uk

Entry 764 Map 7

Conwy

The Groes Inn
Ty'n-y-Groes

The first licensed house in Wales (1573) is splendidly old-fashioned, with rambling bars, nooks and crannies, and low beams and doorways that demand heads be bowed. Painted stonework is hung with local prints and pictures, there are displays of teacups and Victorian postcards, a red carpet, a polished dresser, a wood-burner to keep things toasty. Our pint of Orme's Best – brewed by Justin's cousin – went down a treat, as did the prime-beef burger in its great toasted bap, with a crisp mixed salad and delicious hand-cut chips. In the more elegant restaurant, 32 wines accompany award-winning dishes: baked field mushrooms, Conway crab and Anglesey oysters, sweet Welsh lamb with rich rosemary jus, chocolate-scented pancakes with sumptuous ice cream. For summer there's a pretty garden with mountain views. Top hole!

Meals	Bar meals from £9.65.
	Lunch & dinner from £13.25.
Closed	3pm-6pm.

Dawn & Justin Humphreys
The Groes Inn,
Ty'n-y-Groes LL32 8TN
Tel   +44 (0)1492 650545
Web   www.groesinn.com

Entry 765 Map 7

Conwy

Pen-y-Bryn
Colwyn Bay

Oak floors and bookcases, open fires and Turkey rugs — welcome to the make-believe world of Brunning & Price. Staff are well-informed and never too busy to share their knowledge, of the food and its provenance. Menus are enticing and generously priced: braised shoulder of lamb with dauphinoise potatoes and rosemary gravy; warming leek and potato soup with crusty bread. Pork and lamb is local, cheeses fly the Principality's flag and plump mussels come from down the coast. You're high up on Colwyn Heights here but a few glasses of Purple Moose's Snowdonia or Salopian's Black Heart Stout will soon warm your toes. Sturdy wooden furniture in the garden fits in well with the neighbourhood's residential air... and there are wonderful views over the sea.

Conwy

The Kinmel Arms
St George

In a tiny hamlet — yet easily reachable from the A55 — the Kinmel Arms shines like a culinary beacon. Lynn and Tim arrived a decade ago and the place continues to delight. Walk in to an open-plan space of cool neutral colours, hardwood floors and a central bar with stained-glass above; then through to a conservatory restaurant, painted a cheery yellow and decorated with Tim's photographs. Seasonal brasserie-style menus champion local producers — Welsh beef fillet with Penderyn whisky sauce; Asian-spiced sea bass with crispy squid in a coconut and lentil cream. All is beautifully presented, and the slate-topped bar dispenses top quality local ales and great value bin-end wines. This is a hop from the stunning North Wales coast and Snowdonia; great walks start from the door.

Meals	Bar meals £4.50-£9.25. Lunch & dinner £6.25-£16.95. Sunday roast £10.25.
Closed	Open all day.

Meals	Lunch £6.95-£17.50. Dinner £14.95-£24.95.
Closed	3pm-6pm; Sun & Mon all day.

Andrew Grant
Pen-y-Bryn,
Wentworth Avenue,
Colwyn Bay LL29 6DD
Tel   +44 (0)1352 750500
Web   www.penybryn-colwynbay.co.uk

Entry 766 Map 7

Tim Watson & Lynn Cunnah-Watson
The Kinmel Arms,
The Village, St George,
Abergele LL22 9BP
Tel   +44 (0)1745 832207
Web   www.thekinmelarms.co.uk

Entry 767 Map 7

The Hand at Llanarmon
Llanarmon Dyffryn Ceiriog

Single-track lanes plunge you into the middle of nowhere, lush valleys rise and fall – pull on the boots and scale a mountain. Back at the inn, once frequented by 16th-century drovers, the pleasures of a country local are hard to miss. A coal fire burns on the range in reception, a fire crackles under brass in the front bar and a wood-burner warms the lofty dining room. There are exposed stone walls, low beamed ceilings, old pine settles and candles on the mantelpiece, a games room for darts and pool, a quiet sitting room for maps and books. Delicious food is popular with locals, so grab a table and enjoy seasonal menus – perhaps chicken liver parfait with fruit chutney and toasted homemade bread, duck with pancetta, black pudding and red wine, and autumn berry pudding. Stay and you'll get a lovely cooked Welsh breakfast too. Bedrooms are just as they should be: not too fancy, cosy and warm, with crisp white linen and scrupulously clean. A very friendly place: Jonathan and Jackie are full of passionate enthusiasm and have made their home warmly welcoming. Everyone loves this place.

Rooms	9 doubles, 4 twin/doubles: £90–£128. Singles from £52.50.
Meals	Bar meals from £9.50. Lunch from £4.75. Sunday roast from £15. Dinner, 3 courses, £25–£30.
Closed	Rarely.

Jackie & Jonathan Greatorex
The Hand at Llanarmon,
Llanarmon Dyffryn Ceiriog,
Llangollen LL20 7LD

Tel	+44 (0)1691 600666
Web	www.thehandhotel.co.uk

Entry 768 Map 7

Denbighshire

The Corn Mill
Llangollen

The 18th century has been left far behind in this renovated corn mill beside the swift flowing Dee. Not only is the interior airy and well-designed but the menu is laced with contemporary ideas. There are gorgeous views onto the river whether you're quaffing your pint of Phoenix in the fabulous bar, or sitting down to eat in one of the upper dining areas. The decked veranda-cum-walkway is stunning, built out over cascading rapids with a gangway overhanging one end beyond a revolving water wheel. Watch dippers and wagtails as you tuck into smoked haddock and mozzarella rarebit, Welsh pork sausages with spring onion mash, king prawn salad with chilli dressing – the Brunning & Price formula is known for its 'something-for-everyone' appeal.

Meals	Lunch & dinner £8.95–£16.50.
Closed	Open all day.

Andrew Barker
The Corn Mill,
Castle Street,
Llangollen LL20 8PN
Tel   +44 (0)1978 869555
Web   www.cornmill-llangollen.co.uk

Entry 769 Map 7

Denbighshire

Pant-yr-Ochain
Gresford

A long drive snakes through landscaped parkland to a magnificent multi-gabled country house sheltered by trees, to one side of which a huge conservatory opens up views across terraces to the estate lake. Inside, a jigsaw of richly panelled rooms and drinking areas lures drinkers and diners alike: note the nine real ales. There are intimate corners, comfy alcoves and private snugs, open fires, quarry tiles and bare boards below an eccentric ceiling-line. Everywhere, a cornucopia of bric-a-brac: penny slots and cases of clay pipes, caricatures and prints. It sounds OTT but it fits comfortably here, and the ever-reliable Brunning & Price menus feature enjoyable dishes: venison, orange and thyme burger; smoked haddock and salmon fishcakes. Outside? A flower-filled, lakeside garden.

Meals	Lunch & dinner £5.75–£16.95.
Closed	Open all day.

James Meakin
Pant-yr-Ochain, Old Wrexham Rd,
Gresford, Wrexham LL12 8TY
Tel   +44 (0)1978 853525
Web   www.brunningandprice.co.uk/
pantyrochain

Entry 770 Map 7

Flintshire

Glasfryn
Sychdyn

Drawing a diverse crowd, this solid red brick pub — a former judges' residence with an Arts & Crafts pedigree — sits on a south-facing slope with views over the town to the Clwydian range. A stunning makeover has led to acres of oak flooring, Indian rugs, book-lined walls and locally themed pictures and prints. Real ale aficionados will thrill to eight cask ales. Purple Moose's Snowdonia delivers a crisp, citrus beer; Flowers Original is brewing heritage in a glass. Foodies are not forgotten... find mint-braised shoulder of lamb with mustard mash and broccoli; quiche with roasted squash, goat's cheese and red onion; white chocolate cheesecake. You get 80 malts, every spirit imaginable and coffee made by an Italian — need we say more? It's abuzz, and the staff are attentive and helpful.

Meals	Lunch & dinner £8.50-£15.95.
Closed	Open all day.

Andrew Grant
Glasfryn,
Raikes Lane, Sychdyn,
Mold CH7 6LR
Tel   +44 (0)1352 750500
Web   www.glasfryn-mold.co.uk

Entry 771 Map 7

Flintshire

The Glynne Arms
Hawarden

This handsome Georgian coaching inn was built in 1812 and takes its name from the Glynne family whose ancestral seat was Hawarden Castle. From the outset it was a place for the village, more 'house of refreshment' than drinking den. Today that is as true as ever, with outstanding produce from the estate's farm shop finding its way to the kitchen. There's grilled sea bream on crushed new potatoes with curly kale and a crayfish and thermidor sauce; grills, antipasti and ploughman's platters and more. The pub itself has undergone a stunning renovation and has a retro-quirky character with bold rugs, framed period posters, bills and letters, crossed axes, antlers and a bust encircled with a footy scarf — get the picture? Charming staff make you feel welcome, and being here is a treat.

Meals	Lunch & dinner £6.95-£23.50.
Closed	Open all day.

Martin Hurd
The Glynne Arms,
3 Glynne Way,
Hawarden CH5 3NS
Tel   +44 (0)1244 569988
Web   www.theglynnearms.co.uk

Entry 772 Map 7

Cross Foxes
Brithdir

Nicol and Dewi have worked wonders breathing new life into this stone built former farmhouse. A steel and glass entrance leads through to a modern bar where flagstones, exposed stonework and beams mingle with contemporary sofas, designer bar stools and sleek lighting. In summer, sup Purple Moose's Snowdonia Ale on the terrace and gaze up at lofty Cadair Idris – a giant's seat indeed. Food from the open kitchen comes with impeccable local credentials and the char-grill compliments the meats perfectly. What could be more local than Conwy mussels, leeks and cream followed by confit leg of Welsh lamb, rosemary and honey gravy, potatoes and seasonal vegetables? There are great Sunday roasts too, light bites, and afternoon teas. Upstairs the comfort factor scales new heights as natural stone, beams and antiques blend with a crisp modernity; there are lazy beds for dreaming in and mountain views to gaze on. Gorgeous bathrooms, with Thierry Mugler lotions and thick robes, soothe those who have stretched their muscles in the surrounding hills. A 15-minute drive brings you to delightful Barmouth and the coast.

Rooms	2 doubles, 2 twin/doubles, 2 suites for 2: £90-£135.
Meals	Lunch from £4.95. Dinner & bar meals from £9.95. Sunday lunch, 2 courses, £12.95.
Closed	Rarely.

	Nicol Gwynne
	Cross Foxes,
	Brithdir,
	Dolgellau LL40 2SG
Tel	+44 (0)1341 421001
Web	www.crossfoxes.co.uk

Entry 773 Map 7

Penhelig Arms
Aberdyfi

It all comes together in one of Wales' finest fishing villages; sea, estuary and mountains wait outside the door. From this handsome harbourside coaching inn the views are wide and uplifting. With a salty tang on your cheek, enter the traditional Fisherman's Bar to order a pint of Reverend James – or craft ale, Willy Nilly – and settle into a nautically cosy corner. From kitchen to smartly dressed dining table flow classic Anglo-Welsh dishes that change daily, with the emphasis on fish. Start with pearl las and broccoli soup, then fillet of baked black sea bream infused with chilli, ginger and garlic, served with soy rice and courgettes, then perhaps a slate of Welsh cheeses; there are great wines, too. The jewels in the crown are the light-filled annexe suites perched above, where modern colours, leather sofas, nautical artwork, state of the art gadgets and private balconies or patios. The ten rooms in the hotel are not quite so lavish, but almost all get the views, and Penhelig House is perfect for families. A place run with passion and a welcome for all – including our four-legged friends.

Rooms	9 doubles: £80-£210.
	6 singles: £60-£170.
Meals	Bar meals from £7.95.
	Lunch & dinner £8.95-£15.95.
Closed	Rarely.

Chris Ainsworth
Penhelig Arms,
27-29 Terrace Road,
Aberdyfi LL35 0LT
Tel   +44 (0)1654 767215
Web   www.penheligarms.com

Entry 774 Map 6

Newbridge On Usk
Tredunnock

As darkness falls, the old stone bridge is floodlit, its arches reflected in the waters of the Usk. The setting is seductive, the garden runs down to the river bank, salmon leap in the eddying river outside and the views from the window are stunning. This is what a gastropub should be; warm, inviting and beautifully turned out. In several rooms on several levels, pots of flowers or collections of squashes reflect the seasons, big leather sofas invite you to sit, and the interior reveals the naked beauty of floorboards and beams. You don't have to eat here but you should and the set lunch is a steal. Ingredients are sourced with care; try woodland mushroom and white truffle risotto, Brecon venison wrapped in smoked bacon, a wicked sticky toffee pudding. Groups can sit down to an indulgent feasting menu in an atmospheric wine store. Avoid the dark, windy roads and stay in one of the six inviting purpose-built rooms set away from the pub; rustically styled with solid oak furniture and heavenly bathrooms. Go up a level for a four-poster and a view.

Rooms	5 doubles, 1 four-poster: £77–£235.
Meals	Set lunch, 2 courses, from £15.95.
	Dinner, 3 courses, from £30.
Closed	Rarely.

The Manager
Newbridge On Usk,
Tredunnock,
Usk NP15 1LY
Tel   +44 (0)1633 410262
Web   www.celtic-manor.com/newbridge-on-usk

Entry 775 Map 2

Monmouthshire

The Hardwick
Hardwick

After honing his skills in some of the best kitchens in the world – not least the Walnut Inn near Abergavenny – Stephen Terry then purchased the old Horse & Jockey at Hardwick. The fashionably back-to-basics interior is a modest background for seriously fine wines and astonishingly good food. While some of the ingredients are imported from Italy, most originate from closer to home, including the beers (Hobby Horse, Otley Bitter) on draught. The impressive menu offers the likes of confit duck hash, fried local duck egg with chargrilled endive and blood orange then, perhaps, roast cod with chorizo and saffron risotto cake and romesco sauce. A sleek stylish bar and a function room complete the immaculate picture, and lunch is brilliant value.

Meals	Lunch £19-£24.
	À la carte menu, 3 courses, £40.
	Sunday roast £21-£26.
Closed	Open all day.

Stephen & Jo Terry
The Hardwick,
Old Raglan Road, Hardwick,
Abergavenny NP7 9AA
Tel   +44 (0)1873 854220
Web   www.thehardwick.co.uk

Entry 776 Map 7

Monmouthshire

The Bell at Skenfrith
Skenfrith

The Bell stands by an ancient stone bridge in a little-known valley with beautiful hills rising behind and a Norman castle paddling in the river a hundred yards from the front door. A sublime spot – and the inn is as good. In the locals' bar you find slate floors, open fires, plump-cushioned armchairs and polished oak. In summer, life decants onto the terrace at the back; priceless views of wood and hill interrupted only by the odd chef pottering past on his way to a rather impressive kitchen garden. Stripped boards in the restaurant give an airy feel, so stop for delicious food served by young, attentive staff, perhaps chicken liver parfait, duck with chorizo and mixed bean cassoulet, and chocolate fondant with caramelised banana and white chocolate ice cream. Finish with a fine cognac – the list is long.

Meals	Lunch from £5.95.
	Sunday roast from £12.95.
	Dinner, 3 courses, around £35.
Closed	Tues.
	Nov- Mar.

Richard Ireton & Sarah Hudson
The Bell at Skenfrith,
Skenfrith,
Abergavenny NP7 8UH
Tel   +44 (0)1600 750235
Web   www.skenfrith.co.uk

Entry 777 Map 7

Newport

The Ridgeway Bar & Kitchen
Newport

Minutes from the M4 this former 1960s watering hole has been transformed into a stylish concern in a residential suburb. The bar area is for drink and chat only and has a smart lounge feel, all padded banquettes, polished slate tiles and a mix of wood and painted furniture. Cheery staff dispense Sharps, St Austell and Wye Valley ales, and cocktails are coming soon. The dining areas are spacious and comfortable with New England tones on painted panelling and here you can enjoy chef Rickie's modern British food. There are good old-fashioned methods in the preparation and no corner-cutting. Start with Somerset cider-steamed mussels mopped up with toasted artisan bread, and move on to braised beef shin with chantenay carrots, wilted spinach, fondant potato and roasting jus. Quality is king.

Meals	Lunch & dinner £8.50–£15.
Closed	Open all day.

David Pell
The Ridgeway Bar & Kitchen,
No.2 Ridgeway Avenue,
NP20 5AJ
Tel   +44 (0)1633 266053
Web   www.storyinns.com

Entry 778 Map 2

My Inspected & Selected

The Highlander Pub   ➤ 90mi
45 Upper Tilehouse Street, Hitchin, SG5 2EF
A French twist on British classics, wine by the fire and a frothy pint in the garden – a traditional free house with a modern bistro feel...

Search   Nearby   Favourites   Sawday's

Available on the
App Store

www.sawdays.co.uk/pubs

Pembrokeshire

Stackpole Inn
Stackpole

In the lovely Stackpole National Park, a jolly, thriving, dining pub with infectiously enthusiastic owners and a chef with local food connections: as much as possible is Welsh and all is cooked from scratch. Ramble through several rustic-smart rooms with a mix of exposed wood and stonework, carpets and slate floors, warmed by wood-burners and freshly painted, soft-lit and cosy. Daily specials (fresh sea bass, Welsh Black beef) compete with a sensibly priced menu: perhaps Welsh blue cheese pots with crusty bread and local pork in an apple and cider cream sauce. There are several good single-malt whiskies to choose from, wine is plentiful by the glass and real ales include Rev James and Double Dragon. Bedrooms, in a separate building, are light, airy and beachy; family rooms are excellent value. This is perfect for walking the coastal path, climbing cliff and rock faces, fishing from beach or boat, surfing those tricky beaches... each room has a locker downstairs for outdoor equipment, and there's a cycle rack.

Rooms	2 twin/doubles: £90.
	2 family rooms for 4: £90-£120.
	Singles from £60.
Meals	Dinner, 3 courses, £25-£30
	(not Sundays Oct-Mar).
	Lunch from £5.
	Sunday roast from £9.50.
Closed	Rarely.

Gary & Becky Evans
Stackpole Inn,
Stackpole,
Pembroke SA71 5DF
Tel   +44 (0)1646 672324
Web www.stackpoleinn.co.uk

Pembrokeshire

The Old Point House Inn
Angle

Lonely, windswept, so close to the sea they're cut off at spring tide. Weary fishermen have beaten a path to the inn's door for centuries; part-built with shipwreck timbers, it started life as a bakehouse for ships' biscuits. The tiny, low-beamed bar, its bare walls papered with old navigation charts, is utterly authentic, the restaurant is cosy by night, and in fine weather you can sit out and devour prawn sandwiches. Everyone is welcome here, from weathered regulars meeting over pints of Felinfoel to families in for Sunday lunch. Naturally, menus favours fish, with local Milford cod, sea bass and a delicious peppery fish chowder, all chalked up on the board. Further crowd-pleasers rib-eye steak with red wine sauce and piles of chips.

Meals	Lunch & bar meals £5.50–£10.50. Dinner £5.50–£19.95. Sunday lunch, 3 courses, £12.50.
Closed	3pm-6pm. Closed Mon & Tues in winter. Open all day in summer.

John Noble
The Old Point House Inn,
Angle Village,
Angle,
Pembroke SA71 5AS
Tel   +44 (0)1646 641205

Entry 780 Map 6

Pembrokeshire

Griffin Inn
Dale

Dale's last, very old pub – there were once 15 – sits defiantly close to the water and has seen out some stormy seas. The stone sea wall in front is known as 'the longest bar in Pembrokeshire' and what better place to be on a warm day with a pint of Rev James or Cwrw Haf as you watch the day's catch being unloaded on the jetty from the Griffin's own boat. Fresh fish, lobster and shellfish are hugely popular here and make the short distance from beach to Simon and Sian's home-cooked menus. Inside are red quarry tiles, painted stone, wood panelling and an open fire in the cosy traditional bar. An extension and roof-top terrace are planned, to make the most of the great views across the bay and up the Haven, kids love to play on the pontoon, and the coastal walks are superb.

Meals	Starters from £5.95. Dinner from £9.25.
Closed	Open all day.

Simon & Sian Vickers
Griffin Inn,
Dale,
Haverfordwest SA62 3RB
Tel   +44 (0)1646 636227
Web   www.griffininndale.co.uk

Entry 781 Map 6

Pembrokeshire

The Swan Inn
Little Haven

Little Haven is jumbled into the seaward end of a narrow valley with glorious views across St Bride's Bay. Trek up the cobbled path to reach the Swan, whose fabric and fortunes have been restored by Paul Morris. Original features abound in the uncluttered sideroom snug and the blue-painted dining room, alongside bare boards and stone, simple wood furniture and glowing stoves for wild days. Equally warming is the delicious food: at lunch, homemade sodabread topped with smoked salmon maybe, or a traditional Welsh cawl with Caerfai cheese. In the evening: pan-fried scallops with chorizo, roasted sea bass with caper butter and samphire. For summer there's a broad wall to lounge on and a tiny terrace, so settle in for the day with a foaming pint of Bass and take in the views – they're stupendous.

Meals	Lunch from £5.50.
	Dinner from £12.
Closed	Open all day.

Paul & Tracey Morris
The Swan Inn,
Point Road, Little Haven,
Haverfordwest SA62 3UL
Tel   +44 (0)1437 781880
Web   www.theswanlittlehaven.co.uk

Entry 782 Map 6

Pembrokeshire

The Sloop
Porthgain

Perfectly in keeping with its seawashed setting, the Sloop has been welcoming fisherfolk since 1743. The village remains a fishing harbour – the landlord catches his own lobster, mackerel and crab, and dives for scallops – but, until the 1930s, Porthgain was more famous for bricks and granite. Weatherbeaten on the outside, with a little seating area at the front, the old Sloop is surprisingly cosy within. Expect bare beams, some bare boards, a happy mêlée of furniture, a canoe suspended from the ceiling and a board announcing daily specials. Tuck into homemade mackerel pâté, lobster thermidor or Welsh Black steak; breakfast too (open to all) sounds a treat. Holiday makers descend in summer but the rest of the year this is a community pub, with a proper games room and real fires.

| Meals | Lunch & dinner £5.35–£18. |
| Closed | Open all day. |

Matthew Blakiston
The Sloop,
Porthgain,
Haverfordwest SA62 5BN
Tel   +44 (0)1348 831449
Web   www.sloop.co.uk

Entry 783 Map 6

Pembrokeshire

Tafarn Sinc
Rosebush

The highest pub in Pembrokeshire is the quirkiest pub in the world – a corrugated crimson shed. It was speedily erected in 1876 as a hotel on the GWR railway; now this huge zinc building with a panorama of the Preseli Hills oversees a railway platform complete with mannequin-travellers. It is beautifully tended, with a profusion of planters and picnic sets outside and an arresting Alpine-panelled bar within. Hams and lamps hang from the ceiling, there's sawdust on the floors and two wood-burners that belch out heat. It's warm and welcoming and full of merry walkers. Hafwen the perfect landlady, and husband Brian, oversee the cosy constant buzz and serve a solidly traditional menu (Preseli lamb burgers; faggots with onion gravy), and their own excellent beer. No further introduction is needed – just go.

Pembrokeshire

The Old Sailor's
Dinas Cross

A quick zig and a zag off the coast road and you are rewarded with a sublime waterside setting, a stunning walk around Dinas Head and superb seafood at this 500-year old pub. Formerly called the Sailors' Safety, it once kept a light burning as a guide for ships. Dylan Thomas visited at least once and so must you! It's no beauty from the outside but inside is comfortingly traditional with a dark wood carved bar, quarry tiles, sturdy tables and chairs, rough-rendered white walls and nautical bits: a fitting place for a Felinfoel ale pulled by long-term landlord Langley, who will tell you about the best fish of the day on the specials boards; the shellfish, crabs and lobster are good too. The dining area is more formal and has great views across the garden to Fishguard.

Meals	Lunch & dinner £9.80–£16.50.
	Sunday lunch, 3 courses, £12.95.
Closed	Mon (in winter).

Meals	Starters from £4.95.
	Dinner from £9.
Closed	Mon all day.

Brian & Hafwen Davies
Tafarn Sinc,
Rosebush,
Clynderwen SA66 7QU
Tel   +44 (0)1437 532214
Web   www.tafarnsinc.com

Entry 784 Map 6

Langley Forrest
The Old Sailor's,
Pwllgwaelod, Dinas Cross,
Newport SA42 0SE
Tel   +44 (0)1348 811491

Entry 785 Map 6

Pembrokeshire

Llys Meddyg
Newport

This fabulous restaurant has a bit of everything: cool rooms that pack a designer punch, super food in a sparkling restaurant, a cellar bar for drinks before dinner, a fabulous garden for summer treats. It's a very friendly place with charming staff on hand to help, and it draws in a local crowd who come for the seriously good food, perhaps mussel and saffron soup, rib of Welsh beef with hand-cut chips, cherry soufflé with pistachio ice cream. You eat in style with a fire burning at one end of the restaurant and good art hanging on the walls. Best of all is the back garden with a mountain-fed stream pouring past. In summer, a café/bistro opens up out here — coffee and cake or steak and chips — with doors that open onto the garden. Don't miss Pembrokeshire's fabulous coastal path for its windswept cliffs, sandy beaches and secluded coves.

Meals	Lunch from £7.
	Dinner from £14.
Closed	Open all day.

Louise & Edward Sykes
Llys Meddyg,
East Street,
Newport SA42 0SY
Tel +44 (0)1239 820008
Web www.llysmeddyg.com

Entry 786 Map 6

Pembrokeshire

Nag's Head Inn
Abercych

Behind the vibrant orange exterior is a feast of bare wood and stone. The lighting is soft and warm, there's a rustic chicken-wire sideboard crammed with old beer bottles, a glass cabinet displaying the famous 'rat' of Abercych (a stuffed coypu) and a photo of old Emrys, the treasured regular after whom the home-brew is named. The Nag's Head has a simple, tasteful charm, is full of old tales, curios and quirkery and serves the best kind of hearty food, from whitebait and fresh soups to steak and kidney pudding, treacle tart, and Sunday roasts. Come with the family and explore the pushchair-friendly Clynfyw sculpture trail — it starts from here. There's a play area too, in the lovely riverside garden. By a bridge on the river bank, at the bottom of a steep hill, the setting alone is worth the trip.

Meals	Lunch & dinner £8–£15.
	Sunday lunch, 3 courses, £13.95.
Closed	3pm–6pm.
	Open all day Sun.

Sam Jamieson
Nag's Head Inn,
Abercych,
Boncath SA37 0HJ
Tel +44 (0)1239 841200
Web www.nagsheadabercych.co.uk

Entry 787 Map 6

The Felin Fach Griffin
Felin Fach

It's quirky, homespun, utterly intoxicating and thrives on a mix of relaxed informality and colourful style. The timber-framed bar resembles the sitting room of a small hip country house, with sofas in front of a fire that burns on both sides and backgammon waiting to be played. Painted stone walls throughout come in blocks of colour. An open-plan feel sweeps you through to the restaurant, where stock pots simmer on an Aga; try hake fillet with pernod cream, pheasant rillette, Eve's pudding with cinnamon custard, all of it delicious. Bedrooms above are warmly simple with comfy beds wrapped in crisp linen, making this seductive for those in search of a welcoming billet close to the mountains. There are framed photographs on the walls, the odd piece of mahogany furniture, good books, no TVs (unless you ask). Breakfast is served in the dining room; wallow with the papers and make your toast on the Aga. A road passes outside, quietly at night, lanes lead into the hills, and a small organic kitchen garden provides much for the table. The Beacons are close, so walk, ride, bike, canoe – or head to Hay for books galore.

Rooms	2 doubles, 2 twin/doubles, 2 four-posters: £125–£160. 1 family room for 3: £165. Dinner, B&B £90 per person per night.
Meals	Lunch from £7. Dinner, 3 courses, about £30. Sunday roast from £19.70.
Closed	Christmas Eve & Day (evening). 4 days in January.

Charles & Edmund Inkin
The Felin Fach Griffin,
Felin Fach,
Brecon LD3 0UB
Tel   +44 (0)1874 620111
Web   www.felinfachgriffin.co.uk

Wynnstay Hotel
Machynlleth

In the quaint first capital of Wales, you'll be charmed to discover this old coaching inn. It may be more hotel than pub, but there's a great big bar with old oak floors and beams, scrubbed tables and candles, and it buzzes. Bag a seat by the woodburner in winter and study Gareth Johns's menus over a pint of Welsh ale. He applies his skills to the finest local produce: Conwy mussels, Borth lobster, salmon from the river Dyfi, beef and lamb from the valley. Try scallops with Dijon velouté and truffle dressing, then Marches venison with root vegetables, colcannon, red wine and chocolate; and you can finish with a slate of Welsh cheeses. Some wonderful wines from small producers too, and, surprisingly, a real pizzeria at the back. Stroll off any excess with a walk and the dog.

Meals	Lunch £7.95–£15.95. Dinner from £11.95. Sunday lunch, 3 courses, £16.50.
Closed	2.30pm–6pm (bar only).

Gareth & Paul Johns
Wynnstay Hotel,
Heol Maengwyn,
Machynlleth SY20 8AE
Tel   +44 (0)1654 702941
Web www.wynnstay-hotel.com

Entry 789 Map 7

Riverside Hotel
Pennal

Between the bohemian market town of Machynlleth and charming Aberdyfi by the sea is a handsome village inn, the focal point of little Pennel. New pumps shine behind the well-polished counter, the carpeted lounge is smart with mini sofas. Even the restaurant is spruce with new slate floors and matching tables, and there's a roaring wood-burner between the two. Look forward to great ales and malts, good wines by the glass and delicious food that never lets you down. Whether you go for a Welsh Black sirloin steak or a spicy vegetable stew, you know it's from local suppliers. The fish cakes were spot on and served with skinny fries; the chicken liver pâté, a smooth parfait with a lovely lingering taste, was served with berry chutney. Folks flock for the Sunday lunches, families love the riverside garden.

Meals	Lunch from £5.95. Dinner from £8. Sunday roast from £9.50.
Closed	Mon all day. 3pm–6pm Tues–Thurs. Open all day Sat & Sun.

Glyn & Corina Davies
Riverside Hotel,
Pennal,
Machynlleth SY20 9DW
Tel   +44 (0)1654 791285
Web www.riversidehotel-pennal.co.uk

Entry 790 Map 7

Powys

The Harp
Old Radnor

Chris Ireland and Angela Lyne have taken over this ancient Welsh longhouse, tucked up a dead-end lane near the parish church, and there are no plans to change. The wonderful interior is spick-and-span timeless: 14th-century slate flooring in the bar, tongue-and-groove in a room that fits a dozen diners, crannies crammed with memorabilia, an ancient curved settle, an antique reader's chair, two fires and a happy crowd. Accompany a pint of Wye Valley or Three Tuns bitter with a Welsh Black rump steak with chips, or sea bass with salsa verde. Or take a ploughman's to a seat under the sycamore and gaze on the spectacular Radnor Valley. Life in this tiny village, like its glorious pub, remains delightfully unchanged.

Powys

Nantyffin Cider Mill Inn
Crickhowell

Diners pour in here for menus that spotlight pork, lamb, duck, guinea fowl, beef — exuberantly casseroled in farmhouse cider. A network of small suppliers provides the rest, while autumn brings mushrooms and game from a nearby estate. This roadside pub started life in the 15th century as a more peaceful drovers' inn, and an old cider press occupies one end of the high-raftered restaurant in the old mill room. You can also sit in one of two intimate bars and choose from a bar menu and a specials board that is chalked up daily. Expect country cooking concocted with minimum fuss and maximum flavour — lamb with colcannon mash and rosemary garlic sauce, fish casserole — plus ales and (lots of) ciders on tap, delicious wines by the glass, hot punch in winter and luscious lemonade in summer.

Meals	Lunch from £5.
	Dinner from £10.
	Sunday lunch, 3 courses, from £17.
Closed	Tues-Fri lunch & all day Mon.
	Open 3pm-6pm Sat & Sun.

Meals	Bar meals from £6.95.
	Lunch from £9.50.
	Dinner from £10.95.
	Sunday lunch, 3 courses, £20.50.
Closed	3pm-6pm (7pm Sun).
	Sun evenings in winter & all day
	Mon (except Bank Holidays).

Chris Ireland & Angela Lyne
The Harp,
Old Radnor,
Presteigne LD8 2RH
Tel   +44 (0)1544 350655
Web   www.harpinnradnor.co.uk

Entry 791 Map 7

Sean Gerrard, Glyn and Jess
Bridgeman
Nantyffin Cider Mill Inn,
Brecon Road, Crickhowell NP8 1SG
Tel   +44 (0)1873 810775
Web   www.cidermill.co.uk

Entry 792 Map 7

Swansea

Pen y Cae Inn
Pen-y-Cae

Everything about the Pen y Cae is pristine, from the multi-levelled garden at the back to the claret sofas and wood-burner in the bar. They've even created a new upper floor, reached by a wooden staircase, supported by chunky beams. It's an exceptionally lovely interior, the best of old and new, and you feast under rafters. French windows open to the Brecon Beacons in summer, informed staff are delightful and there's food to match, from classic pub grub at lunch to liver with crispy pancetta on creamed potatoes at dinner. Find too Welsh Black rib-eye steak with dauphinoise potatoes, and rump of Breconshire lamb with chive mash and roasted vegetables. Wash it all down with a bottled beer from Tomos Watkin, Wales's fastest growing brewery, and trundle off home – charmed, well-fed and happy.

Vale of Glamorgan

Plough & Harrow
Monknash

Originally part of a monastic grange, well off the beaten track, the Plough & Harrow is hugely convivial. Ancient low white walls lead to the front door, then you dip into two dim-lit, low-ceilinged, character-oozing rooms, their rustic fireplaces filled with church candles or crackling logs. There are cheerful yellow walls, original floors, church pews, smiling staff and a small bar area with a big array of handpumps – up to 11 ales are served. Traditionalists will smile to see gammon and chips on the lunch menu while the more adventurous may plump for summer crab salad, moules marinière or roast belly pork with mustard mash and sweet cider sauce. A brilliant atmosphere, a great find, the kind of pub you wish was your local – and as friendly to single drinkers as to groups.

Meals	Lunch, bar meals & dinner £4.95. Sunday roast from £9.95.
Closed	3pm-6pm. Sun evenings & Mon all day. Open all day Sat.

Meals	Lunch & dinner £6.95-£13.95.
Closed	Open all day.

	Anthony Christopher Pen y Cae Inn, Brecon Road, Pen-y-Cae SA9 1FA
Tel	+44 (0)1639 730100
Web	www.penycaeinn.com

Entry 793 Map 7

	Paula Jones Plough & Harrow, Monknash, Cowbridge CF71 7QQ
Tel	+44 (0)1656 890209
Web	www.ploughandharrow.org

Entry 794 Map 2

Vale of Glamorgan

The Blue Anchor
East Aberthaw

Inglenooks and open log fires, stories of smugglers and derring-do – it's rich in atmosphere. Inside is a warm warren of little rooms and doorways less than five feet high. The Colemans have nurtured this 700-year-old place for 66 years and restored the pub following a fire in 2004. Dine in winter on pheasant from the shoot, in summer on sewin from Swansea Bay and salads from the vegetable garden. Pop in for a bowl of mussels and a moreish pint of Wye Valley – or dip into the chef's selection of regional cheeses. Under the eaves of a classic thatched roof, the restaurant delivers hake with chorizo and roasted red pepper risotto, duck with savoy cabbage, pancetta and redcurrant jus, lemon and sultana cheesecake, and roasts on Sundays (do book). It's pubby, good looking and wonderful at doing what it knows best.

Meals	Lunch £8.95-£10.95. Dinner £12.50-£17.85.
Closed	Open all day.

	Jeremy Coleman The Blue Anchor, East Aberthaw, Barry CF62 3DD
Tel	+44 (0)1446 750329
Web	www.blueanchoraberthaw.com

Entry 795 Map 2

Wrexham

The Cross Foxes
Erbistock

It's on a travellers' crossroads, as the highway crosses the waters of the Dee and man and fish move in either direction, depending on the season. Rest on the terrace with a pint of Marston's Burton Bitter or Ringwood's Huffkin and soak up the views from this timeless spot. Inside, a log fire throws light on a well-carved bar front, polished wood tables and quarry tiles, while on the shelves glows the finest whisky and armagnac collection for many a mile: cockle-warming stuff. The big blackboard at the end of the bar is scrawled with good things to eat, from Cumberland sausage with black pudding mash to venison and pheasant meat loaf with juniper sauce. Settle into the wood-panelled area, the fireside snug or the conservatory. Enjoy a genuine classic.

Meals	Bar meals from £4.75. Lunch & dinner £9.50-£16.95.
Closed	Open all day.

	Ian Pritchard-Jones The Cross Foxes, Erbistock, LL13 0DR
Tel	+44 (0)1978 780380
Web	www.crossfoxes-erbistock.co.uk

Entry 796 Map 7

Alastair

Sawday's

'More than a bed
for the night…'

Britain
France
Ireland
Italy
Portugal
Spain

www.sawdays.co.uk

Self-Catering | B&B | Hotel | Pub | Treehouses, Cabins, Yurts & More

Bath & N.E. Somerset

797 Gascoyne Place 1 Sawclose, Bath BA1 1EY   +44 (0)1225 445854
Bang opposite the Theatre Royal, Gascoyne Place, steeped in history, is now a thoroughly contemporary place. Food is modern, British and based around produce from local farms – and there are 90 wines to have fun with! Map: 3

798 Graze Bath 9 Brunel Square, Bath BA1 1SX   +44 (0)1225 429392
In a super location alongside Bath Spa station, you can sit upstairs – gleaming central bar, dramatically glass-walled – and watch the trains roll in and out as you tuck into the Bath Ales classic menu, from breakfast until late. Map: 3

799 The Salamander 3 John Street, Bath BA1 2JL   +44 (0)1225 428889
A fine Bath Ales pub without the spittle. The main bar, like a Victorian apothecary, is stacked with bottles on a Welsh dresser and hand pumps gleam under glass fluted lights. Head upstairs for traditional dishes from an open kitchen. Map: 3

800 The Hop Pole 7 Albion Buildings, Upper Bristol Road, Bath BA1 3AR   +44 (0)1225 446327
Gently sophisticated boozer with a polished feel, a verdant summer courtyard and a modern British menu. An easy pedal from the Bristol-Bath cycle path for tip-top Bath ales. Map: 3

Berkshire

801 The Queen's Arms Newbury Road, East Garston, Newbury RG17 7ET   +44 (0)1488 648757
Deep in horse training country, so expect to rub shoulders with owners, trainers, jockeys and locals. Bar snacks are moreish – popcorn cockles with chilli vinegar, macaroni and ham hock croquettes. Gun dogs and pooches are welcome; woods and water meadows radiate from the door, just the thing after an indulgent lunch. Map: 3

802 The Rowbarge Station Road, Woolhampton, Newbury RG7 5SH   +44 (0)1189 712213
A big, historic, characterful pub, fun for families, locals, anyone who fancies a drink on the lawns, and something from a long menu of part pre-prepared dishes. Great ales, decent wines – just off the A4, yet right on the banks of the Kennet river and canal. Map: 4

803 Bladebone Inn Chapel Row, Bucklebury RG7 6PD   +44 (0)118 971 2326
This 17th century inn, all brick and blue shutters, takes it's name from the golden bladebone that hangs proudly above it's doorway. The wine list is remarkable, the roasts are other-worldly, the chocolate rubble with passionfruit sorbet a must-try. Map: 4

804 The Little Angel Remenham Lane, Henley-on-Thames RG9 2LS   +44 (0)1491 411008
A winning combination of good all-day pub food and quirky surroundings works wonders at this spruced-up old pub, a short sprint from the Thames on the edge of top-notch Henley. Map: 4

805 Hinds Head High Street, Bray, Maidenhead SL6 2AB   +44 (0)1628 626151
When the Tudor tavern across the road from his Fat Duck came on the market, Heston Blumenthal snapped it up. Now the old Hinds Head is the poshest of village pubs with terrific food. Book if you want a table in the restaurant, or a private room, suitable for parties. Map: 4

806 The Greene Oak Dedworth Road, Windsor SL4 5UW   +44 (0)1753 864294

With a background in London gastropubbery, Henry and Katherine Cripps could not fail at their first solo venture – this swish dining pub. Most come to eat: ham hock and guinea fowl terrine with piccalilli; beef cheek with beef rump cap; wild seabass fillet with new potatoes and capers. And 18 wines by the glass.   Map: 4

Brighton & Hove

807 The Ginger Dog 12 College Place, Brighton BN2 1HN   +44 (0)1273 620990

Part of Ben McKellar's Ginger Man group, this unpretentious stripped-down gastropub in a residential Kemp Town street is worth knowing for its good beers, wines and decent food.   Map: 4

Bristol

808 Old Duke 45 King Street, Bristol BS1 4ER   +44 (0)1179 277137

There's a New Orleans speakeasy, British-pub feel to this shrine to jazz and blues not far from Bristol Old Vic. Music is served up nightly along with the occasional curry or stew.   Map: 3

809 The Pump House Merchants Road, Hotwells, Bristol BS8 4PZ   +44 (0)117 927 2229

Right on the water, in a former Victorian pump house, this is a gastropub of the highest order but comfy too. Squishy sofas, board games, a terrace where the kids can spill in summer... and great food. Top notch.   Map: 3

Buckinghamshire

810 The Black Horse Windmill Road, Fulmer, Gerrards Cross SL3 6HD   +44 (0)1753 663183

A warren of tiny character-steeped rooms a short hop from London. All is warm and cosy – a charming mix of brocante finds, rich fabrics and heritage colours. Find hand-pulled beers, European wines and robust British cooking. Enjoy the large garden too, with peaceful terrace.   Map: 4

811 Lions of Bledlow Church End, Bledlow, Princes Risborough HP27 9PE   +44 (0)1844 343345

An ideal base for tackling one of the local walks into the Chiltern Hills, this time-worn 16th-century village pub delivers a good range of real ales, a pleasant garden, and hearty pub food.   Map: 4

Cambridgeshire

812 Cambridge Blue 85 Gwydir Street, Cambridge CB1 2LG   +44 (0)1223 471680

Away from the centre, this simple local has a warm atmosphere and stacks of rowing paraphenalia. A wide choice of ales, among them Adnams and Elgoods, and straightforward bar food.   Map: 9

813 The George Inn 7 High Street, Spaldwick, Huntingdon PE28 0TD   +44 (0)1480 890293

The rambling building – 500 years old – overlooks the village green. Find wonky walls, exposed timbers, bare boards, chunky tables and leather sofas, the uncluttered styling blending beautifully with the history. There's classic pub food and Adnams ale to quaff.   Map: 9

814 The Blue Bell 10 High Street, Glinton, Peterborough PE6 7LS   +44 (0)1733 252285

Everything's traditional at this 18th-century pub except the cooking: the menu might include pork and pistachio terrine, potato gnocchi with toasted almonds. It's especially toasty in winter: find yourself an open fire – there are three – and defrost your nose in a mulled cider or whisky mac.   Map: 9

Cheshire

815 Old Harkers Arms Russell Street, Chester CH3 5AL +44 (0)1244 344525
A buzzy atmosphere and a great range of microbrewery ales at this beautifully converted warehouse down by the canal. Run by Brunning & Price pubs – good modern pub food. Map: 7

816 Dusty Miller Cholmondeley Road, Wrentury, Nantwich CW5 8HG +44 (0)1270 780537
Hugely popular pub in a beautifully converted watermill beside the Shropshire Union Canal. Local food is ever-present on the imaginative menus. Super al fresco areas. Map: 7

817 Sutton Hall Inn Bullocks Lane, Sutton, Macclesfield SK11 0HE +44 (0)1260 253211
A rambling place in expansive grounds, this astonishing pub has been fashioned from the family seat of the Earls of Lucan and a former convent. It's a toasty place, with log fires in winter and view-filled terraces in summer, great muskets on the walls and modern British food. Map: 8

818 The Bull's Head Wimslow Road, Mottram Saint Andrew SK10 4QH +44 (0)1625 828111
Brunning & Price rescued this one-time Italian restaurant, and have neatly and cleverly split up into small, private-feeling dining rooms, warm and welcoming with wonderful food. Good walking country all around. Map: 8

819 The Black Swan Manchester Rd, Hollins Green, Warrington WA3 6LA +44 (0)1612 224444
Outside, a sprawling terrace, lawned gardens a duck pond and a playground for children. Inside, six local ales and top-notch pub grub: homemade pies, beer-battered cod, coq au vin, a good steak. The inn has season tickets to Sale Rugby Club and Manchester United; first come, first served. Map: 12

820 The Buffet Bar Stalybridge Station, Rassbottom St, Stalybridge SK15 1RF +44 (0)1613 030007
Only a handful of these charming Victorian establishments survive – this extraordinary, narrow little bar is an integral part of the busy Stalybridge Station. Renowned for its choice of real ale, pies and puddings. Map: 12

Cornwall

821 The Maltsters Arms Chaple Amble, Wacebridge PL27 6EU +44 (0)1208 812473
Inland, away from the busy beaches around Rock, is this inviting 16th-century pub. Fun and funky eating areas and a good all-round menu, with excellent fresh-fish specials. Reports please. Map: 1

822 The Crown Inn Lanlivery, Bodmin PL30 5BT +44 (0)1208 872707
On the bucolic Saint's Way, where Irish drovers took cattle from Padstow to Fowey before setting sail for France. Tuck into crab gratin, braised shoulder of lamb, Cornish rump steak with pepper sauce. Spill outside to a gorgeous sloping garden with a view of the church tower. Map: 1

823 The Blue Peter Quay Road, Polperro, Looe PL13 2QZ +44 (0)1503 272743
Unspoilt little fishing pub built into the cliffside by Polperro's harbour. Dark and cosy wood-floored bar with hidden corners, nautical artefacts, tip-top Cornish ales, and sea views. Map: 1

824 The Old Ferry Inn Bodinnick, Fowey PL23 1LX   +44 (0)1726 870237
Everyone's welcome, including the dog, at this high-up inn with bobbing-boat views. Quaint charm (nautical paraphernalia, wood-burner, slate floors) and terraces for the sun, hearty food and Cornish ciders and ales. Catch the ferry to Fowey!   Map: 1

825 The Rashleigh Inn Polkerris, St Austell PL24 2TL   +44 (0)1726 813991
A pub on the beach, in a tiny cove! The old coastguard station is cosy in winter, unbeatable in summer; down a pint of real ale and watch the sun set across St Austell bay.   Map: 1

826 Cadgwith Cove Inn Cadgwith, Ruan Minor, Helston TR12 7JX   +44 (0)1326 290513
Smack on the coastal path, in a thatched fishing hamlet, sits this old smugglers' inn. Decked with seafaring mementos, there's a fishy menu and five ales on tap. Views reach across the cove from the sun-trap terrace.   Map: 1

827 Halzephron Inn Gunwalloe, Helston TR12 7QB   +44 (0)1326 240406
Sea views from the roadside terrace, a lively courtyard for summer, and a small garden overlooking fields. Lunch on hearty homemade food like fish chowder, cottage pie or chicken stuffed with crab and dill sauce, then walk it all off on the cliffs to Gunwalloe.   Map: 1

828 Godolphin Arms West End, Marazion TR17 0EN   +44 (0)1736 888510
Spruced up in smart contemporary style in 2014, this grand old building stands smack beside the water's edge overlooking St Michael's Mount and Mount's Bay. Walk straight off the beach and tuck into a platter of seafood in the light-bathed glass and zinc dining area, or bag a table on the terrace or balcony and soak up views. Reports welcome.   Map: 1

Cumbria
829 The Cross Keys Inn Carleton, Penrith CA11 8TP   +44 (0)1768 865588
Donald Newton and son Paul, owners of the successful Highland Drove in Great Salkeld, have refurbished this 16th-century roadside inn close to Penrith. It has a super terrace and fine views – reports welcome.   Map: 11

830 The Three Shires Little Langdale, Ambleside CA13 0RU   +44 (0)15394 37215
Walkers love this friendly pub – for its stunning Lakeland setting, and hearty snacks in the slate-walled public bar or carpeted lounge. Worth calling in after journeying over the high Wrynose and Hardknott passes.   Map: 11

831 Old Dungeon Ghyll Great Langdale, Ambleside LA22 9JY   +44 (0)15394 37272
To hikers ruddy from the day's exertions, full of stories of courage in the face of adversity, the infamous Walkers' Bar serves decent grub, mugs of tea, and God's own beer, Yates. The atmosphere is infectious.   Map: 11

832 Britannia Inn Elterwater, Ambleside LA22 9HP   +44 (0)15394 37210
Being everyone's secret, this pub is always busy, with punters spilling onto terrace, garden and maple-shaded village green. At the centre of lovely Elterwater, a brilliant launch pad for walkers.   Map: 11

833 The Eltermere Inn Elterwater, Ambleside LA22 9HY   +44 (0)15394 37207
This elegant building, as old as the hills, is in the stunning Langdales. Wonderful walks start from the door — strolls round Loughrigg or proper climbs up the Old Man of Coniston. Inside, open fires, long views over Elterwater, and venison carpaccio or bangers and mash on the menu.   Map: 11

834 The Sun Hotel & Inn Coniston LA21 8HQ   +44 (0)15394 41248
A no-nonsense little pub at the back of an Edwardian hotel, with stone flags and walls, old settles, local ales from the cask and hearty pub food. Great views from the garden.   Map: 11

835 The Watermill Inn Ings, Kendal LA8 9PY   +44 (0)1539 821309
The draw of this converted old wood mill in prime Windermere country is the mind-boggling range of 16 real ales, including cracking beers brewed in the pub's own microbrewery visible from the bar. Heady farm ciders and 50 malt whiskies, too.   Map: 11

836 Royal Oak Appleby Bongate, Appleby in Westmorland CA166UN   +44 (0)17683 51463
Both the snug and Taproom at this 17th-century coaching inn are pristine examples of the traditional English pub, with oak panelling, stone walls, wonky beams, and glowing log fires setting the scene for savouring a pint of Hawkshead Bitter and some hearty pub food. A handy pit-stop after exploring pretty Appleby.   Map: 12

Derbyshire
837 The Barley Mow Main Street, Kirk Ireton, Ashbourne DE6 3JP   +44 (0)1335 370306
In a gem of a village, a gem of a Jacobean pub. The tiled tap room floor is framed by wall benches, dotted with old stools and barrels of ale are racked behind the bar; it is austere, dimly lit, sheer delight for drinkers, ramblers and historians. Tuck into a lunchtime cob.   Map: 8

Devon
838 Poltimore Arms South Molton EX36 3HA   +44 (0)1598 710381
An isolated old coaching inn, high on the edge of Exmoor with great Devon views. Very rustic with flagstones, lit with a generator, it attracts farmers and huntsmen with its traditional food and ales.   Map: 2

839 The Dartmoor Inn Lydford, Okehampton EX20 4AY   +44 (0)1822 820221
Walkers and dogs stride in from the moors for Dartmoor Best Bitter, Cornish Lager and cider on tap, real homemade crisps and hearty steak sandwiches. And fish and chips; pork belly with celeriac purée and pepper and thyme sauce; chocolate and hazelnut torte. Nearby is the thrilling Lydford Gorge.   Map: 2

840 The Warren House Inn Postbridge, Yelverton PL20 6TA   +44 (0)1822 880208
Old tin miners' pub, high and alone, in a remote part of Dartmoor. No frills, just plain and simple, with Otter on tap and log fires warming the panelled bar. Visit on a clear day — the view sails for 20 miles.   Map: 2

841 The Drewe Arms Drewsteignton, Devon EX6 6QN   +44 (0)1647 281224
Long, low and thatched, an unpretentious and well-loved village local in a pretty square by the church. Local ales still served from hatchways, and home cooking for walkers. Castle Drogo is nearby. Reports welcome.   Map: 2

842 Rose & Crown Market Street, Yealmpton, Plymouth PL8 2EB   +44 (0)1752 880223
Delicious smells tempt you the moment you enter this big, bustling, open-plan pub and people travel miles for the traditional bar meals and roasts on Sunday. Glorious and delicious.   Map: 2

843 Cricket Inn Beesands, Kingsbridge TQ7 2EN   +44 (0)1548 580215
Unassuming outside, open-plan within, but a real local feel. The great seaside location is matched by a good fish menu. Expect jazz with Sunday lunch.   Map: 2

844 The Start Bay Inn Torcross, Kingsbridge TQ7 2TQ   +44 (0)1548 580553
Packed the minute it opens (arrive late at your peril), this modest 14th-century beachside inn serves the best fresh fish and chips in Devon. Arrive hungry.   Map: 2

845 The White Hart Dartington Hall, Dartington, Totnes TQ9 6EL   +44 (0)1803 847111
Down a long drive past farmland and deer, Dartington Hall peeps into view. Tucked into the corner of the courtyard – furnished with picnic tables in summer – is the White Hart. Walk off a lunch of Exmouth mussels or line caught mackerel escabeche with a stroll through the parkland that borders the Dart.   Map: 2

846 The Ferry Boat Inn Manor Street, Dittisham, Dartmouth TQ6 0EX   +44 (0)1803 722368
The only inn on the river – you can still arrive by boat – has big windows, nautical bric-a-brac and a log fire in its unspoilt little bar. You overlook the wooded banks of the Greenway Estate, once Agatha Christie's home – shake the bell and catch the ferry.   Map: 2

847 The Turf Hotel Exminster, Exeter EX6 8EE   +44 (0)1392 833128
Reached only on foot (20-min walk), by bike or by boat, a unique, rambling old pub overlooking Exe estuary mudflats. Bareboard bar with big bay windows for winter wader-watching and top-notch Otter Ales. Closed Dec-Feb.   Map: 2

Dorset
848 The Rose & Crown Trent, Sherborne DT9 4SL   +44 (0)1935 850776
In a sleepy estate village is this 15th-century pub, refreshingly simple inside, with a rug-strewn stone floor, newspapers, books, church candles and log fires. Expect pub classics with a twist at lunch, adventurous evening dishes, and four gleaming handpumps in the bar.   Map: 3

849 Crown Inn Ibberton, Blandford Forum DT11 0EN   +44 (0)1258 817448
True old Dorset local in a sleepy village under Bulbarrow Hill. Kick off your hiking boots in the lovely garden, savour local ciders and real ales, refuel on fabulous, well-priced food.   Map: 3

850 Vine Inn Vine Hill, Pamphill, Wimborne BH21 4EE   +44 (0)1292 882259
Former bakehouse run by the Sweatland family for generations, now National Trust owned. Two timeless bars, London Pride on tap and sandwiches for sustenance. Close to Kingston Lacy House.   Map: 3

Essex

851 The Swan School Road, Little Totham, Maldon CM9 8LB   +44 (0)1621 892689

In a village of 300 souls with no bus, post office or shop, a pretty pub with award-winning ales. No glamour, no frills, just low beams, open fires, soft lighting and happy chatter. A dining room too, ideal for family gatherings, and a beer garden for summer.   Map: 10

Gloucestershire

852 The Kilcot Inn Ross Road, Kilcot, Newent GL18 1NA   +44 (0)1989 720707

Rescued from closure and newly restored, this smart roadside inn is a useful pit-stop after a walk — or drive — through the Forest of Dean. Flagged floors and Tudor beams mix with contemporary art: a comfortable setting for modern British dishes and pints of Wye Valley.   Map: 8

853 The Boat Inn The Quay, Ashleworth, Gloucester GL19 4HZ   +44 (0)1452 700272

This extraordinary, and tiny, pub has been in the family since Charles II granted them a licence — for liquor and exclusive ferrying rights. A peaceful rosy-brick cottage on the banks of the Severn, it's an ale-lover's paradise, an absolute gem.   Map: 8

854 The Royal Exchange Gloucester Rd, Hartpury, Gloucester GL19 3BW   +44 (0)1452 700 273

Perfect spot for a tasty lunch en route to the Forest of Dean: a club sandwich with salad and fries, a toad in the hole made with Old Spot sausages, or a well-priced Sunday roast; it's really popular with the locals. Dine on the heated deck where the views are wide and glorious.   Map: 8

855 The Crown Inn High Street, Kemerton, Tewkesbury GL20 7HY   +44 (0)1386 725020

The prettily planted terrace at the back is a sunny spot for a pint in warmer weather. At one of the polished wood tables inside, tuck into a hearty salad with fresh figs, or Meadow Farm's sausages followed by a fruit crumble. An unpretentious base for exploring the Cotswolds, without the customary price tag.   Map: 8

856 The Gloucester Old Spot Piffs Elm, Tewkesbury Road, Coombe Hill, Cheltenham GL51 9SY +44 (0)1242 680321

A former toll house with a cheery traditional bar for good ales, cider and perry and a baronial dining hall offering modern menus with rare-breed pork as a speciality. Friendly staff and a pretty patio.   Map: 8

857 The White Hart Inn High St, Winchcombe, Cheltenham GL54 5LJ   +44 (0)1242 602359

A stroll from Sudeley Castle is a 16th-century pub for trekkers of the Cotswold Way where the food is a treat. The menu's awash with local produce including sausages and lists its suppliers. If you dine in, there's an organic wine shop that allows you to choose your bottle at cost price, plus corkage.   Map: 8

858 The Plough Inn Ford, Temple Guiting, Cheltenham GL54 5RU   +44 (0)1386 584215

Horses from the stables gallop by, local shoots lunch, race-goers dine — the Plough is dedicated to country pursuits. Bars are darkly cosy with low beams, flagstones and smouldering fires, beers are local and the asparagus suppers are famous. Cheltenham week is bedlam.   Map: 8

859 The Bell at Stow Oddington Road, Stow-on-the-Wold GL54 1AJ +44 (0)1451 870916
Pop in for spicy sweet-potato fries and a pint of Old Hooky, a bottle of champers or a meal. Perhaps chicken liver and pink peppercorn parfait; pan-roast cod fillet with chorizo (the fish specials change daily); marmalade mascarpone. Wines are from a local merchant; the staff are young and exemplary.   Map: 8

860 Inn at Fossebridge Fossebridge, Cirencester GL54 3JS +44 (0)1285 720721
The bar is as authentic as they come (flagstone floors, open fires), the Georgian-style dining room pulls in lovers of good food, and the garden is one of the loveliest in the Cotswolds — a vast lake, a tyre swing, a train for kids, big barbecues. Walk up the Coln valley for glorious countryside.   Map: 8

861 The Colesbourne Inn Colesbourne, Cheltenham GL53 9NP +44 (0)1242 870376
If it's authenticity you seek then look no further: this handsome Cotswolds coaching inn dates back to 1827 and oozes country pub bonhomie — let log fires warm you after a tramp. Expect ales from Wadworth, good wines by the glass and a modern pub menu.   Map: 8

862 Bathurst Arms North Cerney, Cirencester GL7 7BZ +44 (0)1285 831281
Handsome inn on the Bathurst Estate where locals, walkers and travellers drop in for real ale and some very good food. Tuck into the likes of rabbit and hare pie, pork loin with gratin dauphinoise, pumpkin torte with garden-grown quince. The set menu is a steal.   Map: 8

863 The Gumstool Inn Calcot Manor, Calcot, Tetbury GL8 8YJ +44 (0)1666 890391
Quietly civilised bar/brasserie attached to the Calcot Manor Hotel. Cosy up by the log fire in the elegant bar; take your pick of local ales, good wines and imaginative food. Westonbirt Arboretum is up the road.   Map: 3

Hampshire

864 The Royal Oak 19 Langstone High Street, Havant PO9 1RY +44 (0)23 9248 3125
Beat a path to this waterside pub for stunning views across Chichester Harbour and watch the tide ebb and flow. Inside the former 16th-century cottages you'll discover rambling rooms with flagstone and pine floors, beams, open fire, and standard pub food.   Map: 4

865 Hampshire Bowman Dundridge Lane, Bishops Waltham, Southampton SO32 1GD
+44 (0)1489 892940
Rustic, secreted-away country local set beside a winding lane. Draws an eclectic crowd for farm cider and Hampshire ales tapped from the barrel in the time-worn bar, hearty home cooking, and orchard garden.   Map: 4

866 The White Horse Inn Monkey Lane, Priors Dean, Petersfield GU32 1DA +44 (0)1420 588387
This isolated downland pub may be fiendish to find but it's worth the effort. Candlit Jacobean charm (log fires, old tables, ticking clocks) and a mind-boggling choice of eight real ales. Blissfully cosy in winter, and in summer you can sprawl in the garden.   Map: 4

867 The Hawkley Inn Pococks Lane, Hawkley, Liss GU33 6NE   +44 (0)1730 827205
Gritty, earthy, genuine old inn with charming garden. Sample the local beers – Dark Star Winter Meltdown, Palmers Copper Ale, Ballards Best – and tuck into fresh, seasonal, daily-changing pub food. Jane Austen's house at Chawton is close.   Map: 4

868 The Chequers Eversley Cross RG27 0NS   +44 (0)1184 027065
Close to the green, though not in the village – another attractive contemporary refurb of an old inn, with a parasoled front terrace, loads of indoor seating and a youthful vibe. More for diners perhaps than drinkers but Peach Pubs are great at covering all the bases.   Map: 4

869 The Mill House Hook Road, North Warnborough, Hook RG29 1ET   +44 (0)1256 702953
A sympathetic refurb of a wonderful listed water mill with a mill race running beneath the rambling high-raftered bar. Less pub, more dining venue, with a modern please-all repertoire. Good beers, global wines, great garden – just watch kids round the mill pond.   Map: 4

870 The Northbrook Arms East Stratton, Winchester SO21 3DU   +44 (0)1962 774009
Refreshingly traditional estate village pub with a weathered brick exterior that catches the eye and draws you in; it looks and feels unspoilt and authentic. Enjoy the timeless charm and true community vibe in the simply furnished bar, quaff tip-top Hampshire ales and tuck into hearty home-cooked food.   Map: 4

871 The Plough Inn Sparsholt, Winchester SO21 2NW   +44 (0)1962 776353
Walkers drop by for Wadworth ales on draught and children frolic in the flowery garden's wooden chalet and play fort. After 18 years at the helm, Richard and Kathryn continue to run this busy pub with enthusiasm and good humour.   Map: 4

872 The Black Boy 1 Wharf Hill, Winchester SO23 9NQ   +44 (0)1962 861754
A pub with personality, real ales and fine food: just follow the riverside path from the National Trust's Winchester Mill. It's pleasingly off the wall, full of quirky collectibles to catch the eye as you sup a pint of Flower Pots Bitter in a cosy corner by the log fire.   Map: 4

873 No 5 Bridge Street Bridge Street, Winchester SO23 0HN   +44 (0)1962 863838
In a great spot, close to the river Itchen and a stroll from the cathedral, is a new Winchester acquisition for the team behind the White Star Tavern, Southampton. Tuck into crayfish and lemon mayonnaise sandwiches or tapas-style fried squid, or pork belly with watercress champ and cider gravy.   Map: 4

874 The White Horse Main Road, Otterbourne, Winchester SO21 2EQ   +44 (0)1962 712830
An inspired pit stop for the clued-up traveller, barely a mile from the M3. Local ales and good wines accompany small plates such as squid fritto served with smoked paprika aïoli, or pollock fillet served with a warm puy lentil salad. For summer: a terrace and a garden.   Map: 4

875 The Mayfly Chilbolton, Stockbridge SO20 6AX   +44 (0)1264 860283
Unrivalled river scenes draw summer crowds to this beamed old farmhouse on the banks of the fast-flowing Test. Comfortable bar, pubby food, splendid riverside terrace. Arrive on foot (or bike) via the Test Way.   Map: 3

876 The Hawk Inn Amport, Andover SP11 8AE   +44 (0)1264 710371
You could mistake The Hawk for a cool city inn, with its all-day opening hours and its modern makeover: yet it stands in a pretty rural village. British pub classics like sausages and mash stand alongside the likes of herb-crusted sea bream with tomato and olive salsa and roasted Jerusalem artichokes.   Map: 3

Herefordshire
877 The Cottage of Content Carey, Hereford HR2 6NG   +44 (0)1432 840242
With the Wye Valley on the doorstep and miles and miles of footpaths, you are in fine walking country. The main bar oozes authenticity and the name says it all – come and settle in for a couple of hours. You'll be well cared for here.   Map: 7

878 The Tram Eardisley, Hereford HR3 6PG   +44 (0)1544 327251
Find a perfect combination of styles at this 16th-century half-timbered freehouse, where a quarry tiled and beamed bar dispenses Dorothy Goodbody and Reverend James and a large plush dining room serves delicious meals. Genial owners, a great garden and a family-friendly feel.   Map: 7

879 Three Tuns 4 Broad Street, Hay-on-Wye HR3 5DB   +44 (0)1497 821855
Beautifully restored with slate floors, oak beams and exposed stone, following a devastating fire in 2005. Hay's oldest pub (16th-century) draws locals and tourist in for exceptional Wye Valley beers and interesting fresh food. We look forward to your reports.   Map: 7

880 Bull's Head Craswall, Hay-on-Wye HR2 0PN   +44 (0)1981 510616
Gwatkins farmhouse cider comes at you through a 'hole in the wall' – the perfect tonic after a hike. The Mackintoshes bring a dash of the Mediterranean to their unfussy and flavoursome dishes. In season you can sample Black Mountain wimberry tart and double cream. A garden and a field for camping – heaven!   Map: 7

Hertfordshire
881 The Old Mill London Road, Berkhamsted HP4 2NB   +44 (0)1442 879590
A beautifully restored old mill, with natural oak furnishings and deep sofas in classy rooms, and menus to match – a class act from vibrant Peach Pubs. Great canal-side terrace.   Map: 9

882 The Holly Bush Potters Crouch, St Albans AL2 3NN   +44 (0)1727 851792
An immaculate, 18th-century country pub elegantly furnished with antiques and big oak tables candlelit at night. Fabulous Fuller's ales, straightforward food, nice garden.   Map: 9

883 The Brocket Arms Ayot St Lawrence, Welwyn AL6 9BT   +44 (0)1438 820250
Atmospheric medieval inn in a splendid village, close to Shaw's Corner (National Trust): George Bernard Shaw lived here for 40 years. Expect dark beams, a roaring fire, rustic benches and delicious local food.   Map: 9

884 The Rusty Gun London Road, St Ippolyts, Hitchin SG4 7PG   +44 (0)1462 432653
Rejuvenated pub with a food shop in a converted barn, run by a small innovative pub company with a passion for regional, seasonal food. Expect a colourful, funky rustic feel throughout and hearty dishes on monthly menus.   Map: 9

885 The Tilbury Watton Road, Datchworth, Knebworth SG3 6TB   +44 (0)1438 815550

Chef Paul Bloxham and his crew are dedicated to sourcing the best – locally reared meats and game, salt marsh lamb from Wales, Norfolk mussels from Blakeney Point. Unmissable is the delicious treacle-bread pot – and the barbecues in the big garden in summer. Worth going out of your way for.   Map: 9

886 The Hoops Inn Perry Green, Much Hadham SG10 6EF   +44 (0)1279 843568

Henry Moore dropped by on Sundays. Now visitors to the Moore's Sculpture Garden & Studios across the road do likewise. Food is modern: skewered chilli and ginger king prawns, lamb koftas with minted crème fraîche, honeycomb cheesecake; you can get a good ham sandwich, too. Fair prices, real ales, friendly service.   Map: 9

Isle of Wight
887 Spyglass Inn Esplanade, Ventnor PO38 1JX   +44 (0)1983 855338

Famous and fascinating 19th-century inn on Ventnor Esplanade overlooking the sea. Seafaring memorabilia fills rambling rooms; come for seafood specials, local ale and seating by the sea wall.   Map: 4

Kent
888 Shipwright's Arms Hollowshore, Faversham ME13 7TU   +44 (0)1795 590088

Full of character and quirkiness, pub and boatyard are surrounded by salt marshes – a wonderful isolation. Plain and simple are the three tiny bar rooms, warmed by open fires or stoves. Beers from Kent brewers are expertly kept, basic food sustains walkers on the Saxon Shore Way.   Map: 5

889 The Dove Plum Pudding Lane, Dargate, Faversham ME13 9HB   +44 (0)1227 751360

Who could resist a country pub in the gloriously named Plum Pudding Lane? Cosy dining rooms, verdant gardens, great food and pints of Spitfire, this lovely old village inn has long been a popular foodie destination.   Map: 5

890 The Gate Inn Church Lane, Chislet, Canterbury CT3 4EB   +44 (0)1227 860498

A charming rural local, run for years by a landlord who resists change. Two small, well-worn bars, log fires, Shepherd Neame tapped from the cask, and simple hearty food.   Map: 5

891 The Griffin's Head Chillenden, Canterbury CT3 1PS   +44 (0)1304 840325

If you love fizz, you'll feel at home the moment you spot the roll call of champagne: long-standing landlord Jeremy Copestake takes his wines seriously, and offers guests a chance to taste before committing. Good traditional home cooking rules here. An affable and simple country pub.   Map: 5

892 The Duck Inn Pett Bottom Road, Pett Bottom, Canterbury CT4 5PB   +44 (0)1227 830354

The blue plaque says author Ian Fleming wrote the Bond novel You Only Live Twice at this brick-and-tiled pub lost down lanes south of Canterbury. Today, ex-Granville chef Jim Shave is cooking up a different storm, creating exciting dishes from local and seasonal ingredients, best enjoyed by the fire in the timbered bar.   Map: 5

893 The Kings Head Church Street, Wye TN25 5BN   +44 (0)1233 812418

Enterprising newish landlords doing well at this scrubbed village pub set beneath the North Downs in great walking country. Open from 8am for breakfast every day with interesting pub food served all day at weekends. You can stay too… Reports, please.   Map: 5

894 The Tiger Stowting, Ashford TN25 6BA   +44 (0)1303 862130
Lost down winding lanes in rolling Kent, close to the North Downs Way, the Tiger is an unpretentious country local. full of charm with rugs on bare boards, candles on scrubbed tables, roaring winter fires, and cracking local ales.   Map: 5

895 Woolpack inn Church Lane, Warehorne, Ashford TN26 2LL   +44 (0)1303 813334
Ramblinns, who own the Five Bells at Brabourne and the Globe Inn Marsh at Rye (see entries), pushed open the doors of this 16th-century pub in May 2015 following a serious revamp. Seek out sleepy Warehorne, hidden down lanes on the edge of the Romney Marsh, and expect to be wowed by the location (opposite the church), the food and the quirky, hugely individual interior.   Map: 5

896 The Woolpack Brookland, Romney Marsh TN29 9TJ   +44 (0)1797 344321
An isolated medieval pub on the edge of windswept Romney Marsh. Seek refuge and warmth by the log fire in the low-ceilinged bar, quaff Shepherd Neame in tip-top condition, tuck into hearty pub food.   Map: 5

897 Nevill Crest & Gun Eridge, Tunbridge Wells TN3 9JR   +44 (0)1892 864209
Brunning & Price have lavished time and money on restoring and rejuvenating this 500-year-old tile-hung pub on the Eridge Estate. Their winning formula has been replicated so innovative food is served all day, alongside a raft of ales and wines and a laid-back vibe.   Map: 5

898 The Beacon Tea Garden Lane, Rusthall, Tunbridge Wells TN3 9JH   +44 (0)1892 524252
The spacious late-Victorian interior is a work of art and good beers, wines, food and fires lure drinkers to the clubby bar; in summer you take to the terrace with its famed panorama of the Weald of Kent. Everything ticks over beautifully here.   Map: 5

899 The Hare Langton Road, Langton Green, Tunbridge Wells TN3 0JA   +44 (0)1892 862419
On the town green, one of Kent's least well-kept secrets. It may be mighty but it's relaxed and friendly too and the food is some of the best in the area: pub classics and posh sandwiches and wraps. Chirpy staff dispense Greene King Abbot Ale and guest beers and 17 good wines come by the glass.   Map: 5

900 Spotted Dog Smarts Hill, Penshurst, Tonbridge TN11 8EP   +44 (0)1892 870253
Ancient, low-beamed, panelled, nooked, crannied and rambling – everyone loves this country pub and the glorious views across the Medway Valley from its back terrace.   Map: 5

901 The Harrow Common Road, Ightham, Sevenoaks TN15 9EB   +44 (0)1732 885912
This Kent ragstone country pub looks the part: cottage flowers outside, candlelight and winter fire within. Stylish and cosy, with a charming vine-clad conservatory, it has a great reputation for food, local ales and good wines. Check limited opening hours.   Map: 5

902 The Rising Sun Cotmans Ash Lane, Kemsing, Sevenoaks TN15 6XD   +44 (0)1959 522683
Horse brasses hang from the walls, there's a talking parrot in the inglenook, expect the unexpected from this 16th century pub close to the North Downs way. The focus is on real ale and there's a good sized garden perfect for summer.   Map: 5

Lancashire

903 Bay Horse Inn Bay Horse, Lancaster LA2 0HR   +44 (0)1524 791204

Two fires crackle, the atmosphere is easy and Moorhouses Pendle Witches Brew and Black Sheep are on tap. Marvellous Lancashire produce (herbs and veg from the pub garden) and modern British cooking.   Map: 11

904 The Castle Inn Main Street, Hornby, Lancaster LA2 8JT   +44 (0)1524 222279

Wonderfully restored and restorative medieval-village inn, perfect for relaxing in after a stroll by the river Lune. Lounge by the wood-burner on a battered leather sofa with the papers and a pint of Lancaster Blonde, or tuck into tasty pizzas and game-centric dishes.   Map: 12

905 The Waddington Arms Waddington, Clitheroe BB7 3HP   +44 (0)1200 423262

The bar is the hub of the village, bustling with locals, bursting with character. Food is hearty, full-flavoured and fabulous: try ham hock and black pudding terrine, plaice with mussel and leek stew, and a moreish sticky toffee pudding. Ale lovers are spoiled with Tirril Nameless Ale and Bowland Sawley Tempted.   Map: 12

London

906 The Atlas 16 Seagrave Road, Fulham, London SW6 1RX   +44 (0)20 7385 9129

A great little place at the un-posh end of Fulham in which to delve into more modern brews, and 24 wines by the glass. Tasty dishes change twice a day – grilled sardines, Tuscan sausages – and doors lead to a walled beer garden where folk flock under the rain cover.   Map: 15

907 The White Horse 1-3 Parson's Green, Fulham, London SW6 4UL   +44 (0)20 7731 2183

'The Sloany Pony' may be a hotbed of Fulhamites but it's also reputed to have the best-kept beers in Europe. Comfy sofas, log fires, slatted blinds, a big terrace, and a menu that suggests the best accompanying liquor.   Map: 15

908 The Woodman 60 Battersea High St, Battersea, London SW11 3HX   +44 (0)20 722 82968

Imaginatively remodelled, hidden-gem gastropub for all occasions, serving cask-conditioned ales, well-chosen wines and accomplished food in a vaulted restaurant: perhaps slow-braised estate venison cooked with red wine, rosemary and juniper. Bar snacks include wild boar.   Map: 15

909 The Fox & Hounds 66 Latchmere Rd, Battersea, London SW11 2JU   +44 (0)20 7924 5483

A bright little corner pub in Battersea, a foodie destination and a shrine to the golden brew. Mediterranean-style dishes flow from the open-to-view kitchen; a great atmosphere, and a garden for summer.   Map: 15

910 Camberwell Arms 65 Camberwell Church St, Camberwell, London SE5 8TR   +44 0207 358 4364

Alight at Denmark Hill station to find this classic Victorian pub, the new sister pub to London's top gastropub the Anchor & Hope, and the Canton Arms (see entries 410 and 408). Sit at scrubbed wooden tables in the traditional and cosy interior, painted in warm ox-blood magenta, and enjoy some rustic and hearty food (beef, ale and marrow bone pie, lamb neck, creamed spinach and parmesan) delivered from buzzy, open-to-view kitchen.   Map: 15

911 The Narrow 44 Narrow Street, Limehouse, London E14 8DJ   +44 (0)20 7592 7950
An Edwardian dockmaster's house on a gorgeous bend of the Thames. Good range of real ales and ciders and modern British food, with barbecues at weekends. The setting is the thing.   Map: 15

912 Fox and Anchor 115 Charterhouse St, Smithfield, London EC1M 6AA +44 (0)20 7250 1300
The former dawn-drinking hole for Smithfield market has become a gastropub with rather stylish bedrooms and robust English dishes. Ale comes in tankards in the unspoilt Victorian bar.   Map: 15

913 The Eagle 159 Farringdon Road, Clerkenwell, London EC1R 3AL   +44 (0)20 7837 1353
No tablecloths, no reservations, scuffed floors, worn leather chairs, and Mediterranean food – gutsy, delicious – ordered from the bar. With its real ales and decent choice of wines, the appeal is as much for drinkers as for diners. One of the Clerkenwell gastropub originals.   Map: 15

914 The Wilmington 69 Rosebery Ave, Clerkenwell, London EC1R 4RL +44 (0)207 8371384
A bustling, bistro pub in hip Clerkenwell with wooden floors and brick walls. Find fresh flowers, craft brews behind the bar, delicious brunches and lunches – maybe Moroccan pancakes or Hampshire pheasant. Roasts are massive, the music plays and the cocktails are great.   Map: 15

915 The Peasant 240 St John Street, Islington, London EC1V 4PH +44 (0)20 7336 7726
A Victorian gin palace with a reputation for splendid food, wines, beers and cocktails. Tapas, mezze and the daily papers downstairs; pretty restaurant up. Brilliantly positioned for antique shops, the Design Centre and Sadler's Wells.   Map: 15

916 The Albion 10 Thornhill Road, Islington, London N1 1HW   +44 (0)20 7607 7450
Hidden in leafy, well-to-do Islington, this wisteria-clad Georgian jewel has winter fires, period detail and dark woods… and a wonderful big walled garden. The food is wonderful and Sunday lunch is what Sundays were made for. Don't miss the Yorkshire puds.   Map: 15

917 The Salt House 63 Abbey Rd, St John's Wood, London NW8 0AE +44 (0)20 7328 6626
A mere scuttle from the Beatles' zebra crossing, the Salt House brings a taste of sleepy Suffolk to the metropolis. The meats are rare breed, the day-boat fish is caught by Andy in Looe and practically everything is homemade. A very special gastropub.   Map: 15

918 The Junction Tavern 101 Fortess Rd, Kentish Town, London NW5 1AG +44 (0)20 7485 9400
From the open-to-view kitchen flows food that is modern European and wide-ranging. While half the pub is restaurant, the rest is old-fashioned bar, serving over ten real ales a week. A great Saturday brunch, and kid-friendly too. A joy in laid-back Kentish Town.   Map: 15

919 Bull & Last 168 Highgate Road, Gospel Oak, London NW5 1QS +44 (0)20 726 73641
On the Highgate/Kentish Town border: melt-in-your-mouth braised beef cheeks, white parmesan polenta, home-cured meats and amaretti ice cream. Bare boards and bonhomie in the bar, taxidermy in the Stag Room. Avoid if you're in a hurry! Rammed, especially at weekends.   Map: 15

920 Lord Palmerston 33 Dartmouth Park Hill, Archway, London NW5 1HU +44 (0)20 7485 1578
A Youngs/Geronimo gastropub in bustling Archway with a cool bare boards interior. Braised pig cheek appears on the blackboard menu, and ham hock terrine on sourbread toast. Good beers on tap, film nights upstairs and a lovely little garden for summer.   Map: 15

Manchester
921 Circus Tavern 86 Portland Street, Manchester M1 4GX   +44 (0)1612 365818
One of Britain's smallest pubs, thrice as deep as wide, with a tiny under-stairs bar and two
magnificent, panelled roomettes. Twenty punters (supping Tetleys Bitter) is a crowd here.   Map: 12

922 Marble Arch 73 Rochdale Road, Manchester M4 4HY   +44 (0)1618 325914
Marvellous tiled interior, with mosaic friezes high up in the vaulted roof and a deceptively sloping
floor. A microbrewery at the rear produces an enticing array of organic vegan beers.   Map: 12

923 The Parlour 60 Beech Road, Chorlton M21 9EG   +44 (0)161 881 4871
In the leafy Manchester suburb of Chorlton is this 'traditional local with a modern edge'.
Unpretentious to the core, yet full of character with etched windows and eclectic furnishings, it's
THE place in town for craft ales and top-notch pub food from local, independent produce. Book to
savour the award-winning Sunday lunches.   Map: 12

924 Arden Arms 23 Millgate, Stockport SK1 2LX   +44 (0)1614 802185
A superb tiled lobby bar, hidden snug, real fires and sublime Edwardian wood and glass bar, in the
shadow of ASDA. The limited lunchtime food is of restaurant quality.   Map: 12

Merseyside
925 The Philharmonic 36 Hope Street, Liverpool L1 9BX   +44 (0)1517 072837
The Phil was built by Liverpool brewers Robert Cain & Co in the style of a gentlemen's club so
there's Victorian extravagance at every turn and the gents' loos are of historic importance. Popular
with students, this is a great pub serving baked potatoes, fish and chips, beers, wines and whiskies and
a huge dose of cheer.   Map: 11

Norfolk
926 Kings Arms 28 The Green, Shouldham PE33 0BY   +44 (0)1366 347410
Resurrected in 2014 by the community (189 locals chipped in) following a period of closure, this
cottagey old whitewashed village pub creaks with age and is now the hub of Shouldham. Expect beer
from the barrel, hearty home-made food, a cheery 'community café' at one end, and a busy events
calendar – live music, quizzes, open mic nights, and monthly philosophy nights.   Map: 9

927 The Lifeboat Inn Ship Lane, Thornham, Hunstanton PE36 6LT   +44 (0)1485 512236
Glowing lamps and open fires in this bags-of-character inn. It's been an ale house since the 16th
century and they still serve a decent pint along with traditional food; and the rooms have had a
makeover. The sea is a brisk walk across fields.   Map: 9

928 The Crown Inn The Green, East Rudham, King's Lynn PE31 8RD   +44 (0)1485 528530
Smack beside the A148, overlooking the village green – a spot to rest and refuel while exploring
the North Norfolk coast. Fishermen and farmers supply a menu with the likes of Brancaster
mussels, and seafood linguine with garlic, parsley and parmesan cream. All very relaxing and
quietly pleasing.   Map: 10

929 The Lord Nelson Walsingham Rd, Burnham Thorpe, King's Lynn PE31 8HN   +44 (0)1328 738241
Ancient benches and settles, worn brick, tile floors, and a serving hatch instead of a bar
distinguish this marvellous place. Be tempted by a tot of Nelson's Blood or a pint of Woodforde's.
Family-friendly garden.   Map: 10

930 White Horse Hotel 4 High Street, Blakeney, Holt NR25 7AL   +44 (0)1263 740574
With its spruced up bars, airy conservatory and sheltered courtyard, Blakeney's friendly hub is the place to rest and refuel after a bracing coast-path walk. Now with Adnams Brewery — reports please.   Map: 10

931 The Hunny Bell The Green, Hunworth, Melton Constable NR24 2AA +44 (0)1263 712300
Sean & Penny snapped up this North Norfolk beauty in early 2014 — an 18th-century pub on an idyllic green in glorious Glaven Valley. Food is freshly caught and local; King's Lynn shrimps, steaming Brancaster mussels, Norfolk Wherry cod. Delicious.   Map: 10

932 Buckinghamshire Arms Blickling, Norwich NR11 6NF   +44 (0)1263 732133
A Jacobean coaching inn, once the estate builder's house for Blickling Hall; like the Hall, it's owned by the National Trust. Bars are charming in cosy red or bold green, with log fires, leaded windows, scrubbed tables, and a super-snug bar at the front. Reports please.   Map: 10

933 The Ingham Swan Sea Palling Road, Ingham, Norwich NR12 9AB
+44 (0)1692 581099
Down a wilderness of lanes, the Swan pleases foodies and lovers of Woodforde's Best — our Cromer crab with pink grapefruit salad was delicious. Add a dining room of brick, wood-burners, suave leather chairs, a sofa'd snug in the bar and staff who are on the ball, and you have a perfect gastropub.   Map: 10

934 Fat Cat 49 West End Street, Norwich NR2 4NA   +44 (0)1603 624364
Victorian corner pub and beer drinkers' heaven: 30 real ales with some on handpump, others tapped from cask. The owners proudly keep this a traditional and simple drinking pub.   Map: 10

935 King's Head Harts Lane, Bawburgh, Norwich NR9 3LS   +44 (0)1603 744977
The feel is of scuffed-around-the-edges nostalgia, all low beams, horse brasses and old maps — joined by sofas near the fire and tempting blackboards with seasonal specials. Bustle, background music, a welcome for dogs — there's lots of love. Pop in for a pint, take home fish and chips wrapped in proper paper.   Map: 10

Northamptonshire

936 The Althorp Coaching Inn Main St, Great Brington, Northampton NN7 4JA
+44 (0)1604 770651
Decked with flowers inside and out, a popular pub in the heart of a thatched estate village — you can't go wrong with ales from the cask and beef and game from the farm estate. There's an enclosed courtyard and pretty garden, winter fires burn brightly in the restaurant and bar, and Tuesday evenings see live music.   Map: 8

937 The Falcon Fotheringhay, Peterborough PE8 5HZ   +44 (0)1832 226254
Discreetly modernised with an Orangery addition, it keeps its pubby feel — darts in the tap bar, open fire, Digfield Fool's Nook on hand-pump. Cooking is stylishly simple and wines are as good, with a surprising 24 by the glass.   Map: 9

Northumberland

938 The Manor House Inn Shotley Bridge, Consett DH8 9LX +44 (0)1207 255268
Cheerful landlords, tasty food, a good bar with four local cask ales and a cask cider, a raft of malts. Take your pint of Nel's Best into the garden in summer where the eye sweeps over to the Durham moors. Map: 12

939 Dipton Mill Dipton Mill Road, Hexham NE46 1YA +44 (0)1434 606577
Former 18th-century mill house in a deep hollow next to a babbling brook a short drive south of Hexham. Squeeze into the single panelled bar for blazing log fires, top-notch Hexhamshire ales (the pub is the brewery tap), and warming home-cooked food. Super summer garden. Map: 12

940 Northumberland Arms The Peth, West Thirston, Felton, Morpeth NE65 9EE +44 (0)1670 787 370
Having made a huge success of her artisan bakery and café (The Running Fox), Kris Blackburn set to work breathing new life into the Northumberland Arms, beside the River Coquet. Expect chic design, locally sourced food, a rooftop terrace, and opulent bedrooms. The perfect pit-stop 1 mile off the A1. Map: 14

941 The Percy Arms Main Road, Chatton, Northumberland NE66 5PS +44 (0)1668 215244
Pull up a pew next to the pot bellied stove in this turn-of-the-century inn deep in the heart of rural Northumberland. Tuck into boiled ham and Doddington's cheese sandwiches after a boat trip to the Farne Islands, or cosy up by the fire with a pint. Map: 14

Nottinghamshire

942 The Victoria 85 Dovecote Lane, Beeston, Nottingham NG9 1JG +44 (0)1159 254049
Ex-Victorian railway hotel with bags of character and an awesome raft of ales, malt whiskies and wines by the glass. Blackboards give the food and booze headlines and there's a heated marquee area at the back. Catch the summer festival of ale, food and music – service is always efficient and friendly. Map: 8

943 Larwood and Voce Fox Rd, West Bridgford, Nottingham NG2 6AJ +44 (0)1159 819960
Thriving town-centre 'pub and kitchen' next to Trent Bridge cricket ground. Come for the plush modern bar, cricket on the screen, live jazz and superb gastropub food. On match days the bar throngs. Map: 8

944 Bottle & Glass High Street, Harby, Newark NG23 7EB +44 (0)1522 538902
They put the emphasis on fish at this deceptively spacious village gastropub – down to fish and chip takeaways on a Friday night. Good selection of real ales and plenty of wines by the glass. Map: 9

Oxfordshire

945 The Highway Inn 117 High Street, Burford OX18 4RG +44 (0)1993 823661
Alongside 15th-century architectural gems (beams, nooks, flagstones, stairs) are padded window seats, stripped boards, open fires, real ales and good cheer. Tuck into fishcakes with tartare sauce, Cotswold rib-eye steak with béarnaise, apple and blackberry crumble. A treat. Map: 8

946 The Star Inn 22 Market Place, Woodstock OX20 1TA   +44 (0)1993 811373
In perfect Woodstock, the perfect English pub. Settle in to polished wood tables, crackling logs and
wing-back chairs. Ales come from Bedfordshire brewery Wells and Young's, the menu is hale and
hearty (excellent fresh fish and chips), there's a sunny courtyard for loafing.   Map: 8

947 Kings Arms Hotel 19 Market Street, Woodstock OX20 1SU   +44 (0)1993 813636
Standing proud in historic Woodstock — estate village to Blenheim Palace — the Kings Arms is a
refuge from town bustle. Up-to-date are menus offer the likes of Cornish crab and dill omelette
with Lord of the Hundred's cheese, or braised duck leg with rich plum sauce. Staff are great and
locals love it.   Map: 8

948 The Bear 6 Alfred Street, Oxford OX1 4EH   +44 (0)1865 728164
Oxford's oldest boozer, popular with town and gown, has a low-beamed, shambolic interior, many
years' worth of framed, frayed ties (it's a long story) and cracking ale.   Map: 8

949 Rose & Crown 14 North Parade Avenue, Oxford OX2 6LX   +44 (0)1865 510551
No music or mobile phones at this characterful, three-room Victorian city pub — just conversation,
great ales, traditional lunchtime food, and a heated back yard.   Map: 8

950 The Punter 7 South Street, Osney Island, Oxford OX2 0BE   +44 (0)1223 363322
A great little Oxford stop-off if you're strolling along the Thames, with a garden safe for children and
a gorgeous river view. An authentic Victorian pub with a shabby-chic look and a real open fire, decent
ale and a weekly changing menu. Bring the dog.   Map: 8

951 King William IV Hailey, Wallingford OX10 6AD   +44 (0)1491 681845
Take an OS map to locate this rural treat tucked down single-track lanes in the Chilterns. Spick-and-
span traditional interior, the full range of Brakspear ales, grassy front garden with peaceful views —
super after a hike in the hills.   Map: 4

952 The Sweet Olive at The Chequers Inn Baker Street, Aston Tirrold, Didcot OX11 9DD
+44 (0)1235 851272
Expect more than a hint of Gallic charm at this homely village local close to the Ridgeway
Path. Cracking locals' bar with Hooky on handpump; first-class French country cooking in the rustic,
bistro-style dining room. Reports please.   Map: 4

953 Black Horse Checkendon, Reading RG8 0TE   +44 (0)1491 680418
Persevere up the rutted lane to this old-fashioned country local and escape modern-day life.
Run by the same family for over 100 years, with local ales from the cask, filled rolls, pickled eggs and
peaceful garden.   Map: 4

954 The Bull & Butcher Turville, Henley-on-Thames RG9 6QU   +44 (0)1491 638283
This little pub quenches the thirsts of all who come to visit one of the most bucolic film locations in
Britain. A jolly place in which to down a pint of Brakspear's finest and indulge is some good pub food.
Get there early at weekends when Londoners descend.   Map: 4

955 The Three Tuns 5 Market Place, Henley-on-Thames RG9 2AA   +44 (0)1491 411588

The blackboard lists fish from Devon that has the well-heeled Henley crowd hooked, but there's also Middle White pig rillette with pickles and croutons and daube of beef with truffle onions and carrots, tempting choices especially when accompanied by a bottle from a well-researched wine list. Map: 4

Rutland

956 The Wheatsheaf 1 Stretton Road, Greetham, Oakham LE15 7NP   +44 (0)1572 812325

Locals pile in for portions of good value pub food at this large, unpretentious pub just off the A1. Game sausages or beef and mushroom pie fit the bill – and in summer you can drink beside a stream complete with ducks and duck house! Map: 9

Shropshire

957 The Fox Pave Lane, Newport TF10 9LQ   +44 (0)1952 815940

It's huge, this 1920s pub. Fires crackle in magnificent fireplaces, there's a happy mix of furniture, a lively bistro feel and a great big garden with rolling views. It's a grown-ups' pub attracting a civilised crowd, here for the steak and kidney pie, ham, egg and chips, good coffee and regularly changing ales. Map: 8

958 Fighting Cocks 1 High St, Stottesdon, Kidderminster DY14 8TZ   +44 (0)1746 718270

As you tail tractors and horses on the lane to get here, you pass the farm that supplies the kitchen with its meat. You'll love the gamey, spicy casseroles, the organic salmon, scrumptious pies, nursery puddings. A true community pub, with a warm welcome for all . Shropshire's ancient hills beckon. Map: 7

959 Bottle & Glass Picklescott, Church Stretton SY6 6NR   +44 (0)1694 751345

It's properly out in the sticks, a warm and inviting little 17th-century inn run by landlord Jon. Log fires, fresh flowers, candles, low beams and hearty helpings for all, happily ensconced in the wild hills of Shropshire. Kids and dogs are welcome. Map: 7

Somerset

960 The Bridge Inn 20 Bridge Street, Dulverton TA22 9HJ   +44 (0)1398 324130

On the edge of a popular Exmoor village, you're greeted with good food and cask ales. Sip drinks on the terrace or warm up in front of the fire in the bar; dig into homemade pies or a good ploughmans. Map: 2

961 The Farmers Arms Combe Florey, Taunton TA4 3HZ   +44 (0)1823 432267

Several workers' cottages woven together make one simple, charming pub, a place you'll instantly feel at home in. Patterned carpet, polished wood, big inglenook with wood-burner and dogs welcome in the garden and the bar. Come for local ale and cider, and straightforward pub food. Map: 2

962 The Blue Ball Inn Triscombe, Bishops Lydeard, Taunton TA4 3HE   +44 (0)1984 618242

Old thatched buildings and ancient stables were restored some while ago to create the Blue Ball, now a thriving food pub on a dead-end lane below the Quantock Hills. Follow cracking pub food in high-raftered dining rooms with wonderful walks from the door. Map: 2

963 The White Post Rimpton, Yeovil BA22 8AR   +44 (0)1935 851525
Straddling two county borders, the White Post was lovingly refurbished by chef Brett Sutton and his family in 2014. Expect pigs cheek and wild mushroom lasagne, Himalayan salt chamber beef, Madagascan vanilla crème brûlée, all a treat.   Map: 3

964 Wookey Hole Inn Wookey Hole, Wells BA5 1BP   +44 (0)1749 676677
It may look trad but it sure is funky. On the edge of the Mendip hills, close to Wookey Hole, the place throngs, thanks to succulent wild boar burgers and delicious Sunday roasts, paper tablecloths and wax crayons for kids, and a great walled garden replete with quirky sculptures.   Map: 3

965 The Hunters' Lodge Priddy, Wells BA5 3AR   +44 (0)1749 672275
On the windswept crossroads, a stark little treasure. Mr Dors is its proudest fixture, administering ale and just-made bowls of chilli to cavers, pot-holers, hikers and the odd local. An unpretentious treat.   Map: 3

966 Tucker's Grave Inn Faulkland, Radstock BA3 5XF   +44 (0)1373 834230
An unassuming, almost-unsigned 17th-century stone building, Tucker's is a treasure. Few frills, no bar, just four beer casks and containers of local heady cider in the bar, and a stack of crisp boxes against the wall. Defiantly informal.   Map: 3

967 Carpenter's Arms Stanton Wick, Pensford, Bristol BS39 4BX   +44 (0)1761 490202
Beams and stone walls are jazzed up by a tartan carpet, and the gleaming country style bar bristles with beverages at this classy inn set high above the Chew Valley. Good food and fine wines, too.   Map: 3

Suffolk
968 Star Inn The Street, Lidgate, Newmarket CB8 9PP   +44 (0)1638 500275
The pretty Star was built in 1588. Fires blaze in winter, the garden glows in summer and the rich (French/Spanish) aromas that greet you are delicious all year round. Greene King on hand pump, and Newmarket close by. Reports welcome.   Map: 9

969 Old Cannon Brewery 86 Cannon Street, Bury St Edmunds IP33 1JR   +44 (0)1284 768769
Tricky to find down Bury's back streets but well worth it: the Old Cannon is a bright renovation of a Victorian brewhouse pub. The youthful atmosphere is enlivened by pints of own-brew Gunner's Daughter and Blonde Bombshell, and good hearty food. Strolling distance from ancient Bury and its treasures.   Map: 10

970 Queens Head Hawkedon, Bury St Edmunds IP29 4NN   +44 (0)1284 789218
A true community pub lost down lanes amid unspoilt Suffolk farmland. The draw is the unpretentious atmosphere, the huge inglenook that glows in winter, the excellent country cooking (own butcher's shop and livestock) and the six changing regional ales. Don't miss the July beer festival.   Map: 10

971 The Bildeston Crown 104 High Street, Bildeston IP7 7EB +44 (0)1449 740510
Flowers in the courtyard and Suffolk beers to quench your thirst at this civilised village dining pub near Lavenham. Sriking colours, gilded mirrors, and some showy dishes including a theatrically presented eight-course tasting menu in the evening. One for a top occasion. Map: 10

972 The Swan The Street, Monks Eleigh, Ipswich IP7 7AU +44 (0)1449 741391
The team behind the Angel and Anchor at Nayland took over the 16th-century thatched Swan and the village shop (in the car park) as in 2014. Very much a pub at heart, there's a large bar, Adnams on hand pump and a good line in wines by the glass. Children have their own 'Little Cygnets' menu. Map: 10

973 Dove Street Inn 76 St Helens Street, Ipswich IP4 2LA +44 (0)1473 211270
Unassuming, refreshingly traditional town centre corner pub with a rustic bar, cosy snug, an airy conservatory and a cracking summer terrace. Come for the 20 cask ales (over 600 different brews were tapped in 2013), all kept in tip-top condition and don't miss the three annual beer festivals. Map: 10

974 Anchor Inn 26 Court Street, Nayland, Colchester CO6 4JL +44 (0)1206 262313
Welcome to a contemporary gastropub with informal bar and dining areas. You can chill out with a pint of Woodforde's Once Bittern and a brie and bacon sandwich, or tuck into something heartier from the crowd-pleasing menu: perhaps lamb shank with pearl barley broth. Summer barbecues enliven the garden. Map: 10

975 Butt & Oyster Pin Mill, Ipswich IP9 1JW +44 (0)1473 780764
Impossibly charming riverside pub with old settles, tiled floors, fine views across the Orwell and Adnams tapped from the cask. Arrive early if you want a window seat. Map: 10

976 Victoria The Street, Earl Soham, Woodbridge IP13 7RL +44 (0)1723 685758
Inauspicious whitewashed village local by the green, famous for its home-brewed beers (Earl Soham Brewery). Few frills in the main bar but hearty pub food and a proper pint of Victoria Ale. Map: 10

977 The Plough & Sail Snape Maltings, Snape, Saxmundham IP17 1SR −44 (0)1728 688413
In front of the Maltings, next to the road, this busy Adnams pub-restaurant has promising new tenants. Brothers Oliver and Alex, both chefs, have spruced the place up and are delivering exciting modern dishes to an appreciative crowd. Reports please. Map: 10

978 The Crown Inn Bridge Road, Snape, Saxmundham IP17 1SL +44 (0)1728 688324
Garry, forager and lover of the 'good life', shares this Adnam's inn and smallholding with partner Teresa. A timeless interior, roaring log fires and a rare Suffolk settle combine with dayboat fish and their own meats. Families and dogs are encouraged. Map: 10

979 The Bell at Sax 31 High Street, Saxmundham IP17 1AF   +44 (0)1728 602331
Chef Jonny Nicholson gently refurbished this striking building in the heart of Saxmundham in late 2013. More restaurant with rooms, his food is finding favour – white bean and smoked pancetta broth, lamb rump with rosemary jus, buttermilk panna cotta – and there's a small bar serving a decent pint of Adnams.   Map: 10

980 Duke's Head Slugs Lane, Somerleyton, Lowestoft NR32 5QR   +44 (0)1502 730281
Tucked down Slug Lane and part of the Somerleyton Estate, this laid-back, shabby-chic gastropub offers bare boards and beams and roaring log fires in a cosy bar and a rambling dining area. Expect good, gutsy, seasonal food on daily menus, and serene views.   Map: 10

Surrey
981 The White Cross Water Lane, Richmond, Richmond TW9 1TJ   +44 (0)20 8940 6844
Real fires in cosy bars and huge windows overlooking the Thames – what views! Enjoy a pint or three on the river terrace, packed on a summer day. Bar food is swiftly served.   Map: 4

982 The Jolly Farmers Reigate Road, Betchworth, Reigate RH3 7BG   +44 (0)1737 221355
On the A25, and thriving, is Jon and Paula Briscoe's gastropub. Find flagstones, timbers and brown leather sofas in bar and café; tuck into fresh food from meticulously sourced produce: coffee and cakes, lunches, dinners, local wines and superb ales. Don't miss the farm shop.   Map: 4

983 Red Barn Tandridge Lane, Lingfield RH7 6LL   +44 (0)1342 830820
Geronimo Inns has transformed this rambling, former Brewer's Fayre pub. Eat enjoyably at scrubbed tables in the high-raftered barn with its central fire. Reports please.   Map: 4

984 Stephan Langton Friday Street, Abinger Common, Dorking RH5 6JR   +44 (0)1306 730775
Walkers refuel in the unpretentious bar (bare boards, rustic furnishings, open fires), washing down venison cottage pie, hearty sandwiches, a bowl of courgette and coriander soup with a pint of Surrey Hills ale. After tucking into these treats, head off to explore Surrey's beech woods.   Map: 4

985 Punch Bowl Inn Oakwood Hill, Dorking RH5 5PU   +44 (0)1306 627249
15th-century charm: a roaring inglenook, scrubbed tables and wonky flagged floors. The tile-hung pub is in superb walking country. Summer barbecues and Badger beers.   Map: 4

Sussex
986 The Partridge Inn Singleton, Chichester PO18 0EY   +44 (0)1243 811251
Former Ritz chef, Giles Thompson is a man with the Midas touch. Enjoy Harvey's Sussex Best with a traditional ploughman's in the bar, or pan-fried lamb's liver and bacon with onion gravy. Desserts are the best of old British: treacle sponge, spotted dick. The lovely big garden attracts a crowd in summer.   Map: 4

987 The White Horse Inn The Street, Sutton, Pulborough RH20 1PS   +44 (0)1798 869221
Squirrelled away on the South Downs, in the village of Sutton, the White Horse combines an unexpected modernity with a welcoming feel. Now more gastropub than local, it sets much store by its food: regional, seasonal, delicious. Stunning walks from the front door.   Map: 4

988 The Royal Oak Inn The Street, Poynings, Brighton BN45 7AQ +44 (0)1273 857389
A pretty village location below the South Downs for Paul Day's revamped pub. Come for the lovely summer garden (great barbecues), the local Harvey's bitter and the ambitious menus brimming with local foods.   Map: 4

989 The Kings Head 9 Southover High Street, Lewes BN7 1HS +44 (0)1273 474628
The team behind the successful Foragers pub in Brighton have rescued and revamped this unusual gabled corner pub close to Lewes Priory. Come for a great atmosphere, Harvey's ale and short interesting menus that bristle with free range, local and sustainable produce.   Map: 4

990 The Jolly Sportsman Chapel Lane, East Chiltington, Lewes BN7 3BA +44 (0)1273 890400
Deep in Sussex, a little place with a passion for beer, food and wine. In the stylish restaurant, delicious dishes are ferried to oak tables decorated with flowers and candles; outside, ancient trees give shade to rustic tables and the garden has a play area. A team of talented enthusiasts runs this pet-friendly pub.   Map: 4

991 The Hatch Inn Colemans Hatch TN7 4EJ +44 (0)1342 822363
Tiny 15th-century weatherboarded cottage hidden down lanes on the edge of the Ashdown Forest. Worth seeking out for tip-top Larkins' ales, blazing log fires and a big summer garden. Food is hearty and home-cooked; arrive early – the beamed bar fills quickly.   Map: 4

992 Rose Cottage Inn Alciston, Polegate BN26 6UW +44 (0)1323 870377
In walking country close to the South Downs Way, this 17th-century, wisteria-clad cottage is on a quiet lane to nowhere. It's a bolthole for ramblers in search of a decent pint and fresh local fish.   Map: 5

993 The Cricketers Arms Berwick, Polegate BN26 6SP +44 (0)1323 870469
Harveys ales are tapped from the cask and the food is straightforward pub grub – gammon steak and egg, a seafood platter. Try your luck at playing the Sussex coin game, Toad-In-Ye-Hole. Surrounded by a cottage garden resplendent with foxgloves and roses, the Cricketers is equally charming in summer.   Map: 5

994 Six Bells The Street, Chiddingly, Lewes BN8 6HE +44 (0)1825 872227
Led Zeppelin and Leo Sayer have played in this quirky little boozer renowned for its music. Log fires, Harveys on handpump, atmosphere, boules in the garden, and great value food.   Map: 5

995 The Queen's Head Parsonage Lane, Icklesham, Rye TN36 4BL +44 (0)1424 814552
Arrive early to bag a rustic garden bench in summer; in winter retreat to the beamed bar for pints of Dark Star or heady Biddenden cider. Traditional pub food too at this tile-hung 17th-century pub, set on a ridge with spectacular views across the Brede Valley to Rye.   Map: 5

Warwickshire
996 The King's Head 21 Bearley Road, Aston Cantlow B95 6HY +44 (0)1789 488242
They say Shakespeare's parents had their wedding reception at this long, low, rambling country inn with small leaded windows and a log fire in the inglenook. New owners are settling in well and the famous Duck Supper, a house speciality, is still on the menu. More reports, please.   Map: 8

Wiltshire

997 The Compasses Inn Lower Chicksgrove, Tisbury, Salisbury SP3 6NB   +44 (0)1722 714318
A village pub whose thatched roof is like a sombrero, shielding windows that peer sleepily over the lawn. Duck in to a wonderful long, timbered and flagstoned room, its cosy booths divided by farmyard salvage; people come for the welcome and the food.   Map: 3

998 Red Lion Inn Kilmington, Warminster BA12 6RP   +44 (0)1985 844263
The four-centuries-old farmhouse has become a quiet, traditional local. Accompany a great-value homemade cottage pie with a pint of Butcombe Bitter and a fabulous view of the South Wiltshire Downs.   Map: 3

999 The Spread Eagle Church Lawn, Stourton, Warminster BA12 6QE   +44 (0)1747 840587
Peep inside to find slate and coir floors and jugs of garden flowers on old pine tables. In the bar a wood-burning stove is merry, while food is English and local. Make the most of Stourhead's stupendous example of a landscape garden with lake and follies.   Map: 3

1000 The Barge Inn Honeystreet, Pewsey SN9 5PS   +44 (0)1672 851705
The famous canalside pub thrives again. Now community-owned and supported by the BBC Village SOS project, it's become the village hub. This crop-circle enthusiasts' HQ has camping facilities, live music (don't miss Honeyfest), local beers, food and a laid-back vibe. Reports welcome.   Map: 3

1001 Rising Sun 32 Bowden Hill, Lacock, Chippenham SN15 2PP   +44 (0)1249 730363
Unpretentious stone pub high on a hill above Lacock. Escape the crowds for the terrace and unrivalled Avon Valley views, sup a pint of Moles as hot-air balloons drift across the sky on summer evenings.   Map: 3

1002 The Neeld Arms The Street, Grittleton, Chippenham SN14 6AP   +44 (0)1249 782470
True country boozer with friendly locals, two glowing inglenooks, fresh tasty food, good beers and the new function room is popular with village events.   Map: 3

1003 Quarrymans Arms Box Hill, Box, Corsham SN13 8HN   +44 (0)1225 743569
From the tiny terrace at the front you can watch farmers and walkers weave through the hamlet, but it's the big garden at the back where the faithful gather in summer — where better to consume a plate of rare roast beef and a pint of Butcombe on a sunny Sunday?   Map: 3

Worcestershire

1004 The Monkey House Defford, Upton-on-Severn WR8 9BW   +44 (0)1386 750234
One of the last four cider houses in England — a curiosity. No signs guide you to the thatched house set back from the road but the locals will. Try Weston's First Quality or Woodmancote Dry cider served through the hatch, and sit outside; there's a shed if the weather's bad.   Map: 8

1005 The Live & Let Live Bringsty Common, Bringsty WR6 5UW   +44 (0)1886 821462
Well off the beaten track, this 300-year-old thatched pub sits in splendid isolation. On sunny days, outside is best — a pretty little garden with views. Wherever you perch, tuck into beer, cider and perry, and good grub — Bringsty lamb chops, steak and kidney pie, and, more surprisingly, Hungarian goulash.   Map: 8

Yorkshire

1006 The Fat Cat 23 Alma Street, Sheffield S3 8SA +44 (0)1142 494801
In Sheffield and desperate for a pint? Follow signs to the Kelham Island Museum to locate this bustling backstreet boozer. Great home-brewed beers and six guest ales await. Good value pub grub. Map: 12

1007 The Milestone 84 Green Lane at Ball St, Kelham Island, Sheffield S3 8SE +44 (0)1142 728327
Victorian gastropub full of pizzazz. Sup beer from Kelham Island, along with speciality lagers, spirits and wines, before tucking into such delights as sausage casserole with puy lentils, paprika and crispy back fat, followed by wine-poached pear with vanilla panna cotta. One for your foodie map. Map: 12

1008 The Woodman Inn Thunder Bridge Lane, Kirkburton, Huddersfield HD8 0PX
+44 (0)1484 605778
A big welcoming roadside pub in a pretty village, with an oddly urban vibe. Matching upholstered chairs, pale-hued banquettes, a good-looking fricassee of wild mushrooms and a pint of Bradfield's Farmers Blonde. There are a couple of open fires and despite the size it's nice and cosy. Map: 12

1009 The Sair Inn 139 Lane Top, Linthwaite, Huddersfield HD7 5SG +44 (0)1484 842370
A Yorkshire treasure, enhanced by locals and traditional pub games while side rooms allow escape from the hubbub. Beers are to die for, created in the brewhouse behind the pub; eight or more. Not one for shrinking violets, 'grand' in the Wallace and Grommit sense, great value and welcoming to all. Map: 12

1010 The Old White Beare Village St, Norwood Geen, Halifax HX3 8QG +44 (0)1274 676645
Inviting pub in a pretty Pennine village, with flagged floors, oak settles and a fire in the ancient snug. Ales include Timothy Taylor's and Thwaites and the wine list has lots by the glass. Dogs are welcome and the food is good: steak and ale pie, rack of three-Dales lamb, jam roly poly with crème anglais. Map: 12

1011 The Pack Horse Widdop, Hebden Bridge HX7 7AT +44 (0)1422 842803
This old whitewashed inn sags beneath weathered gritstone tiles in a gloriously remote spot favoured by ramblers on the Pennine Way and riders on the Pennine Bridleway. Four or five real ales to enjoy alongside whopping portions of crispy roast duck, rack of lamb, and a whole side of grilled plaice. Map: 12

1012 Whitelocks Turks Head Yard, Leeds LS1 6HB +44 (0)1132 453950
In Leeds centre, an interior barely changed since Victorian times: old button-backed leather banquettes with panelled mirrored dividers in a tiny narrow bar. Come for the history not the food, and the Deuchars. Map: 12

1013 The Fauconberg Arms Coxwold, Thirsk YO61 4AD +44 (0)1347 868214
Settle in a chintz-covered armchair or an antique carriage seat... Honest hearty dishes include homemade pie, ham and eggs and pot-roast partridge. Top tip: have a wander round nearby Shandy Hall then settle in front of the fire for a cracking lunch with a glass of local cider. Map: 12

1014 The George At Wath Main Street, Wath, Ripon HG4 5EN   +44 (0)1765 641324

The handsome Georgian pub in a sleepy Dales village is bright with oak floors and checked wool chairs, and a welcome as warm as the roaring wood stove. Check out the creative menu with a cask ale in your hand, feast on chicken pie or local venison with celeriac purée. Pub as hub (and conveniently close to the A1).   Map: 12

1015 The Bruce Arms Main Street, West Tanfield, Ripon HG4 5JJ   +44 (0)1677 470325

A handsome Dales pub close to Ripon and Fountains Abbey. Traditional meets contemporary with a flagged open-plan bar, a wood-burner in the corner and eye-catching art everywhere (from the great and good as well as interesting new talent). Hugh's kitchen credentials are top-notch, and provenance rules.   Map: 12

1016 The George Kirk Gill, Hubberholme, Skipton BD23 5EJ   +44 (0)1756 760223

Perfectly positioned Dales pub with good beer and food, sunny garden. Child- and dog-friendly too. J B Priestley's favourite watering hole – he's buried in the church opposite.   Map: 12

1017 The Fox & Rabbit Lockton, Pickering YO18 7NQ   +44 (0)1751 460213

This friendly family-run roadside inn is worth stopping for. Look forward to open fires, a series of small rooms and an interesting menu: figs with Parma ham alongside pub classics like gammon and homemade chips and steak and ale pie.   Map: 13

1018 St Vincent Arms Main St, Sutton-upon-Derwent, York YO41 4BN   +44 (0)1904 608349

A great little local that hums with happy chat. A traditional public bar (no music or electronic gadgetry) is at its heart, serving eight cask beers and interesting food: crab sandwiches, chorizo and scallop risotto, lobster with garlic butter, sticky toffee pudding.   Map: 13

Wales

Anglesey
1019 The Seacroft Ravenspoint Rd, Trearddur Bay, Holyhead LL65 2YU   +44 (0)1407 860348

Wonderfully positioned, whitewashed walls sparkling in the summer sun, this is a very happy place, a pub to some (Tuesday night is quiz night) and a restaurant to others (Anglesey lamb, mussels from the Menai Strait). Spin outside to explore the wide sands of Trearddur Bay, the coastal path, the sailing school.   Map: 6

Ceredigion
1020 The Ship Tresaith, Cardigan SA43 2JL   +44 (0)1239 811816

Soften salt-parched lips with refreshing Brains ales, then tuck into a seafood platter on the terrace for splendid sea views – you may spot a dolphin. The fun, surf-chic interior is bright and child-friendly.   Map: 6

Gwynedd
1021 Ty Coch Inn Porthdinllaen, Morfa Nefyn, Pwllheli LL53 6DB   +44 (0)1758 720498

Find time to walk along the beach to the tiny beachside hamlet and this spectacularly sited pub – sup a pint of Purple Moose Bitter with your feet in the sea. A Welsh welcome and simple food await – lovely. Phone for winter opening times.   Map: 6

Monmouthshire

1022 Hunter's Moon Inn Llangattock Lingced, Abergavenny NP7 8RR   +44 (0)1873 821499

Everything a country pub should be: as old as the hills, serving hearty food and immersed in splendid country. The menu of comforting pub classics has a few twists such as sizzling prawn salad. On top of that, you have Granny Beryl's homemade puddings, a pretty garden to sit in, and Offa's Dyke up the lane.   Map: 7

1023 The Crown at Pantygelli Old Hereford Road, Pantygelli, Abergavenny NP7 7HR
+44 (0)1873 853314

Handsome 16th-century roadside pub with glorious rolling country views towards the Skirrid. A true community pub with farmers at the bar, local ales on tap and good food sourced from surrounding farms. Reports welcome.   Map: 7

1024 Llanthony Priory Llanthony, Abergavenny NP7 7NN   +44 (0)1873 890487

Once only walkers knew Llanthony was here, now the abbot's cellar holds an atmospheric hotchpotch of tables and high-backed pews. Simple food, pints of Felinfoel, proper espresso, romantic views.   Map: 7

Vale of Glamorgan

1025 The Bush St Hilary, Cowbridge CF71 7DP   +44 (0)1446 772745

Wonderfully traditional thatched pub in gentle countryside. Cul-de-sac location opposite the church makes outside benches popular in summer. In winter head for the roaring fire, pints of Old Rosie and Speckled Hen, and great food.   Map: 2

Wrexham

1026 The Boat Erbistock, Wrexham LL13 0DL   +44 (0)1978 780666

Arrive on the right bank of the Dee as the winch ferry no longer operates to pull you across to this riverside beauty. In the conservatory extension, daily changing menus reflect a passion for fish and game, with plenty for kids to enjoy too. Arrive early if the sun's shining, and grab a picnic bench by the rushing river.   Map: 7

Photo: The Three Tuns, entry 681

Alastair Sawday has been publishing books for over twenty-one years, finding Special Places to Stay in Britain and abroad. All our properties are inspected by us and are chosen for their charm and individuality and, now, with eleven titles to choose from there are plenty of places to explore. You can buy any of our books at a reader discount of 25%* on the RRP.

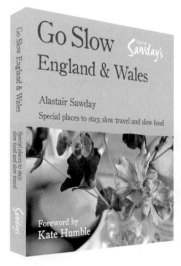
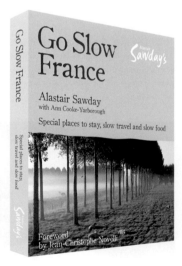

www.sawdays.co.uk/bookshop

List of titles:	RRP	Discount price
British Bed & Breakfast	£15.99	£11.99
British Hotels and Inns	£15.99	£11.99
Pubs & Inns of England & Wales	£15.99	£11.99
Dog-friendly Breaks in Britain	£14.99	£11.24
French Bed & Breakfast	£15.99	£11.99
French Châteaux & Hotels	£15.99	£11.99
Italy	£15.99	£11.99
Portugal	£12.99	£9.74
Spain	£15.99	£11.99
Go Slow England & Wales	£19.99	£14.99
Go Slow France	£19.99	£14.99

*postage and packaging is added to each order

How to order:
You can order online at: www.sawdays.co.uk/bookshop/
or call: **+44(0)117 204 7810**

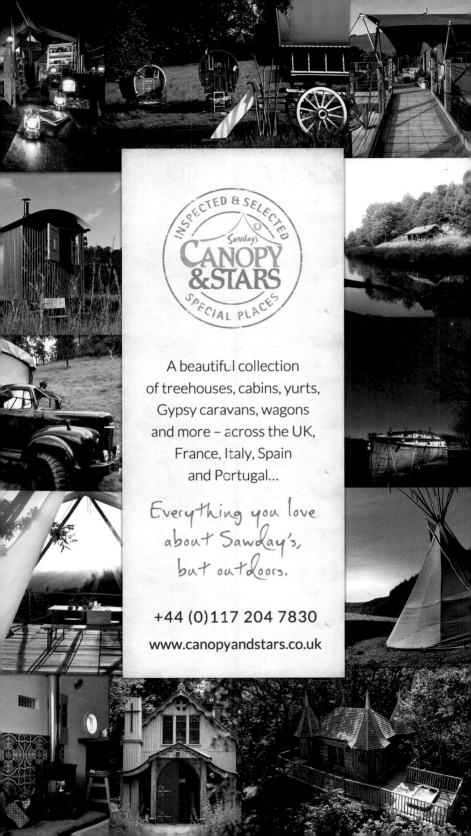

Join us

TIME AWAY IS FAR TOO PRECIOUS TO
SPEND IN THE WRONG PLACE. THAT'S WHY,
BACK IN 1994, WE STARTED SAWDAY'S.

Twenty years on, we're still a family concern – and still
on a crusade to stamp out the bland and predictable,
and help our guests find truly special places to stay.

If you have one, we do hope you'll decide
to take the plunge and join us.

ALASTAIR & TOBY SAWDAY

"Trustworthy, friendly and helpful – with a reputation
for offering wonderful places and discerning visitors."

JULIA NAISMITH, HOLLYTREE COTTAGE

"Sawday's. Is there any other?"

SONIA HODGSON, HORRY MILL

Hampshire

The Wellington Arms
Baughurst

Lost down a web of lanes, the 'Welly' draws foodies from miles around. Cosy, relaxed and decorated in style – old dining tables, crystal decanters, terracotta floor – the newly extended bar-dining room fills quickly, so make sure you book to sample Jason's inventive modern cooking. Boards are chalked up daily and the produce mainly home-grown or organic. Kick off with home-grown courgette flowers stuffed with ricotta, parmesan and lemon zest, follow with rack of home-reared lamb with root vegetable mash and crab apple jelly, finish with elderflower jelly, strawberry and raspberry sorbet. Migrate to the huge garden for summer meals and views of the pub's small holding: handfuls of pigs and sheep, bees, and hens of all sorts; buy the eggs at the bar. Stay over and get cosy in either one of the three rooms, housed in the former wine store and pig shed. Expect exposed brick and beams, vast Benchmark beds topped with goose down duvets, fresh flowers, coffee machines, mini-fridges, and slate tiled bathrooms with underfloor heating and walk-in rain showers. Breakfast too is a treat.

Rooms	3 doubles: £95–£200.
Meals	Set lunch £15.75–£18.75.
	Dinner £11–£21.
Closed	Rarely.

Jason King & Simon Page
The Wellington Arms,
Baughurst Road,
Baughurst RG26 5LP
Tel   +44 (0)118 982 0110
Web   www.thewellingtonarms.com

Entry 274 Map 4

WHY BECOME A MEMBER?

Becoming a part of our 'family' of Special Places is like being awarded a Michelin star. Our stamp of approval will tell guests that you offer a truly special experience and you will benefit from our experience, reputation and support.

A CURATED COLLECTION

Our site presents a relatively small and careful selection of Special Places which helps us to stand out like a brilliantly shining beacon.

QUALITY, NOT QUANTITY

We don't pretend (or want) to be in the same business as the sites that handle zillions of bookings a day. Using our name ensures that you attract the right kind of guests for you.

INSPECT AND RE-INSPECT

Our inspectors have an eagle-eye for the special, but absolutely no checklists. They visit every member, see every bedroom and bathroom and, on the lucky days, eat the food.

VARIETY

From country-house hotels to city pads and funky fincas to blissful B&Bs, we genuinely delight in the individuality of our Special Places.

LOYALTY

Nearly half of our members have been with us for five years or more. We must be doing something right!

GET IN TOUCH WITH OUR MEMBERSHIP TEAM...

+44 (0)117 204 7810
members@sawdays.co.uk

...OR APPLY ONLINE

sawdays.co.uk/joinus

The friendly crew